M000169781

Oracle Press™

Oracle CRM On Demand Reporting

Michael D. Lairson

New York   Chicago   San Francisco
Lisbon   London   Madrid   Mexico City   Milan
New Delhi   San Juan   Seoul   Singapore   Sydney   Toronto

The McGraw-Hill Companies

Library of Congress Cataloging-in-Publication Data

Lairson, Michael D.
  Oracle CRM on demand reporting / Michael D. Lairson.
    p. cm.
  ISBN 978-0-07-159304-5 (alk. paper)
  1. Oracle (Computer file) 2. Business report writing—Data
processing. 3. Relational databases. I. Title.
  QA76.9.D3L343 2008
  005.75'6—dc22

                              2008033332

McGraw-Hill books are available at special quantity discounts to use as premiums and sales promotions, or for use in corporate training programs. To contact a special sales representative, please visit the Contact Us page at www.mhprofessional.com.

Oracle CRM On Demand Reporting

1 2 3 4 5 6 7 8 9 0 FGR FGR 0 1 9 8

ISBN   978-0-07-159304-5
MHID   0-07-159304-7

Sponsoring Editor	**Copy Editor**	**Composition**
Lisa McClain	Bill McManus	International Typesetting and Composition
Editorial Supervisor	**Proofreader**	**Illustration**
Janet Walden	Medha Joshi	International Typesetting and Composition
Project Manager	**Indexer**	
Vastavikta Sharma	Claire Splan	**Art Director, Cover**
Acquisitions Coordinator	**Production Supervisor**	Jeff Weeks
Mandy Canales	George Anderson	**Cover Designer**
Technical Editor		Pattie Lee
Zephrin Pinto		

To Susan, Robbie, and David.
You are the source of my inspiration and motivation.

About the Author

Michael Lairson began his career in 1993 in Charlotte, North Carolina as a technical writer after earning a BA in English at The University of North Carolina Charlotte. Mike moved into the instructional design field in 1995 and prepared training materials that ranged from training manuals to high-end multimedia applications for many companies. During this time, Mike returned to UNC Charlotte to earn an M.Ed. in Instructional Systems Technology. Continuing to broaden his experience and explore professional interests in evaluation and analysis led Mike to Siebel Systems, where he worked as a Certification Exam Developer for several years. In this role, he created the certification exams and the study materials for most of the Siebel Certification exams and performed a large amount of reporting of exam data.

In the process of writing the CRM On Demand exam, Mike began to take great interest in the application and moved to the training team as part of the professional services organization. He has since continued to expand his knowledge of the application and has established himself as an expert resource for Oracle CRM On Demand, and in particular, the reporting tool.

Mike played a key role in the development of the Advanced Analytics Workshop training offered by Oracle, and regularly delivers custom analytics workshops to Oracle CRM On Demand users. Mike works full time as a Principal Consultant supporting Oracle CRM On Demand and, in particular, reporting.

When not working, Mike spends time with his wife and two sons and is an active member of his church, The Knights of Columbus, and Boy Scouts of America.

About the Technical Editor

Zephrin Pinto has over 12 years of experience in all phases of design, development, and implementation of computer applications. His experience spans consulting services, application development, networking, and system implementation in financial services, healthcare, high technology/electronics, manufacturing, and services industries. Zephrin has been at Siebel Systems and Oracle for nine years and specializes in analytics reporting. He is a graduate of Jackson State University with a BS in Computer Science. In his spare time, Zephrin likes to analyze stocks, with a focus on technical analysis. He lives in Massachusetts with his wife and three children.

Contents

Acknowledgments

How can I possibly acknowledge everyone who has made this book possible? Even when you had no idea you were helping, you were supporting, encouraging, challenging, and motivating me. First and foremost, my family was extremely patient in allowing me to neglect my chores and other projects while I worked my regular full-time job by day and wrote by night. I received encouragement from Mom, Dad, Mother, and Father and the rest of the Lairson and Carr families throughout.

I have to give a huge thanks to Zephrin Pinto, Tom Griffin, Binh Le, and Jeff Hunt for the things I learned from them and incorporated into my reporting arsenal. Appreciation goes to Hilary Atkinson, John Durkin, Louis Peters, Laurie Coleman, and Jeff Saenger for entrusting our customers' reports to me. Thanks to all of those with whom I work each day for the questions and challenges, especially Katie Pilcher, Karen Selke, Julie Goughnour, Elizabeth Byron, Jayd McFerson, Jason Newlove, Bob Bray, Erin Wiesley, Assane Faye, Paul Dezzutto, and Brandye Williams. Of course, my customers, who challenged me and forced me to the next level, also deserve some credit.

I also received a lot of encouragement from friends. Thanks to Joe and Kristin Vickery for loaning me a quiet place to work when I needed quiet, and to Chris "The Stonecypher" Vickery for the incredible music when I needed to rock.

I offer a very special thanks and remembrance to my "Holshouser Mafia," their families, and especially our patriarch, Douglas Estes, who passed away during the writing of this book. Doug's encouraging words will always be special to me and part of this work.

Acknowledgments go to local businesses offering free Wi-Fi and a comfortable place to work, especially The Well in Wake Forest, North Carolina, where the great coffee and food kept me going. And finally, I must give appreciation to all of those from McGraw-Hill and International Typesetting and Composition who made creating my first book a great experience.

Introduction

As the business world becomes increasingly competitive and companies look deeper and deeper for a competitive advantage, it is no surprise that the term "business intelligence" (BI) has become part of our normal business speak. Chances are, your employer pines for information about marketing effectiveness, sales efficiency, revenue pipelines, service resolution times, employee utilization, return on investment, and more.

Another growing trend in today's business world is the popularity of *software as a service* (SaaS), whereby companies pay to use software but do not pay to own, install, maintain, or support the software. Companies are realizing significant savings by engaging with software services, because the cost of servers and other hardware is greatly reduced, if not eliminated completely, and the cost of internal IT resources to maintain that hardware is exponentially less as well. The popularity of SaaS and BI has come together in an Oracle product called Oracle CRM On Demand.

About Oracle CRM On Demand

It all started with Sales.com, the first hosted CRM product for Siebel Systems. Siebel Systems, the leader in the CRM industry at the time, found itself a little ahead of its time and Sales.com eventually shut down in 2001 due to a lack of demand. Just two years later, in 2003, Siebel reentered the hosted CRM market with Siebel CRM OnDemand. A short time later, Siebel acquired UpShot, a trailblazer in the hosted CRM industry. Siebel's subsequent acquisition of Ineto added call center hosting to Siebel OnDemand and the climb to industry dominance began.

When Oracle completed the acquisition of Siebel Systems in early 2006, some customers were worried that Siebel CRM OnDemand would get lost in the Oracle enterprise of applications. Quite the opposite happened, however. CRM OnDemand continued to thrive at Oracle, becoming a prominent member of Oracle's rich product line of hosted applications. SaaS is a booming industry to which Oracle has proven a strong commitment. Oracle CRM On

Demand (Oracle added a space to OnDemand) continues to flourish and grow in the marketplace, appealing to companies across many industries and of all sizes.

Oracle CRM On Demand is a full-service suite of hosted CRM that includes core service, sales, and marketing components. Hosted Call Center and Email Marketing are two additional options that fully integrate with the application. The extensive CRM functionality of Oracle CRM On Demand includes marketing campaign management, lead management, revenue forecasting, sales opportunity management, account management, contact management, service request and solution management, and quota management. Offline access and integration with email applications and mobile devices are also available.

Most important to the readers of this book, Oracle CRM On Demand includes the Answers On Demand tool, which offers extensive and powerful embedded analytics functionality. The functionality of the Oracle CRM On Demand reporting tool is the focus of this text. I believe that you will find this book to be not only an informative read, but an indispensable reference as you expand your own report development skills.

It is for this purpose, creating a report development reference, that I write this book. I began this effort by documenting examples of my own experiences with reports development. I found myself so overwhelmed with the features and possibilities of analytics in Oracle CRM On Demand and the functions at my disposal that I wanted a single resource that I could reference as I built reports. I often teach Advanced Reporting workshops. Without fail, a student will present me with one of their most challenging reporting problems and stare at me, waiting for the solution. There I am, in front of a room full of report developers, with all eyes on me to deliver a solution. For those not accustomed to a firing squad, this is not a comfortable position. All of the report developers that I know have the luxury of locking themselves away in a cubicle, office, or basement somewhere while they tackle their most difficult analytical pursuits. No such luxury is afforded to the so-called expert that is teaching a class. I had to come up with some way to cope with this part of my work life.

I started recording as many problems and solutions as I could. I soon found that it is impossible to anticipate every problem, so I turned my focus to mastering the features and functions of Answers On Demand. Then it occurred to me that report development is more than just memorizing the functions and mastering the features. Report development is both art and science. Just knowing every button and function would never be enough. The best report developers employ strategy and a touch of flair. After all, just getting the right data onto a report is only part of the challenge. Reports have a purpose and an audience. There is a design element that must be considered. Reports only become great when they provide the information the user needs in such a way that the user understands the data, and can use the data. Great reports are not always complex, and complex reports are not necessarily great. So this book was born out of frustration and inspiration, and I hope it provides you with some ideas, some strategies, and answers to your reporting questions. My desire is to create a comprehensive guide to the features of Answers On Demand coupled with planning and design strategies that will serve you well as you build reports in Oracle CRM On Demand.

About This Book

Oracle CRM On Demand report developers, from novices to experts, should find something in this book that will make the next report a little easier, and maybe even great. The book begins with a description of the report developer role and the user settings that are required for access to Answers On Demand. Then it explores the prebuilt reports in Oracle CRM On Demand and takes a look at the Answers On Demand tool and the subject areas available for reporting.

Of course, you cannot just jump into Answers On Demand and start building a report without a plan, so Chapter 2 helps you understand the importance of knowing why you need your report, how it will be used, who will use it, and what needs to be in it. It may seem silly or redundant to perform so much analysis before you build your report, but the value of a good plan pays dividends in report development effort and time.

In Chapter 3, you begin basic report building by learning how to format and sort data. This chapter explores adding columns to your report and working with the columns to change the appearance of the data and headings. You discover all the formatting options available, including conditional formats. You also come to appreciate how the order of columns and sorting of data in the report play a role in how your data is presented.

After you have data in your report, you may want to think about excluding data that you do not want in your report. Chapter 4 shows you several methods for ensuring that only the desired data is exposed in your report. You can create your own column filters, use predefined filters, and save and reuse your own filters. I also share more advanced filtering techniques, such as using another report to filter your analysis and inserting a filter right inside the formula of a column in your report. Additional filters known as prompts are brought up in Chapter 14.

Chapters 5 through 9 all focus on the column formula. It is the analytical field reference or formula that controls how data is pulled into the column and how that data is treated. There are so many things that you can do with the formulas in your report. You first learn about changing the column formula, in Chapter 5, which introduces the default behavior of different field types and looks at some simple ways to manipulate column data by changing aggregation rules, changing headers, and blanking out the analytical field reference. Then, before you jump into the functions and writing formulas, Chapter 5 explores session variables and literals.

The "Using Column Formulas" chapters are organized into four categories: metric formulas (Chapter 6), date and time formulas (Chapter 7), string formulas (Chapter 8), and case and conversion formulas (Chapter 9). These chapters examine each and every function individually. In addition to providing an explanation of what each function does and the syntax for including the function in your column formula, I provide one or more examples of actual formulas and their results. Also be on the lookout for some tips and strategies for when and where to use some of the most useful functions.

Following Chapter 9, with your desired data now in the report, it is time to dress the data up a bit. The visual layer of reports is made up of views. Each view has a purpose and a number of formatting options. Chapter 10 introduces the Table and Title views and explores the options available with these default views. The Table view may be the most basic of data views, but there are many things that can be done with value formats, calculations, headings, borders, and colors to bring interest to the Table view.

Have you ever wondered what all those different charts and graphs are good for? In Chapter 11, you will learn how to add these views to your report, and go on to discover some tips and strategies for using the right types of charts. The purpose of your report and the type of data you are representing lend themselves to certain chart types, and eliminate others from consideration. Chapter 11 explains the formatting options for each chart type and provides some great examples.

In Chapter 12, you learn all about the most versatile view in the set. Pivot tables allow you to create multiple views of your data, group data in a variety of ways, and even perform some tricks that might just amaze you and your report users. The Pivot Table view allows you to add depth to your otherwise flat data.

Chapter 13 rounds out your tour with the advanced views and dashboards. You will discover views that enable you to add dynamic and static text to your report. Chapter 13 also covers views that provide some controls to enable your users to manipulate the contents and views of the report data themselves. You will also begin to use the custom dashboards in Oracle On Demand.

Chapter 14 revisits filters by describing filter prompts, which enable your report users to specify the data to include in the analysis. There are two types of prompts: the column filter prompt and the image prompt. I provide instruction on and examples of the many ways you can format the prompts, and I offer some tips on determining the best prompt format for your reports.

Sometimes a single report simply cannot give you all the data you want. In these cases, as you will read in Chapter 15, you may find it necessary to combine two or more analyses. Combining reports is one of the most misunderstood features of Answers On Demand, and this chapter attempts to explain combined analyses in such a way that you will fear them no more.

The last two chapters put the user in mind as you build interactivity into your reports to provide to users links that take them from report to report, report to record, and record to report. Planning navigational features into your report design allows you to control how your users will experience the analysis. You can allow your users to dive deeper into the data of their choosing. Making data accessible is the point of creating powerful analytical reports. Making data accessible to the right people is the point of the final chapter on report management.

How to Use This Book

This book is more than just a detailed explanation of the features of Answers On Demand. It contains valuable experience. You see, the best way to develop your reporting skills is through practice. You hold in your hands hours of the author's own practice. It is not a replacement for your own time, of course, but it certainly is a nice head start. In addition to the strategies for report planning, design, and development, you will find a rich resource of explanations and examples of the many functions available to you in your Oracle CRM On Demand reporting tool. For every function, I provide sample code and the results generated by that code. Use these examples to guide you in your own report development. Additionally, the Appendix contains reference tables that you will find yourself coming back to over and over as you write more complex and exceedingly useful formulas and design high-impact reports that your users will love.

Novice or seasoned veteran, whether you read it to learn or use it as a reference tool, I hope and believe you and your reports will benefit from my own experience that I have recorded here for you.

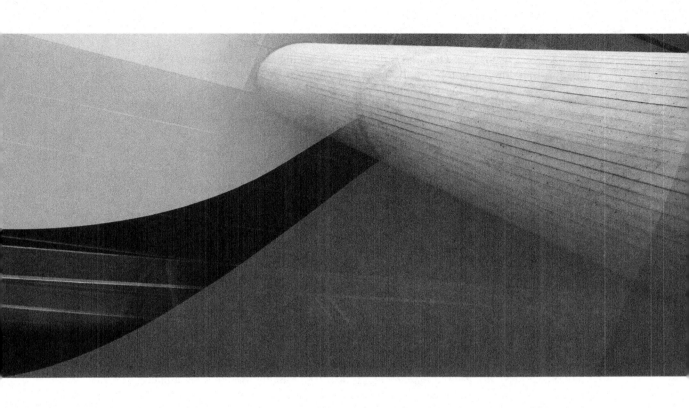

CHAPTER
1

Getting Started with
Answers On Demand

nswers On Demand is the business intelligence tool built into CRM On Demand, and is the topic of this book. Answers On Demand is an extremely powerful analytical tool that, with the proper planning and knowledge, can become the difference between reporting and business intelligence. This chapter looks at the basic requirements for gaining access to Answers On Demand. Chapter 2 covers recommended stages of planning your analysis.

I encourage you to read the first two chapters of this book carefully and give their content some genuine consideration before you jump into the definitions of functions and explanations of views a little deeper into the book. After all, a little planning goes a long way and pays dividends in time when you get things right the first time.

Report Development Privileges

As a user of CRM On Demand, you have access to data and features based on the settings in your assigned role. The roles in CRM On Demand are highly configurable. Many people may share the same role if they all perform the same job. Alternatively, a single person may be the only user assigned to a role. The system administrator is typically responsible for maintaining these roles and providing or revoking certain levels of access and privileges in CRM On Demand.

Before you can go much further in this book and perform the tasks it presents, you need to ensure that you have the necessary access and privilege settings in your assigned role. Figure 1-1 shows a portion of the Role Management window, showing the privileges associated with analytics. Many users will have some of these privileges associated with their roles even if they are not responsible for creating reports. For instance, the Analytics Dashboards Access and Analytics Reports Access privileges simply enable users to view the Dashboard and Reports tabs. The Access Analytics Reports—View Prebuilt Analyses privilege allows user to run the prebuilt reports. Without this privilege, users accessing the Reports tab in CRM On Demand will not see any of the prebuilt reports listed.

The privileges that are critical to the report developer's role are Access All Data in Analytics, Analytics Scripting, Manage Dashboards, Manage Custom Reports, and Manage Personal Reports. Let us examine each of these privileges in a little more detail.

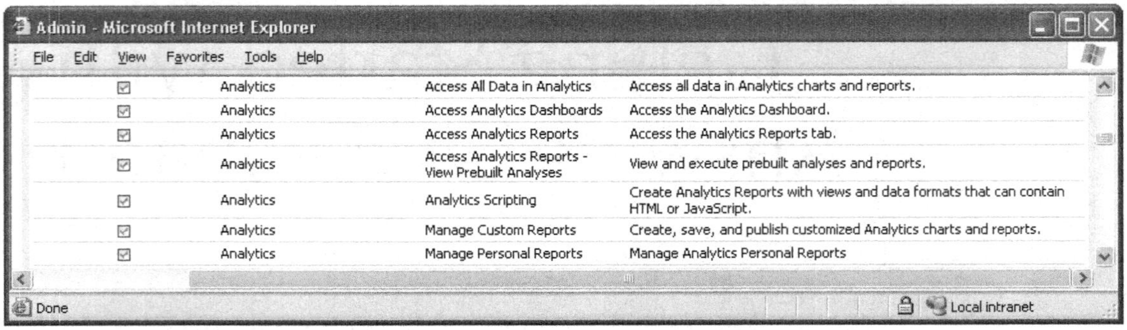

☑	Analytics	Access All Data in Analytics	Access all data in Analytics charts and reports.	
☑	Analytics	Access Analytics Dashboards	Access the Analytics Dashboard.	
☑	Analytics	Access Analytics Reports	Access the Analytics Reports tab.	
☑	Analytics	Access Analytics Reports - View Prebuilt Analyses	View and execute prebuilt analyses and reports.	
☑	Analytics	Analytics Scripting	Create Analytics Reports with views and data formats that can contain HTML or JavaScript.	
☑	Analytics	Manage Custom Reports	Create, save, and publish customized Analytics charts and reports.	
☑	Analytics	Manage Personal Reports	Manage Analytics Personal Reports	

FIGURE 1-1. *Privileges associated with user roles*

The Access All Data in Analytics privilege ensures that you are, while developing reports, able to see all data in the database. Without this privilege, you will have visibility to data based on data access settings in your role and access profile. It would be difficult to develop reports for anyone other than yourself if you are only able to see a limited dataset. If your company is rather liberal with data access, and does not limit visibility, this is not a huge issue. It is still better to have this privilege and know that you have access to data than to assume you do because you believe you are able to see all records by default.

The Analytics Scripting privilege is particularly important for some of the advanced reporting techniques that employ HTML and Java scripting. It is possible to embed scripts in data formats and some view settings. In order to create reports with these capabilities, you will need your role enabled with this privilege. Your users, however, do not need this privilege in order to use reports taking advantage of these features.

The Manage Dashboards, Manage Custom Reports, and Manage Personal Reports privileges are the most important of all of the report developer's privileges. These three privileges work together, and enable you to create new public dashboards and custom reports in the Shared Custom Analyses folder for others to access or in the My Folder directory for your personal use. With the Manage Dashboards privilege, you see the Manage Dashboards link on the Dashboard tab. When you have the Manage Custom Reports and Manage Personal Reports privileges, you are able to see the Design Analyses link on the Reports tab.

Click the Design Analyses link now to open the Answers On Demand application. The first window you see within Answers is the Getting Started with Answers window, described next.

The Getting Started with Answers Window

It is from the Getting Started with Answers window, shown in Figure 1-2, that you create, edit, and maintain your custom reports. Notice that there are three sections to this window. The Create New Analysis section contains the subject areas for creating new custom reports. Before we get into the subject areas, let us look below at the Open Existing Analysis and Manage Analyses sections.

Open Existing Analysis

The Open Existing Analysis section contains the Open Analysis button. Clicking this button allows you to select an existing report to open in the Answers window for editing. You are able to open and work with existing custom reports from your My Folders directory, the Company Wide Shared Folder directory, or the Pre-built Analysis directory. Opening an existing report and saving it with a different name is a great way to create a new report without starting from a blank slate.

Manage Analyses

The Manage Analyses section contains the Manage Analyses button. Clicking this button allows you to copy, move, rename, and delete reports in the My Folders directory or the Shared Folders directory. You cannot access the prebuilt reports here. I describe the reports management features in detail in Chapter 17.

Subject Areas

The Create New Analysis section contains two lists. The first list contains the Analytics subject areas. The other list contains the Reporting subject areas. It is important to understand the

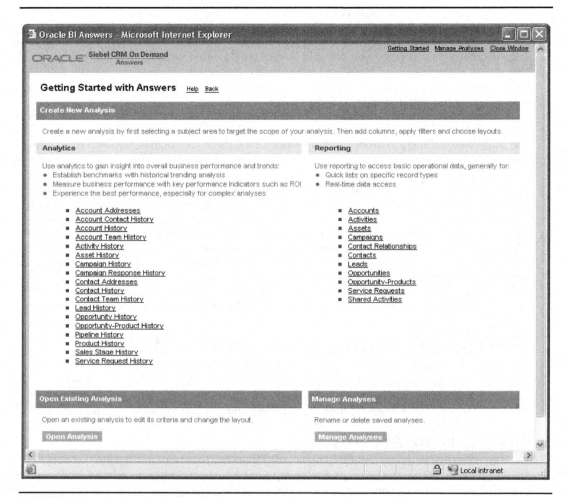

FIGURE 1-2.   *Getting Started with Answers window*

differences between these two subject area classifications. Choosing the correct subject area for your report is critical to the success of your analytic venture.

Analytics Subject Areas

It is highly preferable to select a subject area from the Analytics subject areas, for a number of reasons. You will achieve the best performance from reports built from one of these subject areas. Reports based on Analytics subject areas draw data from a data warehouse. The data warehouse is tuned for maximum report performance. You will also find that data from related records is more often available for reporting as the number of available columns exceeds the columns available for real-time subject areas. Data moves from the operational database daily during an overnight data warehouse refresh. For this reason, reports built in these subject areas contain data that is current as of the previous day.

You will notice, too, that the Analytics subject areas offer several more choices of subject areas. The data warehouse allows you to take full advantage of the reporting capabilities of CRM On Demand with historical analyses, additional metric columns designed to measure key performance indicators, and a more complete library of related data within each subject area.

Reporting Subject Areas

The subject areas under Reporting draw data from the operational database. The users of On Demand are updating this database through the CRM On Demand interface. Users are constantly manipulating and updating this data. The operational database is structured for efficient data creation and management. When used for reporting, it will typically be slower than the data warehouse. You will want to use the Reporting subject areas only when real-time data analysis is a requirement of your report.

Explore the Prebuilt Reports

As you begin to think about the types of reports that you would like to build, the prebuilt reports in CRM On Demand can be a great resource to you. The prebuilt reports are an excellent source for reporting ideas as well as for examples of many of the different functions and views that you will want to include in some of your own reports. By running the prebuilt reports or opening them in Answers On Demand, you can learn a great deal about report design.

The rest of this chapter introduces the various prebuilt reports and identifies what these reports do and, perhaps more importantly, how they do what they do. One thing that you will undoubtedly notice about many of the prebuilt reports is that there is a distinct difference in the report when you run the report from the Reports tab and the design of what appears to be the same report when opened in Answers to examine the design. This is because these reports use dashboard prompts and run in a dashboard view. The preconfigured Dashboard reports visible on the Dashboard tab use many of these reports. Currently, you cannot edit standard dashboards for the Dashboard tab. You can, however, create custom public dashboards, as discussed in Chapter 13.

When you run a prebuilt report and see a separate view at the top of the window with one or more drop-down lists allowing you to filter the report data, this is likely a dashboard prompt that you will not see when you edit the same report in Answers On Demand.

A recurring theme that you should notice as you examine the prebuilt reports is simplicity. Most of these reports are quite simple in structure, and do not attempt to cram as much data as possible onto a single report. There is a clear purpose, or business question, that drives the report. When it comes to reporting, simple is almost always better. The natural trend seems to drive us in the other direction. This personal desire, or corporate directive, to do as much as possible with as few reports as possible may prove to be more difficult for you to overcome than the actual design and development of reports in general. Chapter 2 revisits this concept. For now, let us have a look at the prebuilt reports in CRM On Demand.

Quick Lists

The Quick Lists reports are the most simple of the prebuilt reports library. Their design meets the common needs of many businesses to see a logically organized list of records.

Opportunities By Account

This report provides a list of sales opportunities organized by the accounts to which those opportunities are related. The report uses the Opportunities Reporting subject area. The layout is a simple table, but there are a few features worth mentioning. The Account Name, Opportunity Name, and User Name columns are all action links. I will discuss how to format action links in a future chapter, but if you like to figure things out on your own, it would be easy enough to dig into this report. This report also demonstrates the green-bar formatting in the Table view. Green-bar formatting emulates the old green-bar paper that was once popular for printing vast amounts of data. Every other line has light-green background shading.

Opportunities By Sales Stage

This report is quite similar to the Opportunities By Account report, and also uses the Opportunities Reporting subject area. It contains a simple Table view with action links on the Account Name, Opportunity Name, and User Name columns. One distinct difference is the use of system variables in the report filters. This report only displays records falling within the current fiscal year and quarter. You can see these filters in the Answers Define Criteria window, and I will discuss the use of the system variables beginning in Chapter 5. Notice, too, that an Active Filter view is on the report layout. This view displays all the filters affecting the data in the report.

Activities By Opportunity

The Activities By Opportunity report employs the Activities Reporting subject area. It too is a simple table, as most list reports are. This report employs the ActionLink class and green-bar styling as well. You will also notice that the report uses a filter to display only those activities which take place in the current fiscal year. This particular report makes a nice starting point for a report that provides some aggregated totals of activities. Remove the Subject and Date columns, add a metric column, and you have a completely different but quite useful report that calculates the number of activities by opportunity and type for each user.

Accounts By Sales Rep

The Accounts By Sales Rep report provides sales managers with a list of the accounts that their subordinates own. There are action links to the account record as well as the user record in the table. One interesting feature of this report is the method of limiting the data to the sales reps who report to the manager running the report. Note the filter on the Manager Email column. This session variable, used on User Email and Manager Email columns, compares the current user's email address to the email address listed in the filtered database column.

Contact Mailing List

Sorted by account and built from the Contacts Reporting subject area, this simple report pulls your contact's email, address, and phone number information into a table. Action links will take you to the detail record for an account or contact.

Employee List

Clicking the Employee List link on the Reports Homepage actually runs the Employees and Managers List report and the Employees List report. Running the Employee List report using the link on the Reports Homepage provides a list of all the users and their managers in the top table. The table below that is the Employee List report and provides just a list of the users, without listing the managers for each user.

Service List

This report does not appear on the Reports Homepage in the Quick Lists section; rather, to find it, open Answers, click Open Analysis, and look in the Quick List Reports folder. You will find this report listed further down the Reports Homepage in the Service section.

Pipeline Analysis

The Pipeline Analysis reports provide a great starting place for many of your sales reports. Often, these reports need only minor changes to customize them for your business. This section provides a brief summary of each report and calls out some of the more interesting features. Unlike the Quick Lists reports, the Pipeline Analysis reports tend to employ some more visually stimulating layout elements.

Pipeline Analysis

The Pipeline Analysis report is fantastically simple yet extremely insightful. The report itself contains only two columns. The real magic happens on the report layout. Open this report and have a look at the views in use here. The column selector view, which I describe in detail in Chapter 13, enables the user to specify exactly which two columns of data to examine with the report. By enabling columns with the column selector, this report essentially provides 20 separate reports in one simple report. The chart view below the column selector changes dynamically when you select columns from the selector, as does the table below it.

This report uses the active Opportunities Reporting subject area. Unless you have a real business need for seeing this type of data in up-to-the-second real time, I recommend you build a report like this from the Opportunity History Analytics subject area.

Opportunity Revenue Analysis

The Opportunity Revenue Analysis report is very much like the Pipeline Analysis report, only in this report, the Revenue column is fixed, and you are able to select one of four columns with which to analyze the revenue amounts. Again, this is a real-time report, but is likely just as effective for this type of analysis if built on the Opportunity History subject area.

Pipeline Quality Analysis

The Pipeline Quality Analysis report is a nice example of using the column selector to allow the user to choose the metric examined in the report. This report offers a horizontal bar chart with the sales stages listed in the vertical axis. The horizontal axis dynamically changes to reflect the metric selected in the column selector. This report could easily be adapted for multiple sales stages. You could also enable the Sales Stage column in the column selector view to allow the user to select other ways to organize the data.

Team Pipeline Analysis

The Team Pipeline Analysis report is almost identical to the Pipeline Quality Analysis report, only the fixed value in this report is users. If you run this report and see no results, it may be by design. Open the report and examine the filters. Notice that the Manager Email column filters to match the current user. What that means is that if there are no users reporting to you in the database, then you will see no results on this report. That also means that each manager will see only those users that report to him or her. Notice also that there is a filter on the Reporting Level column. By including only those records where the reporting level is equal to zero, the results of this report are limited to just those users who report directly to the individual running the report.

Top 10 Opportunities

The Top 10 Opportunities report is rather simple. The layout includes a horizontal bar chart and a basic table with revenue and expected revenue. The RANK function on the Revenue column is what limits the data to the top ten. You will find more detail on the RANK function in Chapter 6.

For now, I will just point out that by building off this report, you can very easily modify the filter on the ranked column with any number you like to create your own Top *n* Opportunities report.

Historical Pipeline Analysis
The Historical Pipeline Analysis report takes advantage of the Pipeline History Analytics subject area, which retains historical snapshots of data in order to provide this type of comparative analysis over time. The report itself is quite simple, with a bar chart comparing the metrics chosen in the column selector.

Historical Expected Revenue Quarterly Analysis
This report is essentially a copy of the Historical Pipeline Analysis report with the revenue columns removed from the column selector in favor of including only the Expected Revenue for the previous and current quarter. The column selector allows you to group the data in a number of ways, but only shows the expected revenue.

Historical Opportunity Revenue Quarterly Analysis
This report is identical to the Historical Expected Revenue Quarterly Analysis report, only with the Revenue column rather than Expected Revenue column.

Quarterly Closed Revenue Analysis
The Quarterly Closed Revenue Analysis report allows for the comparison of closed revenue from last quarter to the closed revenue of the current quarter. Again, it is very similar to the previous Pipeline Analysis reports, only the Sales Stage column is not available in the column selector. Because it includes only closed revenues, the only sales stage represented is Closed/Won, so there is no point in including the column in the selector.

Opportunity vs. Expected Revenue vs. Closed Revenue
This report takes your revenue, expected revenue, and closed revenue for each week of the quarter and plots them on a line graph. This is a nice example of another chart type that allows you to compare values visually. Since this report is concerned only with revenues in the current quarter, there is no need to build the report using the Pipeline History Analytics subject area. This report relies on the Opportunity History Analytics subject area.

Sales Stage History Analysis
The Sales Stage History Analysis report draws from the Sales Stage History subject area, as you might expect. The Sales Stage History subject area is a particularly useful Analytics subject area, especially if you are interested in how long sales opportunities are in a particular sales stage.

When you run the Sales Stage History Analysis report, you are actually running the Sales Stage History Analysis in the Sales Stage History Analytics folder rather than a report from the Pipeline Analytics folder. Looking in the Sales Stage History Analytics folder, you will notice that there are actually three reports there. There are no direct links to those other two reports from the Reports Homepage. These other two reports, Team Sales Stage History Analysis and Sales Stage History Detail, are actually targets of navigation links. Clicking a Sales Stage column value in the Sales Stage History report will navigate you to the Team Sales Stage History Analysis report. To see how this is accomplished, you can examine the column properties for the Sales Stage column. On the Column Format tab, you will see that the Value Interaction is "Navigate" with the target report identified in the Target field. The Sales Stage value that you click passes to the target report as a filter.

Open the Team Sales Stage History Analysis report and you will see that there are filters on Sales Stage and Date set equal to "is prompted." This instructs the report to look for values passed from the initiating report. Have a look at the column properties on the User Name field and you will discover that clicking a value in the User Name column of the Team Sales Stage History report navigates you to the Sales Stage History Detail report.

I explain adding interactivity, like navigation between reports, in detail in Chapter 16.

Sales Effectiveness

The Sales Effectiveness reports provide insight into your sales teams. With these reports, you can examine how sales teams are performing using a variety of different metrics. If your organization is using the sales modules of CRM On Demand, you will surely find some useful reports here that you can use to build some custom reports of your own.

Top Performers List

The Top Performers List report is a simple list report that shows the top 20 sales people and their total revenue, closed revenue, number of opportunities, and number of wins. The ranking is on the Revenue column, so it is possible that the number of opportunities, for instance, can be a small number but still show on this report if the revenue associated with those opportunities is large enough to be in the top 20. If you prefer to measure your sales people with number of opportunities or number of wins, you would need only to modify the filter so that the RANK function applies to one of the other metric columns.

Quarterly Sales Effectiveness Analysis

This report provides a quarterly breakdown of opportunity win rate, average deal size, or average sales cycle. This is another example of using a column selector to provide users control over what data they see. Suppose you need to see this type of information broken down by month. You could simply enable the Fiscal Qtr/Yr column in the column selector and add the Fiscal Mth/Yr column. This would enable users to select the time unit. Another option would be to replace the Fiscal Qtr/Yr column in the report and save the report as a new analysis.

Team Sales Effectiveness Analysis

The Team Sales Effectiveness Analysis report is another example of using the column selector view. If you are not seeing data on this report, it is likely due to the filter on the Manager Name column. This report presents an opportunity to provide a caution about the column selector view, however. Notice that the columns available here are the same in both selectors, and contain different value types. The Opportunity Loss Rate and Opportunity Win Rate columns are percentage values. The Average Deal Size column is a currency value. Finally, the Average Sales Cycle column reports a number of days. The following are a couple of things that, in my opinion, you should avoid for clarity of the report's purpose and data reported:

■ When you provide the same values in multiple column selector columns, your users may select the same value in each column, eliminating the comparative function of the report.

■ When you select the same column in both column selector fields, the chart becomes no more useful than a chart of a single value, and the data table repeats the same value in multiple columns.

When there are differing value formats, take caution with the type of chart you use to illustrate the selected data. For instance, if you compare deal size to sales cycle, which is a perfectly valid analysis, you run the risk of having such a large variance between the two data elements that the smaller elements practically disappear from the chart. Suppose you have an average deal size of $800,000 with an average sales cycle of 24 days. These two measurements side by side on a chart would hardly provide a helpful visual comparison.

Team Activity Analysis

This team report shows the number of open and closed activities for each employee reporting to the manager running the report. This report employs the Activity History Analytics subject area. This means that any activities created today will not appear on this report. Any activity that closes today would still show as open on this report. If up-to-the-minute accuracy is important to your analysis, build a report like this using the Activities Reporting subject area.

Team Win Rate Analysis

The Team Win Rate Analysis report provides managers with a quick summary of their team members' win or loss rate. The Win Rate and Loss Rate columns are metric columns available in the Opportunity History Analytics subject area. These columns do not appear as fields in the database. The win and loss rates are calculated and stored as metric columns in the analytics data warehouse. While it would be possible to calculate these values with the data from the database, the Analytics subject areas provide a number of precalculated metric columns for your reports.

Team Average Sales Cycle Analysis

The Team Average Sales Cycle Analysis report provides managers with a quick summary of their team members' average sales cycle or average deal size. Again, these columns are metric columns available in the Opportunity History subject area.

Customers

A customer relationship management system is all about knowing your customer. How many of your customers have purchased your products or services? How many customers do you have? How many contacts have you made? Who are your best customers? You are likely to have some reporting needs regarding customer activity. The prebuilt reports in this area provide a great starting point for this type of report.

Number of Accounts Opportunity Analysis

The Number of Accounts Opportunity Analysis report provides a count of accounts that have one or more related opportunities. A column selector allows you to select from a number of groupings by which to view the data. Without modification, you are able to view this data by Annual Revenue Tier, Region, State, Industry, and Account Type. In many cases, companies will not track all of these data points, and often create custom fields on their accounts. By modifying the Column Selector view, you can add your custom columns and remove any columns you are not using. Bear in mind that this report draws from the Account History Analytics subject area, so custom fields will not be available until the day after you create them in CRM On Demand.

Also, notice that the first column in the report is set to navigate to the Opportunities By Account report from the Quick Lists section. The value of the column passes to the target report when clicked. Interestingly, you can change this column using the column selector, so the value passed to the target report is from the active column selected from the column selector.

Number of Accounts Analysis

The Number of Accounts Analysis report is exactly like the Number of Accounts Opportunity Analysis report, only this report counts all accounts rather than just those with related opportunities. This report also allows for navigation to another report. In this case, clicking the first column value in either the table or the chart navigates you to the Accounts By Sales Rep report in the Quick Lists section. The filter value passed to the target report depends on the value clicked and the active column selected in the column selector.

Contact Analysis By Opportunity

The Contact Analysis By Opportunity report provides a count of contacts that have one or more related opportunities. Like the Number of Accounts Opportunity Analysis report, a column selector allows you to select from a number of groupings by which to view the data. In this case, you can choose from Sales Stage, Deal Size, and (Opportunity) Status. By modifying the Column Selector view, you can add your custom columns and remove any columns you are not using. This report also uses the Opportunity History Analytics subject area, so custom fields are not available until the day after you create them in CRM On Demand. The report data is accurate as of the previous day's analytics refresh. Clicking the data in this report takes you to the Contact Mailing List report in the Quick Lists section.

Contact Analysis By Account

The Contact Analysis By Account report provides a count of contacts for each of your accounts. You are able to see these counts by State, Region, or Industry. Clicking one of these columns in this report takes you to the Contact Mailing List report in the Quick Lists section.

Top 10 Customers

The Top 10 Customers report is another simple ranking report. The layout includes a horizontal bar chart and a basic table with Account Name, Revenue Tier, Account Type, and Closed Revenue columns. The RANK function is on the Closed Revenue column. (Chapter 6 provides more detail on the RANK function.) The Account Name column is an action link that navigates to the detail window for the selected account.

Account Analysis

The Account Analysis report includes a Column Selector view that allows you to select the columns you want to analyze with this report. You may choose to view the number of accounts with opportunities or closed revenue by selecting one of these columns in the Column Selector view. You can also choose the column by which you want to group the measurement. The columns available are State, Account Type, Region, Industry, and Annual Revenue Tier. With just two columns in the column selector, this report will produce ten combinations. Adding to this is as simple as adding additional columns to the report. Clicking one of the hyperlinks in the report will navigate you to the Opportunities By Account report.

Closed Revenue By Account Analysis

The Closed Revenue By Account Analysis report gives you the breakdown of closed revenue across one of five account variables. You can see the closed revenue by Account Type, State, Region, Industry, or Annual Revenue Tier. This report also provides navigation to the Account By Sales Rep report.

Service

The prebuilt reports in the Service section examine the Service Request object in CRM On Demand. You will find that the design of these reports is very similar in concept to the reports in the other sections of the prebuilt reports. There is a heavy use of the column selector view, and the overall design of the reports is simple and quite focused.

Service Analysis

The Service Analysis report is one of the many simple yet extremely insightful reports among the prebuilt reports. The report itself contains only two columns. The metric column that this report analyzes is the number of service requests, and with the column selector view, you are able to view this data by User Name, Industry, Area, Source, Region, or Priority. This report uses the active Service Request History Analytics subject area, so the data returned is current as of the previous day.

Service Report List

This is a quick list report that provides a table displaying SR Number, Source, Status, Priority, Account Name, Date, and Fiscal Year for each user. You will find this report listed in the Service section on the Reports tab, but if you want to open the report in Answers, you need to look in the Quick Lists folder.

This report would be a good candidate for a pivot table. Of course, you might want to add a metric column. You can use a pivot table view, for example, to group the data differently or to provide counts for each user across source. Pivot tables add an almost infinite set of possibilities. Learn more about pivot tables in Chapter 12.

Current Service Request Aging Analysis

The Current Service Request Aging Analysis report provides a visual analysis of how long the currently open service requests have been open. You can see this data grouped by source, priority, or area. I would like to use this report to illustrate a couple of points. First, notice that the metric column in this report is Avg Open SR Age. This column does not exist in the functional CRM On Demand database. You will not see this column exposed on any layout in the application. The column exists only in Answers as a calculated field.

In addition, if you examine the filter used on this report you will see a session variable there named NQ_SESSION.SR_OPEN. This system variable is one of many. You will not find a complete list documented in the Online Help. Having command of all the system variables is not necessary to be a successful reports developer. You can calculate all the system variable values using other functions in column formulas. You may see system variables in predefined reports, and I document some of them for you in this book.

Open Service Request Analysis

The Open Service Request Analysis report is similar to the Current Service Request Aging Analysis report, except that this report is concerned with the number of open service requests rather than how long they have been open. You can see how many open service requests there are by User Name, Source, Priority, or Area. This report also uses the NQ_SESSION.SR_OPEN system variable. You can just as easily filter on the Status column, including only the open service requests.

Number of Service Request Analysis

The Number of Service Request Analysis report is almost exactly like the Service Analysis report. This report also contains two columns. The metric column that this report analyzes is also the number of service requests, and with the column selector view, you are able to view this data by User Name, Status, Area, Source, or Priority. This report draws from the active Service Request History subject area, so the data returned is current as of the previous day.

Team Service Analysis

Like the other "Team" reports, this one provides managers a means for examining a number of different metrics for each of their subordinates. You may need to remove the Manager Email column filter to see data in this report if you are not a service manager. Managers are able to see the average age of open service requests, the number of open service requests, the number of closed service requests, the number of pending service requests, the number of cancelled service requests, and the number of service requests regardless of status for each of their subordinates.

Notice that the report filters to show only direct reports by including only those records where the reporting level is "0."

Marketing Effectiveness

You use the prebuilt reports in this final group to analyze your marketing data. These reports focus primarily on campaign records, but rely on relationships between campaigns and leads and opportunities to determine how effective campaigns are. The Marketing Effectiveness reports are also a treasure trove of interesting report elements. Dig into them and you will see many undocumented session variables, use of images with conditional data, multiple layers of navigation, and the use of narrative report views.

You will find that beyond the nine reports listed on the Reports tab, when you look inside the Marketing Effectiveness folder from Answers, there are a dozen additional reports. These reports make up the dashboards targeted by the navigation links in the listed reports. I encourage you to explore these reports from within the CRM On Demand user interface as well as with Answers.

Active Campaign Status

The Active Campaign Status report examines all of your currently active campaigns and allows you to view statistics on those campaigns. There is a wealth of information available through this report. The metrics available here are Return on Investment (ROI), Cost Per Lead, Lead Conversion Rate, Cost Per Closed Sale, Opportunity Win Rate, Opportunity Revenue, Closed Revenue, Number of Wins, Number of Opportunities, and Number of Leads.

This report also has navigation built into the Campaign Name column that takes you to a dashboard containing a number of other campaign reports. You will also notice that the filters include a session variable named NQ_SESSION.ACTIVE_CAMPAIGN. This variable obviously limits the data to only those campaigns that are active. You can easily accomplish this with a filter on the status column that identifies all of the appropriate active status values.

Another interesting feature of this report is the dynamic sort ability on the ROI column. You can provide users with this dynamic sorting ability on columns in a table by enabling the sort on the Table View.

Completed Campaign Results

The Completed Campaign Results report examines all of your closed campaigns and allows you to view statistics on those campaigns. This is the same report as the Active Campaign Status report for your closed campaigns. The metrics included in this report, like the previous report, are Return on Investment (ROI), Cost Per Lead, Lead Conversion Rate, Cost Per Closed Sale,

Opportunity Win Rate, Opportunity Revenue, Closed Revenue, Number of Wins, Number of Opportunities, and Number of Leads.

This report also navigates to a dashboard containing a number of other campaign reports. One of the filters in this report compares the Status field with the session variable NQ_SESSION. COMPLETED_CAMPAIGN. This variable is the inverse of the variable used in the active report, and limits the data to only those campaigns that are not active.

Campaign Effectiveness By Campaign Name

The report that you are able to open in Answers is a simple table report that lists completed activities organized by type and shows metrics for each. The metrics include Actual Cost, Number of Leads, Number of Opportunities, Number of Wins, Closed Revenue, Cost Per Lead, Cost Per Closed Sale, and Return on Investment. Clicking a campaign name in this report will navigate you to the same dashboard that the previous two reports target.

If you run this same report from the Reports tab, you will notice that there is more than meets the eye compared to looking at the design of the report. Running this report exposes a number of additional embedded reports, many of which are described individually further down this list. The report makes use of a dashboard view that is currently only available on the Dashboard tab for your custom dashboards.

Campaign Effectiveness By Campaign Type

This report is the same as the Campaign Effectiveness By Campaign Name report with the Campaign Name column removed. The navigation on this report is on the Campaign Type column. This report is also quite different when run from the Reports tab.

Lead Followup Analysis

Use this report to analyze the status of your leads dated within the last 90 days. The report displays the number of leads within each stage by Fiscal Year, Fiscal Half Year, Fiscal Quarter and Year, Fiscal Month and Year, Fiscal Week and Year, Lead Owner, or Sales Person based on a selection from the column selector.

Examine the filter on this prebuilt report and you will see a great example of the TIMESTAMPADD function along with the CAST and CURRENT_DATE functions. Detailed information on these functions is provided in upcoming chapters, but in summary, this filter limits data to dates between the current date minus 90 days and the current date.

The data table on the report is not a regular table. This report uses a pivot table to group the measurements into columns for each status value. The pivot table view is the most versatile of all views in Answers On Demand, which you will discover in Chapter 12.

Lead Source Analysis

The Lead Source Analysis report displays the number of leads dated within the last 90 days organized by source, lead owner, sales person, or campaign name. This report also uses the TIMESTAMPADD filter to limit data to the past 90 days.

Opportunity Source Analysis By Close Date

The Opportunity Source Analysis By Close Date report analyzes opportunities that closed in the previous 90 days. You are able to see the number of opportunities by lead source, campaign name, owner, or territory.

Opportunity Source Analysis By Create Date

The Opportunity Source Analysis By Create Date report analyzes opportunities with a create date within the previous 90 days. You are able to see the number of opportunities by lead source, campaign name, owner, or territory.

Projected Revenue

You will not find the Projected Revenue report on the Reports tab. This report is a subreport that is part of another report. This report shows revenue data based on leads created in the last 90 days, and compares lead potential revenue to actual closed opportunity revenue.

The report filter uses the TIMESTAMPDIFF function to limit the number of days between lead creation and the last data refresh.

Campaign Activity

This report provides a line graph of number of leads, number of new opportunities, and number of wins by fiscal week. You will find this chart embedded in other prebuilt reports; it is visible when you run those reports from the Reports tab.

Campaign Averages

This small report simply calculates the average time it takes to convert a lead and close an opportunity and the average revenue amount. The interesting element in this report is the use of conditional formatting to include a small flag icon next to the values in the columns.

Campaign Detailed Results

This report is nothing more than a narrative view designed to display a campaign name as part of one of the dashboard-style reports described earlier.

Campaign Leads

This report provides a bar chart that graphs the number of leads by lead status. This report is also part of the dashboard reports described earlier.

Campaign Opportunities

The Campaign Opportunities report is another one of those simple reports that serves as an element of the dashboard reports. This report contains a bar chart that graphs the number of opportunities by sales stage.

Campaign Revenue

The Campaign Revenue report contains a bar chart that graphs revenue by opportunity sales stage.

Campaign Performance Summary—Averages

This report provides 16 separate averages using session variables in the formula for each column. The metrics provided are averages of actual campaign cost, budgeted campaign cost, percentage of budget, number of leads, lead conversion rate, cost per lead, number of leads targeted, percentage of leads achieved, revenue target, percentage of revenue target achieved, opportunity revenue, closed revenue, return on investment percentage, number of wins, opportunity win rate, and cost per closed sale.

Lead Conversion Metrics

The Lead Conversion Metrics report provides a table with conditional formatting that displays the number of accounts, contacts, leads, and opportunities for campaigns.

Accounts List, Contact List, Lead Lists, and Opportunity Lists

The List reports in the Marketing Effectiveness folder provide basic tables designed to list the accounts, contacts, leads, or opportunities associated with a particular campaign. You will find these reports embedded in other dashboard-style reports.

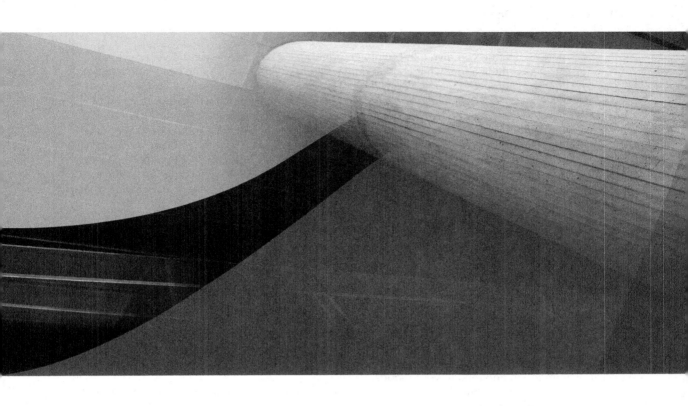

CHAPTER
2

Planning Your Reports

efore you dive into building reports, take a step back, take a deep breath, and think about what you are doing. The Analytics pool is quite deep, and without proper planning, you will quickly find yourself drowning in columns, fields, views, calculations, charts, and interactivity. So often, we receive that call to produce something quickly for that executive meeting that should have started ten minutes ago. Sometimes we have no choice but to dive in and hope for the best. My hope with this chapter is to prepare you for those times when you do have time to plan. I believe that once you become skilled at planning reports, you will find yourself anticipating reporting needs and producing powerful and meaningful business intelligence before it becomes an emergency.

Planning and Report Validity

Like most creative processes, creating great reports takes a little planning. The array of features and functions in Answers On Demand is vast. This book will certainly help you master those features, but knowing how to create column formulas, complex filters, impressive charts, and highly interactive elements within your reports will not guarantee a report that is informative, useful, or effective.

This chapter examines the effort that you should make before beginning your report-building work. I encourage you to consider the advice in this chapter carefully. Having built many reports, and in teaching others how to build reports, I have found that these initial steps pay dividends in time and effort. If you do not take the time to plan your reporting effort, you are likely to need time to redesign and rebuild your reports.

Whether you are building reports for yourself or at the request of someone else, it is important to have a complete understanding of the report's purpose. Reporting without direction or reason is usually a fruitless effort. Reports should answer a business question. How much revenue did each sales team generate last month? What is the average service request volume by product type? What percentage of my customers is located in Texas? Having a question in mind and identifying what you need in order to answer that question will better enable you to build effective custom analyses using Answers On Demand that meet the unique reporting needs of your company.

Proper planning leads to report validity. There are different types of validity, all of which are affected by planning. A great report has the following:

- **Face validity** A report that has face validity looks like it measures what you intend to measure. The purpose of face validity is to win acceptance among report users. Users are likely to reject a report if they do not recognize the report as a valid measurement instrument that answers a business question. The question the report answers should be obvious to the user, and the report should clearly deliver the answer. Face validity alone does not make for a valid report. After all, a report can appear to be valid without actually delivering accurate data.

- **Content validity** A report achieves content validity when a subject matter expert reviews the report and certifies that it measures and reports the correct data. Someone intimately familiar with the data should review the report and validate the results. Proper planning and consideration of content validity before building a report helps to ensure that the content of your report is what it needs to be. Identifying the empirical data to include in the report is, of course, critical. An oft-overlooked element is how your user will use that data to make judgments and draw conclusions. Perhaps you will even find it is possible to automate those decisions within the report itself based on these criteria. Any time you can transform qualitative information into valid quantitative report data, you add value to your report. More than anything else, a report with content validity ties directly to your business question.

■ **Construct validity**   A report has construct validity (my personal favorite) when it is formatted in such a way that it delivers the intended message in as accurate and useful a way as possible. It is the "quality of quantity" principal applied to reporting. A great report does not need to employ every flashy feature. Excessive formatting usually distracts from the data rather than clearly delivering the report's intended message. As you saw with many of the prebuilt reports in Chapter 1, simple reports containing only the information required can be very useful and very powerful business tools. Charts and graphs should be simple and focused. Several views, each with a single objective, are more effective than a single view that attempts to deliver on multiple objectives at once.

Construct validity is not just about keeping your reports simple. You must also take care to identify the correct data elements. Verifying that you are targeting the most relevant data and the data required to answer the business question is critical to construct validity. If you do not start with the correct data elements, it hardly matters how you format the report. No matter how engaging and well designed your report layouts are, if the report does not provide an answer to the business question, it has failed, and is not valid.

■ **Predictive validity**   The holy grail of report validity is predictive validity. When your report has the ability to accurately predict future results, it is exhibiting predictive validity. This is often the goal of historical reporting. A report on the average win rate versus the win rate over the last few quarters may exhibit an ability to predict the win rate over the next few quarters. Predictive reports are extremely difficult to design. With so many variables affecting business outcomes, to accurately predict results is closer to impossible than we would like to admit. If a predictive quality in your report is a goal, you may want to seek the assistance of someone who has a degree in mathematics, actuarial science, statistics, or a business-related discipline such as economics, finance, or accounting.

You likely are beginning to sense how difficult it would be to build a valid report without a little planning. Before you can design and build a report, you need a plan. This plan begins as a question that you want to answer using the data in the CRM On Demand database.

First, you need to identify your business question. Developing reports without having first identified the business question is inefficient, and often ineffective. I have mentioned this repeatedly. It is not enough, however, to simply answer the question. A report is a business tool that you need to carefully design for a specific job. This takes planning.

I will illustrate this planning effort in the form of four questions that you should ask about every report that you build:

■ Why do you need a report?

■ How will you use this report?

■ Who will use the report?

■ What should the report contain?

Why Do You Need a Report?

This seems like such a simple question, one that someone requesting a report should answer easily. The answer, however, is often not so clear. Performing a simple needs analysis to determine the need for a report will save you the time and effort involved in creating reports that will not get much or any use. It is easy to lose sight of your objective in the excitement of having so much data at your disposal in CRM On Demand. Too often, report developers answer the call to create reports because they can, not because there is a real need for a report.

I encourage you to question requests for reports to separate the "wants" from the "needs," even if that means you risk appearing hard to get along with. Ideally, all of your reports will support a specific business goal and answer a specific business question. If you are unable to identify these things, you do not have a legitimate need for your report.

Let us look at two different reports as an example. Suppose the marketing manager requests a report of the campaigns closed over the last 12 months. She wants to see the actual costs and the revenue generated from those campaigns, grouped by campaign type. When you ask this marketing manager why she needs such a report, she explains that the board has asked for a marketing plan for the next year, and she wants to maximize the return by making marketing channel decisions based on past performance.

This request certainly sounds legitimate. You have a clear business question and business goal. "Which campaigns were the most successful over the last 12 months?" The marketing department measures success of their campaigns by comparing cost and revenue.

You receive another request, this time from the service manager. He wants to have a real-time report that displays the number of service requests opened each week, organized by department. This initially sounds like a legitimate request. When you ask him why he needs this report, his justification is that he likes to know how many requests the department opens. Digging a little more, you find out that the company evaluates service representatives on the number of issues closed by priority. The risk of creating this report is that the service manager will soon stop using the report because there is no real value in it, or he will make business decisions based on the wrong data.

You may not be in a position to challenge every report request, but as a report developer, you certainly should be able to make some recommendations. I would like to offer you some strategies for working with superfluous report requests. Depending on the personalities you are working with, and your corporate environment, you may want to try one or more of these.

- **Redirect the request by making suggestions of your own** Do not be afraid to say something if you have an idea for a report that appears to fit the business requirements better than the report the requestor suggested. Often, the person making the request does not fully understand what is and is not possible with Reports in CRM On Demand. As the report developer, you have valuable knowledge to offer. Other times, someone may request a report just because it is flashy or looks impressive.

- **Develop or sketch out alternatives** It is usually easier to describe ideas when you can show someone the idea. It is also easier to understand what the individual making the request is looking for if you collaborate over a sketch. If there is truly no need for the report, and you are unable to redirect the request to a more useful alternative, explain why you think the report is not necessary. Recommend some alternatives such as using a custom list in CRM On Demand or using the printer-friendly link on a record to send the data to a printer. You might be surprised at how often a printout of a single record from the database will satisfy a "reporting" need.

Another very powerful tool that often helps people put their needs in perspective is the use of measurable objectives. Asking those who request reports to express their needs in measurable objectives tends to provide perspective for both you and the one requesting the report. The next section discusses this in more detail.

Finally, it is important to admit that it is not always possible to say "no" or suggest other options. In these times, you may need to go ahead and create a report that you are sure is unnecessary. When this happens, offer to follow up with the person who requested the report in a couple of months to see that it is still meeting the needs. This approach appears impressively proactive and gives the report user time to really evaluate the usefulness of the report.

How Will You Use This Report?

This question is twofold. You are asking about both physical use of the report and cognitive use of the report. Printing and mailing a report is physical use. Making marketing decisions is an example of cognitive use. Both of these have a profound impact on your report design. By conducting a little analysis before you begin building your report, you will spend less time struggling with design decisions and revising reports that do not fit the needs of your business.

Physical Use

Regarding the physical use of your report, there are several different options, and each option has implications. Users of CRM On Demand can view reports online, print reports, save reports as a PDF or HTML file, and download the data from reports to Microsoft Excel, a text file, or an HTML file. Each option is described in turn next.

Online Reports

Viewing reports online may seem like an obvious thing to a user of CRM On Demand. After all, there is some form of analytics on almost every homepage and an entire tab dedicated to nothing but reports. This use of reports, however, is a very important characteristic that the report developer needs to consider when designing a new report. There are features of analytics specifically designed for online use that would be pointless in a report that is only used offline.

- **Page size and line breaks** With a report that your users will view online, you do not need to worry too much about page size and page breaks. A report that stretches beyond the margins of the computer screen will have scroll bars.

NOTE
The report elements that I mention in this section are all described in detail in this book. I offer much more detail on their use in future chapters.

- **Drill downs** Many columns have drill-down interactivity by default. These columns allow users to click a value to further filter a report. It is also possible to change the default interactivity settings to add drill-down capability to your report. This interactivity is only available online.

- **Navigation** Another interactivity setting that you obviously can take advantage of only while online is the navigational interaction. With the navigational interactivity setting on a column, you have the ability to move from the active report to another report. The value that you click on the active report passes to the target report as a filter value.

- **Action link**   Another navigational element that you can take advantage of with online reports is the action link. Using the custom ActionLink class, you are able to create a hyperlink in a column that navigates the user to the detail screen for the clicked value.

In addition to the navigational features of online reports, there are several report layout views impacted by your decision to design a report for online use. Most of the prebuilt reports feature the Column Selector view. The Column Selector view enables the report user to choose which columns to view in the analysis. As the report developer, you determine which columns to make available. This view is obviously interactive only on the online reports.

Another view that is rather pointless outside of an online report is the Ticker view. A Ticker view scrolls data across the report. The Ticker view will only perform as designed when you view the report online.

Some views have elements that work best when online. You can, and often should, use these views on your reports even when the reports are not designed specifically for online use. The page selector on the pivot table view allows report users to select a value from a column placed in this section. The pivot table limits the values in the view to the data related to the selected page. This is but one element of the pivot table view. If you do not need to provide users with this ability, then online use of the report has no bearing on your decision to use a pivot table view.

The chart property that causes the chart values and value names to appear when you place your mouse cursor over the chart element is only effective online. This does not preclude you from using the chart view on other types of reports.

Clearly, there are some great interactive elements available for your CRM On Demand reports. When you are designing a report that users will view exclusively online, you have the ability to make your analysis more dynamic and personalized with these interactive options. It would be unusual for a company to have a set of reports that are never printed or downloaded. Think about how printing your report affects these interactive elements.

Printed Reports

When you design a report for printing, you have some other considerations. Rather than focus on how the interactivity affects your reports, as with online reports, you need to consider the implications of printing a report. Printing a report is akin to taking a snapshot. The printed report is a frozen image of your data. You still want that image to be useful, so you need to make some design decisions to maximize that potential usefulness.

When you know that you are designing a report for print, you want to consider what that report will look like when it rolls off the printer. You need to think about page margins and orientation. How will page breaks affect your report? You may find that you need to manually set column widths to keep tables on a single page.

Give some thought to colors and shading in your report. While colors may look great online, when a report is printed, they can render the report unreadable if poorly designed. Consider using a shading pattern rather than color for one-color printing of charts. Conditional formats (color changes based on data values) is another area that can cause problems with printing.

There are other considerations beyond readability of printed reports. When you run a report online, you can be certain that you are seeing current information. When you pick up a printed report, you may not have the same confidence. Consider adding a date or time stamp to your reports. You can show the date or date and time for a report within the title view or with a session variable.

You also need to consider the nature of the data you are exposing on your report. Is the information sensitive? Should the user shred this report within a specified period, or retain the report for a particular length of time? Is the report for internal or external use? Using a static text or narrative view on your report, you can provide instructions, a confidentiality statement, copyright, or any other text that you would like to include on the printed report.

As discussed for online reports, several interactive elements allow users to filter data or select the data on the report that they want to see. These elements are still effective for reports destined for the printer. The users just have to be sure to select options prior to printing. If you need to provide for user-controlled filtering of a report, but want to avoid adding drop-down fields to your report, consider setting up column filter prompts. These prompts allow users to make decisions about the data to include in their report without affecting the report layout.

Saved Reports

Online and print reports probably comprise a majority of your reports. There are, however, other options to consider. Suppose you are designing a report that users will save and retain. What about a report that users will attach to email messages? Many of the print considerations apply. One consideration may be the ability to modify the report after saving it. The Print view provides an option for PDF format or HTML format. If a user selects HTML format and saves the file, the user can edit and change the saved file. When a user selects PDF format and saves a copy of the report, it saves as a PDF file, which is not editable.

If this is a concern for your company, you need to consider access to your custom reports carefully. You do not have the ability to disallow saving the report or downloading the report. For this reason, it is best to restrict access to reports that are this sensitive.

Another common use of saved reports is inclusion of the report in presentations. Often managers will want reports to embed in their executive presentations, for example, to present business data to executives, partners, customers, investors, and employees. If this is the purpose of your report, consider keeping the report very simple. For example, add a chart view to your report and remove all other views. The user can then access the print view and save the report to create a chart file that they can embed into their presentation or document files.

Downloaded Reports

Finally, downloading data is a very common use of CRM On Demand reports. Users download report data for a number of different reasons. Users may be interested in opening the resulting data file in a spreadsheet program to further manipulate the data, performing offline analysis. Users may want to import the data into a table of another database application.

When you download a report from CRM On Demand, the only element of the report that downloads is the data table. That fact alone eliminates the need for any other views. The data table probably does not need much formatting, if any at all, since the data is destined for another file format.

If users plan to import the data into another application, be sure to identify any data requirements of the target application. Things to consider are column order, field length, number formats, date and time formats, column header names, and sort order. It is also important to ensure that the rows are not grouping. Set each column to repeat values in order to eliminate blanks.

Determining how your users intend to physically use the reports you create clearly gives you a lot of direction and certainly sets some parameters for your report development. Of course, you need to also give some thought to the way your users are planning to use the data within the report.

Cognitive Use

Now that you know what the users plan to physically do with the report, it is important to know what sort of decisions the report will influence. You may find that well-defined business objectives are helpful with this analysis. When answering the question "why do you need the report?" it makes perfect sense to put together some measurable objectives.

If a user plans to use a report to realign territories based on volume, for instance, it is helpful to express this in some sort of measurable objective. "I need to identify the average volume of sales for each territory, broken down by state, in order to realign territories into five territories, each with 20 percent of the average volume." This is a very useful objective. Now, you know that you need sales volume data grouped by territory and state within each territory.

Suppose a user is interested in a sales revenue report to determine bonus amounts for each sales team. This seems like a straightforward request. Now consider the reports you would build based on each of the next two objectives:

- I need to identify the sales teams that met the team sales quota in order to distribute the bonus pool evenly across qualified teams.

- I need to identify and rank the sales volumes for each sales team in order to distribute the bonus pool according to the overall percentage of total volume across all sales teams.

The reports you build to satisfy these objectives would be very different.

What should you do if it is difficult to write a measurable objective? While it is preferable to work toward a very specific and measurable objective, the reality of the business world does not always fall so neatly into place. It is not unusual to receive a report request third or fourth hand. Often the report request passes from senior management to middle management to the report developer. For example, the best objective you might get could be something like this: "I need a report to summarize our business unit's quarterly activity to executive management." You have to work with the information you have at your disposal, and you cannot expect to get everything you need laid out for you so precisely. My favorite strategy for overcoming a lack of detail is the sketch. Ask the person requesting the report to sketch out what he or she has in mind for the report. This often exposes those expectations that you need to understand to develop a useful report.

Who Will Use the Report?

Knowing the users of the report is as important as knowing what they plan to do with the report. You will design a report differently for different users. For instance, a report for all users of CRM On Demand is likely quite different from a report for your business partners. A report designed for you will be different from a report designed for the officers of the company. Among the design considerations are level of data access, volume of data based on that access, type of information included, and the detail granularity of that information.

Let us consider a simple opportunity list report that displays some key details of opportunities visible to the sales employee running the report. A report of this kind may contain very useful information for a sales representative, but that same report would likely contain too much information for a senior-level sales manager who has visibility to all of the opportunities across all of the sales teams.

Consider also the type of information that you include in a report. At the risk of applying a stereotype, most senior-level executives do not have a need or interest in the minutia of every record in the database. These individuals tend to prefer summary data. I would even venture that these individuals will often prefer a visual chart that reflects the data to seeing actual numbers in a table. On the other end of the data granularity spectrum, we have our team leaders, the operational managers. These individuals need the details in order to make day-to-day decisions that keep the customers happy.

There is also a difference in the information you include on a report for internal use and one destined for public display. You would not likely send a detailed report about your accounts and contacts outside the company, but you may display a chart of the percentage of customers you serve in each industry.

A safe position to take regarding report design is to always assume that your report will be printed and left on the copier at the local 24-hour copier establishment. If you have any concern about data privacy, consider the design of your report, who is going to have access to that report, and what they are likely to do with that report.

Chapter 17 looks at organizing reports into folders and limiting access to those folders. This is a good way to ensure that the only people who *can* access a report are those who *should* access the report. It does not keep those individuals from leaving a printout of the report in the copier, but it is a start.

What Should the Report Contain?

Now that you have a handle on who the users are and how they intend to use the report, you can begin to think about getting the correct data into the report. This is more complicated than you might think. To make the decisions necessary to populate your report with the correct data, you need to consider which type of subject area to use, Analytics or Reporting, which subject area contains the fields you need, the data visibility implications, and, finally, which columns to include.

Analytics Subject Area Versus Reporting Subject Area

The first choice here is whether to use a subject area from the Analytics list or from the Reporting list. In most cases, an Analytics subject area is the best choice. In general, these subject areas result in better report performance and provide a more complete dataset with which to work. The only thing gained from using a Reporting subject area is that it offers real-time data. If you must have real-time data in your report, you must use a subject area from the Reporting section. Table 2-1 compares the pros and cons of the two types of subject areas.

Selecting a Subject Area

Before you begin building your report, you should give some thought to the most appropriate subject area for the report. You typically want to use a subject area that reflects the main topic of your report—that is, the thing you intend to measure.

The best subject area is not always obvious, and may require some trial and error depending on the details you want in your report. Consider a report that shows the amount of revenue generated by each sales team last month. Depending on the data you need, you could use one of the Analytics subject areas: Opportunity History, Opportunity-Product History, or Pipeline History.

	Analytics	**Reporting**
Pros	Better performance More complete dataset available Additional metric columns available	Up-to-the-minute data if needed
Cons	Data created or modified since the last overnight data update is not available for reporting	Much slower performance Data changes constantly, resulting in different report results for different people at different times

TABLE 2-1. *Pros and Cons of Analytics and Reporting Subject Areas*

Sometimes the best subject area is obvious, but depends on how current the data needs to be. A report that shows the average service request volume by product type might use the Service Request History (Analytics) or Service Requests (Reporting) subject area.

Determining Data Visibility

Different users may see different data in the same reports due to the rules that govern analytics visibility. There are several visibility controls in place in CRM On Demand. Users see data in reports based on their role privileges, shared folder role associations, Analytics Visibility settings in the user and company profiles, and the book or user selected in the Book of Business Look In selector field.

The Access All Data in Analytics role privilege overrides all other visibility settings and provides the user with complete visibility to all of the data in the entire organization, including records marked Private. If the user role does not have this privilege, the Analytics Visibility setting specified in the company or user profile determines which data the user sees in reports.

The Manage Custom Reports privilege provides access to create custom reports. With this privilege, a user has access to Answers On Demand and the ability to publish reports to a personal report folder and to the Company Wide Shared Folder. To provide access to create personal custom reports, but not shared reports, the user needs the Manage Personal Reports privilege.

When you associate a role to a shared folder, only users assigned to the role have access to the reports saved in that folder. Users with the Manage Custom Reports privilege or the Access All Data in Analytics privilege are still able to access these restricted folders.

The Analytics Visibility setting within the company and user profiles affects visibility for all other users in the organization. This setting is available on both the company and user profiles. If the user profile does not have this setting defined on a user's profile, then the company profile setting applies.

The Analytics Visibility setting has three available settings:

- **Manager visibility** Allows users to see their own data and all the data directly owned by their subordinates, including records marked private.

- **Team visibility** Allows users to see their own data and all data shared with them by membership in account and opportunity teams and through group assignment.

- **Full visibility** Affects only historical reports, and combines Manager and Team Visibility.

If you are using the Full Visibility setting, the Book of Business feature allows additional control of which data you see in reports. Use the Look In selector on the report pages to restrict, or filter, the data to the selected book and any subbooks. This feature is only available to users assigned to one or more books of business. If the user has added another user to their Delegated User list, the delegated user can select the username from the Look In selector to see report data for that user. The delegated user does not gain a higher level of visibility through delegation. In other words, a user who does not have manager visibility does not gain manager visibility when delegated to by a user with that level of access.

Locating Columns for Your Report

The next step in designing the report is to think about what specific data columns you need in the report. It is often tempting to include "everything" or "as much as possible" but this is risky. You can easily lose sight of the question you are trying to answer by cluttering the report with nonessential data. Return to the business question and think about what data is essential to answering the question.

It is not unusual to refine your question at this point, now that you are beginning to see what the report contains and which data elements are available. Remember that the goal is to build a report that answers the question, not to come up with a question that fits your report.

Folders within each subject area contain the data columns. Folders represent data on the primary object and related objects. Usually, the correct folder can be identified using some simple logic, but you may have to do some searching if it is not obvious where the data would be held.

Column order is roughly the same order as appears on your default layouts. Custom fields are included in subfolders by field category. Measured data (or metrics) are available in the Metrics folder for the subject area. The Metrics folder is always at the end of the list, and contains not columns, but some common calculations based on numerical fields.

You may find it very useful, especially for more complex analysis, to sketch your report out on paper before you begin building it in Answers. As you become more familiar with Answers and report building, this may not be as necessary, but still having a clear picture of what your question is and what the report that answers that question looks like will save you time and frustration as you build the report.

If you are building a report for someone else, having that person sketch their idea out will often lead you to a refinement of the business question and help you both determine the best design for the report before digging into the details of building a report.

Without that question to guide you, you can get lost in all of the fantastic features of Answers and end up creating a report that has no business use.

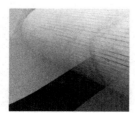

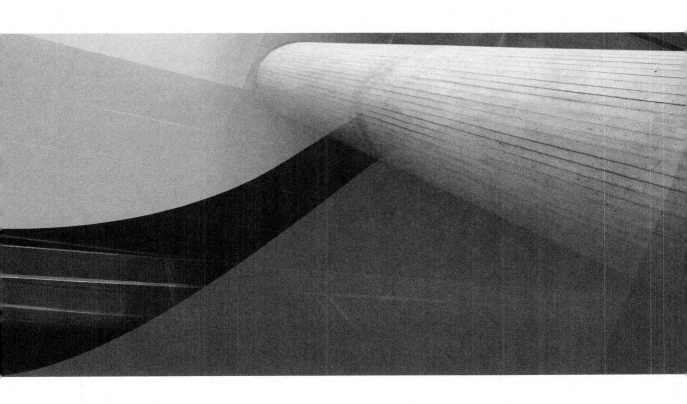

CHAPTER
3

Formatting and Sorting
Report Data

n this chapter, you begin developing reports by learning how to add, format, and sort columns. By this point in the report development process, you have identified the purpose and use of your report. One universal truth to report development, particularly for a new user of CRM On Demand, is to not fear the trial-and-error method. First, you will not damage any data in your On Demand database by playing with reports. Secondly, the more you poke around in the reporting area, the more you will learn and develop your own reporting style. This book can give you the specifics on how to build a report, but style is all up to you.

Build and View Analyses

The first step is to open Answers On Demand. To access Answers On Demand, navigate to the Reports tab and click the Design Analysis link. This action opens the Getting Started with Answers window (examined in Chapter 1). Click the subject area you selected for your report, which opens the Build and View Analysis window, shown in Figure 3-1.

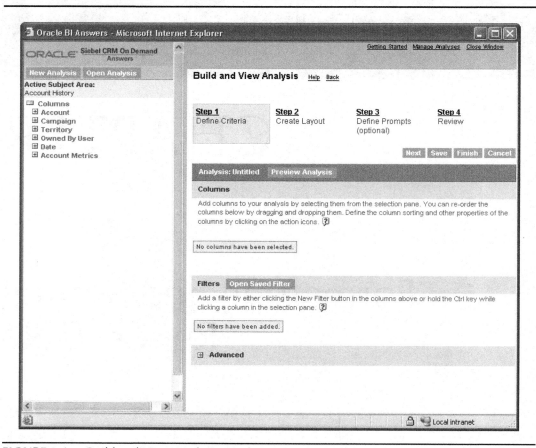

FIGURE 3-1. *Build and View Analysis window*

Let us take a moment to examine the Build and View Analysis window. In the upper-left corner, you see the current subject area identified (which is the Account History Analytics subject area in Figure 3-1). Below the subject area name are all the columns available within the subject area. You will find each column listed inside one of the folders in this tree view. The folder names refer to the source data table of the enclosed columns or the type of columns it contains. For instance, you will always find the Metrics folder at the bottom of this list. The columns inside this folder are calculated metric columns and do not come from a specific data table in the database or data warehouse.

Across the very top of the Build and View Analysis window, you see three links. The Getting Started link returns you to the Getting Started window. The Manage Analyses link takes you to the Manage Analyses window (discussed in Chapter 17). The Close Window link simply closes the Build and View Analysis window.

The Preview Analysis button located in the header below the step number indicators allows you to have a look at your report in its current state. You will find yourself using this preview function frequently. When you click this button, a new window opens and generates your report. This is very helpful as you experiment with different formatting and column arrangements.

In the main body of the window, you see that we are on the first of four steps. As you move through the report development process, you will progress through these steps. Clicking the Next button moves you to the next step in the process. The Save button allows you to save your current report edits without closing the report. The Finish button also allows you to save the report, but then closes the report and returns you to the Getting Started window. The Cancel button allows you to exit from the current report without saving any changes you have made.

The Columns section of the window is where columns that you add to the report will appear. Once you add columns to the report, you can configure exactly how you want the data in those columns to appear in your report. The Filters section shows all of the active filters affecting your report. Finally, the Advanced section allows you to combine two or more reports.

NOTE
Chapter 4 discusses filtering data, and Chapter 15 covers combining reports.

Adding Columns

Chapter 2 discussed the necessity of determining what data should go into your report. It is important to know this in order to select the correct subject area for your report. Choosing a subject area is usually easier than identifying and locating the columns for your report.

Within each subject area, folders contain the available columns. Once you understand the organizational system at work here, finding the columns for your report will be a little easier. The columns that appear through the CRM On Demand user interface are listed in folders by the name of the source table. The columns in the Owned By User folder are from the Employee table. There are also two special folders below these record type folders. The columns located in the Date and Metrics folders are not fields in the database. Answers On Demand calculates these columns for reporting.

The Date folder contains a variety of calculated dates. You will find columns for fiscal and calendar year quarters, months, weeks, and days. The Metrics folder contains additional calculated fields based on the record type.

Once you locate a column that you want to include in your analysis, simply click the column name to add the column to the report. The column will appear in the Columns section of the Build and View Analysis window. Each column has a table heading and a column heading. For example, as shown in Figure 3-2, if you add the Account Name column to your report, the top heading is Account and refers to the table name. The second heading on the column is Account Name, referencing the column name. (You can change these headings, as you will soon learn.) The Answers On Demand tool will do some automatic grouping of the columns as you add them to your report. For instance, if I continued to add columns, adding the full name of the primary contact first, and then the account location, the Location column appears in the second position rather than the third. Since the Account Name and Location columns are both from the Account table, Answers On Demand automatically arranges them together, as shown in Figure 3-2. You can change the order of the columns by clicking and dragging. Click the column heading and drag to move just that column. Click the table heading and drag to move all of the columns under that heading at once.

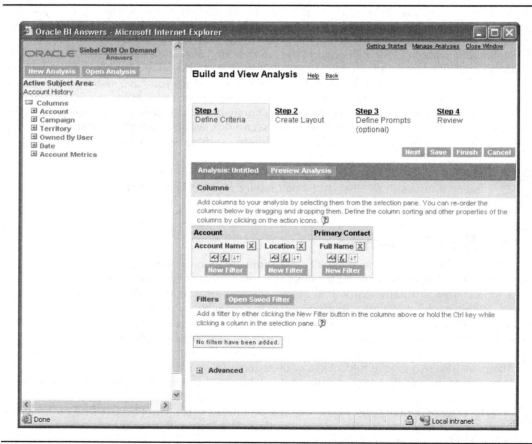

FIGURE 3-2.   *Account columns grouped under the Account table heading*

It is possible to add multiple instances of the same column to your report. You will find yourself doing this quite a lot, actually, when you begin editing column formulae. To remove a column from your analysis, click the X button next to the column name.

Formatting Columns

Once you have columns added to your analysis, you can begin formatting those columns. If at any point you want to see how the table looks with your formatting, click the Preview Analysis button to run the report. Before I begin discussing the formatting options, look at the three buttons under the column name of each column. The button on the left, which bears an icon of a hand, is the Column Properties button. The center button, which has the letters fx on it, is the Edit Formula button. The right button, with the up and down arrows, is the Order By button. If you have trouble remembering what these buttons are, move your mouse pointer over each one to see pop-up text of the button name.

This section discusses use of the Column Properties button, and the "Sorting Columns" section later in the chapter discusses use of the Order By button. (The Edit Formula button is introduced in Chapter 4.) When you click the Column Properties button, the Column Properties window opens. As you can see in Figure 3-3, this window contains four tabs—Style, Column Format, Data Format, and Conditional Format. The following sections examine in turn each of these tabs and the formatting options available on each.

FIGURE 3-3. *Column Properties window—Style tab*

Style Tab

The Style tab of the Column Properties window allows you to make decisions about the way the fonts and table cells appear on your report. The font settings available here allow you to set the font family, size, color, style, and effects. The default font is 10-point Arial and the color is black with regular styling and no effects.

Your font options are Arial, Arial Black, Arial Narrow, Courier New, Garamond, Lucida Sans Unicode, Microsoft Sans Serif, Times New Roman, Tahoma, and Verdana. If your company has a standard for which fonts to use, you may want to select a font for your reports that adheres to this standard.

To change the font color, click the white box to open the color selector. There are 48 standard colors available from which to choose. Alternatively, if you know the HTML color code for your desired color, you can enter # and the six-digit code in the field at the bottom of the color selector pop-up menu. This is true for all of the color options throughout Answers On Demand, enabling you to match your company colors precisely. You may also make your font bold, italic, or both using the Style field. The available effects are underlined and strikethrough.

Within the Cell section of the Style tab, you are able to apply horizontal and vertical alignment and add a background color to the cell. The default horizontal alignment is left for text fields and right for numeric data. The default vertical alignment is center. To apply a background color, click the white box next to Background Color and select the desired color. Also available here is an option to include an image in the cell. Bear in mind that adding an image to the cell here will repeat the image on every row of your table. To add an image, click the white box next to Image. Click one of the images in the list representing the available image categories. Select the image you want to add to the cell. The selector at the bottom of this window allows you to designate that the image should be to the left or right of the value in the cell, or you may choose to display the image rather than the value. Again, there is little practical application to adding an image to the cell in a table that will contain multiple rows.

In the Border section of the Style tab, you can add single, double, or thick borders to one or more sides of your cell. You may select only one style of border for the cell. You apply the selected style to any side of the cell to which you add a border. To add a border, you can choose All in the Position drop-down list to apply a border to all four sides, or you can click one or more sides of the cell in the diagram below the Position field. The color selector beside Border Color works exactly like the others on this tab and allows you to change the color of all borders applied to this cell.

Expand the Additional Formatting Options section and you find fields that allow you to adjust the size of your column cell and the padding around the value within the cell. The Height and Width fields allow you to adjust the size of the cell by entering a desired size in points. Adjusting the height of a column cell will affect cells across all columns because the table will adjust to the height of the largest cell in order to align the data in the table.

Cell padding provides space between the sides of the cell and the value in the cell. Adding padding around the cell values will override any specified height or width if the padding results in a larger cell size than the cell size setting. The inverse is also true. If the specified cell height and width settings result in a larger cell than the padding would cause, the height and width measurements apply.

If you happen to be knowledgeable about using cascading style sheets (CSS), you can apply your custom cascading style sheet using the cascading style sheets fields. You can use a cascading style sheet to apply font formats to the cell.

There are three small icons in the upper-right corner of the Style tab. The left icon, an eraser, resets all of the style settings to the default values. The copy icon copies all of the style settings so that you can access the column properties of another column and paste (the right icon) the settings to that column in one click.

Column Format

The Column Format tab (see Figure 3-4) permits you to change the way values in the column repeat or group together across related rows of data, change the way the column heading and data react to a user's click of the mouse, or even hide the column from view. Let us begin with hiding the column. There are many reasons why you might want to hide a column from view but include it in your analysis. One of the most popular columns to hide in a report is the ID column for the particular record type you are reporting on.

It is often beneficial to include the ID column on your report. Doing so enhances the performance of the report because the ID column is an indexed field and your report queries will run more efficiently when looking up records by their unique ID. The unique row IDs, however, are not very interesting data to the typical user of CRM On Demand. The series of characters and numbers making up the ID are system generated and are usually not useful to users.

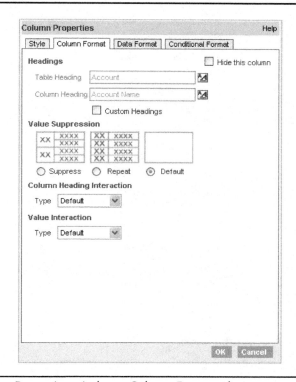

FIGURE 3-4. *Column Properties window—Column Format tab*

To hide a column, check the Hide This Column check box. The column will still be part of the report, and will affect the data on the report as if you are displaying the column. The default action of a report table is to group data from left to right. For instance, an activity report that displays Type in the first column, Subject in the second column, and Due Date in the third would look like the report in Figure 3-5. If you add the Activity ID column to the report and place it in the first column, you get a report like the one shown in Figure 3-6. Notice how the report without the Activity ID column groups the activities by type and the type does not repeat in every row. When you add the Activity ID column, the values repeat. If we hide the Activity ID column, we get the result shown in Figure 3-7. Notice that the data in the report remains organized as if the ID column is visible. The Activity ID column is still part of the report and affects the report data, even when hidden.

If you want to change the grouping behavior of your columns, you can adjust the value suppression settings on the Column Format tab. The default suppression setting for most columns, if not every column, is Suppress. To force values to repeat, select the Repeat radio button in the Value Suppression section. You should make this change to all columns that you want to repeat.

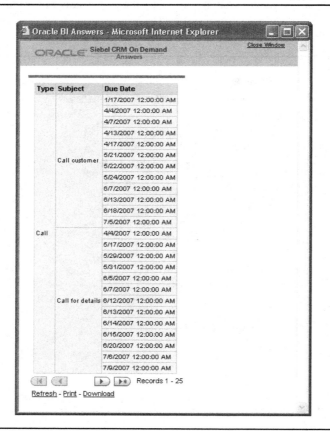

FIGURE 3-5. *Activity report data grouped by type*

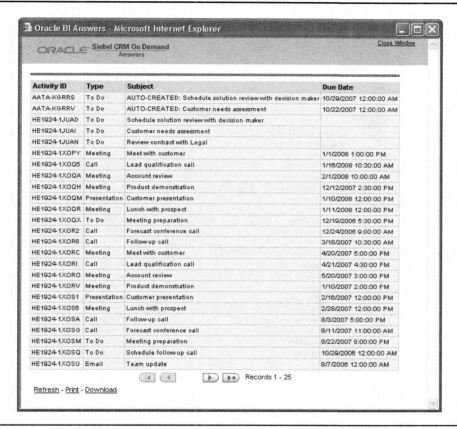

FIGURE 3-6.   *Activity report with Activity ID column*

In Figure 3-8, the Activity ID column is not present, and the value suppression on the Type and Subject columns is set to Repeat. Notice that the data in this report appears in the same order as in Figure 3-5, only with the values in the first two columns repeated rather than grouped, or suppressed. The most common reason to force values to repeat in your report is to facilitate downloading the report data.

Often, the field name in CRM On Demand just does not fit your report. In these cases, you can change the headings to whatever pleases you by clicking the Custom Headings check box and typing the headings of your choice in the fields above it. The column headings appear in your reports. The table headings typically do not. When I discuss formatting the Table view in a later chapter, you will see that it is possible to display the table heading. These headings, if showing the default table name, may not prove very useful to your users. You can modify these headings to provide meaningful information to your users.

Another handy use of the table heading has more to do with how you build the report than how your users benefit. If you will recall, when dragging columns to adjust the order in which the columns appear in the report, it is possible to click the table heading and drag a group of columns

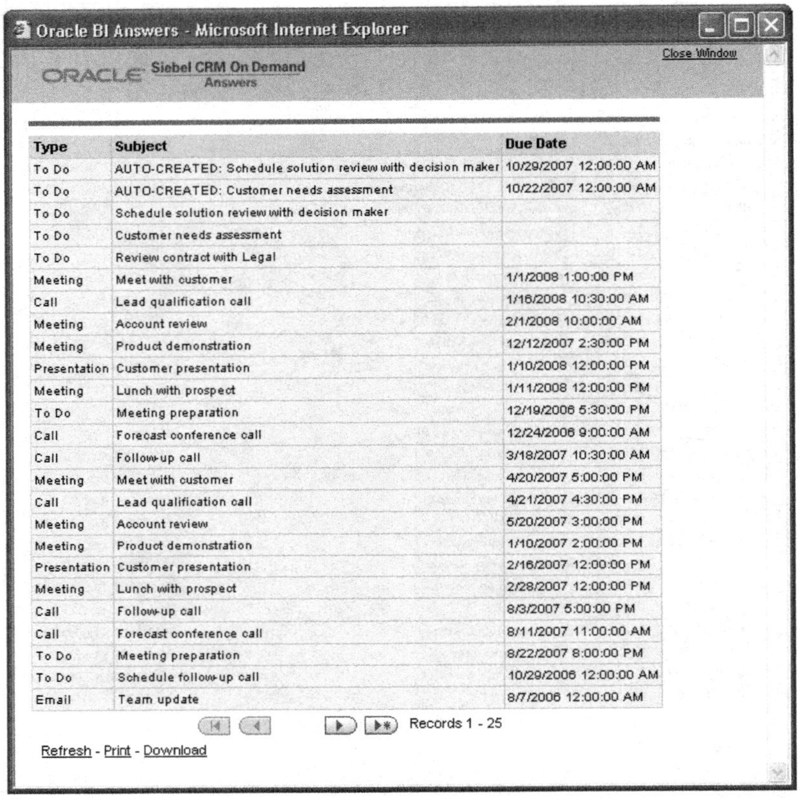

Type	Subject	Due Date
To Do	AUTO-CREATED: Schedule solution review with decision maker	10/29/2007 12:00:00 AM
To Do	AUTO-CREATED: Customer needs assessment	10/22/2007 12:00:00 AM
To Do	Schedule solution review with decision maker	
To Do	Customer needs assessment	
To Do	Review contract with Legal	
Meeting	Meet with customer	1/1/2008 1:00:00 PM
Call	Lead qualification call	1/16/2008 10:30:00 AM
Meeting	Account review	2/1/2008 10:00:00 AM
Meeting	Product demonstration	12/12/2007 2:30:00 PM
Presentation	Customer presentation	1/10/2008 12:00:00 PM
Meeting	Lunch with prospect	1/11/2008 12:00:00 PM
To Do	Meeting preparation	12/19/2006 5:30:00 PM
Call	Forecast conference call	12/24/2006 9:00:00 AM
Call	Follow-up call	3/18/2007 10:30:00 AM
Meeting	Meet with customer	4/20/2007 5:00:00 PM
Call	Lead qualification call	4/21/2007 4:30:00 PM
Meeting	Account review	5/20/2007 3:00:00 PM
Meeting	Product demonstration	1/10/2007 2:00:00 PM
Presentation	Customer presentation	2/16/2007 12:00:00 PM
Meeting	Lunch with prospect	2/28/2007 12:00:00 PM
Call	Follow-up call	8/3/2007 5:00:00 PM
Call	Forecast conference call	8/11/2007 11:00:00 AM
To Do	Meeting preparation	8/22/2007 8:00:00 PM
To Do	Schedule follow-up call	10/29/2006 12:00:00 AM
Email	Team update	8/7/2006 12:00:00 AM

FIGURE 3-7. *Activity report with Activity ID column hidden*

at one time. If you are building a report on which you have groups of columns that should stay together, try changing the table heading to name the group of columns. All columns arranged together with the same table heading will move as one when you click and drag the table heading.

You can apply custom formatting to each of your headings. Click the Edit Format button, located to the right of each field, to open the Edit Format window. This window should look familiar. It is exactly the same as the Style tab with the same options that you can apply to the table or column heading.

The final two fields on the Column Format tab allow you to adjust the interactivity of the column heading and column value. The values in each of these fields are Default, None, Drill, and Navigate. Columns have different default interactivity behaviors depending on the column and the subject area you are using. If you know that you do not want any interactivity, select the None option. This will remove any default interactivity that may exist.

The Drill interactivity setting allows users to drill down to see additional detail by filtering data on the value that the user clicks in the report. The behavior of the drill interactivity, in my

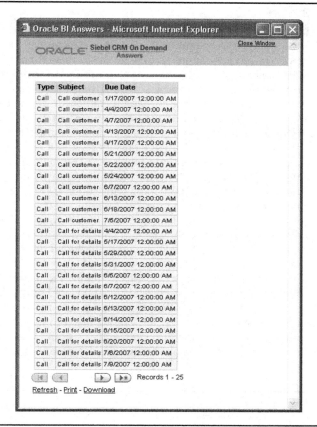

FIGURE 3-8. *Activity report without Activity ID column—value suppression set to Repeat*

experience, is rather sporadic. I have had very limited success with the Drill interactivity setting, and prefer the control that the Navigate interactivity setting offers.

The Navigate interactivity setting allows users to click a value in your report to navigate to another report. The report passes the value that the user clicks to the target report. When you select Navigate for the Interaction field, a new Select Navigation Target button becomes available. Clicking this button opens up two additional fields. These fields are the Target field, to identify the target report, and the Caption field, to provide the value that will appear in the pop-up menu that appears when there are multiple target reports available. To identify a target report, click the Browse button and navigate through the report folders to select the target report. Add a suitable caption to the Caption field if you are planning to add additional targets. If identifying only one target, the caption is not necessary.

Navigating to other reports, of course, requires that the target report exists and is set up properly to receive the passed value. I will revisit this topic in more detail in Chapter 16.

Data Format

The Data Format tab allows you to transform the data in the column into another format. This tab changes depending on the type of column. Let us begin with a numeric column. Figure 3-9 shows the Data Format tab of a numeric column. To change the format of the data in the column, click the Override Default Data Format check box. Doing so activates the fields on the tab, allowing you to select the format in the Treat Numbers As field. The values available in this field are Number, Currency, Percentage, Month Name, Month Name (Abbreviated), Day Name, Day Name (Abbreviated), and Custom. Based on the value you select in the Treat Number As field, additional fields may become available for setting additional options. For example, if you select Currency, additional fields appear for setting the currency symbol, the format for negative values, the number of decimal places, and the option to include a comma separator for thousands.

The Month Name and Day Name options translate the values 1–12 as the months of the year and values 1–7 as the days of the week, beginning with Sunday. The Custom format allows you to create your own special treatment of the numeric data. For instance, if you were to select Custom in the Treat Number As field and enter "Chapter - "# in the Custom Numeric Format field, this would cause the value 3 to display as Chapter - 3 in your report. The pound sign (#) is the placeholder for the numeric value. Static text should be included inside of double quotes.

The Data Format tab for a date or date/time, shown in Figure 3-10, has a different set of fields and options. The Date Format field contains dozens of different date and time formats and the option to create a custom format of your own. The Custom Date Format displays the format code for the chosen Date Format value. If you select Custom, you use this field to input your own custom format. You can most easily discover the valid codes for the Custom Date Format field by selecting different formats and comparing the code in the Custom Date Format field with the chosen format. You may also refer to the appendix for a complete listing of these codes.

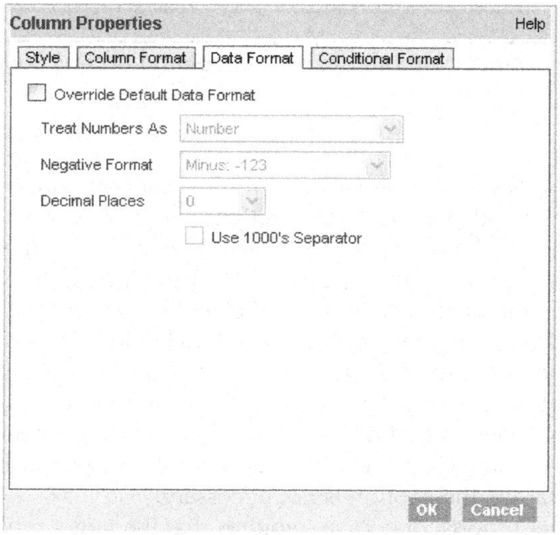

FIGURE 3-9. *Column Properties window—Data Format tab for a numeric column*

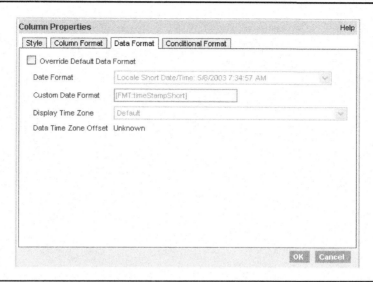

FIGURE 3-10. *Column Properties window—Data Format tab for a date column*

The Display Time Zone field allows you to select a specific time zone for the time values in the column. CRM On Demand stores all dates and times in Greenwich Mean Time and displays dates and times in the default time zone of your company or the time zone of the user's locale, if different. This default time zone is a setting on the company profile established when Oracle provisions your company's On Demand database. The user's locale is a setting on the user profile for each user.

The Data Format tab for a text field, shown in Figure 3-11, has yet another set of fields and options that pertain to text formats. When you click the Override Default Data Format check box, the Treat Text As field becomes available, with a number of formatting options. The choices available are Plain Text, Plain Text (Don't Break Spaces), HTML, HyperText Link, HyperText Link (Prepend http://), Mail-To Address, Image URL, and Custom Text Format.

Each of these formatting options allows you to take the data from the field and append additional static text before and after the field content. An ampersand (@) represents the field content within the Custom Text Format field. Since CRM On Demand operates using a browser interface, On Demand windows and reports are essentially web documents that use HTML and JavaScript to render. This means that you can take advantage of HTML code to modify text in your report. For instance, you can format the text of a field that contains an email address using the Mail-To Address custom text option to insert HTML code around the email address. The result is that clicking the email address in the report will initiate a new email message in the user's default email application. You can use this feature to create hyperlinks to web sites, display images, or simply display some static text to the contents of the field.

In Chapter 8, which discusses string functions, you will learn that there are other ways to make these formatting customizations using column formulas. You will find that using the Data Format tab is usually the easiest and least complex method.

FIGURE 3-11.   *Column Properties window—Data Format tab for a text column*

Conditional Format

A common request of report developers is to highlight data in a report that is below or above a particular threshold, or meets some other criteria that makes the data special in some way. Perhaps you want to assign a color to every sales person and highlight their opportunity data in their color. Perhaps you want to call out service requests that have been open for longer than a week. You might even want to display some sort of graphic next to records that meet some requirement.

You can accomplish all of these things with conditional formatting. The Conditional Format tab in the Column Properties window, shown in Figure 3-12 with a few conditions already added, allows you to add formatting to column data that meets a defined condition. To add a conditional format, you access this tab for the column you wish to apply the formatting to, but you may base the condition on another column in the report.

To add a condition, click the Condition button on the tab, and select the column on which you want to base the condition. You will notice that you are able to select from any of the columns present in your report, including the column you are formatting. Upon selecting a column, the Create/Edit Filter window opens. Here, you select the condition and enter the value with which to compare the column data. Upon clicking OK, the already familiar Edit Format window appears for you to define the format for data meeting the condition. This formatting applies only to the column you are currently editing. If you want to apply a background color for an entire row, for instance, you will need to replicate your conditional formatting for each column.

You may continue to add additional conditions to the column to set formatting options for multiple conditions. When multiple conditions exist, the report evaluates the conditions beginning with the first condition in the list. When the report encounters data that meets a condition, it applies the conditional formatting and evaluates no additional conditions for that data cell.

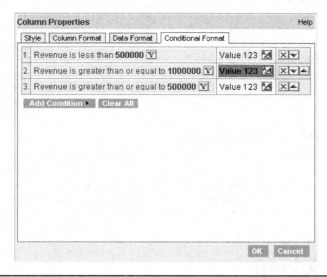

FIGURE 3-12. *Column Properties window—Conditional Format tab*

This means that the order of your conditions is very important. Suppose we have two conditions. The first applies a background color to revenue amounts greater than $1,000. The second applies a font color to revenue amounts greater than $10,000. The report will never apply the formatting of this second condition. Any revenue amount that would qualify, one that is greater than $10,000, would have already met the first condition of being greater than $1,000 and would receive that formatting. If we were to change the order and put the $10,000 condition first, then we would see the formatting for the $10,000 condition applied to any revenue amount of $10,000.01 and up, and the $1,000 formatting on revenue amounts between $1,000.01 and $10,000.

After adding conditions to the Conditional Format tab, you can change the order of your conditions by using the up and down arrow buttons next to each condition. Use these buttons to adjust the order to get the behavior you desire, remembering that for each row, the report evaluates the conditions starting with the first in the list, and once a matching condition applies, no further evaluation occurs for that row.

You can remove conditions by clicking the X button next to the condition. If you have added a condition, but now want to change that condition, you can click the funnel icon next to that condition to alter the conditional requirements. This reopens the Create/Edit Filter window with your previous settings. Alter the filter and click OK to submit new conditional requirements.

You can change the formatting for the conditions by clicking the Edit Format button on the condition listed on the tab. This allows you to change only the formatting, not the condition requirements. Note that you see a small representation of the formatting for each condition on the tab. This allows you a small preview of the formatting, but to really see how the conditional formatting affects your report, use the Preview button. I, on many occasions, felt good about my format choices when viewing a single formatted row, but did not like the way the report appeared with many of its rows formatted according to my condition rule.

Chapter 5 discusses a method for adding a blank column to your report. Why would you want a blank column? Well, one reason might be to contain a graphic based on data conditions using conditional formatting. You already know that you can add graphics to data columns using the Edit Format window by clicking the Image button. When you add a graphic to a column that contains data, the image simply appears before the data in the column. This tends to look messy and throws off the data alignment. If you have a blank column in your table with a conditional format based on another column in the report, there is no data in the column to disrupt the images. The image appears in the column on its own based on the conditional formatting.

Apply Formatting Changes

Once you have made the desired changes on each tab of the Column Properties window, you apply these changes to the column by clicking on the OK button. You may find that this is an iterative process, and you will return to this window many times during your report development. Regardless of how many or few modifications you make here, you must click OK to apply them to the column on your report. Clicking Cancel, of course, ignores your changes and reverts to the previous settings.

Sorting Columns

Back on Step 1 of the Build and View Analysis window, each column that you have added to your report also has those three buttons mentioned earlier, at the beginning of the "Formatting Columns" section. The previous section examined use of the Column Properties button; this section examines use of the rightmost of the three column buttons, the Order By button.

The Order By button initially appears with two small arrows, one pointing up and the other pointing down, which indicates the initial state of the sort on each column that you add to your report: unsorted. Thereafter, the appearance of the Order By button indicates how the report is currently sorting the data. Clicking the Order By button toggles the sort direction. Click once for an ascending sort. The single arrow on the button now points up. Click the button again and the column changes to a descending sort. The arrow now points down. Click the button a third time and you return to the initial unsorted state, with both up and down arrows displayed on the button.

The sorts are alphanumeric sorts, with numbers coming before letters. Text fields, for instance, will sort beginning with leading numeric characters and then alphabetical. An ascending sort on a date or date/time field will bring the oldest date to the top of the list and then sort chronologically. Check box fields contain an N character for the unchecked state and a Y character for the checked state; therefore, an ascending sort on a check box field will list all of the unchecked records before the checked records. An ascending sort on a column that contains null values within the data will move the null values to the bottom of the list. Symbol characters (anything that is neither number nor letter) appear in an ascending sort before numbers.

Sorting Multiple Columns

You can sort by multiple columns in your reports. There is a bit of a trick to setting the sort order so that the report sorts first by one column, then by a second, then by a third, and so on. The column you specify a sort on first will be the primary sort. The column you specify a sort on next will be your secondary sort. A small numeral 2 appears in the lower-right corner of the Order By button, indicating that this column is the secondary sort. Likewise, the next column you set sort on is the tertiary sort, and the button shows a small numeral 3 in the lower-right corner.

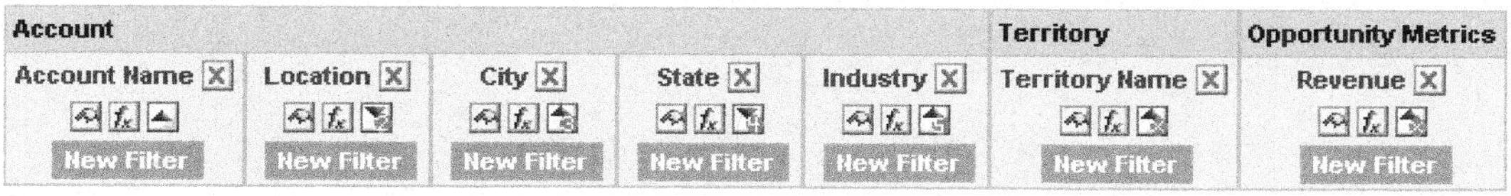

Account					Territory	Opportunity Metrics
Account Name X	Location X	City X	State X	Industry X	Territory Name X	Revenue X
New Filter	New Filter	New Filter	New Filter	New Filter	New Filter	New Filter

FIGURE 3-13. *Report columns with multiple sorts applied*

This pattern continues until you reach your sixth sort. Your sixth or greater sort will cause the Order By button to display an X in the lower-right corner rather than a number. Figure 3-13 illustrates the way the Order By button changes when you add multiple sorts. While there is no limit to the number of sorts you can use in your report, I would venture that you will see little difference in a data set sorted by 3 columns and one sorted by 13 columns.

Now, while setting the initial sort order for multiple columns is relatively simple, changing that sort order can become akin to a logic problem. Consider a report that contains the Account Name, City, State, and Number of Opportunities columns. Your initial sort specifications have an ascending sort on City, then a secondary ascending sort on State, and finally a tertiary ascending sort on Number of Opportunities. You decide that it makes more sense to sort first by State and then by City. In order to get to this sort order, you must remove the sort from City. This causes the primary sort to be on State and the secondary sort on Number of Opportunities. Next, you would need to remove the sort on Number of Opportunities. Why would you need to do this? Because if you reapply the sort to the State column, it becomes your tertiary sort rather than your secondary sort. Remove the sort from Number of Opportunities and then apply the sort to City. This way, the State column is your primary sort and the City column is your secondary sort. At this point, you can reapply the sort to the Number of Opportunities column for your tertiary sort.

Could you have used another pattern of removing and adding sorts to achieve this? Sure, but none of them would be any more efficient. As a rule, it generally works best to remove all but your intended primary sort and reapply the sorts in your desired order.

Data Grouping and Default Sorts

By default, data in your report will sort in ascending order by the first column in the report. If this is the only sort you desire for your report, then it is not necessary to specify a specific sort on the first column. However, if you want your data sorted by the first column, and then the second column, you need to explicitly set the sort on the first and then the second column.

Data in your report also groups from left to right. In other words, the rows of data associated with the first column group together. Your sorting decision can and often will affect this grouping. If you want data grouped by a particular column, you need to include that column in your sort specification. For example, the report with Account Name, City, State, and Number of Opportunities with the primary sort on State will group data by State. The State value will not repeat in the table unless you explicitly set that column's setting to repeat values, on the Column Format tab of the Column Properties window.

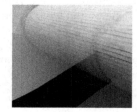

CHAPTER
4

Filtering Report Data

f you were unable to filter data, your reports would not be much more useful than simply exporting data from the database into your favorite spreadsheet program. Filtering is a critical component of reporting. Analysis often requires that we focus on very specific segments of data. That could be data related to a particular group of users, a specific territory, a certain timeframe, or any of the nearly limitless views and classifications of data.

There are many ways to filter data in a report. This chapter explores some of those methods. Here we will examine column filters, predefined filters, saving and reusing these filters, and even using another report as a filter. In future chapters, we will explore filters within column formulas, filter prompts, and a few other tricks that control which data appears in your report.

Filtering Data

Applying filters to your report allows you to control which data you use to populate your report. You can think of a filter as a method of identifying which data the report will use, or identifying the data that your report will not use. Each filter is made up of three components: a column to filter, the value you want to use within the filter, and the condition that describes how the filter value is applied to the filter column. There are many of these conditions, called *operators*, available for your filters, and they are outlined in Table 4-1.

Operator	Valid Column Types	Usage
is equal to or is in	Text, numbers, or dates	Limits results to records where the column matches the filter value(s).
is not equal to or is not in	Text, numbers, or dates	Limits results to records where the column does not match the filter value(s).
is less than	Numbers or dates	Limits results to records where the column is lower (or earlier for date values) than the filter value.
is greater than	Numbers or dates	Limits results to records where the column is higher (or later for date values) than the filter value.
is less than or equal to	Numbers or dates	Limits results to records where the column is the same as or lower (or earlier for date values) than the filter value.
is greater than or equal to	Numbers or dates	Limits results to records where the column is the same as or higher (or later for date values) than the filter value.
is between	Numbers or dates	Limits results to records where the column is the same as or falls between the two filter values.
is null	Text, numbers, or dates	Limits results to records where the specified column contains no data.

TABLE 4-1. *Filter Operators*

is not null	Text, numbers, or dates	Limits results to records where the specified column contains any data.
is in top	Text, numbers, or dates	Limits results to records where the column contains the top-ranked records. The filter value is a number indicating how many records to return. When used on text columns, the ranking is the inverse of alphabetical order. Date ranking evaluates the latest date being first. Number ranking is highest to lowest value.
is in bottom	Text, numbers, or dates	Limits results to the bottom-ranked records. Filter value(s) is a number indicating how many records to return. When used on text columns, the ranking is the inverse of alphabetical order. Date ranking evaluates the latest date being first. Number ranking is highest to lowest value.
contains all	Text, numbers, or dates	Limits results to records where the column contains all of the one or more filter values.
contains any	Text, numbers, or dates	Limits results to records where the column contains any of the one or more filter values.
does not contain	Text, numbers, or dates	Limits results to records where the column does not contain any of the one or more filter values.
begins with	Text, numbers, or dates	Limits results to records where the column data begins exactly as described by the filter value.
ends with	Text, numbers, or dates	Limits results to records where the column data ends exactly as described by the filter value.
is LIKE (pattern match)	Text	Limits results to records where the column data matches the pattern described in the filter. You may use a single filter value, and that value may contain up to two percent-sign wildcard characters (%) to define the pattern.
is not LIKE (pattern match)	Text	Limits results to records where the column data does not match the pattern described in the filter. You may use a single filter value, and that value may contain up to two percent-sign wildcard characters (%) to define the pattern.
is prompted	Text, numbers, or dates	Limits results to records where the column data matches values passed to the report from another report. Use this operator when linking reports using report navigation.

TABLE 4-1. *Filter Operators*

You can apply filters to one or more columns. These columns may or may not be included in your report results. Filters may be connected with an AND or an OR statement to affect the logic of how multiple filters work together. You can group filters together to create more complex filter logic. Converting filters to SQL statements allows for functions embedded in your filters for even more advanced filtering.

The options and possible combinations are plentiful and range from very simple to extremely complex. The remainder of this chapter examines the functionality of report filters.

Column Filters

The most common way to initiate the creation of a filter is by clicking the New Filter button on the column you intend to filter. Doing so opens the Create/Edit Filter window, shown in Figure 4-1. You use this method to create a column filter on a column that you have included in your report. Of course, it is possible, and often desirable, to filter a report on a column not visible in the report. This method is discussed a bit later in the chapter.

You will create most of your filters using the Create/Edit Filter window. On this window, you see the three basic components of the column filter. At the top of the window, you find the filter column. Below that is the Operator field, where you select one of the operators (listed in Table 4-1) for your filter. In the Value field, you enter the filter value, or select the value from the right to populate the Value field. With a text column, you have the option of displaying the possible values in a list, and then clicking the value in the list to add it to the filter.

To display values to choose from, you have several options. Click the All Choices hyperlink to display all valid values for the current field. This often results in a lengthy list with multiple pages. Each page of this list displays ten values, and you are able to scroll through the pages using the number bar and arrows at the bottom of the window. If displaying all of your choices is a little too much, you have the option of clicking the Limited Choices hyperlink. The resulting list of values is dependent on any other filters already added to the report. For instance, suppose you have a report on accounts with a filter of Territory Is Equal To Southeast. When you add a second

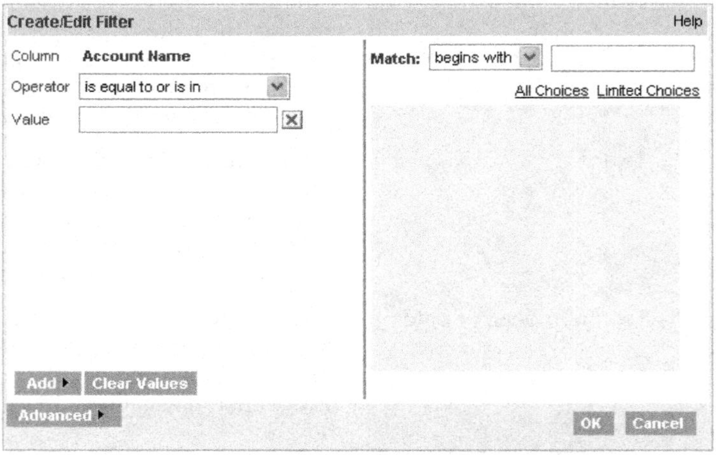

FIGURE 4-1. *Create/Edit Filter window for a text column*

filter on State and click the Limited Choices link, you will see only states that are valid for accounts in the southeast territory. Clicking All Choices would display a list of all states.

It is important to note that elements such as data rules, territory boundaries, and reporting structure have no bearing on the values available in these lists. The actual data present in the column you are filtering governs what Answers considers a value choice in your filter. You may also perform a search on the valid values using the fields just above the All Choices and Limited Choices hyperlinks. Select Begins With, Ends With, or Contains from the Match drop-down list, and enter a search value in the field to its right. Then click All Choices to see all values that meet your criteria or click Limited Choices to see a list of values that both meet your criteria and are valid values given any other filters in place on the report.

So far, we have examined the Create/Edit Filter window for text columns. The Create/Edit Filter window for numeric or date columns is quite similar. Figure 4-2 shows the Create/Edit Filter window for a numeric field. Notice that the options to show the available values are not part of this window. To create a filter on a numeric column, you simply select the operator and enter the value. Some operators accept only one value, while others require two.

The Create/Edit Filter window for a date column, shown in Figure 4-3, is almost identical to the Create/Edit Filter window for a text column. The primary difference has to do with the date selector fields on the right side of the window. Rather than a Match field, you can limit the list of available values to dates within a range. Notice the calendar icons to simplify selecting dates. The All Choices and Limited Choices links perform the same function as they do with text column filters.

If you want to filter data on a column that you do not want in your report, you can add a column filter using that column by holding down your CTRL key while clicking the column name. This action opens the Create/Edit Filter window for the selected column. After selecting your operator and values for your filter and clicking the OK button, the filter appears in the Filters section of the Build and View Analysis window. To reopen the Create/Edit Filter window for a filter that you have added to your report, click the Filter Options button to the right of the filter. This opens a menu. Select Edit Filter to open and make changes to the filter. You will notice that you also have the option to cut or copy the filter. To remove a filter, click the Delete button to the far right of the filter.

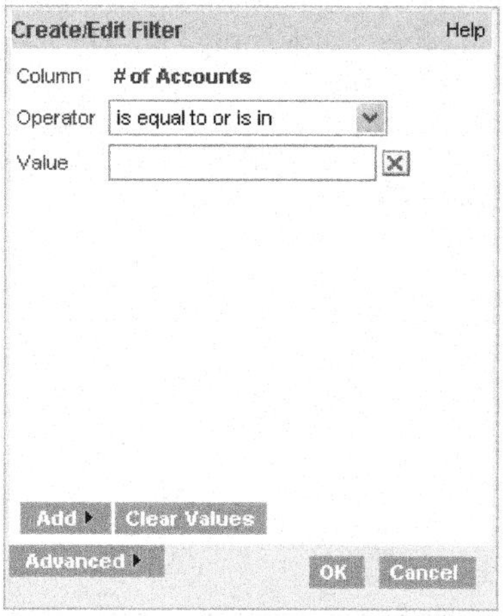

FIGURE 4-2.   *Create/Edit Filter window for a numeric column*

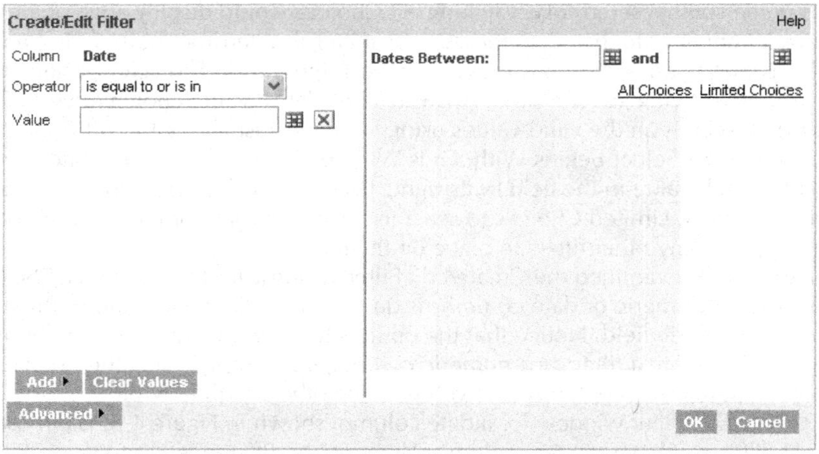

FIGURE 4-3. *Create/Edit Filter window for a date column*

Filter Groups

As you continue to add filters to the report, Answers ties these filters together with the AND statement. This is the default setting, but you can change the way your filters work together. I can best illustrate this concept with an example. Suppose you are creating a report on activities. You add three filters to this report. Filter number one is Activity Type Is Equal To Or Is In Task. Filter number two indicates that the Owner Is Equal To Or Is In Paul D. The third and final filter limits the records to those with Due Dates During The Last Quarter. I will refer to these three filters as F1, F2, and F3.

Without any changes from the default, the configuration of these filters is F1 AND F2 AND F3, as shown in Figure 4-4. The result of this filter configuration will include records where all three filters apply to each record—in other words, only Paul D's tasks with due dates in the last quarter.

With these same three filters in place, if you click the AND statement between F2 and F3, that statement changes to an OR statement. This also causes a new filter group, as shown in Figure 4-5. Now this report will include tasks owned by Paul D and tasks with a due date in the previous quarter. The data must meet the criteria of F1 AND either F2 OR F3. Notice that a new button

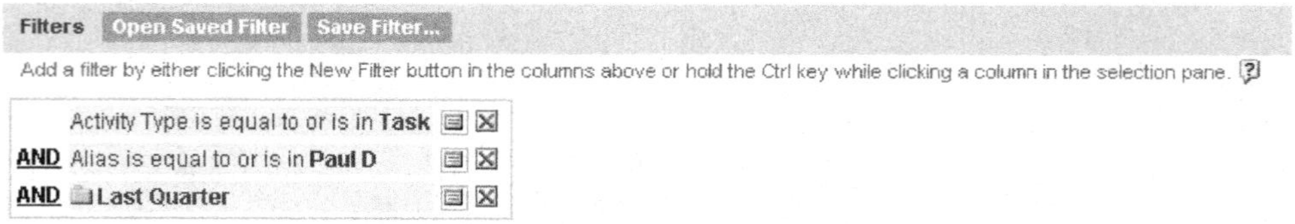

FIGURE 4-4. *Three filters connected with AND statements*

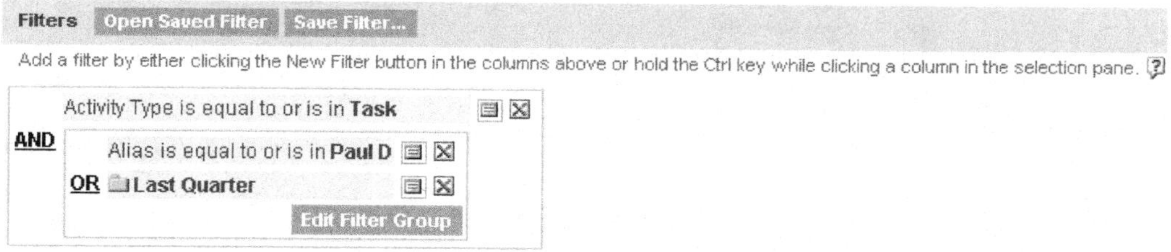

FIGURE 4-5.   *Three filters with a filter group*

appears within the filter group. This Edit Filter Group button enables you to cut and copy this entire filter group as you would a single filter. The other option available by clicking the Edit Filter Group button is to ungroup the filter. Ungrouping the filter shown in Figure 4-5 returns the filters to the configuration shown in Figure 4-4.

Continuing to click the AND/OR statements and ungrouping filters enables you to configure your filters to get the data you want in your reports. Often, report developers mistakenly think that it takes more than one report to collect different sets of data, when perhaps a report with the appropriate groups of filters will do exactly what they need.

One final example using the three filters in the earlier examples, shown in Figure 4-6, connects all of the filters with the OR statement. This report would return all tasks, regardless of owner or date, AND all activities owned by Paul D, regardless of activity type or date, AND all activities from the previous quarter, regardless of type or owner. Essentially, this report would not filter any records out of your report.

Predefined Filters

You may have noticed that the third filter in the preceding example looks a little different from the others. The filter for previous quarter is an example of a predefined filter. Each subject area contains a set of predefined filters that you may use on your reports. These filters are typically time-based and differ from one subject area to another.

To add a predefined filter to your report, click the Open Saved Filter button. This opens a window displaying the folder structure. Drill down into the Filters folders by double-clicking the folders to display the contents, as shown in Figure 4-7. Select from one of the available filters.

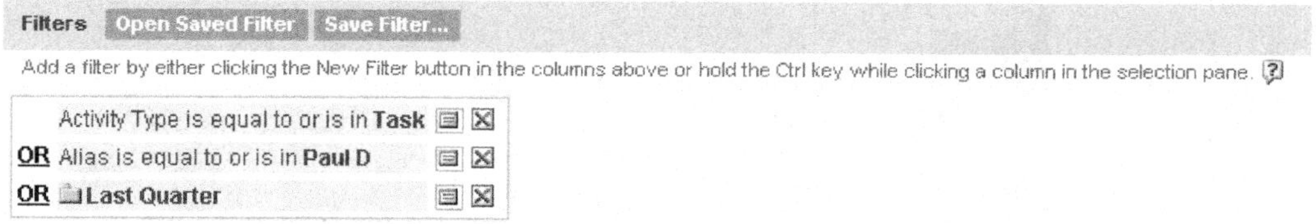

FIGURE 4-6.   *Three filters connected with OR statements*

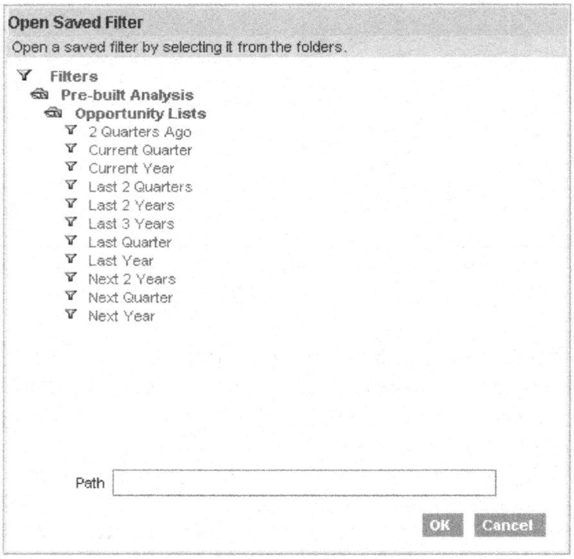

Open Saved Filter
Open a saved filter by selecting it from the folders.

- Filters
  - Pre-built Analysis
    - Opportunity Lists
      - 2 Quarters Ago
      - Current Quarter
      - Current Year
      - Last 2 Quarters
      - Last 2 Years
      - Last 3 Years
      - Last Quarter
      - Last Year
      - Next 2 Years
      - Next Quarter
      - Next Year

Path [   ]

OK   Cancel

FIGURE 4-7. *Open Saved Filter window showing available filters*

You will notice that each of these prebuilt filters has something to do with time. Each subject area within Answers contains some prebuilt time-based filters that you can use, and even modify, on your reports. To add a prebuilt filter to your report, select it from the list and click the OK button. Answer reacts by displaying the Apply Saved Filter window, shown in Figure 4-8. This window shows you the location of the filter and, more importantly, the contents of the filter.

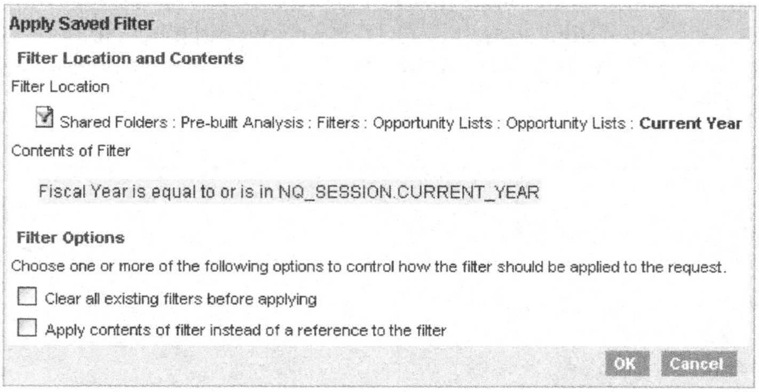

Apply Saved Filter

Filter Location and Contents

Filter Location

☑ Shared Folders : Pre-built Analysis : Filters : Opportunity Lists : Opportunity Lists : **Current Year**

Contents of Filter

Fiscal Year is equal to or is in NQ_SESSION.CURRENT_YEAR

Filter Options

Choose one or more of the following options to control how the filter should be applied to the request.

☐ Clear all existing filters before applying

☐ Apply contents of filter instead of a reference to the filter

OK   Cancel

FIGURE 4-8. *Apply Saved Filter window*

The check boxes under Filter Options give you a couple options when applying this filter to your report. You may choose one or both of these options. Let us examine each and talk about why you would choose each:

- **Clear all existing filters before applying** This option might suit you if you're working on building filters for your report and, after trying a filter or two, determine that a prebuilt filter would better serve your purpose. After you check this box, when you add the predefined filter to your report, it replaces all other filters already on your report. If you leave this box unchecked, this filter appears at the end of the list of filters already on your report, if any.

- **Apply contents of filter instead of a reference to the filter** This visible or aesthetic difference may be one reason you want to use a reference to the filter. When I discuss the report layout later in the book, you will see that it is possible to display the active filters on your report. If you are using a reference to a predefined filter, your report will display something like "Current Year" rather than "Fiscal Year is equal to or is in NQ_SESSION.CURRENT_YEAR." Most users will understand the reference to a filter before they comprehend its contents. One significant difference between the reference and the contents is the ability to edit the filter. When you add the reference to the filter, your options are limited to copying, removing, or viewing the filter. You are not able to edit the filter. If you want to use a predefined filter as a starting point for a filter you are creating, you need to include the contents of the filter rather than just a reference, by checking this box.

Saving Filters

When you opened the Open Saved Filter window (see Figure 4-7) by clicking the Open Saved Filter button in the Build and Analysis window (see Figure 4-6), you may have noticed that the Open Saved Filter window listed prebuilt filters but not predefined filters. The reason is that you haven't yet created and saved your own filters. To save your own filters, you click the Save Filter button (next to the Open Saved Filter button) in the Build and Analysis window to open the Save Filter window, shown in Figure 4-9, which allows you to save the filter in your My Filters folder or the Public Filters/Company Wide Shared Folder.

The prebuilt filters are saved filters, of course. You are also able to create and save your own filters. Saved filters are only available within the subject area in which you initially create the filters. Filters saved in the My Filters folder are available only for your use. Filters saved in the Public Filters folder are available to anyone with the necessary report development privileges.

There are two reasons you might want to save filters. The more obvious reason is to use the same filter on multiple reports. When you click the Save Filter button, the Save Filter window appears (see Figure 4-9), allowing you to save the filter in your My Filters folder or Public Filters/Company Wide Shared Folder. The filter that you save includes the entire filter group. This is particularly helpful when you have a complex filter that you want to use repeatedly for other similar reports. This also brings us to the other compelling reason for saving your filters. Suppose you are developing a series of activity reports. These reports should include activities for only active users with the Field Sales role and activities with a type of Ssales Call, Quote Preparation, Sales Presentation, Negotiation, and Customer Appreciation. Now, you certainly could easily create this filter on every report. You also know you could save yourself some time and effort by saving and reusing the filter.

The benefit I want to mention takes us back to the options available to you when applying a saved filter. When you save this filter, you give it a name. That name will reference the filter and,

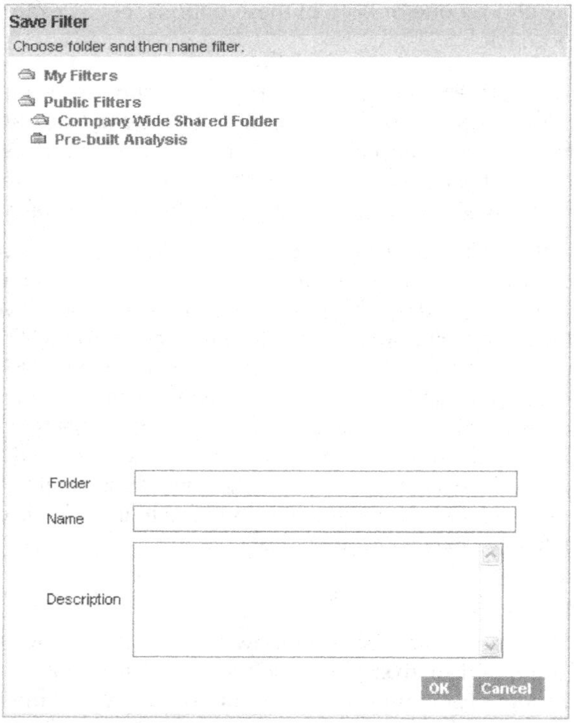

FIGURE 4-9. *Save Filter window*

when you apply the filter, will display on the report rather than the complex contents of the filter. This allows you to create some complex filters and then mask that complexity with a simple reference.

Advanced Filtering

This section describes some more advanced filtering techniques. The methods described in the prior section will satisfy a vast majority of your filtering needs, but it would be a disservice to you to not describe these additional filtering methods.

I will start by describing how to use expressions in your filters, and then move into system variables. If you are familiar with writing SQL statements, you may want to take advantage of the ability to convert your filters to SQL and modify the filter query directly. Finally, I will show you how to make use of another report as a filter.

Expressions

An expression is a bit of SQL that returns some value. Most expressions of any use in a filter are date expressions. The chapters that follow describe each expression available in Answers On Demand in detail. For now, I will explain how to use the expressions in a filter.

You begin, as before, in the Create/Edit Filter window. The filters examined thus far identify the column, condition, and value for the filter. In place of the value, you can use an expression to retrieve a value dynamically when the report generates. For instance, the NOW() expression returns the current date and time. Thus, you can build a filter on your report that retrieves data by applying the condition using the expression to return the current date and time. This is quite handy when you want a report that returns data such as open activities with a due date prior to the current date.

To use an expression rather than a value in your filter, click the Add button at the bottom of the Create/Edit Filter window. Notice in the pop-up menu that you can add a value, SQL expression, or variable to the filter. Select the SQL Expression option and the Value field is replaced by a SQL Expression field. It is in this field that you build your expression.

Figure 4-10 shows a useful example of using expressions in a column filter. This filter limits data to activities with a due date between the current date/time and seven days from the current date/time. The resulting filter appears in the Build and View Analysis window as "Due Date Is Between NOW() and TIMESTAMPADD(SQL_TSI_DAY, 7, NOW())" in the Filters section of the window. To build this filter, I added a filter on the Due Date column and selected the Is Between operator. I then added two SQL expressions to the filter. In the first, I input the expression NOW(), which returns the current date and time. In the second, I input TIMESTAMPADD(SQL_TSI_DAY, 7, NOW()), which adds seven days to the current date and time. These expressions may be foreign to you now, but in the next few chapters you will learn these and many more expressions and functions.

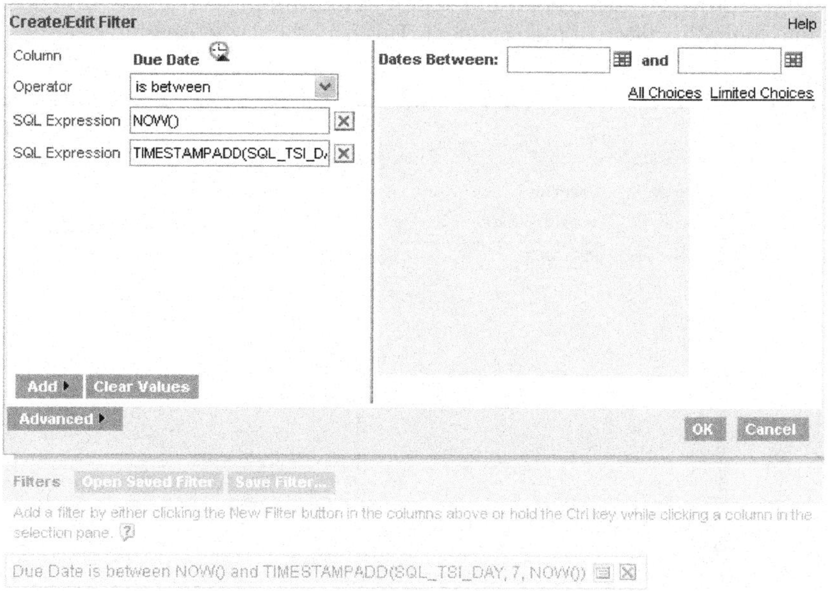

FIGURE 4-10. *Filter using SQL expressions*

Variables

Similar to the use of expressions, session variables in filters generate values with which the filter works. For the most part, the values generated by the session variables can be derived by other means through column formulae. You will find many of these session variables in the prebuilt reports. I also describe each of the session variables in the next chapter.

To use a session variable in your filter, click the Add button in the Create/Edit Filter window and select Variable. There is a small Variable submenu that contains the options of Session, Repository, and Presentation. Select Session from this menu to add the Session Variable field to the filter. The other two Variable options, Repository and Presentation, are currently not functional in the On Demand version of Analytics.

While most variables are of little use in a column filter, there is one session variable that is quite useful. REPLUSER returns the current user's email address. An example use of this simple variable is to create a report that filters to records owned by the individual running the report.

To add a session variable to your filter, simply type the variable name in the Session Variable field of the Create/Edit Filter window, as shown in Figure 4-11. When the filter content displays in the Build and View Analysis window, you will notice that the filter adds NQ_SESSION to the front of the variable, as shown in Figure 4-12. This is the full name of the session variable. If you enter the session variable in the Value or SQL Expression field on a filter, you will not receive the results you are hoping to receive.

It is possible to use a system variable as part of an expression. If you call a system variable within an expression, you must use the VALUEOF() function to draw the value out of the variable. To accomplish the same results as the previous example using an expression, you would filter on the expression VALUEOF(NQ_SESSION.REPLUSER). The end result is the same.

Another nice use of the REPLUSER variable involves applying the filter to the Manager Email field. Doing so provides managers with a report that lists records that are owned by only users that fall into their direct line of management. This is particularly useful in cases where your

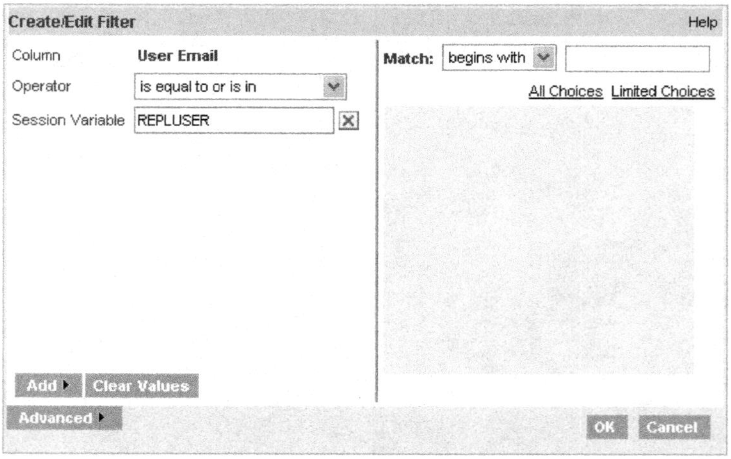

FIGURE 4-11. *Create/Edit Filter window using the REPLUSER variable*

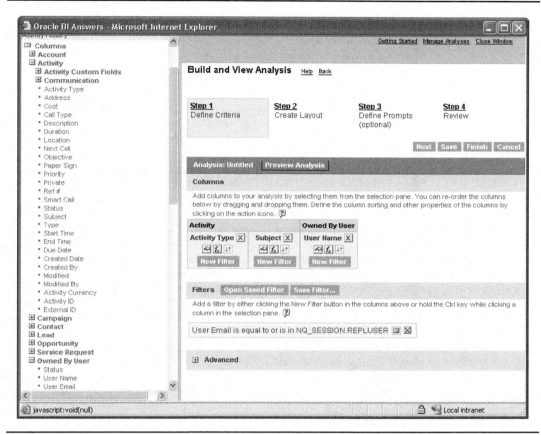

FIGURE 4-12. *Build and View Analysis window with session variable*

visibility structure allows managers to view data across teams but you want to limit the report data to a single manager's team.

SQL Filters

If you are familiar with the SQL query language, you may find the ability to convert filters to SQL quite useful. To convert and edit a column filter with SQL, click the Advanced button at the bottom of the Create/Edit Filter window and select Convert This Filter to SQL. You must have a filter defined in order to convert to SQL. When you convert your filter to SQL, the Advanced SQL Filter window opens displaying your filter in SQL format. It is in this window that you will modify the filter using the SQL query language.

The filter I described earlier using the REPLUSER variable appears as Employee."Employee Login" = VALUEOF(NQ_SESSION.REPLUSER) in SQL format. This is shown in Figure 4-13. The portion of this expression before the equal sign references the column that filter is filtering on. This is also referred to as the analytical field reference for the column.

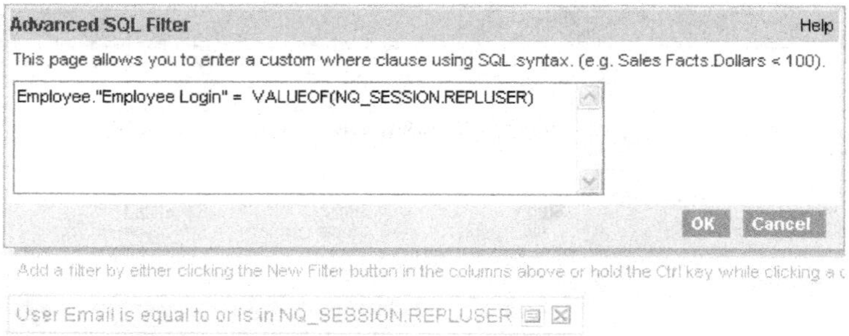

FIGURE 4-13. *Advanced SQL Filter window*

Notice that the other side of the expression (after the equal sign) is using the VALUEOF() function on the NQ_SESSION.REPLUSER session variable. Using SQL, you can alter this filter as you so choose, then click OK to save the filter on your report.

This particular method of creating a report filter is a great way to create a comparison between two columns. Suppose you want to create a report that displays only pending opportunities where the total revenues of open opportunities is greater than 5 percent of the account's annual revenues. In this case, your filter value is different for each account, so a simple filter just will not do. You want to compare the Opportunity Revenue column to the Account Annual Revenues column of each record to determine if the record should or should not appear in the report results.

The first step is to find the analytical field reference for the Annual Revenues column. To do this, add the column to your report, then click the Edit Formula button on the column. The Edit Formula button is between the Column Properties and Sort buttons, and bears the letters fx. We will do much more with the Edit Column Formula window (see Figure 4-14) in the next several chapters. For now, simply highlight the analytical field reference shown in the window and press CTRL-C to copy the reference to your clipboard.

Next, you click the Filter button on the column you want to filter. You need to input something in the Value field before you can convert the filter to SQL. For the example of comparing the Opportunity Revenue column to the Account Annual Revenues column of each record , I would go ahead and select the Is Greater Than or Equal to condition and then type any number in the Value field. With all three components of a filter in place, you can click the Advanced button and choose the Convert This Filter to SQL option.

In the Advanced SQL Filter window, shown in Figure 4-15, remove the value you had typed in the Value field and paste (CTRL-V) the analytical field reference of the other column from your clipboard. You can continue to edit this SQL expression now. For my example, I would type *.05 at the end of the filter expression. My completed filter expression will cause my report to show only those records where the opportunity revenue is greater than 5 percent of the account revenue. In Figure 4-15, you can see the completed filter expression in the Advanced SQL Filter window and how it appears on the Build and View Analysis window in the background.

It is certainly possible to create a filter that accomplishes this same objective in other ways. One method would be to change a column formula to calculate the percentage of the account revenue represented by the opportunities and then filter the report to include only columns where the result of this calculation is greater than or equal to 0.05.

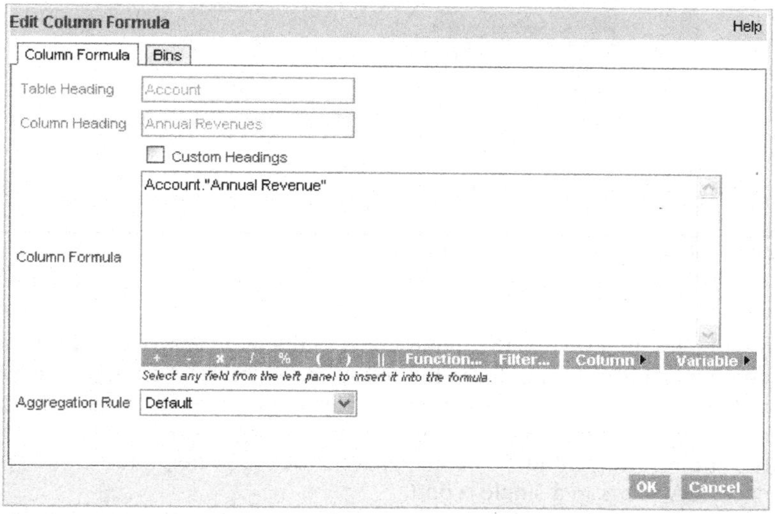

FIGURE 4-14. *Edit Column Formula window*

Another way is by modifying a column formula to calculate the 5 percent of account revenue and use a conditional to return a YES if the opportunity revenue amount is greater than the calculated account revenue, and a NO if it is not. Then a simple filter to only include the YES records would return the same dataset. The SQL filter is a much simpler solution.

Reports as Filters

I have one last advanced filtering method to offer. The Filter Based on the Results of Another Request option accessed by clicking the Advanced button, allows you to filter your report to include only the records from another report. This essentially creates a subquery for the report

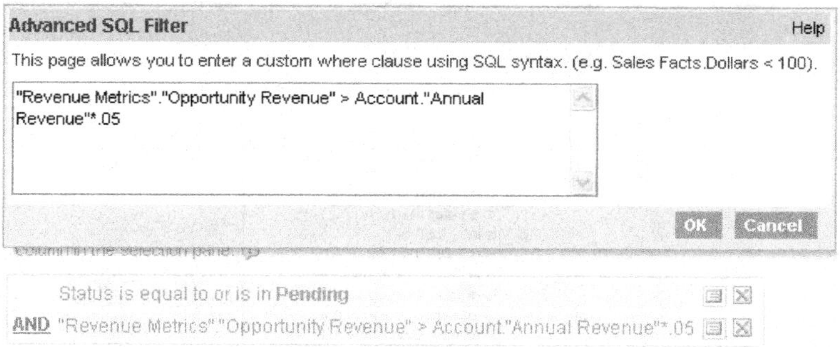

FIGURE 4-15. *Example of a SQL filter comparing two columns*

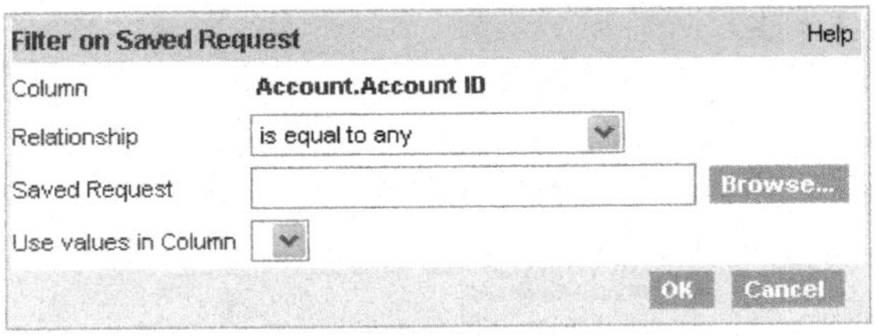

FIGURE 4-16. *Filter on Saved Request window*

you are building. In other words, the request sent to the analytics server contains not only the primary query from this report, but also the query generated by the filtering report as a subquery.

This method of filtering can be useful if you need to pull together a set of records from one subject area and then build a report in another subject area that references that dataset. Using two reports from the same subject area is typically not overly helpful since it is possible to just build the necessary filters in a single report.

To add a filter based on another report, click the Advanced button in the Create/Edit Filter window and select the Filter Based on the Results of Another Request option. This opens the Filter on Saved Request window (see Figure 4-16), in which you identify the report you want to filter with, the columns that you want to compare, and what their relationship should be.

Both reports must have a common column, or at least columns of the same type, to compare within the filter definition. Usually an ID column makes the most sense to satisfy this requirement if your intention is to report on records that are in the filter report (is equal to any) or do not appear (is not equal to any) in the filter report. You may also find use for comparing metric columns. The available relationships between your two reports (see Figure 4-17) include greater than, less than, greater than or equal to, and less than or equal to. You may apply one of these conditions to all records (only include records where the revenue is greater than all of the revenue fields in the other report, for example) or to any record (only include records that are greater than any of the revenue fields on the other report).

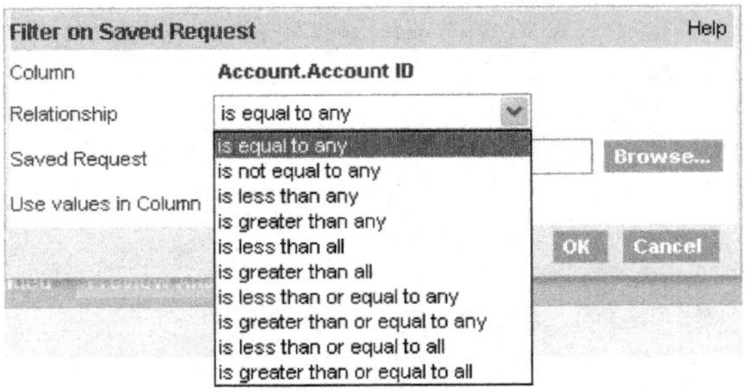

FIGURE 4-17. *Filter on Saved Request Relationship options*

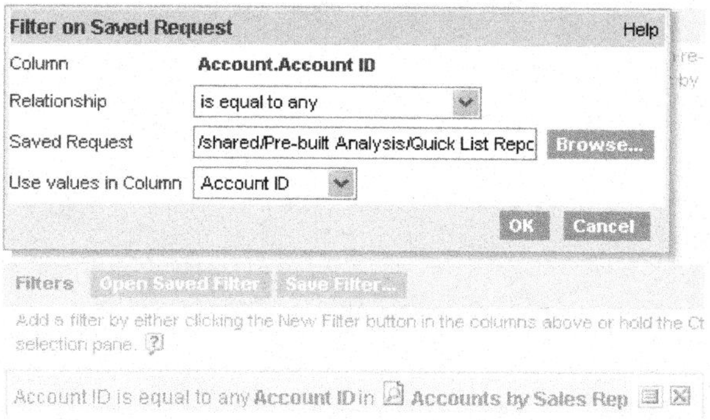

FIGURE 4-18. *Completed Filter on Saved Request window*

In the Filter on Saved Request window, the analytical field reference for the column on which you clicked the Filter button appears at the top. This is the first part of your query. Next, you identify the relationship that you want that column to have with the similar column in the filter report. Next, in the Saved Request field, you browse for and select the report that you want to use for your filter. This report, of course, must already exist. The Use Values in Column field will contain choices based on this report selection. Select the column from the filter report that you are using to relate the two reports.

Figure 4-18 shows a completed Filter on Saved Request window and, in the background, the way that the filter appears in the Build and View Analysis window. If your report is intended for other users of CRM On Demand, you need to ensure that both reports are saved in locations that are available to the intended users. It is not necessary to save them both in the exact same location, but if your filter report is in a restricted folder or in your My Folder directory, someone without access to those locations will not be able to successfully run the report.

I recommend that you avoid using this filtering method with reports that involve very large datasets. When Answers On Demand runs a report with this type of filter, the analytics server attempts to send the entire query, including the subquery for the filter report, to the database. This is not always possible, so the server will attempt to execute the subquery first and then repackage the result into the main query. If the result of the subquery is too large, the main query becomes larger than Answers On Demand is able to handle. When this happens, the report results in an error. A general guideline is to use a report as a filter only if you are certain that the result set generated by the report will be fewer than 1,000 records.

CHAPTER
5

Modifying Data
with Formulas

n this chapter we begin to explore column formulas. The column formula in its simplest form is an analytical field reference that identifies the column in the database that the report column queries to extract the report data. You can modify these analytical field references to change the data in your report. There are countless reasons why you may want to change the formula that drives the content of a column in a report. From performing simple mathematical calculations to adding conditional logic to a column, there are many methods available for manipulating column formulas to meet your reporting needs. This chapter lays some groundwork for the upcoming modules, all dedicated to working with column formulas.

Changing Column Formulas

All the work you will do on your column formulas will take place in the Edit Column Formula window (see Figure 5-1). Open this window by clicking the Edit Formula button, which is the center of the three small buttons on each column. The Edit Column Formula window allows you to not only modify the column formula, but also see exactly where the column data comes from, modify the column headers that appear in your report, and adjust how the data aggregates (combines) when grouped together across multiple records.

It is in this window that you will also group data into bins or filter data from within the column formula, or even eliminate the formula all together to create a blank column. In order to perform these tasks, you need some understanding of the way analytical field references work and how you can transform column data with functions, variables, and literals.

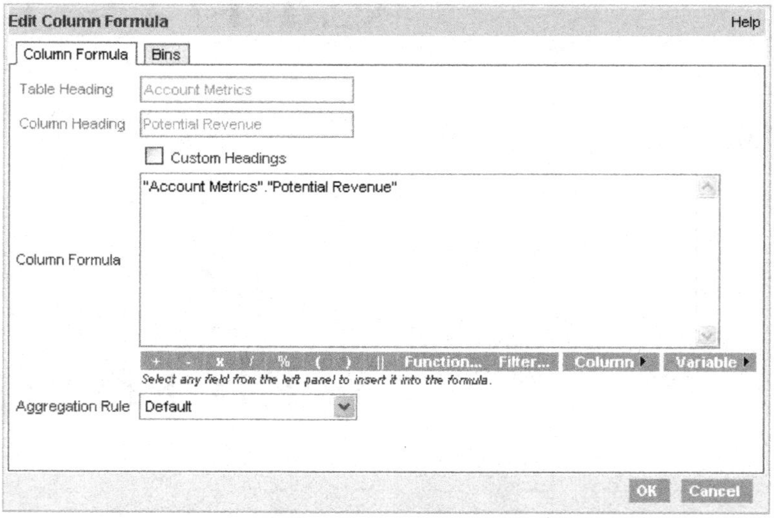

Edit Column Formula	Help
Column Formula | Bins	
Table Heading	Account Metrics
Column Heading	Potential Revenue
	☐ Custom Headings
Column Formula	"Account Metrics"."Potential Revenue"
	+ - x / % ( ) || Function... Filter... Column ▶ Variable ▶
	Select any field from the left panel to insert it into the formula.
Aggregation Rule	Default
	OK Cancel

FIGURE 5-1. *Edit Column Formula window*

Knowing something about the columns, their data types, and from where the data that they contain comes is also quite helpful in working with column formulas. Most columns in your reports are not likely to need formula modifications. Some columns you use are calculated values that come not from the data tables, but from the analytics data warehouse. But for those columns that just don't quite give you what you want, you can modify or write a formula to create the column that you need for your report.

Custom Headers

Let us start with the simplest of changes you can make with the Edit Column Formula window. Each column has a default table name and column name associated with it. Table names usually do not appear in your reports. It is possible to display them, but this is not the default behavior. The column names, on the other hand, are typically very prominent elements in your reports. Regularly, the default column name does not reflect exactly what you want as a column heading on your report.

You will find that as you change column formulas the default column name changes to reflect the content of that column formula. This typically is not the header you want displayed in your report. To make a change to the table and column headers, first check the Custom Headings check box. This makes the Table Heading and Column Heading fields editable. Overwrite the current headers with the text of your choice.

Analytical Field References

When you initially open the Edit Column Formula window, the contents of the Column Formula field references the table and column in which the data resides, either in the database (Reporting subject areas) or the data warehouse (Analytics subject areas). It is not possible for you to view the data tables that make up the On Demand database or to draw data from or update these tables through tools other than On Demand applications or web services. For this reason, the analytical field references themselves provide little information.

The structure of the analytical field reference is rather simple. A table reference and a column reference separated by a period make up the analytical field reference. Account."Account Name" is the analytical field reference for the Account Name column in the Account table. The analytical field reference for a calculated metric column, one that is available in Answers On Demand, follows the same pattern even though it is not available for display on a layout in CRM On Demand. "Account Metrics"."Opportunity Revenue (000)" is the analytical field reference for a metric column that contains the opportunity revenue in thousands for each account. If either the table name or column name contains a space, it must be enclosed in quotation marks.

To change a column's formula, you do not change the analytical field reference. You may remove the reference or include the entire reference in a function statement, but the analytical field reference itself should not be altered.

Using Special Columns

While on the subject of what defines report columns, let us take a moment to discuss some of the special columns available in Answers On Demand. While most columns are simply direct reflections of the data stored in the database, there are some columns that exist in Answers On

Demand only for reporting, either because they are frequently used calculations or because they are necessary to support a specific type of field. These special columns include:

- Multi-Select Picklist Values
- Metric Columns
- Date Dimension Columns

Multi-Select Picklist Values

If your On Demand application is making use of the multiple-selection picklist field type that one field on the application layout creates an interesting set of columns in Answers On Demand. In the example shown in Figure 5-2, I have a multi-select picklist for personal technology. There are eight values available in this field. Values added to this field appear in the CRM On Demand application field separated by commas.

Multi-select picklists are not available in the Reporting subject areas. That means you are not able to include multi-select picklist data on a real-time report. These fields are available in the Analytics subject areas, so including them in your historical reports is possible. My sample field, shown in Figure 5-2, results in nine columns in Answers On Demand. These columns are located in a column folder named with the multi-select field name located in the object folder. For example, the columns for our example are located in the Personal Technology subfolder of the Contact folder (see Figure 5-3). Notice that we have a column named Personal Technology. This column contains the data that is visible through the user interface—values separated with a comma. The other columns in this folder are the actual values available in the picklist. These are Yes/No columns. For each record, a "Y" appears in each column corresponding to a value selected in the multi-select picklist. An "N" appears in those columns corresponding to values that are not selected for each record.

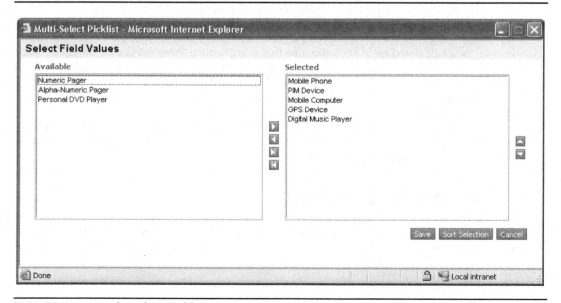

FIGURE 5-2. *Multi-Select Picklist window*

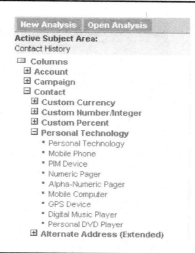

FIGURE 5-3. *Personal Technology multi-select picklist columns*

One important benefit of this structure for the multi-select picklist is performance. If I am interested in building a report containing my contacts who own a mobile computer, I can filter on the Mobile Computer column equal to "Y" rather than filter on the Personal Technology column using a "contains" condition. A query that must dig through the contents of a field on each record to identify those that contain a bit of text takes a bit longer than a binary query on a Yes/No field.

Metric Columns

The last column folder in most subject areas contains metrics. The columns in the Metrics folder provide aggregated measurements for the records in your report. These metric columns are typically record counts or totals of currency columns, but you will also find percentages and averages among the metrics, depending on the subject area. Your custom metric fields are also available for reporting. With perhaps the exception of a simple list report, most every report you create will contain some sort of metric. After all, analytics is all about measuring things.

Not all metric columns in Answers On Demand are part of the CRM On Demand database. For instance, in Answers you will find Opportunity History columns such as Revenue (000), which returns revenue totals in thousands, or Avg # Days in Stage, which provides the average number of days that opportunities remained in each sales stage, but you will not find these columns in CRM On Demand.

Metric columns will aggregate to the constraint of the row, meaning the measurements that make up the amount displayed in your report results will be based on the records included in the row in your results. If you include the Sales Stage column and # of Opportunities column in a report, the total shown in each row of the # of Opportunities column is the total number of opportunities within the sales stage displayed in that row (see Figure 5-4). Replace the Sales Stage column with the Opportunity Type column, and the metric changes to display the number of each type of opportunity (see Figure 5-5).

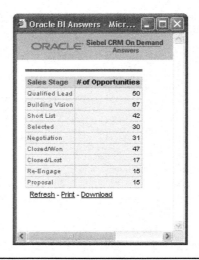

FIGURE 5-4. *Number of Opportunities by Sales Stage*

Date Dimension Columns

Near the end of the Columns list of many of the subject areas you will find a Date folder. This folder contains date dimension columns that work in conjunction with metrics on your reports. As shown in Figure 5-6, the Date folder contains a Date column and a series of Fiscal and Calendar columns for day, week, month, quarter, and year. These date columns have no real meaning without a metric column. They provide a date dimension for the measurements returned by a metric column. For instance, an activity report with the Calendar Mth/Year column along with # of Open Activities and # of Closed Activities columns would produce results similar to those shown in Figure 5-7.

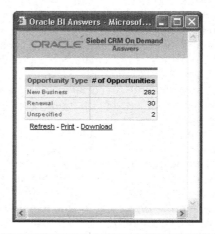

FIGURE 5-5. *Number of Opportunities by Type*

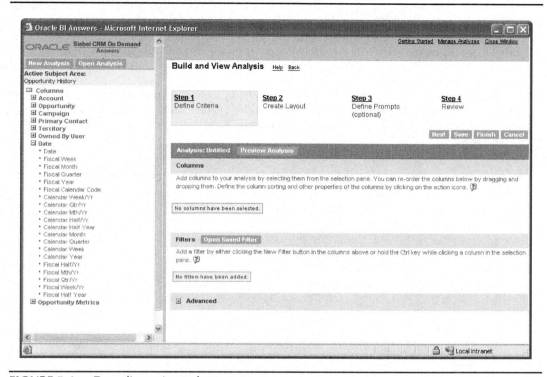

FIGURE 5-6.   *Date dimension columns*

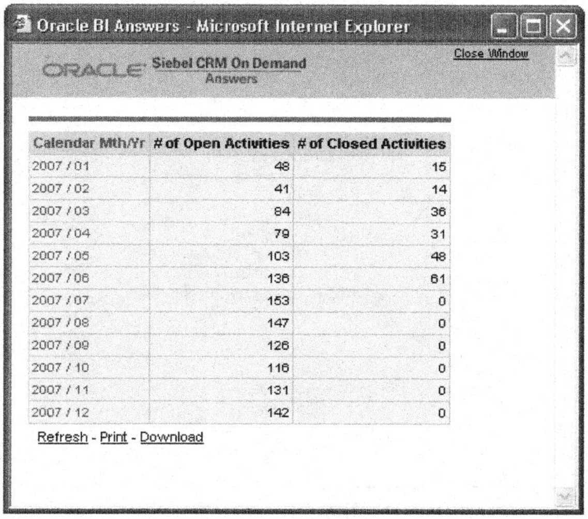

Calendar Mth/Yr	# of Open Activities	# of Closed Activities
2007 / 01	48	15
2007 / 02	41	14
2007 / 03	84	36
2007 / 04	79	31
2007 / 05	103	48
2007 / 06	136	61
2007 / 07	153	0
2007 / 08	147	0
2007 / 09	126	0
2007 / 10	116	0
2007 / 11	131	0
2007 / 12	142	0

Refresh - Print - Download

FIGURE 5-7.   *Activity report—dates based on due date*

What this report is telling us is that there were 48 open activities with a due date in January 2007. We also see that 15 completed activities' due dates fell in January 2007. The dates used for each metric is dependent on what it measures. Notice in Figure 5-8 that the Activity History subject area contains metrics tied to different dates on the record. You can choose to see the number of activities, open activities, or closed activities by the date they were created rather than the due date for example.

If you are ever unsure of which date is referenced by the date dimension, you can create a report similar to the one shown in Figure 5-9, which includes the date dimension and the date fields on the record. In my example, I have filtered by the record ID to limit the report to a single record, for convenience.

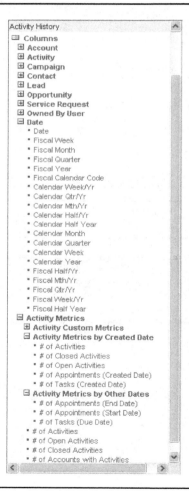

FIGURE 5-8. *Date-based metric columns*

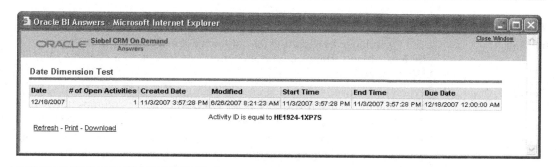

FIGURE 5-9. *Date Dimension Test report*

Setting Aggregation Rules

Aggregation rules define how data in a column calculates when shown in a subtotal or grand total. The aggregation rule defines how this amount is calculated. To set the aggregation rule on a column, select a value from the Aggregation Rule drop-down list in the Edit Column Formula window (see Figure 5-1). Figure 5-10 illustrates the way aggregation rules affect the way total values are calculated. You can see the aggregation rule I used for each column in the table header over each column. The bottom row shows the results of the column values totaled with each aggregation rule.

There are ten values available in the Aggregation Rule drop-down list. Based on my testing and research in Answers On Demand, Table 5-1 offers some generalizations regarding each of the aggregation rules. My research, though extensive, was certainly not inclusive of every column, possible combination of columns, and possible treatments of those columns in a report.

This is not the final discussion on aggregation rules. The use of aggregation rules will be covered when discussing the report layout, particularly in Chapter 12.

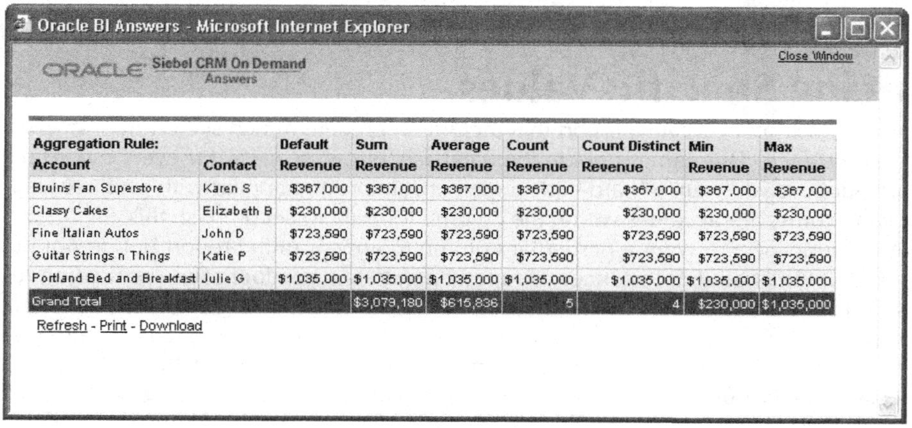

Aggregation Rule: Account	Contact	Default Revenue	Sum Revenue	Average Revenue	Count Revenue	Count Distinct Revenue	Min Revenue	Max Revenue
Bruins Fan Superstore	Karen S	$367,000	$367,000	$367,000	$367,000	$367,000	$367,000	$367,000
Classy Cakes	Elizabeth B	$230,000	$230,000	$230,000	$230,000	$230,000	$230,000	$230,000
Fine Italian Autos	John D	$723,590	$723,590	$723,590	$723,590	$723,590	$723,590	$723,590
Guitar Strings n Things	Katie P	$723,590	$723,590	$723,590	$723,590	$723,590	$723,590	$723,590
Portland Bed and Breakfast	Julie G	$1,035,000	$1,035,000	$1,035,000	$1,035,000	$1,035,000	$1,035,000	$1,035,000
Grand Total			$3,079,180	$615,836	5	4	$230,000	$1,035,000

Refresh - Print - Download

FIGURE 5-10. *Aggregation Rules Sample report*

Aggregation Rule	Effect
Default	The Default aggregation rule for columns not listed in any of the Metrics folders is None. The Default aggregation rule for columns from the Metrics folders is Sum.
Server Determined	When I have used this setting on nonmetric columns, the result is always the value in the first row of my table. Used with metric columns, the Server Determined aggregation rule returns a sum of column values in the table.
Sum	The Total row gives you the total of the column values in the table. Attempting to apply the Sum aggregation rule on a text or date/time column results in an error.
Average	The Total row gives you the average value of the column values in the table. Attempting to apply the Average aggregation rule on a text or date/time column results in an error.
Count	The Total row gives you the total number of values in the table column.
Count Distinct	The Total row gives you the total number of unique values in the table column.
Min	The Total row gives you the lowest value in the table column. For text values, this is the first value when sorted alphabetically. For date and time values, this is the earliest date and time in the column.
Max	The Total row gives you the largest value in the table column. For text values, this is the last value when sorted alphabetically. For date and time values, this is the latest date and time in the column.
None	Prevents a value in the Total row for the column.
Server Complex Aggregate	Returns the sum of column values from all records in the database. This aggregation rule ignores report filters.

TABLE 5-1. *Aggregation Rules*

Forcing Specific Values

Suppose you want to create a report that includes a predetermined static value—a commission rate, for instance. This value is not in the database, but is the same for every record on your report. Suppose you want to hard-code a date or some text to appear with each record in the report. You can express literal values within the column formula to accomplish this.

Now suppose you want a particular column to appear in the report but do not want it to display a value at all. For instance, you might generate a product sales verification report that your users will print and on which they will be required to sign off on each row to confirm the shipped count. Or suppose you simply want to include a space between columns. You might even format this column to create a thick border between vertical sections of your report. This too is possible through the expression of a literal value—that value being no value at all.

Expressing Literals

A literal is a value corresponding to a given data type that you want displayed in your report. Literal values are constants that are taken literally as is, without changing them. Any literal value must comply with the data type it represents. The three data types are character, date/time, and numeric. In this section, we primarily examine the expression of literals as stand-alone expressions to define the contents of a column. You will see the literals in action many times throughout the book, however, because they also play an important role in many functions and formulas.

To add a literal value to your report, you first add any column to your report and delete the column formula. At this point, go ahead and check the Custom Headings check box and enter a new column heading for your literal column.

Character Literals

A character literal contains letters, numbers, and/or symbols. To express a character literal, replace the analytical field reference with the character string enclosed in single quotation marks. The literal value is all the text between the single quotes. The following is an example of a literal expression of a character value:

```
'Ship to 2000 Griffin Street, Thomasville, GA 31757'
```

This string results in the column displaying the same text in every row of the report. Notice that this literal value has a combination of letters, numbers, and symbols. One obvious issue comes into play if your literal value happens to have a single quote within the value. For instance, if I wanted to display "Customer's Signature:" as a literal value, inserting this string between two single quotes would result in an error. Answers look for the values between single quotes to define the literal value. The apostrophe in "Customer's" interprets as the second single quote, and the rest of the string does not follow any approved syntax and errors out.

If you absolutely must include an apostrophe in a character literal, you may use an ASCII code representing the character you want to include. You will also use the CHAR function and the concatenate operator to convert the ASCII code and tie it in with the strings of text. Functions and operators are covered in detail in subsequent chapters, but for the purpose of expressing literal values, the following code serves as an example of their use:

```
'Customer' || CHAR(39) || 's Signature'
```

The double pipe characters cause the parts of this string to concatenate, or come together. The CHAR function converts the ASCII code of 39 to a single quote. Refer to the CHAR function description in Chapter 8 for other useful ASCII characters.

Date/Time Literals

There are three types of date/time literals. You have one format for expressing a date, one for expressing a time, and one for expressing a date timestamp. The expressed literal of a date, time, or timestamp must conform to the field type of the column you are modifying.

Below, you see the format and an example of each date/time literal type. These formats are fixed, and you cannot express dates in any other way. This does not mean that the date must display in this format. When you express a date literal, you must comply with the data format in the database, but you can format these values to display in any of the other date formats by formatting the column data. To express a date/time literal, use the keywords DATE, TIME, or

TIMESTAMP followed by a date or time string enclosed in single quote marks. You must use four digits for the year and two digits for all other components, even if the value is a single digit.

```
DATE 'yyyy-MM-dd'
DATE '1972-05-17'

TIME 'hh:MM:ss'
TIME '07:22:00'

TIMESTAMP 'yyyy-MM-dd hh:mm:ss'
TIMESTAMP '1972-05-17 07:22:00'
```

Numeric Literals

To express a numeric literal in a numeric column, simply include the number. Do not surround numeric literals with single quotes; doing so expresses the literal as a character literal.

You may preface a number with either a plus sign (+) or minus sign (–) to indicate a positive or negative number, respectively. Numbers can contain a decimal point and decimal numbers.

To express floating point numbers as literal constants, enter a number followed by the letter *E* (either uppercase or lowercase) and followed by a plus sign or minus sign to indicate a positive or negative exponent. No spaces are allowed between the integer, the letter *E*, and the sign of the exponent. Table 5-2 offers some tips on the various formats of numeric literal values.

Inserting Blank Columns

There are times when you want to insert a blank column in your report. Simply removing the analytical field reference from a column is not enough to create a blank column. You are essentially expressing a literal value of nothing. Using either a text or date field, replace the column's analytical field reference with two single quotes (' '). This replaces the column value with nothing.

Desired Output	Numeric Literal	Notes
10	10	Do not use single quotes. Doing so will express the number as a character.
3.75	3.75	Be sure you are not using an Integer field, and format the column to show the decimal places.
1,943,325	1943325	Do not use commas. If you want commas in the value, format the column display.
–76 (76)	–76	Enter negatives with the minus sign. If you prefer negative numbers inside parentheses, format the column display.
0.0000000001	1e–10	Be sure you format the column to display enough decimal places.

TABLE 5-2. *Numeric Literals*

You cannot create a blank column using a numeric column while retaining its numeric format. If you need to create a numeric column with no value, replace the analytical field reference with a zero.

Changing Column Formulas

The analytical field reference is the default formula for a column. You can add to, change, or delete this analytical field reference to obtain the data you need for your report. There is a very wide range of complexities that your column formulas can take on. In addition to analytical field references, column formulas may contain operators, functions, variables, and literals.

The Edit Column Formula window contains a series of buttons that help you to build your formulas without requiring you to memorize all of the specific syntax requirements. It is, however, quite useful to make yourself familiar with the operators, functions, literal formats, and variables available to you. Having a strong working knowledge of these will assist you not only in designing and developing reports, but also with troubleshooting reporting issues and testing assumptions about your data.

The remainder of this chapter is dedicated to some basic formula writing and use of the tools in the Edit Column Formula window. The four chapters following this chapter are focused on the vast collection of functions in Answers On Demand.

Simple Column Formulas

Let us begin our foray into column formulas with some simple calculations. With some familiar operators, you can perform calculations. A commission report that multiplies sales revenue by .05 to calculate commission amounts is an example of a simple formula that includes one analytical field reference, an operator, and an expressed constant. The structure of these simple calculation formulas follows the normal rules of mathematical structure that we all learned in school:

```
"Revenue Metrics"."Opportunity Revenue" * .05
```

Operators may also be used to perform a calculation using multiple analytical field references. Comparing the number of opportunity activities to opportunity revenue to get some idea of the value of level of effort would be one example of this type of formula:

```
Opportunity."Opportunity Revenue" / "Activity Metrics"."# of Activities"
```

To build a formula like these, you should first add a column to your report. This is the column of which you will edit the formula, so it usually makes sense to select the column that will be first identified in the formula. Open the Edit Column Formula window and add the desired operator. You can add some of these operators by clicking one of the buttons just below the Column Formula field (see Figure 5-1).

To insert the analytical field reference of another column, simply click the name of the column in the Columns list on the left while your cursor is in the Column Formula field.

Table 5-3 identifies all of the available operators, with a definition and sample formula for each. More complex formulas may include several of these operators.

Other operators exist for comparison operations and use with filters and functions within a column formula. You will use the comparison operators primarily in CASE and FILTER statements. You will see both of these later in this chapter, and I cover CASE statements in detail in Chapter 9, but in the spirit of completeness, Table 5-4 describes the remainder of the operators.

Operator	Description
+	The plus sign for addition. Type it into your formula or click the + button beneath the Column Formula field. Use + to add numeric column values or literals to other numeric column values or literals. "Revenue Metrics"."Expected Revenue" + "Revenue Metrics"."Closed Revenue" "Revenue Metrics"."Closed Revenue" + 1000
–	The minus sign for subtraction. Type it into your formula or click the – button beneath the Column Formula field. Use – to calculate the difference between numeric column values or literals and other numeric column values or literals. "Revenue Metrics"."Opportunity Revenue" – "Revenue Metrics"."Closed Revenue" "Revenue Metrics"."Closed Revenue" – 250
*	Use an asterisk to multiply. Type it into your formula or click the × button beneath the Column Formula field. Use * to multiply numeric column values or literals by other numeric column values or literals. "Revenue Metrics"."# of Wins" * "Revenue Metrics"."Average Deal Size" "Revenue Metrics"."Closed Revenue" * .025
/	Use a forward slash to divide. Type it into your formula or click the / button beneath the Column Formula field. Use / to divide numeric column values or literals by other numeric column values or literals. The dividend is before the / and the divisor is after the / in the formula. "Revenue Metrics"."Closed Revenue" / "Revenue Metrics"."Average Deal Size" "Revenue Metrics"."Closed Revenue" / 100 The % button below the Column Formula field inserts /100 to divide by 100 to reach a percentage value.
||	The double pipe concatenates character strings. Type it into your formula or click the || button beneath the Column Formula field. Use || to tie character strings together. Strings may be column values or literals in a formula result. 'You have '||"Revenue Metrics"."# of Opportunities" || 'Opportunities' Contact."Contact Name" || ': Please sign here. _____'
( )	Use the open and close parentheses to begin and end a group for grouping operations. Type them into your formula or click the (and) buttons beneath the Column Formula field. ("Revenue Metrics"."Opportunity Revenue" – "Revenue Metrics"."Closed Revenue") / 50 (10 * ("Revenue Metrics"."Closed Revenue" * .025)) / ("Revenue Metrics"."# of Opportunities")

TABLE 5-3. *Math Operators*

Operator	Description
>	The greater than sign, indicating values higher than the comparison
<	The less than sign, indicating values lower than the comparison
=	The equal sign, indicating the same value
>=	The greater than or equal to sign, indicating values the same or higher than the comparison
<=	The less than or equal to sign, indicating values the same or lower than the comparison
<>	The not equal to sign, indicating values higher or lower, but not the same
AND	AND connective, indicating intersection with one or more conditions to form a compound condition
OR	OR connective, indicating the union with one or more conditions to form a compound condition
NOT	NOT connective, indicating a condition is not met
,	Comma, used to separate elements in a list

TABLE 5-4.   *Comparison and Connective Operators*

We will see more of these formulas, and examine how to create and use them, in the coming sections. You will find many of the operators from Table 5-4 in the following examples:

```
FILTER(Employee."Employee Name" USING (((Territory."Territory Name" = 'Central')
AND ("Revenue Metrics"."Opportunity Revenue" >= 100000)) OR ((Territory."Territory
Name" = 'Central') AND ("Revenue Metrics"."Opportunity Revenue" < 500000))))
CASE
WHEN Account."Account State / Province" IN ('FL', 'GA', 'NC', 'SC', 'VA') THEN
'Eastern Accounts'
WHEN Account."Account State / Province" IN ('AZ', 'CA', 'MO', 'NV', 'OR', 'WA')
THEN 'Western Accounts'
WHEN Account."Account State / Province" IN ('DE', 'KY', 'MD', 'DC', 'NH', 'PA')
THEN 'Northeast Accounts'
ELSE 'Central Accounts'
END
CASE
WHEN Account."Annual Revenue" <= 1000000 THEN 'Large Account'
WHEN Account."Annual Revenue" < 100000 THEN 'Small Account'
ELSE 'Medium Account'
END
```

Bins

A common task when working with reports is to group and label records that fit a certain criteria. Doing so can result in a much cleaner report (see Figure 5-11). A CASE statement in the column

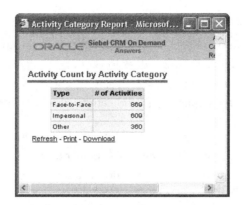

FIGURE 5-11. *Activity Category report*

formula makes this possible. The bins functionality makes creating the column formula to do this very easy.

The report in Figure 5-11 shows an example of using bins to group records. The database does not include a field to categorize activities as Face-to-Face, Impersonal, or Other. We can create these categories on our report using bins to create the CASE statement that groups and labels the activities for our report:

```
CASE
WHEN Activity.Type IN ('Demonstration', 'Meeting', 'Presentation') THEN 'Face-to-
Face'
WHEN Activity.Type IN ('Call', 'Email') THEN 'Impersonal'
ELSE 'Other'
END
```

It is not important that you understand the structure of the resulting CASE statement generated using bins. To use bins on a report column, access the Edit Column Formula window for the column you wish to group. Click the Bins tab. Click the Add Bin button. The Create/Edit Filter window, with which you should be familiar from the previous chapter, opens for you to create the criteria for the first bin.

Designate the condition and value for your bin. Continue adding bins as necessary until you have identified all of your bin groups. You may also add a bin for all values that do not meet the criteria of any of the other bins. Notice that each of these filters is added to the Bins tab in the order that you create them. These filters are evaluated in the order listed here, so order may be important if you have any overlapping criteria. Use the up and down arrow buttons beside each filter to modify their order as necessary. Figure 5-12 shows the Bins tab for the Activity Category Report example above.

After creating your bins, if you return to the Column Formula tab, you can see the CASE statement generated by your bin settings. At this point, the CASE statement is not directly editable. You can make changes by returning to the Bins tab and modifying the filters. If you use bins to generate your CASE statement, but want to make some more complex changes to the CASE

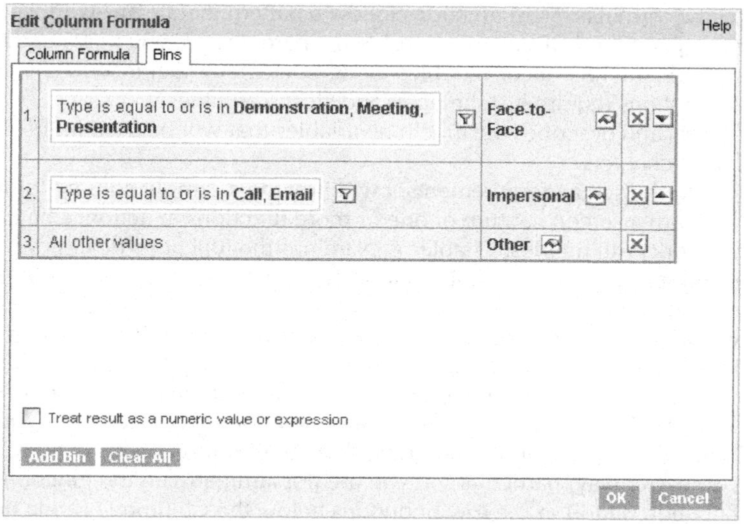

FIGURE 5-12. *Bins tab*

statement, click the Clear All button on the Bins tab. This opens the Clear Bins message shown in Figure 5-13. Click the Yes button here and the CASE statement remains in the Column Formula tab and the bin definitions clear from the Bins tab. Now, you can return to the Column Formula tab and edit the CASE statement directly. Click the No button on the Clear Bins message and both the CASE statement and bin definitions clear from the Edit Column Formula window, and the original analytical field reference for the column returns to the Column Formula field.

There are many other uses for CASE statements that I will discuss in Chapter 9, but to quickly create a simple grouping CASE statement, there is no quicker or easier method than using bins.

Functions

Nearly everything you do in Answers On Demand generates some SQL, whether you see it or not, that performs a query operation against the database to build your report. Answers On Demand recognizes many SQL functions, or commands, if you prefer. Among the functions available, there are aggregate, string, math, calendar date/time, conversion, and system functions. The four chapters that follow this one describe each function in detail with examples of its use.

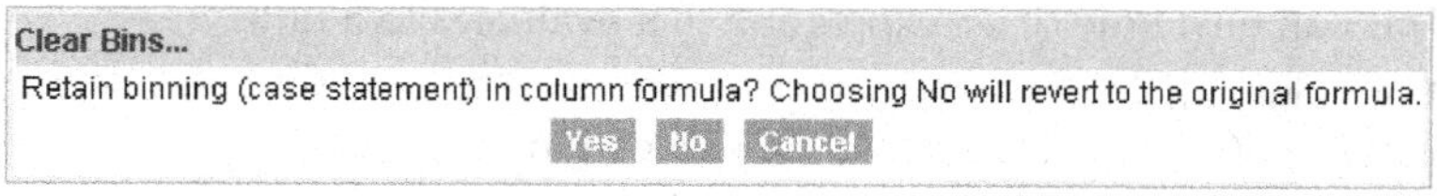

FIGURE 5-13. *Clear Bins message*

For now, take a look at the basic structure of functions and how you can insert these functions into your column formulas. Most functions follow a pattern that begins with the function name and is followed by a parenthetical statement. Inside the parentheses, you may need to designate a column analytical field reference, variables, or other elements that instruct the function on the data to use. Some functions require just the open and close parentheses.

Table 5-5 lists and describes the function variables that will be used in the syntax for functions in this and future chapters.

In addition to the syntax requirements, I will provide a sample column formula using the function along with a screen capture of one or more functions in action. Chapter 6 examines the functions that work with metrics. Chapter 7 examines the functions dealing with dates and times. Chapter 8 examines the functions that work with character strings. Chapter 9 examines the CASE function and functions that convert data.

Before we dig into the specific functions, let us have a look at how we can add functions to our column formulas. Begin by adding a column to your report that is the appropriate format. If your function is going to include a reference to a column, it often makes sense to start with that column. Access the Edit Column Formula window for your chosen column. On the Column Formula tab, you can type your function directly in the Column Formula field.

There is an easier way, particularly if you are not familiar with the function you want to use. Notice the Function button in the row of buttons below the Column Formula field. Click the

Variable	Description
m-exp	Metric expression. This is an analytical field reference or expression built off of any column located in a Metrics folder of the current subject area.
n-exp	Numeric expression. This can be anything that evaluates as a number or a literal number.
N	Integer. This can be any whole number or expression that results in a whole number.
string	Character string. This can be any string of characters, or a reference to a text field.
expression	Any expression. This can be any numeric or text expression.
char-exp	Character expression. This can be any single character or expression that evaluates to a single character.
date-exp	Date expression. This can be a date or an expression that evaluates to a date.
time-exp	Time expression. This can be a time or an expression that evaluates to a time.
interval	Time interval. This is a SQL Time Stamp Interval expression.

TABLE 5-5. *SQL Function Variables*

FIGURE 5-14. *Insert Function window*

Function button to open the Insert Function window (see Figure 5-14). The content of the Insert Function window includes an organized list of most available functions. Expand a category to see the functions included within. Click a function and the function's syntax and a brief description display below the Functions list.

Click the OK button to insert the selected function into the column formula. If you have highlighted the column formula before clicking the Function button, when you click OK the function and current formula come together so that the function statement is in front with the formula inside the parentheses. If the function requires nothing inside the parentheses, the selected function will overwrite the highlighted formula.

To insert a column reference for a column not included in your report, place your cursor in the Column Formula field and click the column name from the Columns list on the left of the window. The analytical field reference for the column you click inserts into the Column Formula field. If you have a need to insert the formula from another column in the report, you can click the Column button and select the desired column. Inserting a column using this method drops the entire content of the selected column's Column Formula field into the current folder. This allows you to reuse formulas from other columns or nest formulas together very easily.

Session Functions and Variables

Session functions and session variables are bits of SQL code that result in values that you can reference within other functions. This section describes two session functions and a number of session variables. Most of these variables arrive at results that you can easily derive from other functions and, in some cases, data that frankly is not very useful.

Session Functions

In Answers On Demand, I have encountered only two session functions, DATABASE() and USER(). Their usefulness is limited, but I include them here in hopes that you will find a use for them. You use a session function the same way you will use all other functions. Add a column to your report and replace the column formula with the session function. Session functions operate on server information rather than column data.

DATABASE()

The DATABASE() session function returns the name of the On Demand database that you are currently logged in to. This really does not do much to help you since Answers On Demand is primarily a hosted service. In the future, on-premise versions of CRM On Demand may change how useful this information is to an administrator.

USER()

The USER() session function returns the current user's login ID. In recent implementations of CRM On Demand, a company identifier followed by a slash mark is part of a user's ID. USER() in these instances replaces the slash with the pound sign, rendering it somewhat less useful. The REPLUSER session variable returns the same information with the slash intact.

Session Variables

Session variables in Answers On Demand are much more useful than the session functions. Having made that statement, I should reiterate that most of these variables return data that you can also generate with other functions, though sometimes not as easily. You can use session variables in filters and formulas to insert values. All session variables are called with the VALUEOF function and have a prefix of NQ_SESSION. In this section, I give a brief description of each of the session variables of which I am aware. There may be other, undocumented session variables.

VALUEOF

The VALUEOF function extracts the value of a session variable within a column formula or filter. Use the VALUEOF function for all session variables, which begin with NQ_SESSION and provide information relevant to the current CRM On Demand session for the user running the report.

Function Syntax

```
VALUEOF(session variable)
VALUEOF(NQ_SESSION.REPLUSER)
```

The syntax for the VALUEOF function requires that you include a complete session variable inside of the parentheses. A complete session variable always begins with NQ_SESSION followed by a period and the name of the variable. Session variables are occasionally added to Answers On Demand, and often go undocumented. The list of session variables in this text will continue to grow after printing.

REPLUSER

```
VALUEOF(NQ_SESSION.REPLUSER)
```

This may be the most useful of all the session variables. It certainly is my favorite, at least. Just like the USER() session function, the REPLUSER session variable returns the login ID of the person currently logged into the session. This variable correctly returns the slash character, unlike the session function. In other words, it identifies the person running the report. A filter on the Owned By User/User Email column set to equal the REPLUSER session variable will limit the data in the report to only records owned by the user running the report.

Another favorite use of this session variable is to filter on the Manager Email column. A report limited to records where the manager email is equal to the current user will actually include all records owned by the current user and those records owned by any subordinates of that individual. This works due to the combination of the Manager Email and Reporting Level fields. Answers On Demand identifies each user as their own manager with reporting level 0, their immediate manager with reporting level 1, and continues this pattern for the entire reporting hierarchy.

Figure 5-15 shows an example of using the REPLUSER system variable.

DISPLAYNAME

VALUEOF(NQ_SESSION.DISPLAYNAME)

This session variable returns the username of the person currently logged into the session. This value is on the User Name column of the user record. You could potentially use this session variable to limit the data to records owned by the current user based on username. The primary issue with this use is that users may have the same name in CRM On Demand. The user email address (or login ID) must be unique for each user, so the REPLUSER session variable is more reliable for this use.

A more valid use of this variable would be as part of a column formula to return the current user's name in a column of your report. You could then expose this column in a view on the report to indicate the name of the user who generated the report. This can be particularly useful for reports designed for printing and distribution.

Figure 5-16 shows an example of using the DISPLAYNAME system variable.

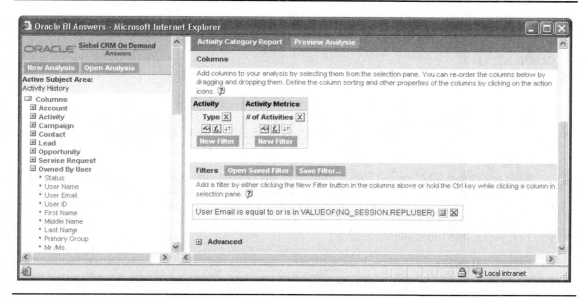

FIGURE 5-15. *Adding the REPLUSER system variable to a column filter*

FIGURE 5-16. *Current user's display name exposed in a report*

CURRENT_YEAR

VALUEOF(NQ_SESSION.CURRENT_YEAR)

The CURRENT_YEAR session variable returns the current four-digit fiscal year. For instance, if your fiscal year begins on the first day of July, and you run a report with this variable on November 4, 2008, the result of the CURRENT_YEAR variable would be 2009. If you need to use the current calendar year in a formula, you should use the YEAR function, described in Chapter 7.

In Figures 5-17 and 5-18 I have created a report using several of these date-based session variables. Figure 5-17 shows the Build and View Analysis window with the formulas showing in the column headers. Figure 5-18 shows the results of this report. Note that the values returned are just numbers. This is important because one of these session variables can serve as a numeric expression in another formula.

CURRENT_QTR

VALUEOF(NQ_SESSION.CURRENT_QTR)

The CURRENT_QTR session variable returns the current one-digit fiscal quarter. For instance, if your fiscal year begins on the first day of July, and you run a report with this variable on November 4, 2008, the result of the CURRENT_QTR variable would be 2. If you need to use the current calendar year in a formula, you should use the QUARTER_OF_YEAR function, described in Chapter 7.

Refer to Figures 5-17 and 5-18 for a sample of this session variable. This variable assumes that you use calendar months for your quarter. If your company uses a 4-5-4 or 4-4-5 quarter where the fiscal months and quarters are determined by the number of weeks, the quarter start and end dates will vary slightly from year to year. This variable may not return an accurate result for you if you find yourself in this situation.

CURRENT_MONTH

VALUEOF(NQ_SESSION.CURRENT_MONTH)

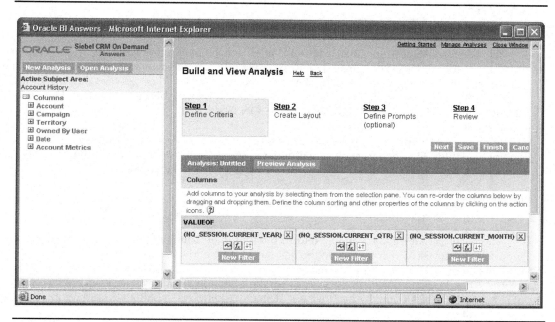

FIGURE 5-17.   *Date Session Variables—Build and View Analysis window*

The CURRENT_MONTH session variable returns the current one- or two-digit fiscal month. For instance, if your fiscal year begins on the first day of July, and you run a report with this variable on November 4, 2008, the result of the CURRENT_MONTH variable would be 5. If you need to use the current calendar month in a formula, you should use the MONTH function, described in Chapter 7.

Refer to Figures 5-17 and 5-18 for a sample of this session variable. This variable assumes that you use calendar months for your quarter, so the same caveat as described in the preceding section applies if your company uses a 4-5-4 or 4-4-5 calendar.

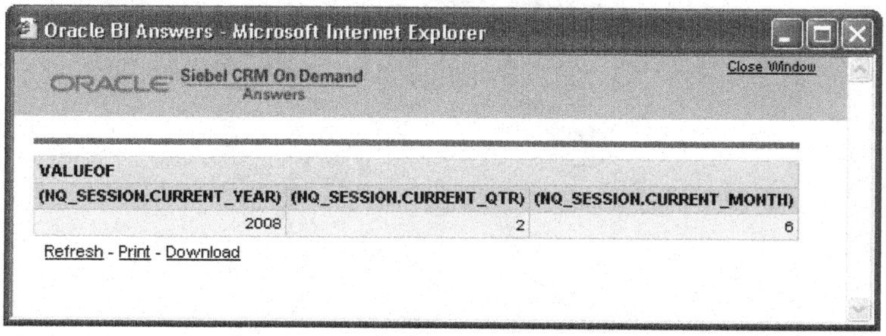

FIGURE 5-18.   *Date Session Variables report*

LAST_YEAR

VALUEOF(NQ_SESSION.LAST_YEAR)

The LAST_YEAR session variable returns the four-digit value of the previous fiscal year. For instance, if your fiscal year begins on the first day of July, and you run a report with this variable on November 4, 2008, the result of the LAST_YEAR variable would be 2008 as the current fiscal year is 2009. You can use math operators with these session variables as well, so VALUEOF(NQ_SESSION.LAST_YEAR) and VALUEOF(NQ_SESSION.CURRENT_YEAR)–1 would return the exact same result.

In Figures 5-19 and 5-20 I have created a report using the LAST_YEAR and NEXT_YEAR session variables. Figure 5-19 shows the Build and View Analysis window with the formulas showing in the column headers. Figure 5-20 shows the results of this report.

NEXT_YEAR

VALUEOF(NQ_SESSION.NEXT_YEAR)

The NEXT_YEAR session variable returns the four-digit value of the coming fiscal year. For instance, if your fiscal year begins on the first day of July, and you run a report with this variable on November 4, 2008, the result of the NEXT_YEAR variable would be 2010, as the current fiscal year is 2009. You can use math operators with these session variable as well, so VALUEOF(NQ_SESSION.NEXT_YEAR) and VALUEOF(NQ_SESSION.CURRENT_YEAR)+1 would return the exact same result.

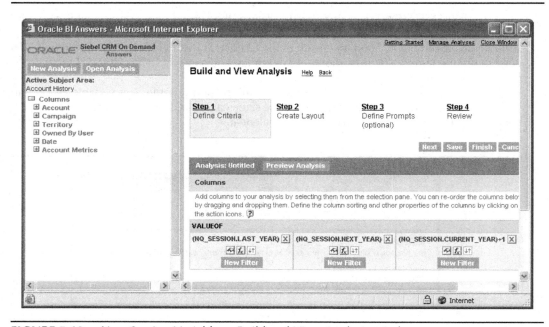

FIGURE 5-19. *Year Session Variables—Build and View Analysis window*

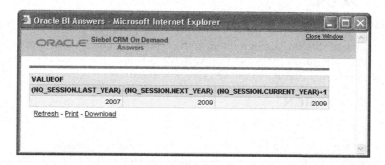

FIGURE 5-20. *Year Session Variables report*

Again, Figures 5-19 and 5-20 show a report using the LAST_YEAR and NEXT_YEAR session variables. Figure 5-19 shows the Build and View Analysis window with the formulas showing in the column headers. Figure 5-20 shows the results of this report. Notice that the third column uses the CURRENT_YEAR variable to calculate next year by adding one to the value.

COMPANY_TIMEZONE

```
VALUEOF(NQ_SESSION.COMPANY_TIMEZONE)
```

The COMPANY_TIMEZONE session variable returns the value in the Default Time Zone field on the company profile window. This can be particularly useful if timestamp values are present in your report, because reports reflect times in the default time zone for the company. Figure 5-21 shows a sample result from this session variable.

Campaign Session Variables

The remaining session variables documented in this chapter are all specific to campaigns. You can find sample uses of each of these session variables in the Campaign Management prebuilt reports.

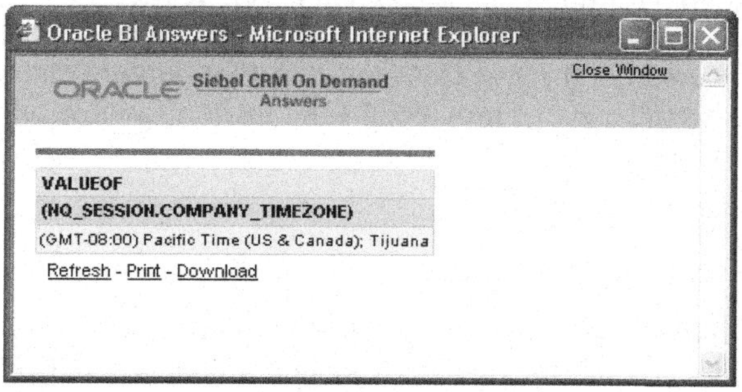

FIGURE 5-21. *COMPANY_TIMEZONE session variable result*

ACTIVE_CAMPAIGN

VALUEOF(NQ_SESSION.ACTIVE_CAMPAIGN)

This session variable is used in a filter on the Marketing Effectiveness report named Active Campaign Status. The result of this session variable is simply the word "Active" and does not appear to be tied to any metrics in the On Demand database.

COMPLETED_CAMPAIGN

VALUEOF(NQ_SESSION.COMPLETED_CAMPAIGN)

This session variable is used in a filter on the Marketing Effectiveness report named Completed Campaign Results. The result of this session variable is simply the word "Completed" and does not appear to be tied to any metrics in the On Demand database.

AVG_COST_PER_CLSD_SALE_PER_CMPGN

VALUEOF(NQ_SESSION.AVG_COST_PER_CLSD_SALE_PER_CMPGN)

This session variable is used in the Marketing Effectiveness report named Campaign Performance Summary – Averages. This variable provides the overall average campaign cost per closed sale per campaign, and is the same value returned by the Avg Cost Per Closed Sale metric column in the Campaign History subject area if applied to all campaigns. A comparison of this metric applied to a subset of campaigns and the overall average provided by the session variable provides insight into how that set of campaigns is performing compared to historical averages.

AVG_DAYS_TO_CONVERT_LEAD_PER_CMPGN

VALUEOF(NQ_SESSION.AVG_DAYS_TO_CONVERT_LEAD_PER_CMPGN)

This session variable is used in the Marketing Effectiveness report named Campaign Averages. This variable provides the overall average number of days it took to convert leads tied to campaigns. A comparison of the Avg Days to Convert Lead metric applied to a subset of campaigns and the overall average provided by the session variable provides current performance against historical averages.

AVG_DAYS_TO_CLOSE_OPTY_PER_CMPGN

VALUEOF(NQ_SESSION.AVG_DAYS_TO_CLOSE_OPTY_PER_CMPGN)

This session variable is used in the Marketing Effectiveness report named Campaign Averages. This variable provides the overall average number of days it took to close opportunities tied to campaigns. A comparison of the Avg Days to Close Opportunity metric applied to a subset of campaigns and the overall average provided by the session variable provides current performance against historical averages.

AVG_ACT_COST_PER_CMPGN

VALUEOF(NQ_SESSION.AVG_ACT_COST_PER_CMPGN)

This session variable is used in the Marketing Effectiveness report named Campaign Detailed Results. This variable provides the overall average from the Actual Cost field on all campaigns. There is also a column named Avg Actual Cost available in the Campaign History subject area in the Campaign/Actual Cost folder. Compare the results of the variable and this column to judge a subset of campaigns against the overall average.

AVG_BDGT_COST_PER_CMPGN

VALUEOF(NQ_SESSION.AVG_BDGT_COST_PER_CMPGN)

This session variable is used in the Marketing Effectiveness report named Campaign Detailed Results. This variable provides the overall average from the Budgeted Cost field on all campaigns. There is also a column named Avg Budgeted Cost available in the Campaign History subject area in the Campaign/Budgeted Cost folder. Compare the results of the variable and this column to judge a subset of campaigns against the overall average.

AVG_LEAD_TGT_PER_CMPGN

VALUEOF(NQ_SESSION.AVG_LEAD_TGT_PER_CMPGN)

This session variable is used in the Marketing Effectiveness report named Campaign Detailed Results. This variable provides the overall average from the Leads Targeted (#) field on all campaigns. There is also a column named Avg Leads Targeted (#) available in the Campaign History subject area in the Campaign/Leads Targeted (#) folder. Compare the results of the variable and this column to see how aggressive your targets today are compared to the overall average.

AVG_REVN_TGT_PER_CMPGN

VALUEOF(NQ_SESSION.AVG_REVN_TGT_PER_CMPGN)

This session variable is used in the Marketing Effectiveness report named Campaign Detailed Results. This variable provides the overall average from the Revenue Target field on all campaigns. There is also a column named Avg Revenue Target available in the Campaign History subject area in the Campaign/Revenue Target folder. Compare the results of the variable and this column to see how aggressive your targets today are compared to the overall average.

AVG_PCT_LEAD_TGT_ACHVD_PER_CMPGN

VALUEOF(NQ_SESSION.AVG_PCT_LEAD_TGT_ACHVD_PER_CMPGN)

This session variable is used in the Marketing Effectiveness report named Campaign Detailed Results. This variable provides the overall percentage of campaigns that achieved their targeted number of leads. This calculation comes from dividing the targeted number of leads by the count of leads tied to campaigns. You can include this calculation in your report using the % of Lead Target Achieved metric in the Campaign History subject area. You can use this session variable to compare that success rate metric with the overall success rate.

AVG_PCT_REVN_TGT_ACHVD_PER_CMPGN

VALUEOF(NQ_SESSION.AVG_PCT_REVN_TGT_ACHVD_PER_CMPGN)

This session variable is used in the Marketing Effectiveness report named Campaign Detailed Results. This variable provides the overall percentage of campaigns that achieved their targeted revenue amount. This calculation comes from dividing the targeted number of leads by the count of leads tied to campaigns. You can include this calculation in your report using the % of Revenue Target Achieved metric in the Campaign History subject area. You can use this session variable to compare that success rate metric with the overall success rate.

AVG_PCT_BDGT_PER_CMPGN

VALUEOF(NQ_SESSION.AVG_PCT_BDGT_PER_CMPGN)

This session variable is used in the Marketing Effectiveness report named Campaign Detailed Results. This variable provides the overall percentage of campaign budget used. This calculation comes from dividing the actual cost amount by the budget cost amount for all campaigns. You can include this calculation in your report using the % of Budget metric in the Campaign History subject area. You can use this session variable to see how well your current campaigns are staying within budget compared to the overall percentage.

AVG_COST_PER_LEAD_PER_CMPGN

VALUEOF(NQ_SESSION.AVG_COST_PER_LEAD_PER_CMPGN)

This session variable is used in the Marketing Effectiveness report named Campaign Detailed Results. This variable provides the overall average of campaign cost compared to the number of leads generated by those campaigns. This calculation comes from dividing the actual cost amount by the number of leads tied to campaigns. You can include this calculation in your report using the Avg Cost Per Lead metric in the Campaign History subject area. You can use this session variable to see how well your current cost-to-lead ratio is stacking up to the overall average.

AVG_COST_PER_CLSD_SALE_PER_CMPGN

VALUEOF(NQ_SESSION.AVG_COST_PER_CLSD_SALE_PER_CMPGN)

This session variable is used in the Marketing Effectiveness report named Campaign Detailed Results. This variable provides the overall average of campaign cost compared to the number of closed sales generated by those campaigns. This calculation comes from dividing the actual cost amount by the number of closed sales tied to campaigns. You can include this calculation in your report using the Avg Cost Per Closed Sale metric in the Campaign History subject area. You can use this session variable to see how well your current cost-to-closed sale ratio compares to the overall average.

AVG_ROI_PER_CMPGN

VALUEOF(NQ_SESSION.AVG_ROI_PER_CMPGN)

This session variable is used in the Marketing Effectiveness report named Campaign Detailed Results. This variable provides the overall average return on investment per campaign using all campaigns. Return on investment is calculated by dividing the difference between cost and revenue by the cost of the campaign. You can include this calculation in your report using the ROI (%) metric in the Campaign History subject area. You can use this session variable to see how well your current return on investment compares to the overall average.

AVG_NUM_LEADS_PER_CMPGN

VALUEOF(NQ_SESSION.AVG_NUM_LEADS_PER_CMPGN)

This session variable is used in the Marketing Effectiveness report named Campaign Detailed Results. This variable provides the overall average number of leads generated per campaign across all campaigns. This is a useful indicator for marketing organizations that tie the success of their campaigns to lead generation. This calculation is also available as a metric column named # of Leads for Campaign if you apply the aggregation rule to average the values across a subset of campaigns. Comparing the metric results to the session variable provides a view of how well your campaigns are generating leads against the overall average.

AVG_LEAD_CONV_RATE_PER_CMPGN

`VALUEOF(NQ_SESSION.AVG_LEAD_CONV_RATE_PER_CMPGN)`

This session variable is used in the Marketing Effectiveness report named Campaign Detailed Results. This variable provides the overall average lead conversion rate across all campaigns. This takes the previous metric one step further and, in addition to the number of leads generated per campaign, calculates the rate of conversion of these leads. When generating leads is not enough, but the conversion of leads to accounts, contacts, and/or opportunities is the result you are after, this metric is for you. Lead Conversion Rate for Campaign is the comparable metric in the Campaign History subject area. Comparing the metric results to the session variable provides a view of how well your campaigns are generating converted leads against the overall average.

AVG_NUM_WINS_PER_CMPGN

`VALUEOF(NQ_SESSION.AVG_NUM_WINS_PER_CMPGN)`

This session variable is used in the Marketing Effectiveness report named Campaign Detailed Results. This variable provides the overall average number of wins across all campaigns. Since a converted lead does not guarantee a win, this variable takes the previous metric to the next step and, in addition to the rate of leads converted per campaign, calculates the number of opportunities resulting in a Closed/Won sales stage. Wins means revenue, and having some idea of the number of wins generated by your campaigns leads to analytical proof of the financial success of your campaigns. Use the Campaign History metric named # of Wins for Campaign. Comparing the metric results to the session variable provides a view of how well your campaigns are generating converted leads against the overall average.

AVG_OPTY_WIN_RATE_PER_CMPGN

`VALUEOF(NQ_SESSION.AVG_OPTY_WIN_RATE_PER_CMPGN)`

This session variable is used in the Marketing Effectiveness report named Campaign Detailed Results. This variable provides the overall average opportunity win rate across all campaigns. This takes the previous metric one step further and, in addition to the number of wins generated per campaign, calculates the rate of successful opportunity wins. Knowing how many opportunities you receive from campaigns only tells part of the story. Showing the percentage of these opportunities that make it to the Closed/Won sales stage ties real success to your campaigns. Opportunity Win Rate for Campaign is the comparable metric in the Campaign History subject area. Comparing the metric results to the session variable provides a view of how well your campaigns are leading to sales wins against the overall average.

AVG_OPTY_REVN_PER_CMPGN

`VALUEOF(NQ_SESSION.AVG_OPTY_REVN_PER_CMPGN)`

This session variable is used in the Marketing Effectiveness report named Campaign Detailed Results. This variable provides the overall average revenue on opportunities tied to your campaigns. Knowing how many wins you can track back to your campaign is useful, but attributing revenue to campaigns is even better. With this variable, you continue to take your campaign analysis to the next level. Use the Campaign History metric named Opportunity Revenue for Campaign. Comparing the metric results to the session variable provides a view of how well your campaigns are leading to opportunity revenue against the overall average.

AVG_CLSD_REVN_PER_CMPGN

```
VALUEOF(NQ_SESSION.AVG_CLSD_REVN_PER_CMPGN)
```

This session variable is used in the Marketing Effectiveness report named Campaign Detailed Results. This variable provides the overall average closed revenue on opportunities tied to your campaigns. Knowing how many wins you can track back to your campaign is useful, but attributing revenue to campaigns is even better. Since not all revenue on opportunities is realized with a closed sale, the average amount of closed revenue is more telling of campaign success. With this variable, you reach the marketing analysis pinnacle and show real financial results tied all the way back to the campaign that generated the leads that converted to the opportunities that successfully closed and generated revenue. Use the Campaign History metric named Avg Closed Revenue for Campaign. Comparing the metric results to the session variable provides a view of how well your campaigns are leading to opportunity revenue against the overall average.

Filter Function

The FILTER function is like any other function that you use in an expression in the column formula to modify the data returned by the column. The syntax of the filter expression includes a metric column and filter detail:

```
FILTER(m-exp USING (filter detail))
```

Expressions using the FILTER function provide a means for filtering a single column in your report. This makes it possible to create a matrix-style table with categories in the left columns and different segments of the same metric in the columns to the right. Suppose, for instance, that you are interested in knowing how many opportunities your sales people have in each state. Using the FILTER function, you can easily create a report that lists the territories on the left and the number of accounts categorized by owner with the total for each owner in a separate column (see Figure 5-22).

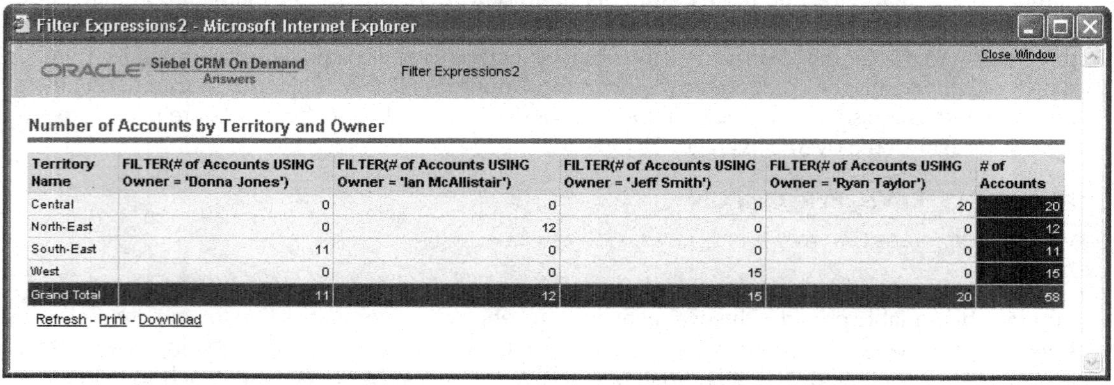

Number of Accounts by Territory and Owner

Territory Name	FILTER(# of Accounts USING Owner = 'Donna Jones')	FILTER(# of Accounts USING Owner = 'Ian McAllistair')	FILTER(# of Accounts USING Owner = 'Jeff Smith')	FILTER(# of Accounts USING Owner = 'Ryan Taylor')	# of Accounts
Central	0	0	0	20	20
North-East	0	12	0	0	12
South-East	11	0	0	0	11
West	0	0	15	0	15
Grand Total	11	12	15	20	58

Refresh - Print - Download

FIGURE 5-22.   *Accounts by Territory and Owner report*

The expression uses a FILTER function to restrict the data in a column based on one or more filters applied to just that column. The expression itself can be somewhat complicated, but Answers On Demand provides a very simple method for applying the FILTER function to your column formula. You can apply the filter expression to metric columns only. That means you must start with a column from the Metrics folder in your subject area. Open the Edit Column Formula window for your metric column. Ensure that you have highlighted the column formula, and then click the Filter button located below the Column Formula field. This opens the Insert Filter window (see Figure 5-23). At the top of this window, you can see the filter expression taking shape.

To add the filter details to the expression, you click the column from the Columns list on the left that you want to use to filter your data. For instance, if you are creating a report like the one shown in Figure 5-22, you would add the Owner column to your filter expression. Clicking on a column opens the Create/Edit Filter window examined in the previous chapter. Define your filter as you would for a report column filter. When you click OK, you return to the Insert Filter window with the newly defined filter's contents displayed in the window.

From here, you can continue to add additional columns to your filter to create a filter group. You can also edit or remove filter details here. When you are satisfied with your filter details, click the OK button to apply the filter expression to the column formula. Repeat this process with the same column multiple times using different filter values with each, and you will soon have a matrix table in your report.

FIGURE 5-23. *Insert Filter window*

You may combine the use of column filters that affect the entire report and filter expressions within specific columns to draw out the data you need for your report. The effect of using filter expressions to create a matrix is very similar to the effect of formatting your data with a pivot table view. When deciding which method you should use, consider that pivot tables have limitations on the number of metric columns you are able to include. On the other hand, pivot tables are very feature-rich and the metric columns are dynamic, meaning that the collection of metric columns present in the table is determined by the data present in the dataset.

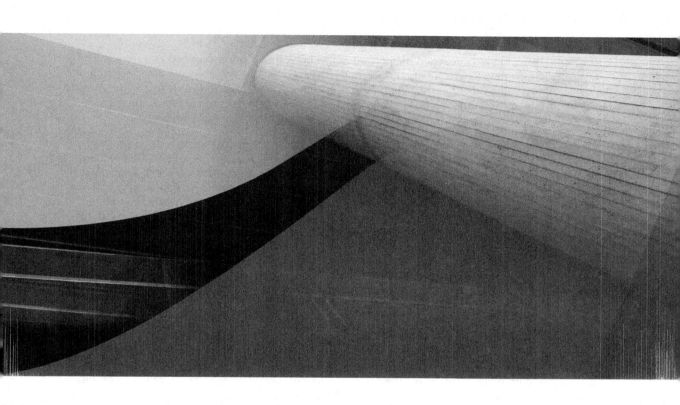

CHAPTER
6

Using Column Formulas
with Numeric Data

ou have reached the portion of this book that is best described as a report developer's function reference. This and the next few chapters describe each of the functions available in Answers On Demand. I provide an explanation of what each function does along with the proper syntax for utilizing each function in column formulas. I also show you the functions in action in reports.

I have organized these functions into chapters according to data type: numeric data (this chapter), date and time data (Chapter 7), character string data (Chapter 8), and finally functions that provide logic and data conversions (Chapter 9). Numbers are probably the first thing you think about when you think of formulas. The functions that modify numeric data are the most plentiful, and usually some of the most useful for analysis of business data. Within this chapter, I have organized the numeric functions into aggregate, running aggregate, and mathematical functions. There are four Answers On Demand field types that contain numeric data. The Number, Integer, Percent, and Currency field types all contain numeric data with which these functions are primarily used.

You will find that most functions may be nested inside of one another to perform multiple functions at once. You may also use some of these aggregate functions with other data types.

Aggregate Functions

We can easily extract detailed data from CRM On Demand with a simple report. This level of minutia is usually not very interesting, insightful, or useful in analyzing large amounts of data. Executives hardly ever want to see the detail of every service request or every sales opportunity. What our decision makers need is a summary of data from CRM On Demand. Aggregate functions work with a set of values, but return a single value. Using aggregate functions in our column formulas allows us to summarize our data in limitless ways.

AVG

The AVG function calculates the average (mean) value of a dataset returned by a numeric expression. For instance, you can use this function to determine the average number of activities completed each week by the sales team.

Applying the AVG function to a numeric column provides the average of all values in that dataset, not necessarily the entire database. For example, in Figure 6-1, the AVG function is applied to the # of Contacts metric. In the results, the average number of contacts represented in

Edit Column Formula	Help

Column Formula | Bins

Table Heading: Contact Metrics

Column Heading: Average # of Contacts

☑ Custom Headings

Avg(Metrics."# of Contacts")

FIGURE 6-1. *Edit Column Formula window—AVG function*

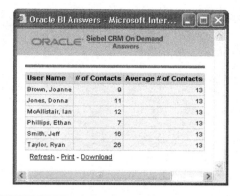

FIGURE 6-2. *Report showing Average # of Contacts*

the report is indicated in the corresponding column (see Figure 6-2). If there are other users who own contacts in my database, but I have filtered them out of this report, the average will change to reflect the average number of contacts owned by the users shown in the report (see Figure 6-3).

Function Syntax

```
AVG(n-exp)
AVG("Revenue Metrics"."Opportunity Revenue")
AVG("Revenue Metrics"."Opportunity Revenue"*.12)
```

The syntax for the AVG function requires that you include a numeric expression in the parentheses. This numeric expression can be any column or formula that results in numeric data. Figure 6-1 shows the AVG function applied to a single metric column.

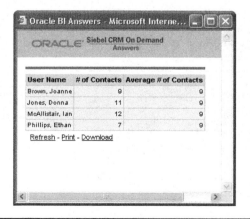

FIGURE 6-3. *Report showing Average # of Contacts with some users filtered out*

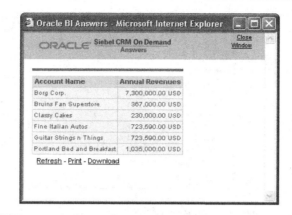

FIGURE 6-4. *Report of account annual revenue*

AVG(DISTINCT)

The AVG(DISTINCT) function calculates the average (mean) value of unique (distinct) values in a dataset returned by a numeric expression. For instance, you can use this function to determine the average number of distinct products purchased by a set of customers.

Applying the AVG(DISTINCT) function to a numeric column provides the average of all unique values in that dataset. For example, in Figure 6-4, I have a set of accounts with their respective revenue amounts. In Figure 6-5, I have another report with the AVG(DISTINCT) function applied to the Annual Revenue column. In Figure 6-6 you will notice that the average annual revenue amount in the third column differs from the average of distinct annual revenue amounts in the fourth column. This is because the revenue for two of my accounts is exactly the same, and that amount is included in the distinct average calculation only once.

Function Syntax

```
AVG(DISTINCT n-exp)
AVG(DISTINCT "Revenue Metrics"."Opportunity Revenue")
AVG(DISTINCT COUNT("Account Metrics"."# of Open SRs"))
```

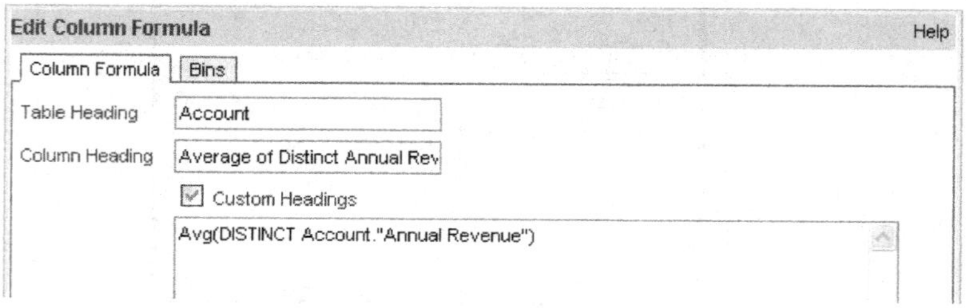

FIGURE 6-5. *AVG(DISTINCT) function applied to Annual Revenue column*

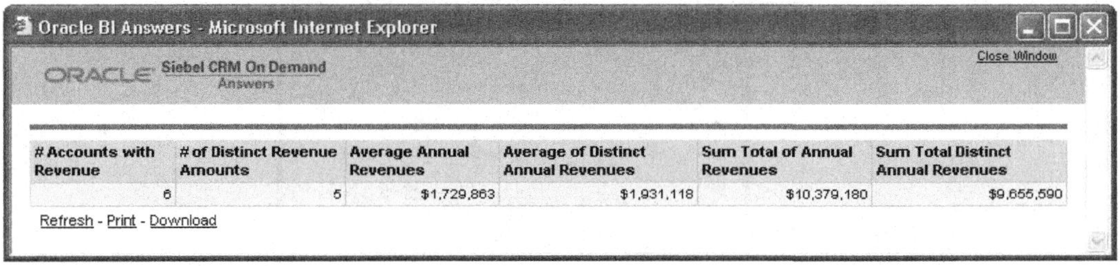

FIGURE 6-6. *Aggregate report on account annual revenue*

The syntax for the AVG(DISTINCT) function is the same as the AVG function with the addition of the DISTINCT modifier before the numeric expression in the parentheses. This numeric expression can be any column or formula that results in numeric data. Figure 6-5 shows the AVG(DISTINCT) function applied to a single metric column.

BOTTOMN

The BOTTOMN function returns the rank from lowest to highest for a designated number of values based in a dataset. The lowest value receives a rank value of 1. The BOTTOMN function works only with numeric data.

Applying the BOTTOMN function to a numeric column provides a rank from the bottom and returns only the number of rows that you designate within the function, unless there is a tie in the ranking. For example, back in Figure 6-4, I have a set of accounts with their respective revenue amounts. In Figure 6-7, I have another report where I have applied the BOTTOMN function to the Annual Revenue column. In Figure 6-8 you will notice that the lowest three annual revenue amounts are returned in this report and the BOTTOMN column in the report displays a numerical rank where 1 is the lowest number in the dataset. The report displays four records because the third-lowest annual revenue amount is on two different accounts. You may use only one BOTTOMN function on any single report.

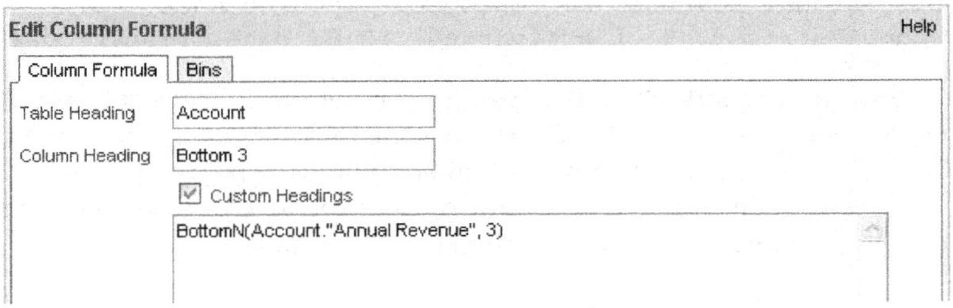

FIGURE 6-7. *BOTTOMN function applied to Annual Revenue column*

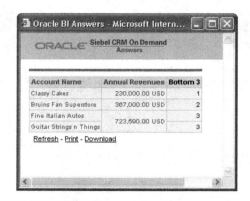

FIGURE 6-8. *Bottom Three Annual Revenue report*

Function Syntax

```
BOTTOMN(n-exp,N)
BOTTOMN("Revenue Metrics"."Opportunity Revenue",10)
BOTTOMN(AVG("Revenue Metrics"."Opportunity Revenue")*
("Revenue Metrics"."# of Opportunities"),20)
```

The syntax for the BOTTOMN function requires that you include a numeric expression in the parentheses, a comma, and the number of rankings to return. The numeric expression can be any column or formula that results in numeric data. Figure 6-7 shows the BOTTOMN function applied to a single numeric column.

BY

Not a function that works alone, BY is a modifier that is quite handy with many of the aggregate functions. You can include BY in a column formula to apply a grouping to your aggregation. For example, you may want to sum activities by month or average revenues by salesperson.

Function Syntax

```
SUM(Account."Annual Revenue" BY Employee."Employee Name")
TOPN("Account Metrics"."# of Activities", 5 BY Date."Fiscal Quarter")
```

Figure 6-9 shows a report where the average number of service requests (SR) by user and the overall average appear. Notice that each user has their own average and that individual average may span multiple rows depending on what other columns appear in the report. The last column shows the overall average, which is the same for each row because the overall average does not consider any other factors and calculates using the entire dataset.

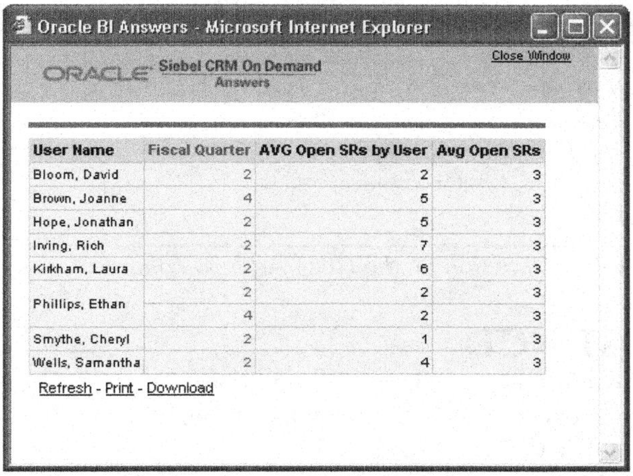

User Name	Fiscal Quarter	AVG Open SRs by User	Avg Open SRs
Bloom, David	2	2	3
Brown, Joanne	4	5	3
Hope, Jonathan	2	5	3
Irving, Rich	2	7	3
Kirkham, Laura	2	6	3
Phillips, Ethan	2	2	3
	4	2	3
Smythe, Cheryl	2	1	3
Wells, Samantha	2	4	3

FIGURE 6-9. *Report of average number of SRs by user and overall*

COUNT

The COUNT function returns a count of the number of rows that contain data. Null records are not counted. The expression is typically a column name, but the expression can be anything. The result is always an integer.

There are many built-in metric columns that provide a count of records, usually records related to the record type you are reporting on. The COUNT function enables you to count records that contain data in any field you choose within the subject area. Counts are often used as part of mathematical operations as well. With a count, you can provide a quantitative value to otherwise qualitative data.

Function Syntax

```
COUNT(expression)
COUNT("Revenue Metrics"."Opportunity Revenue")
COUNT(Contact."Contact Name") - COUNT(Contact."Email Address")
```

The syntax for the COUNT function allows for any expression of any data type. The result of the count is always a number. Best practice for counting nonnumeric values is to insert a metric column and replace the analytical field reference with your COUNT formula. Doing so ensures that the field type is numeric and can therefore be aggregated properly in a table.

Figure 6-10 shows the COUNT function applied to a single column. The report in Figure 6-11 has three columns using the COUNT function. The first and second columns are counts of contacts and contact email addresses. The third column subtracts the count of email addresses from the count of contacts, resulting in the count of contacts without email addresses. The formula I used for this is shown in the preceding syntax samples.

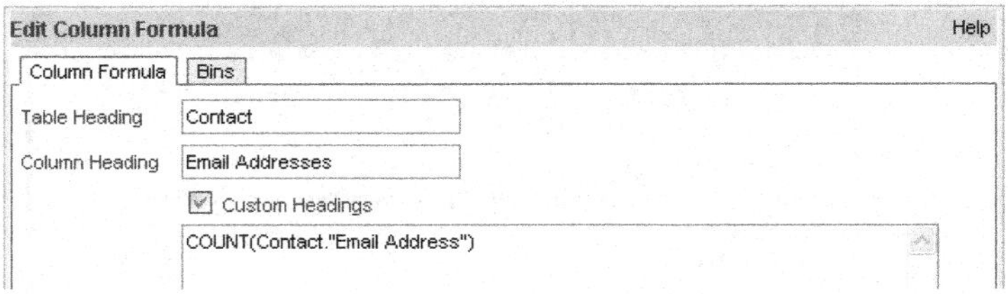

FIGURE 6-10. *COUNT function on the Email Address column*

COUNT(DISTINCT)

The COUNT(DISTINCT) function returns a count of distinct values in a column. Null records are not counted. The expression is typically a column name, but the expression can be anything. The result is always an integer.

The COUNT(DISTINCT) function enables you to count unique records in any field you choose within the subject area. Distinct counts are used to determine how many of something there are, regardless of how many times the same thing appears in the dataset.

Function Syntax

```
COUNT(DISTINCT expression)
COUNT(DISTINCT Lead.Company)
COUNT(Lead.Company)- COUNT(DISTINCT Lead.Company)
```

The syntax for the COUNT(DISTINCT) function allows for any expression of any data type. The result of the count is always a number. Best practice for counting nonnumeric values is to insert a metric column and replace the analytical field reference with your COUNT(DISTINCT) formula. Doing so ensures that the field type is numeric and can therefore be aggregated properly in a table.

Figure 6-12 shows the COUNT(DISTINCT) function applied to a single column. The report in Figure 6-13 has three columns using the COUNT(DISTINCT) function. The first column is a count of the Company field on the Lead record. The second column is the count of distinct company values on the Lead record. The third column subtracts the distinct count from the count of the

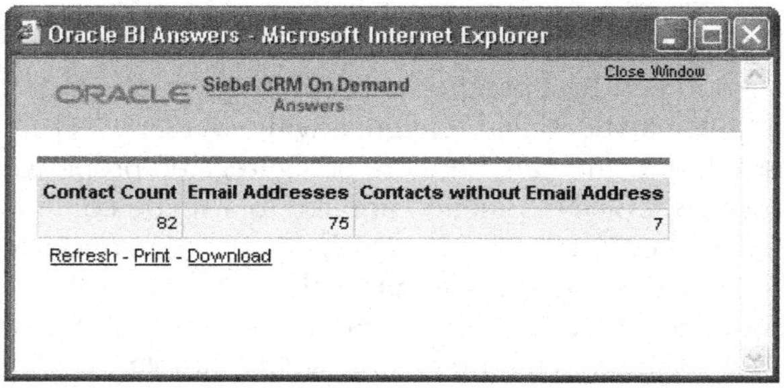

FIGURE 6-11. *Report with count of contacts who have and do not have an email address*

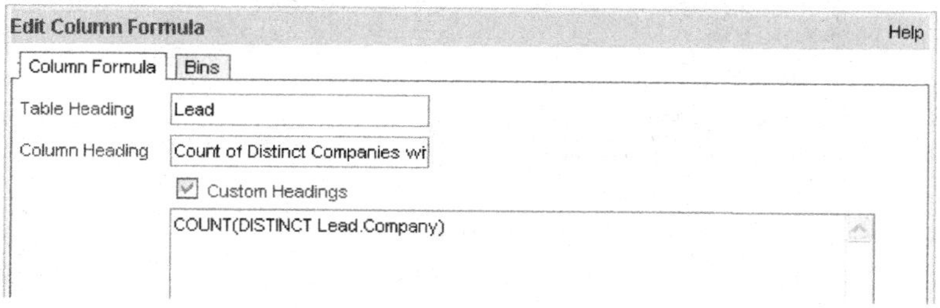

Edit Column Formula   Help

| Column Formula | Bins |

Table Heading   Lead

Column Heading   Count of Distinct Companies wi

☑ Custom Headings

COUNT(DISTINCT Lead.Company)

FIGURE 6-12. *COUNT(DISTINCT) function on the Lead Company column*

Company field, resulting in the number of companies with multiple leads. The formula I used for this is shown in the preceding syntax samples.

COUNT(*)

The COUNT(*) function returns a count of the number of rows in a table. COUNT(*) does not take an expression, so the contents of the columns of the table do not affect the outcome. You may want to use COUNT(*) to get a total of all records, regardless of null values, but a count on one of the key columns, such as Account ID, should return the same count.

Function Syntax

COUNT (*)

MAX

The MAX function returns the largest value from the column in the dataset. For numeric data, this is the largest number in the set. For text string data, the maximum value is the value that would appear at the end of an alphabetical sort. The MAX function applied to date and date/time data returns the latest date or date/time in the dataset.

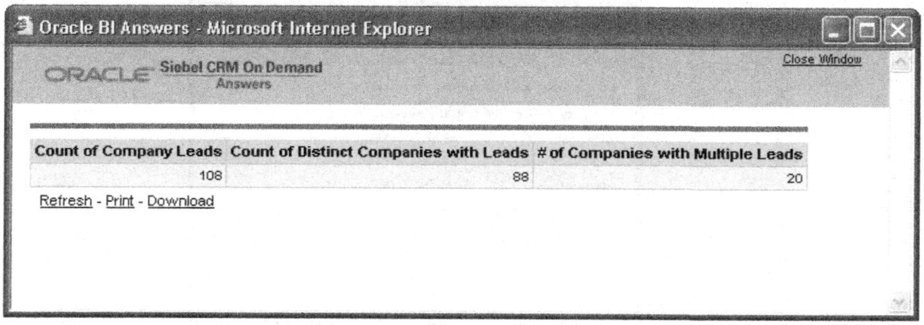

🔳 **Oracle BI Answers - Microsoft Internet Explorer**   🔲🔳❌

ORACLE Siebel CRM On Demand   Close Window
                Answers

Count of Company Leads	Count of Distinct Companies with Leads	# of Companies with Multiple Leads
108	88	20

Refresh - Print - Download

FIGURE 6-13. *Count report of companies named on lead records*

Edit Column Formula   Help

| Column Formula | Bins |

| Table Heading | Account |
| Column Heading | Highest Annual Revenue |

☑ Custom Headings

MAX(Account."Annual Revenue")

FIGURE 6-14. *MAX function applied to the Annual Revenue column*

Any column containing both text and numbers is sorted so that the values beginning with numerals have the lowest value and the values beginning with letters at the end of the alphabet have the highest value. The MAX function on such a column will return a value found at the end of an alphabetical sort.

Function Syntax

```
MAX(expression)
MAX("Account Metrics"."Opportunity Revenue")
MAX("Date Created".Date)
```

Figure 6-14 shows the MAX function applied to the Annual Revenue column. The result in Figure 6-15 illustrates how the MAX function returns the highest value in the column by priority. If your report is grouping data like this, the MAX function will show the highest value in each group.

MEDIAN

The MEDIAN function returns the middle value in a list of column values in the dataset. The size or value of the data does not directly impact the median value, except in that the middle value is arrived at after sorting the data. When your dataset contains an even number of rows, the median

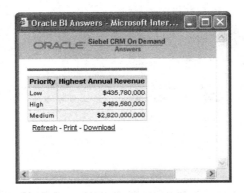

Priority	Highest Annual Revenue
Low	$435,780,000
High	$489,580,000
Medium	$2,820,000,000

Refresh - Print - Download

FIGURE 6-15. *Highest Annual Revenue by Account Priority report*

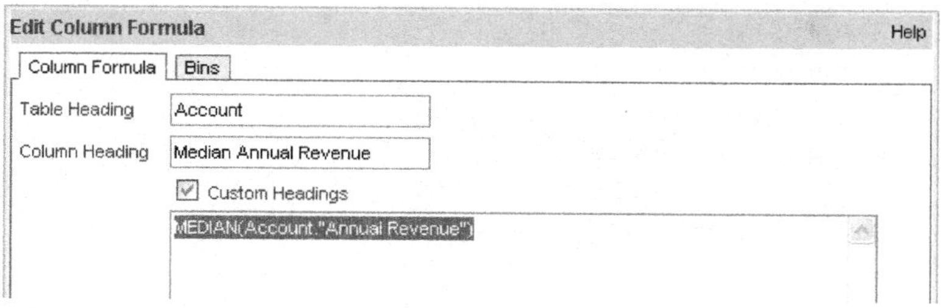

FIGURE 6-16.   *MEDIAN function applied to the Annual Revenue column*

is the mean of the two middle rows. The default numerical format of the value returned by the MEDIAN function is a number with two decimal places.

Function Syntax

```
MEDIAN(expression)
MEDIAN("Account Metrics"."Opportunity Revenue")
MEDIAN("Date Created".Date)
```

Figure 6-16 shows the MEDIAN function applied to the Annual Revenue column. The result in Figure 6-17 shows the median revenue value for each priority value. If your report is grouping data like this, the MEDIAN function will show the middle value in each group.

MIN

The MIN function returns the lowest value from the column in the dataset. For numeric data, this is the smallest number in the set. For text string data, the minimum value is the value that would appear at the beginning of an alphabetical sort. The MIN function applied to date and date/time data returns the earliest date or date/time in the dataset.

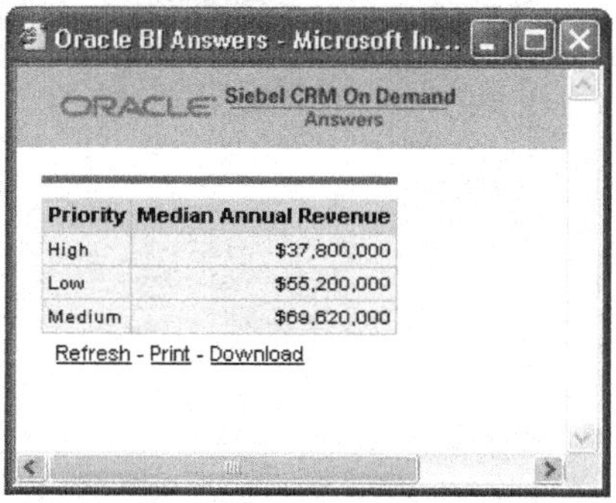

FIGURE 6-17.   *Median Annual Revenue by Account Priority report*

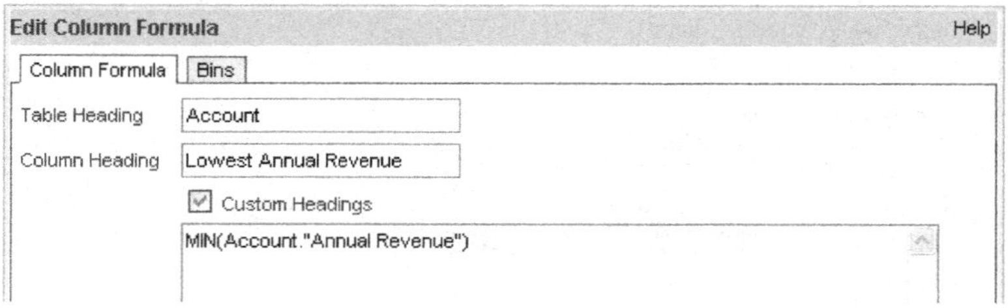

FIGURE 6-18. *MIN function applied to the Annual Revenue column*

Any column containing both text and numbers is sorted so that the values beginning with numerals have the lowest value and the values beginning with letters at the end of the alphabet have the highest value. The MIN function on such a column will return a value that begins with a number before one that begins with a letter.

Function Syntax

```
MIN(expression)
MIN("Account Metrics"."Opportunity Revenue")
MIN("Date Created".Date)
```

Figure 6-18 shows the MIN function applied to the Annual Revenue column. The result in Figure 6-19 illustrates how the MIN function returns the lowest value in the column by priority. If your report is grouping data like this, the MIN function will show the lowest value in each group.

NTILE

The NTILE function determines the rank of a value in terms of a user-specified segment of the dataset. For instance, a list of 1,000 values sorted and divided into 10 segments or tiles, contains

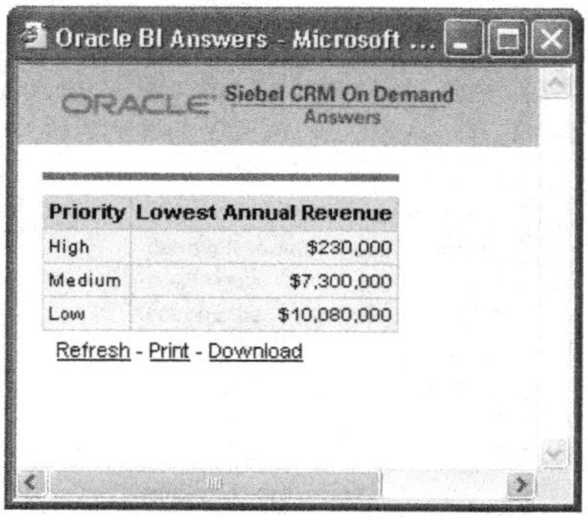

FIGURE 6-19. *Lowest Annual Revenue by Account Priority report*

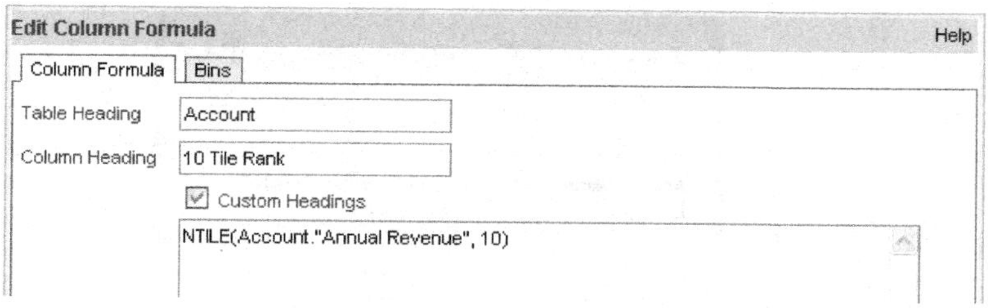

FIGURE 6-20. *NTILE function applied to the Annual Revenue column*

100 values per tile. NTILE returns integers to represent the number of the tile in which the value falls. The sorted dataset is broken into a number of tiles where there are roughly an equal number of values in each tile.

An NTILE function with 100 tiles results in a percentile (with numbers ranging from 1 to 100, with 100 representing the high end of the sort). This value is different from the results of the PERCENTILE function (discussed next), which returns values from 0 to 1.

Function Syntax

```
NTILE(expression,N)
NTILE(Account."Annual Revenue", 10)
NTILE("Revenue Metrics"."Closed Revenue"*.1, 100)
```

In Figure 6-20 I have applied the NTILE function to the Annual Revenue column using ten tiles. This will return numbers falling between 1 and 10 according to the tile in which the account's annual revenue falls. Figure 6-21 shows the result of this analysis. Notice that the smaller revenue amounts are in the lower numbered tiles and the larger revenue amounts are in the higher numbered tiles.

PERCENTILE

The PERCENTILE function calculates a percent rank for each resulting value in a numeric expression column. The percent rank ranges are from 0.00 to 1.00 (1st percentile to the 100th percentile). The PERCENTILE function calculates the percentile based on only the values in the result dataset.

Function Syntax

```
PERCENTILE(expression)
```

Figure 6-22 applies the PERCENTILE function to the Closed Revenue column. In the resulting report (see Figure 6-23), the Percentile column contains the percentile rank for each opportunity by closed revenue amount. The largest amount in the dataset will always have a percentile rank of 1.00 (100th percentile) and the smallest amount will always have a percentile rank of 0.00 (1st percentile).

Account Name	Annual Revenue	10 Tile Rank
Action Rentals	$124,800,000	8
Armex Corp.	$238,400,000	10
BJC, Inc.	$134,400,000	8
Barber Design	$31,008,000	4
Bay Advertising	$10,080,000	2
Bay Delivery	$196,800,000	9
Bayfair Brothers	$66,000,000	6
Bayview Corp.	$17,680,000	2
Blue Lake Services	$408,000,000	10
Bobcat Solutions	$2,820,000,000	10
Borg Corp.	$7,300,000	1
Bruins Fan Superstore	$367,000	1
Canterbury Tech	$95,472,000	7
Carters Graphics	$44,660,000	6
Cartwright Printing	$187,200,000	9
Cattington Equipment	$122,616,000	8
Chanson Company	$66,960,000	6
Classy Cakes	$230,000	1
Coast Company	$23,100,000	3
Coastal Company	$27,160,000	4
Deep Basin Inc.	$44,400,000	5
Desert Industries	$71,920,000	7
Diamond Corp.	$26,160,000	3
Fine Italian Autos	$723,590	1
GC Corporation	$22,140,000	3

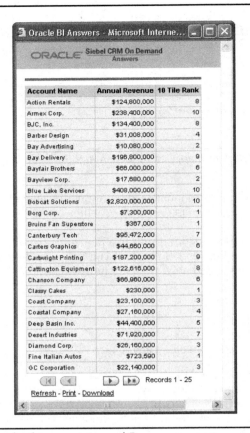

FIGURE 6-21. *10 Tile Rank of Account Annual Revenues report*

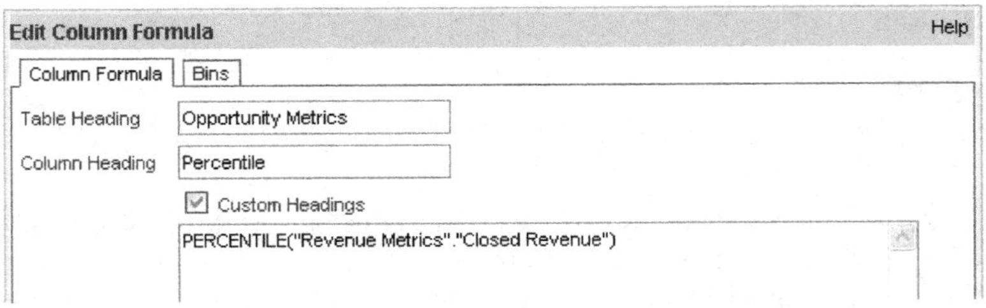

FIGURE 6-22. *PERCENTILE function applied to the Closed Revenue column*

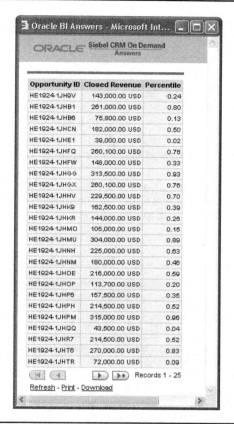

FIGURE 6-23.   *Closed Revenue Percentile Ranking report*

RANK

The RANK function calculates the rank for each value in a numeric expression or column. The highest number is assigned a rank of 1, and each successive rank is assigned the next consecutive integer (2, 3, 4...). If some values are equal, they are assigned the same rank (1, 1, 1, 4, 5, 5, 7...). Notice in the previous example the ranks of 2, 3, and 6 are not present. You can use the RANK function on multiple columns in the same report to create a ranking across multiple columns.

Function Syntax

```
RANK(expression)
RANK("Revenue Metrics"."Opportunity Revenue")
```

In Figure 6-24 I have applied the RANK function to the Opportunity Revenue column. I also sorted the ranked column so the values would be listed from highest rank (1) to lowest (see Figure 6-25).

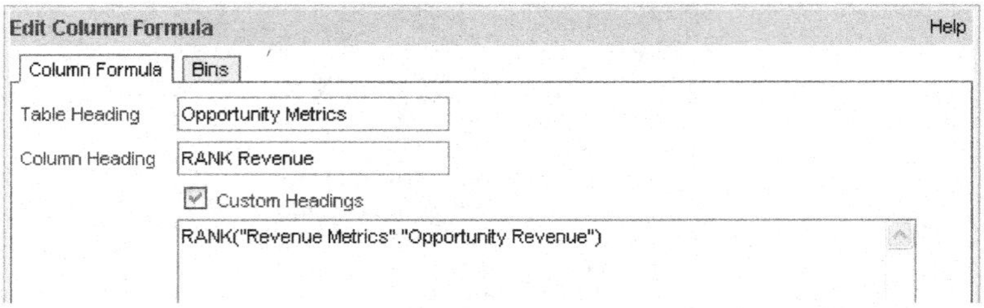

Edit Column Formula   Help

| Column Formula | Bins |

Table Heading   Opportunity Metrics

Column Heading   RANK Revenue

☑ Custom Headings

RANK("Revenue Metrics"."Opportunity Revenue")

FIGURE 6-24. *RANK function applied to the Opportunity Revenue column*

If you want a top ten list of records, you can place a filter on the report to limit data to records where the rank value is equal to or less than ten. This may result in more than ten records if there is a tie for the tenth rank. You could also nest your RANK formula inside of a BOTTOMN function:

```
BOTTOMN(RANK("Revenue Metrics"."Opportunity Revenue"),10)
```

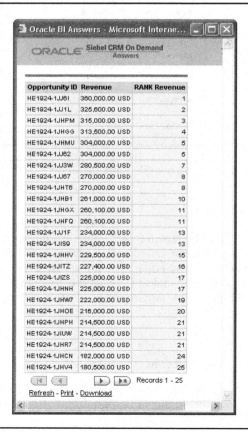

FIGURE 6-25. *Opportunity Revenue RANK report*

Suppose you want to rank opportunity revenue, but you want to see a ranking by the opportunity owners as well. For this you can use the BY function inside of your formula. You can use the BY function with many other functions to create subgroupings within the data. This function is inserted inside the parentheses of the primary function and precedes the analytical field reference or column formula you want to group by: In Figure 6-26 the RANK function is applied to the Opportunity Revenue column with the results organized by Opportunity Owner.

```
RANK("Revenue Metrics"."Opportunity Revenue" BY Opportunity.Owner)
```

STDDEV and STDDEV_SAMP

The STDDEV function calculates the standard deviation for a set of values in a dataset. The standard deviation formula applied here is the standard deviation of a sample, which uses N-1 as the denominator to provide an estimator for population. The result of STDDEV will always be the same as the result of the STDDEV_SAMP function. These two functions are synonymous. The result is always a number with two decimal places.

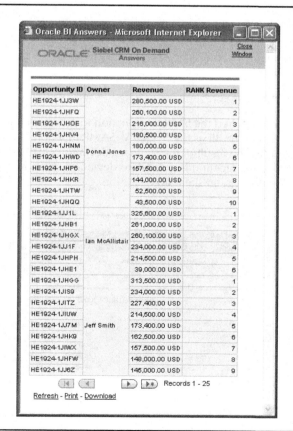

FIGURE 6-26. *Opportunity Revenue RANK by Owner report*

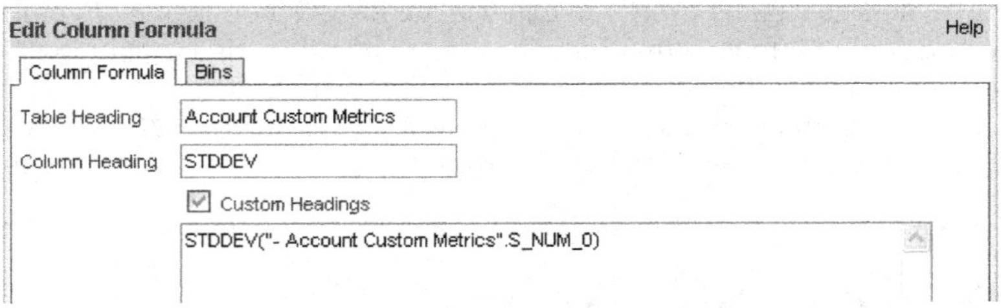

FIGURE 6-27. *STDDEV function*

These functions also take a modifier of ALL or DISTINCT. If you use no modifier or the modifier ALL, the calculation uses the entire dataset in the standard deviation calculation. If you use the DISTINCT modifier, duplicate values are ignored in the calculation.

Function Syntax

```
STDEV(n-exp)
STDEV(ALL n-exp)
STDEV(DISTINCT n-exp)
STDDEV_SAMP(n-exp)
STDDEV_SAMP(ALL n-exp)
STDDEV_SAMP(DISTINCT n-exp)
```

In Figure 6-27 I have applied the STDDEV function to a custom number column. This function generates the same result as the STDDEV_SAMP function.

In Figure 6-28 you see the result of the standard deviation calculation on a custom Satisfaction Score field. This function is a standard deviation on a sample. Next we examine the similar function for the population standard deviation.

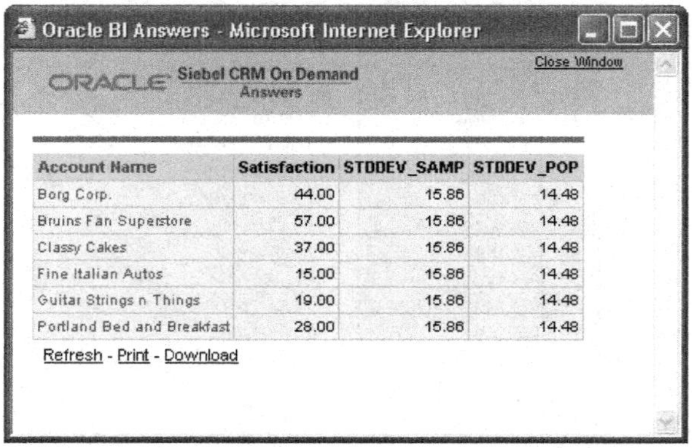

Account Name	Satisfaction	STDDEV_SAMP	STDDEV_POP
Borg Corp.	44.00	15.86	14.48
Bruins Fan Superstore	57.00	15.86	14.48
Classy Cakes	37.00	15.86	14.48
Fine Italian Autos	15.00	15.86	14.48
Guitar Strings n Things	19.00	15.86	14.48
Portland Bed and Breakfast	28.00	15.86	14.48

FIGURE 6-28. *Standard Deviations of Satisfaction Scores report*

STDDEV_POP

The STDDEV_POP function calculates the population standard deviation for a set of values in a dataset. The standard deviation formula applied here is the standard deviation of a population, which uses N rather than N–1 as the denominator because no estimator is required. The result is always a number with two decimal places.

This function also takes a modifier of ALL or DISTINCT. If you use no modifier or the modifier ALL, the calculation uses the entire dataset in the standard deviation calculation. If you use the DISTINCT modifier, duplicate values are ignored in the calculation.

Function Syntax

```
STDDEV_POP(n-exp)
STDDEV_POP(ALL n-exp)
STDDEV_POP(DISTINCT n-exp)
```

In Figure 6-29 I have applied the STDDEV_POP function to the custom Satisfaction column. Refer to Figure 6-28 to see the result of the standard deviation calculation on a custom Satisfaction Score field. The last column shows the population standard deviation.

SUM

The SUM function provides a total of all values in a dataset column. If displayed in the report table, the total sum repeats in each row. SUM is particularly handy within a formula as part of a mathematical equation.

Function Syntax

```
SUM(n-exp)
SUM("Activity Metrics"."# of Open Activities")
"Activity Metrics"."# of Open Activities" /
SUM("Activity Metrics"."# of Open Activities") * 100
```

The SUM function is one of the most commonly used aggregate functions in Answers On Demand, and will find its way into many of your more complex formulas. In its most simple application, as shown in Figure 6-30, the SUM function calculates the total of all values in the

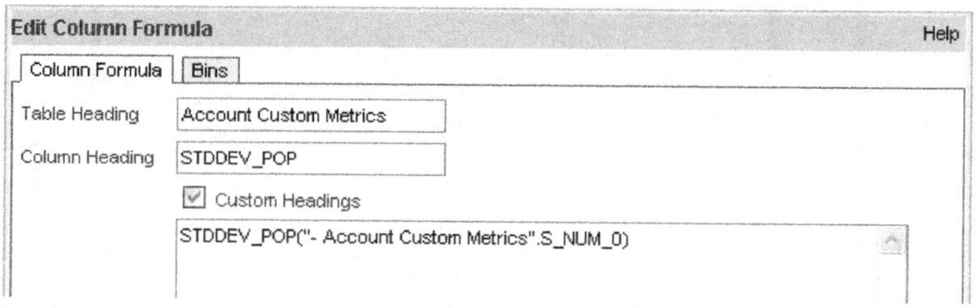

FIGURE 6-29. *STDDEV_POP function applied to column*

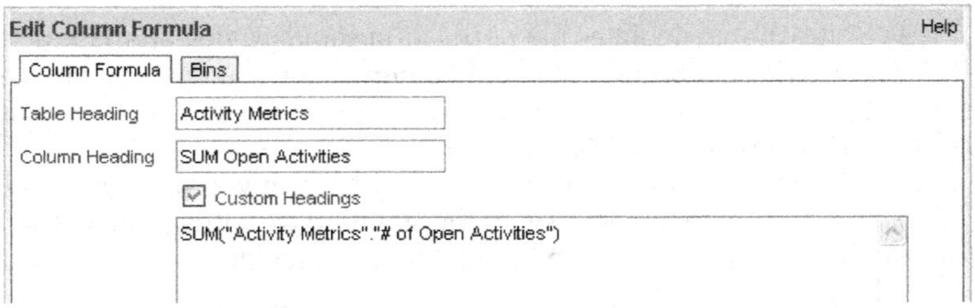

FIGURE 6-30. *SUM function applied to a column*

dataset for the designated column. The result of this calculation is not usually very useful in a table of values, as shown in Figure 6-31. The total amount repeats in every row, but by using the SUM function as part of a mathematical equation, you are able to create a column that provides some useful information, such as the percentage of total for each row.

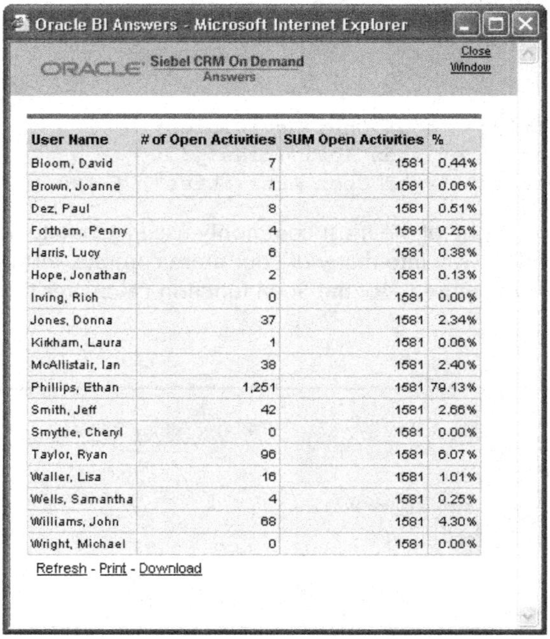

User Name	# of Open Activities	SUM Open Activities	%
Bloom, David	7	1581	0.44%
Brown, Joanne	1	1581	0.06%
Dez, Paul	8	1581	0.51%
Forthem, Penny	4	1581	0.25%
Harris, Lucy	6	1581	0.38%
Hope, Jonathan	2	1581	0.13%
Irving, Rich	0	1581	0.00%
Jones, Donna	37	1581	2.34%
Kirkham, Laura	1	1581	0.06%
McAllistair, Ian	38	1581	2.40%
Phillips, Ethan	1,251	1581	79.13%
Smith, Jeff	42	1581	2.66%
Smythe, Cheryl	0	1581	0.00%
Taylor, Ryan	96	1581	6.07%
Waller, Lisa	16	1581	1.01%
Wells, Samantha	4	1581	0.25%
Williams, John	68	1581	4.30%
Wright, Michael	0	1581	0.00%

Refresh - Print - Download

FIGURE 6-31. *Open Activity report with total and percent of total*

SUM(DISTINCT)

The SUM(DISTINCT) function provides a sum total of distinct values within a dataset. Like other functions with a DISTINCT modifier, the "distinct" portion of the function goes inside the parentheses with the numeric expression.

Function Syntax

```
SUM(DISTINCT n-exp)
SUM(DISTINCT "Account Metrics"."# of Leads")
SUM(DISTINCT Metrics."# of Contacts" BY Account."Account Type")
```

In Figure 6-32 my formula is totaling the distinct number of contacts by account type organized by state. In this formula I am using the BY function to perform the calculation by account type. The report in Figure 6-33 shows the results of this formula.

TOPN

The TOPN function returns the rank from highest to lowest for a designated number of values in a dataset. The highest value receives a rank value of 1. This function works exactly like the BOTTOMN function only in the other direction. The TOPN function works only with numeric data.

Applying the TOPN function to a numeric column provides a rank from the top and returns only the number of rows that you designate within the function, unless there is a tie in the ranking.

Function Syntax

```
TOPN(n-exp,N)
TOPN("Revenue Metrics"."Opportunity Revenue",10)
TOPN(AVG("Revenue Metrics"."Opportunity Revenue")*
("Revenue Metrics"."# of Opportunities"),20)
```

For example, in Figure 6-34, I have applied the TOPN function to the Annual Revenue column. In Figure 6-35 you will notice that the top three annual revenue amounts are returned in this report and the TOPN column in the report displays a numerical rank, where 1 is the highest number in the dataset. The report displays four records because the third-highest annual revenue amount is on two different accounts. You may use only one TOPN function on any single report.

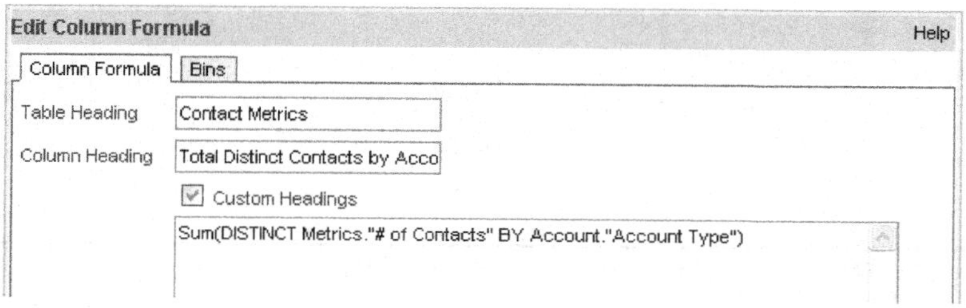

FIGURE 6-32. *SUM(DISTINCT) function totaling contact numbers by Account Type*

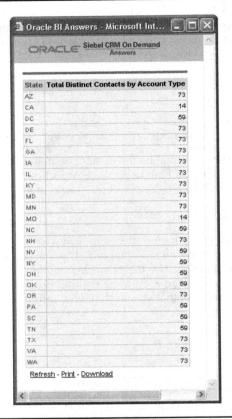

FIGURE 6-33. *Report of contacts by Account Type by State*

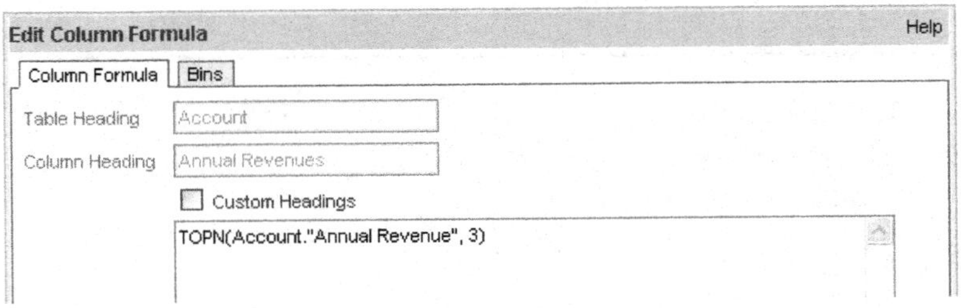

FIGURE 6-34. *TOPN function applied to Annual Revenue column*

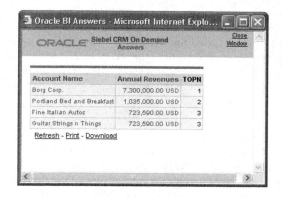

FIGURE 6-35.   *Top three Annual Revenue report*

Running and Moving Aggregate Functions

This section provides information on the running and moving aggregate functions. With running aggregates, the calculation includes increasingly more rows of data as it moves down the column. With moving aggregates, you can identify the number of rows that you want to include in your calculation, and as you move down the column of data, the calculation considers the current row and the number of previous rows designated within the formula.

If your data changes over time, a moving average or moving sum or other moving or running aggregation may provide more useful information than an overall aggregation. Moving aggregates provide insight into a subseries of data, rather than analyzing the entire series. A comparison of running aggregates to all-inclusive aggregates can also provide some useful information for trending analysis. Running aggregate functions show a trend over time or across a sorted dataset.

MAVG

The MAVG function calculates a moving average (mean) using the specified number of rows of data, inclusive of the current row. A moving average of three rows includes the current row and the previous two. The average for the first row is equal to the numeric expression for the first row, the average for the second row is calculated by taking the average of the first two rows of data, and the average for the third row is calculated by taking the average of the first three rows of data. When the required number of rows is reached, the average is calculated based on the number of rows of data that you indicated in the function.

Function Syntax

```
MAVG(n-exp,N)
MAVG("Activity Metrics"."# of Activities",5)
MAVG("Activity Metrics"."# of Activities",5) -
"Activity Metrics"."# of Activities"
```

Moving averages are popular with analysts of the stock market and financial instruments. The moving average is a rather useful calculation when performing trending analysis or other sorts of time-based analyses. In Figure 6-36 I have applied the MAVG function to the # of Activities column. Notice that I have included the number 5 in the formula, indicating that I want to see the average over the last five rows of data. In Figure 6-37 you see the results of this formula. Each row shows the number of activities in the dataset for a week along with the moving average of the number of activities over the current and previous four weeks.

MSUM

The MSUM function calculates a moving total using the specified number of rows of data, inclusive of the current row. A moving sum of three rows includes the current row and the previous two. The total for the first row is equal to the numeric expression for the first row, the total for the second row is calculated by taking the sum of the first two rows of data, and the total for the third row is calculated by taking the sum of the first three rows of data. When the required number of rows is reached, the sum is calculated based on the number of rows of data that you indicated in the function.

Function Syntax

```
MSUM(n-exp,N)
MSUM("Service Request Metrics"."# of Open SRs",10)
MSUM("Service Request Metrics"."# of Open SRs",5) -
"Service Request Metrics"."# of Closed SRs"
```

Moving sums are useful for a number of analyses, such as inventory control or service volume analysis. The moving sum allows you to calculate a total for a subset of sorted data. In Figure 6-38 I have applied the MSUM function to the # of Open SRs column. Notice that I have included the number 4 in the formula, indicating that I want to see the total over the last four rows of data. In Figure 6-39 you see the results of this formula along with the result of the same function applied to closed SRs. Building on an analysis like this can lead me to some conclusions about how the service team is keeping up with the volume of service issues. Each row shows the total number of open and closed service requests in the dataset for a week over the current and previous three weeks.

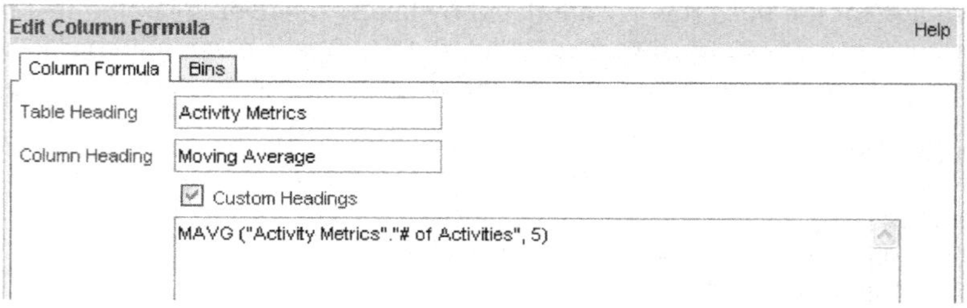

FIGURE 6-36. *MAVG function applied to # of Activities column*

Calendar Week/Yr	# of Activities	Moving Average
2006 Week27	1	1
2006 Week28	2	1
2006 Week29	1	1
2006 Week30	1	1
2006 Week31	1	1
2006 Week32	3	1
2006 Week33	5	2
2006 Week34	5	3
2006 Week35	3	3
2006 Week36	3	3
2006 Week37	5	4
2006 Week38	6	4
2006 Week39	5	4
2006 Week40	2	4
2006 Week41	6	4
2006 Week42	3	4
2006 Week43	4	4
2006 Week44	8	4
2006 Week45	4	5
2006 Week46	4	4
2006 Week47	4	4
2006 Week48	6	5
2006 Week49	8	5
2006 Week50	4	5
2006 Week51	9	6

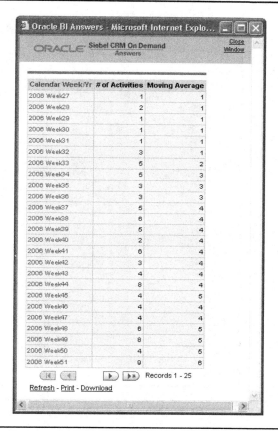

FIGURE 6-37. *Moving Average Activity Volume report*

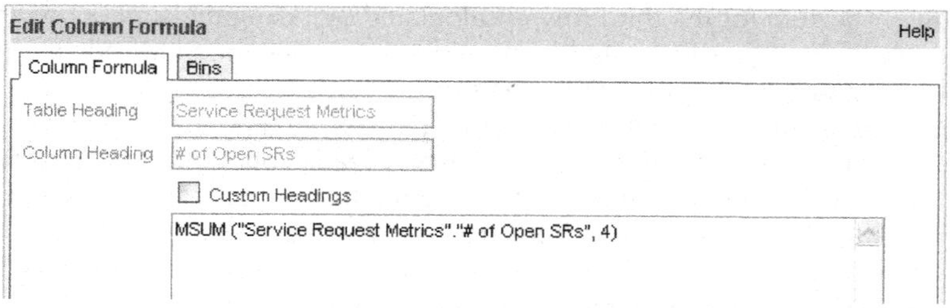

FIGURE 6-38. *MSUM function applied to # of Open SRs column*

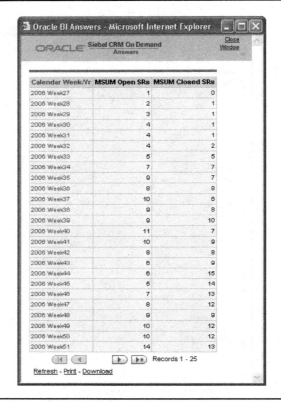

FIGURE 6-39. *Total Open and Closed SRs During Last Four Weeks report*

RSUM

The RSUM function calculates a running sum in a report column. The total includes the current row and all previous rows in the dataset. The total for the first row is equal to the numeric expression for the first row. The total for the second row is calculated by taking the sum of the first two rows. The sum for the third row is calculated by taking the sum of the first three rows of data. This pattern continues through the entire dataset so that the total shown in the last row of your report is the sum total of the entire column.

A running sum is a useful metric for anything that is accumulated over time. Perhaps you are interested in knowing how many service requests or leads your company has processed over the course of a year. The running sum provides not only the final total for the year, but also totals along the way at increments of your choosing. For instance, a report that shows the data by week would give you a running sum at one-week increments. The same data organized by month would provide the total at monthly increments.

Function Syntax

```
RSUM(n-exp)
RSUM("Activity Metrics"."# of Closed Activities")
```

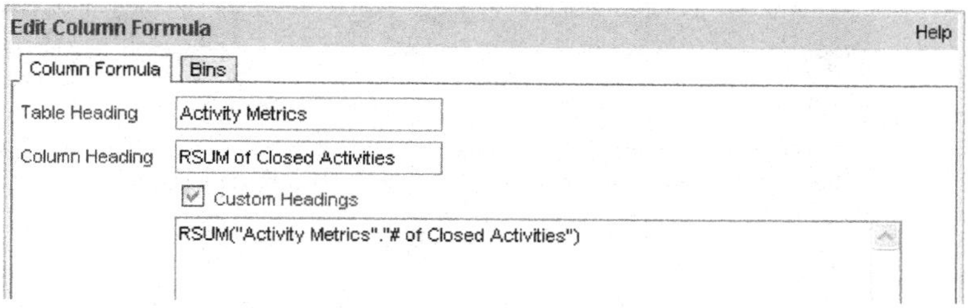

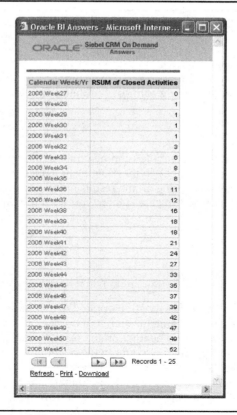

FIGURE 6-40. *RSUM function applied to # of Closed Activities column*

```
FILTER(RSUM("Activity Metrics"."# of Closed Activities") USING
(Employee."Employee Name" = "Bob B"))
```

In Figure 6-40 I have applied the RSUM function to the # of Closed Activities column. This, in combination with the Calendar Week/Yr column, will provide a running total of the closed activities by week, as shown in Figure 6-41.

Calendar Week/Yr	RSUM of Closed Activities
2006 Week27	0
2006 Week28	1
2006 Week29	1
2006 Week30	1
2006 Week31	1
2006 Week32	3
2006 Week33	6
2006 Week34	8
2006 Week35	8
2006 Week36	11
2006 Week37	12
2006 Week38	16
2006 Week39	18
2006 Week40	18
2006 Week41	21
2006 Week42	24
2006 Week43	27
2006 Week44	33
2006 Week45	35
2006 Week46	37
2006 Week47	39
2006 Week48	42
2006 Week49	47
2006 Week50	49
2006 Week51	52

FIGURE 6-41. *Running Sum of Closed Activities report*

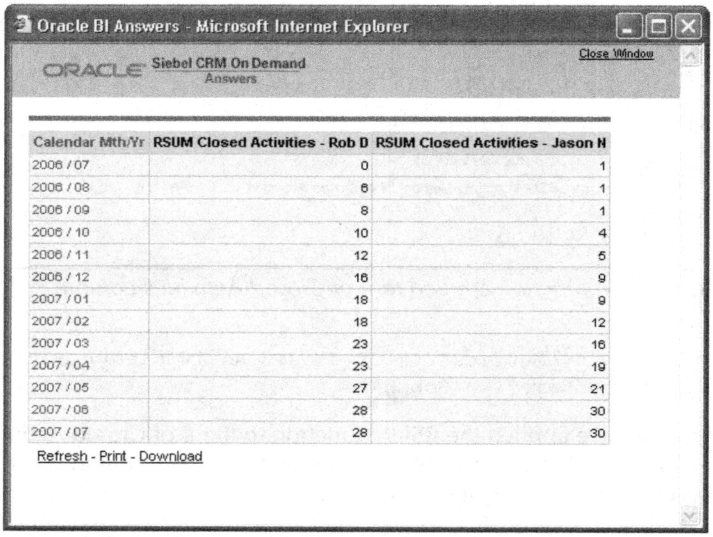

Calendar Mth/Yr	RSUM Closed Activities - Rob D	RSUM Closed Activities - Jason H
2006 / 07	0	1
2006 / 08	6	1
2006 / 09	8	1
2006 / 10	10	4
2006 / 11	12	5
2006 / 12	16	9
2007 / 01	18	9
2007 / 02	18	12
2007 / 03	23	16
2007 / 04	23	19
2007 / 05	27	21
2007 / 06	28	30
2007 / 07	28	30

FIGURE 6-42. *Closed Activity by User and Week report*

Another interesting use of the running sum uses the FILTER USING function to provide a running sum, side-by-side comparison of a measure for multiple users or other category. In Figure 6-42 I have created a running sum of completed activities by week for two different users.

RCOUNT

The RCOUNT function provides a simple running count of the rows in the first column. In fact, unlike the COUNT function described in the "Aggregate Functions" section, the equation you provide in the function has no bearing on the results of the formula. The RCOUNT function can be a useful addition to your report in cases where you want to number your table rows.

Function Syntax

```
RCOUNT(expression)
RCOUNT(1)
RCOUNT("Associated Contacts"."Contact Last Name")
```

Figure 6-43 shows the RCOUNT function applied to a column. This could be any column from the subject area, or could be a literal such as a number or text value. The expression you use in the RCOUNT function has no bearing on the results of the formula, because the RCOUNT function provides a simple running row count in the result table. The only situation where the expression influences the results of the RCOUNT function is when you have only one column in your report, and you apply the RCOUNT function to that column. Figure 6-44 shows a sample report with the RCOUNT function providing numbered rows.

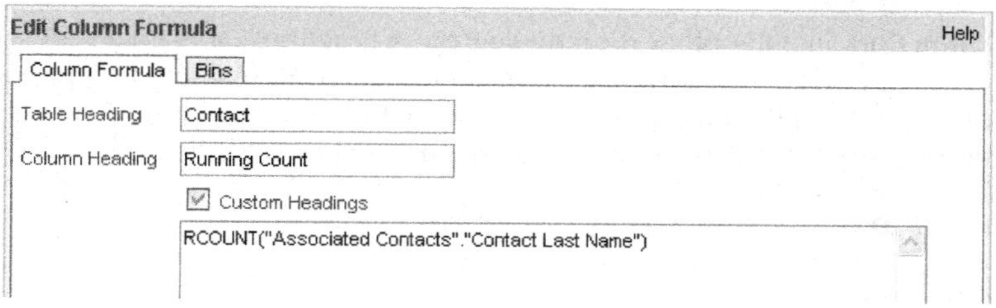

Edit Column Formula   Help

| Column Formula | Bins |

Table Heading   Contact

Column Heading   Running Count

☑ Custom Headings

RCOUNT("Associated Contacts"."Contact Last Name")

FIGURE 6-43. *RCOUNT function applied to the Contact Last Name column*

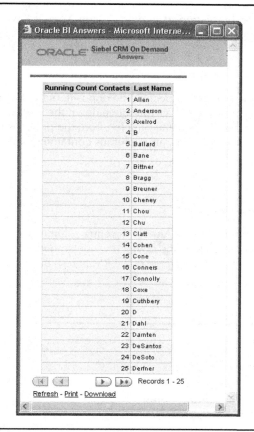

FIGURE 6-44. *Numbered Contact Last Name report*

RMAX

The RMAX function, like the other running aggregate functions, acts on a set of records one at a time. As you move down the rows of the result table, the RMAX function provides the largest value encountered from the previous rows. This function works with numeric as well as text columns, and columns containing both numeric and text data.

Function Syntax

```
RMAX(expression)
RMAX(Account."Annual Revenue")
```

The RMAX function applied to the Annual Revenue column (see Figure 6-45) provides a list of annual revenue amounts that reflects the highest revenue amount encountered within all of the previous rows of the report table. A sample of the RMAX result is shown in Figure 6-46. Be careful with this function, because it can appear misleading. For instance, if the Account Name column appeared in this report in place of the Annual Revenue column, one might presume that the revenue amount listed in the RMAX column is associated with the account on the same row.

RMIN

The RMIN function, as you might suspect, is the opposite of the RMAX function. RMIN also acts on a set of records one at a time, but as you move down the rows of the result table, the RMIN function provides the smallest value encountered from the previous rows. This function works with numeric as well as text columns, and columns containing both numeric and text data.

Function Syntax

```
RMIN(expression)
RMIN(Account."Annual Revenue")
```

The RMIN function applied to the Annual Revenue column (see Figure 6-47) provides a list of annual revenue amounts that reflects the lowest revenue amount encountered within all of the previous rows of the report table. A sample of the RMIN result is shown in Figure 6-48. As explained

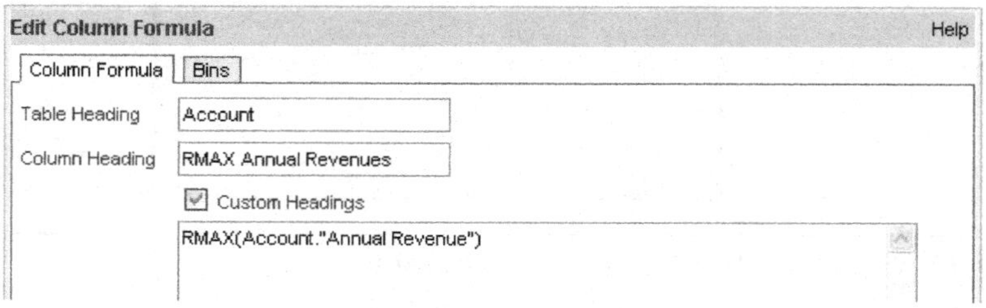

FIGURE 6-45. *RMAX function applied to Annual Revenue*

State	Annual Revenues	RMAX Annual Revenues
AZ	27,840,000.00 USD	$27,840,000
	196,800,000.00 USD	$196,800,000
	245,196,000.00 USD	$245,196,000
CA	7,300,000.00 USD	$245,196,000
	31,008,000.00 USD	$245,196,000
	32,320,000.00 USD	$245,196,000
	37,960,000.00 USD	$245,196,000
	98,800,000.00 USD	$245,196,000
	139,200,000.00 USD	$245,196,000
	273,408,000.00 USD	$273,408,000
	435,780,000.00 USD	$435,780,000
DC	27,160,000.00 USD	$435,780,000
	67,320,000.00 USD	$435,780,000
DE	21,120,000.00 USD	$435,780,000
	408,000,000.00 USD	$435,780,000
FL	7,952,000.00 USD	$435,780,000
	2,820,000,000.00 USD	$2,820,000,000
GA	35,760,000.00 USD	$2,820,000,000
	44,400,000.00 USD	$2,820,000,000
IA	23,100,000.00 USD	$2,820,000,000
	30,240,000.00 USD	$2,820,000,000
	489,580,000.00 USD	$2,820,000,000
IL	25,200,000.00 USD	$2,820,000,000
	66,000,000.00 USD	$2,820,000,000
	90,200,000.00 USD	$2,820,000,000

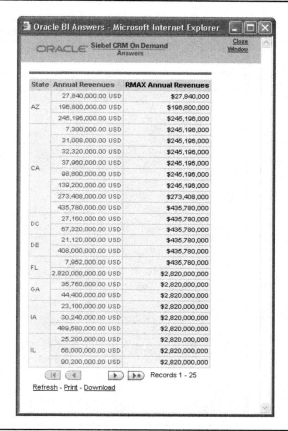

FIGURE 6-46. *Annual Revenues by State with Running Max report*

previously with the RMAX function, you should consider how the results may be interpreted, because it is possible that an amount displayed in a row might be mistaken as directly related to the other data in the row.

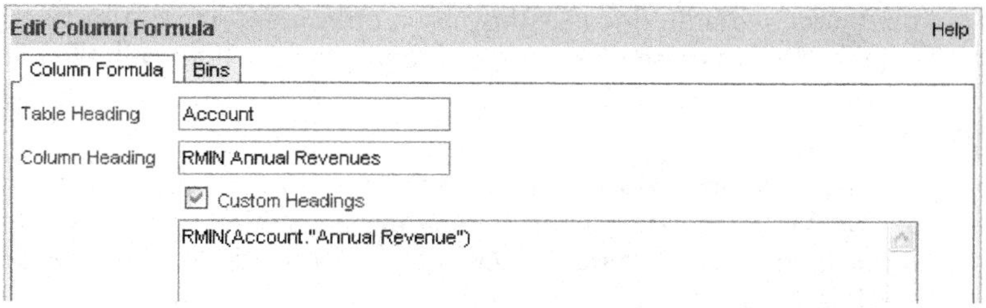

FIGURE 6-47. *RMIN function applied to Annual Revenue column*

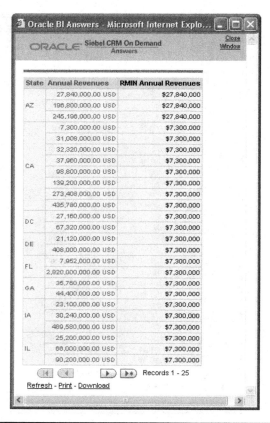

FIGURE 6-48. *Annual Revenue by State with Running Min report*

Math Functions

Aggregate functions operate in multiple records to provide a calculation across many records. The functions that I describe in this section operate within a single record to perform a mathematical calculation using one or more numeric expressions. Chapter 5 described the mathematical operators in detail. Because they are a prominent part of most calculations, I will first provide a brief review of these operators and then describe the available math functions.

Operators

Operators are used to combine expression elements to perform a calculation or make certain types of comparisons between expressions. While operators often work alone in a simple mathematical formula, they are also quite prevalent in many other useful formulas. Table 6-1 lists and describes the basic math operators (see Table 5-2 for an expanded version of this table).

Operator	Description
+	The plus sign for addition
–	The minus sign for subtraction
*	The asterisk to multiply
/	The forward slash to divide
( )	Open and close parentheses to begin and end a group for grouping operations

TABLE 6-1.   *Math Operators*

When using operators in your column formulas, you should construct your formula with a structure based on order-of-operation rules. Answers will follow the same order-of-operation rules we learned in grade school:

1. Perform any calculations inside of parentheses.

2. Perform multiplication and division operations working from the left to the right.

3. Perform addition and subtraction operations working from the left to the right.

Suppose you want to add the number of open tasks and the number of future appointments and divide by the number of users. You are using two operators here, so structure is important. Suppose also that you have 100 open tasks, 50 future appointments, and 25 users. The structure of this formula will affect the outcome, as the following examples demonstrate:

100 + 50 / 25 = 100 + 2 = 102

(100 + 50) / 25 = 150 / 25 = 6

The more complex the formula becomes, the more difficult it is to construct the formula in such a way that you receive the desired outcome. At the end of this chapter, I have included a section on nesting formulas, with some tips for building complex calculations.

ABS

The ABS function calculates the absolute value of a numeric expression. Absolute value can be described as the distance from 0. The numbers 10 and –10 are both the same distance from 0, so ABS(–10) and ABS(10) are both 10.

Function Syntax

```
ABS(n-exp)
ABS("- Account Custom Attributes".INTEGER_1 -
"- Account Custom Attributes".INTEGER_2)
```

My favorite application of the ABS function is to determine the difference between two values. Suppose I track two key values on an opportunity. Either value can be larger than the

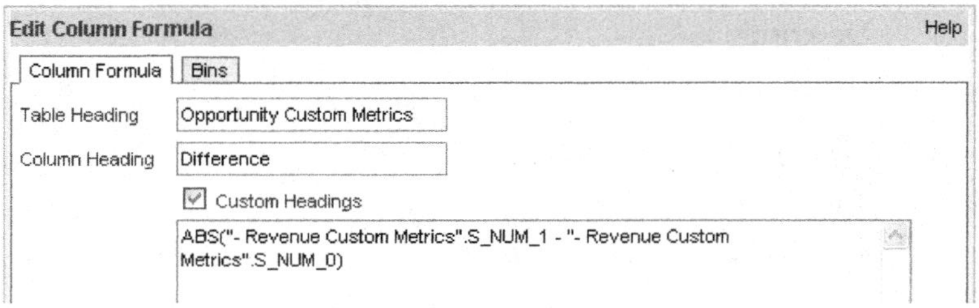

FIGURE 6-49. *ABS function applied to calculation formula*

other, but I want to know the difference between the two. That is the example shown in Figures 6-49 and 6-50, in which I have applied the ABS function to a calculation that subtracts one value from the other.

CEILING

The CEILING function rounds a noninteger number or numeric expression to the next highest integer. If the numeric expression evaluates to an integer, the CEILING function returns that integer. This function always rounds up. For instance, CEILING(5.17) = 6.

Function Syntax

```
CEILING(n-exp)
CEILING("Revenue Metrics"."Average Deal Size")
CEILING("Revenue Metrics"."Opportunity revenue (000)" *
"Revenue Metrics"."Opportunity Win Rate"
```

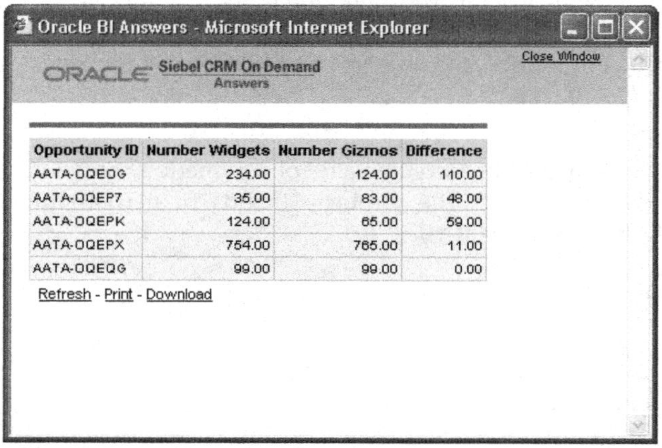

Opportunity ID	Number Widgets	Number Gizmos	Difference
AATA-0QEDG	234.00	124.00	110.00
AATA-0QEP7	35.00	83.00	48.00
AATA-0QEPK	124.00	65.00	59.00
AATA-0QEPX	754.00	765.00	11.00
AATA-0QEQG	99.00	99.00	0.00

FIGURE 6-50. *Difference Between Widgets and Gizmos report*

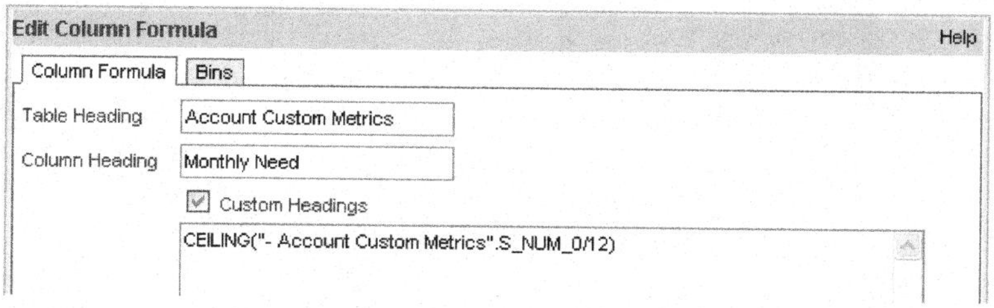

FIGURE 6-51. *CEILING function applied to equation*

You will hardly ever use the CEILING function on a single column from your On Demand application. After all, if you need an integer to describe that field, wouldn't you just use an integer field? You will find applications for the CEILING function when performing calculations. For instance, suppose your company sells hydraulic fluid. You sell and ship your product by the gallon. Your customer uses 159 gallons a year, but signs up for a monthly delivery. Figure 6-51 applies the CEILING function to the annual volume field divided by 12 to determine the appropriate amount of fluid to send to the customer each month. As you see in the results, shown in Figure 6-52, you need to ship 14 gallons each month.

FLOOR

The FLOOR function rounds a noninteger number or numeric expression to the next lowest integer. If the numeric expression evaluates to an integer, the FLOOR function returns that integer. This function always rounds down. For instance, FLOOR(9.8) = 9.

Function Syntax

```
FLOOR(n-exp)
FLOOR("Revenue Metrics"."Average Deal Size")
FLOOR("Revenue Metrics"."Opportunity revenue (000)" *
"Revenue Metrics"."Opportunity Win Rate"
```

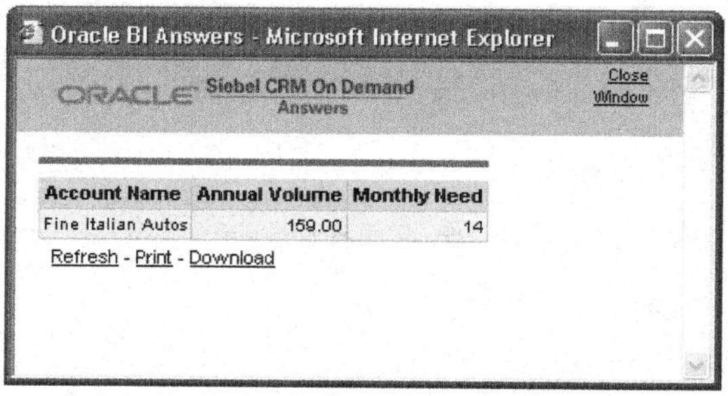

FIGURE 6-52. *Monthly Need Based on Annual Volume report*

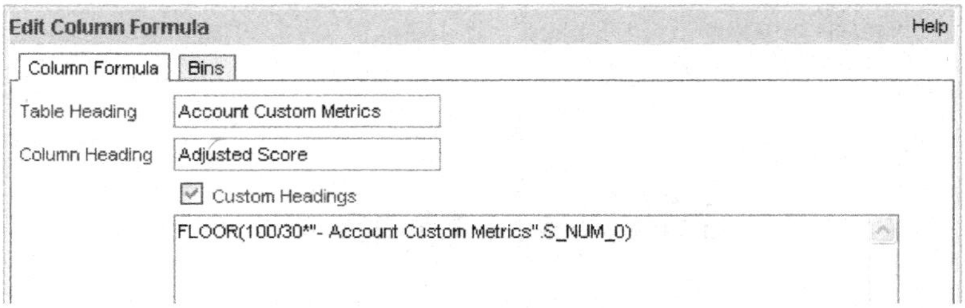

FIGURE 6-53. *FLOOR function applied to a column formula*

Like the CEILING function, you will rarely use FLOOR on a single column from your On Demand application. You will find applications for the FLOOR function when performing calculations. For instance, suppose you use On Demand to calculate and track test results. Your test scores must be whole numbers, because your policy forbids partial credit. On a 30-question quiz, your customer answers 23 correctly. As shown in Figure 6-53, you apply the FLOOR function to calculate the adjusted score. As you see in the results, shown in Figure 6-54, this person fails the test by one point, even though she was technically .23 points from passing. Had you used a regular rounding function, Katie would have passed her test.

MOD

The modulo (MOD) function performs a division calculation and returns the remainder portion of the quotient. This function requires two numeric expressions. MOD divides the first number (the dividend) by the second number (the divisor). MOD(8,3) = 2 because 3 goes into 8 twice, leaving 2 as the remainder. You can calculate MOD(8,3) manually with the equation $8 - (3*FLOOR(8/3)) = 8 - (3*2) = 8 - 6 = 2$.

In cases where the divisor is larger than the dividend, the MOD function always returns a value equal to the dividend. In cases where the divisor is 0, the function returns the value of the dividend. If your dividend is 0, MOD always returns a 0. Your inputs into the MOD function may be noninteger values, but the result will always be an integer.

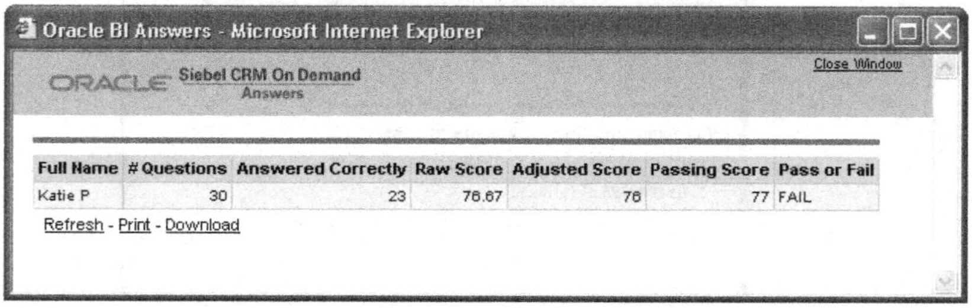

FIGURE 6-54. *Test Results report*

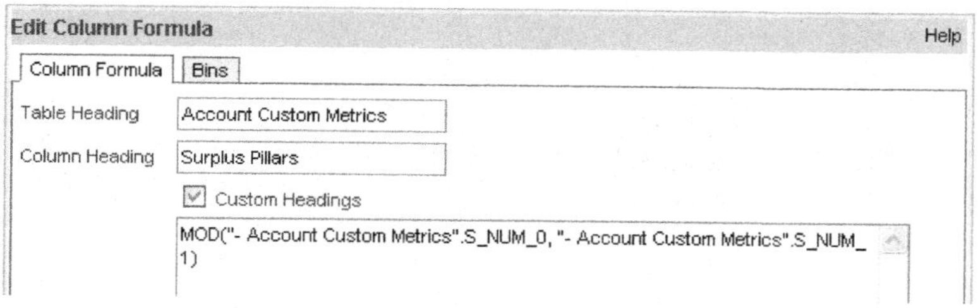

FIGURE 6-55. *MOD function applied to a column formula*

Function Syntax

```
MOD(n-exp, n-exp)
MOD(145, 12)
MOD("- Account Custom Metrics"."S_NUM_0", "- Account Custom Metrics"."S_
NUM_0")
```

Calculating the modulo of two numbers might be useful in cases where the first number indicates a count of units and the second number indicates the number of units used per component. To provide a more realistic example, suppose I produce wedding cakes that require eight cake pillars per cake. I ordered 300 pillars and want to know how many I will have left over after producing as many cakes as possible. In Figure 6-55 I am using the MOD function to help me with this analysis. According to the analysis shown in Figure 6-56, I will have four pillars left.

PI

The PI function returns the value of pi (3.14). The constant pi plays a role in many equations, and you can include pi in your report formulas. While it is possible to calculate pi to an endless number of digits, Answers On Demand uses only the first 12 digits (3.14159265359) which is usually more than necessary for most any equation.

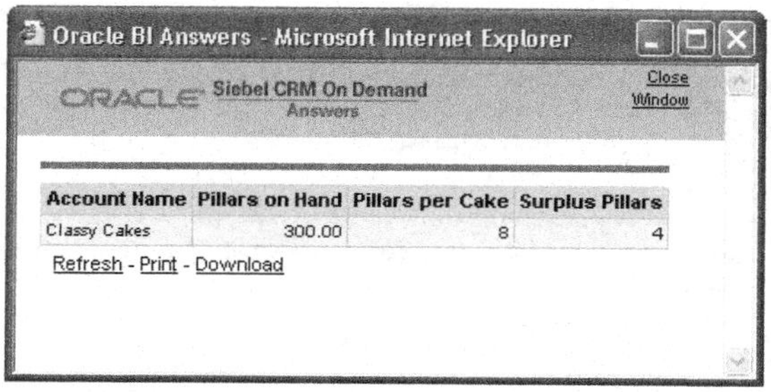

FIGURE 6-56. *Surplus Supplies report*

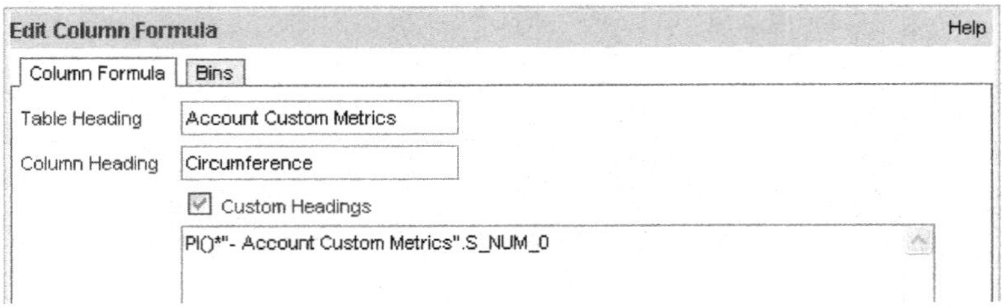

FIGURE 6-57. *PI function in a column formula*

Function Syntax

```
PI()
```

Going back to the example of the cake maker, suppose I need to calculate the circumference of cake to determine how much ribbon I need for my cakes. I capture the diameter and quantity of each tier in my On Demand application when inputting an order. So in a report, I need to calculate the supplies necessary to make the cake. In this report, I will use the diameter measurement to calculate the length of ribbon necessary to circle the cake. In Figure 6-57 I am using the PI function in the circumference calculation, the results of which are shown in Figure 6-58. I can encircle a 24-inch-diameter cake tier with 75.4 inches of ribbon, or a little over 226 inches for all three tiers.

POWER

The POWER function raises a numeric value to a specified power. For instance, if you needed to take a measurement stored in your database to the third power, you would use the POWER function to raise the result of your measurement column to the power of three.

Function Syntax

```
POWER(n-exp,N)
POWER(Opportunity.S_NUM_0,3)
(PI()*POWER(Opportunity.S_NUM_0,2)*(Opportunity.S_NUM_1)) * 7.48
```

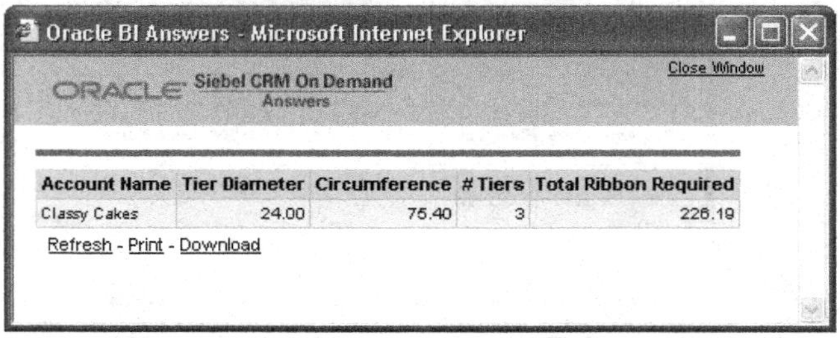

FIGURE 6-58. *Cake Circumference report*

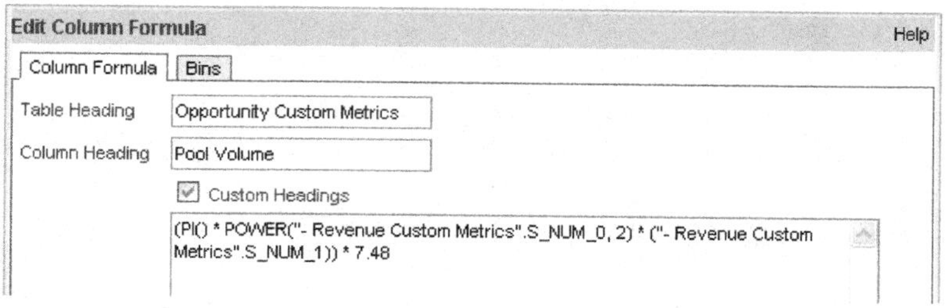

Edit Column Formula   Help

| Column Formula | Bins |

Table Heading   Opportunity Custom Metrics

Column Heading   Pool Volume

☑ Custom Headings

(PI() * POWER("- Revenue Custom Metrics".S_NUM_0, 2) * ("- Revenue Custom Metrics".S_NUM_1)) * 7.48

FIGURE 6-59. *Volume formula using PI and POWER functions*

Suppose you are in the custom pool business, and you have configured your opportunity records to store the radius and depth of your circular pools. Since every pool is custom, you decide to produce a report that describes the measurements of the pool along with the maximum volume of water each pool can hold. You can calculate the volume using a mathematical formula that takes pi times the radius of the pool squared times the depth of the pool ($\pi r^2 d$). This formula will give you the cubic feet of water needed to fill the pool. If you multiply that result by 7.48, you get the measurement in gallons.

As shown in Figure 6-59, you apply the POWER function as part of the calculation to determine the gallons of water needed to fill a round pool. The results are shown in Figure 6-60 for a five-foot-radius pool of five feet in depth.

RAND

The RAND function generates a pseudo-random number between 0 and 1. A random number generated by a computer is called *pseudo*-random because a truly random number cannot come from a logic-based system like a computer. If a computer generates a number, another computer can replicate the process. Random numbers are used in some statistical processes and cryptographic systems. RAND used without a numeric expression inside the parentheses generates a random number based on a randomization algorithm only. Place a numeric

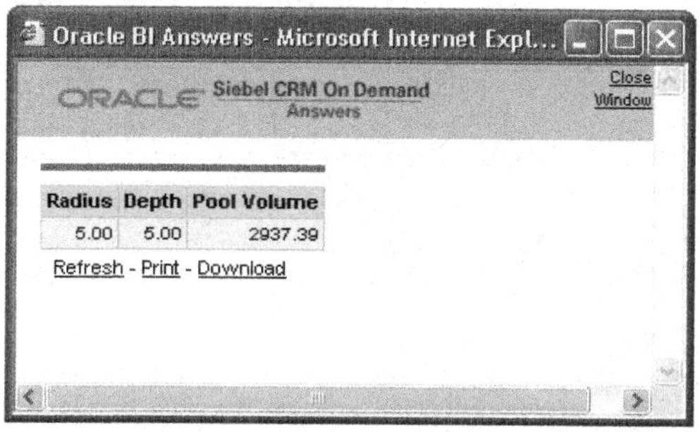

Oracle BI Answers - Microsoft Internet Expl...

ORACLE   Siebel CRM On Demand   Answers   Close Window

Radius	Depth	Pool Volume
5.00	5.00	2937.39

Refresh - Print - Download

FIGURE 6-60. *Pool Volume report*

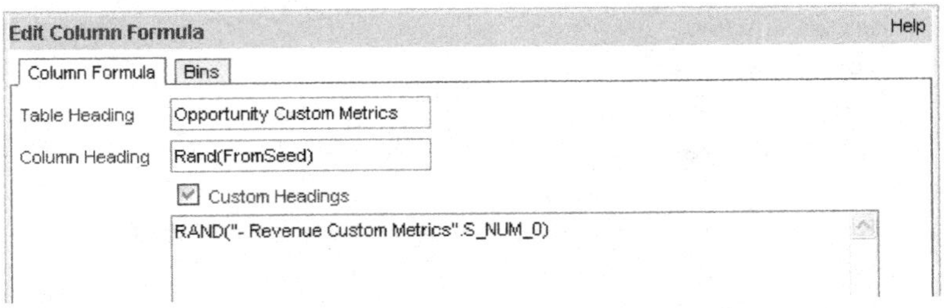

FIGURE 6-61. *Column formula with RANDFROMSEED function*

expression in the parentheses and the function generates a random number based on your seed data. The RAND function will generate the same set of random numbers for the same seed value.

Function Syntax

```
RAND()
RAND(n-exp)
```

I do not know of any compelling business reasons for using a random-number generator within Analytics. I do not recommend using the RAND function to generate numbers for a unique ID, as there is no way to guarantee uniqueness, and the numbers will change each time your report runs or is refreshed. The default format for the random number is a hundredth between 0.00 and 1.00. You can override this format to generate a random number with up to 15 decimal places.

If you insert the function using the Function button in the Edit Column Formula window, you will notice that RAND and RANDFROMSEED are listed here separately. The difference between the two is in how the function inserts itself into the column formula. If you highlight the contents of the Column Formula field in the Edit Column Formula window and then select the RandFromSeed function in the function selector, the content of the column formula will be placed inside the parentheses of the RAND function (see Figure 6-61). Select the Rand function from the function selector and the RAND function overwrites the highlighted column formula (see Figure 6-62).

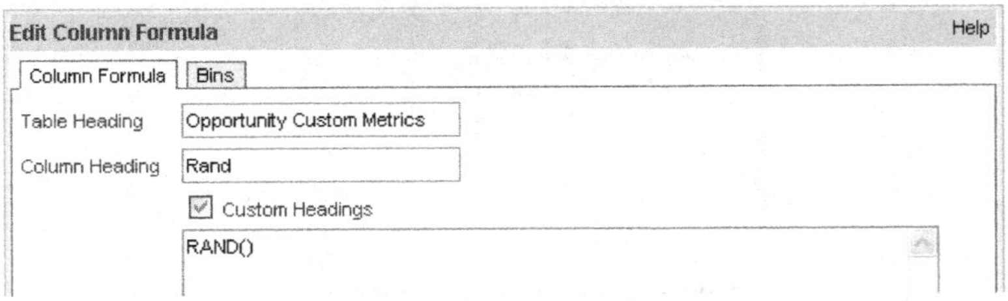

FIGURE 6-62. *Column formula with RAND function*

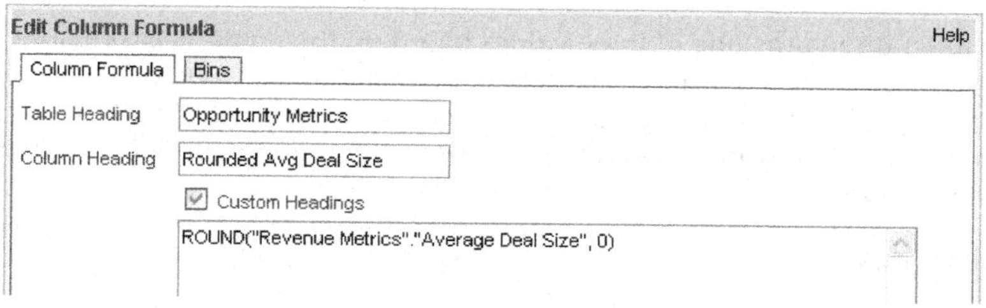

FIGURE 6-63. *ROUND function applied to the Average Deal Size column*

ROUND

The ROUND function rounds a numeric value to a prescribed number of digits. The ROUND function follows the normal rounding rule of 0 through .499 rounds down to 0 and .500 through 1 rounds up to 1 when the level of precision is set to 0. When you use the ROUND function, you designate the level of precision with an integer within the column formula. A precision value of 0 will round your number to the nearest whole number. A precision value of 1 will round your number to the nearest tenth. There is no limit on the precision level, but Answers On Demand can only display up to 15 decimal places—a precision of 16.

Function Syntax

```
ROUND(n-exp,N)
ROUND("- Activity Custom Metrics".A_NUM_0, 0)
```

A typical use of the ROUND function is to round off aggregated values, such as an average number of service issues or percentage of revenue amounts. In Figure 6-63 I have applied the ROUND function to an average metric column with a precision of 0 to arrive at the nearest whole number. The report in Figure 6-64 shows the original values and the rounded values at different precision levels.

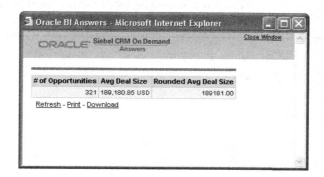

FIGURE 6-64. *Average Deal Size report*

SIGN

The SIGN function returns one of three values based on the numeric expression it is evaluating. If the numeric value of the column is less than 0, SIGN returns a value of −1. If the column value is greater than 0, SIGN returns a value of 1. A 0 evaluates as a 0 with the SIGN function. This can be a useful function if you don't need to know the actual result value of a calculation but you do need to know whether the result is less than or greater than 0.

Function Syntax

```
SIGN(n-exp)
SIGN("- Activity Custom Metrics".S_NUM_1 +
"- Activity Custom Metrics".S_NUM_2 +
"- Activity Custom Metrics".S_NUM_3)
```

Suppose you are tracking a series of evaluation scores in CRM On Demand. Your scoring scale ranges from −5 to 5, and you want to determine how many of the overall scores are negative, positive, and neutral. Applying the SIGN function to the total score result changes the scores to −1, 0, and 1 (see Figure 6-65). Now you can use those values to categorize and count the results in a chart or pivot table on your report (see Figure 6-66) without concern for the actual calculated values from your evaluations.

SQRT

The SQRT function calculates the square root of your numeric expression. The numeric expression in your SQRT formula cannot be a negative value. If the expression you are working with may evaluate to a negative number, and it is appropriate to do so, you may want to use the ABS function to ensure that the number is positive.

Function Syntax

```
SQRT(n-exp)
SQRT(Opportunity.Revenue)
SQRT(ABS(Activity.S_NUM_1 * Activity.S_NUM_3))
```

The square root calculation is an integral part of many calculations in mathematics, and you can construct any of these calculations in Answers On Demand by using the functions

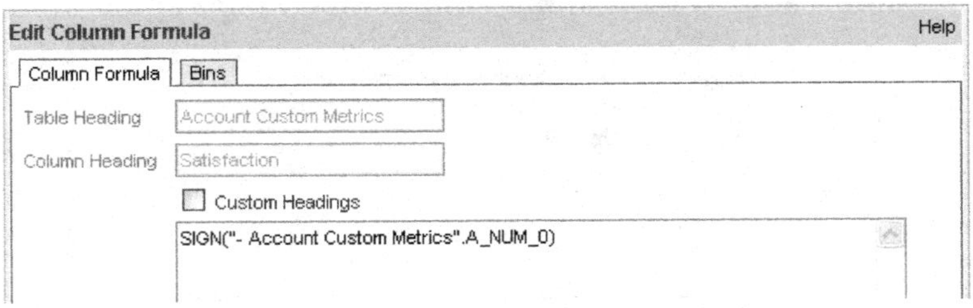

FIGURE 6-65. *SIGN function applied to the Average Satisfaction column*

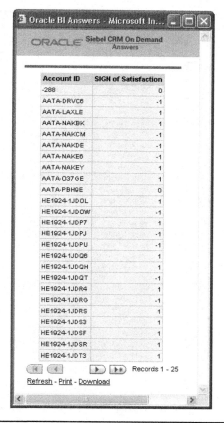

FIGURE 6-66. *SIGN of Satisfaction report*

and operators described in this book. In Figure 6-67 I have applied the SQRT function to a custom field in my CRM On Demand application. Figure 6-68 shows the result of this calculation.

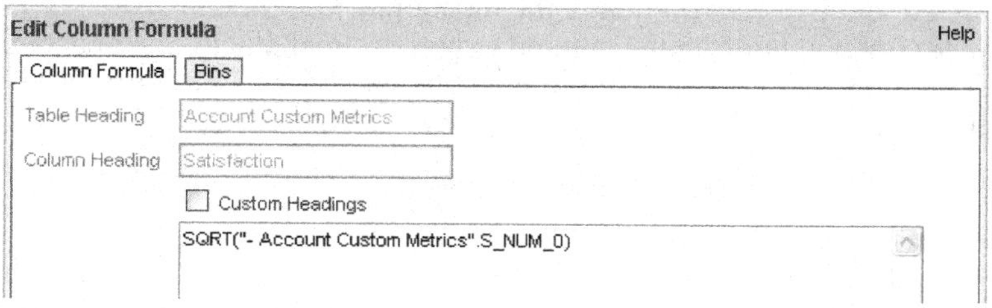

Edit Column Formula Help

Column Formula | Bins

Table Heading Account Custom Metrics

Column Heading Satisfaction

☐ Custom Headings

SQRT("- Account Custom Metrics".S_NUM_0)

FIGURE 6-67. *SQRT function applied to column*

FIGURE 6-68. *SQRT Example report*

TRUNCATE

The TRUNCATE function allows you to return a number up to a specified number of decimal places. This is different from the ROUND, FLOOR, and CEILING functions. TRUNCATE does not round a number up or down, but rather simply cuts the number off at the number of decimal places specified in the integer portion of the function. If your column is set to display four decimal places but you truncate the column to two decimal places, the final two digits in each row of the column will be zeroes. For example, the numbers 1.111 and 1.119 will both truncate at two decimal places to 1.11.

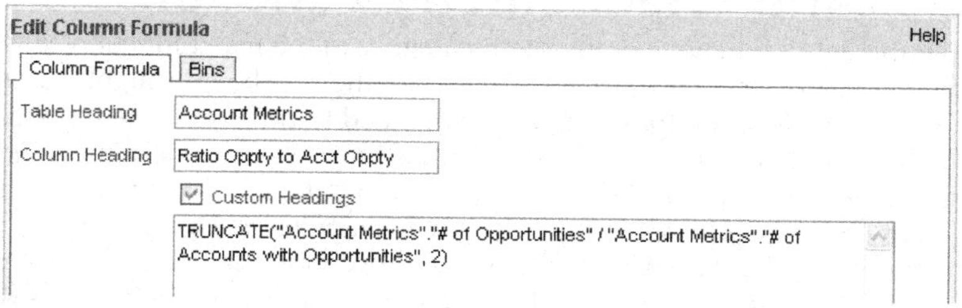

FIGURE 6-69. *TRUNCATE function applied to calculation*

Function Syntax

```
TRUNCATE(n-exp,N)
TRUNCATE("Account Metrics"."Avg Minutes to Close SRs",3)
TRUNCATE(("Account Metrics"."# of Opportunities") /
("Account Metrics"."# of Accounts with Opportunities"),2)
```

In Figure 6-69 I have applied the TRUNCATE function to a formula that divides the number of opportunities by the number of accounts with opportunities. I have indicated that the result should be truncated to two decimal places. The truncated and nontruncated results are shown in Figure 6-70.

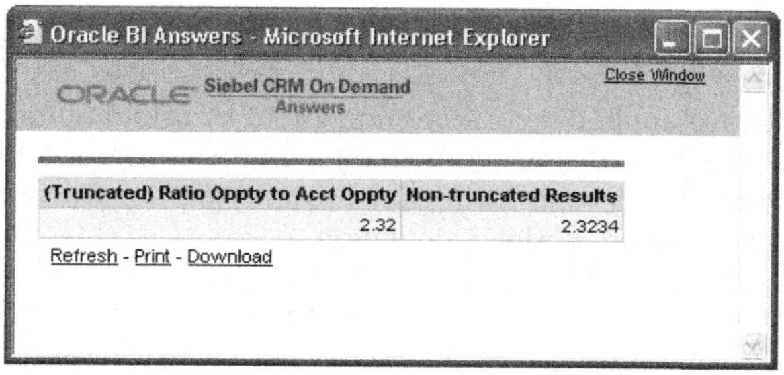

FIGURE 6-70. *Truncated and Nontruncated results*

Calculus and Trigonometry Functions

You can find this set of functions in the Math category in the insert function selector, but I have categorized them separately here because I consider them to be in a slightly different class of functions. These functions are for those of us who need to perform some high math in our reports. Frankly, I have never needed any of these functions in my years of designing and building reports in Answers On Demand, but this book simply would not be complete without them. Who is to say that you, my readers, will not need to do a little calculus or trigonometry in your reports.

Trigonometry is really quite simple once you understand the concepts, but there is not much call for it in business unless you happen to be in the civil engineering business or something that uses a lot of angles and circles. A brief explanation of trigonometry may be necessary in order to properly discuss these functions. There are three basic measurements in trigonometry: sine, cosine, and tangent. These three measurements and their inverses make up the trigonometry functions. The results of these calculations are given in radians or degrees, and Answers On Demand provides functions to convert between these two types of values.

Also included in this section are functions for exponents and logarithms. These functions are particularly useful for modeling and predicting behavior such as population growth or compounding interest. Clearly, there are some great math applications for major number crunching, but if you just need to include some calculations like this in your reports, Answers On Demand can certainly deliver.

ACOS

The ACOS function calculates the arc cosine of a numeric expression. The arc cosine is the radian measure of the arc on a circle corresponding to a given value of cosine. In other words, the arc cosine is the inverse of cosine. The ACOS function requires a numeric expression or literal between –1 and 1. The arc cosine result will be a number between 0 and pi.

Function Syntax

```
ACOS(n-exp)
ACOS("- Activity Custom Metrics".S_NUM_1)
DEGREES(ACOS("- Activity Custom Metrics".S_NUM_1))
```

In Figure 6-71 I have applied the ACOS function to a custom numeric field. When using the ACOS function, be sure the numeric expression for which you calculate the arc cosine falls within the valid range, or your report will generate an error message and fail to run. Figure 6-72 shows a sample result of an arc cosine calculation.

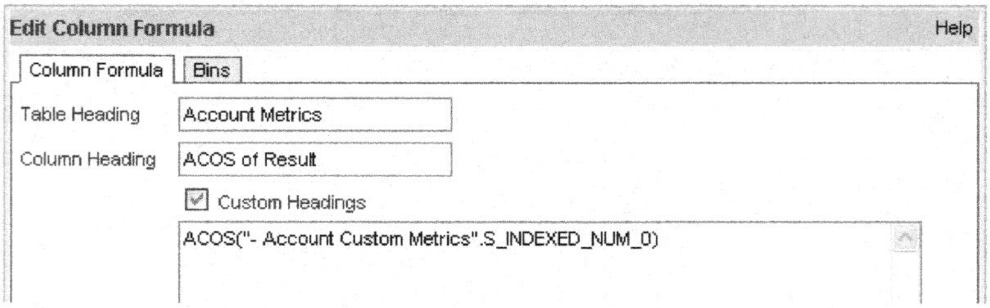

FIGURE 6-71. *ACOS function applied to column formula*

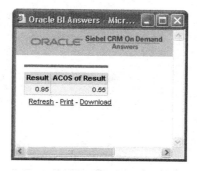

FIGURE 6-72. *Sample ACOS result*

ASIN

ASIN calculates the arc sine of a numeric expression or literal. The arc sine is the radian measure of the degrees of an angle that has a sine equal to a given number. In other words, the arc sine is the inverse of sine. The ASIN function requires a numeric expression or literal between –1 and 1. The arc cosine result will be a radian measure between –1.57 and 1.57 (or –pi/2 and pi/2).

Function Syntax

```
ASIN(n-exp)
ASIN("- Activity Custom Metrics".S_NUM_1)
DEGREES(ASIN("- Activity Custom Metrics".S_NUM_1))
```

In Figure 6-73 I have applied the ASIN function to a custom numeric field. Remember that the result of the ASIN function is in radians. You can convert radians to degrees with the DEGREES function. Figure 6-74 shows a sample result of an arc sine calculation.

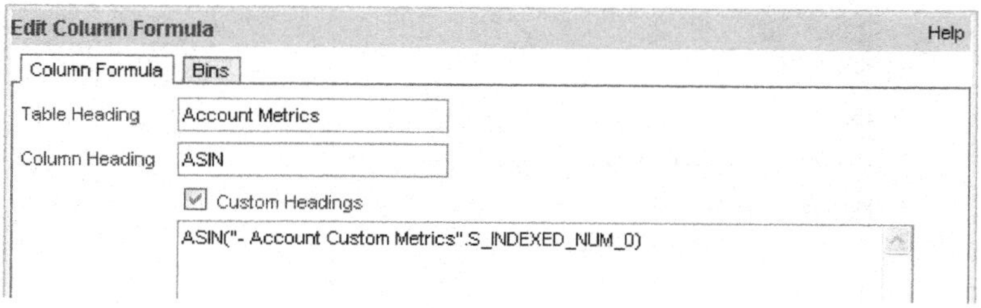

Edit Column Formula   Help

| Column Formula | Bins |

Table Heading   Account Metrics

Column Heading   ASIN

☑ Custom Headings

ASIN("- Account Custom Metrics".S_INDEXED_NUM_0)

FIGURE 6-73. *ASIN function applied to column formula*

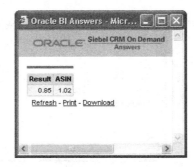

FIGURE 6-74. *Sample ASIN result*

ATAN

ATAN calculates the arc tangent of a numeric expression or literal. The tangent of an angle in a triangle is the ratio of the opposite side of the angle to the adjacent side. The arc tangent, then, is the inverse of this ratio. The ATAN function requires a numeric expression or literal. The arc tangent result will be a radian measure between –1.57 and 1.57 (or –pi/2 and pi/2).

Function Syntax

```
ATAN(n-exp)
ATAN("- Activity Custom Metrics".S_NUM_1)
DEGREES(ATAN("- Activity Custom Metrics".S_NUM_1))
```

In Figure 6-75 I have applied the ATAN function to a custom numeric field. The result of the ATAN function is in radians. You can convert radians to degrees with the DEGREES function. Figure 6-76 shows a sample result of an arc tangent calculation.

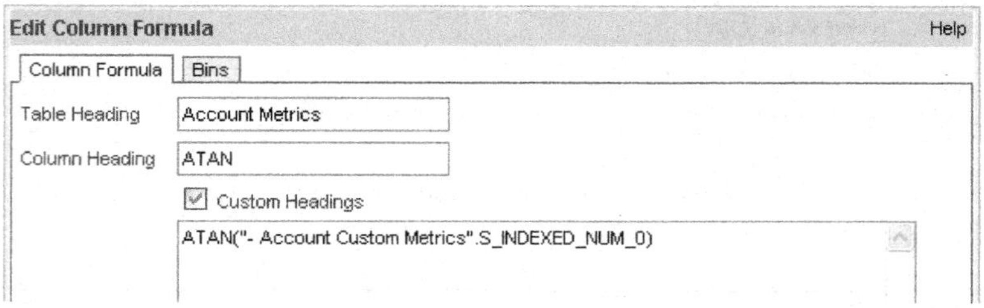

Edit Column Formula   Help

Column Formula | Bins

Table Heading   Account Metrics

Column Heading   ATAN

☑ Custom Headings

ATAN("- Account Custom Metrics".S_INDEXED_NUM_0)

FIGURE 6-75. *ATAN function applied to column formula*

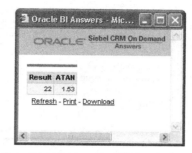

FIGURE 6-76. *Sample ATAN result*

ATAN2

ATAN2 calculates the arc tangent of one numeric expression divided by a second numeric expression. The results of this calculation will fall within the range of –3.14 and 3.14 (–pi – pi). This function is useful if you happen to have a need to convert a two-dimensional vector expressed in Cartesian coordinates (x, y) into polar coordinates (rho, theta). Essentially, ATAN2 calculates the counterclockwise angle between the X axis and the provided vector. The results, like the other functions, are in radians.

Function Syntax

```
ATAN2(n-exp, n-exp)
ATAN2("- Activity Custom Metrics".S_NUM_1, 0)
ATAN2("- Account Custom Metrics".S_NUM_1, "- Account Custom Metrics".S_NUM_3)
```

Figure 6-77 shows the ATAN2 function in a column formula. The resulting radian measure appears in Figure 6-78.

Edit Column Formula		Help
Column Formula	Bins	
Table Heading	Account Custom Metrics	
Column Heading	ATAN2	
	☑ Custom Headings	
	ATAN2("- Account Custom Metrics".S_INDEXED_NUM_0,"- Account Custom Metrics".S_NUM_0)	

FIGURE 6-77. *ATAN2 function applied to column formula*

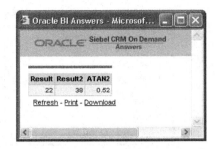

FIGURE 6-78. *Sample ATAN2 result*

COS

The COS function calculates the cosine of a numeric expression. The cosine of an angle in a right triangle is the measure of the adjacent side divided by the measure of the hypotenuse. The COS function produces a radian result –1 and 1. Since the period of cosine is 6.28 (2*pi), the cosine of a number is the same value as the cosine of the same number plus 6.28.

Function Syntax

```
COS(n-exp)
COS("- Activity Custom Metrics".S_NUM_1)
DEGREES(COS("- Activity Custom Metrics".S_NUM_1))
```

In Figure 6-79 I have applied the COS function to a custom numeric field. Figure 6-80 illustrates how COS(x) = COS(x + 2pi). Notice that the results of each calculation are the same.

COT

The COT function returns the cotangent of a numeric expression or numeric constant. Cotangent is not to be confused with arctangent. Arctangent is the inverse of tangent, and cotangent is cosine divided by sine. If that makes any sense to you, then you will know what to use this function for.

Edit Column Formula		Help
Column Formula	Bins	

Table Heading	Account Metrics
Column Heading	COS

☑ Custom Headings

COS("- Account Custom Metrics".S_INDEXED_NUM_0)

FIGURE 6-79. *COS function applied to column formula*

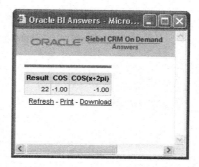

FIGURE 6-80. *Sample COS results*

Function Syntax

```
COT(n-exp)
COT("- Activity Custom Metrics".S_NUM_3)
```

In Figure 6-81 I have applied the COT function to a custom numeric field. Figure 6-82 shows the results of that calculation.

DEGREES

You may have noticed this function in some of the syntax examples earlier in this section. The DEGREES function converts a numeric expression of radians to its equivalent in degrees. Many of the trigonometric functions produce results in radians, and this function converts those results to the equivalent in degrees.

Function Syntax

```
DEGREES(n-exp)
DEGREES(COS(n-exp))
DEGREES(SIN("- Activity Custom Metrics".S_NUM_4))
```

Edit Column Formula		Help
Column Formula Bins		
Table Heading	Account Metrics	
Column Heading	COT	
	☑ Custom Headings	
	COT("- Account Custom Metrics".S_INDEXED_NUM_0)	

FIGURE 6-81. *COT function applied to column formula*

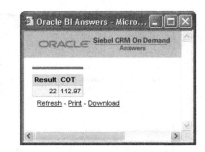

FIGURE 6-82. *Sample COT result*

In Figure 6-83 I am using the DEGREES function to convert an arc sine calculation from radians to degrees. The DEGREES function is most useful in this type of formula, where your result would otherwise be in the form of radians but you want your data in degrees. Of course, if you are storing radian measures in your database, you would be able to use the DEGREES function on its own. Figure 6-84 shows three columns, the second with the result in radians and the third in degrees.

EXP

The value 2.718281828459 is the irrational number *e*, which is the base of the natural logarithm. The EXP function raises the value *e* to the power specified. The natural logarithm of a number *x* is the power to which you must raise *e* to equal *x*. For example, the natural log of 2.71828 is 1, since $e^1 = 2.71828$.

Function Syntax

```
EXP(n-exp)
EXP(2.5)
EXP("Account Metrics"."# of Opportunities")
```

Edit Column Formula	Help

Column Formula | Bins

Table Heading — Account Metrics

Column Heading — DEGREES - ASIN

☑ Custom Headings

DEGREES(ASIN("- Account Custom Metrics".S_INDEXED_NUM_0))

FIGURE 6-83. *DEGREES function applied to a calculation*

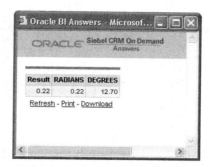

FIGURE 6-84.   *Results in radians and degrees*

If you use the EXP function, it will most likely be with a literal value, but any numeric expression will work. Figure 6-85 shows the EXP function applied to a numeric column, and Figure 6-86 shows the result of that calculation.

LOG

The LOG function calculates the natural logarithm of a numeric expression. The natural log describes the power to which the exponent e must be raised to obtain the given value, and is typically depicted as *ln* in mathematical equations. For instance, the natural log of 100 is 4.6052 because $e^{4.6052}$ is 100. Remember that e is 2.71828. Given this, we know that POWER(2.71828, 4.6052) gives us a result of 100 and that EXP(4.6052) also gives us 100.

Function Syntax

```
LOG(n-exp)
LOG(50)
LOG("Account Metrics"."# of Opportunities")
```

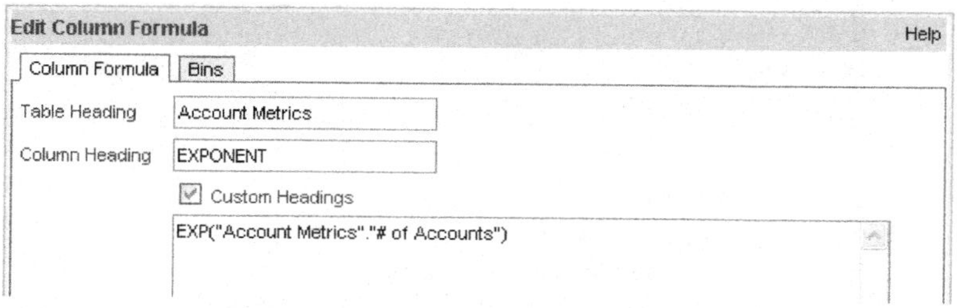

FIGURE 6-85.   *EXP function applied to column*

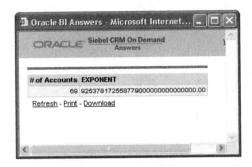

FIGURE 6-86. *Exponential calculation on of Accounts*

Figure 6-87 shows the formula to calculate the natural logarithm of a metric in my database. I plan to plot these values on a chart and want to use a logarithmic scale, so I have decided to calculate the natural log of each value. Figure 6-88 shows the result of this calculation in my report. In Chapter 11, which discusses adding charts to a report, you will see how to use a logarithmic scale in your charts.

LOG10

While the natural log is probably the most commonly used logarithm in scientific circles, logarithms using other bases are sometimes favored by mathematicians. The most common of these is the base 10 log, usually represented as Log_{10}. This often makes the manual calculation of a logarithm a bit simpler, and base 10 is the predominant base of our counting system. Using the same example as with the LOG function, the base 10 log of 100 or LOG10(100) is 2 because 10^2 or POWER(10,2) is 100.

Function Syntax

```
LOG10(n-exp)
LOG10(300)
LOG10("Account Metrics"."# of Opportunities")
```

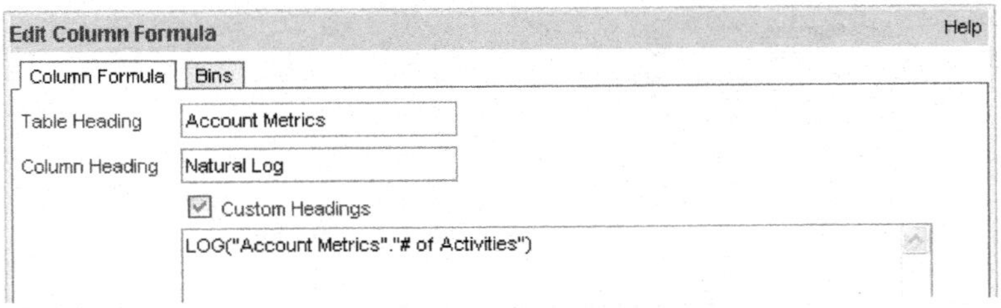

Edit Column Formula		Help
Column Formula | Bins		
Table Heading	Account Metrics	
Column Heading	Natural Log	
	☑ Custom Headings	
	LOG("Account Metrics"."# of Activities")	

FIGURE 6-87. *LOG function applied to column formula*

Account Type	Natural Log
Customer	0.69
Competitor	0.00
Prospect	3.26
Customer	3.04
Customer	3.14
Prospect	2.83
Customer	3.04
Prospect	3.09
Customer	3.30
Prospect	3.26
Prospect	3.00
Prospect	3.18
Customer	3.09
Prospect	2.94
Customer	3.40
Customer	3.43
Prospect	3.18
Customer	3.26
Prospect	3.00
Customer	3.18
Customer	3.37
Prospect	3.09
Customer	3.18
Prospect	3.04
Prospect	2.83

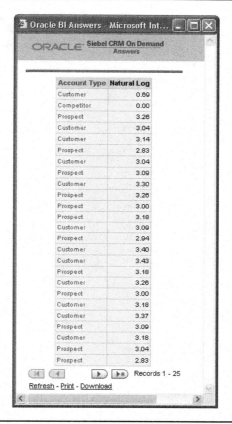

FIGURE 6-88. *Sample Natural Log result*

Figure 6-89 shows the formula to calculate the base 10 logarithm of a metric in my database. Figure 6-90 shows the result of this calculation in my report.

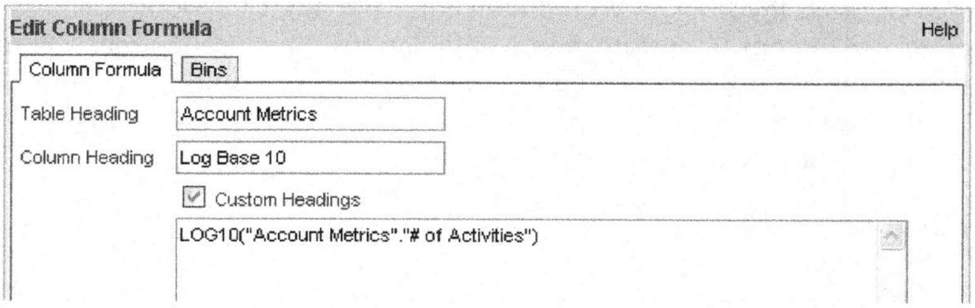

FIGURE 6-89. *LOG10 function applied to column formula*

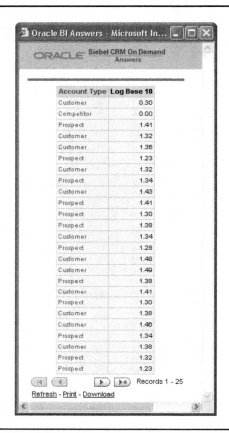

FIGURE 6-90. *Sample Log Base 10 result*

RADIANS

The RADIANS function converts degrees to radians. You may recall that the DEGREES function does just the opposite. If you work with dimensions and angles in your business, you probably have a need to use radians to perform some calculations. Because degrees is a more common measurement and is likely the measurement your customers would use to describe an angle, it is more likely the measurement you would then store in your database. If this is the case, the RADIANS function may be quite useful.

Function Syntax

```
RADIANS(n-exp)
RADIANS(180)
RADIANS("- Account Custom Metrics".S_NUM_1)
```

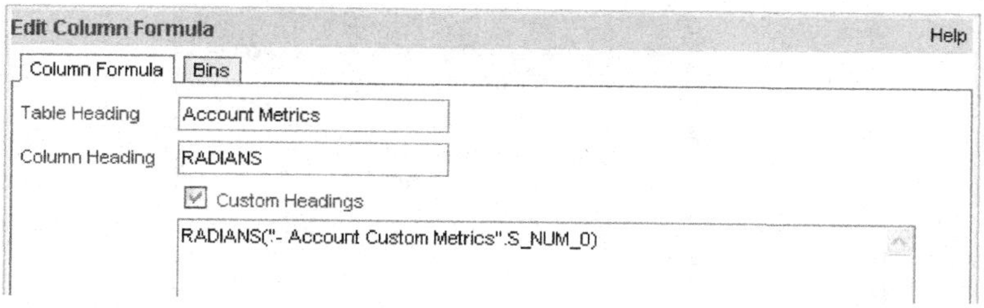

FIGURE 6-91. *RADIANS function applied to column formula*

Since a single degree is 1/360th of a full turn of two pi radians, using a function that converts degrees to radians is much easier than doing the necessary math for this conversion. In Figure 6-91 I have a column formula that converts data from a custom degrees field in my database to radians. The result in Figure 6-92 shows the radian equivalent of several common degree measures.

SIN

SIN calculates the sine of a numeric expression or constant. The sine of an angle is calculated by finding the ratio of the opposite side and the hypotenuse of the right triangle formed by the angle. The result of the SIN function will always fall between –1 and 1.

Function Syntax

```
SIN(n-exp)
SIN(45)
SIN("- Opportunity Custom Metrics".S_NUM_1)
```

In Figure 6-93 I am using the SIN function to calculate the sine of a numeric value. Figure 6-94 shows the result of this calculation.

TAN

The final function to introduce in this chapter is the tangent calculation. TAN provides the tangent of a numeric expression or constant. The tangent of x is equivalent to the sine of x over the cosine of x. The two formulas TAN(25) and SIN(25)/COS(25) give the same result.

Function Syntax

```
TAN(n-exp)
TAN("- Account Custom Metrics".S_NUM_1)
TAN("- Opportunity Custom Metrics".S_NUM_1 +
"- Opportunity Custom Metrics".S_NUM_3)
```

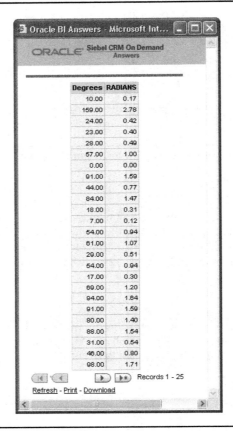

FIGURE 6-92. *Degrees converted to Radians report*

In Figure 6-95 I have created a formula that gives the tangent of the sum of two values from my database. Notice that the equation is written to add two numeric columns together, and then give the tangent of that result. The report in Figure 6-96 shows this result.

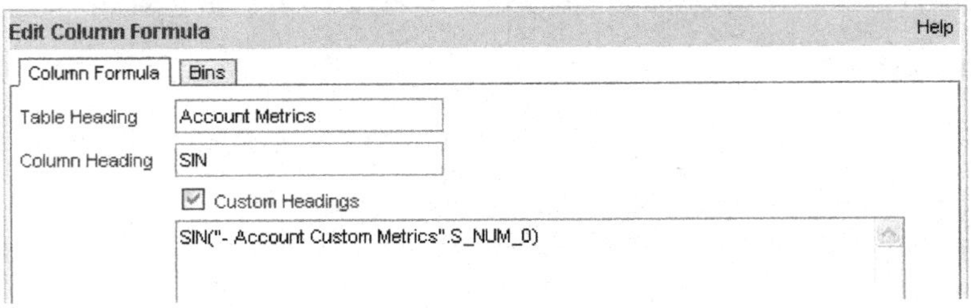

Edit Column Formula   Help

| Column Formula | Bins |

Table Heading   Account Metrics

Column Heading   SIN

☑ Custom Headings

SIN("- Account Custom Metrics".S_NUM_0)

FIGURE 6-93. *SIN function applied to column formula*

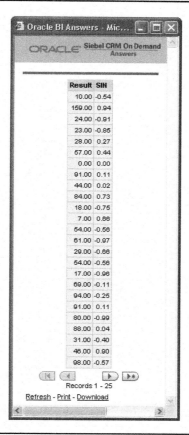

FIGURE 6-94. *Sample SIN result*

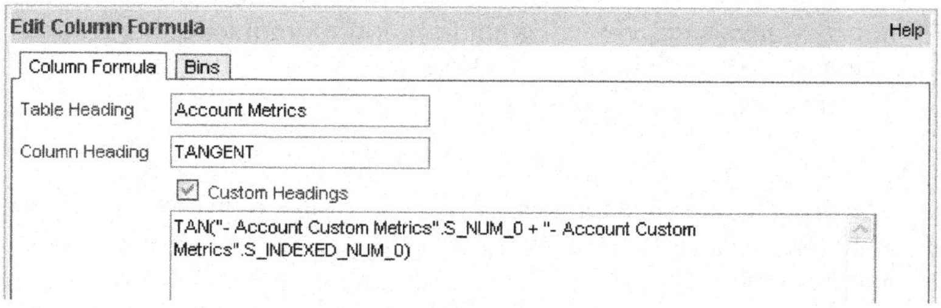

Edit Column Formula

Column Formula | Bins

Table Heading | Account Metrics
Column Heading | TANGENT

☑ Custom Headings

TAN("- Account Custom Metrics".S_NUM_0 + "- Account Custom Metrics".S_INDEXED_NUM_0)

FIGURE 6-95. *TAN function applied to column formula*

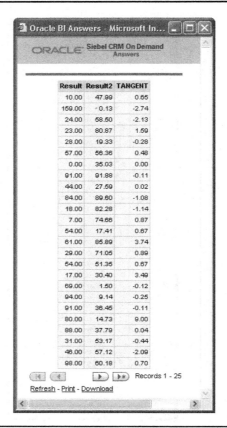

FIGURE 6-96. *Sample TANGENT result*

Organizing Complex Formulas

Now that we have walked through all the aggregate, running aggregate, and math functions, let us examine how we can use several of these functions and operators together to build more complex formulas. Many things we will want to report on require either a series of several functions or a single complex formula using several functions. This section offers some useful information on constructing such formulas.

Expressions

Nearly every function requires an expression within the syntax of the formula. It is important to understand what constitutes an expression. Table 6-2 lists and gives examples of numeric expressions.

In short, any number or formula that results in a number is considered a numeric expression for the purposes of using functions in Answers On Demand. In more complex formulas, this can get very confusing, and your attention to detail becomes a critical success factor for your reports. I have four suggestions for working with complex formulas: use parenthetical expressions carefully, add white space to your long formulas, nest formulas by combining columns, and add comments to your formula code.

Numeric Expression Style	Example
Numeric literal	3.14
Column field reference	"– Opportunity Custom Metrics".S_NUM_1
Simple math equation	724/56
Field and literal equation	"– Account Custom Metrics".S_NUM_10 * 1.15
Multifield equation	("– Opportunity Custom Metrics".S_NUM_1 + "– Opportunity Custom Metrics".S_NUM_2) / 100
Single function	PI()
Combination of any of the above	((3.14 * "– Opportunity Custom Metrics".S_NUM_1) + ("– Opportunity Custom Metrics".S_NUM_10 * 1.15)) / SUM("Revenue Metrics"."Opportunity Revenue")

TABLE 6-2. *Variations of Numeric Expressions*

Nesting Formulas with Parenthesis

When combining or nesting formulas, your use of parentheses becomes very important. Any one of three mistakes in your use of parentheses will drive you crazy trying to figure out why your column formula is not working or is returning an inaccurate result.

- If you are missing one or more opening or closing parentheses, Answers gives you an error message when you try to save the formula.

- If you have the correct number of parentheses but have inserted one or more of them in an incorrect position, either you will get an error or your result will not be accurate.

- Finally, it is possible to write a formula with perfect syntax, but find that the formula you have written is not the formula you intended to write because you failed to put the necessary parentheses in place to force the correct order of operations.

Remember that Answers follows the order of operations and evaluates operations inside of parentheses first. Thus, the following expressions differ only in the placement of (or lack of) parentheses but produce different results:

- $1 + 2 * 3 - 4 = 3$
- $(1 + 2) * 3 - 4 = 5$
- $(1 + 2) * (3 - 4) = -3$
- $1 + 2 * (3 - 4) = -1$

Although each of these expressions contains the same numbers and operators, each expression produces very different results because of the addition or lack of parentheses. When you start creating very complex equations featuring many columns from the database and many functions, the task of identifying the individual expressions and properly placing the parentheses becomes quite a challenge. Fortunately, Answers On Demand ignores extra spaces and line breaks in formulas. You can use this to your advantage.

Use White Space

Take the following real-life example of a formula, for instance:

```
(CASE WHEN Opportunity."Sales Stage" NOT IN ('Closed/Won', 'Closed/Lost') THEN
(SUM((((CASE WHEN Opportunity.PICK_1 = "- Owned By User"."Employee Name" THEN
"- Custom Number/Integer (Opty)".NUM_14 ELSE 0 END / SUM ("Activity Metrics"."#
of Activities" by Opportunity.Name)) + (CASE WHEN Opportunity.PICK_21 =
"- Owned By User"."Employee Name" THEN "- Custom Number/Integer (Opty)".NUM_6
ELSE 0 END / SUM ("Activity Metrics"."# of Activities" by Opportunity.Name)) +
(CASE WHEN Opportunity.PICK_20 = "- Owned By User"."Employee Name" THEN "- Cus-
tom Number/Integer (Opty)".NUM_13 ELSE 0 END / SUM ("Activity Metrics"."# of
Activities" by Opportunity.Name)) + (CASE WHEN Opportunity.PICK_50 = "- Owned
By User"."Employee Name" THEN "- Custom Number/Integer (Opty)".NUM_4  ELSE 0
END / SUM ("Activity Metrics"."# of Activities" by Opportunity.Name)) + (CASE
WHEN Opportunity.PICK_3 = "- Owned By User"."Employee Name" THEN "- Custom
Number/Integer (Opty)".NUM_3 ELSE 0 END/ SUM ("Activity Metrics"."# of Activi-
ties" by Opportunity.Name)) )) + CASE WHEN "- Custom Number/Integer".S_NUM_0 <
0 THEN (CASE WHEN Opportunity.PICK_1 = "- Owned By User"."Employee Name" AND
Activity.Type IN ('PM-Configuration', 'PM-Review/Validation', 'Change Consult-
ing', 'Report Requirements', 'Report Development' ) THEN ABS ( "- Custom Num-
ber/Integer".S_NUM_0) ELSE 0 END + CASE WHEN Opportunity.PICK_21 = "- Owned By
User"."Employee Name" AND Activity.Type = 'Project Management' THEN ABS
( "- Custom Number/Integer".S_NUM_0) ELSE 0 END + CASE WHEN Opportunity.PICK_20
= "- Owned By User"."Employee Name" AND Activity.Type = 'PM-Business Require-
ments' THEN ABS ( "- Custom Number/Integer".S_NUM_0) ELSE 0 END + CASE WHEN
Opportunity.PICK_50 = "- Owned By User"."Employee Name" AND Activity.Type =
'Import Consulting' THEN ABS ( "- Custom Number/Integer".S_NUM_0) ELSE 0 END +
CASE WHEN Opportunity.PICK_3 = "- Owned By User"."Employee Name" AND Activity.
Type IN ('Training Development', 'Training Requirements', 'Training Delivery')
THEN ABS ( "- Custom Number/Integer".S_NUM_0) ELSE 0 END ) ELSE 0 END BY Op-
portunity.Name ) - SUM ( CASE WHEN "- Custom Number/Integer".S_NUM_0 < 0 THEN
0 WHEN Activity.Type = 'Customer Satisfaction' THEN 0 ELSE "- Custom Number/
Integer".S_NUM_0 END BY Opportunity.Name)) / SUM ("Activity Metrics"."# of
Activities" by Opportunity.Name) ELSE 0 END) + (CASE WHEN (CASE WHEN CAST ( "-
Due Date"."Task Due Date" as DATE) BETWEEN date '2006-05-27' AND date '2006-
08-25' THEN 'Fiscal 2007 Q1' WHEN CAST ( "- Due Date"."Task Due Date" as DATE)
BETWEEN date '2006-08-25' AND date '2006-11-24' THEN 'Fiscal 2007 Q2' WHEN CAST
( "- Due Date"."Task Due Date" as DATE) BETWEEN date '2006-11-24' AND date
'2007-02-23' THEN 'Fiscal 2007 Q3' WHEN CAST ( "- Due Date"."Task Due Date"
as DATE) BETWEEN date '2007-02-23' AND date '2007-05-25' THEN 'Fiscal 2007
Q4' WHEN CAST ( "- Due Date"."Task Due Date" as DATE) BETWEEN date '2007-05-
25' AND date '2007-08-31' THEN 'Fiscal 2008 Q1' WHEN CAST ( "- Due Date"."Task
Due Date" as DATE) BETWEEN date '2007-08-31' AND date '2007-11-30' THEN 'Fis-
cal 2008 Q2' WHEN CAST ( "- Due Date"."Task Due Date" as DATE) BETWEEN date
'2007-11-30' AND date '2008-02-29' THEN 'Fiscal 2008 Q3' WHEN CAST ( "- Due
Date"."Task Due Date" as DATE) BETWEEN date '2008-02-29' AND date '2008-05-30'
THEN 'Fiscal 2008 Q4' ELSE NULL END) = (CASE WHEN Current_DATE BETWEEN date
```

```
'2006-05-27' AND date '2006-08-25' THEN 'Fiscal 2007 Q1' WHEN Current_DATE
BETWEEN date '2006-08-25' AND date '2006-11-24' THEN 'Fiscal 2007 Q2' WHEN Cur-
rent_DATE BETWEEN date '2006-11-24' AND date '2007-02-23' THEN 'Fiscal 2007 Q3'
WHEN Current_DATE BETWEEN date '2007-02-23' AND date '2007-05-25' THEN 'Fiscal
2007 Q4' WHEN Current_DATE BETWEEN date '2007-05-25' AND date '2007-08-31' THEN
'Fiscal 2008 Q1' WHEN Current_DATE BETWEEN date '2007-08-31' AND date '2007-11-
30' THEN 'Fiscal 2008 Q2' WHEN Current_DATE BETWEEN date '2007-11-30' AND date
'2008-02-29' THEN 'Fiscal 2008 Q3' WHEN Current_DATE BETWEEN date '2008-02-
29' AND date '2008-05-30' THEN 'Fiscal 2008 Q4' ELSE NULL END) THEN CASE WHEN
"- Custom Number/Integer".S_NUM_0 < 0 THEN 0 ELSE "- Custom Number/Integer".S_
NUM_0 END ELSE 0 END)
```

Can you tell exactly what is missing from this formula by looking at it like this? I'm assuming that you took one look at that formula and decided that it was not something you were interested in troubleshooting. If so, you are not alone. Formulas like this one are nearly impossible to troubleshoot when they appear like this.

There is no reason for you to leave lengthy formulas jammed together like the preceding one. Because Answers On Demand ignores extra spaces and line breaks, for complex formulas such as the preceding one with nested functions and many column references, you can make it much easier to read, as follows:

```
(CASE
WHEN Opportunity."Sales Stage" NOT IN ('Closed/Won', 'Closed/Lost')
THEN (SUM((((
 CASE
 WHEN Opportunity.PICK_1 = "- Owned By User"."Employee Name"
 THEN "- Custom Number/Integer (Opty)".NUM_14
 ELSE 0
 END
/ SUM ("Activity Metrics"."# of Activities" by Opportunity.Name))
+ (CASE
 WHEN Opportunity.PICK_21 = "- Owned By User"."Employee Name"
 THEN "- Custom Number/Integer (Opty)".NUM_6
 ELSE 0
 END
/ SUM ("Activity Metrics"."# of Activities" by Opportunity.Name))
+ (CASE
 WHEN Opportunity.PICK_20 = "- Owned By User"."Employee Name"
 THEN "- Custom Number/Integer (Opty)".NUM_13
 ELSE 0
 END
/ SUM ("Activity Metrics"."# of Activities" by Opportunity.Name))
+ (CASE
 WHEN Opportunity.PICK_50 = "- Owned By User"."Employee Name"
 THEN "- Custom Number/Integer (Opty)".NUM_4
 ELSE 0
 END
/ SUM ("Activity Metrics"."# of Activities" by Opportunity.Name))
+ (CASE
 WHEN Opportunity.PICK_3 = "- Owned By User"."Employee Name"
 THEN "- Custom Number/Integer (Opty)".NUM_3
```

```
  ELSE 0
  END
/ SUM ("Activity Metrics"."# of Activities" by Opportunity.Name)) ))
+ CASE
 WHEN "- Custom Number/Integer".S_NUM_0 < 0
 THEN
  (CASE
  WHEN Opportunity.PICK_1 = "- Owned By User"."Employee Name"
   AND Activity.Type IN ('Configuration', 'Review', 'Consulting', 'Reports')
   THEN ABS ( "- Custom Number/Integer".S_NUM_0)
   ELSE 0
   END
 + CASE
  WHEN Opportunity.PICK_21 = "- Owned By User"."Employee Name"
   AND Activity.Type = 'Management'
   THEN ABS ( "- Custom Number/Integer".S_NUM_0)
   ELSE 0
   END
 + CASE
  WHEN Opportunity.PICK_20 = "- Owned By User"."Employee Name"
   AND Activity.Type = 'Business Requirements'
   THEN ABS ( "- Custom Number/Integer".S_NUM_0)
   ELSE 0
   END
 + CASE
  WHEN Opportunity.PICK_50 = "- Owned By User"."Employee Name"
   AND Activity.Type = 'Importing'
   THEN ABS ( "- Custom Number/Integer".S_NUM_0)
   ELSE 0
   END
 + CASE
  WHEN Opportunity.PICK_3 = "- Owned By User"."Employee Name"
   AND Activity.Type IN ('Training', 'Training Delivery')
   THEN ABS ( "- Custom Number/Integer".S_NUM_0)
   ELSE 0
   END )
  ELSE 0
  END BY Opportunity.Name )
 - SUM
  (CASE
  WHEN "- Custom Number/Integer".S_NUM_0 < 0 THEN 0
  WHEN Activity.Type = 'Other' THEN 0
  ELSE "- Custom Number/Integer".S_NUM_0
  END BY Opportunity.Name))
 / SUM ("Activity Metrics"."# of Activities" by Opportunity.Name)
ELSE 0
END)
+
(CASE
WHEN
 (CASE
```

```
WHEN CAST ( "- Due Date"."Task Due Date" as DATE)
  BETWEEN date '2006-05-27' AND date '2006-08-25' THEN 'Fiscal 2007 Q1'
WHEN CAST ( "- Due Date"."Task Due Date" as DATE)
  BETWEEN date '2006-08-25' AND date '2006-11-24' THEN 'Fiscal 2007 Q2'
WHEN CAST ( "- Due Date"."Task Due Date" as DATE)
  BETWEEN date '2006-11-24' AND date '2007-02-23' THEN 'Fiscal 2007 Q3'
WHEN CAST ( "- Due Date"."Task Due Date" as DATE)
  BETWEEN date '2007-02-23' AND date '2007-05-25' THEN 'Fiscal 2007 Q4'
WHEN CAST ( "- Due Date"."Task Due Date" as DATE)
  BETWEEN date '2007-05-25' AND date '2007-08-31' THEN 'Fiscal 2008 Q1'
WHEN CAST ( "- Due Date"."Task Due Date" as DATE)
  BETWEEN date '2007-08-31' AND date '2007-11-30' THEN 'Fiscal 2008 Q2'
WHEN CAST ( "- Due Date"."Task Due Date" as DATE)
  BETWEEN date '2007-11-30' AND date '2008-02-29' THEN 'Fiscal 2008 Q3'
WHEN CAST ( "- Due Date"."Task Due Date" as DATE)
  BETWEEN date '2008-02-29' AND date '2008-05-30' THEN 'Fiscal 2008 Q4'
ELSE NULL
END)
=
(CASE
WHEN Current_DATE
  BETWEEN date '2006-05-27' AND date '2006-08-25' THEN 'Fiscal 2007 Q1'
WHEN Current_DATE
  BETWEEN date '2006-08-25' AND date '2006-11-24' THEN 'Fiscal 2007 Q2'
WHEN Current_DATE
  BETWEEN date '2006-11-24' AND date '2007-02-23' THEN 'Fiscal 2007 Q3'
WHEN Current_DATE
  BETWEEN date '2007-02-23' AND date '2007-05-25' THEN 'Fiscal 2007 Q4'
WHEN Current_DATE
  BETWEEN date '2007-05-25' AND date '2007-08-31' THEN 'Fiscal 2008 Q1'
WHEN Current_DATE
  BETWEEN date '2007-08-31' AND date '2007-11-30' THEN 'Fiscal 2008 Q2'
WHEN Current_DATE
  BETWEEN date '2007-11-30' AND date '2008-02-29' THEN 'Fiscal 2008 Q3'
WHEN Current_DATE
  BETWEEN date '2008-02-29' AND date '2008-05-30' THEN 'Fiscal 2008 Q4'
ELSE NULL
END) THEN
  CASE
  WHEN "- Custom Number/Integer".S_NUM_0 < 0 THEN 0
  ELSE "- Custom Number/Integer".S_NUM_0
  END
ELSE 0
END)
```

I almost always dissect and analyze my complex formulas in a simple text editor. This is particularly helpful when troubleshooting or tweaking a complex column formula. I have even used a word processing program to gain the capability to color code, underline, bold, italicize, and change fonts of parts of my formula to help me see the various parts of the formula. Now that I have organized the elements of this formula, I can begin to see the functions and expressions involved and understand how the formula is working.

So, how do we wind up with such lengthy and complex column formulas? You will find that it is really not very difficult to build a formula like this. In fact, I would venture that troubleshooting or updating someone else's column formulas is much more difficult than building one yourself.

Build the Small Formulas First

Now for my next tip for complex nested formulas: create the parts and then put them together to form the whole formula. In other words, add all the columns that you need and create the individual expressions and formulas that will ultimately make up your larger formula. You can remove the unneeded columns later.

Perhaps an example will help make this clear. Suppose we want to write a formula that will calculate the difference between the average commissions earned on opportunities where products were sold and the average commissions earned on services opportunities by month for each salesperson. Since this data is somewhat sensitive, we want our report to show only the individual differences for each salesperson each month, not salesperson names or the specific commission amounts. Everyone earns the same commission rate of 3 percent on all sales.

First, we should identify all of our data points. For this example, we need the following columns:

- Opportunity Type
- Opportunity Revenue
- Sales Stage
- Opportunity Close Date
- Opportunity Owner

After adding these columns to our report, it is time to design the formula and identify all of its parts. On our report, we will include the Close Date column, showing only the month, and include a column with our commission difference calculation. The owner field needs to be in the report also, but should be hidden from view. To ensure that we are working with only closed opportunities, we will filter on the Sales Stage column.

For this example, our formula should be

```
(FILTER(AVG(Revenue * .03 USING (Type = Product)))) -
(FILTER(AVG(Revenue * .03 USING (Type = Service))))
```

So, the individual expressions that make up this simple formula are

- Average "Revenue Metrics"."Opportunity Revenue" * .03
- Filter Using Opportunity."Sales Type" = 'Product'
- Filter Using Opportunity."Sales Type" = 'Service'

Now, when we put it all together, we build the following formula:

```
FILTER(AVG("Revenue Metrics"."Opportunity Revenue" * .03)
USING (Opportunity."Sales Type" = 'Product')) -
FILTER(AVG("Revenue Metrics"."Opportunity Revenue" * .03)
USING (Opportunity."Sales Type" = 'Service'))
```

There are essentially three methods for building this formula in the Column Formula field:

■ Type it all directly into the field. For some short formulas, this is easy enough to do.

■ Click the column name in the Columns list on the left side of the window to insert the necessary column field references, and then type in the parentheses, operators, and functions necessary to build the formula. This method is easy as long as you are working with only a few columns.

■ For those formulas that are very long and require nesting of several functions, build each piece of your formula in separate columns and then pull them together by using the Column button.

I find that the last method helps to keep everything straight and allows me to test the pieces before I assemble the whole. Take the following formula, for instance. This formula is long and complex. To build this formula, I started with a column for each of the nested functions (see Figure 6-97).

```
IFNULL(FILTER(FILTER("- Activity Custom Metrics".S_NUM_0 USING
(CASE MONTH(Activity."Due Date") WHEN 6 THEN
```

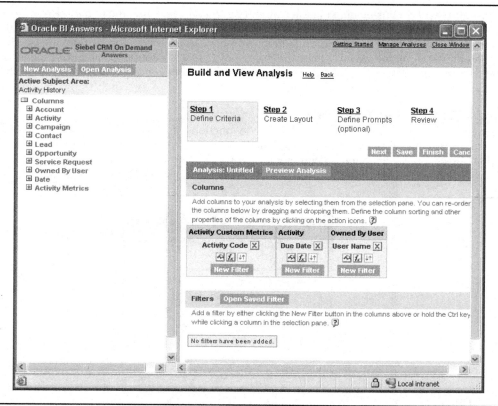

FIGURE 6-97. *Step 1 of activity report*

```
CAST(YEAR(Activity."Due Date")+1 AS CHAR) || ' Q 1' WHEN 7 THEN
CAST(YEAR(Activity."Due Date")+1 AS CHAR) || ' Q 1' WHEN 8 THEN
CAST(YEAR(Activity."Due Date")+1 AS CHAR) || ' Q 1' WHEN 9 THEN
CAST(YEAR(Activity."Due Date")+1 AS CHAR) || ' Q 2' WHEN 10 THEN
CAST(YEAR(Activity."Due Date")+1 AS CHAR) || ' Q 2' WHEN 11 THEN
CAST(YEAR(Activity."Due Date")+1 AS CHAR) || ' Q 2' WHEN 12 THEN
CAST(YEAR(Activity."Due Date")+1 AS CHAR) || ' Q 3' WHEN 1 THEN
CAST(YEAR(Activity."Due Date") AS CHAR) || ' Q 3' WHEN 2 THEN
CAST(YEAR(Activity."Due Date") AS CHAR) || ' Q 3' WHEN 3 THEN
CAST(YEAR(Activity."Due Date") AS CHAR) || ' Q 4' WHEN 4 THEN
CAST(YEAR(Activity."Due Date") AS CHAR) || ' Q 4' WHEN 5 THEN
CAST(YEAR(Activity."Due Date") AS CHAR) || ' Q 4' ELSE NULL END =
(CAST(VALUEOF(NQ_SESSION.CURRENT_YEAR) AS CHAR) ||' Q '||
CAST(VALUEOF(NQ_SESSION.CURRENT_QTR) AS CHAR))))
USING (Employee."Employee Name" IN ('Robert', 'Mike', 'David', 'Susan'))), 0)
```

Creating first the individual columns allows me to test the pieces of the formula before I assemble the entire string of code. It is much easier to troubleshoot individual functions and small operations than to determine why a 40-line formula is not working.

Now that I am satisfied that all of the individual components of my formula perform as expected, I can add another column to my report and begin the process of building the final formula. I will do this by clicking the Column button and selecting the column I want to insert into my column formula. Upon selecting a column, the entire formula for the selected column inserts itself into the Column Formula field. All I have to do is type the appropriate operators and parentheses along the way to create the proper syntax for the formula. After building the formula and testing it with the preview, I can delete any of the unneeded columns from my report. Figure 6-98 shows the resulting report.

Add Comments to Your Code

As you continue to expand your mastery of the functions of Answers On Demand, you will find yourself nesting functions and building lengthy formulas. My final tip for lengthy formulas is to do yourself a favor and include comments in your code. Months later when you need to make

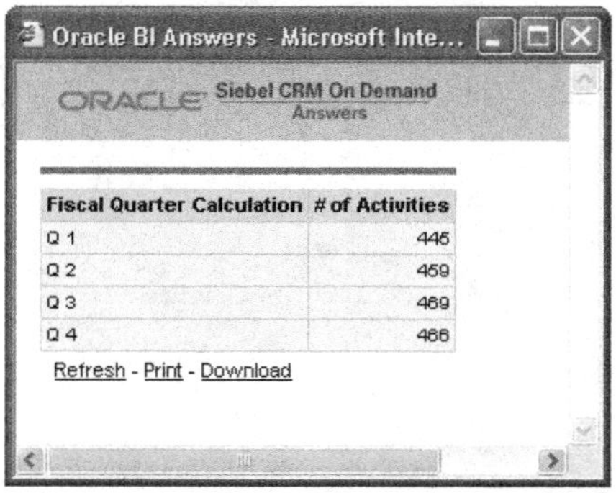

FIGURE 6-98. *Activities by Fiscal Quarter with Custom Quarter Calculation*

a change to your report, you will be glad you took the time to leave yourself some notes on exactly what you were thinking when you created that four-page formula.

To add comments anywhere in your code, start with a forward slash and asterisk, enter your comment, and end with an asterisk and forward slash. Answers On Demand completely ignores everything between the /* and */ symbols.

```
/* This formula calculates the average commission with the
current commission rate of 5% */
(AVG("Revenue Metrics"."Opportunity Revenue" * .05)
/* Identify the average by the month that opportunity closed */
BY MONTH(Opportunity."Close Date"))
```

This chapter took you through the mathematical functions. With these, you can take the metrics provided by CRM On Demand and Answers On Demand and create analyses that move your reports a little closer to business intelligence.

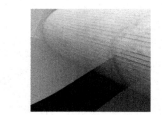

CHAPTER
7

Using Column Formulas
with Date and Time Data

n most cases, when you are analyzing your business data, you are interested in seeing a specific portion of the data rather than every record in your database. One element that is commonly of interest to all users of On Demand, regardless of industry, sale process, service methodologies, or size, is the element of time. Everyone has at least one report need that examines data based on time.

The most important thing to be aware of when working with date and time fields is that there are two distinct types of fields. The Date field type contains only a date. The Timestamp field type contains both a date and time.

Whether you are comparing sales data from one quarter to the next or examining how long it takes to resolve your service requests, the date/time functions are instrumental in your report development. This chapter provides explanations and examples for each of the date/time functions available in Answers On Demand, organized into three categories:

- Functions that describe current date and time

- Functions that extract date and time information from date and date/time expressions

- Two special functions that allow you to add and subtract units of time and calculate the difference between two timestamps

This chapter examines the available date and time functions and literals in Answers On Demand. These functions and literal values will prove indispensable in your report column formulas and report filters as you design your business analyses. At the end of the chapter, I have included some useful date and time formula samples.

Date/Time Literals

When working with date and time functions, you often need to express a specific date, time, or timestamp as a literal value. There are three types of date/time literals. You have one format for expressing a date, one for expressing a time, and one for expressing a date timestamp. This section shows the format and an example of each date/time literal type. These formats are fixed, and you cannot express dates in any other way. This does not mean that the date must display in this format. When you express a date literal, you must comply with the data format in the database, but you can format these values to display in any of the other date formats by formatting the column data.

To express a date/time literal, use the keyword DATE, TIME, or TIMESTAMP followed by a date or time string enclosed in single quote marks. You must use four digits for the year and two digits for all other components, even if the value is a single digit.

Date literals must contain a valid date. You cannot express September 31 as a literal date, because September contains only 30 days. Answers On Demand does recognize leap years, so a literal date of February 29 in 2008 is acceptable, but would fail with the year 2007.

```
DATE 'yyyy-MM-dd'
DATE '1972-05-17'
```

Time literals use the 24-hour clock format. A value of 01:00:00 is 1:00 A.M. and a value of 13:00:00 is 1:00 P.M. Even if you include AM or PM in your time literal, the 24-hour clock is used to identify the time. In other words, TIME '01:00:00 PM' is still going to result in 1:00 A.M. in your report.

```
TIME 'hh:mm:ss'
TIME '07:22:00'
```

The timestamp literal must comply with the rules for dates and times just described.

```
TIMESTAMP 'yyyy-MM-dd hh:mm:ss'
TIMESTAMP '1972-05-17 07:22:00'
```

Current Date/Time Functions

The four functions described in this section return information on the moment in time that your user runs a report. These functions can stand on their own or you can use them as expressions in other functions.

CURRENT_DATE

The CURRENT_DATE function returns the current date that you run your report. This allows you to include a variable date in your report so that your report is based on the date that the report runs. The CURRENT_DATE value does not contain a time component.

Function Syntax

```
CURRENT_DATE
TIMESTAMPDIFF(SQL_TSI_DAY, Account."Created Date", CURRENT_DATE)
```

Replacing the entire column formula with CURRENT_DATE instructs Answers to replace the function with today's date in mm/dd/yyyy format. You may also use this function in place of any date expression within other functions. In Figure 7-1, I have inserted the CURRENT_DATE function into a column in my report. This will insert the current date into every row of my report, which is not entirely useful. However, in this case I am going to use the column to display the report date in a narrative view, as shown in Figure 7-2.

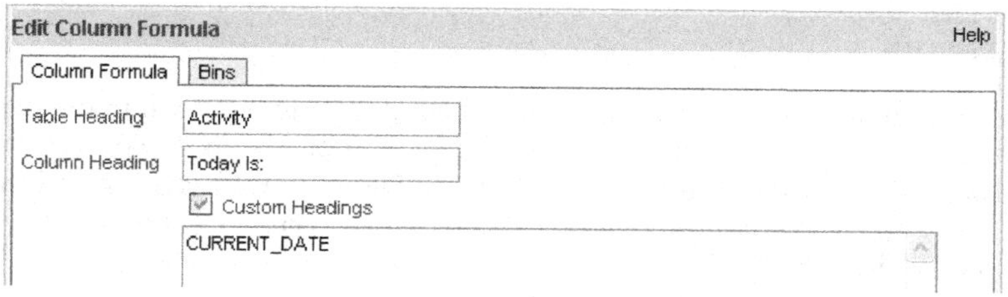

FIGURE 7-1. *CURRENT_DATE column*

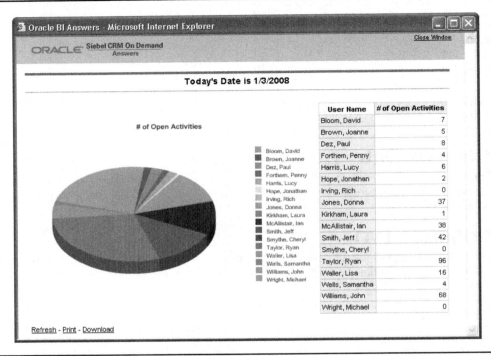

FIGURE 7-2. *Current date's Activity Count report*

CURRENT_TIME

The CURRENT_TIME function returns the time that you run your report. This allows you to include a variable time in your report so that your report is based on the time that the report runs. The CURRENT_TIME value does not contain a date component.

Function Syntax

```
CURRENT_TIME
CURRENT_TIME(N)
```

If you examine the online help for this particular function, you will find a description of this function with the use of an integer to specify the level of precision down to fractions of a second. I have not had much luck with this functionality. In Figure 7-3, I have inserted the CURRENT_ TIME function into a column in my report. This will insert the current time into every row of my report, as shown in Figure 7-4.

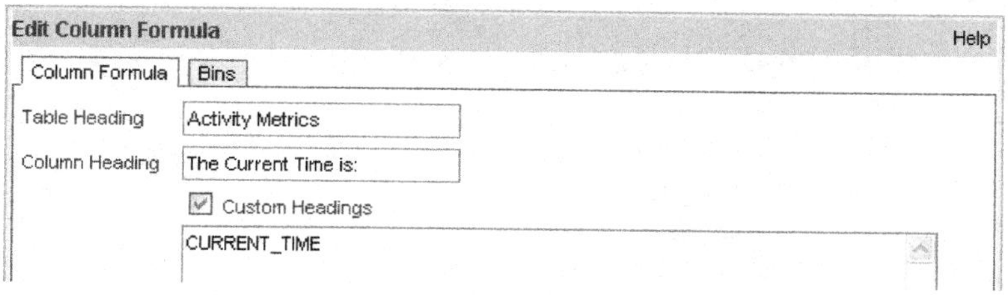

Edit Column Formula   Help

Column Formula	Bins

Table Heading   Activity Metrics

Column Heading   The Current Time is:

☑ Custom Headings

CURRENT_TIME

FIGURE 7-3. *CURRENT_TIME column*

CURRENT_TIMESTAMP

The CURRENT_TIMESTAMP function returns the current date and time that you run your report. The time zone is based on the system where the On Demand Answers data warehouse resides, which is Central U.S. time for most CRM On Demand customers. The CURRENT_TIMESTAMP value contains the date and time component.

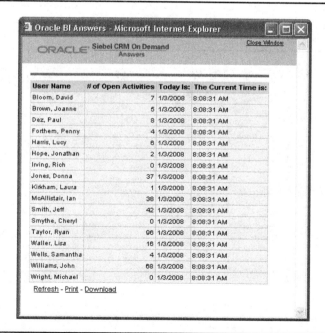

FIGURE 7-4. *Current Activity Count report*

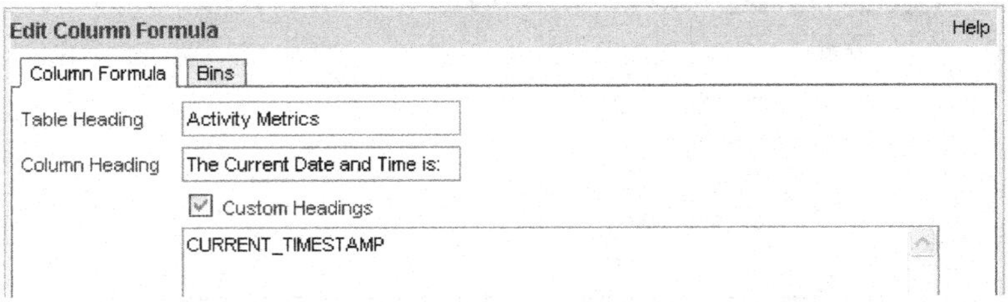

FIGURE 7-5. *CURRENT_TIMESTAMP column*

Function Syntax

```
CURRENT_TIMESTAMP
CURRENT_TIMESTAMP(N)
```

Replacing the entire column formula with CURRENT_TIMESTAMP instructs Answers to replace the function with today's date and current time in mm/dd/yyyy hh:mm:ss tt format. In Figure 7-5, I have inserted the CURRENT_TIMESTAMP function into a column in my report. This will insert the current date and time into every row of my report, as shown in Figure 7-6.

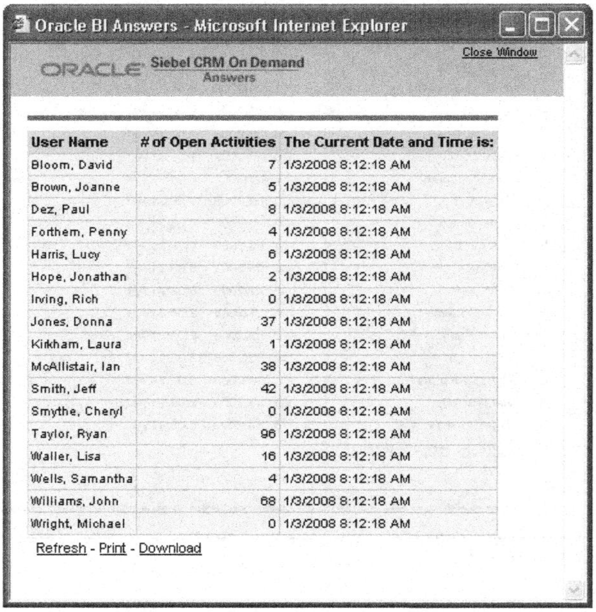

User Name	# of Open Activities	The Current Date and Time is:
Bloom, David	7	1/3/2008 8:12:18 AM
Brown, Joanne	5	1/3/2008 8:12:18 AM
Dez, Paul	8	1/3/2008 8:12:18 AM
Forthem, Penny	4	1/3/2008 8:12:18 AM
Harris, Lucy	6	1/3/2008 8:12:18 AM
Hope, Jonathan	2	1/3/2008 8:12:18 AM
Irving, Rich	0	1/3/2008 8:12:18 AM
Jones, Donna	37	1/3/2008 8:12:18 AM
Kirkham, Laura	1	1/3/2008 8:12:18 AM
McAllistair, Ian	38	1/3/2008 8:12:18 AM
Smith, Jeff	42	1/3/2008 8:12:18 AM
Smythe, Cheryl	0	1/3/2008 8:12:18 AM
Taylor, Ryan	96	1/3/2008 8:12:18 AM
Waller, Lisa	16	1/3/2008 8:12:18 AM
Wells, Samantha	4	1/3/2008 8:12:18 AM
Williams, John	68	1/3/2008 8:12:18 AM
Wright, Michael	0	1/3/2008 8:12:18 AM

FIGURE 7-6. *Current Activity Count report with timestamp*

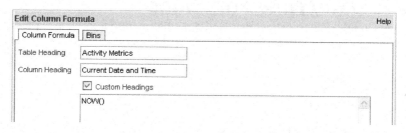

FIGURE 7-7. *Current Timestamp column using NOW()*

NOW

The NOW function is equivalent to the CURRENT_TIMESTAMP function, as it too returns the current timestamp.

Function Syntax

NOW ( )

For the sake of comparison, I have added two columns to a report, one with the CURRENT_TIMESTAMP function and the other using the NOW function (see Figure 7-7). Notice in Figure 7-8 that the result is exactly the same for both columns.

User Name	# of Open Activities	The Current Date and Time is:	Current Date and Time
Bloom, David	7	1/3/2008 8:17:28 AM	1/3/2008 8:17:28 AM
Brown, Joanne	5	1/3/2008 8:17:28 AM	1/3/2008 8:17:28 AM
Dez, Paul	8	1/3/2008 8:17:28 AM	1/3/2008 8:17:28 AM
Forthem, Penny	4	1/3/2008 8:17:28 AM	1/3/2008 8:17:28 AM
Harris, Lucy	8	1/3/2008 8:17:28 AM	1/3/2008 8:17:28 AM
Hope, Jonathan	2	1/3/2008 8:17:28 AM	1/3/2008 8:17:28 AM
Irving, Rich	0	1/3/2008 8:17:28 AM	1/3/2008 8:17:28 AM
Jones, Donna	37	1/3/2008 8:17:28 AM	1/3/2008 8:17:28 AM
Kirkham, Laura	1	1/3/2008 8:17:28 AM	1/3/2008 8:17:28 AM
McAllistair, Ian	38	1/3/2008 8:17:28 AM	1/3/2008 8:17:28 AM
Smith, Jeff	42	1/3/2008 8:17:28 AM	1/3/2008 8:17:28 AM
Smythe, Cheryl	0	1/3/2008 8:17:28 AM	1/3/2008 8:17:28 AM
Taylor, Ryan	96	1/3/2008 8:17:28 AM	1/3/2008 8:17:28 AM
Waller, Lisa	16	1/3/2008 8:17:28 AM	1/3/2008 8:17:28 AM
Wells, Samantha	4	1/3/2008 8:17:28 AM	1/3/2008 8:17:28 AM
Williams, John	68	1/3/2008 8:17:28 AM	1/3/2008 8:17:28 AM
Wright, Michael	0	1/3/2008 8:17:28 AM	1/3/2008 8:17:28 AM

Refresh - Print - Download

FIGURE 7-8. *Current Activity Count report with CURRENT_TIMESTAMP and NOW()*

Extract Date/Time Functions

The functions in this section extract date and time information from date expressions. The syntax of these expressions does not include the EXTRACT SQL command, but the command sent to the database is EXTRACT(Function name FROM (date exp)). The column formula

```
DAY_OF_QUARTER(NOW())
```

sends a SQL command of

```
EXTRACT(DAY_OF_QUARTER FROM NOW())
```

Of course, you could type the EXTRACT command in the Column Formula field directly if you are more comfortable with that syntax, but I will define the functions in this section with the shorter syntax, not using the EXTRACT command.

DAY

To get the day number within a month for a given date, you may use either the DAY or the DAYOFMONTH function. These functions are identical in that they both return the numerical day of the month for a date expression. The result is given as an integer with a value of 1 to 31.

Function Syntax

```
DAY(date_exp)
DAY(CURRENT_DATE)
DAY(Activity."Due Date")
```

Using the DAY function, I can identify the day within the month for a given date or perform some basic calculations using this number. For instance, in Figures 7-9 and 7-10, I am determining the day within the month that leads were created.

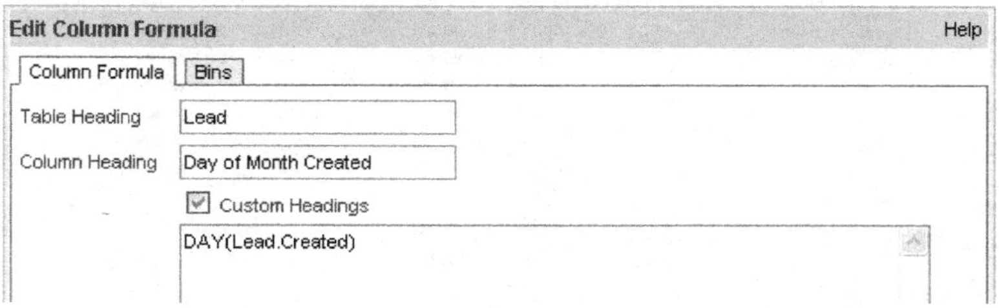

FIGURE 7-9. *DAY function on Lead Created date column*

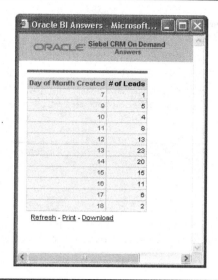

FIGURE 7-10. *Number of Leads Created by day of month*

DAY_OF_QUARTER

The DAY_OF_QUARTER function returns a number that corresponds to the day of the quarter for a date expression. This can be quite helpful if you want to include some metrics in your reports based on when the current quarter ends, for instance. The numeric value returned by this expression will fall between 1 and 92, where 1 is the first day of the quarter.

The DAY_OF_QUARTER function bases its results on the calendar year. Answers On Demand determines the start and end of your quarters based on your Fiscal Year Begins setting on the company profile only if you use the session variables to determine this value. Review Chapter 5 for information about the session variables and their usage.

Function Syntax

```
DAY_OF_QUARTER(date-exp)
DAY_OF_QUARTER(CURRENT_DATE)
DAY_OF_QUARTER(Account."Created Date")
```

In Figure 7-11, I have written a column formula that determines the day of the quarter that opportunities were created. I plan to use this data to plot the number of opportunities created each day of the quarter. The result is an integer indicating the day of the quarter that each opportunity was created (see Figure 7-12).

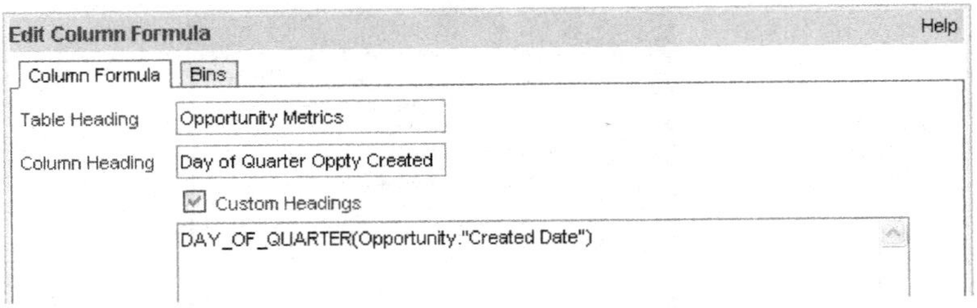

FIGURE 7-11. *DAY_OF_QUARTER applied to the Opportunity Created Date column*

DAYNAME

The DAYNAME function returns the English name of the day of the week for a given date. The days are named with the three-character abbreviation for the day name (Sun, Mon, Tue, Wed, Thu, Fri, and Sat).

Function Syntax

```
DAYNAME(date_exp)
DAYNAME(CURRENT_DATE)
DAYNAME(Lead."Created Date")
```

One interesting use of the DAYNAME function is to create more user-friendly views of date data. In the examples shown in Figures 7-13 and 7-14, I have applied the DAYNAME function to the Activity Due Date column to build a simple calendar view of the number of activities due on a given day. The view I am using here is a pivot table with the day names as column headings. Of course, a similar effect can be achieved by modifying the Column Data Format as described in Chapter 3.

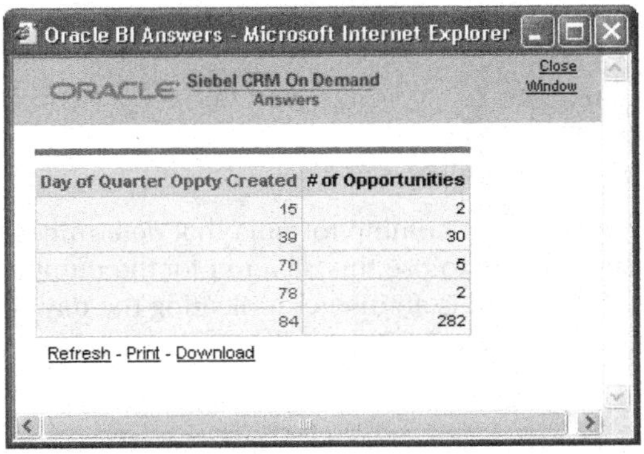

FIGURE 7-12. *Day of Quarter Opportunities Created report*

Edit Column Formula   Help

| Column Formula | Bins |

| Table Heading | Activity |
| Column Heading | Day |

☑ Custom Headings

DAYNAME(Activity."Due Date")

FIGURE 7-13. *DAYNAME function applied to Activity Due Date column*

Oracle BI Answers - Microsoft Internet Explorer

Year 2007   Year 2007   Year 2007   Year 2007
Qtr 1   Qtr 2   Qtr 3   Qtr 4

Jan

| | # of Activities | | | | | | |
Week	Sun	Mon	Tue	Wed	Thu	Fri	Sat
1	1	4	1	3	4	1	3
2	3	1	1	1	2	2	1
3		2	1	3			4
4	2	3	2	3	2	5	3
5	2	1	2				

Feb

| | # of Activities | | | | | | |
Week	Sun	Mon	Tue	Wed	Thu	Fri	Sat
5					2		1
6	2	2	2			1	4
7	3	1	2	4	3	5	2
8	2	3	3	1	5		2
9			3	2			

Mar

| | # of Activities | | | | | | |
Week	Sun	Mon	Tue	Wed	Thu	Fri	Sat
9	7				5	5	6
10	3	2	3	3	4	3	5
11	8	4	5	4	4	2	2
12	4	5		7	4	3	2
13		2	4	2	3	7	2

Apr

| | # of Activities | | | | | | |
Week	Sun	Mon	Tue	Wed	Thu	Fri	Sat
13	3						
14	4	4	2	5	2	5	4
15	3	5	3		2	4	4
16	1		4	5	4	4	3
17	9	7	5	2	4	5	3
18		4					

May

| | # of Activities | | | | | | |
Week	Sun	Mon	Tue	Wed	Thu	Fri	Sat
18	3		4	3	2	8	5
19	2	5	4	3	2	2	6
20	12	10	4	6	4	2	4
21	6	6	6	7	8	3	3
22		3	8	7	3		

Jun

| | # of Activities | | | | | | |
Week	Sun	Mon	Tue	Wed	Thu	Fri	Sat
22	6					4	4
23	4	8	8	5	6	7	15
24	3	6	11	10	13	10	9
25	4	5	4	9	5	4	4
26		5	5	6	4	6	7

Jul

| | # of Activities | | | | | | |
Week	Sun	Mon	Tue	Wed	Thu	Fri	Sat
26	7						
27	3	8	6	6	9	8	3
28	4	3	3	7	4	4	3
29	4	3	1	5	7	6	8
30	8	4	7	3	3	6	3
31		4	3				

Aug

| | # of Activities | | | | | | |
Week	Sun	Mon	Tue	Wed	Thu	Fri	Sat
31	5			2	6	7	5
32	8	6	5	4	4	3	10
33	5	3	3	5	6	4	6
34	6	4	3	10	5	3	3
35		7	2	2	3	2	

Sep

| | # of Activities | | | | | | |
Week	Sun	Mon	Tue	Wed	Thu	Fri	Sat
35	6						3
36	6	5	5	6	8	2	5
37	4	5	1	7	4	5	3
38	4	4	3	6	3	1	6
39	2	3	2	6	6	2	3

Oct

| | # of Activities | | | | | | |
Week	Sun	Mon	Tue	Wed	Thu	Fri	Sat
40	5	3	3	2	4	6	5
41	5	7	6	2	2	6	2
42	3	3	3	3	7	1	4
43	3	5	3	5	1	2	5
44		4	4	2			

Nov

| | # of Activities | | | | | | |
Week	Sun	Mon	Tue	Wed	Thu	Fri	Sat
44	5				1	9	5
45	4	2	5	3	5	3	4
46	5	6	4	6	3	2	6
47	4	2	4	5	5	2	8
48		4	6	3	5	5	

Dec

| | # of Activities | | | | | | |
Week	Sun	Mon	Tue	Wed	Thu	Fri	Sat
1		2					
48	1						10
49	5	6	5	6	6	5	6
50	5	3	6	7	3	6	4
51	3	7	3	7	6	1	5
52	4	2	4	8	2	2	6

Refresh - Print - Download

FIGURE 7-14. *Calendar report with number of activities by day*

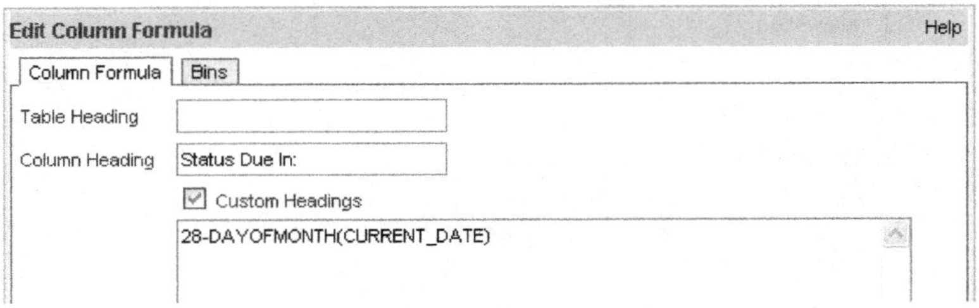

FIGURE 7-15. *Column with 28-DAYOFMONTH(CURRENT_DATE) formula*

DAYOFMONTH

The DAYOFMONTH function, like the DAY function, returns the day number within a month for a given date. This function returns the numerical day of the month for a date expression. The result is given as an integer with a value of 1 to 31.

Function Syntax

```
DAYOFMONTH(date_exp)
DAYOFMONTH(CURRENT_DATE)
DAYOFMONTH(Activity."Due Date")
```

Using the DAYOFMONTH function, I can identify the day of the month for a given date or I can perform some basic calculations using this number. For instance, in Figures 7-15 and 7-16, I am calculating the number of days until I must submit my monthly status report, which is due on the 28th of every month.

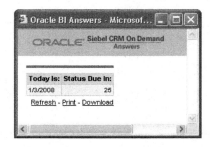

FIGURE 7-16. *Days Until Status Due report*

DAYOFWEEK

The DAYOFWEEK function returns a number between 1 and 7, corresponding to the day of the week, for a specified date. The number 1 corresponds to Sunday, and the number 7 corresponds to Saturday.

Function Syntax

```
DAYOFWEEK(date_exp)
DAYOFWEEK(DATE '2008-09-08')
DAYOFWEEK(Activity."Due Date")
```

I typically use this function to provide a column on which to sort my data when I want to display data within a particular week in date order. Since sorting on the name of the day would provide an alphabetical order (Fri, Mon, Sat, Sun, Thu, Tue, Wed), I often use the DAYOFWEEK function in a hidden column with an ascending sort to get the proper order of days in a week. Figure 7-17 shows the DAYOFWEEK function with the activity due date expression. Figure 7-18 shows my data sorted by the DAYOFWEEK results, but displaying day names rather than the number.

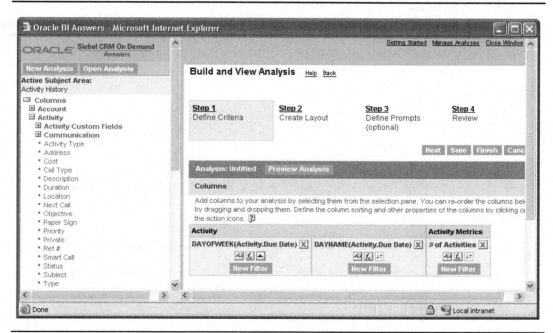

FIGURE 7-17. *Report design with DAYOFWEEK column sorted*

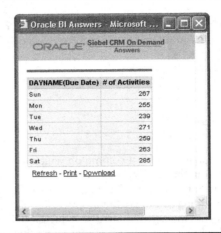

FIGURE 7-18. *Number of Activities by Day report*

DAYOFYEAR

If you are interested in knowing the number of a particular day within the calendar year, use the DAYOFYEAR function. This function returns the number (between 1 and 366) corresponding to the day of the year for a specified date. January 1 is day number 1 and December 31 is either day 365 or 366 depending on the year.

Function Syntax

```
DAYOFYEAR(date_exp)
DAYOFYEAR(DATE '2008-11-04')
DAYOFYEAR(Activity."Due Date")
```

The DAYOFYEAR function can be useful for building a simple timeline of some business data or comparing particular metrics from year to year. In Figure 7-19, I have applied the DAYOFYEAR function to today's date and a date literal to calculate the number of days remaining in the current year. The result is shown in Figure 7-20.

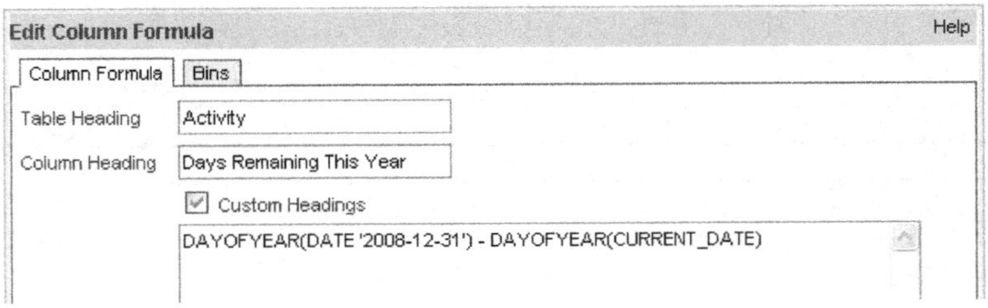

Edit Column Formula   Help

Column Formula | Bins

Table Heading   Activity

Column Heading   Days Remaining This Year

☑ Custom Headings

DAYOFYEAR(DATE '2008-12-31') - DAYOFYEAR(CURRENT_DATE)

FIGURE 7-19. *DAYOFYEAR used in simple calculation*

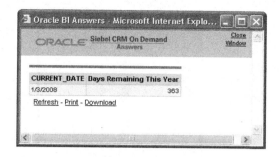

FIGURE 7-20. *Number of Days Left in Year report*

Consider that with many of these functions that return a number representing a date, they do not consider the differences in week, month, or year. For instance, simply subtracting the day of year of December 25, 2007 (359) from the day of the year from December 31, 2008 (366) will give you a result of 7, not 372.

HOUR

The HOUR function extracts the hour from a time expression. The number is between 0 and 23. Numbers 0 through 11 correspond to 12:00 A.M. through 11:00 A.M., and 12 through 23 correspond to 12:00 P.M. through 11:00 P.M.

Function Syntax

```
HOUR(time_exp)
HOUR(CURRENT_TIME)
HOUR(Activity."Planned Start Time")
```

The HOUR function works with both time and timestamp expressions. This function could prove useful in your activity reports to determine which hours are the busiest for your users. For example, I have used the HOUR function on the Activity Start Time column (see Figure 7-21) with a count of activities to determine which times my users use when scheduling appointments (see Figure 7-22).

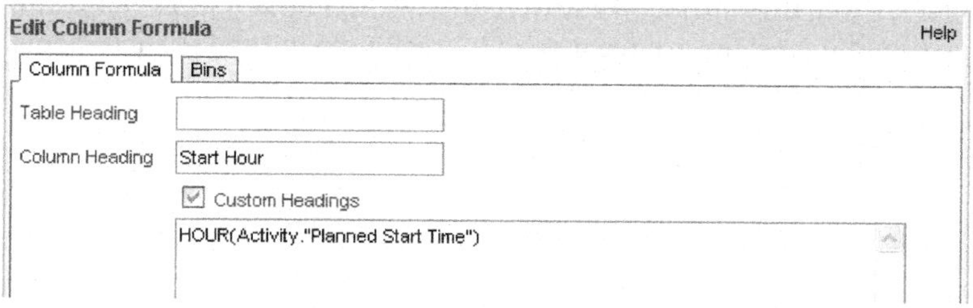

FIGURE 7-21. *HOUR function on Activity Start Time column*

FIGURE 7-22. *Hour of Scheduled Activities report*

MINUTE

The MINUTE function extracts the minute from a time expression. The number is between 0 and 59, corresponding to the minute within the time expression. The number 0 corresponds to 0 through 59 seconds past the hour.

Function Syntax

```
MINUTE(time_exp)
MINUTE(CURRENT_TIME)
MINUTE(Activity."Planned End Time")
```

The MINUTE function also works with both time and timestamp expressions. This function could prove useful if your users have a need to track time in smaller increments. Call centers often have such a requirement. In Figure 7-23, I am using the MINUTE function on the current time. Figure 7-24 shows the results.

Edit Column Formula   Help

Column Formula	Bins

Table Heading   Activity

Column Heading   Current Minute

☑ Custom Headings

MINUTE(CURRENT_TIMESTAMP)

FIGURE 7-23. *MINUTE function*

MONTH

The MONTH function returns a number between 1 and 12 indicating the calendar month of the specified date. The MONTH function works with both date and timestamp expressions, extracting only the month information in numerical form.

Function Syntax

```
MONTH(date_exp)
MONTH(NOW())
MONTH(Opportunity."Close Date")
```

I find that this function is most useful for sorting data by month, since an alphabetical sort on the month name would not produce the desired chronological results. In Figure 7-25, I have applied the MONTH function to the Opportunity Close Date column. My report in Figure 7-26 shows the number of opportunities with a close date in each month.

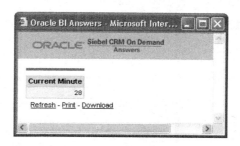

FIGURE 7-24. *MINUTE function result*

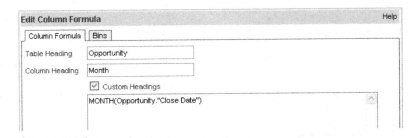

FIGURE 7-25. *MONTH function applied to Opportunity Close Date column*

MONTH_OF_QUARTER

The MONTH_OF_QUARTER function returns a number between 1 and 3 indicating the first, second, or third month of the calendar quarter for a specified date. The MONTH_OF_QUARTER function works with both date and timestamp expressions, extracting only the month information in numerical form.

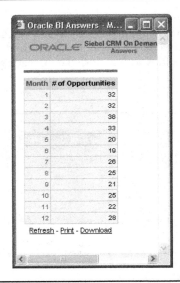

FIGURE 7-26. *Opportunities Closing Each Month report*

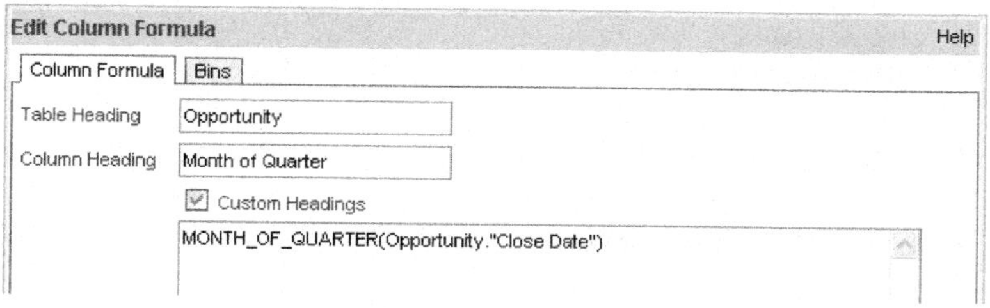

FIGURE 7-27. *MONTH_OF_QUARTER function applied to Opportunity Close Date column*

Function Syntax

```
MONTH_OF_QUARTER(date_exp)
MONTH_OF_QUARTER(NOW())
MONTH_OF_QUARTER(Opportunity."Close Date")
```

This is particularly useful when you are organizing dates by quarter, but also want to identify where within a quarter that your date expression falls. In Figure 7-27, I have applied the MONTH_OF_QUARTER function to the Opportunity Close Date column. My report in Figure 7-28 shows the number of opportunities with a close date by month and quarter.

If your fiscal year does not follow the calendar year, you will want to use a session variable rather than a column function to identify the quarter. Review Chapter 5 for the appropriate session variables and their usage.

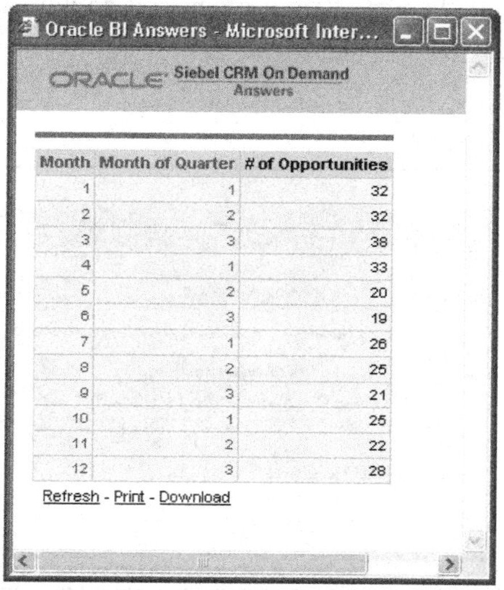

Month	Month of Quarter	# of Opportunities
1	1	32
2	2	32
3	3	38
4	1	33
5	2	20
6	3	19
7	1	26
8	2	25
9	3	21
10	1	25
11	2	22
12	3	28

FIGURE 7-28. *Opportunities Closing Each Month report*

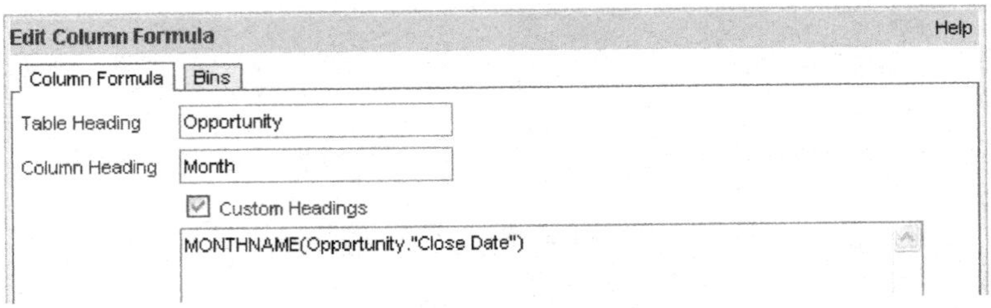

FIGURE 7-29. *MONTHNAME function applied to Opportunity Close Date column*

MONTHNAME

The MONTHNAME function returns the English name of the month for a given date. The dates are named with the three-character abbreviation for the month name (Jan, Feb, Mar, Apr, May, Jun, Jul, Aug, Sep, Oct, Nov, and Dec).

Function Syntax

```
MONTHNAME(date_exp)
MONTHNAME(CURRENT_DATE)
MONTHNAME(Lead."Created Date")
```

One use of the MONTHNAME function is to create a month-by-month view of data. In the examples shown in Figures 7-29 and 7-30, I have applied the MONTHNAME function to the Opportunity Close Date column to build a simple monthly total of the number of opportunities closing during each month. The view I am using here is a pivot table with the month names as column headings.

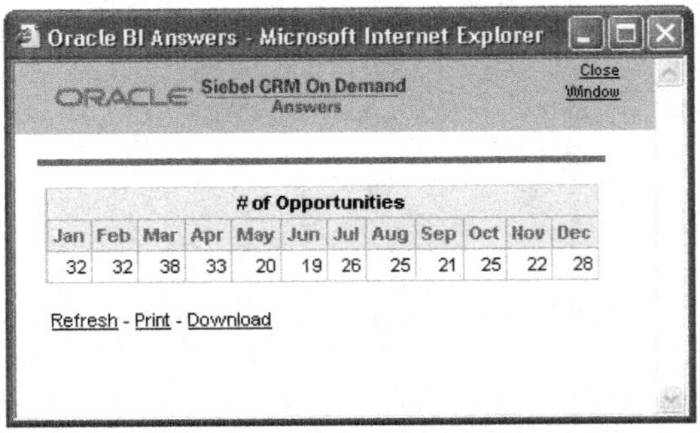

FIGURE 7-30. *Opportunities Closing Each Month report*

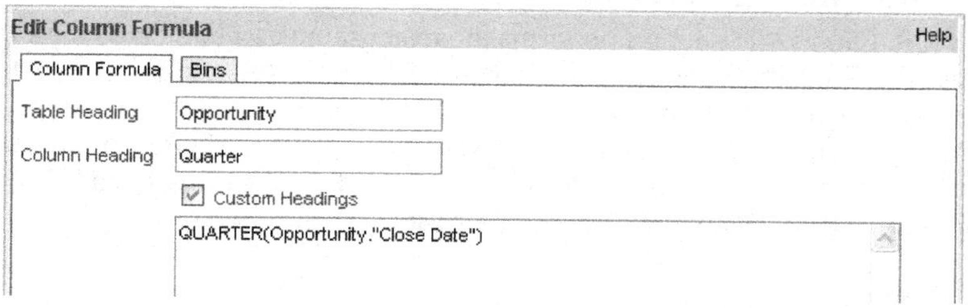

FIGURE 7-31. *QUARTER function applied to Opportunity Close Date column*

QUARTER

The QUARTER function identifies the calendar quarter in which a specified date falls. The result is given as a number (1 through 4) that corresponds to the quarter. Quarters are defined as three months, where January 1 through March 31 is quarter 1, April 1 through June 30 is quarter 2, July 1 through September 30 is quarter 3, and October 1 through December 31 is quarter 4.

Function Syntax

```
QUARTER(date_exp)
QUARTER(NOW())
QUARTER(Account."Created Date")
```

This function is particularly useful when you are organizing dates by quarter to identify where within a calendar year your date expression falls. In Figure 7-31, I have applied the QUARTER function to the Opportunity Close Date column. My report in Figure 7-32 shows the number of opportunities with a close date by month and quarter.

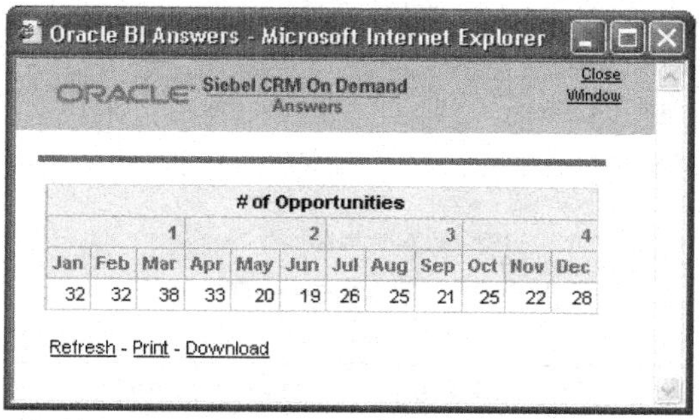

FIGURE 7-32. *Opportunities Closing Each Month and Quarter report*

QUARTER_OF_YEAR

The QUARTER_OF_YEAR function performs the exact same calculation as the QUARTER function. You may use these two functions interchangeably to identify the quarter in which a specified date falls. The result is given as a number (1 through 4) that corresponds to the calendar quarter. If your fiscal year does not follow the calendar year, this function will still return the calendar quarter. You can use a session variable to identify quarters based on your fiscal year. Review Chapter 5 for more information on session variables and their usage.

Function Syntax

```
QUARTER_OF_YEAR(date_exp)
QUARTER_OF_YEAR(NOW())
QUARTER_OF_YEAR(Account."Created Date")
```

Again, this function is useful when you are organizing dates by quarter to identify where within a calendar year your date expression falls. Also, if the start of my fiscal year differs from the calendar year by 3, 6, or 9 months, a simple mathematical equation can shift the result of this function to an appropriate quarter. In Figure 7-33, I have applied the QUARTER_OF_YEAR function to the Opportunity Close Date column and subtracted 1 from the result if the result is greater than 1 and changed a result of 1 to 4 because my fiscal year actually begins April 1. My report in Figure 7-34 shows close dates and their adjusted quarter.

SECOND

The SECOND function extracts the second from a time expression. The number is between 0 and 59, corresponding to the second value within the time expression.

Function Syntax

```
SECOND(time_exp)
SECOND(CURRENT_TIME)
SECOND(Activity."Planned End Time")
```

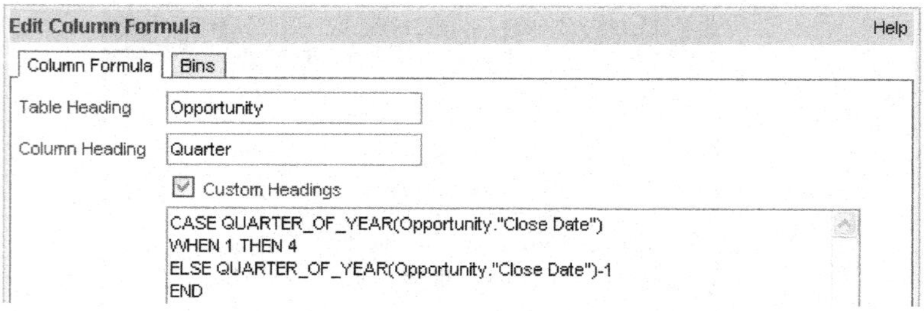

FIGURE 7-33. *QUARTER_OF_YEAR function in an equation*

Close Date	Quarter	# of Opportunities
2/4/2007	4	1
2/25/2007	4	1
3/6/2007	4	1
3/16/2007	4	1
3/26/2007	4	2
3/30/2007	4	1
3/31/2007	4	1
4/2/2007	1	1
4/4/2007	1	2
4/9/2007	1	1
4/10/2007	1	1
4/13/2007	1	1
4/15/2007	1	1
4/16/2007	1	1
4/19/2007	1	1
4/20/2007	1	1
4/21/2007	1	1
4/23/2007	1	1
4/24/2007	1	1
4/26/2007	1	1
4/29/2007	1	1
4/30/2007	1	2
5/2/2007	1	2
5/6/2007	1	1
5/8/2007	1	1

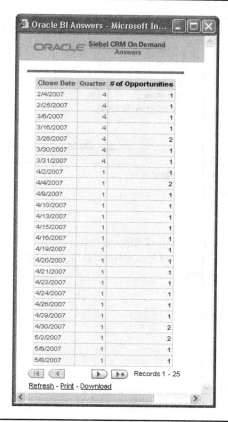

FIGURE 7-34. *Opportunity Close Dates with Adjusted Quarter*

The SECOND function works with both time and timestamp expressions. This function could prove useful if your users have a need to track time in very small increments. Call centers often have such a requirement. In Figure 7-35, I am using the SECOND function on the Current Time column. Figure 7-36 shows the results.

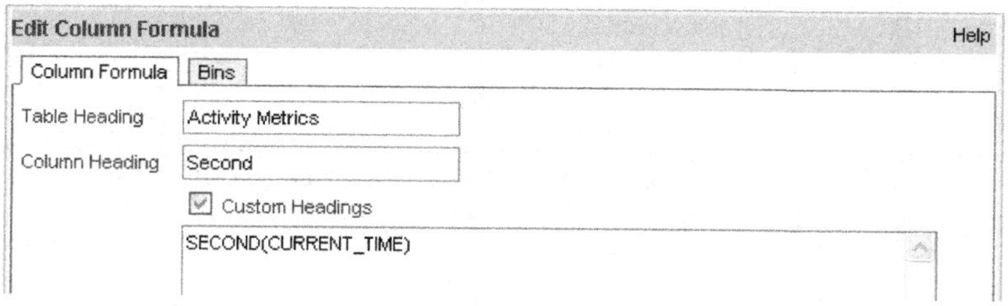

FIGURE 7-35. *SECOND function applied to Current Time column*

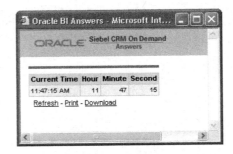

FIGURE 7-36. *Current time example with seconds*

WEEK

The WEEK function returns a number (1 through 53) corresponding to the week of the calendar year for the specified date. Answers On Demand defines a week as a period beginning with Sunday and ending with Saturday.

Function Syntax

```
WEEK(date_exp)
WEEK(DATE '2010-04-22')
WEEK(Activity."Due Date")
```

The WEEK function sometimes evaluates December 31 as week 52 or 53 and January 1 as week 1 even when they both fall in the same week, because they cross the year boundary. In Figure 7-37, I have applied the WEEK function to the Activity Create Date column. Figure 7-38 shows a simple report where I see the weeks that activities are created.

FIGURE 7-37. *WEEK function applied to Activity Create Date column*

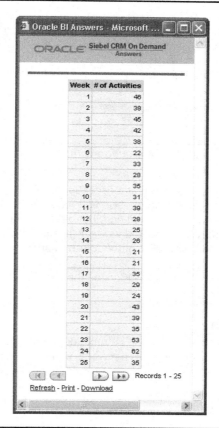

FIGURE 7-38. *Activities Created Each Week report*

WEEK_OF_QUARTER

Using the WEEK_OF_QUARTER function gives you a number (1 through 14) corresponding to the week of the calendar quarter for the specified date. Answers On Demand defines a week as a period beginning with Sunday and ending with Saturday.

Function Syntax

```
WEEK_OF_QUARTER(date_exp)
WEEK_OF_QUARTER(CURRENT_DATE)
WEEK_OF_QUARTER(DATE '2004-03-19')
```

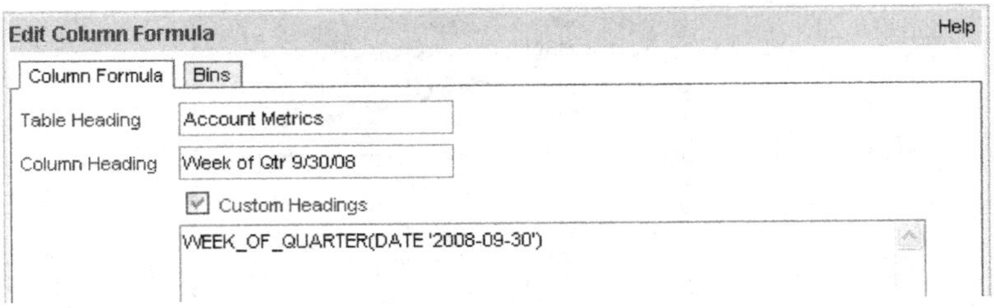

FIGURE 7-39. *WEEK_OF_QUARTER function with a literal date*

One interesting distinction here is that a fiscal quarter will only have 13 weeks, but some dates using the WEEK_OF_QUARTER function will return a value of 14 based on calendar quarters defined not by the week start and end, but by the month start and end. For instance, Tuesday, September 30, 2008 is evaluated as week 14 of the third quarter, and Wednesday, October 1, 2008 is evaluated as week 1 of the fourth quarter. Both dates fall in the same calendar week (week 40).

I illustrate this in Figures 7-39 and 7-40 using the WEEK_OF_QUARTER and WEEK_OF_YEAR functions on the date literals.

WEEK_OF_YEAR

The WEEK_OF_YEAR function and the WEEK function are the same. WEEK_OF_YEAR also returns a number (1 through 53) corresponding to the week of the calendar year for the specified date. Answers On Demand defines a week as a period beginning with Sunday and ending with Saturday.

Function Syntax

```
WEEK_OF_YEAR(date_exp)
WEEK_OF_YEAR(DATE '2010-04-22')
WEEK_OF_YEAR(Activity."Due Date")
```

The same rule that I mentioned for the WEEK_OF_QUARTER function holds true for the WEEK_OF_YEAR function that it will sometimes evaluate December 31 as week 52 or 53 and

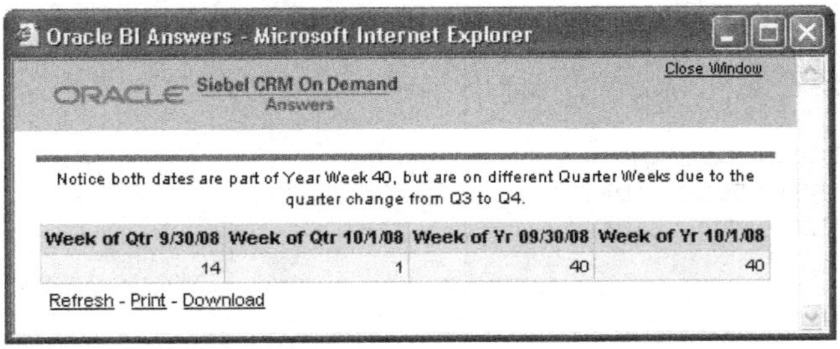

FIGURE 7-40. *Week of quarter comparison*

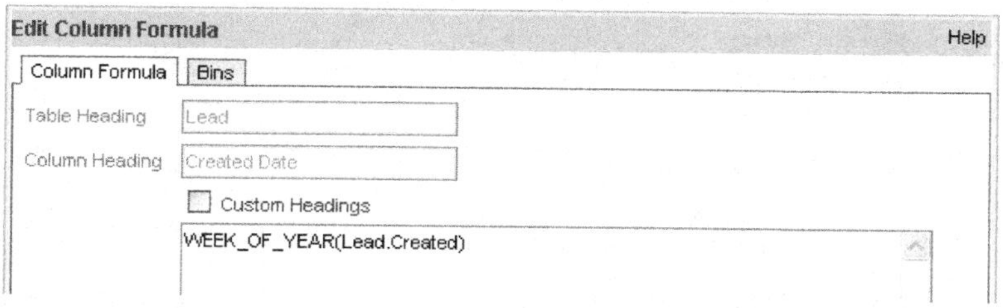

FIGURE 7-41. *WEEK_OF_YEAR function applied to Lead Create Date column column*

January 1 as week 1 even when they both fall in the same week. In Figure 7-41, I have applied the WEEK_OF_YEAR function to the Lead Create Date column. Figure 7-42 shows a simple report that displays the weeks that leads are created and converted.

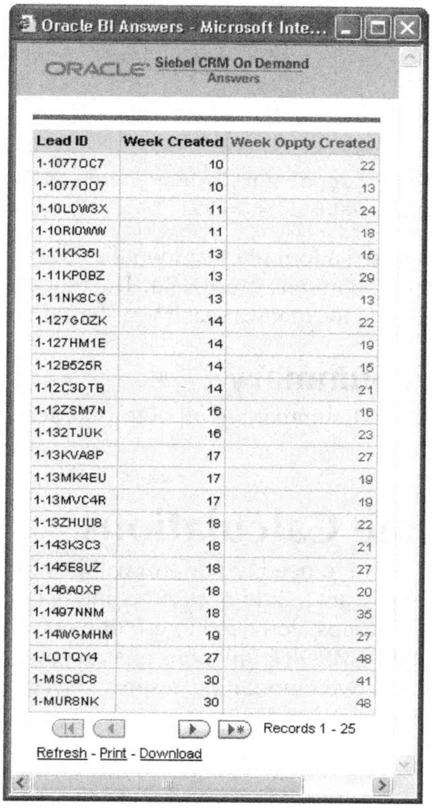

Lead ID	Week Created	Week Oppty Created
1-1077OC7	10	22
1-1077OO7	10	13
1-10LDW3X	11	24
1-10RIOWW	11	18
1-11KK35I	13	15
1-11KP0BZ	13	29
1-11NK8CG	13	13
1-127GOZK	14	22
1-127HM1E	14	19
1-128525R	14	15
1-12C3DTB	14	21
1-12ZSM7N	16	16
1-132TJUK	16	23
1-13KVA8P	17	27
1-13MK4EU	17	19
1-13MVC4R	17	19
1-13ZHUU8	18	22
1-143K3C3	18	21
1-145E8UZ	18	27
1-146A0XP	18	20
1-1497NNM	18	35
1-14WGMHM	19	27
1-LOTQY4	27	48
1-MSC9C8	30	41
1-MUR8NK	30	48

Records 1 - 25

Refresh - Print - Download

FIGURE 7-42. *Comparison of lead creation and an opportunity creation dates*

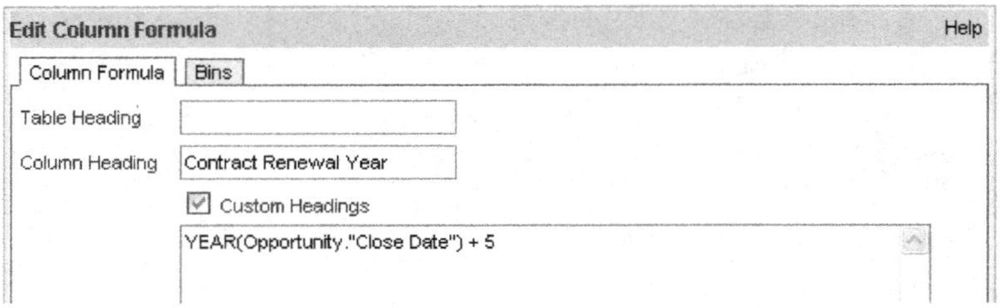

FIGURE 7-43. *Formula to add five years to close date*

YEAR

The final extract date/time function is the YEAR function. This function returns the four-digit calendar year for the specified date. If your fiscal calendar does not follow the calendar year, you will want to use a session variable to identify your fiscal year. I described session variables and their usage in Chapter 5.

Function Syntax

```
YEAR(date_exp)
YEAR(Opportunity."Close Date")
FILTER("Revenue Metrics"."Opportunity Revenue" USING
(YEAR(Opportunity."Close Date") = 2007))
```

In Figure 7-43, I have written a formula that identifies the year that five-year contracts come up for renewal based on the opportunity close date. The report shown in Figure 7-44 tells me how many contracts are eligible for renewal each year based on past sales.

Extract Functions Summary

For your convenience, Table 7-1 summarizes all of the extract date/time functions for November 21, 2008 03:42:23 A.M.

Performing Time Calculations

It is a very common requirement to need to perform within your reports calculations that involve dates and times. Whether you want to add or subtract intervals of time or determine the difference between two timestamps, you need to use one of two special functions. The TIMESTAMPADD and TIMESTAMPDIFF functions enable you to add or subtract time intervals and calculate the difference in two timestamps, respectively.

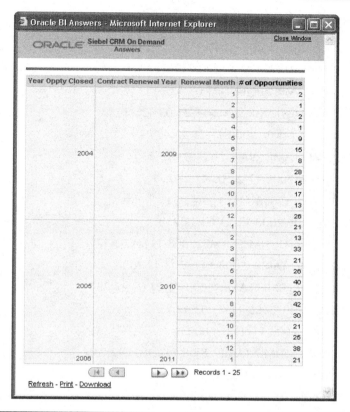

FIGURE 7-44. *Contract Renewal report*

A requirement of both functions is the use of an interval. You must identify the type of interval you want to use in your date/time calculation. In other words, if you are determining the difference between two timestamps, do you want to know the difference in days, hours, or seconds? If you are adding time to a timestamp, are you adding months, weeks, or minutes?

The intervals are identified with a very specific syntax of their own. Each interval value begins with SQL_TSI_, which stands for Structured Query Language and Time Stamp Interval. Table 7-2 shows the available intervals and their syntax.

Function	Result
DAY(TIMESTAMP '2008-11-21 03:42:23')	21
DAY_OF_QUARTER(TIMESTAMP '2008-11-21 03:42:23')	52
DAYNAME(TIMESTAMP '2008-11-21 03:42:23')	Fri
DAYOFMONTH(TIMESTAMP '2008-11-21 03:42:23')	21
DAYOFWEEK(TIMESTAMP '2008-11-21 03:42:23')	6
DAYOFYEAR(TIMESTAMP '2008-11-21 03:42:23')	326
HOUR(TIMESTAMP '2008-11-21 03:42:23')	3
MINUTE(TIMESTAMP '2008-11-21 03:42:23')	42
MONTH(TIMESTAMP '2008-11-21 03:42:23')	11
MONTH_OF_QUARTER(TIMESTAMP '2008-11-21 03:42:23')	2
MONTHNAME(TIMESTAMP '2008-11-21 03:42:23')	Nov
QUARTER_OF_YEAR(TIMESTAMP '2008-11-21 03:42:23')	4
SECOND (TIMESTAMP '2008-11-21 03:42:23')	23
WEEK(TIMESTAMP '2008-11-21 03:42:23')	47
WEEK_OF_QUARTER(TIMESTAMP '2008-11-21 03:42:23')	8
WEEK_OF_YEAR(TIMESTAMP '2008-11-21 03:42:23')	47
YEAR(TIMESTAMP '2008-11-21 03:42:23')	2008

TABLE 7-1. *Extract Date/Time Functions—Sample Results*

TIMESTAMPADD

The TIMESTAMPADD function adds a number of intervals to a specified timestamp, returning a single timestamp reflecting the added time.

Function Syntax

```
TIMESTAMPADD(interval, integer, timestamp)
TIMESTAMPADD(SQL_TSI_MONTH, 6, TIMESTAMP '2009-03-19 12:00:00')
TIMESTAMPADD(SQL_TSI_MINUTE, -45, Activity."Start Time")
```

Interval	Syntax
Second	SQL_TSI_SECOND
Minute	SQL_TSI_MINUTE
Hour	SQL_TSI_HOUR
Day	SQL_TSI_DAY
Week	SQL_TSI_WEEK
Month	SQL_TSI_MONTH
Quarter	SQL_TSI_QUARTER
Year	SQL_TSI_YEAR

TABLE 7-2. *Timestamp Intervals*

The TIMESTAMPADD function multiplies the designated interval by the provided integer and adds the product to the specified timestamp expression. If you fail to include either the integer or the timestamp in the TIMESTAMPADD function, the result will also be null.

It is important to appreciate how performing computations involving time is quite different from other calculations. The most basic calculation simply adds the specified integer value to the appropriate component of the timestamp, based on the interval. This is very simple when there is no overflow to consider. For instance, the following column formula generates the result of 2008-05-17 01:50:01 P.M.:

```
TIMESTAMPADD(SQL_TSI_MINUTE, 30, TIMESTAMP '2008-05-17 13:20:01')
```

You can also subtract time using the TIMESTAMPADD function by using a negative integer in your expression. In the following example, I am subtracting three days by adding negative 3 to a timestamp. The result is 2008-05-14 01:20:01 P.M.

```
TIMESTAMPADD(SQL_TSI_DAY, -3, TIMESTAMP '2008-05-17 13:20:01')
```

Adding years, months, days, hours, minutes, and seconds is fairly straightforward since these are the units included in the timestamp. Adding a week is the equivalent of adding seven days. Adding a quarter is like adding three full months. The following pairs of formulas give the exact same result:

```
TIMESTAMPADD(SQL_TSI_WEEK, 2, TIMESTAMP '2008-05-17 13:20:01')
TIMESTAMPADD(SQL_TSI_DAY, 14, TIMESTAMP '2008-05-17 13:20:01')
TIMESTAMPADD(SQL_TSI_QUARTER, 2, TIMESTAMP '2008-05-17 13:20:01')
TIMESTAMPADD(SQL_TSI_MONTH, 6, TIMESTAMP '2008-05-17 13:20:01')
```

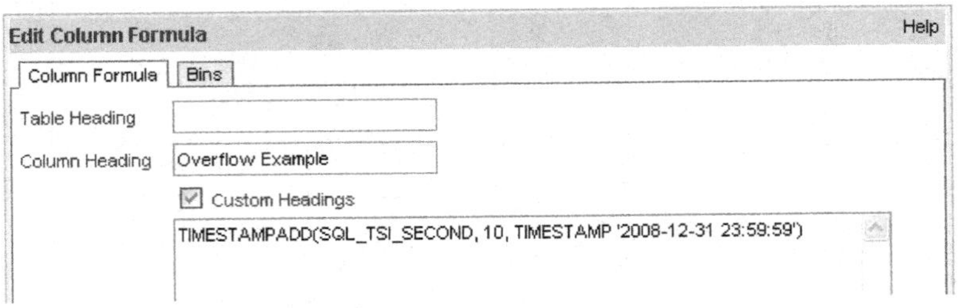

Edit Column Formula		Help

Column Formula | Bins

Table Heading

Column Heading | Overflow Example

☑ Custom Headings

TIMESTAMPADD(SQL_TSI_SECOND, 10, TIMESTAMP '2008-12-31 23:59:59')

FIGURE 7-45. *TIMESTAMPADD function*

When an addition to a timestamp results in an overflow of one or more of the timestamp elements (such as more than 60 seconds, 24 hours, 12 months), an appropriate amount propagates to the next component. For example, when adding to the day component of a timestamp, the TIMESTAMPADD function considers overflow and takes into account the number of days in a particular month (including leap years when February has 29 days). In Figure 7-45, I have written a TIMESTAMPADD formula that adds ten seconds to 2008-12-31 23:59:55. Notice how the overflow caused by the additional ten seconds of time rolls all the way up across the timestamp in Figure 7-46.

When adding months to a timestamp, the TIMESTAMPADD function verifies that the resulting timestamp is a valid date. For example, adding four months to 2010-05-31 does not result in 2010-09-31 because September does not have 31 days. This function instead reduces the day element of the timestamp to the last day of the month, 2010-09-30 in this example.

The TIMESTAMPADD function also considers leap years when performing a calculation. For instance, when adding a year to 2008-02-29 12:00:00, the result will be 2009-02-28 12:00:00 P.M. because February of 2009 has only 28 days (2009 is not a leap year). If you add two days to 2007-02-27 12:00:00, your result is 2007-03-02 12:00:00, but add two days to 2008-02-27 12:00:00 and your result is 2008-03-01 12:00:00.

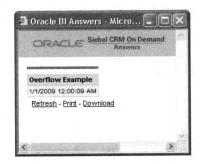

FIGURE 7-46. *TIMESTAMPADD Overflow Example report*

When adding in intervals of year, quarter, or month, the TIMESTAMPADD function will select the valid date based on the interval. In other words, adding one year to 2009-08-13 results in 2010-08-13 because August 13 is a valid date one year later. If adding one quarter to 2009-01-31, the result will be 2009-04-30 because April 31 is not a valid date. Adding one month to 2009-01-31 will result in 2009-02-28 by the same rule.

The intervals of days, hours, minutes, and seconds have the expected overflow reaction to time calculations. Adding 30 days rather than one month to 2009-01-31 will generate a result of 2009-03-02 instead of 2009-02-28.

Advanced Timestamp Calculations

With a little logic and ingenuity, the TIMESTAMPADD function can provide the flexibility of rolling time, use variable numbers of time units, and even filter reports to include data within certain time ranges. By nesting other functions inside of the TIMESTAMPADD function, you can have your calculations react based on the current date, for instance.

Here is a sample calculation that returns the beginning of the current month by determining what the current day of the month is, then subtracting one less of that number from the current date. So if the report is run on June 11, the TIMESTAMPADD function subtracts ten days from the current date to return June 1.

```
TIMESTAMPADD(SQL_TSI_DAY, -(DAYOFMONTH(CURRENT_DATE) -1), CURRENT_DATE)
```

Thinking through the preceding calculation, and assuming that today is June 11, 2009, you can see exactly how this logic works:

1.   Replace CURRENT_DATE with the date, 2009-06-11:

```
TIMESTAMPADD(SQL_TSI_DAY, -(DAYOFMONTH(2009-06-11 00:00:00)-1,
2009-06-11 00:00:00)
```

2.   Perform the 11-1 calculation:

```
TIMESTAMPADD(SQL_TSI_DAY, -(11)-1, 2009-06-11 00:00:00)
```

3.   Subtract ten days from 2009-06-11:

```
TIMESTAMPADD(SQL_TSI_DAY, -10, 2009-06-11 00:00:00)
```

4.   The result:

```
2009-06-1 00:00:00
```

How would you get the last day of the month? You can use the same logic to determine the last day of the previous month and then add a month to that result. The formula would look like this:

```
TIMESTAMPADD(SQL_TSI_MONTH, 1, (TIMESTAMPADD(SQL_TSI_DAY, -
(DAYOFMONTH(CURRENT_DATE)), CURRENT_DATE)))
```

The bold portion of the formula subtracts a number of days equivalent to today's date. This provides the timestamp for the primary TIMESTAMPADD function, which adds one month to the date.

If your company has a weekly deadline, such as a regular shipment date or a weekly invoice date, you may want to identify the date that something occurs based on the current date or based on another key date in your database. Take a look at how you might identify the Monday of the previous week based on a date on your opportunity object:

```
TIMESTAMPADD(SQL_TSI_DAY, -5 -(DAYOFWEEK(CURRENT_DATE)), CURRENT_DATE)
```

How would you go about finding the Sunday of the current week? The formula is quite similar:

```
TIMESTAMPADD(SQL_TSI_DAY, 1 -(DAYOFWEEK(CURRENT_DATE)), CURRENT_DATE)
```

Filtering with Timestamp Calculations

You will also find the TIMESTAMPADD function quite useful for filtering reports. You may know how to filter a report to include data between two dates or after a particular date. You may also know how to use prebuilt filters to restrict data to the current quarter or some other predetermined setting. Neither of these filters gives you much control or flexibility in your report design. What if you want to see the last six weeks of data or three weeks before today and four weeks after today? The standard filters just will not do.

To add a filter using the TIMESTAMPADD function to create a "rolling" filter, begin like you normally would. Click the New Filter button on your date column to access the Create/Edit Filter window. Select your desired operator and then click the Add button at the bottom of the window. From the Add menu, select SQL Expression. It is in this SQL Expression field that you will write your timestamp formula.

Suppose you want to build a report that shows the last 20 days of activity data and the next 10 days of planned activities. The filter for this report will need to determine the current date and subtract 20 days for the start date and add 10 days to determine the end date for the report. To accomplish this, you will use two timestamp formulas with the "Is Between" operator. Figure 7-47 shows the Create/Edit Filter window with the following formulas:

```
TIMESTAMPADD(SQL_TSI_DAY, -20, (CURRENT_DATE))
TIMESTAMPADD(SQL_TSI_DAY, 10, (CURRENT_DATE))
```

Now, suppose you want to create a filter to show only last month's data. You might think you could use a simple MONTH(CURRENT_DATE)-1 formula, but this would not work if your current month is January and the previous month is December of the previous year. Also, you must consider how you will limit your data to the correct year for the rest of your data. After all, every year contains the same months, so you need a year component in your filter. There are a few different ways to accomplish this with multiple filters and multiple functions or a lengthy CASE statement (see Chapter 9).

The solution I have decided to use here is rolled up into a single filter on a single column in my report. The first step is to include a column in your report that identifies the year and month of a custom date column in my database. The column formula takes the year of the date and multiplies it by 100 to add a couple of zeroes to the result—for example, 2009 becomes 200900. The next part of the formula takes the month number and adds this to the year calculation. For example, October 2009 becomes 200910. The multiplier on the year is important because simply adding the year and month would not reliably identify both the year and month. February 2008, January 2009, and other combinations all add up to 2010. The following is the formula:

```
YEAR(Opportunity.DATE_2)*100 + MONTH(Opportunity.DATE_2)
```

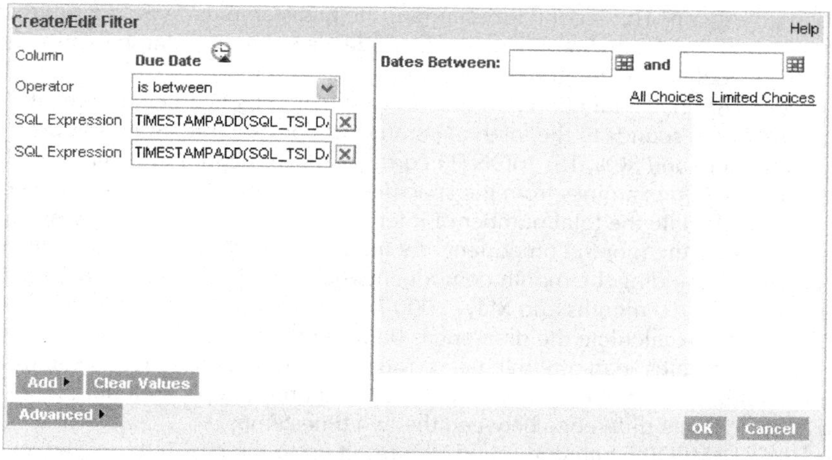

FIGURE 7-47.   *TIMESTAMPADD filter*

The filter for this column performs the same calculation on today's date. This way, you can use the "is equal to or is in" operator to match the current year/month with the data from that year/month in the database. Create your filter by clicking the New Filter button on your new column, selecting your operator, and adding a SQL expression value. Add the following calculation to your filter:

```
YEAR(TIMESTAMPADD(SQL_TSI_MONTH, -1, CURRENT_DATE))*100 +
MONTH(TIMESTAMPADD(SQL_TSI_MONTH, -1, CURRENT_DATE))
```

What I especially like about this example is that it illustrates how, with a little creativity and ingenuity along with a working knowledge of the Answers On Demand functions, you can solve almost any business problem. Every company has different ideas and different needs for their reporting, but one common theme is time. I have not encountered any company using CRM On Demand that does not have reporting requirements for analyses based on time.

TIMESTAMPDIFF

The TIMESTAMPDIFF function provides a measurement of time between two timestamps. This function uses the same intervals as the TIMESTAMPADD function to identify the unit of measurement for the result value.

Function Syntax

```
TIMESTAMPDIFF(interval, timestamp1, timestamp2)
TIMESTAMPDIFF(SQL_TSI_MONTH, NOW(), TIMESTAMP '2009-03-19 12:00:00')
TIMESTAMPDIFF(SQL_TSI_MINUTE, Activity."Start Time", Activity."End Time")
```

The first timestamp in the function syntax is the timestamp from which you want to subtract the second timestamp. The second timestamp is the timestamp that you are subtracting from the first timestamp to determine the difference. If you leave either timestamp expression null in this function, the calculation will return a null value.

The TIMESTAMPDIFF function performs its calculation by first determining the part of the timestamp that corresponds to the interval parameter. For example, SQL_TSI_DAY corresponds to the day component and SQL_TSI_MONTH corresponds to the month component.

The function then examines from the specified interval up to the highest level of both timestamps to calculate the total number of intervals for each timestamp. For example, if the specified interval is the month component, the function calculates the total number of months for each timestamp by adding the month component and 12 times the year component. So October, 2000 represents 24010 months and May, 2000 is 24005 months. 24010 – 24005 = 5 months. By using this method to calculate the differences between dates and times, the calculation is not affected when the dates span multiple years, months, or days. The function subtracts the first timestamp's total number of intervals from the second timestamp's total number of intervals arriving at an accurate difference between the two timestamps.

The TIMESTAMPDIFF function rounds the result up to the next integer whenever fractional intervals result from the calculation due to crossing interval boundaries. For example, the difference in years between 2007-12-31 and 2008-01-01 is one year because the fractional year represents a crossing from one year to the next. By contrast, the difference between 2007-01-01 and 2007-12-31 is zero years because the fractional interval falls entirely within a particular year.

Since the timestamp includes only components for year, month, day, hour, minute, and second, when calculating the difference in weeks or quarters, the function needs to convert weeks to days and quarters to months. When you use the week interval, TIMESTAMPDIFF calculates the difference between the two timestamps in days and then divides by seven before rounding. When using the quarter interval, the function calculates the difference in months and divides by three before rounding.

The following code example asks for a difference in days between timestamps 1998-07-31 23:35:00 and 2000-04-01 14:24:00. It returns a value of 610. Notice that the leap year in 2000 results in an additional day.

```
TimestampDIFF(SQL_TSI_DAY, TIMESTAMP'1998-07-31 23:35:00',
TIMESTAMP'2000-04-01 14:24:00')
```

Let us examine the TIMESTAMPDIFF calculation between two timestamps using each of the available intervals in Table 7-3. For this example, we want to find out the difference between May 17, 2008 07:58:52 and September 8, 2007 08:15:00.

Clearly, using the TIMESTAMPDIFF function is much easier than performing the calculations one step at a time. It certainly is not necessary to understand the calculation that Answers On Demand performs when you use the TIMESTAMPDIFF function, but it is necessary if you are accountable for the accuracy of these calculations and your rounding methodology is different from the method that the function employs.

Let us examine the formula for calculating the time difference in seconds, as it contains all of the elements present in the formulas for the other internals. In order to calculate the difference in seconds, we first need to convert our timestamps to seconds. Take the equation for converting timestamp number one in our TIMESTAMPDIFF function, May 17, 2008 07:58:52:

```
( ( ( ( (\( ( (2007*365)+50+136) *24) *60) *60)+((7*60) *60)+(58*60)+52)
```

Interval	Result	Formula Behind the Function
SQL_TSI_SECOND	21771832	$((((((2007 * 365) + 50 + 136) * 24) * 60) * 60) +$ $((7 * 60) * 60) + (58 * 60) + 52) -$ $((((((2006 * 365) + 50 + 249) * 24) * 60) * 60) +$ $((8 * 60) * 60) + (15*60)) =$ $(63308822400 + 25200 + 3532) -$ $(63287049600 + 28800 + 900) =$ $63308851132 - 63287079300 = 21771832$
SQL_TSI_MINUTE	362864	$(((((2007 * 365) + 50 + 136) * 24) * 60) + (7 * 60) + 59) -$ $(((((2006 * 365) + 50 + 249) * 24) * 60) + (8 * 60) + 15) =$ $(1055147040 + 420 + 52) - (1054784160 + 480 + 15) =$ $1055147519 - 1054784655 = 362864$
SQL_TSI_HOUR	6048	$((((2007 * 365) + 50 + 136) * 24) + 8) -$ $((((2006 * 365) + 50 + 249) * 24) + 8) =$ $17585792 - 17579744 = 6048$
SQL_TSI_DAY	252	$((2007 * 365) + 50 + 136) -$ $((2006 * 365) + 50 + 249) =$ $732741 - 732489 = 252$
SQL_TSI_WEEK	36	$(((2007 * 365) + 50 + 136) -$ $((2006 * 365) + 50 + 249)) / 7 =$ $(732742 - 732489) / 7 =$ $252 / 7 = 36$
SQL_TSI_MONTH	8	$(2008 * 12) + 5 - (2007 * 12) + 9 =$ $24101 - 24093 = 8$
SQL_TSI_ QUARTER	3	$((2008 * 12) + 5 - (2007 * 12) + 9) / 3 =$ $(24101 - 24093) / 3 =$ $8/3 = 2.666$ rounds up to 3
SQL_TSI_YEAR	1	$2008 - 2007 = 1$

TABLE 7-3.   *TIMESTAMPDIFF Calculations*

First, we need to convert the years to days. There were 2,007 complete years prior to 2008, so we multiply 2,007 by 365 to get the days. There were also 50 leap years during that period with one extra day, so we add 50 days. Next we add the number of days that have passed in 2008. May 16 is the 136th day of the year. May 17 is not yet complete, so we take the day of the year value for May 16 (which includes February 29 since 2008 is a leap year). At this point we have calculated a total of 732,741 days in 2008-05-16. Next, we convert days to hours by multiplying days by 24, then hours to minutes by multiplying hours by 60, then to seconds by multiplying minutes by 60. Now we have determined that there are 63,308,822,400 seconds in 2008-05-16.

Now we move on to the partial day. We need to determine the number of seconds in 07:58:52. Start with the hour component. Seven hours multiplied by 60 gives us minutes. Minutes then multiplied by 60 gives us seconds. We need to add to this the minute component of the timestamp converted to seconds and then add the second component. At this point we have determined that 2008-05-16 07:58:52 contains a total of 63,308,851,132 seconds.

Repeat this process for the other timestamp, and we arrive at a total of 63,287,079,300 seconds in 2007-09-08 08:15:00. Finally, a bit of simple subtraction gives us the solution:

```
TIMESTAMPDIFF(SQL_TSI_SECOND, TIMESTAMP '2008-05-16 07:58:52',
TIMESTAMP '2007-09-08 08:15:00') = 21,771,832
```

Continuing our examination of the TIMESTAMPDIFF function, as we move up the timestamps and the calculations at the other levels, we begin to see the rounding that takes place. The time portion of the first timestamp 07:58:15, for instance, becomes 07:59:00 in the minute interval calculation and 08:00:00 in the hours calculation. The 08:15:00 time of the second timestamp does not round up on the hour calculation, becoming 08:00:00.

Ultimately, the result of your TIMESTAMPDIFF calculation is a number value for the interval you selected. You can include this calculation, therefore, in any other function that operates on a numeric expression or as part of a mathematical calculation.

CURRENT_DATE or NOW()?

Have a look at the difference between the output of the CURRENT_DATE function and the NOW() function in Figure 7-48. The CURRENT_DATE function provides just that: today's date. The NOW() function gives you not only today's date, but the current time down to the second.

If you were to write a TIMESTAMPDIFF function to find the difference between a date in your database and the present, which function would you use in your calculation? Both work in certain situations, but with a different degree of accuracy. If you are calculating the difference between a date field and the current date, then CURRENT_DATE works fine for intervals of day, week, month, quarter, and year. In fact, attempting to use the hour, minute, or second intervals will cause an error if one or both date expressions are dates rather than timestamps. CURRENT_DATE is not a timestamp.

When calculating the difference between two timestamps, you may use any of the interval values without generating an error. However, you will want to consider the effects of rounding, particularly at the larger intervals. If comparing a date/time field and the present, you will want to use the NOW() (or CURRENT_TIMESTAMP) function for the best accuracy.

Comparing two date values or two date/time values is fairly straightforward. What if you have a date column and a date/time column of which you need to calculate the difference? That gets a little trickier, since there is a time element and the rounding effect on the date/time side of the

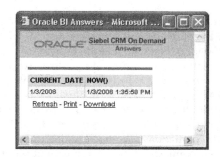

FIGURE 7-48. *Comparison of CURRENT_DATE and NOW() functions*

equation. When you want to know the difference in days or larger intervals, you will want to negate the time portion of the date/time column to eliminate the rounding or force it to round up the way you need. The following two samples show how to set the timestamp either to 00:00:00 to remove it from the equation or to 23:59:59 to ensure that the date rounds up.

You use a CAST function to convert a date field to a timestamp. I discuss the CAST function in detail in Chapter 9. For now, all you really need to know is that casting a date to a timestamp adds a timestamp of 00:00:00 or 12:00 A.M. to the date.

```
CAST(Opportunity."Close.Date" AS TIMESTAMP)
```

The TIMESTAMPDIFF function in this case would be in the following format:

```
TIMESTAMPDIFF(SQL_TSI_DAY, Opportunity."Created Date",
CAST(Opportunity."Close Date" AS TIMESTAMP))
```

If your need is to change the date value to one that has a 23:59:59 timestamp to include the entire day, you need to include a TIMESTAMPADD function in your equation to add the necessary time to the timestamp. Note that there are 86,399 seconds between midnight and 11:59:59 P.M. The following is an example that results in a time of 23:59:59:

```
TIMESTAMPADD(SQL_TSI_SECOND, 86399,
CAST(Opportunity."Close Date" AS TIMESTAMP))
```

The TIMESTAMPDIFF function in this case would be in the following format:

```
TIMESTAMPDIFF(SQL_TSI_DAY, Opportunity."Created Date",
TIMESTAMPADD(SQL_TSI_SECOND, 86399,
CAST(Opportunity."Close Date" AS TIMESTAMP)))
```

Filtering with TIMESTAMPDIFF

Suppose you want to create a report that includes only records created in the last ten days. You could use either the TIMESTAMPADD or TIMESTAMPDIFF function to accomplish this. Either should work just fine, and the choice between them has more to do with the design of your report than the effectiveness of the timestamp functions.

In the first example of this report, I want to show the create date for activity records along with the owner and number of activities. I only want to show the activities created within the last ten days. For this report, I am going to use the TIMESTAMPADD function in my filter on the Created Date column. That filter, shown in Figure 7-49, is set to allow only activities with a create date greater than or equal to:

```
TIMESTAMPADD(SQL_TSI_DAY, -10, CURRENT_DATE)
```

Here is another method for arriving at the same report. The easiest method for filtering using the TIMESTAMPDIFF function involves the addition of another column. I'll call this column Activity Age and set the column formula to the following:

```
TIMESTAMPDIFF(SQL_TSI_DAY, CURRENT_DATE, Activity."Created Date")
```

Now I have a column in my report that shows the age in days of my activity records. I can choose to display or hide this column, or even remove it after I set my filter on the column to less than or equal to 10. Figure 7-50 shows this filter in place. Notice that the filter contains the TIMESTAMPDIFF function.

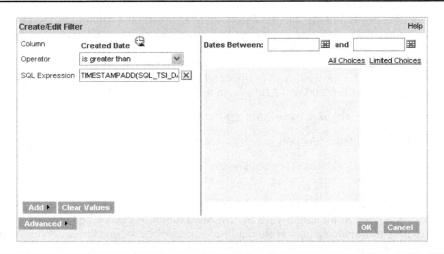

FIGURE 7-49. *Filter for activities created in last ten days*

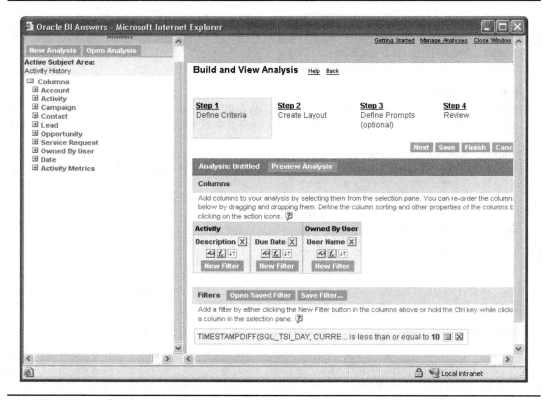

FIGURE 7-50. *Filter for activities created in last ten days using TIMESTAMPDIFF*

Useful Samples

In this final section, I want to offer you a small selection of some sample expressions using the date and time functions. These samples represent some of the reporting challenges that I and others have overcome. It is my hope that you will be able to either use these in your own reports or at least get some ideas for how you might overcome some of your own reporting challenges. These samples and others are compiled in the appendix for your reference as well.

Upcoming Dates Report

Do you track special dates for your contacts, like birthdays or anniversaries? How about contract end dates or any other date that you would like to have on a monthly, weekly, or daily report based on the current date?

On the date column in your report, click the New Filter button and type any valid date in the value field. Next, click the Advanced button and select Convert This Filter to SQL. Type over the filter text with a statement of this nature:

```
MONTH(Contact."Date of Birth") = MONTH(CURRENT_DATE)
```

With this filter, your report will display all records where the month of the birthday is the same as the current month. You could add the DAY function to the filter as well with a statement like this:

```
MONTH(Contact."Date of Birth") = MONTH(CURRENT_DATE) AND
DAY(Contact."Date of Birth") = DAY(CURRENT_DATE)
```

Current Week Filter

Yes, this filter seems very simple. Hopefully, your first instinct is to use the WEEK function in some way to match the week of your filtered date field with the current week. Fifty-one weeks out of the year, that method would be perfectly acceptable. But Tom, a good friend of mine, discovered the flaw in this method when suddenly the filter stopped working the week of a year change.

December 31 is week 52, and the next day, January 1, is week 1 of the new year. The innovative solution that Tom crafted uses the TIMESTAMPADD function along with the DAYOFWEEK function to identify Sunday and Saturday of the current week, regardless of year. Add a filter to your date column and select the "Is Between" operator. Add the following equations to two SQL Expression fields on the filter:

```
TIMESTAMPADD(SQL_TSI_DAY, -(DAYOFWEEK(CURRENT_DATE) -1), CURRENT_DATE)
TIMESTAMPADD(SQL_TSI_DAY, 7-DAYOFWEEK(CURRENT_DATE), CURRENT_DATE)
```

This filter works by subtracting from the current date a number of days equivalent to one less than the current day of the week. So if the current day is Wednesday, the day of the week is 4. Subtract three days from Wednesday and you get Sunday's date. The other end of the between filter adds seven days to the current date and then subtracts the number of the current day of the. If the current day is Wednesday, the filter subtracts four from seven to get three days. Adding those three days to Wednesday gives us the date for Saturday.

Rolling Date Filter

One of the most common reporting needs that date and time functions address is the rolling date filter. Hard-coding dates into your report is simply not effective, because you would need to modify the report each day that you run the report. As I discuss in a later chapter, it is certainly possible, and sometimes preferable, to use a column filter prompt in your report that allows users to identify the filter dates for the report. For now, we will examine some regular column filters.

With a filter on a date or date/time column, you can easily create a rolling date filter that will keep your report current. To add a filter to your date column click the New Filter button and select the "Is Between" operator. Enter you filter expressions in the SQL Expression fields on the filter.

I will start with date (not date/time) column filters. For these, you will notice that I am using a CAST function to convert timestamps to date values.

Opportunities That Will Close in the Next 30 Days

This filter is on the Date Column in the Date dimension column folder. The analytic field reference for this column is Date.Date:

```
CAST(TIMESTAMPADD(SQL_TSI_DAY,-1,CURRENT_DATE) AS DATE)
CAST(TIMESTAMPADD(SQL_TSI_DAY,30,CURRENT_DATE) AS DATE)
```

Opportunities That Will Close in the Next 60 Days

This filter is also on the Date Column in the Date dimension folder:

```
CAST(TIMESTAMPADD(SQL_TSI_DAY,-1,CURRENT_DATE) AS DATE)
CAST(TIMESTAMPADD(SQL_TSI_DAY,60,CURRENT_DATE) AS DATE)
```

Activities During Previous and Next 7 Days

This filter is on the Activity Due Date column, which is a timestamp column. I do not need to convert the timestamp to a date value.

```
TIMESTAMPADD(SQL_TSI_DAY,-8,CURRENT_DATE)
TIMESTAMPADD(SQL_TSI_DAY,7,CURRENT_DATE)
```

Opportunities with a Close Date in the Next Four Full Months

This filter is a little different, as we want to identify records that fall within the next three calendar months, including all dates in the third month. For instance, if you are running a report on December 15, you want records with dates through March 31 on your report. Your filter needs to pull records in that include the last day of the month that includes three full months.

My friend Tom came up with this strategy. This filter adds four months to the current date and subtracts the number of days equal to the day of the month your four-month addition ended on. If, however, we run this report on the first day of the month, we need to only add three months. For this filter, we will also use a CASE function, which I describe in detail in Chapter 9.

This "Is Between" filter is on an Opportunity Close Date column:

```
CURRENT_DATE
CASE WHEN DAY(CURRENT_DATE) = 1
THEN CAST (TIMESTAMPADD (SQL_TSI_MONTH, 3, CURRENT_DATE) AS DATE)
WHEN DAY(CURRENT_DATE) <> 1
THEN TIMESTAMPADD (SQL_TSI_MONTH, 4,TIMESTAMPADD
(SQL_TSI_DAY, -DAY(CURRENT_DATE), CURRENT_DATE)) END
```

Calculating Differences in Business Days

A common request for date calculations in reports is to determine the number of business days between two dates. Answers On Demand does not contain any functions of variables that identify business versus non-business days. The following sample code calculates the business day difference between open and close dates on service request records. I have included comments in the formula that explain what each portion of the formula does.

```
(CASE
/* Convert Sunday to the Business Day Of the Year */
WHEN DAYOFWEEK("Service Request"."Closed Date and Time") = 1
THEN (DAYOFYEAR("Service Request"."Closed Date and Time") -
WEEK("Service Request"."Closed Date and Time")) -
(WEEK("Service Request"."Closed Date and Time") - 2)
/* Convert Saturday to the Business Day Of the Year */
WHEN DAYOFWEEK("Service Request"."Closed Date and Time") = 7
THEN (DAYOFYEAR("Service Request"."Closed Date and Time") -
WEEK("Service Request"."Closed Date and Time")) -
(WEEK("Service Request"."Closed Date and Time") - 1)
/* Convert Mon-Fri to the Business Day Of the Year */
ELSE (DAYOFYEAR("Service Request"."Closed Date and Time") -
WEEK("Service Request"."Closed Date and Time")) +
(2 - WEEK("Service Request"."Closed Date and Time")) END) -
(CASE
/* Convert Sunday to the Business Day Of the Year */
WHEN DAYOFWEEK("Service Request"."Opened Date") = 1
THEN (DAYOFYEAR("Service Request"."Opened Date") -
WEEK("Service Request"."Opened Date")) -
(WEEK("Service Request"."Opened Date") - 2)
/* Convert Saturday to the Business Day Of the Year */
WHEN DAYOFWEEK("Service Request"."Opened Date") = 7
THEN (DAYOFYEAR("Service Request"."Opened Date") -
WEEK("Service Request"."Opened Date")) -
(WEEK("Service Request"."Opened Date") - 1)
/* Convert Mon-Fri to the Business Day Of the Year */
ELSE (DAYOFYEAR("Service Request"."Opened Date") -
WEEK("Service Request"."Opened Date")) +
(2 - WEEK("Service Request"."Opened Date")) END) +
/* Adjust for Year Change */
(365 * (YEAR("Service Request"."Closed Date and Time") -
YEAR("Service Request"."Opened Date")))
```

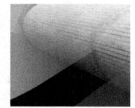

CHAPTER
8

Using Column Formulas
with Text Data

ost of your reporting probably involves quantitative information that you use to measure your business in some way. If all you are interested in is numbers, this chapter will either sorely disappoint you or lead you to discover a whole new world of reporting. We are now entering into the realm of qualitative analysis and leveraging reports for more than a measurement.

You have probably discovered that you keep a lot of information in your database that is beyond numerical and date/time data. Subjects of activities, names of customers, types of opportunities, and descriptions of leads are all examples of useful information that you may want to include in your reports. Often, you will find that this data is stored in a format that you want to change for the report, or you have data stored in several fields and really want to smash all of those fields together in the report. The possibilities here are as endless as with numeric data.

The string functions described in this chapter are all about manipulating textual data, and you might just be surprised at the things you can do with letters rather than numbers.

String Functions

Functions that manipulate textual data are called string functions. As in previous chapters, I will describe each of these functions and offer some examples and tips for their use. Note that you may use string functions with *any* column in the database, even numeric data, but you may need to change the format of the data to a character format first. Keep this in mind as you go into the next chapter, which discusses the CAST function that allows you to change data properties within your report.

ASCII

The ASCII function converts a single character to its corresponding ASCII code. Table 8-1 shows the standard ASCII table. Review the CHAR function for the extended ASCII characters. If you attempt to use the ASCII function on a string with more than one character, the function returns the ASCII code for only the first character in the string.

CHAR	ASCII	CHAR	ASCII	CHAR	ASCII
Null	0	+	43	V	86
Start of Heading	1	,	44	W	87
Start of Text	2	-	45	X	88
End of Text	3	.	46	Y	89
End of Transmission	4	/	47	Z	90
Enquiry	5	0	48	[	91
Acknowledge	6	1	49	\	92
Bell	7	2	50	]	93
Backspace	8	3	51	^	94
Tab	9	4	52	_	95

TABLE 8-1. *Standard ASCII Table*

CHAR	ASCII	CHAR	ASCII	CHAR	ASCII
Line Feed	10	5	53	`	96
Vertical Tab	11	6	54	a	97
Form Feed	12	7	55	b	98
Carriage Return	13	8	56	c	99
Shift Out	14	9	57	d	100
Shift In	15	:	58	e	101
Data Link Escape	16	;	59	f	102
Device Control 1	17	<	60	g	103
Device Control 2	18	=	61	h	104
Device Control 3	19	>	62	i	105
Device Control 4	20	?	63	j	106
Negative Acknowledge	21	@	64	k	107
Synchronous Idle	22	A	65	l	108
End Transmission Block	23	B	66	m	109
Cancel	24	C	67	n	110
End of Medium	25	D	68	o	111
Substitute (EOF)	26	E	69	p	112
Escape	27	F	70	q	113
File Separator	28	G	71	r	114
Group Separator	29	H	72	s	115
Record Separator	30	I	73	t	116
Unit Separator	31	J	74	u	117
Space	32	K	75	v	118
!	33	L	76	w	119
"	34	M	77	x	120
#	35	N	78	y	121
$	36	O	79	z	122
%	37	P	80	{	123
&	38	Q	81	|	124
'	39	R	82	}	125
(	40	S	83	~	126
)	41	T	84		
*	42	U	85		

TABLE 8-1. *Standard ASCII Table*

Use of the ASCII function in a report is unusual, and I can think of no reason to use the function on its own. If it is used at all, it would be as part of a larger formula. I imagine there could be a use for this function if you needed to convert a unique text string into a unique numeric value, perhaps for the purposes of importing into another system that required a numeric ID.

Function Syntax

```
ASCII(char-exp)
ASCII('O')
ASCII(Account."Account ID")
```

I can think of only a few times I have used the ASCII function in a report, but I do have one very compelling use for the ASCII function. If you find a need to move data from one system to another, Answers On Demand permits you to develop a table and export that data to a file. If you should need to import your data into a system that requires a unique numeric identifier, the ID column in CRM On Demand, being an alphanumeric column, would not comply with this requirement.

You can use the ASCII function to convert the characters in your unique ID to their ASCII numeric equivalent without losing the uniqueness of the ID. Since the ASCII function works on one character at a time, you need to build a formula that converts one character at a time. The following formula actually uses several functions you will find described in this chapter, but the ASCII function is the central component of the formula:

```
RIGHT(REPLACE
(CAST(ASCII(SUBSTRING(Account."Account ID" FROM 3 FOR 1)) AS CHAR)||
CAST(ASCII(SUBSTRING(Account."Account ID" FROM 4 FOR 1)) AS CHAR)||
CAST(ASCII(SUBSTRING(Account."Account ID" FROM 5 FOR 1)) AS CHAR)||
CAST(ASCII(SUBSTRING(Account."Account ID" FROM 6 FOR 1)) AS CHAR)||
CAST(ASCII(SUBSTRING(Account."Account ID" FROM 7 FOR 1)) AS CHAR)||
CAST(ASCII(SUBSTRING(Account."Account ID" FROM 8 FOR 1)) AS CHAR)||
CAST(ASCII(SUBSTRING(Account."Account ID" FROM 9 FOR 1)) AS CHAR)||
CAST(ASCII(SUBSTRING(Account."Account ID" FROM 10 FOR 1)) AS CHAR)||
CAST(ASCII(SUBSTRING(Account."Account ID" FROM 11 FOR 1)) AS CHAR)||
CAST(ASCII(SUBSTRING(Account."Account ID" FROM 12 FOR 1)) AS CHAR)
,' ',''), 16)
```

This chapter provides detailed explanations of the RIGHT, REPLACE, and SUBSTRING functions, and the next chapter explains the CAST function. Figures 8-1 and 8-2 show a similar application of this formula column and the result of the conversion from an alphanumeric unique record identifier to a unique numeric record identifier. In the example, I am taking the last 16 digits of the result to create a 16-digit unique numerical identifier.

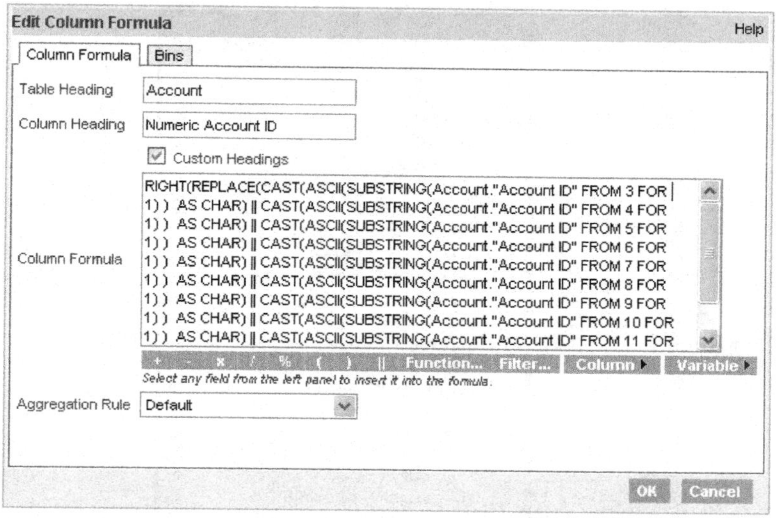

FIGURE 8-1.   *ASCII function in unique numeric ID formula*

BIT_LENGTH

There are 8 bits in a byte, and each Unicode character is 2 bytes in length, or 16 bits. If you need to determine the length of a character string in bits to evaluate string size for compliance with other systems or as part of a larger formula that uses bit length as a condition, then this function can be very helpful.

This function is related to the CHAR_LENGTH and OCTET_LENGTH functions, which are described a little later in the chapter.

Function Syntax

```
BIT_LENGTH(char_exp)
BIT_LENGTH(Account."Account Name")
BIT_LENGTH(Account."Account Name" || Account."Location")
```

In Figure 8-3, I am using the BIT_LENGTH function on a custom field for account numbers. Account numbers should be 12 digits (or 192 bits), but I am having problems with people entering spaces and dashes into the database. Using the BIT_LENGTH function and a simple filter, I can identify those accounts that have a bit length different from 192 (see Figure 8-4).

FIGURE 8-2. *Account IDs converted to numeric IDs*

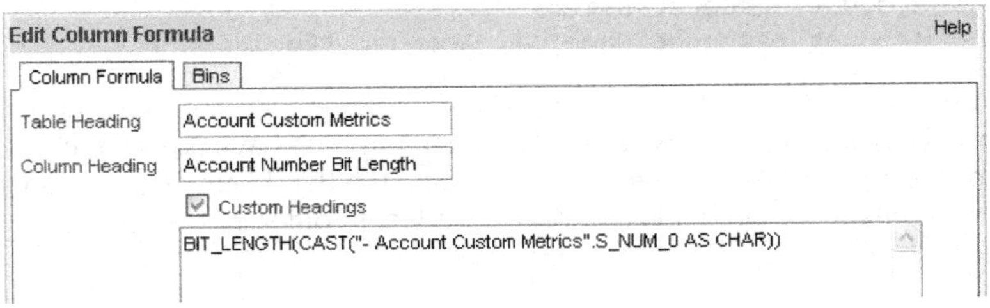

FIGURE 8-3. *BIT_LENGTH function*

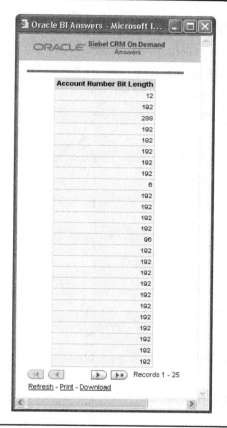

FIGURE 8-4.   *Bit Length report on account numbers*

CHAR

The CHAR function converts a numerical value to the character corresponding to the ASCII code. You may use CHAR to insert any character into your report. Refer to Table 8-1 for the standard codes and Table 8-2 for extended ASCII codes that you can use with the CHAR function. Any integer value is acceptable to the CHAR function, but only the numbers on these two tables will generate a character other than a null value or a small square character.

Function Syntax

```
CHAR(N)
CHAR(10)
'Mike||CHAR(49810)||s Book Emporium'
```

Character	CHAR Command	Character	CHAR Command
•	CHAR(14844066)	Ä	CHAR(50052)
€	CHAR(14844588)	Å	CHAR(50053)
‚	CHAR(49794)	Æ	CHAR(50054)
ƒ	CHAR(49795)	Ç	CHAR(50055)
„	CHAR(49796)	È	CHAR(50056)
…	CHAR(49797)	É	CHAR(50057)
†	CHAR(49798)	Ê	CHAR(50058)
‡	CHAR(49799)	Ë	CHAR(50059)
ˆ	CHAR(49800)	Ì	CHAR(50060)
‰	CHAR(49801)	Í	CHAR(50061)
Š	CHAR(49802)	Î	CHAR(50062)
‹	CHAR(49803)	Ï	CHAR(50063)
Œ	CHAR(49804)	Ð	CHAR(50064)
Ž	CHAR(49806)	Ñ	CHAR(50065)
'	CHAR(49809)	Ò	CHAR(50066)
'	CHAR(49810)	Ó	CHAR(50067)
"	CHAR(49811)	Ô	CHAR(50068)
"	CHAR(49812)	Õ	CHAR(50069)
–	CHAR(49814)	Ö	CHAR(50070)
—	CHAR(49815)	×	CHAR(50071)
˜	CHAR(49816)	Ø	CHAR(50072)
™	CHAR(49817)	Ù	CHAR(50073)
š	CHAR(49818)	Ú	CHAR(50074)
›	CHAR(49819)	Û	CHAR(50075)
œ	CHAR(49820)	Ü	CHAR(50076)
ž	CHAR(49822)	Ý	CHAR(50077)
Ÿ	CHAR(49823)	Þ	CHAR(50078)
¡	CHAR(49825)	ß	CHAR(50079)

TABLE 8-2. *Extended Character Codes*

Character	CHAR Command	Character	CHAR Command
¢	CHAR(49826)	À	CHAR(50080)
£	CHAR(49827)	Á	CHAR(50081)
¤	CHAR(49828)	Â	CHAR(50082)
¥	CHAR(49829)	Ã	CHAR(50083)
¦	CHAR(49830)	Ä	CHAR(50084)
§	CHAR(49831)	Å	CHAR(50085)
¨	CHAR(49832)	Æ	CHAR(50086)
©	CHAR(49833)	Ç	CHAR(50087)
ª	CHAR(49834)	È	CHAR(50088)
«	CHAR(49835)	É	CHAR(50089)
¬	CHAR(49836)	Ê	CHAR(50090)
®	CHAR(49838)	ë	CHAR(50091)
¯	CHAR(49839)	ì	CHAR(50092)
°	CHAR(49840)	í	CHAR(50093)
±	CHAR(49841)	î	CHAR(50094)
²	CHAR(49842)	ï	CHAR(50095)
³	CHAR(49843)	ð	CHAR(50096)
´	CHAR(49844)	ñ	CHAR(50097)
µ	CHAR(49845)	ò	CHAR(50098)
¶	CHAR(49846)	ó	CHAR(50099)
·	CHAR(49847)	ô	CHAR(50100)
¸	CHAR(49848)	õ	CHAR(50101)
¹	CHAR(49849)	ö	CHAR(50102)
º	CHAR(49850)	÷	CHAR(50103)
»	CHAR(49851)	ø	CHAR(50104)
¼	CHAR(49852)	ù	CHAR(50105)
½	CHAR(49853)	ú	CHAR(50106)
¾	CHAR(49854)	û	CHAR(50107)

TABLE 8-2. *Extended Character Codes (Continued)*

Character	CHAR Command	Character	CHAR Command
¿	CHAR(49855)	ü	CHAR(50108)
À	CHAR(50048)	ý	CHAR(50109)
Á	CHAR(50049)	þ	CHAR(50110)
Â	CHAR(50050)	ÿ	CHAR(50111)
Ã	CHAR(50051)		

TABLE 8-2. *Extended Character Codes (Continued)*

Occasionally you will find that, instead of typing a character, you need to use the CHAR function to insert that character. For instance, if you are concatenating a string of text such as in the following example, you may find that the addition of an apostrophe causes your formula to error because of the additional single quote:

```
'Today's Goal is '||("- Account Custom Metrics".S_NUM_0)||',. Good Luck!'
```

The preceding formula will cause an error because Answers reads the apostrophe in "Today's" as the end of the string. A solution to this problem is to incorporate the CHAR function into the statement to provide the apostrophe:

```
'Today'||CHAR(49810)||'s Sales Goal is '||
("- Account Custom Metrics".S_NUM_0)||',. Good Luck!'
```

Another of my favorite uses of the CHAR function is to use it in a REPLACE function to replace line breaks in a Description field with HTML line breaks, so that my data appears on my report with the line breaks. Suppose I want to display the contents of a Description field in my report. I have noticed that simply adding the column to the report does not give me the format I want, because the line breaks are ignored and all of the text runs together. If this is a challenge you have faced, try the solution I have used in Figure 8-5 to produce the desired results (see Figure 8-6). You will need to change the data format on the column to HTML so that the report recognizes the HTML tags.

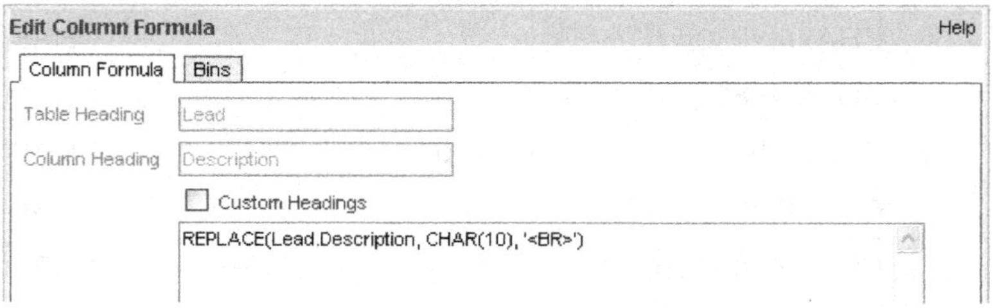

FIGURE 8-5. *Formula to replace line breaks with HTML break tags*

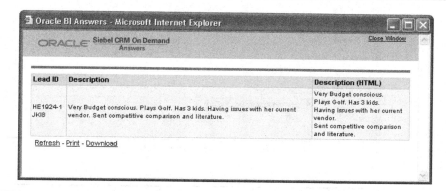

FIGURE 8-6. *Comparison of Description columns*

CHAR_LENGTH or CHARACTER_LENGTH

The CHAR_LENGTH function returns the length, in number of characters, of a string expression. Leading and trailing spaces are not included in the character count. You can get the same results from the LENGTH function as well. The CHAR_LENGTH function is related to the BIT_LENGTH and OCTET_LENGTH functions. You may recall that each character is 2 bytes (16 bits) in length. If you need to determine the length of a character string, any of these three functions can serve the purpose, but each provides a different measurement increment.

Function Syntax

```
CHAR_LENGTH(string_exp)
CHAR_LENGTH(Account."Account Name")
CASE
WHEN CAST(CHAR_LENGTH(CAST("- Account Custom Metrics".S_NUM_0 AS CHAR))
AS INTEGER) = 12 THEN 'Number OK'
WHEN CAST(CHAR_LENGTH(CAST("- Account Custom Metrics".S_NUM_0 AS CHAR))
AS INTEGER) <12 THEN 'Number Too Short'
WHEN CAST(CHAR_LENGTH(CAST("- Account Custom Metrics".S_NUM_0 AS CHAR))
AS INTEGER) >12 THEN 'Number Too Long'
ELSE NULL END
```

The CHAR_LENGTH function does require a text string column. If you need to know the character length of a numeric column, you need to convert that number to a character string before calculating the character length.

In Figure 8-7, I have included the CHAR_LENGTH function on a description field to determine the average length of descriptions. In Figure 8-8, I have put my data into a table and aggregated the values to an average.

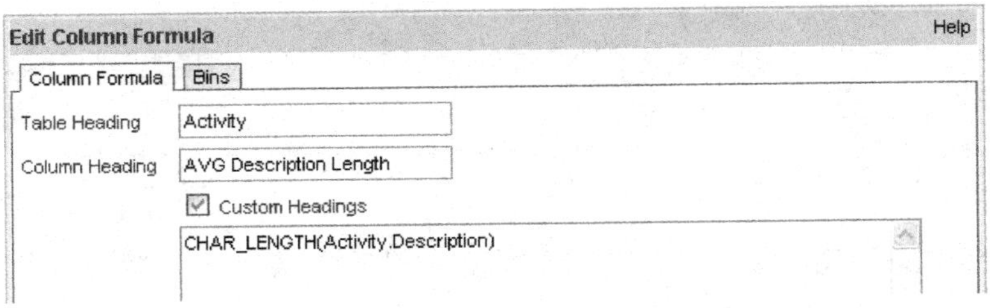

FIGURE 8-7. *CHAR_LENGTH function applied to description field*

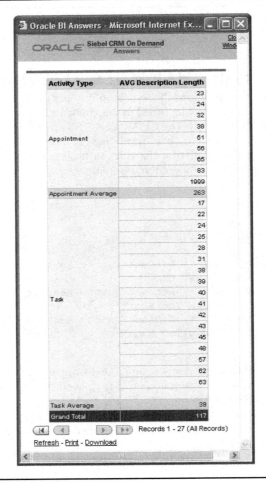

FIGURE 8-8. *Average Description Length report*

CONCAT

There are two forms of the concatenation (CONCAT) function. The first form concatenates only two character strings. The result of this function is a text string made up of the two text strings in the formula.

Function Syntax First Form

```
CONCAT(string_exp1, string_exp2)
CONCAT(Contact."Contact First Name", Contact."Contact Last Name")
CONCAT('Employee Name: ', Employee."Employee Name")
```

Two string expressions are concatenated together to form a new single string expression with this form of the CONCAT function. Limitations of this form often lead report developers to the second CONCAT format. With the first form of the CONCAT function, you are limited to two strings, and those two strings are smashed together with no separator. If this is exactly what you need, CONCAT is great, but if you need a little more flexibility, you will want to use the second form.

Function Syntax Second Form

```
string_exp1 || string_exp2 || string_exp...
Contact."Contact First Name"|| ' ' || Contact."Contact Last Name"
'Contact your sales representative ' || Employee."Employee Name" || ' for more
information about Wonder Widgets.' || CHAR(49817)
```

The double pipe between strings indicates that the strings should concatenate into a single string. You are not limited by the number of strings that you can tie together with this concatenation form. You may only concatenate character strings, so if you want to concatenate any nontext columns, you must convert them to a text string using the CAST function.

In Figure 8-9, I am building an address label using a combination of both forms of the CONCAT function, using the following formula:

```
CONCAT(Contact."Contact Name",'<BR>') ||
CONCAT(Contact."Primary Address",'<BR>') ||
Contact.City || ', ' || Contact.State || ' ' || Contact."Postal Code"
```

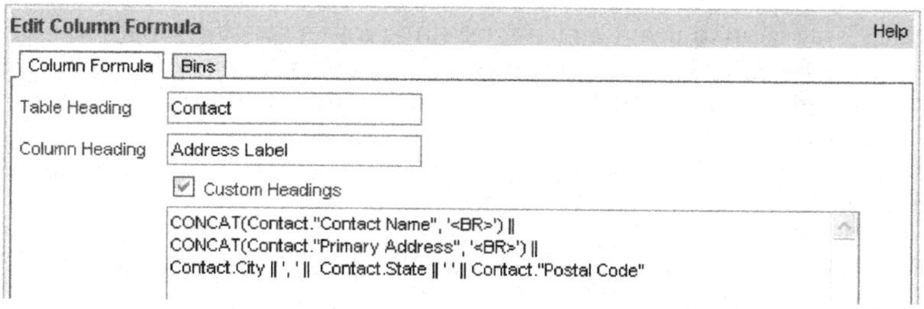

FIGURE 8-9.   *CONCAT functions used to build address labels*

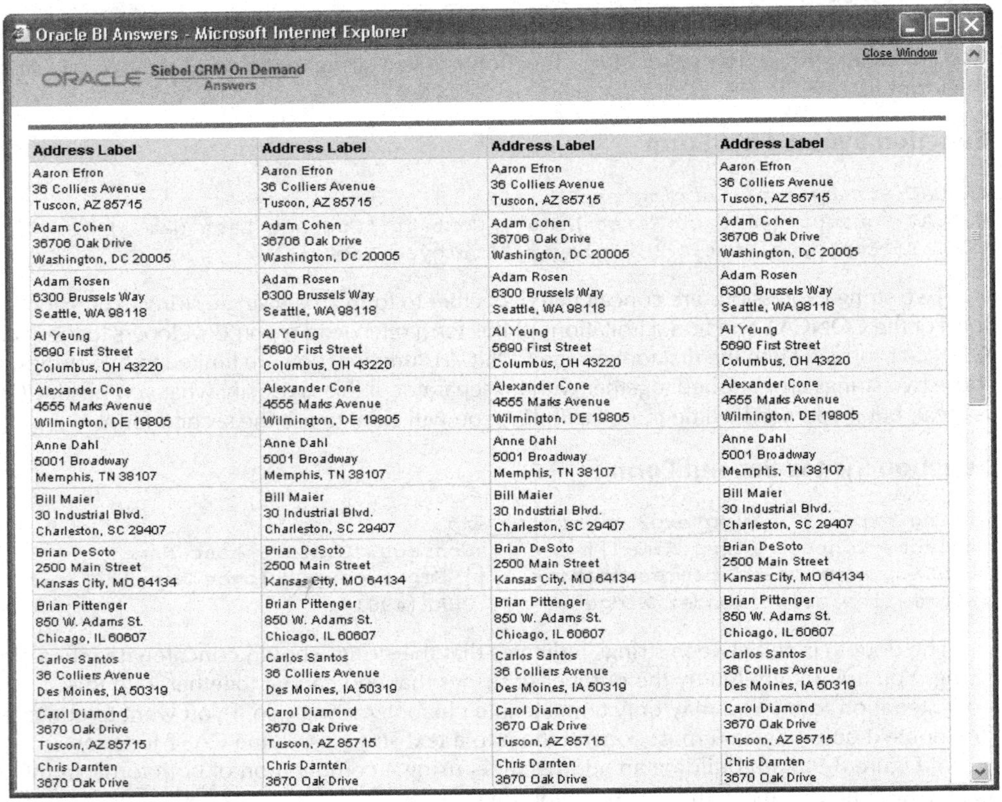

Address Label	Address Label	Address Label	Address Label
Aaron Efron 36 Colliers Avenue Tuscon, AZ 85715	Aaron Efron 36 Colliers Avenue Tuscon, AZ 85715	Aaron Efron 36 Colliers Avenue Tuscon, AZ 85715	Aaron Efron 36 Colliers Avenue Tuscon, AZ 85715
Adam Cohen 36706 Oak Drive Washington, DC 20005	Adam Cohen 36706 Oak Drive Washington, DC 20005	Adam Cohen 36706 Oak Drive Washington, DC 20005	Adam Cohen 36706 Oak Drive Washington, DC 20005
Adam Rosen 6300 Brussels Way Seattle, WA 98118	Adam Rosen 6300 Brussels Way Seattle, WA 98118	Adam Rosen 6300 Brussels Way Seattle, WA 98118	Adam Rosen 6300 Brussels Way Seattle, WA 98118
Al Yeung 5690 First Street Columbus, OH 43220	Al Yeung 5690 First Street Columbus, OH 43220	Al Yeung 5690 First Street Columbus, OH 43220	Al Yeung 5690 First Street Columbus, OH 43220
Alexander Cone 4555 Marks Avenue Wilmington, DE 19805	Alexander Cone 4555 Marks Avenue Wilmington, DE 19805	Alexander Cone 4555 Marks Avenue Wilmington, DE 19805	Alexander Cone 4555 Marks Avenue Wilmington, DE 19805
Anne Dahl 5001 Broadway Memphis, TN 38107	Anne Dahl 5001 Broadway Memphis, TN 38107	Anne Dahl 5001 Broadway Memphis, TN 38107	Anne Dahl 5001 Broadway Memphis, TN 38107
Bill Maier 30 Industrial Blvd. Charleston, SC 29407	Bill Maier 30 Industrial Blvd. Charleston, SC 29407	Bill Maier 30 Industrial Blvd. Charleston, SC 29407	Bill Maier 30 Industrial Blvd. Charleston, SC 29407
Brian DeSoto 2500 Main Street Kansas City, MO 64134	Brian DeSoto 2500 Main Street Kansas City, MO 64134	Brian DeSoto 2500 Main Street Kansas City, MO 64134	Brian DeSoto 2500 Main Street Kansas City, MO 64134
Brian Pittenger 850 W. Adams St. Chicago, IL 60607	Brian Pittenger 850 W. Adams St. Chicago, IL 60607	Brian Pittenger 850 W. Adams St. Chicago, IL 60607	Brian Pittenger 850 W. Adams St. Chicago, IL 60607
Carlos Santos 36 Colliers Avenue Des Moines, IA 50319	Carlos Santos 36 Colliers Avenue Des Moines, IA 50319	Carlos Santos 36 Colliers Avenue Des Moines, IA 50319	Carlos Santos 36 Colliers Avenue Des Moines, IA 50319
Carol Diamond 3670 Oak Drive Tuscon, AZ 85715	Carol Diamond 3670 Oak Drive Tuscon, AZ 85715	Carol Diamond 3670 Oak Drive Tuscon, AZ 85715	Carol Diamond 3670 Oak Drive Tuscon, AZ 85715
Chris Darnten 3670 Oak Drive	Chris Darnten 3670 Oak Drive	Chris Darnten 3670 Oak Drive	Chris Darnten 3670 Oak Drive

FIGURE 8-10. *Address Label report*

Notice that I have inserted the HTML line break tag <BR> into the address. By changing the data format on this column to HTML, my report will insert line breaks wherever the <BR> tag is encountered in the text. Figure 8-10 shows the result of this column formula.

INSERT

Use the INSERT function to insert a character string into a specific location within another character string. This function also allows you to replace a specified number of characters in the target string. This function is particularly useful when you need to build a character string using data from your database.

Function Syntax

```
INSERT(string_exp1, location N, replace N, string_exp2)
INSERT(Employee."Job Title", 1, 0, 'CRM On Demand ')
INSERT('Thank you for attending our PRODUCT workshop!', 29, 7,
Product."Product Name")
```

There are often many ways to accomplish a task in Answers On Demand. At times, you will have questions about using the CONCAT function rather than the INSERT function. Both functions only work with text strings and have the ability to bring strings together. The INSERT function, however, enables you to place one string inside of another, optionally replacing part of the first string.

In Figure 8-11, I use the following function to build a date literal by inserting the current year and month into my target string of "DATE 0000-00-15" to get the 15th day of the current month:

```
CASE
WHEN MONTH(CURRENT_DATE) < 10
THEN INSERT(INSERT ('DATE 0000-00-15',6,4,CAST(YEAR(CURRENT_DATE) AS CHAR)),
12,1, CAST(MONTH(CURRENT_DATE)AS CHAR))
WHEN MONTH(CURRENT_DATE) > 9
THEN INSERT(INSERT ('DATE 0000-00-15',6,4,CAST(YEAR(CURRENT_DATE) AS CHAR)),
11,2, CAST(MONTH(CURRENT_DATE)AS CHAR))
ELSE NULL
END
```

Let us examine the INSERT portion of this formula for single-digit months:

```
(INSERT(INSERT ('DATE 0000-00-15',6,4,CAST(YEAR(CURRENT_DATE) AS CHAR)),
12,1, CAST(MONTH(CURRENT_DATE)AS CHAR)))
```

Notice that I have actually nested an INSERT function inside of another. The interior INSERT is taking the current year cast as a character and inserting it in the "DATE 0000-00-15" string at position 6, replacing four characters. This replaces the "0000" portion of my string with the current year. The outer INSERT places the current month in my newly created string containing the year. This function inserts the number of the month cast as a character into position 12, replacing one character. Because the DATE literal needs a two-digit month, the INSERT function for October through December starts at position 11 and replaces two characters.

Now, as shown in Figure 8-12, I have a column containing the DATE literal string that I can potentially insert in another column for a time calculation.

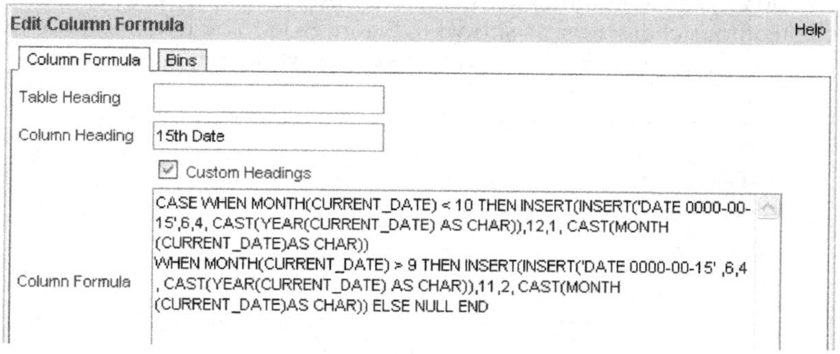

FIGURE 8-11. *Using INSERT function to build date literal*

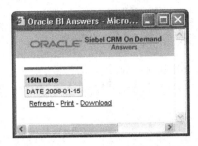

FIGURE 8-12. *Date literal created with INSERT function*

LEFT

The LEFT function extracts a specified number of characters from the left (beginning) of a character string. There are several uses for the LEFT function, but it is imperative that your data is consistent to ensure that the function returns the data you expect.

Function Syntax

```
LEFT(string_exp, N)
CONCAT(LEFT(Contact."Contact First Name",1), Contact."Contact Last Name")
LEFT("- Contact Custom Attributes".TEXT_22,
(LOCATE(' ', "- Contact Custom Attributes".TEXT_22)))
```

Suppose you have a product code field on all of your opportunity records, where the first two characters indicate the product family, the next two characters indicate the product category, and the last four characters identify the product. You need a report that calculates opportunity revenues based on product family, category, or product based on user-selected parameters.

One possible solution is to use the LEFT function, since your data is very consistent and you can reliably identify family, category, and product based on the characters of the product code. You can add to your report a column in which the LEFT function retrieves the first two characters of the product code to identify the product family:

```
LEFT("- Opportunity Custom Attributes".TEXT_30,2)
```

You can add another column to identify the product category, with the same function retrieving the first four characters, as shown in Figure 8-13. You can use these two columns to provide some grouping and subtotals in your report, as shown in Figure 8-14.

Edit Column Formula		Help
Column Formula | Bins		
Table Heading		
Column Heading	Product Prefix	
	☑ Custom Headings	
	LEFT("- Opportunity Custom Attributes".TEXT_30, 4)	

FIGURE 8-13. *LEFT function*

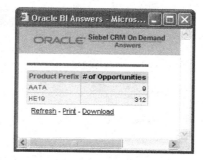

FIGURE 8-14. *Number of Opportunities by Product Prefix report*

LENGTH

The LENGTH function returns the length, in number of characters, of a string expression. Leading and trailing spaces are not included in the character count. You will get the same results from the CHAR_LENGTH function.

Function Syntax

```
LENGTH(string_exp)
LENGTH(Account."Account Name")
LENGTH(CONCAT("- Account Custom Atttributes".TEXT_43,
(CONCAT(SPACE(1), "- Account Custom Atttributes".TEXT_13))))
```

The LENGTH function does require a text string column. If you need to know the character length of a numeric column, you need to convert that number to a character string before calculating the length.

In Figure 8-15, I have included the LENGTH function on a description field to determine the length of activity descriptions. In Figure 8-16, you see the results of this calculation sorted with the longest descriptions at the top.

Edit Column Formula		Help
Column Formula	Bins	
Table Heading	Activity	
Column Heading	Description Length	
	☑ Custom Headings	
	LENGTH(Activity.Description)	

FIGURE 8-15. *LENGTH function on Activity Description column*

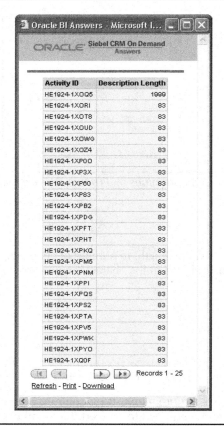

FIGURE 8-16. *Activities sorted by length of description*

LOCATE

Use the LOCATE function to determine the numerical position of one string within another string. If the string is not found, the LOCATE function returns a value of 0. You may also use the LOCATEN function (described next) if you want to specify a starting position within the string to begin the search. This is one method for flagging records in your report that contain a certain bit of text.

An important note here is that the LOCATE function is case sensitive. The function will return the location of the first string in the second string only if there is an exact match, which includes capitalization and punctuation.

Function Syntax

```
LOCATE(string_exp1, string_exp2)
LOCATE('opportunity',Activity.Description)
LOCATE('service', Lead."Product Interest")
```

In Figure 8-17, I have written a column formula that examines a multi-select picklist field to locate those records that contain a particular picklist value. For this example, my picklist has

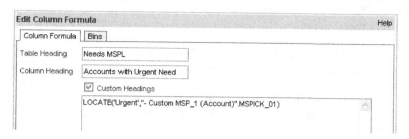

Edit Column Formula   Help

| Column Formula | Bins |

Table Heading   Needs MSPL

Column Heading   Accounts with Urgent Need

☑ Custom Headings

LOCATE('Urgent',"- Custom MSP_1 (Account)".MSPICK_01)

FIGURE 8-17.   *LOCATE function on a multi-select picklist column*

more than 20 possible values, so I do not have the benefit of a separate yes/no field for all of the available values. My report in Figure 8-18 uses the LOCATE function to flag the records that contain any value from the picklist containing the word "Urgent" and uses conditional formatting to flag the records returning a number greater than 0.

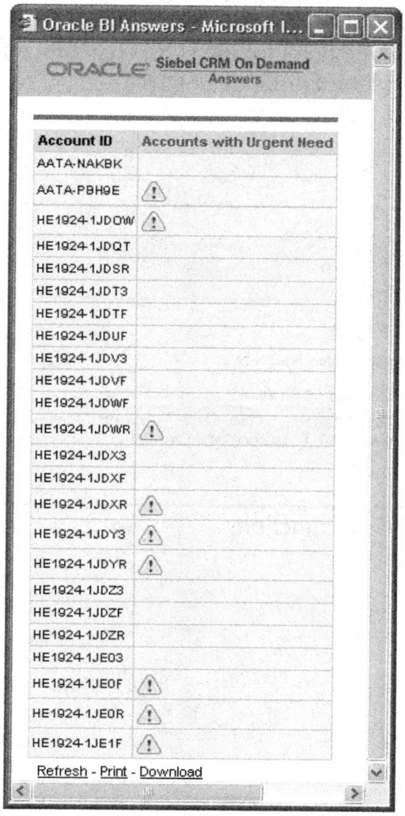

FIGURE 8-18.   *Accounts with Urgent Needs report*

LOCATEN

The LOCATEN function returns the numerical position of one string within another string. This is identical to the LOCATE function, except that the search begins at a specified position. If the string is not found, the LOCATEN function returns a value of 0. The numerical position to return is determined by counting the first character in the string as occupying position 1, regardless of the starting position.

If you insert the LOCATEN function using the Function button on the Edit Column Formula window, the function is inserted as LOCATEN, but it really should be LOCATE, without the "N," because using LOCATEN is not recognized and causes an error. The only difference is that you are including the optional starting point argument.

Function Syntax

```
LOCATE(string_exp1, string_exp2, N)
LOCATE('opportunity',Activity.Description, 5)
LOCATE('service', Lead."Product Interest", 10)
```

In Figure 8-19, I have devised a method for finding a duplicate string inside of another string by nesting a LOCATE function inside of a LOCATEN function. Since I know that the LOCATE function will return an integer indicating the start position of the search string, I am using that result plus 1 to provide a starting point for the LOCATEN function. The result shown in Figure 8-20 provides the location of the second instance of the string.

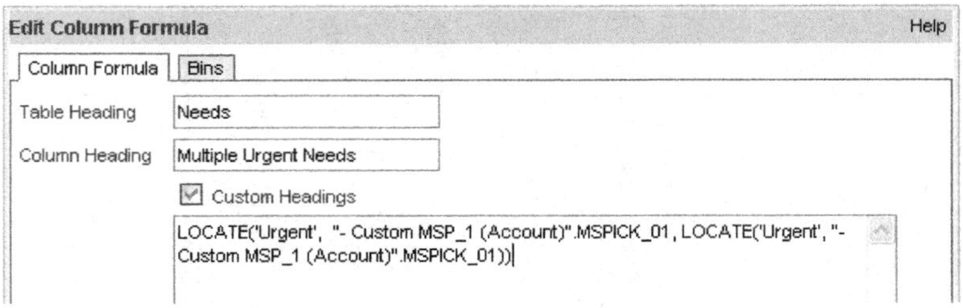

FIGURE 8-19. *Nested LOCATE functions*

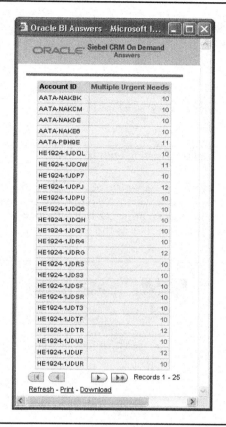

FIGURE 8-20. *Starting location of second urgent need*

LOWER or LCASE

The LOWER and LCASE functions both convert a string to all lowercase letters. This is particularly helpful when your data does not follow a consistent capitalization rule. Numbers within the string are not affected.

Function Syntax

```
LOWER(string_exp)
LOWER(Activity.Description)
LCASE(CONCAT("- Account Custom Attributes".TEXT_05,
"- Account Custom Attributes".TEXT_06))
```

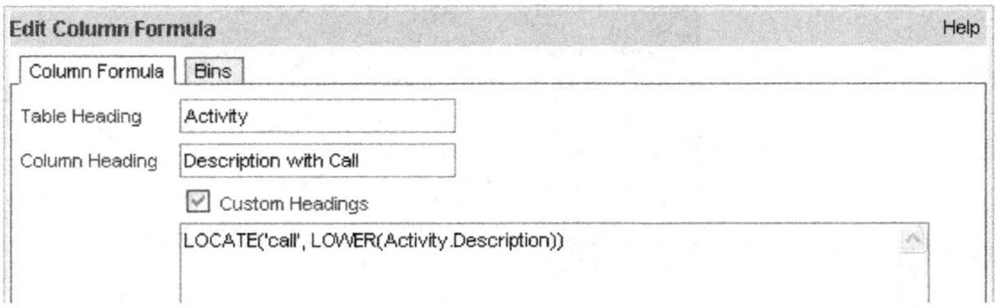

Edit Column Formula Help

| Column Formula | Bins |

Table Heading — Activity

Column Heading — Description with Call

☑ Custom Headings

LOCATE('call', LOWER(Activity.Description))

FIGURE 8-21. *LOWER function assisting with LOCATE*

Since the LOCATE function is case sensitive, in Figure 8-21 I am using the LOWER function to ensure that the string I search is lowercase, so that my LOCATE function will find the search string regardless of case. Notice in Figure 8-22 that although my search string appears in various cases, the LOCATE function returns the correct results thanks to the LOWER function.

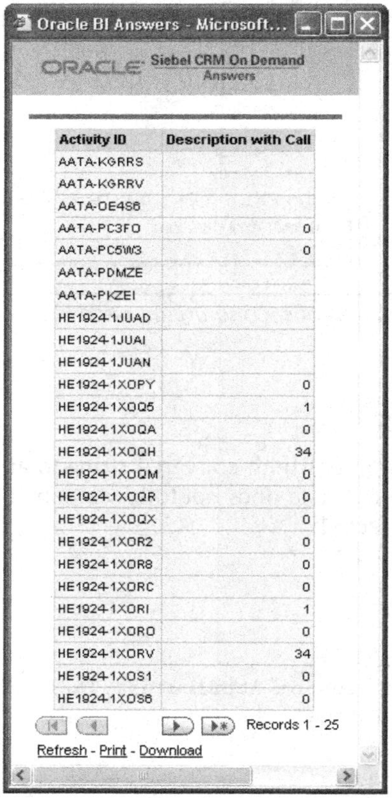

Oracle BI Answers - Microsoft...

ORACLE Siebel CRM On Demand Answers

Activity ID	Description with Call
AATA-KGRRS	
AATA-KGRRV	
AATA-OE4S6	
AATA-PC3FO	0
AATA-PC5W3	0
AATA-PDMZE	
AATA-PKZEI	
HE1924-1JUAD	
HE1924-1JUAI	
HE1924-1JUAN	
HE1924-1XOPY	0
HE1924-1XOQ5	1
HE1924-1XOQA	0
HE1924-1XOQH	34
HE1924-1XOQM	0
HE1924-1XOQR	0
HE1924-1XOQX	0
HE1924-1XOR2	0
HE1924-1XOR8	0
HE1924-1XORC	0
HE1924-1XORI	1
HE1924-1XORO	0
HE1924-1XORV	34
HE1924-1XOS1	0
HE1924-1XOS6	0

Records 1 - 25

Refresh - Print - Download

FIGURE 8-22. *Location of call in activity description*

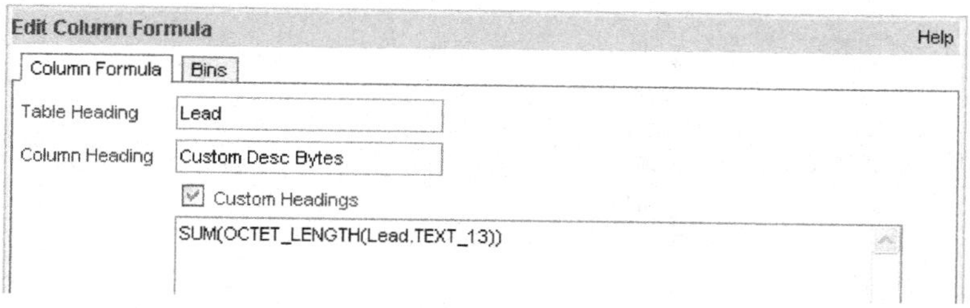

Edit Column Formula   Help

Column Formula | Bins

Table Heading   Lead

Column Heading   Custom Desc Bytes

                   ☑ Custom Headings

                   SUM(OCTET_LENGTH(Lead.TEXT_13))

FIGURE 8-23.   *SUM of OCTET_LENGTH*

OCTET_LENGTH

There are 8 bits in a byte, and each Unicode character is 2 bytes in length, or 16 bits. If you need to determine the length of a character string in bytes (octets) to evaluate string size for compliance with other systems or as part of a larger formula that uses length as a condition, then using this function is one of several options.

This function is related to the CHAR_LENGTH and BIT_LENGTH functions described earlier in this chapter.

Function Syntax

```
OCTET_LENGTH(char_exp)
OCTET_LENGTH(Account."Account Name")
OCTET_LENGTH(Account."Account Name" || Account."Location")
```

In Figure 8-23, I am using the OCTET_LENGTH function on a custom long-text field to determine how many bytes are required to store this information. Using the OCTET_LENGTH function, I can calculate the byte size of this data (see Figure 8-24).

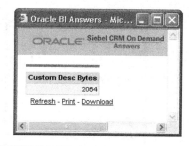

FIGURE 8-24.   *Bytes required to store custom descriptions*

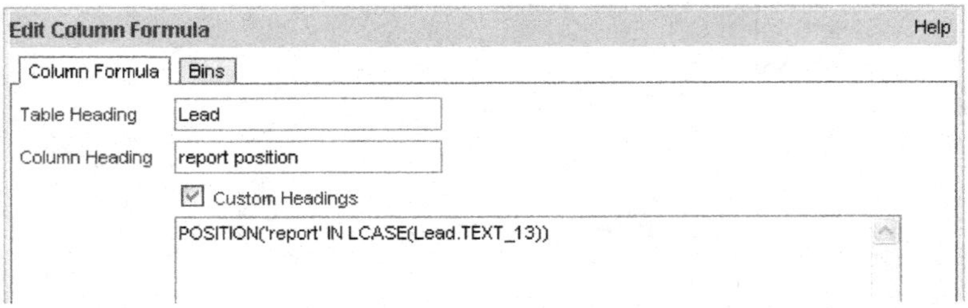

FIGURE 8-25. *POSITION function*

POSITION

Use the POSITION function to determine the numerical position of one string within another string. This function provides the exact same result as the LOCATE function. If the string is not found, the POSITION function returns a value of 0. This is another of several methods for flagging records in your report that contain a certain bit of text.

An important note here is that, just like the LOCATE function, the POSITION function is case sensitive. Refer to the description of the LOWER function for a strategy for overcoming this restriction.

Function Syntax

```
POSITION(string_exp1 IN string_exp2)
POSITION('opportunity' IN Activity.Description)
POSITION('service' IN LOWER(Lead."Product Interest"))
```

In Figure 8-25, I have written a column formula that examines a custom text field for the presence of the word "report." My report flags the records that contain this value (see Figure 8-26).

FIGURE 8-26. *Position of "report" in description*

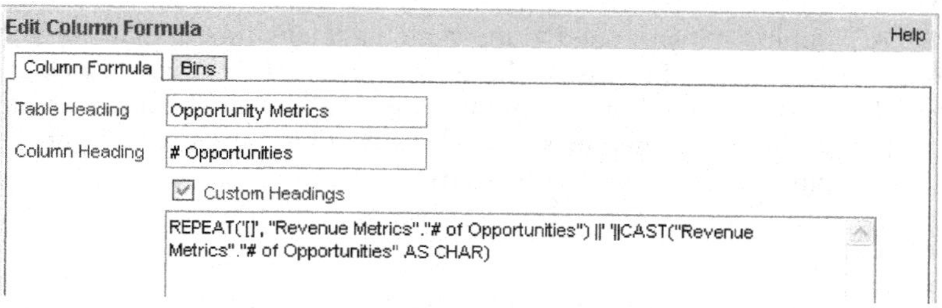

FIGURE 8-27. *REPEAT function to show of Opportunities*

REPEAT

The REPEAT function simply repeats a character string. How many times the string is repeated is based on a specified integer. This is a surprisingly useful function, especially if you want to create simple horizontal bar charts or even a rudimentary Gantt chart that you can download into a text or Excel file. Sure, the chart view in Answers On Demand is much flashier, but charts do not download.

Function Syntax

```
REPEAT(string_exp, N)
REPEAT(CHAR(49799), "Activity Metrics"."# of Activities")
```

I want to create right in my table a simple bar chart showing the number of opportunities that each of my sales reps owns. In Figure 8-27, I have written a column formula that will repeat my character string, made up of open and close square brackets, for each opportunity. I could also enhance my report (see Figure 8-28) with some conditional formatting to change the color of the bars at specified thresholds.

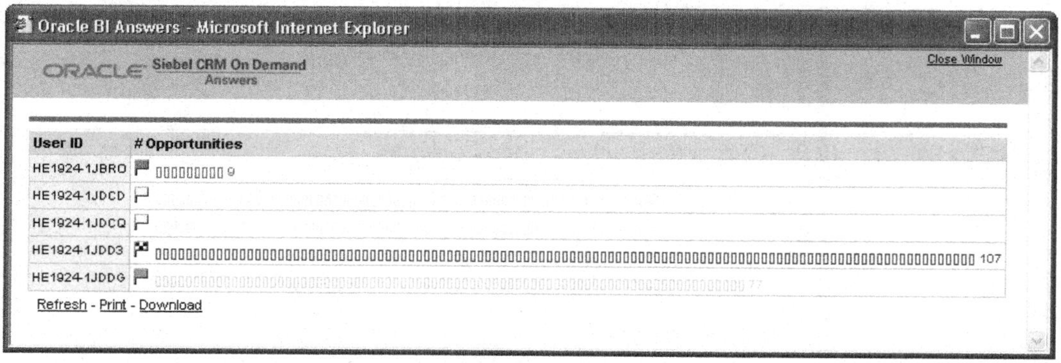

FIGURE 8-28. *Simple text bar chart for opportunity numbers*

REPLACE

Use the REPLACE function if you need to insert a character string in place of another character string. This can be quite useful in cases where you capture data in your database using a particular word, phrase, or abbreviation but want to represent that data some other way on your report. The REPLACE function identifies the exact substring to find within another string and the substring that should replace the original substring.

Function Syntax

```
REPLACE(string_exp, string_exp to change, new string_exp)
REPLACE(Opportunity."Opportunity Product", 'CLP2000', 'Color Printer 2000')
REPLACE(Activity.Description, 'TSP Report', 'Technical Specifications
Preparation
Report')
```

One of my favorite uses of the REPLACE function is to add line breaks to a description column in a report. I simply set the column's data format to HTML and then add the REPLACE function to the column formula, as you saw back in Figures 8-5 and 8-6 when I used REPLACE to replace the line breaks (CHAR(10)) in a column with an HTML break tag (<BR>). The result is a description field that includes the user's line breaks in the report.

Figure 8-29 shows another REPLACE formula that replaces all instances of "training" with "user adoption" in opportunity descriptions on my report. Figure 8-30 shows a side-by-side comparison of a row with the same column using and not using the REPLACE function.

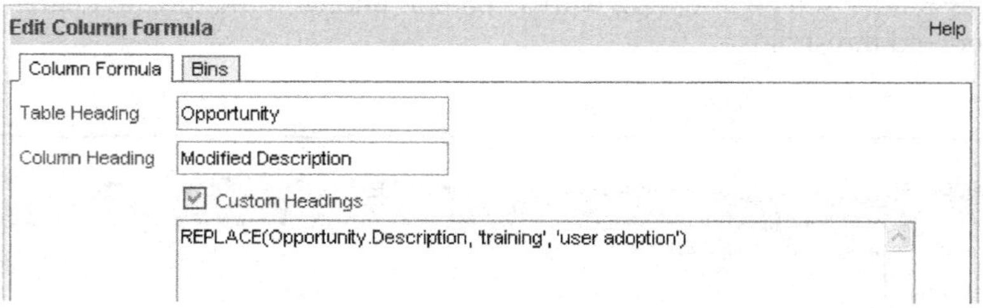

FIGURE 8-29. *REPLACE function on Description column*

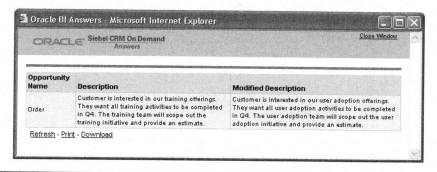

FIGURE 8-30. *Comparison of original description and new description*

RIGHT

The RIGHT function extracts a specified number of characters from the right (end) of a character string. Just as I mentioned with the LEFT function, you may find many uses for the RIGHT function, but it is imperative that your data is consistent to ensure that the function returns the data you expect.

Function Syntax

```
RIGHT(string_exp, N)
CONCAT("XXX-XX-",RIGHT("- Contact Custom Attributes"."TEXT_9",4))
RIGHT("- Contact Custom Attributes".TEXT_22,
(LOCATE(',', "- Contact Custom Attributes".TEXT_22)))
```

Suppose you have a Social Security Number or Account Identifier field on all of your records but do not want to display the entire number on reports for the security and privacy of your customers. You decide to display the last four characters of the ID and replace the rest of the ID with some sort of mask.

In this case you may choose to use the RIGHT function to extract the last bit of the data and concatenate that with a series of characters to mask the leading characters:

```
CONCAT("**********",RIGHT("- Contact Custom Attributes"."TEXT_9",4))
```

This formula will give a result such as "**********1234" in your report rather than exposing the entire contact text column. Refer to Figures 8-31 and 8-32 to see how I have used the RIGHT function to protect my customers' identities.

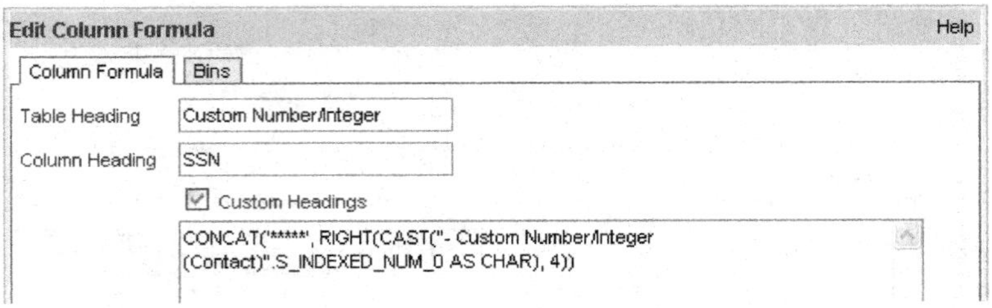

Edit Column Formula   Help

| Column Formula | Bins |

Table Heading   Custom Number/Integer

Column Heading   SSN

☑ Custom Headings

```
CONCAT("*****", RIGHT(CAST("- Custom Number/Integer
(Contact)".S_INDEXED_NUM_0 AS CHAR), 4))
```

FIGURE 8-31. *RIGHT function to get last four digits*

FIGURE 8-32. *Masked SSN list*

SPACE

The SPACE function adds a specified number of space characters. Inserting the SPACE function with an integer of 1 is equivalent to a literal text string of ' '. When you create a string of multiple spaces, by default, Answers On Demand truncates the display down to a single space. Of course, if you are purposely inserting multiple spaces in your column, you probably want to display those spaces. Change the column's data format to "Plain Text (don't break spaces)" and your spaces will appear in the report.

Function Syntax

```
SPACE(N)
SPACE(10)
```

There are not very many uses for the SPACE function that readily come to mind, but I have used it to create a simple Gantt chart–type visual within a report table. The concept is to calculate the difference between the current date and the start date of a task, and represent that number with spaces. Then, concatenated behind the spaces, a REPEAT function repeats a character a number of times equivalent to the difference between the start and end of the task.

In Figure 8-33, you see a formula that performs this series of calculations. Notice that I am really just concatenating two string functions. The first is the SPACE function with the result of a TIMESTAMPDIFF calculation providing my integer argument. I use a similar strategy with a REPEAT function to build the bar representing the task. Figure 8-34 shows a sample of this type of report.

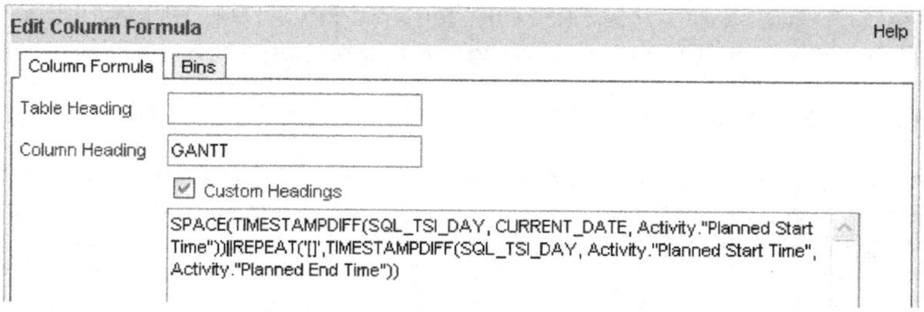

Edit Column Formula		Help
Column Formula	Bins	

Table Heading

Column Heading GANTT

☑ Custom Headings

```
SPACE(TIMESTAMPDIFF(SQL_TSI_DAY, CURRENT_DATE, Activity."Planned Start
Time"))||REPEAT('[]',TIMESTAMPDIFF(SQL_TSI_DAY, Activity."Planned Start Time",
Activity."Planned End Time"))
```

FIGURE 8-33.   *SPACE and REPEAT functions to build Gantt chart*

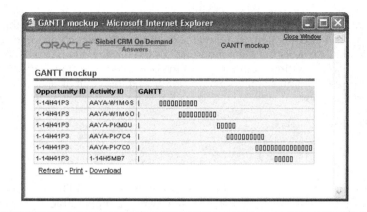

FIGURE 8-34. *Sample text Gantt chart*

SUBSTRING

The SUBSTRING function is similar to the RIGHT function. Using the SUBSTRING function, you are able to create a new character string using a portion of another string beginning with a specified position in that string. For instance, SUBSTRING('Oracle CRM On Demand' FROM 12) returns the substring "On Demand" beginning with the 12th character in the string. As with other functions, you can use any expression that results in an integer for the integer argument.

The SUBSTRING function also includes an optional argument for the length of the substring. For instance, SUBSTRING('Oracle CRM On Demand' FROM 9 FOR 3) will return the substring "CRM" by beginning with the ninth character and extracting three characters.

Function Syntax

```
SUBSTRING(string_exp FROM N FOR N)
SUBSTRING("- Account Custom Attributes".TEXT_0 FROM 5)
SUBSTRING(Opportunity.Description FROM
LOCATE('units',Opportunity.Description)-4)
```

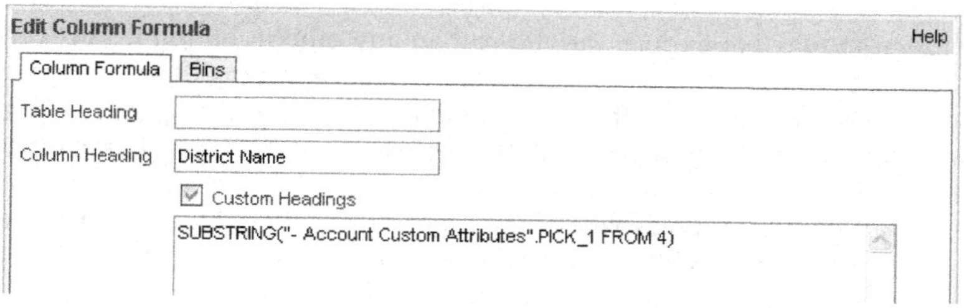

Edit Column Formula   Help

| Column Formula | Bins |

Table Heading   [   ]

Column Heading   [District Name   ]

☑ Custom Headings

SUBSTRING("- Account Custom Attributes".PICK_1 FROM 4)

FIGURE 8-35. *SUBSTRING function to extract portion of picklist*

In my example, I have a picklist in my database that contains a state abbreviation followed by a space and district name (NC Central Piedmont). I want to display just the names of the districts in my report. The RIGHT function will not work for me, since each value is potentially a different length. I do know, however, that the name of the district will always start in the fourth position of my string. Figure 8-35 shows the column formula to extract the district name from my picklist column. The result is shown in Figure 8-36.

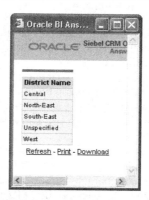

FIGURE 8-36. *District Name list*

TRIM

The TRIM function may have more variations than any other function in Answers On Demand. With this function, you are able to remove leading and/or trailing characters from character strings. There are six variations of the TRIM function. You can trim spaces from the front of a string, back of a string, or both. You are also able to trim specified characters from the front, back, or both ends of a string.

I want to start with trimming spaces from a character string. Occasionally, you will find that the result of some functions will have a trailing space. One such function is the YEAR function, which produces a result that is actually four digits followed by a space.

Syntax

```
LTRIM(string_exp)
RTRIM(string_exp)
TRIM(string_exp)
LTRIM(Activity.Description)
RTRIM(CAST(YEAR(CURRENT_DATE) AS CHAR))||'-'||
RTRIM(CAST(MONTH(CURRENT_DATE) AS CHAR))||'-28'
CONCAT(TRIM("- Account Custom Attributes".TEXT_13),
TRIM("- Account Custom Attributes".TEXT_14))
```

When users enter text into free-form text fields in CRM On Demand, you are pretty much guaranteed to have stray spaces in those fields. Usually these spaces do no harm. Occasionally you may need to concatenate some of these fields or create some sort of condition in a report based on these fields. It is on those occasions when you may find it necessary to clean up the spaces in order to manipulate the data in your report as you like.

The LTRIM function trims any leading spaces in a column field. Any spaces located within or after the text are unaffected. The RTRIM function trims any trailing spaces in a column field without affecting spaces before or within the text. If you need to eliminate both leading and trailing spaces, use the TRIM function. This function removes spaces before and after the text string without affecting spaces within the text.

The YEAR and MONTH functions leave a space at the end of the result. This is problematic if you are trying to build a date or timestamp using these functions. You can use one of the TRIM functions to help resolve this issue. Note that it is necessary to convert the result of the YEAR and MONTH functions to a character string before you can administer the TRIM function, because this function works only on string expressions.

In Figure 8-37, I have written a column formula that creates a date equivalent to the 28th day of the current month and year. Notice that I include the CAST function, which is discussed in the next chapter, to convert the data to a character string. I also apply the TRIM function to the YEAR and MONTH expressions separately. If I applied the TRIM to the result of the entire concatenation, the spaces would remain because they would then be inside the text string rather than trailing.

```
CAST(YEAR(CURRENT_DATE) AS CHAR)||'-'||
CAST(MONTH(CURRENT_DATE) AS CHAR)||'-28'

RTRIM(CAST(YEAR(CURRENT_DATE) AS CHAR))||'-'||
RTRIM(CAST(MONTH(CURRENT_DATE) AS CHAR))||'-28'
```

Edit Column Formula   Help

| Column Formula | Bins |

Table Heading   TRIMMED

Column Heading   28TH OF MONTH

☑ Custom Headings

Column Formula
```
CASE WHEN MONTH(CURRENT_DATE) >9 THEN
RTRIM(CAST(YEAR(CURRENT_DATE) AS CHAR))||'-'||RTRIM(CAST(MONTH
(CURRENT_DATE) AS CHAR))||'-28'
WHEN MONTH(CURRENT_DATE) <10 THEN
RTRIM(CAST(YEAR(CURRENT_DATE) AS CHAR))||'-0'||RTRIM(CAST(MONTH
(CURRENT_DATE) AS CHAR))||'-28'
ELSE NULL END
```

FIGURE 8-37. *RTRIM function to create date*

In Figure 8-38, you can see the result of both of the preceding formulas. Notice that the first result contains spaces after the year and month. Seeing this result, I know I need to add the RTRIM function to the formula to remove those spaces before each is concatenated into the final outcome.

So, trimming space characters is pretty simple, but what if you need to trim off some other characters? There may be some common bits of text that find their way into your data that you are not interested in displaying in your report. This next set of TRIM functions enables you to trim off any character you like. Of course, you certainly could trim spaces with these forms of the TRIM function as well.

Function Syntax

```
TRIM(LEADING char FROM string_exp)
TRIM(TRAILING char FROM string_exp)
TRIM(BOTH char FROM string_exp)
TRIM(LEADING '#' FROM "- Account Custom Attributes".TEXT_2)
TRIM(TRAILING '.' FROM Activity.Description)
TRIM(BOTH '%' FROM Opportunity."- Opportunity Custom Attributes".PICK_7)
```

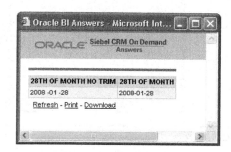

FIGURE 8-38. *Date comparison with and without trim*

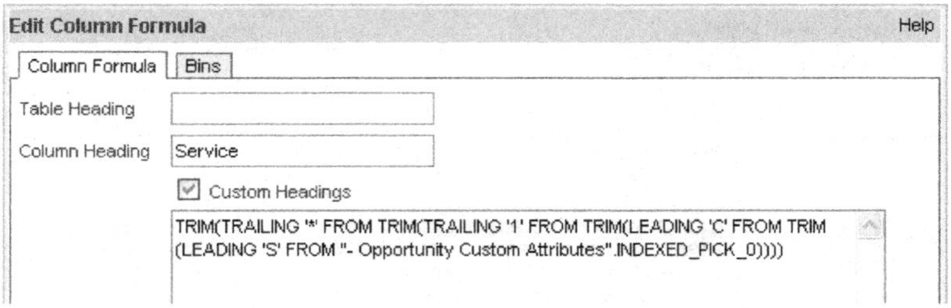

Edit Column Formula   Help

| Column Formula | Bins |

Table Heading

Column Heading   Service

☑ Custom Headings

TRIM(TRAILING '*' FROM TRIM(TRAILING '1' FROM TRIM(LEADING 'C' FROM TRIM
(LEADING 'S' FROM "- Opportunity Custom Attributes".INDEXED_PICK_0))))

FIGURE 8-39. *TRIM LEADING and TRAILING*

Suppose you have a list of service codes in your database. The length and format of these service codes varies, but all codes are prefaced by SC and end with *1. For instance, SCINSTALL*1 and SCFORMAT*1 are codes in this list. While the SC and *1 mean something to someone in the company, you do not want them in your report.

Unfortunately, the TRIM functions allow only a single character. In a case like this, you need to nest several TRIM functions together, as I have done in the following formula and in Figure 8-39:

```
TRIM(TRAILING '*' FROM TRIM(TRAILING '1' FROM TRIM(LEADING 'C' FROM TRIM
(LEADING 'S' FROM Opportunity."- Opportunity Custom Attributes".PICK_1))))
```

Since the formula executes the innermost function first and works its way to the outside, this formula first trims the S from the front of the string. Next, it trims the C that is now at the front of the resulting string from the first trim. It then moves to the end of the string and removes the 1. Finally, the outermost TRIM function takes off the * character. In Figure 8-40, you can see the result of this formula.

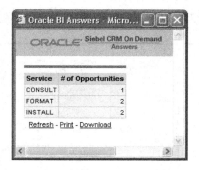

FIGURE 8-40. *Service Codes report*

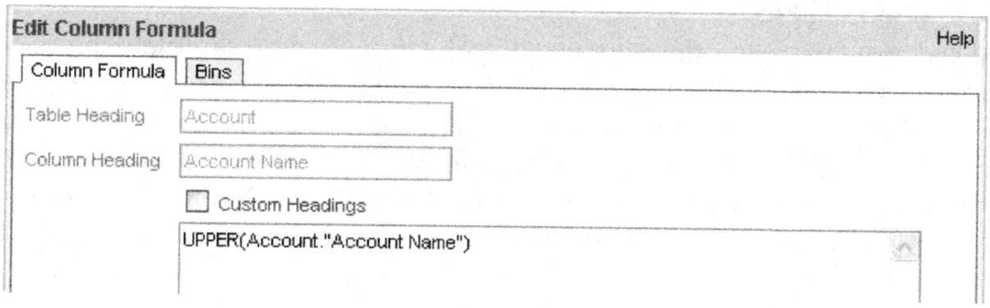

FIGURE 8-41. *UPPER function applied*

UPPER or UCASE

Some people are of the opinion that uppercase text carries some sort of negative connotation. Others feel that the readability and uniformity of uppercase text is much more appealing. Regardless of how you feel on the topic, the UPPER and UCASE functions both convert a character string to all uppercase letters. This is particularly helpful when your data does not follow a consistent capitalization rule. Numbers within the string are not affected.

Function Syntax

```
UPPER(string_exp)
UPPER(Activity.Description)
UCASE(CONCAT("- Account Custom Attributes".TEXT_05,
"- Account Custom Attributes".TEXT_06))
```

One interesting application of the UPPER function is to apply it to every column in a report to generate a data table that you intend to download and import back into On Demand or into another system. You may do so to comply with a business practice of using uppercase text or even a system requirement due to some sort of integration with a mainframe system. In Figures 8-41 and 8-42, you see a before and after screenshot of a report converting the data to all uppercase.

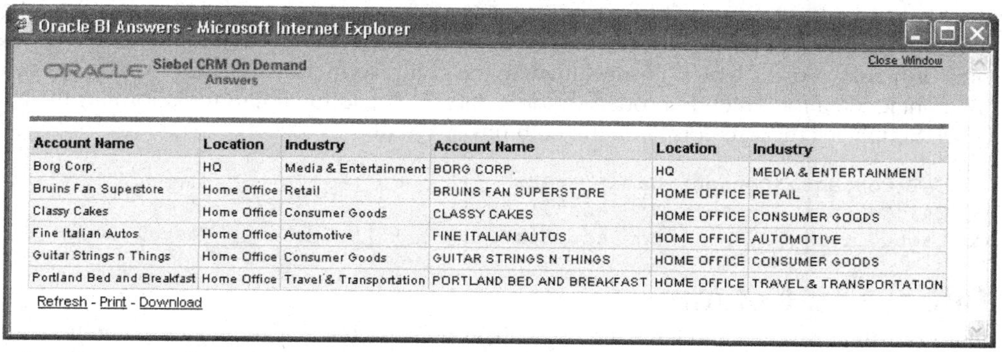

FIGURE 8-42. *Before and after case conversion*

Useful Samples

In this final section, I want to offer you a small selection of some sample expressions using the string functions. These samples represent some of the reporting challenges that I and others have overcome. Unlike some of the other types of data, character strings vary a great deal from company to company. While dates and metrics generally follow some standard formatting and structure, text data varies widely between companies using Oracle CRM On Demand. The unique qualities of text data makes it difficult to offer ready-to-use code samples, but I hope that a few examples of how these functions may be used will prove to be useful fodder for your own reporting.

Build an Email Address

Most companies have a standard format for their email addresses. You may use this to your advantage if you need to craft an email address when an email address field is not available or is not populated. For instance, suppose you have fields for First Name and Last Name of an internal resource, but you are not keeping contact records for these individuals and these individuals are not users of the On Demand application. The following formula takes the content of two custom text fields (First Name and Last Name) and builds a complete email address:

```
UPPER(TRIM(LEFT("- Opportunity Custom Attributes".TEXT_30,1))||
TRIM("- Opportunity Custom Attributes".TEXT_31)||'@mycompany.com')
```

Line Breaks in a Report

Answers On Demand strips line breaks and extra spaces out of description fields in reports. If you want to retain the line breaks, you can use a combination of string function and data formatting to ensure that your report appears exactly as you want. Recall that you can change the data format of a column. Change the data format of the description column to HTML. This will cause Answers On Demand to read HTML tags and display the data as HTML. The following formula replaces the line breaks CHAR(10) with the equivalent HTML line break <BR>:

```
REPLACE(Opportunity.Description, char(10), '<BR>')
```

Address Labels

There are a few different ways to produce address labels with CRM On Demand. You could use the Mail Merge tool. You might even export data and use another application. You can also, with a little ingenuity and formatting, develop a report in Answers On Demand that produces very nice printable address labels. I especially like the ability to modify the filter to extract a subset of my contact data for which to produce address labels. The following formula formats the address label. Simply set the data format of the columns to HTML.

```
CONCAT(Contact."Contact Name",'<BR>') ||
CONCAT(Contact."Primary Address",'<BR>') ||
Contact.City || ', ' || Contact.State || ' ' || Contact."Postal Code"
```

Initial Cap Column

Unfortunately, Answers On Demand does not contain an Initial Capitalization function. I have a strategy for capitalizing the first letter of a column. The first step is to isolate the first character and make that letter uppercase. Then, take the rest of the text in the column and convert it to lowercase text. Finally, concatenate the two pieces together. I have provided a sample of this formula below:

```
CONCAT((UPPER(LEFT(Contact."Contact Last Name",
1))),(LOWER(SUBSTRING(Contact."Contact Last Name" FROM 2))))
```

With this formula, "Atkinson," "atkinson," and "ATKINSON" all display as "Atkinson" in your report.

Additional Tips

The text data you store in your database is going to be quite different in form and substance from anyone else's data. The string functions are quite useful for extracting text from the database for your reports, especially when the string data does not exist in the database exactly as you would have it on your report. Of course, this means that one person's formula will not likely be entirely useful to another, so it is in your best interest to learn these functions independently and challenge yourself to think outside of the box to overcome your specific challenges in your reporting.

The other critical element to successful implementation of string functions is the consistency of your data. When data items in a column share the same format and structure, it becomes very easy to extract pieces of that text or manipulate specific portions of data within a column. So, use whatever influence you have within your organization or with your customers to encourage consistency and structure of data for the sake of good reporting.

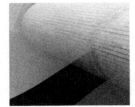

CHAPTER
9

Using Column Formulas
to Apply Logic and
Transform Data

his chapter has two distinct topics—adding logic to your report and changing the format of data in report columns. I considered putting this chapter in front of the other function chapters, because it seems that nearly every column formula I write includes one or more of the functions described in this chapter. I ultimately decided that this should be the final chapter on functions because you will rarely use any of these functions entirely on their own.

With CASE statements, you are instructing Answers On Demand to react to specific conditions and perform a certain calculation in one case and another calculation in other cases. These calculations inevitably include functions discussed in earlier chapters.

With the conversion functions, you are instructing Answers On Demand to take data of one format and either display it in another format or use it in another format in a calculation.

CASE Statements

CASE statements are perhaps the most useful and pervasive element of complex column formulas. Logical processing is often a critical element of reporting, and CASE statements provide this logic. Without logic, many reporting needs would simply go unmet.

There are two forms of the CASE statement:

- The CASE Switch, or lookup, form is typically much shorter, and therefore easier to write. This form of the CASE statement does have some limitations, though.

- The CASE If form can become rather lengthy, but provides the ability to evaluate multiple expressions.

CASE statements can be relatively simple, or they can become quite complex by nesting multiple CASE statements inside of one another. Before discussing the specific types of CASE statements, I want to familiarize you with the different elements of the CASE statement. Table 9-1 describes each element of the CASE statement.

CASE	Every CASE statement begins with CASE. CASE opens the statement.
WHEN	WHEN introduces the condition. In a CASE Switch statement, the field reference is before the WHEN elements. In a CASE If statement, each WHEN element introduces a conditional expression.
THEN	THEN introduces the action expression for the associated WHEN element. A CASE statement contains one THEN element for each WHEN element.
ELSE	ELSE is an optional element that allows you to include an action expression for instances when none of your conditions are met.
END	END closes the CASE statement.

TABLE 9-1. *CASE Statement Elements*

CASE Switch

I am sure you have encountered a reporting requirement that includes some sort of conditional logic. If a report requirement includes the word "if" followed within a phrase or two by the word "then," you are likely to need a CASE statement to meet this reporting request. The CASE statement is a variation of the classic IF-THEN-ELSE programming logic, but allows you to include several "ifs" within the same statement.

The CASE Switch form of the CASE statement performs a single lookup and evaluates a series of WHEN expressions, applying the THEN expression upon encountering a WHEN expression that evaluates as true.

Function Syntax

```
CASE exp1
WHEN exp2 THEN exp2
{WHEN exp... THEN exp...}
ELSE exp
END

CASE Account.Industry
WHEN 'Automotive' THEN 1000
WHEN 'Manufacturing' THEN 750
WHEN 'Consumer Goods' THEN 750
WHEN 'Retail' THEN 600
WHEN 'Financial Services' THEN 500
ELSE 400
END
```

Of the two forms of the CASE statement, the CASE Switch is the least elaborate and is typically the shorter of the two. The CASE Switch form is limited in that the WHEN expression does not perform any sort of operation or calculation.

In this type of statement, the WHEN expression must be a simple binary decision. In a CASE Switch statement, the WHEN expressions must reflect an equality. An expression such as WHEN > 0 THEN 'Positive' is illegal. Comparison operators are not allowed. The WHERE expression will match the result of the CASE expression and continue on to the THEN expression, or it will not match the CASE expression and will move to the next WHEN expression in the statement.

Answers On Demand evaluates CASE statements from the top. It evaluates the first WHEN expression, and if it is not a match, it moves on to the next WHEN expression. Once Answers On Demand encounters a WHEN expression that matches the CASE expression, it executes the associated THEN expression and stops processing the CASE statement. If none of the WHEN expressions evaluate as a match, Answers On Demand moves on to the ELSE expression. The ELSE expression is optional, so if the CASE statement does not contain an ELSE expression, Answers On Demand will assume an ELSE expression of NULL.

The CASE Switch statement is most effective for simply transforming one result value to another in a report. An example of this type of logical process will help demonstrate the CASE Switch statement. Suppose I want to show the commission rate for each territory in a report. My commission rate is different for each territory, so a conversion of this type is quite useful for my commission calculation report. If an opportunity is in the West territory, the sales rep earns a .5 percent commission. In the Central territory, the commission rate is 0.75 percent. The South-East earns a .8 percent commission, and the North-East gets a full 1 percent. Any opportunity outside of these four main territories earns a .25 percent commission. I want the report to provide a calculation of the commission based on the territory without displaying all of the details of the commission rates. The CASE Switch statement for this example follows:

```
CASE Territory."Territory Name"
WHEN 'West' THEN .005 * "Revenue Metrics"."Opportunity Revenue"
WHEN 'Central' THEN .0075 * "Revenue Metrics"."Opportunity Revenue"
WHEN 'South-East' THEN .008 * "Revenue Metrics"."Opportunity Revenue"
WHEN 'North-East' THEN .01 * "Revenue Metrics"."Opportunity Revenue"
ELSE .0025 * "Revenue Metrics"."Opportunity Revenue"
END
```

As you can see in Figure 9-1, the result of this CASE Switch is a calculated commission amount for each territory. This satisfies the requirement of determining the territory and calculating the commission based on the commission rate of each territory.

You may also perform a calculation in the CASE expression. For instance, suppose I want to calculate the number of crates that I need to ship to my customer based on the total number of widgets and gizmos the customer ordered. I will assume that no one can order more than a dozen pieces combined and that I can ship four pieces in a crate. My CASE statement would look something like this:

```
CASE "- Revenue Custom Metrics".S_NUM_0 + "- Revenue Custom Metrics".S_NUM_1
WHEN 1 THEN 1
WHEN 2 THEN 1
WHEN 3 THEN 1
```

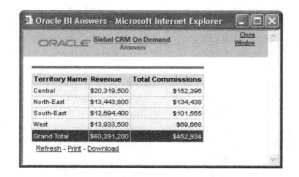

Territory Name	Revenue	Total Commissions
Central	$20,319,500	$152,396
North-East	$13,443,800	$134,438
South-East	$12,694,400	$101,555
West	$13,933,500	$69,668
Grand Total	$60,391,200	$452,934

FIGURE 9-1. *Commission amounts by territory*

```
WHEN 4 THEN 1
WHEN 5 THEN 2
WHEN 6 THEN 2
WHEN 7 THEN 2
WHEN 8 THEN 2
WHEN 9 THEN 3
WHEN 10 THEN 3
WHEN 11 THEN 3
WHEN 12 THEN 3
ELSE 4 END
```

This is an example of a problem that may be solved a number of ways. I certainly could write a mathematical calculation that would do what I need here by taking the total divided by 4 and rounding up:

```
ROUNDUP(("- Revenue Custom Metrics".S_NUM_0 + "- Revenue Custom
Metrics".S_NUM_1)/4,0)
```

My point here is twofold. First, there is often more than one way to accomplish the same result. Second, use the method with which you are most comfortable so long as that solution is valid.

My final example of the CASE Switch statement is a simple translation of data from one value to another using a date/time function. You may recall that it is possible to determine the month of a given date using either the MONTH function or the MONTHNAME function. MONTH returns the number of the month, 1 through 12. MONTHNAME returns the three-character abbreviated month name. What if I want to show the full name of the month in my report? I can use a CASE Switch statement to do just that. I will start with the MONTH function to determine the month, and then change the number to the name with my WHEN/THEN expressions. I could use either MONTH or MONTHNAME, but MONTH requires less effort in crafting the CASE statement:

```
CASE MONTH(Opportunity."Close Date")
WHEN 1 THEN 'January'
WHEN 2 THEN 'February'
WHEN 3 THEN 'March'
WHEN 4 THEN 'April'
WHEN 5 THEN 'May'
WHEN 6 THEN 'June'
WHEN 7 THEN 'July'
WHEN 8 THEN 'August'
WHEN 9 THEN 'September'
WHEN 10 THEN 'October'
WHEN 11 THEN 'November'
WHEN 12 THEN 'December'
END
```

Figure 9-2 shows the number of opportunities closed by the month of the year. I have a hidden MONTH(Opportunity."Close Date") statement that I am using to sort the data by month.

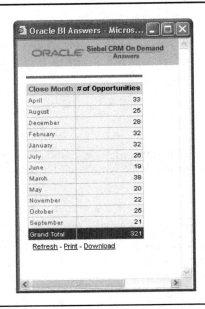

FIGURE 9-2. *Opportunities by Month report*

CASE If

This form of the CASE statement is most like the classic IF-THEN-WHEN statement. The CASE If statement evaluates each WHEN condition and, if satisfied, assigns the value prescribed in the related THEN expression. If none of the WHEN conditions are satisfied, Answers On Demand assigns the default value specified in the ELSE expression. If no ELSE expression is specified, Answers On Demand assumes an ELSE NULL.

The CASE If statement is the most flexible and often the most complex of the two CASE statement formats. With CASE If statements, more so than any other formula in Answers On Demand, you are able to express decisions based on your CRM On Demand data. For example, suppose you are tracking your sales staff's productivity and have decided to implement an incentive plan for the top 10 percent of your staff based on several criteria. Sorting through a report of raw data to determine which of your sales team members are on track to make the top 10 percent would be a tedious, manual process. With CASE statements in combination with other Answers On Demand functions, you not only can automate this decision, you can do so in real time so your employees know exactly where they stand.

Function Syntax

```
CASE
WHEN condition1 THEN exp1
{WHEN condition... THEN exp...}
ELSE exp
END
```

```
CASE
WHEN "Opportunity Metrics"."Opportunity Revenue (000)"<= 25 THEN '0-25'
WHEN "Opportunity Metrics"."Opportunity Revenue (000)"<= 50 THEN '25-50'
WHEN "Opportunity Metrics"."Opportunity Revenue (000)"<= 75 THEN '50-75'
WHEN "Opportunity Metrics"."Opportunity Revenue (000)"<= 100 THEN '75-100'
WHEN "Opportunity Metrics"."Opportunity Revenue (000)"<= 250 THEN '100-250'
WHEN "Opportunity Metrics"."Opportunity Revenue (000)"<= 500 THEN '250-500'
WHEN "Opportunity Metrics"."Opportunity Revenue (000)"<= 750 THEN '500-750'
WHEN "Opportunity Metrics"."Opportunity Revenue (000)"<= 1000 THEN '750-1000'
ELSE '1000+'
END
```

Unlike the Switch form of the CASE statement, the WHEN condition is in the "if" form and allows comparison operators. A legal WHEN condition follows the following syntax:

```
...WHEN exp operator exp {operator exp...} THEN...
```

This allows you to build some rather complex logic into your formulas by nesting expressions and operators inside of the WHEN condition. All of the following are perfectly acceptable WHEN conditions, ranging from simple to complex:

```
...WHEN Account.NUM_0 = 5 THEN...
...WHEN Account.NUM_0 = Account.NUM_1 THEN...
...WHEN Account.NUM_0 > (Account.NUM_1 + Account.NUM_2) THEN...
...WHEN (Account.NUM_0 / Account.NUM_9 )*100 <
(Account.NUM_1 + Account.NUM_2)/Account.NUM_10 THEN...
...WHEN Account."Account Type" = 'Prospect' AND Account."Account Priority" <>
'Low' THEN...
...WHEN (Account.NUM_4 * Account.NUM_0) /
COUNT(Account."Account ID" BY Account."Account Priority") >
(Account.NUM_4 * Account.NUM_1) /
COUNT(Account."Account ID" BY Account."Account Priority")THEN...
```

As with the CASE Switch, Answers On Demand evaluates CASE If statements from the top. Each value within a column is evaluated and acted on based on the first WHEN condition that it meets within your CASE statement. Answers On Demand evaluates the first WHEN expression, and if the condition is not met, it moves on to the next WHEN condition. Once Answers On Demand encounters a WHEN condition that agrees with the value it is evaluating, it executes the associated THEN expression and stops processing the CASE statement. If none of the WHEN conditions are met, Answers On Demand moves on to the ELSE expression. The ELSE expression is optional, so if the CASE statement does not contain an ELSE expression, Answers On Demand will assume an ELSE expression of NULL.

Some common examples of useful CASE If statements include changing the value of a field to another value, grouping data into categories based on column values, calculating an amount based on specific criteria, and extracting data from the database based on a time calculation. Of course, every CASE statement is different, but the following examples illustrate some common forms of the CASE If statement.

I am often asked to sort data in a report, not alphabetically or numerically, but with a custom sort order. I accomplish this with a CASE statement in a column that I will sort and hide. The following CASE statement provides an example of this type of formula:

```
CASE
WHEN "- Account Custom Attributes".PICK_1 = 'Consulting' THEN 1
WHEN "- Account Custom Attributes".PICK_1 = 'Analysis' THEN 2
WHEN "- Account Custom Attributes".PICK_1 = 'Project Management' THEN 3
WHEN "- Account Custom Attributes".PICK_1 = 'Training' THEN 4
WHEN "- Account Custom Attributes".PICK_1 = 'Programming' THEN 5
WHEN "- Account Custom Attributes".PICK_1 = 'Other' THEN 6
END
```

Another common need is to group data in the report into categories that are not explicitly defined within the database. A CASE statement is one way to do this, as the following example shows:

```
CASE
WHEN Product."Product Name" IN ('CX2000', 'CZ1050', 'CX2500') THEN 'Blue'
WHEN Product."Product Name" IN ('UT60', 'GS23', 'FF01') THEN 'Green'
WHEN Product."Product Name" IN ('PO99', 'GH10', 'XT00') THEN 'Red'
WHEN Product."Product Name" IN ('VH3000', 'VH4000', 'VV2000') THEN 'White'
WHEN Product."Product Name" IN ('RT', 'RT002', 'RT012') THEN 'Ruby'
ELSE CONCAT(Product."Product Name", '-Clear')
END
```

This and the previous example are CASE statements that you could easily create using the bin functionality on the column. The next couple of examples are a little too complex for bins, but are not nearly as complex as CASE statements can become.

Here I am interested in performing a few different calculations based on some compound criteria from my database. Notice that I am using the AND and OR statements in some of my WHEN statements. I am also demonstrating use of the FILTER function in one of my WHEN statements.

```
CASE
WHEN ("- Revenue Custom Metrics".S_NUM_0 >
"- Revenue Custom Metrics".S_NUM_1) AND
"Revenue Metrics"."Opportunity Revenue" > 500000
THEN "Revenue Metrics"."Opportunity Revenue" /
"- Revenue Custom Metrics".S_NUM_0
WHEN ("- Revenue Custom Metrics".S_NUM_0 <
"- Revenue Custom Metrics".S_NUM_1) AND
"Revenue Metrics"."Opportunity Revenue" > 500000
THEN "Revenue Metrics"."Opportunity Revenue" /
"- Revenue Custom Metrics".S_NUM_1
WHEN ("- Revenue Custom Metrics".S_NUM_0 >
"- Revenue Custom Metrics".S_NUM_1) AND
"Revenue Metrics"."Opportunity Revenue" < 500000
THEN ("Revenue Metrics"."Opportunity Revenue" +
"Revenue Metrics"."Opportunity Revenue") /
"- Revenue Custom Metrics".S_NUM_0
WHEN ("- Revenue Custom Metrics".S_NUM_0 <
"- Revenue Custom Metrics".S_NUM_1) AND
"Revenue Metrics"."Opportunity Revenue" < 500000
```

```
THEN ("Revenue Metrics"."Opportunity Revenue" +
"Revenue Metrics"."Opportunity Revenue") /
"- Revenue Custom Metrics".S_NUM_1
WHEN "- Revenue Custom Metrics".S_NUM_0 IS NULL OR
"- Revenue Custom Metrics".S_NUM_1 IS NULL
THEN "Revenue Metrics"."Opportunity Revenue"
WHEN FILTER("- Revenue Custom Metrics".S_NUM_0 USING
(Opportunity."Sales Type" = 'Renewal')) > 100
THEN "Revenue Metrics"."Opportunity Revenue" * .5
ELSE "Revenue Metrics"."Opportunity Revenue"
END
```

My final example in this section involves some time calculations. Using the CASE function with date/time calculations is a popular reporting tactic. In this example, I am calculating the difference in days between the opportunity create date and today and displaying "Old," "New," "Working," or "Error" based on the result of that calculation:

```
CASE
WHEN TIMESTAMPDIFF(SQL_TSI_DAY, Opportunity."Created Date", CURRENT_DATE)>
90 THEN 'Old'
WHEN TIMESTAMPDIFF(SQL_TSI_DAY, Opportunity."Created Date", CURRENT_DATE)<=
14 THEN 'New'
WHEN TIMESTAMPDIFF(SQL_TSI_DAY, Opportunity."Created Date", CURRENT_DATE)<=
90 THEN 'Working'
ELSE 'Error'
END
```

Nesting CASE Statements

Like other functions, you can nest CASE statements inside one another. This can add a lot of power to your report logic, but can also be quite complex and confusing. I highly recommend, whenever possible, to create your CASE statements separately and then use the Column button to insert the CASE statement into another CASE statement. A simple nested CASE statement would look something like the following. Note that I have formatted the formula to enhance the readability, but Answers On Demand ignores extra spaces and line breaks.

```
CASE
WHEN "Close Date"."Calendar Month" = MONTH(CURRENT_DATE) THEN
     CASE
     WHEN "Opportunity"."Lead Source" = 'Partner'
     THEN "Opportunity Metrics"."Expected Revenue"/2
     ELSE "Opportunity Metrics"."Expected Revenue"
     END
ELSE 0
END
```

You may also embed a CASE statement inside the WHEN condition:

```
CASE
WHEN  (CASE
     WHEN "Opportunity"."Lead Source" = 'Partner'
     THEN "Opportunity Metrics"."Expected Revenue"/2
```

```
      ELSE "Opportunity Metrics"."Expected Revenue"
      END) > 100000
THEN 'Large Deal'
ELSE 'Small Deal'
END
```

You do not have to stretch your imagination very much to realize how quickly a simple reporting IF-THEN-WHEN type query can grow into a complex CASE statement. In the following CASE statement, I total a custom number field for open opportunities divided by the number of activities based on the username, and then add a custom number based on an activity type. To this I add a custom number field on the activity record for those activities that have a due date in the current customized fiscal quarter.

```
(CASE
WHEN Opportunity."Sales Stage" NOT IN ('Closed/Won', 'Closed/Lost')
THEN (SUM((((
  CASE
  WHEN Opportunity.PICK_1 = "- Owned By User"."Employee Name"
  THEN "- Custom Number/Integer (Opty)".NUM_14
  ELSE 0
  END
/ SUM ("Activity Metrics"."# of Activities" by Opportunity.Name))
+ (CASE
  WHEN Opportunity.PICK_21 = "- Owned By User"."Employee Name"
  THEN "- Custom Number/Integer (Opty)".NUM_6
  ELSE 0
  END
/ SUM ("Activity Metrics"."# of Activities" by Opportunity.Name))
+ (CASE
  WHEN Opportunity.PICK_20 = "- Owned By User"."Employee Name"
  THEN "- Custom Number/Integer (Opty)".NUM_13
  ELSE 0
  END
/ SUM ("Activity Metrics"."# of Activities" by Opportunity.Name))
+ (CASE
  WHEN Opportunity.PICK_50 = "- Owned By User"."Employee Name"
  THEN "- Custom Number/Integer (Opty)".NUM_4
  ELSE 0
  END
/ SUM ("Activity Metrics"."# of Activities" by Opportunity.Name))
+ (CASE
  WHEN Opportunity.PICK_3 = "- Owned By User"."Employee Name"
  THEN "- Custom Number/Integer (Opty)".NUM_3
  ELSE 0
  END
/ SUM ("Activity Metrics"."# of Activities" by Opportunity.Name))))
+ CASE
  WHEN "- Custom Number/Integer".S_NUM_0 < 0
  THEN
    (CASE
    WHEN Opportunity.PICK_1 = "- Owned By User"."Employee Name"
```

```
        AND Activity.Type IN ('Configuration', 'Review', 'Consulting', 'Reports')
        THEN ABS ("- Custom Number/Integer".S_NUM_0)
        ELSE 0
        END
      + CASE
        WHEN Opportunity.PICK_21 = "- Owned By User"."Employee Name"
        AND Activity.Type = 'Management'
        THEN ABS ("- Custom Number/Integer".S_NUM_0)
        ELSE 0
        END
      + CASE
        WHEN Opportunity.PICK_20 = "- Owned By User"."Employee Name"
        AND Activity.Type = 'Business Requirements'
        THEN ABS ("- Custom Number/Integer".S_NUM_0)
        ELSE 0
        END
      + CASE
        WHEN Opportunity.PICK_50 = "- Owned By User"."Employee Name"
        AND Activity.Type = 'Importing'
        THEN ABS ("- Custom Number/Integer".S_NUM_0)
        ELSE 0
        END
      + CASE
        WHEN Opportunity.PICK_3 = "- Owned By User"."Employee Name"
        AND Activity.Type IN ('Training', 'Training Delivery')
        THEN ABS ("- Custom Number/Integer".S_NUM_0)
        ELSE 0
        END)
      ELSE 0
      END BY Opportunity.Name)
    - SUM
      (CASE
      WHEN "- Custom Number/Integer".S_NUM_0 < 0 THEN 0
      WHEN Activity.Type = 'Other' THEN 0
      ELSE "- Custom Number/Integer".S_NUM_0
      END BY Opportunity.Name))
    / SUM ("Activity Metrics"."# of Activities" by Opportunity.Name)
    ELSE 0
    END)
    +
    (CASE
    WHEN
      (CASE
      WHEN CAST ("- Due Date"."Task Due Date" as DATE)
      BETWEEN date '2006-05-27' AND date '2006-08-25' THEN 'Fiscal 2007 Q1'
      WHEN CAST ("- Due Date"."Task Due Date" as DATE)
      BETWEEN date '2006-08-25' AND date '2006-11-24' THEN 'Fiscal 2007 Q2'
      WHEN CAST ("- Due Date"."Task Due Date" as DATE)
      BETWEEN date '2006-11-24' AND date '2007-02-23' THEN 'Fiscal 2007 Q3'
      WHEN CAST ("- Due Date"."Task Due Date" as DATE)
      BETWEEN date '2007-02-23' AND date '2007-05-25' THEN 'Fiscal 2007 Q4'
```

```
WHEN CAST ("- Due Date"."Task Due Date" as DATE)
BETWEEN date '2007-05-25' AND date '2007-08-31' THEN 'Fiscal 2008 Q1'
WHEN CAST ("- Due Date"."Task Due Date" as DATE)
BETWEEN date '2007-08-31' AND date '2007-11-30' THEN 'Fiscal 2008 Q2'
WHEN CAST ("- Due Date"."Task Due Date" as DATE)
BETWEEN date '2007-11-30' AND date '2008-02-29' THEN 'Fiscal 2008 Q3'
WHEN CAST ("- Due Date"."Task Due Date" as DATE)
BETWEEN date '2008-02-29' AND date '2008-05-30' THEN 'Fiscal 2008 Q4'
ELSE NULL
END)
=
(CASE
WHEN Current_DATE
BETWEEN date '2006-05-27' AND date '2006-08-25' THEN 'Fiscal 2007 Q1'
WHEN Current_DATE
BETWEEN date '2006-08-25' AND date '2006-11-24' THEN 'Fiscal 2007 Q2'
WHEN Current_DATE
BETWEEN date '2006-11-24' AND date '2007-02-23' THEN 'Fiscal 2007 Q3'
WHEN Current_DATE
BETWEEN date '2007-02-23' AND date '2007-05-25' THEN 'Fiscal 2007 Q4'
WHEN Current_DATE
BETWEEN date '2007-05-25' AND date '2007-08-31' THEN 'Fiscal 2008 Q1'
WHEN Current_DATE
BETWEEN date '2007-08-31' AND date '2007-11-30' THEN 'Fiscal 2008 Q2'
WHEN Current_DATE
BETWEEN date '2007-11-30' AND date '2008-02-29' THEN 'Fiscal 2008 Q3'
WHEN Current_DATE
BETWEEN date '2008-02-29' AND date '2008-05-30' THEN 'Fiscal 2008 Q4'
ELSE NULL
END)
THEN
  CASE
  WHEN "- Custom Number/Integer".S_NUM_0 < 0 THEN 0
  ELSE "- Custom Number/Integer".S_NUM_0
  END
ELSE 0
END)
```

Clearly, CASE statements can be a very powerful and useful reporting tool. I have some tips on building CASE statements.

- Write down the question you are trying to answer with the CASE statements and identify the columns that contain the data needed to arrive at the answer to that question.

- Add to a report all the columns that you have identified.

- If your CASE statement includes calculations, such as a date/time formula, create columns for each of these calculations.

- Once you have all the elements of your CASE statement, begin building the formula by using the Column button on the Edit Column Formula window to insert the column formulas into your CASE statement.

If your CASE statement is going to include a lot of repetitive statements with a slight difference or two in each, it is easier to copy the beginning of the CASE statement and paste it into a text editor, where you can see more of the formula onscreen at once, copy and paste portions of the formula, and even use the search-and-replace capabilities to assist you with building the CASE statement.

Converting Data with the CAST Function

Sometimes, you may want to use data in a report for a calculation or for a concatenated value, only to learn that the data is not in the proper format for what you want to do. The CONCAT function works only with character data, for instance. With the CAST function, you can change the data type of a column in your report. The data type changes only in the report and not in the database.

The CAST function changes the data type of either a value or a null value to another data type. This change is required before you can use values of one data type in a function or operation that expects another data type.

Function Syntax

```
CAST(exp|NULL AS datatype)
CAST("- Account Custom Metrics".S_INT_0 AS FLOAT)
CAST(Account."Created Date" AS DATE)
```

You will find many instances where the CAST function is necessary to complete an operation successfully. Consider that there are three basic data type categories: numeric, string, and date/time. Within each category, you have particular data types that you can use with the CAST function to convert data from one type to another.

Table 9-2 defines the data types that are available to you for casting data into another data type. This list is not all-inclusive. It includes only the data types that are valid in Answers On Demand and have an application within CRM On Demand data. The BIT string, for instance, is not included because I have never found a successful use for it within the database.

Each data type may be converted to a limited number of other data types. Table 9-3 shows valid conversions between source types and target types using the CAST function. The first column of the table lists the source data types. The first row lists the target data types. An "X" indicates that a conversion is valid.

If a conversion is valid, CAST functions are allowed. Size incompatibilities between the source and target types can still cause run-time errors.

Converting Numeric Types

You can convert a numeric data type to any other numeric type. If the target data type is unable to represent the fractional portion of the source data, the source data is automatically truncated to fit into the target. For example, if you cast 123.4567 as an integer, the integer result is 123.

You may also cast numeric data as a character string. Doing so allows you to concatenate the data with other string data. Numeric data that you have converted to a character string cannot be referenced in a mathematical calculation until it is converted back to a numeric data type.

Data Type	Definition
INT or INTEGER	The Integer data type is a whole number between –2,147,483,648 and 2,147,483,647.
SMALLINT	The Small Integer data type is a whole number between –32,768 and 32,767.
FLOAT	The Float data type is a floating precision number with an accuracy up to seven significant decimal places. Decimal places beyond seven are rounded and not reliable.
REAL	The Real data type is a floating precision number that stores up to 12 significant decimal places. Decimal places beyond 12 are truncated.
DOUBLE or DOUBLE PRECISION	The Double Precision data type is a floating precision number that stores up to 12 significant decimal places. Decimal places beyond 12 are truncated.
CHAR CHARACTER	The Character data type is a character string. Numeric data converted to the Character date type behaves as a string, and mathematical functions are not valid. A column with the Character data type is a fixed-length column in the database with up to 8,000 characters. The fact that a column is fixed or variable length has little bearing on your reports.
VARCHAR	The Variable Character data type is a character string, just like the Character data type. The difference between VARCHAR and CHAR is really on the database table side. A column with the Variable Character data type is a variable-length column with up to 8,000 characters.
DATE	The Date data type contains a date with the month, day, and year. If you format a date value to show the date and time, the default time of 12:00:00 displayed.
TIME	The Time data type contains the hours, minutes, and seconds.
TIMESTAMP	The Timestamp data type is a combination of the Date and Time data types in that it contains both date and time information.

TABLE 9-2. *Data Types for Converting with the CAST Function*

Converting Strings

You can cast strings to any other character string. You can also, if the data matches the necessary format, cast character strings into integer numeric data and date/time data.

Data Types	SMALLINT	INTEGER	FLOAT	REAL	DOUBLE PRECISION	CHAR	VARCHAR	DATE	TIME	TIMESTAMP
SMALLINT		X	X	X	X	X	X			
INTEGER	X		X	X	X	X	X			
FLOAT	X	X		X	X	X	X			
REAL	X	X	X		X	X	X			
DOUBLE PRECISION	X	X	X	X		X	X			
CHAR	X	X					X	X	X	X
VARCHAR	X	X				X		X	X	X
DATE						X	X			X
TIME						X	X			X
TIMESTAMP						X	X	X	X	

TABLE 9-3.   *Valid CAST Conversions*

Converting Date/Time Data

You can cast any date value to and from a timestamp. If you cast a date to a timestamp, the time component is always 12:00:00. If you cast a time value to a timestamp, Answers On Demand will return a run-time error.

If you cast a timestamp to a date, the time is simply truncated from the timestamp. If you are converting to a time, the date component is truncated.

Converting a NULL Value
with the IFNULL Function

The IFNULL function evaluates a column to determine if the value in the column is null; if it is null, IFNULL assigns the provided value. When the IFNULL function encounters a record that contains a value in the column, the function returns the value in the column. This is a particularly useful function when your report data contains both populated and unpopulated fields. Often, null fields will cause your report to return incomplete results.

Function Syntax

```
IFNULL(exp, value)
IFNULL("Account Metrics"."Potential Revenue", 0)
IFNULL(Account.Industry, 'Not Provided')
```

I often use the IFNULL function to populate null fields to ensure that my calculations are completed properly. When my formula is a multiplication or division calculation, I convert null values to 1. If I am adding and subtracting, then a 0 replaces my null values. This ensures that my calculations are completed properly.

I also like to use the IFNULL function to insert a string into a null field, especially when I plan to group or chart data based on the column that contains null values.

Occasionally, you will encounter a situation where a field in a record is null, causing the record to not appear in your report. This often happens when you are including fields across multiple record types. The IFNULL function will not change this behavior. If you feel you are missing data in your report due to null fields, you will want to read Chapter 15 on combining reports.

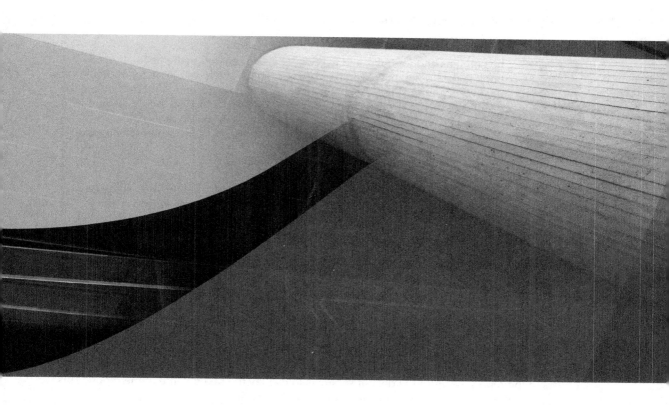

CHAPTER
10

Formatting Report Title
and Table Views

he columns and formulas and everything else discussed in the first half of this book make up the inner workings of your report. We have the motor of the report, if you will grant me the use of the analogy, and now it is time to start building the exterior of this analytics vehicle. Step 2 of the Build and View Analysis window in Answers On Demand is "Create Layout." The report layout, or visual layer, of the report is made up of views. Every visual element of your report, such as the report title, a table, and a chart, is a separate view.

By default, every report begins with two views—a Title view and a Table view. These two basic views are the topic of this chapter, within which I will discuss every feature and function of each view, and offer some tips for formatting these views to enhance your reports.

Formatting the Title View

Your Title View has some default formatting applied before you begin making any edits to the view. The default font is Arial and has a HEX color code of #6666CC, which happens to not be one of the 140 web-safe colors with a name, so I will call it On Demand Blue. The default font size for the title is 13 points. Your default title also has a thick bottom border at the Format Title View layer.

Initially, when you move to Step 2 of the Build and View Analysis window, your Title view appears to be nothing more than a blue line. Once you save and name your report, the title appears in the report, because the default setting is to display the saved name of the report. This setting and others may be changed by formatting and editing the Title view.

Within the descriptions of the various views that make up a report, I reference three different layers. You will find that there are essentially three layers that make up each view. The "base layer" is the bottom-most of the three layers. When you format a view, you are affecting the base layer. The "middle layer" is where the contents of the view reside. Editing the view and changing the content is affecting the middle layer. Finally, the "top layer" is essentially the formatting of the content of the middle layer.

Format View

In the Layout Views section of the Create Layout window, you see three buttons in the upper-right corner of the Title View (see Figure 10-1). The left button is the View Format button. Clicking this button opens an Edit Format window, shown in Figure 10-2, where you may set some formatting variables for the view base layer. (I am calling this the "base layer" because it is the bottommost of the three layers of the Title view that you can format.) As you see in Figure 10-2, at this level you can change the alignment and background color of the Title view, add a border and set the border thickness and color, and, under the Additional Formatting Options, change the sizing and padding of the view.

These settings should look familiar to you if you have done any formatting of your columns during Step 1. You can also erase, copy, and paste your settings from one view to another. In the Cell section, you have the option of left (Default), center, or right horizontal alignment, and top (Default), center, or bottom vertical alignment. These alignment settings affect the placement of the upper layers of the view on this base layer. The Background Color setting here affects only the base layer.

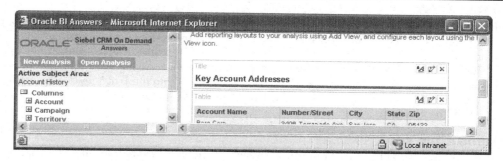

FIGURE 10-1. *Title View*

In the Border section, you can add a border to one or more sides. The Default setting at this layer is no borders. You can add borders by either selecting All in the Position field or clicking on the sides represented by the box below the Position field. Your options in the Border Style drop-down list are Single, Double, or Thick. The Default border style is thin, which applies if you make no selection.

You can set the color of the background and border for this layer by clicking the Border Color box and then clicking one of the 48 colors in the color selector window. You may also enter the HTML color code in the field to the immediate left of the Restore Default button. (You can find HTML color codes through a simple Internet search.) The default setting is the absence of color.

The Additional Formatting Options section contains fields that allow you to set the height, width, and padding of the base layer. These settings affect the base layer, so adding padding, for example, adds space between the border of the base layer and the upper layers.

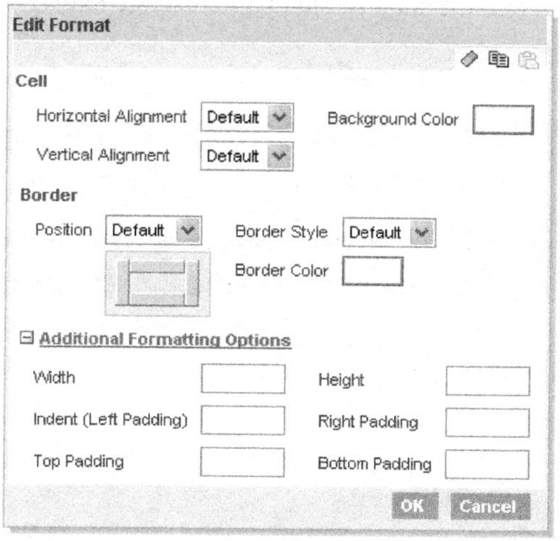

FIGURE 10-2. *Title View—Edit Format window*

Edit View

Back in the main Create Layout window (refer to Figure 10-1), the second of the three buttons on the title view is the Edit View button. Clicking this button opens the Edit View: Title window, where you can adjust the settings for the middle layer of the title. This layer identifies the various components of the Title view. By default, the only elements of the title are the saved name of your report and the bottom border on the layer. From the Edit View: Title window, you add, edit, and format the elements of the Title view. Here you are affecting the middle and top layers of the view.

Format Title View

The light-blue bar at the top of the Edit View section includes two buttons: the Format Title View button and the Import Format button. Using the Import Format button is a great shortcut for making all of your title views appear the same. Click the Import Format button, browse to the report you want to import from, and select the report. The format settings on the middle layer of the Title View are set to match the source report.

The Format Title View button opens an Edit View window that looks and acts very much like the Edit View window from the base layer. If you did not resize your base layer, any formatting you add here to the middle layer will cover, not replace, the formatting on the base layer. In other words, if you add a background color of blue on the base layer, and then add a white background to the middle layer, your title's background will appear white. With no resizing or padding, the only visible element from the base layer would be a border.

Resizing or adding padding to this middle layer affects the layer itself, not the text that you add to the text layer on top of this middle layer. The title view elements are placed on top of the middle layer and may contain formatting of their own. Notice in Figure 10-3 that I have added a dark color to my base layer with some padding on all sides. To my middle layer, I have added a light color.

Add Title View Elements

If you want to show a custom title rather than the saved report name, type in the Title field the title that you want to appear and then uncheck the Display Saved Name check box. If you add

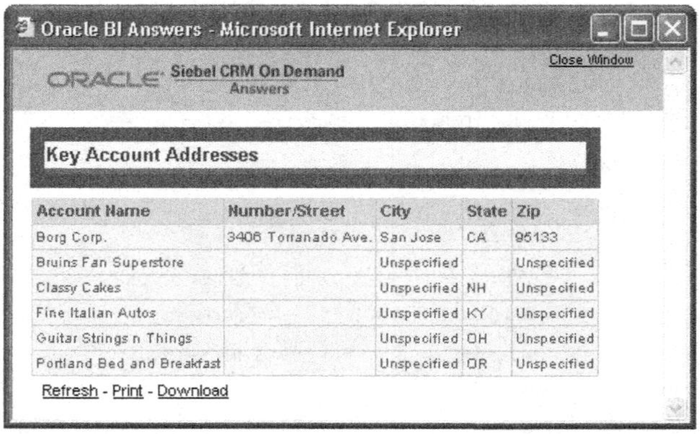

FIGURE 10-3. *Example of formatting title layers*

a custom title and do not uncheck the Display Saved Name check box, both your custom title and the report title will be displayed on your report.

Place an image URL in the Logo field to include a logo or other graphic in your Title view. The logo is placed to the immediate left of your title text.

If you want a subtitle on your report that appears just below the title, add your subtitle text to the Subtitle field. Only text may be included in the Title and Subtitle fields.

It is often helpful to include information about when the report was run. In the Started Time field, you have the option of selecting Date, Time, or Date and Time for display in your title view. Of course, you may leave the default setting of Do Not Display if you do not want to display a date or time in your title view.

The final field is for a URL to a custom online help link. You may reference only custom help files that are located on the Analytics server. Enter the URL in this field, prefaced with **FMAP:** to link to the help file. A question mark icon appears in your title view on your report. Clicking this icon will access the designated file. Contact Customer Care to discuss adding files to the appropriate location on the server if you want to use this feature.

Format Values

Most of the Title view elements have their own formatting settings. You will find a Format Values button next to the Title, Logo, Subtitle, and Started Time fields. Within each of these Edit Title windows, you can apply formatting to each individual element. In Figure 10-4, I have added every element to a title view, with a different shade of background and some padding to make the edges of each layer visible. The relative location of each element is fixed, though it is possible to change alignment, size, and colors.

As you adjust the settings for this and other views, you see a preview of how the view will appear on your report. The Display Results section at the bottom of the edit windows usually

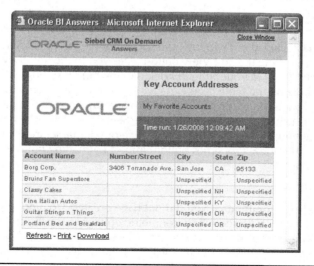

FIGURE 10-4. *Title View showing all elements*

updates automatically as you make changes to the view format. You may also refresh the preview by clicking the Display Results link. If you do not want to see the preview, you can remove the check mark from the corresponding check box and the preview will not show. With some complex views, you may find it helpful to turn off the Display Results preview, for better performance during your layout edits.

Formatting the Table View

Every report also starts with a basic table view, which includes all visible columns that you have included in your report. The formatting of the cell values in the table view is based on the column formatting set in Step 1. The header row displays the column name of each column. If you set a custom name for any columns in Step 1, those custom names are applied on the table view. The sort order set in Step 1 also controls the sort order of the data in the table view. If no specific sorts are set, the table sorts data in ascending order, beginning with the leftmost column.

Paging controls appear in the table view if there are more than 25 records in the result set. These paging controls provide navigation buttons to page through the results one page at a time and buttons to display all pages and to return to the first page of results. The default location for these paging controls is below the table. You can change this setting and others by formatting and editing the Table view.

Format View

Like the Title view, the Table view has a base layer on which the table sits. You may apply some formatting to this base layer to change the default settings. Click the Format View button on the Table view from the Step 2 window to open the Edit Format window. Similar to the Edit Format window for formatting titles, here you may set the horizontal and vertical alignment to adjust how the table appears on top of the base layer, as well as choose settings for background color, borders, size, and padding.

Edit View

Back in the main Create Layout window, the second of the three buttons on the Title view is the Edit View button. Clicking the Edit View button takes you to the Edit View: Table window, where you can apply formatting to your table. By default, any format settings you made to your columns in Step 1 are set here on the table. You can change your column formatting here using the same format tools that you used in Step 1. You can also add, move, and remove columns while editing your table, but it is usually easier to do this in the Step 1 window. The elements of the Edit View: table window that you use to affect the appearance of your table are the Grand Total and Total By buttons, Edit Table View Properties button, Import Formatting button, Refresh button, and the Display selector.

Totals

A new element on the column that you did not have on Step 1 of your report development is the presence of the Total By button on your nonmetric columns. This button has a Greek sigma (S) on it and appears to be grayed out or unavailable. This simply indicates that you have not added a subtotal for that column. Click a column's Total By button to activate totaling and include a subtotal in all metric columns for each value in the column. The aggregation rules on the metric columns dictate how the values are aggregated. Once you have activated totaling on a column, if you click the Total By button again, you receive a pop-up menu with some additional settings (see Figure 10-5).

Select None on the pop-up menu to remove the subtotals from your report column. The only location option for the subtotals is After, so you always see a check mark next to After on this menu. Likewise, the Report-Based Total selection has a check mark next to it by default. This indicates that the total will include only the values that appear in the report. In rare instances, if you feel that relevant values are being excluded from your total, you may try clicking this menu item to remove the check mark and see how it affects your report.

Click the Format Labels menu item to apply formatting to the subtotal measurement label. The default value is the value in the column field followed by "Total." If you would rather have some other label for your subtotals or would like to apply a new format to the label cell in the table, click Format Labels to open the Edit Format window. The Edit Format window is one you should be familiar with at this point in the book, but you will see a new field here. The Folder field, the name of which is misleading, is actually the measurement label; entering a new value into this field changes your measurement label.

Click the Format Measure Values menu item to open the Edit Format window and adjust the format settings of the column subtotal values.

Moving up to the title bar above the columns, you will find another button with S on it. This is the Grand Total button, and it functions the same as and contains the same options as the Total By button. The difference is that the Grand Total button adds a Total row at the bottom of your table.

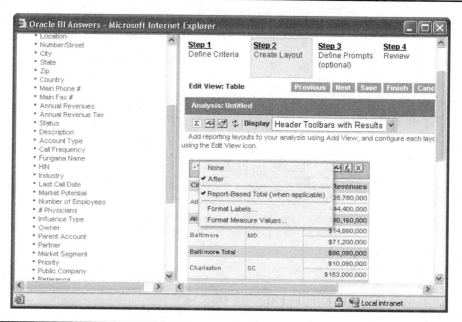

FIGURE 10-5. *Total By menu*

Edit Table View Properties

To the immediate right of the Grand Total button is the Edit Table View Properties button. Clicking this button opens the Edit View window, shown in Figure 10-6. The lower half of this window should be familiar to you. The five fields at the top of this window are properties specific to the Table View.

The Paging Controls field allows you to control if and where the table paging controls will appear. Paging controls are the navigation arrows that appear in a table view when the result data contains more than 25 records. You can choose to display the paging controls at the top or bottom of the table view. If you select Hide This Column in the Paging Controls field, the paging controls will not appear on your report.

CAUTION
If your result data contains more than 25 records and you have hidden the paging controls, your users will not be able to access the records beyond the first 25, unless you have changed the number of rows displayed on each page.

The Rows per Page field is a free-form numeric field in which you can set the number of rows to include on each table page. The minimum value accepted is 1.

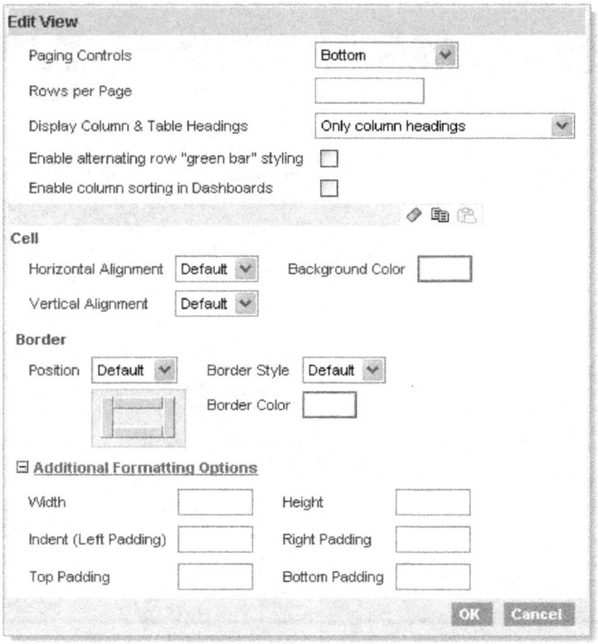

FIGURE 10-6. *Edit View window*

The Display Column & Table Headings field gives you control over which values appear in the column headings and how they should appear. The default setting is to display only column headings. You may also choose to display both column and table headings. You can display the table headings as a separate row or before the column heading on the same row. The As Table.Column (Where Needed) option results in both the table name and column name to appear in the column heading for those columns that have the same name. You also have the option to not display a heading row on the table, by selecting No Column or Table Headings.

Checking the Enable Alternating Row "Green Bar" Styling check box applies light-green background shading to every other row in the table. This can enhance readability of tabular reports that have many rows. If you want to use the green-bar styling, be sure to set your table columns to repeat values rather than suppress values. (This setting is on the Column Format tab of the Column Properties window.) I make this suggestion because when values in a column group across rows, this can throw off the green-bar styling, causing the shading to occur in different rows, as shown in Figure 10-7.

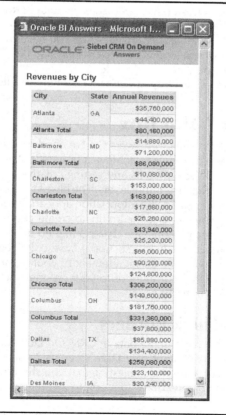

FIGURE 10-7. *Green-bar styling with grouped data*

Choosing the Enable Column Sorting in Dashboards option activates column sorting in your table. Users will be able to click a column header to sort the data by that column. This feature works very much like the column sorting in a record list.

Import Formatting

If you have formatted a table in another report and want to apply the same formatting to tables in a new report, you do not have to do all of that formatting over again to apply consistent formatting to all of your report tables. Clicking the Import Formatting from Another Analysis button enables you to apply all the table formatting from another report to your current table. This overwrites all the formatting on the columns and the table that you have set using the Column Properties and Edit Table View Properties buttons, including borders, backgrounds, fonts, and sizing.

To import table formatting from another report, simply click this button and select the report that contains the formatting you want to duplicate. If you have applied formatting to the base level of the view, that formatting is not affected by importing a format from another report.

Refresh and Display Selector

The next two tools in this view affect only the way your table appears in the preview in the Edit View: Table window. The Refresh button refreshes the data in the table. Do not use the browser refresh while editing your table. Doing so will return you back to Step 1 of the Build and View Analysis window and you will lose any changes that you have made.

The Display field allows you to control what displays in the preview in the Edit View: Table window. By default, the display includes Header Toolbars with Results. You may choose to display Header Toolbars Only or Results Only by selecting a different value from the Display field.

"LayOUTside" the Box

One of my favorite things to do with Answers On Demand in my CRM On Demand implementations is to figure out ways to achieve a unique look for a report. This often means stepping outside the normal design habits and getting creative.

The title and table views have multiple layers. The base layer usually goes unnoticed and unused. After all, the data layer is where all of the information appears. Table columns usually come from the database, but they do not have to. Use the ability to create your own column formulas to enhance your design. When it comes to reports, the data is king, no doubt, but the design makes a report more interesting and more usable. In this section, I have collected a handful of some of my favorite tricks and tips for taking the design element of your reports to the next level. I hope that you not only apply some of these design tips to your reports, but also expand on them to come up with your own favorite design tricks.

Applying Extra-Thick Borders

If you define a report as a picture of the data in CRM On Demand, then why not put that picture in a frame? With this tip, you can put your table view inside of a virtual frame, as shown in the example in Figure 10-8. No, I am not suggesting that you should frame all of your tables in this way, but if you ever need to really draw attention to an element of your report, this is one way to do just that.

To create this effect, apply a background color to the base layer of your title or table view. Remember, you format the base level of your views in the Step 2 window, where all the views on your report are visible. Click the Format View button to open the Edit Format window. Select the

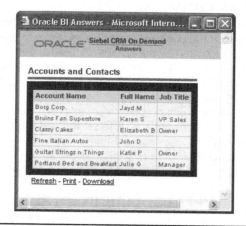

FIGURE 10-8.   *Thick table-border trick*

background color of your choice. Next, determine how thick you want your frame. The thickness I used in Figure 10-8 is 10 points. Expand the Additional Formatting Options section and add padding to all four sides of the base view layer, as shown in Figure 10-9.

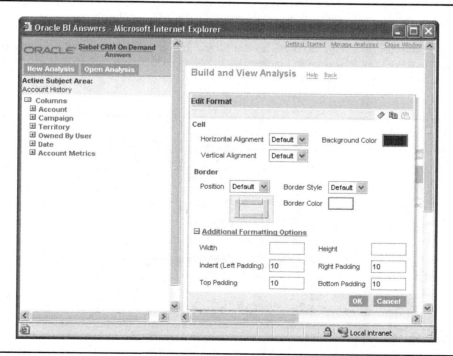

FIGURE 10-9.   *Configuring a thick table border in the Edit Format window*

Displaying Totals Only

Sometimes the sum of the parts is more important than the parts, but you may still want to see some information about what the parts are. Take, for example, a team of sales associates. Suppose that these salespeople are rewarded by the team's total sales, but you don't want the salespeople to know the individual sales of their teammates. It is important, however, to show the accounts involved in those sales. So, you want to see the total but not the numbers that make up that total, as shown in Figure 10-10.

There is actually quite a lot going on here to get this final look. The primary thing that you must do to make the row values "disappear" is to set the column background and font to the same color. Some other adjustments you might like to make include changing the cell borders to the same color to make them not visible as well. In the example shown in Figure 10-10, I also changed the Display Column & Table Headings setting to remove the column headings.

Applying a Thick Vertical Line in a Table

Sometimes you may want to separate groups of data in your table. It is quite easy to insert a column in your table and convert that column to a thick vertical line, like those shown in Figure 10-11.

The first step is to add a column to you report. Any column will do, because you are going to strip it of its identity by replacing the column formula with two single quotes. This changes the column to a character string, because the first single quote indicates the beginning of a string and the second single quote indicates the end of the string. You will also want to replace the table and column heading with a space, to blank those out as well. These steps give you a blank column in your report. Next, apply a background color to the column. You then have a thick vertical line in your table.

Combine this trick with the thick-border trick and you can create an interesting view of the data, as in the example shown in Figure 10-12.

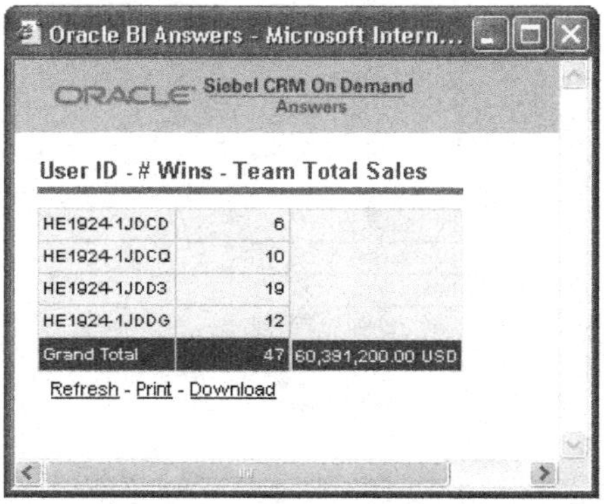

FIGURE 10-10.   *Team Total Sales report with individual total sales hidden*

Account ID	Account Type	Priority	Full Name	Job Title	Work Phone #	SR Number	Area	Status
HE1924-1JDP7	Prospect	High	Jeremy Phishman	Sales Manager	+1 302 9464802	SR-5802	Installation	Open
			Leonard McDonald	Vice President	+1 302 9464801	SR-5801	Maintenance	Open
HE1924-1JDPJ	Customer	Medium	Adam Cohen	Service Manager	+1 202 9927701	SR-5701	Installation	Cancelled
HE1924-1JDPU	Customer	High	David Murray	CEO	+1 878 3822601	SR-5601	Maintenance	Open
HE1924-1JDQ6	Prospect	High	Al Yeung	President	+1 614 5877501	SR-5501	Training	Closed
HE1924-1JDQH	Customer	High	Chris Darnten	Sales Manager	+1 410 6977401	SR-5401	Product	Closed
HE1924-1JDQT	Prospect	High	Rebecca Milstein	Service Manager	+1 212 7244301	SR-5301	Product	Open - Escalated
HE1924-1JDR4	Customer	High	Alexander Cone	Vice President	+1 302 4842201	SR-5201	Installation	Open
HE1924-1JDRG	Prospect	High	Jennifer Miller	President	+1 202 7632101	SR-5101	Training	Closed
HE1924-1JDRS	Prospect	High	Russell Graham	Sales Manager	+1 878 7352001	SR-5001	Training	Closed
HE1924-1JDS3	Prospect	High	Jason Cheney	Service Manager	+1 614 2265901	SR-4901	Training	Cancelled
HE1924-1JDSF	Customer	High	Marianne Pok	Marketing Manager	+1 410 4725801	SR-4801	Product	Open
HE1924-1JDSR	Prospect	Medium	James Mills	President	+1 212 7467701	SR-4701	Training	Cancelled
HE1924-1JDT3	Customer	Low	Mark Clatt	Sales Manager	+1 470 5236601	SR-4601	Maintenance	Closed
HE1924-1JDTF	Customer	Medium	Robin Coxe	Service Manager	+1 305 4347501	SR-4501	Installation	Closed
HE1924-1JDTR	Prospect	Medium	Bill Maier	Sales Manager	+1 843 2953402	SR-4402	Installation	Open
			Ruth Chou	CEO	+1 843 2953401	SR-4401	Product	Closed
HE1924-1JDU3	Customer	High	Anne Dahl	Vice President	+1 901 7633301	SR-4301	Product	Closed
HE1924-1JDUF	Customer	Medium	Travis Matthews	Sales Manager	+1 704 6237201	SR-4201	Product	Closed
HE1924-1JDUR	Customer	Low	Joel Derfner	Service Manager	+1 804 3377101	SR-4101	Product	Open
HE1924-1JDV3	Customer	Low	Mark Kotter	Sales Manager	+1 470 2237001	SR-4001	Maintenance	Closed
HE1924-1JDVF	Prospect	Medium	Jane Markson	Sales Manager	+1 305 9932901	SR-3901	Maintenance	Closed
HE1924-1JDVR	Customer	Low	David Cuthbery	Service Manager	+1 843 9823801	SR-3801	Product	Closed
HE1924-1JDW3	Prospect	Low	Sean Desmond	CEO	+1 901 9565701	SR-3701	Maintenance	Open
HE1924-1JDWF	Prospect	Low	Joseph Mullin	President	+1 704 6848601	SR-3601	Installation	Closed

Records 1 - 25

FIGURE 10-11. *Account Contact SR report with thick vertical lines*

Displaying Images in the Table Row

Using different data formats really opens up a lot of possibilities with your table. One of the data format options is the HTML image tag. Place an image URL in a column of your report and set the data type to image URL. Be sure that the image is located somewhere on a Web server accessible to your users, such as the company web site. The image will appear in your table cell.

There are not too many situations in which you would want to display an image in a report, but it is quite effective in those situations when you want to add a visual element to your report. I can imagine a report that you would print that includes a company logo or a product snapshot or a photograph of the customer's account representative. With the ability to print in color becoming more and more affordable, images in a table can be quite engaging.

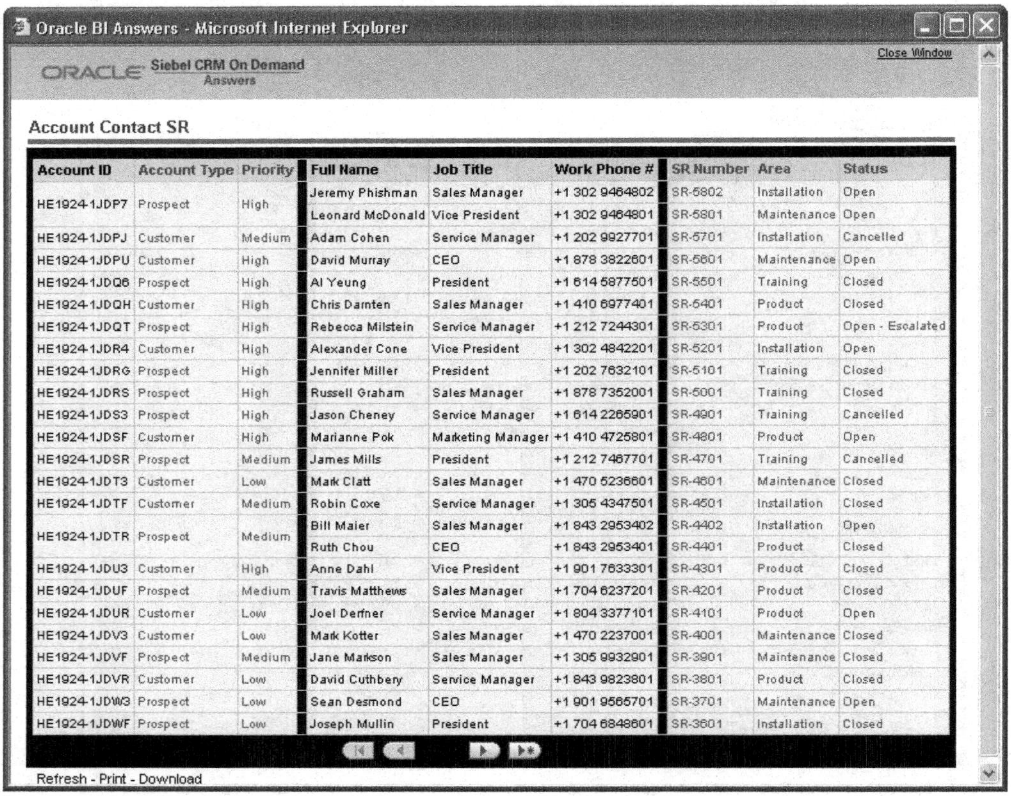

FIGURE 10-12. *Account Contact SR report with thick border*

Figure 10-13 is a simple report that shows property information along with an image of the home design. The simple addition of an image adds interest and provides information that just words and numbers cannot provide.

Formatting with HTML

The great thing about working in a hosted, browser-based application like CRM On Demand is that you can take advantage of HTML within your reports. Simply change the Data Type on your column to HTML and you can use many of the common HTML tags to format the text within the table column. For instance, suppose you want to apply a format to only part of your column text.

10_13 - Microsoft Internet Explorer
ORACLE Siebel CRM On Demand Answers
10_13
Property Information
Neighborhood Name | Lot # | Plan Name | Layout
Estes Estates East | 49 | Hickory
Refresh - Print - Download

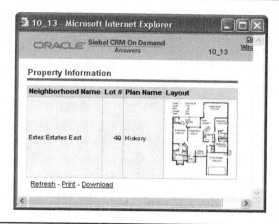

FIGURE 10-13. *Property Information report*

The standard formatting controls are all or nothing. Everything in the column is bold or everything in the column is not bold. In Figure 10-14, I have used the CONCAT function to bring some data into my report, but have applied some character formatting to only the data I am pulling from the database.

I encourage you to get creative when you are designing your reports—to "LayOUTside" the box.

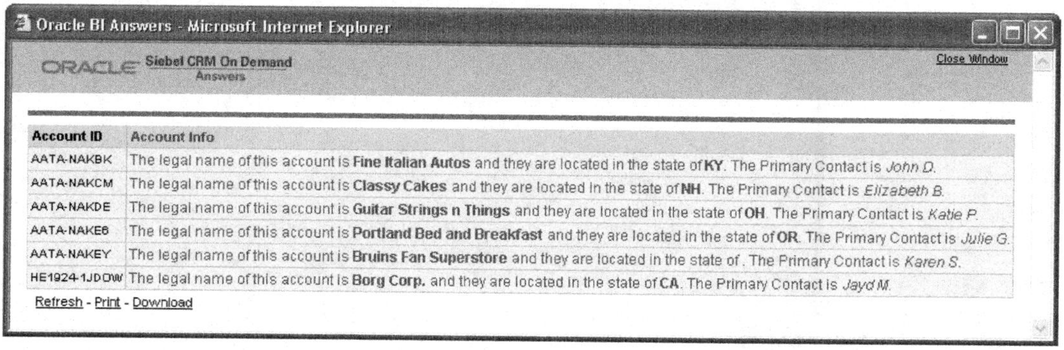

Oracle BI Answers - Microsoft Internet Explorer
ORACLE Siebel CRM On Demand Answers
Close Window
Account ID | Account Info
AATA-NAKBK | The legal name of this account is Fine Italian Autos and they are located in the state of KY. The Primary Contact is John D.
AATA-NAKCM | The legal name of this account is Classy Cakes and they are located in the state of NH. The Primary Contact is Elizabeth B.
AATA-NAKDE | The legal name of this account is Guitar Strings n Things and they are located in the state of OH. The Primary Contact is Katie P.
AATA-NAKE6 | The legal name of this account is Portland Bed and Breakfast and they are located in the state of OR. The Primary Contact is Julie G.
AATA-NAKEY | The legal name of this account is Bruins Fan Superstore and they are located in the state of . The Primary Contact is Karen S.
HE1924-1JDOW | The legal name of this account is Borg Corp. and they are located in the state of CA. The Primary Contact is Jayd M.
Refresh - Print - Download

FIGURE 10-14. *Account Information report with HTML formatting*

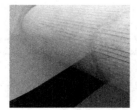

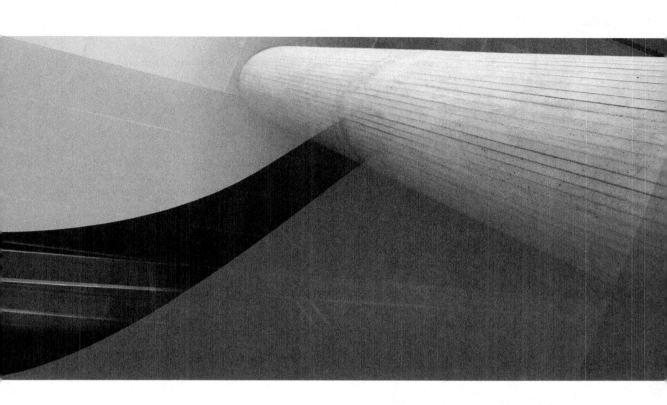

CHAPTER
11

Adding Charts and
Graphs to Reports

picture is worth a thousand words." This common quotation, the origin of which is uncertain though often misattributed as a Chinese proverb, has come to be a staple of justification for adding visuals to the print medium. Regardless of how many words a picture can replace, there certainly seems to be a number of advantages to visually enhancing your reports.

Executives are stereotyped, and often live up to the stereotype, as individuals who want to know everything but want to get the information quickly and at a glance. It is hard to deny that charts and graphs are powerful allies to the report developer in summarizing data and delivering a message quickly.

Introduction to Chart Views

As I was completing my graduate degree, I took a few statistics classes and, much to my surprise, enjoyed them. One of my favorite exercises in one class was to explore printed materials for charts that provided a poor or misleading (often purposely) picture of statistical data. One daily nationwide newspaper provided a daily source of classroom examples. The purpose of the exercise was to demonstrate that charting not only is a very effective and efficient means of delivering analytical data within your report, but also a very effective and efficient means for delivering misleading data within your report. The lesson is that you must choose your charts wisely and format them with usability and understandability in mind.

Using the Chart View

On Step 2 of the Build and View Analysis window, you will find the Add View button just above the preview of your report views. Clicking this button opens a menu of views that you can insert into your report (see Figure 11-1). One of these options is Chart. Selecting Chart inserts a basic chart into your report.

NOTE
Among the options in the Add View menu are two other views, Gauge view and, under the Advanced submenu, Funnel Chart view. Because these views are basically charts, they are described later in this chapter, in the "Advanced Charts" section.

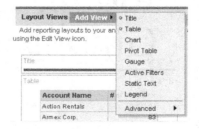

FIGURE 11-1. *Add View menu*

Chart Controls

On Step 2 of the Build and View Analysis window, you always start with a Title view and a Table view. To add additional views, you click the Add View button and select a view type from the list. Selecting Chart takes you to the Chart Edit View (see Figure 11-2) with a default chart type of Vertical Bar.

The buttons and fields in the header bar above the chart allow you to set the properties and chart type for your Chart view. These charting controls are very similar across all chart types. I normally skip past the six buttons and go straight to the Graph, Type, and Style fields to identify the type of chart I want to insert into my report, so those fields are described first, followed by the six buttons.

Graph, Type, and Style Fields

In the Graph drop-down list (see Figure 11-3), select the form of chart that you want to insert into your report. Your options include Area, Horizontal Bar, Bubble, Vertical Bar, Line, Line Bar Combo, Pareto, Pie, Radar, Scatter, and Step. When you select a value from the Graph drop-down list, the chart preview updates to display the selected graph with the current settings.

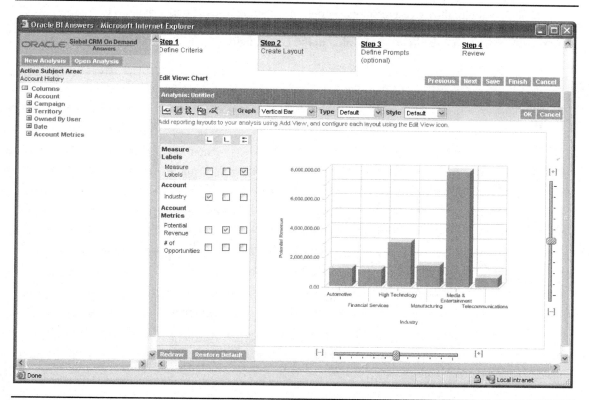

FIGURE 11-2.   *Edit View: Chart*

FIGURE 11-3. *Graph options*

The Type field varies slightly depending on the value you have selected in the Graph field. In most cases, you can choose a three-dimensional or two-dimensional appearance for your chart. The bar-style graphs (horizontal bar, vertical bar, and line bar combo) have added options for two- and three-dimensional stacked types. The Scatter graph Type values are Scatter and Scatter with Lines. When you select a value from the Type drop-down list, the chart preview updates to display the chart with the selected type.

The Style field allows you to select shapes and shading formats depending on the graph selected. Not every graph has options available in the Style field. Table 11-1 describes the Type and Style options available for each value in the Graph field.

Graph	Type	Style
Area	Default (3D)	Default (Solid Fill)
	3D	Solid Fill
	2D	Pattern Fill
Horizontal Bar	Default (3D)	Default (Rectangle)
	3D	Rectangle
	2D	Cylinder
	3D Stacked	Gradient
	2D Stacked	Triangle
		Diamond
		Pattern Fill (Rectangle Shape)
Bubble	N/A	N/A
Vertical Bar	Default (3D)	Default (Rectangle)
	3D	Rectangle
	2D	Cylinder
	3D Stacked	Gradient
	2D Stacked	Triangle
		Diamond
		Pattern Fill (Rectangle Shape)

TABLE 11-1. *Graph, Type, and Style Options*

Graph	Type	Style
Line	Default (3D) 3D 2D	N/A
Line Bar Combo	Default (3D) 3D 2D 3D Stacked 2D Stacked	Default (Rectangle) Rectangle Cylinder Gradient Triangle Diamond Pattern Fill (Rectangle Shape)
Pareto	Default (3D) 3D 2D	Default (Rectangle) Rectangle Cylinder Gradient Triangle Diamond Pattern Fill (Rectangle Shape)
Pie	Default (3D) 3D 2D	Default (Solid Fill) Solid Fill Pattern Fill
Radar	N/A	N/A
Scatter	Default (Scatter) Scatter Scatter with Lines	N/A
Step	Default (3D) 3D 2D	N/A

TABLE 11-1. *Graph, Type, and Style Options*

General Chart Properties Button

The leftmost button on the title bar is the General Chart Properties button. The icon for the General Chart Properties button is very similar to the Column Properties icon you are accustomed to seeing on the columns in Step 1. Click this button and the General Chart Properties dialog box opens (see Figure 11-4).

In the General Chart Properties dialog box, you can format the title, data labels, and chart size. By default, your chart does not have a title. To add a title, check the Custom Title check box and type your desired title in the Title field. Click the Text Format button next to the Title field to set the font family, color, style, and font size for your title in the Text Format dialog box (see Figure 11-5). You may also indicate the number of characters to display in your title by using the Truncate field (of course, you could simply enter the title in truncated form in the Title field and ignore the Truncate field).

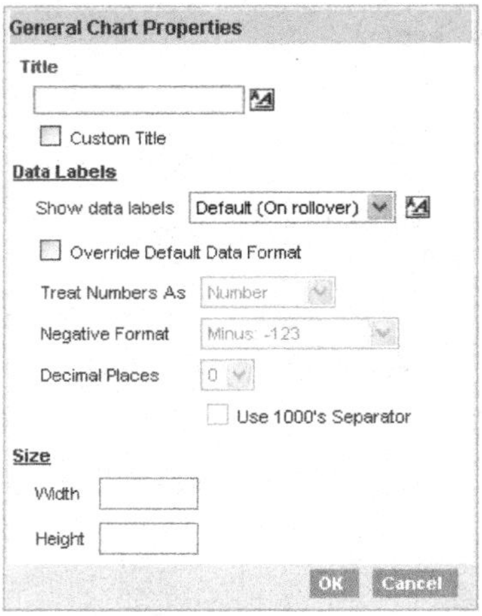

FIGURE 11-4. *General Chart Properties dialog box*

In the Data Labels section of the General Chart Properties dialog box, you can set how and when data labels appear in your chart. The default setting for showing data labels is to show them on rollover, which means an element's data label is displayed whenever the mouse pointer moves over that element. You may click the Text Format button next to your chosen data label setting to modify the font appearance.

Check the Override Default Data Format check box if you want your values to display in a different format. In the Treat Numbers As drop-down list, your choices are to display your numbers as numbers, currency, or percentages. You may also adjust the format for negative values, in the Negative Format field. Finally, you may select the number of decimal places to include in the data values and choose whether to use a thousands separator within the values.

If you have identified a new data format on the columns already, then that selected format is used by default. You can change that format by using the fields just described.

The Size section of the General Chart Properties dialog box allows you to adjust the overall size of the chart in your report. To set the chart size, you may enter values (in points) in the Height and Width fields or use the sliders beneath and to the right of the chart preview. The benefit of using the Height and Width fields is that you can set the size very precisely and beyond the limits of the sliders. Using the sliders, the width range is 90 to 810 points and the height range is 60 to 540 points.

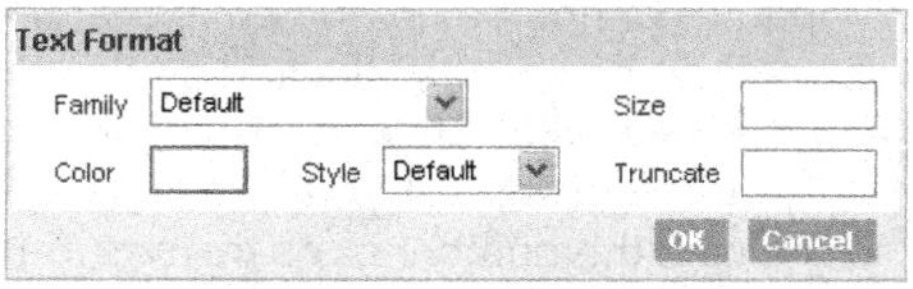

FIGURE 11-5. *Text Format dialog box*

Axis Titles & Labels Button

The next button (second from left) on the title bar is the Axis Titles & Labels button. Clicking this button opens the Axis Titles & Labels dialog box, which contains two or three tabs, depending on the chart type. The Left tab (and Right tab for some charts) allows you to configure the title and label formats of the vertical axis (see Figure 11-6). The Title section controls the axis title, which defaults to the column name for the values displayed along that axis. You can change the title by checking the Custom Title check box and typing a new value in the Title field. Format the title's appearance by using the Text Format button next to the Title field.

The Labels section of the Left or Right tab contains a series of fields allowing you to format the scale labels. Unchecking the Display Scale Labels check box turns the labels off. If you want to keep the labels (by leaving the box checked), you can format the appearance of those labels by clicking the Text Format button next to the field (to open a Text Format dialog box similar to Figure 11-5) and by using the remaining check boxes and fields on the Left or Right tab.

Which fields appear on the tab depends on whether your scale labels are text or numbers. When formatting either text or numeric scale labels, you can choose to rotate those labels by checking the Rotate Labels check box and select the angle you want to use. Your options range from 90 to –90 degrees. Answers On Demand may only rotate the values if space constraints make it necessary.

Two options for text scale labels are to stagger the labels or to skip labels if necessary. These two check boxes appear on the tab when the scale labels are alphanumeric. When your scale labels are numeric, you have the option of abbreviating the number by percentage, thousands, millions, billions, and trillions. Check the Abbreviate check box and select the abbreviation type from the drop-down list. You can also override the numeric data format by checking the Override Default Data Format check box and then identifying how you want to treat the numbers, which negative format you want to use, and how many decimal places you want to include. You also have the option of using the thousands separator.

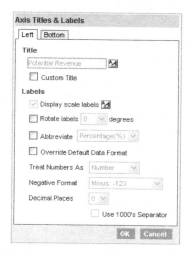

FIGURE 11-6.   *Axis Titles & Labels dialog box*

The Bottom tab also has a Title section and a Labels section for modifying the title and scale labels of the bottom axis. The options are exactly the same as those on the Left tab for an alphanumeric data type.

Axis Scaling Button

The next button (with the green double-headed arrow) is the Axis Scaling button. Clicking this button takes you to the Axis Scaling dialog box (see Figure 11-7), where you find, in my opinion, some of the most dangerous options within charting. The Axis Scaling dialog box has one or two tabs, depending on the type of chart you have selected. A line bar combo chart, for instance, has a scale on the left vertical axis and on the right vertical axis. Both the Left and Right tabs in the Axis Scaling dialog box contain the same fields but may have different settings within those fields.

The Axis Limits section allows you to control the value range for your chart axis. This is where you can really damage the validity of your analysis. You can consider a report valid when it accurately measures what it is intended to measure. This level of validity will have both construct validity and content validity. A properly constructed report has construct validity. A report that contains the correct data has content validity. It is possible to have construct validity without content validity if data is missing. It is also possible to have content validity without construct validity if you have all the correct data but your report does not analyze that data properly.

One other very important type of validity that is often not considered is face validity. An analysis has face validity if it appears to measure data accurately. It is entirely possible to create a report that appears to include all the data and to analyze data properly but that does neither. This report may still have face validity if your user accepts that it is complete and accurate, even though it is a completely invalid report.

A dishonest report developer may even focus on creating face validity while knowingly disregarding content and construct validity. An honest report developer could very easily unknowingly do the same. Axis scaling is one of the favorite tools of dishonest report developers looking for face validity and nothing more. By tweaking the scales on the chart, small bits of data can look large and huge numbers can appear insignificant.

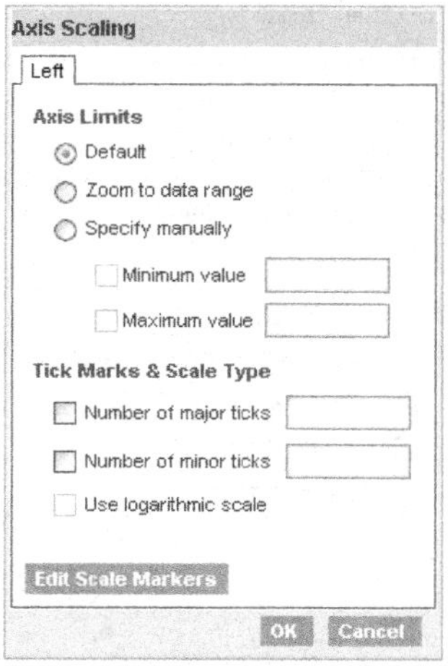

FIGURE 11-7. *Axis Scaling dialog box*

Within the Axis Limits section, you have three choices:

- **Default** The scale is determined dynamically based on the upper and lower numbers within the data you are charting.

- **Zoom to Data Range** Similar to the Default scale but adjusts the axis scale so that the data represented in the chart occupies roughly three-quarters of the scale.

- **Specify manually** Use the Minimum Value and Maximum Value check boxes and fields to manually set the upper, lower, or both thresholds of the chart. This is where you risk skewing the perception of the data significance. It is very easy to include a large maximum value and cause the data to appear small and insignificant, or to set a maximum value too low and cause small insignificant data to appear large and significant. Of course, you can also set the minimum value in order to change the appearance of your data. Examine Figures 11-8 through 11-11. All four of these charts show the exact same data but only Figure 11-11 reflects the data honestly.

The next section in the Axis Scaling dialog box, Tick Marks & Scale Type, allows you to adjust the number of horizontal major and minor ticks present on your axis scale. The easiest way to figure out how many ticks you should insert is to take the top number of the scale and divide by the size of each major section of your scale, and then add one. So, if your maximum scale value is 200 and you want a major tick at every five units, you would set the number of major ticks to 41 (200 / 5 = 40 + 1 = 41).

You may also specify the number of minor ticks. This number is the number of ticks between your major ticks. To determine the number of minor ticks, divide the span between major ticks by the size of your desired minor tick and then subtract one. For instance, if your chart has a major tick at every 40 units and you want a minor tick at every 5 units, you need seven minor ticks (40 / 5 = 8 − 1 = 7).

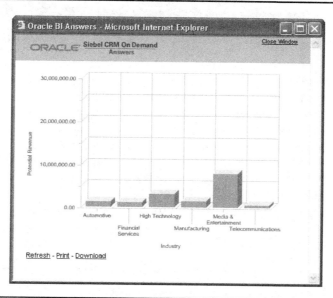

FIGURE 11-8. *Chart with increased maximum value*

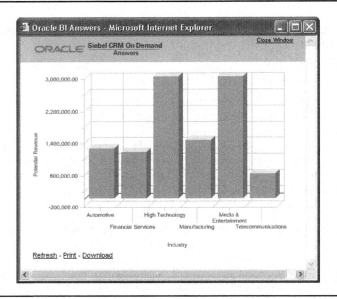

FIGURE 11-9. *Chart with reduced maximum value*

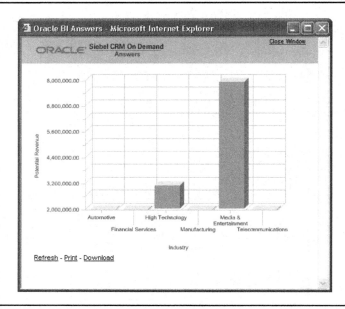

FIGURE 11-10. *Chart with increased minimum value*

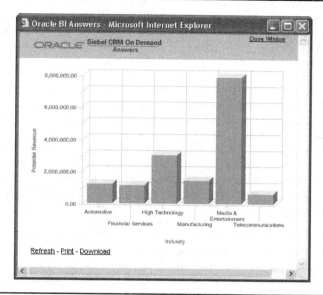

FIGURE 11-11. *Chart with appropriate scale*

Checking the final check box in this dialog box, Use Logarithmic Scale, changes your scale from a standard scale to a logarithmic scale. The logarithmic scale of measurement uses the logarithm of a physical measurement rather than the measurement itself. Logarithmic scales have very specific applications, usually with datasets that have very large ranges or some statistical analyses.

Click the Edit Scale Markers button at the bottom of the Axis Scaling dialog box to open the Scale Markers dialog box (see Figure 11-12), where you can add to your chart markers in the form of lines or ranges. To add a marker, click the Add button. Give the marker a name in the Caption field. This caption will appear in the chart's legend. Select the type of marker, either Line or Range, in the Type drop-down list. The purpose of next two fields depends on your selection in the Type field.

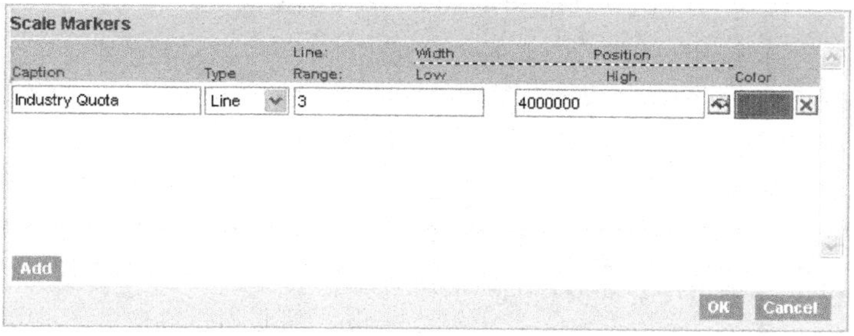

FIGURE 11-12. *Scale Markers dialog box*

For a line marker, the first field is the width of the line, in points. The second field identifies the position of the marker line on your axis scale. The Advanced Options button to the right of the Position field opens an Advanced Options dialog box that allows you to use a column value to position your marker line. For instance, if you have included a column that calculates an average value, you could use that column to locate your marker in order to identify the average value on your chart. If you identify a column for your marker that contains different values across the rows of your table, the marker will appear at the first value that it encounters in the table. Sorting your data may affect which record determines the marker position. I find that using a column that contains a consistent value across all rows usually makes the most sense. An example might be a total or average aggregated amount.

The variable and SQL options for the marker within the Advanced Options dialog box are carry-overs from the enterprise version of Analytics and are not functional in Answers On Demand. You can also set the color for your marker line by clicking the color selector and selecting a new color from the palate or entering an HTML color code and clicking OK.

For a range marker, the first field identifies the low end of the range and the second field identifies the high end of the range. The Advanced Options dialog box for each of these fields is the same as I described for the line marker. A range marker applies shading on the background across the width of your chart between the marker amounts specified.

Figure 11-13 shows a chart with a line marker and a range marker. Notice that a line marker appears in the foreground of the chart and the range marker appears in the background.

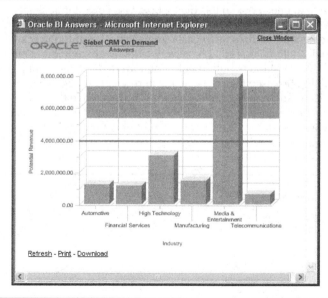

FIGURE 11-13. *Line marker and range marker*

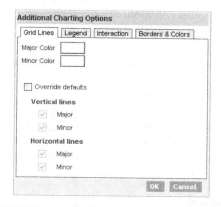

FIGURE 11-14. *Additional Charting Options dialog box—Grid Lines tab*

Additional Charting Options Button

To the right of the Axis Scaling button is the Additional Charting Options button. Clicking this button opens the Additional Charting Options dialog box (see Figure 11-14). This dialog box contains four tabs, each dedicated to a different element of your chart:

- **Grid Lines** Allows you to change the color of the major and minor grid lines. Checking the Override Defaults check box enables the check boxes on the tab that allow you to disable vertical and horizontal grid lines, both major and minor.

- **Legend** Provides some control over if and where your chart legend appears (see Figure 11-15). You can choose to display your legend on the right (default), left, top, or bottom of your chart. You may also select None in the Location field to remove the legend from your chart. The Text Format button next to the Location field provides

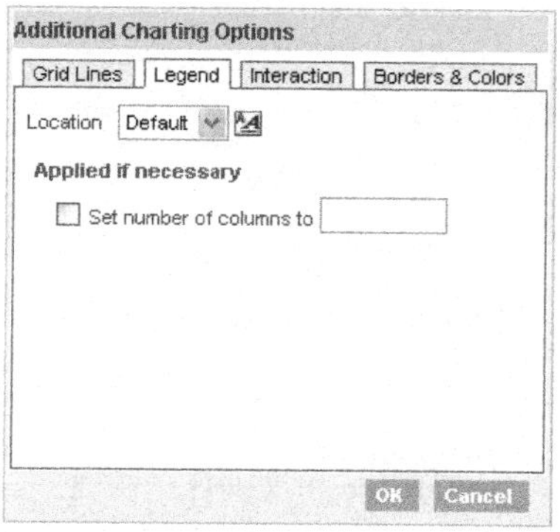

FIGURE 11-15. *Additional Charting Options dialog box—Legend tab*

some typical text formatting controls. You may also indicate the number of columns that your legend should contain if there are enough items in the legend to spread the items across more than one column.

- ■ **Interaction** Allows you to select the type of interaction that will occur when a user clicks on part of the chart. The default setting is to Drill. You may disable interactivity or set up a navigation path to another report. For more information on adding interactivity to your reports, refer to Chapter 16.

- ■ **Borders & Colors** Allows you to set a color for your chart's background, text, and border. To change the color for any of these, click the color selector next to its label and select a new color from the palate or enter an HTML color code. The border and background encompass the entire chart, including the title and legend. The text elements that the color setting affects are the axes titles.

Format Chart Data Button

Clicking the Format Chart Data button opens the Format Chart Data dialog box, where you can format the appearance of your chart components. You can specify the color and style for each series and each chart component. The appearance of this dialog box differs for different chart types. The Format Chart Data dialog box for basic bar charts (see Figure 11-16) is the least complex. To change the color of the bars in your chart, uncheck the Use Default check box for the series position you want to recolor, and then click the color selector and select or enter your new color.

In the Format Chart Data dialog box for a line chart (see Figure 11-17), you have the same color settings plus some additional settings for the line type and width. For each series, you can choose a plain (default) line, a dotted line, a dashed line, or a dashed and dotted line. You can set the width of your line from zero to six points. Lines may also have symbols at each data point. You can select the symbol shape from the Symbol Type field. Your choices of symbols are squares, triangles, rounds, diamonds, or plus signs. You can also choose to turn the symbols off.

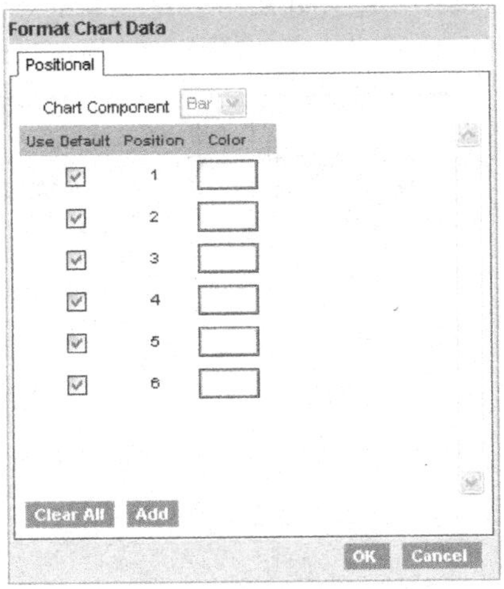

FIGURE 11-16. *Format Chart Data dialog box for a bar chart*

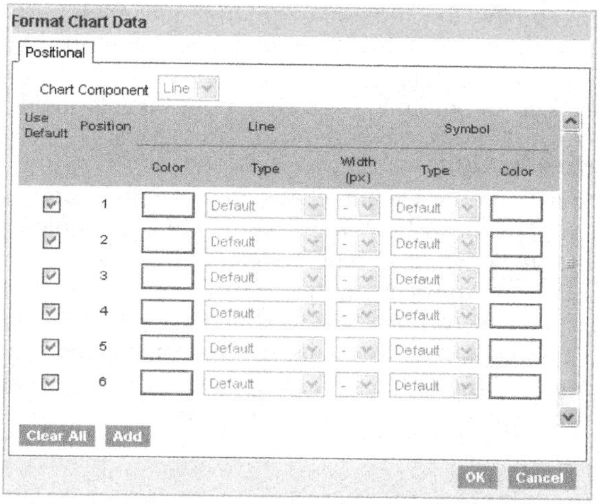

FIGURE 11-17. *Format Chart Data dialog box for a line chart*

The line bar combo chart uses both the line and bar versions of the Format Chart Data dialog box. The Chart Component field allows you to switch between formatting your lines and your bars.

The Format Chart Data dialog box for the Pareto chart (see Figure 11-18) combines the line and bar formatting fields on one screen, allowing you to set the color of the bar with the upper color selector at each position and set the line formatting with the lower set of fields at each position.

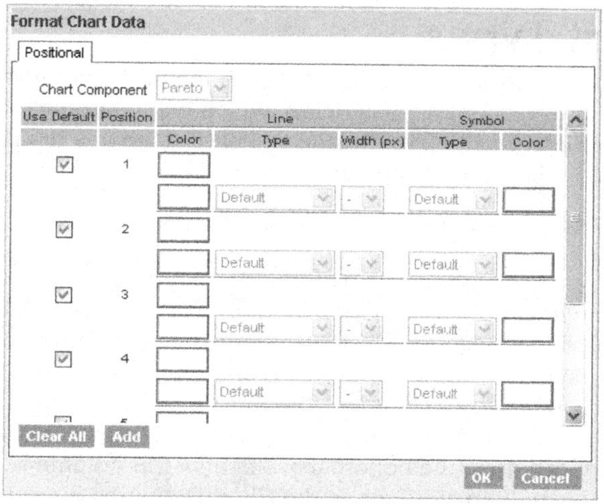

FIGURE 11-18. *Format Chart Data dialog box for a Pareto chart*

With a pie chart, you have the option of exploding one of the chart wedges out of the circle. With a bubble chart, you have the additional option of making the bubbles appear three- or two-dimensional. Regardless of the chart type, one final common element in the Format Chart Data dialog box is the Clear All button. Any time you feel you have gone a little too far with your formatting, click the Clear All button to reset all options back to their default values.

Advanced Properties Button

With the bubble, line bar combo, and pie charts, you can make additional special formatting changes by clicking the Advanced Properties button. On the bubble chart, clicking this button opens the Chart Type Special window, which contains a slider for adjusting the bubble size percentage. On the line bar combo chart, the Chart Type Special window contains a single check box that allows you to synchronize the line and bar axis scales. Finally, clicking the pie chart's Advanced Properties button permits you to format the data values as a percentage of the total or the actual value represented by each wedge. You can also define what information is included in the data label. You can display the value only, the name only, or both the name and value.

Identifying Chart Columns

Each Edit View for charts contains on the left side a series of check boxes that you use to indicate which columns to include in your chart and where the column data should appear (refer to Figure 11-2 for an example). I will refer to this section as the Chart Definition area. Depending on the chart type, you will see a column of check boxes beneath icons representing chart elements. You will have two to five columns of these check boxes. Some charts also allow you to identify if and where to apply measure labels. The specific requirements of each chart type are described in the following section.

To the right of these check box controls is a preview of your chart. This preview may update automatically as you make changes, but you will find that you need to click the Redraw button at times to refresh the preview. If you ever feel like you have gone too far with your chart formatting, you can click the Restore Default button to return to the default format for the current chart.

Basic Chart Types

Answers On Demand charting includes a number of the most common chart formats. This section describes each of these "basic" charts in detail, which were introduced earlier in Table 11-1. Not all charts are appropriate for all types of data, so I encourage you to consider your charting choices carefully and with usability and understandability of the data in mind.

Area Chart

An area chart displays quantitative data by filling in an area under a series line. Area charts are good for showing the total of two or more quantities over a series of time, for instance, while representing the individual quantities that make up that total. Figure 11-19 shows an example of an area chart.

The area chart requires you to identify columns for the bottom and left axes. To populate your area chart, you need to identify the column by which to segment the data in the chart. The values from this column appear along the bottom axis. Identify this column by checking the column's check box beneath the bottom axis icon in the Chart Definition area. This is usually a nonmetric column.

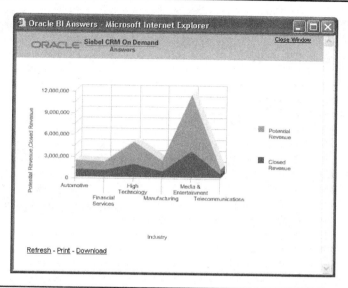

FIGURE 11-19. *Example area chart*

Next you identify one or more metric columns to include on the left (measure) axis. Check the Measure Labels check box under the legend icon and you get a nice area chart with different color areas for each metric and a legend that identifies the metric associated with each color (see Figure 11-20).

I encourage you to experiment with different combinations. For instance, adding a column to the legend further segments the data so that there is a data series in your chart for each combination of metric and nonmetric columns. You must identify at least one column for the measure axis, and you cannot set your measure labels to the measure axis. If you fail to designate a column for the bottom axis, the report will use a combination of all unused columns on the bottom axis.

Horizontal Bar Chart

A horizontal bar chart displays quantitative data represented by horizontal bars extending from the left axis. The chart displays series as sets of horizontal bars grouped by category. Metric values are represented by the length of the bars as measured by the bottom axis. Category labels appear on the left axis. You normally use a bar chart when you want to compare values between categories.

There are two types of horizontal bar charts:

- **Standard**   Represents each metric as an individual bar
- **Stacked**   Displays all metric series stacked into a single column for each category

Figure 11-21 shows the same data in both a standard horizontal bar chart (left) and a stacked horizontal bar chart (right).

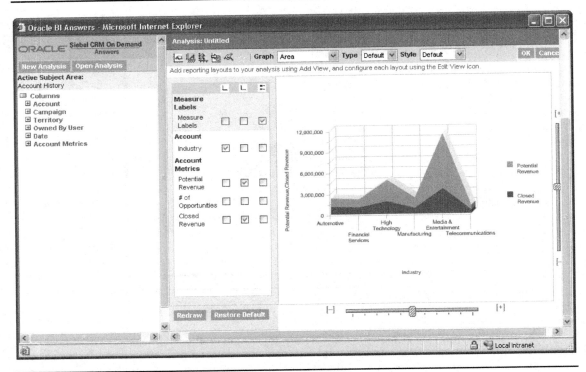

FIGURE 11-20. *Chart Edit View—area chart*

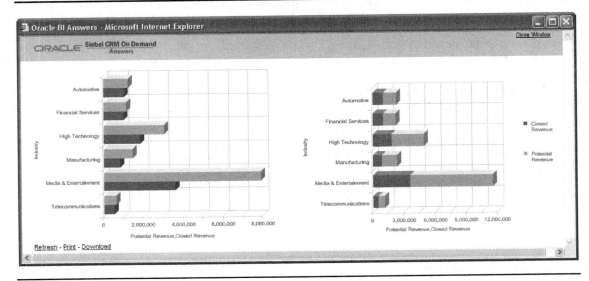

FIGURE 11-21. *Horizontal bar charts*

The horizontal bar chart requires you to identify columns for the bottom and left axes. You must identify the column by which to segment the data in the chart. The values from this column appear along the left axis. Identify this column by checking the column's check box beneath the left axis icon in the Chart Definition area. This is usually a nonmetric column.

Next you identify one or more metric columns to include on the bottom axis. Check the Measure Labels check box under the legend icon in the Chart Definition area if you want the legend to identify what the different color bars represent.

You must identify at least one column for the measure axis, and you cannot set your measure labels to the measure axis. If you fail to designate a column for the left axis, the report will use a combination of all unused columns on the left axis.

Bubble Chart

A bubble chart displays data series as a set of circles (bubbles). Metric values are represented by the position of the point in the chart corresponding to the left and bottom axes and by the size of the bubble. Categories are represented by different colored bubbles in the chart. There is only one type and style of bubble chart.

To display meaningful data in a bubble chart, you need to identify a category, represented by the diagonal axis, or chart area. The location of the bubble for each value is based on its relationship to the metric values on the bottom and left axes. The fourth element is size. A metric value assigned to this element in the bubble chart determines the size of each point in the chart. Adding a column to the legend causes the bubble chart to show different color-coded series of bubbles.

Figure 11-22 shows a preview of a bubble chart in the Chart Edit View window. Notice how each selected column on the left is represented in the chart on the right. All three axes and the size element are required in the bubble chart. Only the legend element in the Chart Definition area is optional.

Vertical Bar Chart

The vertical bar chart is the default chart type. Every time you add a Chart view to your report, you always start with a vertical bar chart. A vertical bar chart displays quantitative data represented by vertical bars extending from the bottom axis. The chart displays series as sets of bars grouped by category. Metric values are represented by the height of the bars as measured by the left axis. Category labels appear on the bottom axis. You normally use a bar chart when you want to compare values between categories.

As with its horizontal bar chart sibling, there are two types of vertical bar charts. The standard vertical bar chart represents each metric as an individual bar. The stacked bar chart displays all metric series stacked into a single column for each category. Figure 11-23 shows the same data in both a standard vertical bar chart (left) and a stacked vertical bar chart (right).

The vertical bar chart requires you to identify columns for the bottom and left axes. You must identify the column by which to segment the data in the chart. The values from this column appear along the bottom axis. Identify this column by checking the column's check box beneath the bottom axis icon in the Chart Definition area. This is usually, but not necessarily a nonmetric column.

Next you identify one or more metric columns to include on the left (measure) axis. Check the Measure Labels check box under the legend icon if you want the legend to identify what the different color bars represent.

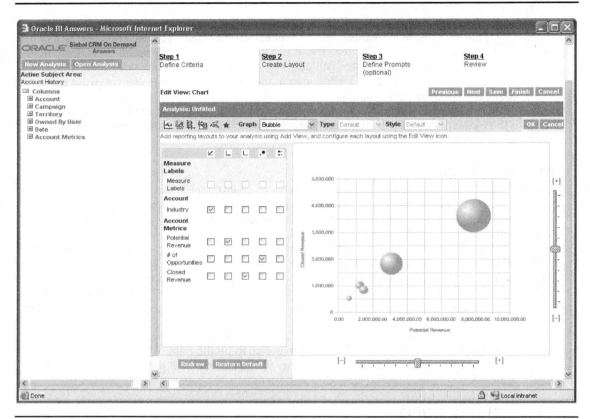

FIGURE 11-22. *Chart Edit View—bubble chart*

You must identify at least one column for the measure axis, and you cannot set your measure labels to the measure axis. If you fail to designate a column for the left axis, the report will use a combination of all unused columns on the bottom axis.

Line Chart

A line chart displays categories of data as points connected by lines. Measure values along the left axis determine the height of each point along the line. The line contains a point for each value in the category series displayed along the bottom axis. You typically use a line chart to compare values over time.

For each measure column you identify on the left axis, your chart will display a line of a different color. You may also manually set the line colors in the Format Chart Data dialog box, perhaps even make all the lines the same color but different types, as shown in Figure 11-24.

You are required to designate at least one column on the left axis. The bottom axis and legend elements are optional, but at least one is needed to display anything meaningful in your line chart.

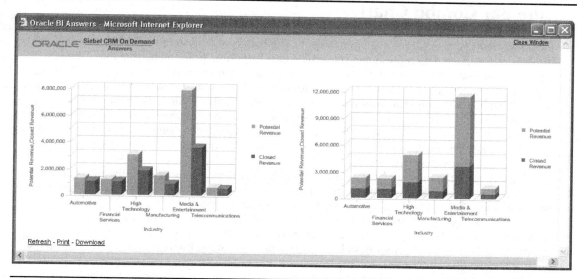

FIGURE 11-23. *Vertical bar charts*

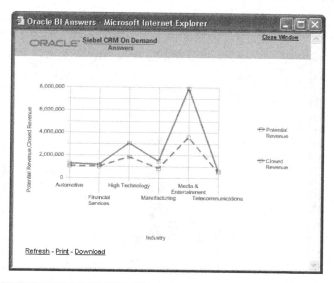

FIGURE 11-24. *Example line chart*

Line Bar Combo Chart

The line bar combo chart, as you might expect, is a combination of the vertical bar chart and the line chart, with all the options available in each. The bar chart portion of the line bar combo chart displays quantitative data represented by vertical bars extending from the bottom axis. The line chart portion displays another metric as points connected by lines with the measure values scale along the right axis determining the height of each point in the line. The line chart contains a point for each value in the same category series as the bar chart displayed along the bottom axis.

The line bar combo chart permits you to show a relationship between metric series, even when the scales are vastly different. This strategy is often used when comparing two different data types to identify correlations between them. Your bars may represent numeric data, for instance, while the line represents currency data.

You still have the option of a standard vertical bar chart representing each metric as an individual bar or a stacked bar chart displaying all metric series stacked into a single column for each category. Figure 11-25 shows a sample line bar combo chart.

The line bar combo chart requires you to identify columns for the bottom and left axes. You must identify the column by which to categorize the data. The chart will use this column to segment the data in the chart for both bar and line portions along the bottom axis. This is usually, but not necessarily a nonmetric column.

Next you identify one or more metric columns to include on the left (measure) axis. If you select only one column, the resulting chart will appear as a line chart, even if you select the column under the left axis. If you select two columns on the left axis and none on the line element in the Chart Definition area, the chart will display the first column as a line and the second as bars. Of course, you can designate which columns to show as lines and which to show as bars by clicking the column's check box under the icons in the Chart Definition area according to your preference.

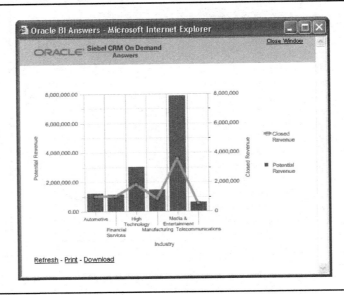

FIGURE 11-25. *Example line bar combo chart*

Pareto Chart

A Pareto chart (see Figure 11-26) is a special line bar chart in which the bars are arranged in descending order according to value. The bar on the far left is the largest and the bar on the far right is the smallest. The line shows a running aggregate of the percentage of the total so that the line always ends at 100 percent in the upper-right corner of the chart. The steeper the angle of this line the more evenly spread are the values across the segments in your chart. A relatively flat line would indicate that one segment contains a vast majority of the value in the dataset.

Pareto charts are often used to analyze the frequency of issues. If you do any work in quality control, you are very likely to have seen many Pareto charts in action. To set up a Pareto chart in CRM On Demand, you need to identify the bottom axis, which is the segmentation of your data, and the left axis, which is the measure to evaluate. You can measure only one column at a time on the measure axis. If you select more than one column on the left axis, the chart will reflect only the first measure column it encounters. The scale on the left axis is based on the column values. The right axis will always be 0 to 100 percent.

Pie Chart

Perhaps the most popular multicolored circle in the charting world, the pie chart is a common choice for showing proportions within data. Despite its popularity, the pie chart is actually not terribly useful. It is difficult to compare multiple segments within a pie chart or compare value across multiple pie charts. The sizes of the wedges in a pie chart are proportional within that single chart according to data values, but the size of the pie can be misleading across multiple charts.

Your pie chart requires you to identify two elements for your chart. The column you choose for the legend element determines the number of wedges present in your pie chart. The other

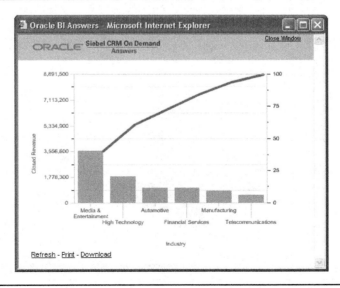

FIGURE 11-26. *Example Pareto chart*

element is the measure, and the column you select for this element determines the size of each wedge. Unlike bar charts and line charts, the scale for a pie chart is not obvious. The data is represented only by a wedge, and if your chart includes several very similarly sized wedges, it would be very difficult to determine at a glance which wedge is bigger. In my opinion, pie charts are most effective if there are no more than four or five segments.

If you want to deliver more detail, you can display the percentages or actual values using the Advanced Properties button. In the General Chart Properties dialog box, set the chart to always show the values or show them when the user moves the mouse over a wedge. Another option for drawing the user's attention to a particular portion of the data is to explode one of the wedges out of the chart, as shown in Figure 11-27. Do this by clicking the Explode Wedge radio button for the segment in the Format Chart Data dialog box.

Radar Chart

The radar chart, also known as a spider chart or spider web chart, is a very interesting and informative chart for comparing at a glance multiple attributes of several different values on the same scale. For instance, suppose you have a team of six sales people, each with a goal of 20 sales per month. With the radar chart, you can graphically represent each sales person's goal, current number of opportunities, and number of wins as shaded areas on the chart. Zero on the scale is the center of the chart. Figure 11-28 shows a sample radar chart. Notice that it is quite easy to tell which user is excelling and which is struggling. You can also tell very quickly which user has the most potential for picking up more wins as the number of opportunities is much greater than the number of wins. The radar chart combines the benefits of bar charts and pie charts.

To configure your radar chart, you identify the column whose value will occupy the points around the outside of the chart. These are the segments into which you will organize the values.

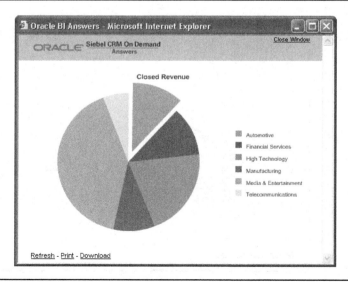

FIGURE 11-27. *Example pie chart*

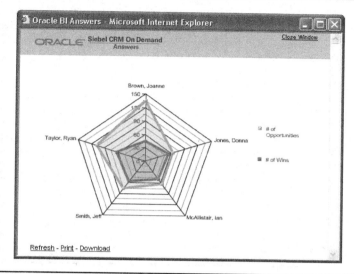

FIGURE 11-28. *Example radar chart*

You can then identify one or more columns for the measures. Each column is assigned a color and appears as a shaded area inside the radar.

On the down side, you are rather limited in regard to the customization of a radar chart. You cannot change the gridlines, for instance. You also have no control over the scale and cannot add a scale marker in the normal fashion. You can, however, add a new column to your report and hard code a value to force a marker into the radar chart.

One configuration that I am fond of making is to format the chart data to choose my own colors and set the line thickness to one or two points, as I find the default is a little too thick for my liking.

Scatter Chart

The scatter chart plots data points on a grid and is a perfect solution for recognizing trends in a very large dataset. Correlations between two different metrics become clear on a well-designed scatter chart. Consider the chart in Figure 11-29. This scatter chart shows a very high positive correlation between number of opportunities and opportunity revenue. You see this correlation on the scatter chart as a cluster that moves from the lower left to the upper right of the chart. In other words, as the number of opportunities increases, so does the revenue amount. A negative correlation would show as a cluster arranged roughly from the upper left to the lower right. As one measure increases the other measure decreases.

Configuring your scatter chart is very similar to configuring a bubble chart, only the element of size is not present. Assign your two measure columns to the bottom and left axes. Assign the segment column—the column to which the two measures are attributed—to the body of the chart represented by the diagonal line icon in the Edit View window. Measure labels are not a valid part of a scatter chart, as the segment values are not identified by different-colored dots.

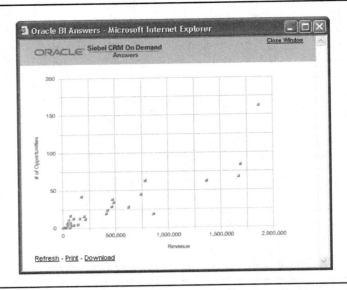

FIGURE 11-29. *Example scatter chart*

The sizing of the scatter chart affects its interpretability more significantly than sizing affects any other chart. If you adjust the height or width of the chart so that one is much larger than the other, the cluster of dots appears skewed as the dots are smashed either vertically or horizontally.

Step Chart

A step chart is quite similar to a line chart. The step chart plots the data point on the chart grid, and connects these points with straight lines, just like a line chart. The difference here is that the data points are connected by horizontal and vertical lines. The data points are actually platted as horizontal lines between two segments. The segments on the bottom axis are assigned to the space between the vertical gridlines rather than to a point on the grid line. The end of each horizontal line is connected to the start of the next horizontal line by a vertical line.

If you sort your data by the measure value, your step chart becomes quite easy to read and the length of the lines gives some insight into trends within the data. For instance, long horizontal lines that span multiple segments indicate that several segments contain equal measures. Long vertical lines indicate a large jump or drop in the data, depending on how you sorted the values.

Figure 11-30 shows a step chart of data that I have sorted. Notice that the chart seems to draw a staircase, lending to its name, and that irregularities in the lengths of lines make variations in the data quite obvious. Like a line chart, each measure column you identify on the left axis is represented as a line of a different color.

You are required to designate at least one column on the left axis. The bottom axis and legend elements are optional, but at least one is needed to display anything meaningful in your line chart.

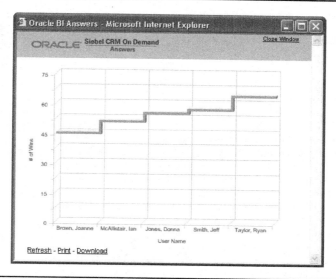

FIGURE 11-30. *Example step chart*

Advanced Charts

There are two additional views that I want to describe in this chapter on charts. Though they are not considered Chart views in Answers On Demand, I consider them to be advanced charts. The configuration of these advanced charts is only slightly different from the configuration of the chart types within the Chart view.

Gauge View

Gauge view is a very impressive visual element that you can add to your charts. The clarity of the data is not necessarily enhanced, but the visual interest of your report may be enhanced greatly. Figure 11-31 shows a sample set of gauges on a report. This type of view on a real-time report showing data that changes often can be fun to watch and informative as the user refreshes the report.

To add gauges to your report, click the Add View button in Step 2 of the Build and View Analysis window and select Gauge (refer to Figure 11-1). The Gauge Edit View window (see Figure 11-32) is quite similar to the Chart Edit View window described earlier. The buttons in the header are different and are specific to the Gauge view. These buttons are described in the sections that follow.

Most of the following examples and explanations assume you are working with dial gauges, but the Gauge drop-down list also gives you options of bar and bulb gauges as well, which are described toward the end of this section.

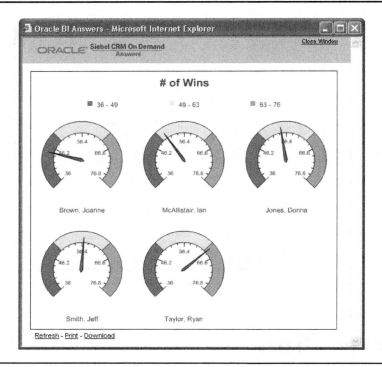

FIGURE 11-31. *Gauge view*

Gauge Canvas Properties Button

The first (leftmost) button on the title bar is the Gauge Canvas Properties button. The icon is the same as the General Chart Properties button in the Edit View for charts. Click this button and the Gauge Canvas Properties dialog box opens (see Figure 11-33).

In the Gauge Canvas Properties dialog box, you can format the title, legend location, borders and colors, and the gauge layout. By default, your Gauge view title will reflect the name of the measure displayed on the gauges. To change the title, check the Override Default check box and type your desired title in the Title field. Click the Text Format button next to the Title field to set the font family, color, style, and font size for your title in the Text Format dialog box.

The Legend Location field provides some control over if and where your gauge legend appears. You can choose to display your legend on the top (default), left, right, or bottom of your chart. You may also select None to remove the legend from your chart. The Text Format button next to the Legend Location field provides some typical text formatting controls.

In the Borders & Colors section, there are color selectors for both the background and the text. The text color does not appear to affect the text in a Gauge view, but the background color is effective and really highlights the gauges on the canvas, because the background color affects all of the background except for the circular area around each gauge. You also see a Border Color selector here. You may uncheck the Show Border check box to disable the border. You may also use the Border Color selector to set the border color for your Gauge view.

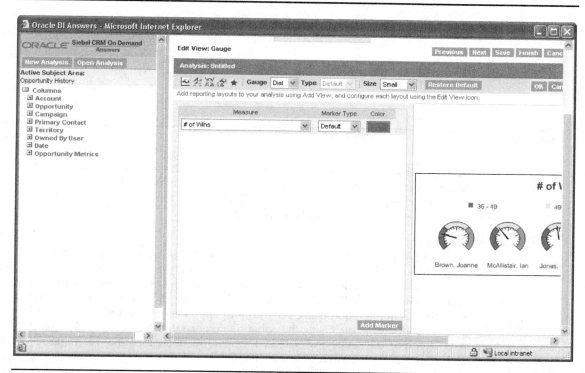

FIGURE 11-32. *Edit View: Gauge*

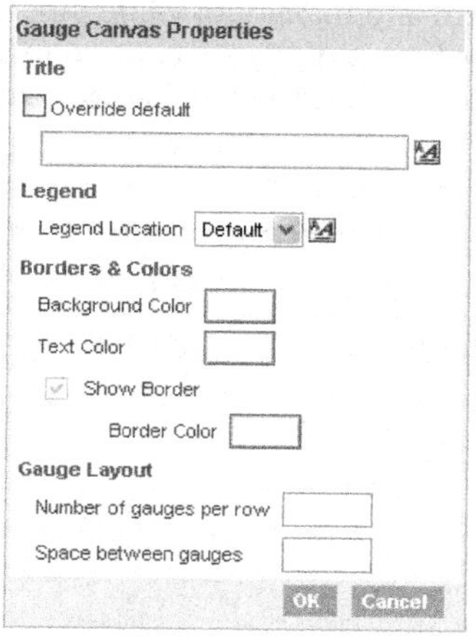

FIGURE 11-33. *Gauge Canvas Properties dialog box*

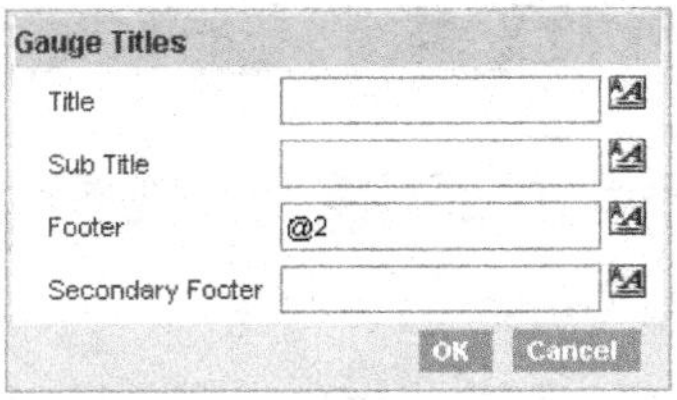

FIGURE 11-34. *Gauge Titles dialog box*

Gauge Layout, the final section of this window, contains two fields for adjusting the number of gauges that appear in each row on the gauge canvas and the amount of space between the gauges. Experiment with adding values to these two fields. The Space Between Gauges field is measured in points and affects both horizontal and vertical spacing.

Gauge Titles Button

The next button on the title bar is the Gauge Titles button. Clicking this button opens the Gauge Titles dialog box, which contains four fields and Text Format buttons (see Figure 11-34). Each gauge can have a title and subtitle above the gauge and a footer and secondary footer below the gauge. Text that you type into any of these fields will appear on every gauge in the canvas. You may also reference columns in the report using a bit of shorthand, where @1 is the first column in the report, @2 is the second, and so on. Using the column reference in the Title fields gives you the value from that column on the gauge associated with each row of data. Format each title's appearance using the Text Format button next to the Title field.

Gauge Ranges Button

The next button is the Gauge Ranges button. Clicking this button takes you to the Gauge Ranges dialog box (see Figure 11-35), where you can identify the size and number of segments that your gauge scales display. The default is a scale of 0 to 100 percent split into three even segments. You can manually change the minimum and maximum value ranges for each section. You may also change the caption of the sections by typing a new caption in the Caption field. This caption appears in the legend on the gauge canvas. Click the color selector to change the default color for the gauge segments.

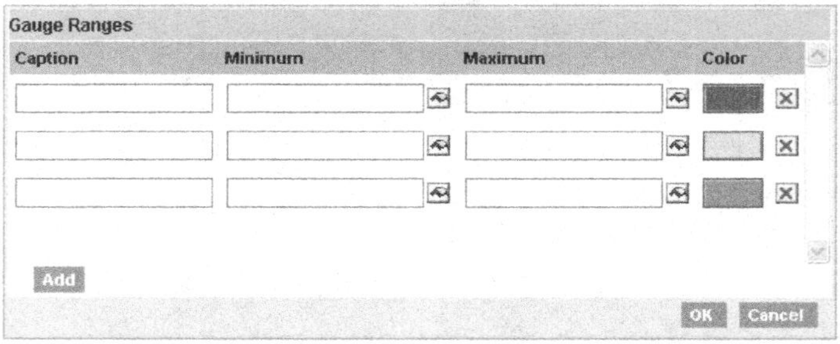

FIGURE 11-35. *Gauge Ranges dialog box*

If you want more than three segments on your gauges, click the Add button to insert an additional segment. One really convenient feature here is that by leaving the Minimum and Maximum fields blank, the gauge will automatically divide into even sections with the specified number of segments. Removing a segment is as simple as clicking the × button to the right of the segment.

Additional Gauge Properties Button

To the right of the Gauge Ranges button is the Additional Gauge Properties button. Clicking this button opens the Additional Gauge Properties dialog box (see Figure 11-36), which contains three tabs, each dedicated to a different element of your chart.

On the Appearance tab, you can specify if and when data labels appear on your gauges and specify their format. In the Borders & Colors section, you can set the background color and text color for your gauges. The background color in this case is the background of the gauge itself, not the canvas. The Text Color option is misleading. The color you select here affects only the tick marks on the gauge. Check the Show Border check box to add a border that encircles each gauge. Once activated, you can use the color selector to specify a color for your border.

In the Size section, you can customize the width and height of your gauges. Since the gauges are circular, specifying either a height or width will change the size of the gauge evenly. If you enter different numbers in the Width and Height fields, your gauges will stretch into an oval shape rather than maintain their circular shape.

The next tab, Scale (see Figure 11-37), allows you to set the upper and lower limits of your gauge scale. The buttons next to the Minimum and Maximum fields open the Advanced Options window, allowing you to identify a column to set your gauge limit on.

Also on this tab, you can change the number of major or minor tick marks. These are the marks around the inside of your dial gauge. In the Labels section, you can format the scale labels by selecting a font family, color, text style, and font size.

The Interaction tab allows you to select the type of interaction that will occur when a user clicks the gauge. You may disable interactivity or set up a navigation path to another report. For more information on adding interactivity to your reports, refer to Chapter 16.

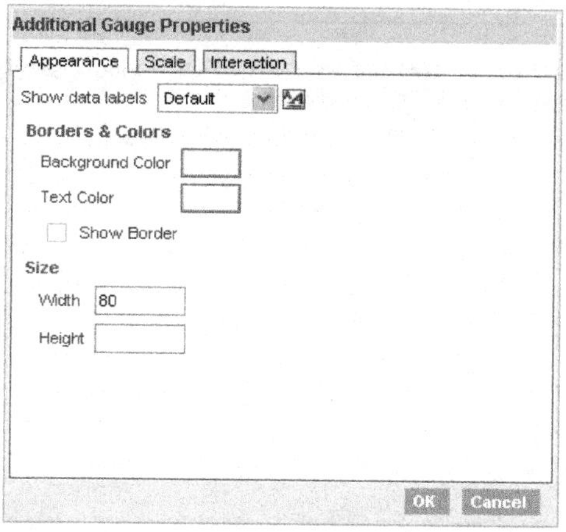

FIGURE 11-36. *Additional Gauge Properties dialog box—Appearance tab*

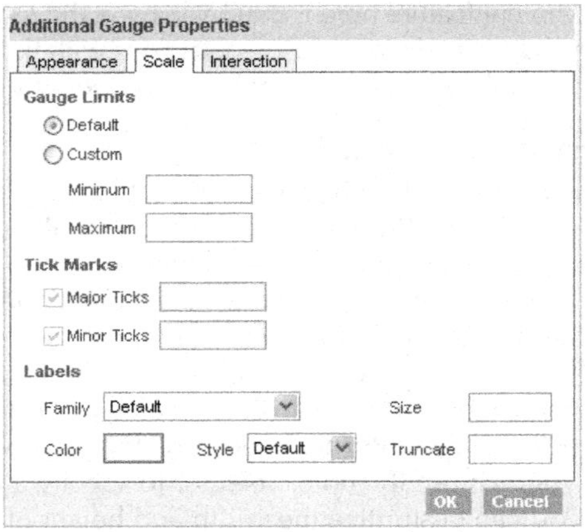

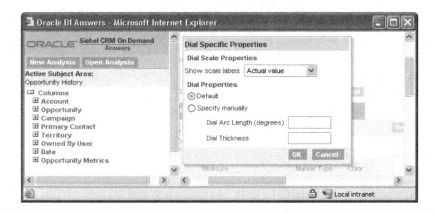

FIGURE 11-37. *Additional Gauge Properties dialog box—Scale tab*

Advanced Properties Button

The final button, in the shape of a star, is the Advanced Properties button. Clicking this button opens a properties window that is specific to the gauge type selected in the Gauge field to the right of the button. Within the Gauge field, you can select Dial, Bar, or Bulb. The Advanced Properties button is available for the dial and bar gauge types.

With the dial gauge, the Dial Specific Properties dialog box (see Figure 11-38) opens when you click the Advanced Properties button. Here you can specify how the scale labels should appear inside the dial. Your options are to show the percentage of total (default) or the actual measure values. You can also choose to not display scale labels. You can also adjust the arc length and thickness of your dial gauge. The dial arc length is measured in degrees, so the valid

FIGURE 11-38. *Dial Specific Properties dialog box*

FIGURE 11-39. *Bar Specific Properties dialog box*

range of values in this field is 0 to 360. A number over 360 will cause a display error. Enter a thickness in points if you want to thicken your dial.

If you are working with bar gauges, clicking the Advanced Properties button opens the Bar Specific Properties dialog box (see Figure 11-39). Your options here are to enable or disable the color bar and scale below the bar gauges.

Gauge, Type, and Size Fields

To the right of the buttons in the title bar, you have three fields. The Gauge field allows you to select one of three gauge styles. The dial gauge is the default, but you also have the option of using a bar gauge or a bulb gauge. The bar gauge fills from left to right according to the measure for the gauge (see Figure 11-40). The bulb gauge simply changes color according to the measure for the gauge (see Figure 11-41). The bar and bulb gauges permit only one measure.

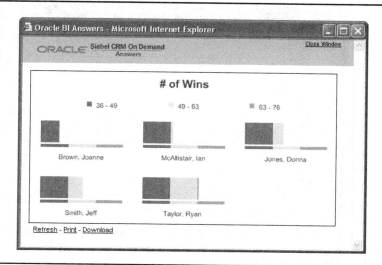

FIGURE 11-40. *Bar gauge*

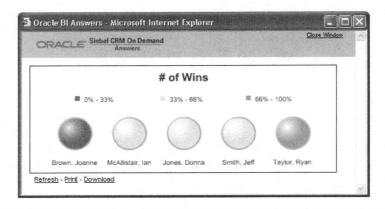

FIGURE 11-41. *Bulb gauge*

The Type field, which is available only with the bar and bulb gauges, allows you to select the fill type (default) or the LED type (see Figure 11-42) for the bar gauge. The Type field for the bulb gauge gives you the option of a two- or three-dimensional appearance for your gauges.

The Size field gives you the option of small, medium (default), large, or custom size gauges. If you select Custom in the Size field, the Additional Gauge Properties dialog box (refer to Figure 11-36) opens, where you may set the size of the gauges. You can make additional special formatting changes by clicking the Advanced Properties button. The small size gauge is preset to an 80-point width. Medium is 150 points wide, and large is 200 points wide.

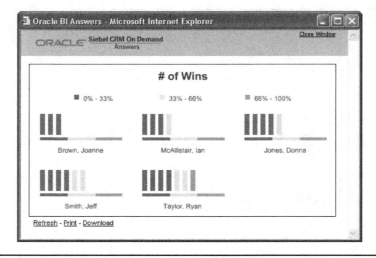

FIGURE 11-42. *Bar gauge, LED type*

Identify and Format Measure Columns

The area to the left of the gauge canvas preview identifies the current measure columns for your Gauge view. The dial gauges permit more than one measure column on each gauge. With the dial gauges, you may select the measure column using the Measure drop-down list. In the Marker Type drop-down list, you can select the Compass (default), Arrow, or Line Marker types. This setting changes the pointer in the dial. The color selector allows you to set a specific color for each measure column. The Marker Type and Color fields are disabled for the bar and bulb gauges. To add an additional marker to your dial gauge, click the Add Marker button and set the Measure, Marker Type, and Color attributes for the new marker. Remove markers by clicking the × button next to the measure column you wish to remove.

Funnel Chart

The final chart in this chapter is the funnel chart. If you are in sales, you either cringed or felt your heart race at the thought of a funnel chart. Funnel charts are most popular among this segment of the corporate world because they provide an interesting view of how sales deals at different stages are performing against goals. Funnel charts have rather limited applicability and require a very specific type of data to be meaningful, but, when placed in the right type of report, can be very informative.

To add a funnel chart to your report, click the Add View button and choose Advanced | Funnel Chart. The Edit View window for the funnel chart is relatively simple, without an abundance of formatting options.

To add a title to your funnel chart, enter your desired chart title in the Chart Title field. (Notice that the Format Text button is not present here, as it is with other text fields.) Three columns are required to build a funnel chart. The Stage element defines the segments of the funnel. Actual Value and Target Value identify the metric columns that are compared within the funnel. The funnel chart will fill and color each portion of the funnel according to the relationship between these two values, and the threshold percentages. Any segment of the funnel where the percentage of the target value represented by the actual value is less than the minimum threshold percentage appears in red on the funnel. If this calculation falls between the minimum and maximum threshold percentages, the segment is colored yellow. Values above the maximum threshold appear green on the funnel. You can adjust these thresholds in the Minimum Threshold and Maximum Threshold fields.

Your funnel chart can reflect the number of records in each stage by making the segments wider for more records and narrower for fewer records. If you want your chart to look more like a funnel, check the Force Standard Shape and Equal Stage Widths check box. The chart will show each segment with the same width, so you lose the perception of size of each stage segment, but your chart looks a bit neater.

The Size field allows you to scale the entire chart with sizes between 10 and 100 in increments of 10. Again, your options to customize this chart are quite limited compared to the options available for other charts. Notice there is no way to adjust the text, colors, borders, or backgrounds.

For certain datasets, you may want to identify your target value only in the final stage. If so, check the Target Value for Final Stage Only check box. This makes the Factor Required to Meet Target field available for edit. I recommend using these options only if you already understand the advanced accounting concepts that go into factoring data in the funnel.

"LayOUTside" the Box

Charts are by nature visually stimulating, so there are not too many tricks to taking them to the next level above the formatting options already described in this chapter. I do want to offer one of my favorite tips for using only charts to create a report that looks a lot like a dashboard. Of course, this is a single report built on a single subject area, so all the data comes from the same report table. The Table view, however, is removed from the report.

Figure 11-43 is an example of what I call the Management Command Center report—a bunch of charts arranged on a report based on Account History that shows high-level information about many different record types associated with accounts in my database. Once you have a few views added to your report, arranging them on the "page" is a simple matter of dragging and dropping the views into place. As you drag a view around the screen, you will see a yellow line indicating where the view will position itself when you drop the view.

As you will see in the remaining chapters, there are many other very useful views to mix in with your tables and charts. Keep in mind as you proceed that simple is usually better than complex, and thus going crazy with the formatting can hinder rather than enhance the usefulness of your reports.

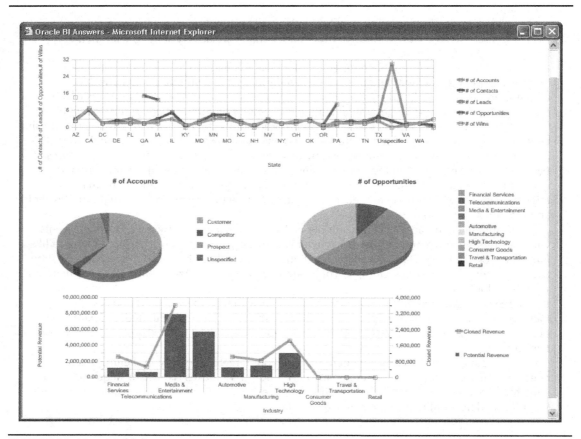

FIGURE 11-43. *Multichart report*

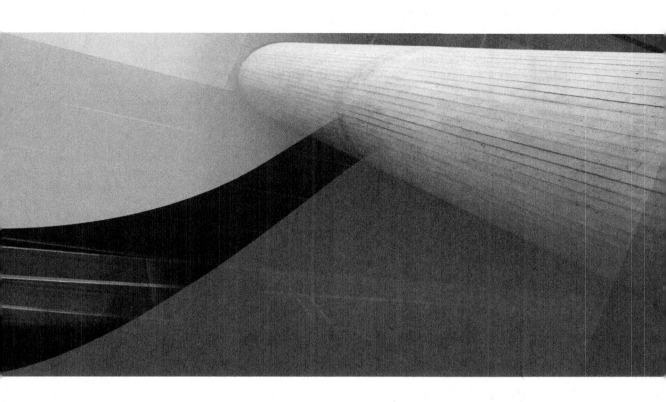

CHAPTER
12

Adding Pivot Tables to Reports

he Pivot Tables view is by far the most flexible, most configurable, and most complex view in Answers On Demand. It's also my favorite view. A pivot table can take on so many forms and display your report data in so many different ways, that all of the combinations would be impossible to comprehend, much less document.

In addition to a table, the Pivot Table view can include a chart based on the data in the pivot table. Pivot charts may be included along with a pivot table or appear on their own in a Pivot Table view. In this chapter I will describe every feature of the Pivot Table view and share my most useful tips for formatting and using pivot tables in your reports.

Introduction to Pivot Tables

Unlike a normal Table view, the Pivot Table view allows you to move data around, organize metrics into columns, create sections of data by segment, and create separate pages for data based on a particular column value. Pivot tables can take on many different forms and serve a multitude of purposes. I like to categorize the Pivot Table view into two different utilities. The basic pivot table is a data summarization tool that is useful for creating cross-tab tables and segmenting data. The Pivot Table view, when used creatively, is also a powerful data formatting and organization tool that gives you the flexibility to do things with your report data that you simply wouldn't expect is possible.

Basic Pivot Tables

A Pivot Table view is made up of six different layout areas into which you can place your data columns. Each area serves a specific purpose and has a different set of formatting options, as described in the following subsections. Your data columns make up the data layer. You can also apply some special formatting to this layer. The most basic pivot table is a simple reorganization of report data into the pivot table layout areas.

When you initially add a Pivot Table view to your report by clicking the Add View button and selecting Pivot Table (from Step 2 of the Build and View Analysis window), you see the Edit View window for your pivot table (see Figure 12-1). By default, the nonmetric columns in your report are located in the Rows area and your metric columns are located in the Measures area. The preview at the bottom of the window shows a table that looks very much like your normal Table view. As you move columns in and out of these areas, the preview below refreshes to show the new arrangement.

Rows Area

The Rows area organizes data into rows, grouping the data from left to right, very much like a normal Table view. You can change this horizontal grouping by changing the order of the columns in the Rows area.

Measures Area

The Measures area typically contains metric columns. This area is where any measures associated with the values in the Rows and Columns areas are located. You may also place nonmetric data in the Measures area. You will notice that the column values appear null when in the Measures area. This is because nonmetric columns have a default aggregation rule of "none."

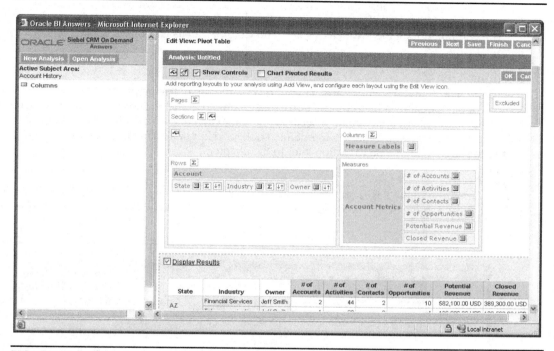

FIGURE 12-1. *Edit View: Pivot Table window*

Columns Area

You create a cross-tab matrix by adding database columns to the Columns area. Your pivot table will have a column for each value in the database column. The values in the Measures area will relate to both the rows and columns where each row intersects each column. Figure 12-2 shows

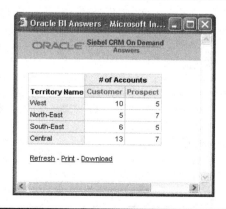

FIGURE 12-2. *Cross-tab pivot table*

a simple cross-tab pivot table showing the number of accounts by territory and account type. For each territory row, you see the number of accounts for each account type.

The combination of the Rows, Measures, and Columns areas is considered the content area of the pivot table.

Sections Area

Placing a column in the Sections area in your pivot table separates the pivot table content into a separate table for each value in the Sections area column. For instance, placing the User Name column in the Sections area creates a separate table for each user. Figure 12-3 shows a pivot table split into separate section tables by username. Look for other interesting uses for the Sections area in the "'LayOUTside' the Box" section later in the chapter.

Pages Area

Placing a column in the Pages area has a similar effect as placing a column in the Sections area, only the Pivot Table view will show only one table at a time based on the column value selected

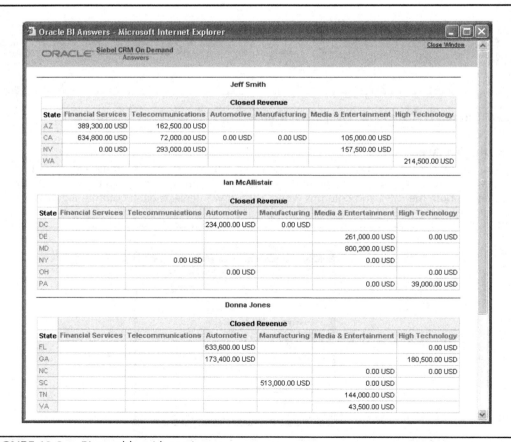

FIGURE 12-3. *Pivot table with sections*

from a drop-down list above the table. Each value in the column is a value in the drop-down list, and selecting a new value in this field changes the pivot table below to show only data related to the selected value. The same pivot table from Figure 12-3 is shown in Figure 12-4 with the User Name field in the Pages area rather than in the Sections area.

Excluded Area

The Excluded area is a place to put any columns that you do not want to affect your pivot table. Any columns placed in this area are removed from the Pivot Table view, but not the report. The ability to exclude columns makes it possible to include multiple Pivot Table views with different content in your report.

For instance, if you wanted to build a report that analyzes the number of activities, opportunities, and contacts associated with each account by territory, you could add all of the necessary columns to a single report. Using a Pivot Table view, you are able to focus the data in the pivot table on activities by adding the opportunity and contact columns into the Excluded area. Adding additional Pivot Table views, you can do the same for opportunities and contacts.

Formatting Pivot Table Areas

The Pivot Table view is rather useful, even without a lot of formatting. The ability to rearrange the data and show multiple views of the same data is a great asset to your reporting design, but that is only the beginning. With some basic formatting and a little creative formatting, the Pivot Table view can take on appearances well beyond the basics.

Changing View Properties

Most of the formatting of pivot tables takes place within the pivot table areas and on the columns themselves. There is a single property affecting the entire pivot table that you can modify. In the title bar of the Edit View window for your pivot table, the leftmost button is the Pivot Table View Properties button. Clicking this button opens the Edit View dialog box (see Figure 12-5). The only property you can edit here is the "green-bar" styling. Clicking the check box enables this styling

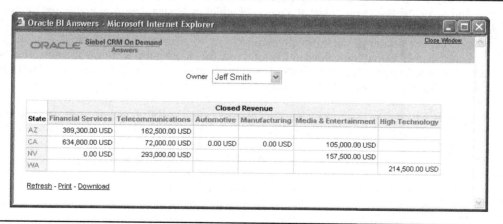

FIGURE 12-4.   *Pivot table with drop-down page selector*

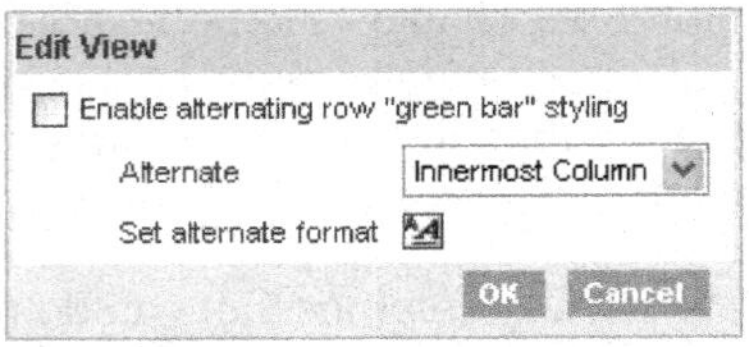

Edit View

☐ Enable alternating row "green bar" styling

Alternate   [Innermost Column ▼]

Set alternate format 🅰

[OK] [Cancel]

FIGURE 12-5. *Edit View dialog box*

and causes every other row in the pivot table to take on a light-green background. The Alternate field lets you choose to shade every other row beginning with the innermost column or to alternate the rows across the entire table. The innermost column is the last column in the Rows area of your pivot table. The rows in the Measures area are given the alternating style when you set the Alternate field to either Innermost Column or All Columns.

You do not have to accept the default format of the "green-bar" styling. You can make the alternating rows any color you please by clicking the Set Alternate Format button. This button opens the standard Edit Format window, allowing you to set the format for the font, cell, and border of every other row.

Adding Totals and Formatting the Rows Area

In the Rows area, click the S button (a mathematical symbol for sum) to open the Totals menu (see Figure 12-6). Initially, the None option is checked, indicating that no totals are included in the pivot table for the rows. To add totals, select either the Before or After option. The Before option creates a Grand Total row at the top of your pivot table (see Figure 12-7) and the After option gives you a Grand Total row at the bottom of your pivot table. The total of the metric columns appears and aggregates the data across all rows based on the aggregation rule for the metric column. You can display this Grand Total row before or after the measure values, not both.

The default label for the row total is "Grand Total." You can change this if you like, along with the format of the label, by again clicking the S button and selecting Format Labels. A typical Edit Format window opens, but with the addition of a Folder field at the very top of the window (see Figure 12-8). The Folder field, the name of which is misleading, is actually tied to the label for the row total. Enter a new label into this field. You may also apply any formatting options to the font, cell, or border as you normally would.

You can also format the values in the total row by clicking the S button and selecting Format Values. Again, a typical Edit Format window opens, where you can format the font, cell, and border for the measure values in the total row.

FIGURE 12-6. *Rows area Totals menu*

State	Closed Revenue					
	Financial Services	Telecommunications	Automotive	Manufacturing	Media & Entertainment	High Technology
Grand Total	**1,024,100.00 USD**	**527,500.00 USD**	**0.00 USD**	**0.00 USD**	**262,500.00 USD**	**214,500.00 USD**
AZ	389,300.00 USD	162,500.00 USD				
CA	634,800.00 USD	72,000.00 USD	0.00 USD	0.00 USD	105,000.00 USD	
NV	0.00 USD	293,000.00 USD			157,500.00 USD	
WA						214,500.00 USD

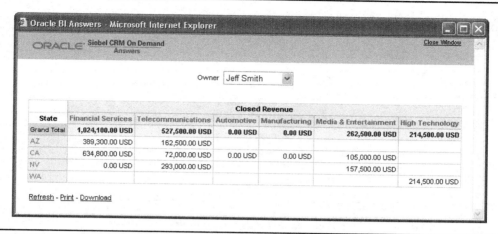

FIGURE 12-7. *Pivot table with Grand Total row at the top*

Adding Totals and Formatting the Columns Area

You may have noticed that your Columns area contains a Measure Labels object. The Measure Labels object contains two buttons. The first is a More Options button and the second is a Totals button. You will also notice a Totals button (S) to the right of "Columns" in the Columns area, just like the one in the Rows area. These two Totals buttons are redundant, except that the Totals button on the Measure Labels object is fully functional whereas the other will insert a total

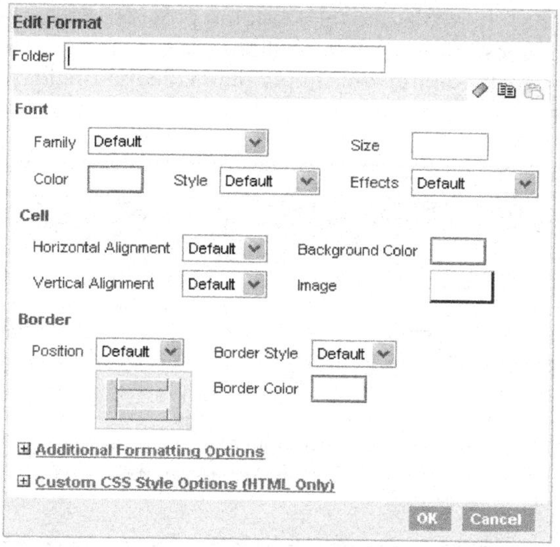

FIGURE 12-8. *Edit Format window*

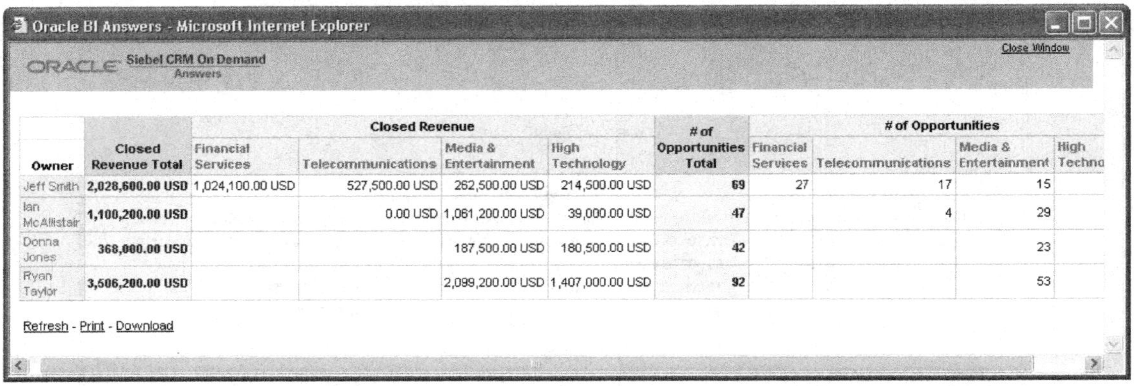

| | | Closed Revenue | | | | # of Opportunities Total | | # of Opportunities | | | |
Owner	Closed Revenue Total	Financial Services	Telecommunications	Media & Entertainment	High Technology		Financial Services	Telecommunications	Media & Entertainment	High Techno
Jeff Smith	2,028,600.00 USD	1,024,100.00 USD	527,500.00 USD	262,500.00 USD	214,500.00 USD	69	27	17	15	
Ian McAllistair	1,100,200.00 USD		0.00 USD	1,061,200.00 USD	39,000.00 USD	47		4	29	
Donna Jones	368,000.00 USD			187,500.00 USD	180,500.00 USD	42			23	
Ryan Taylor	3,506,200.00 USD			2,099,200.00 USD	1,407,000.00 USD	92			53	

Refresh - Print - Download

FIGURE 12-9. *Pivot table with column label totals before metric columns*

column but does not have functional formatting options. For this reason, we will ignore the S button on the Columns area and use only the buttons on the Measure Labels object to insert and format totals in the Columns area.

Click the S button to open the Totals menu on the Measure Labels object in the Columns area. The default option of None is initially selected here too. To add a total column, select the Before, After, At the Beginning, or At the End option. The total column will contain a total of each metric across all columns in each row.

The Before option creates a total column before each set of individual metric columns, as shown in Figure 12-9. The After option places the total columns after each set of individual metric columns, as shown in Figure 12-10.

It is important to note here that the total column provides a total of each single metric, not the total of all different metrics in the pivot table. For instance, if you have not placed any columns in the Columns area, the total column will simply duplicate the single measure column, as shown in Figure 12-11.

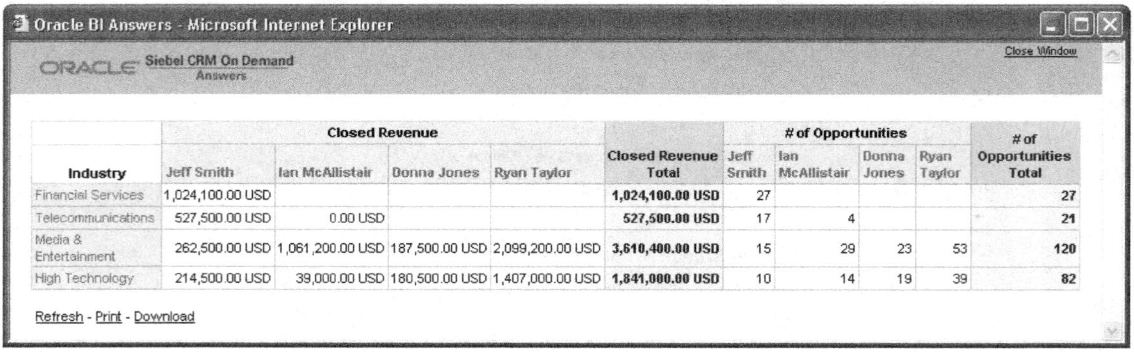

| | Closed Revenue | | | | Closed Revenue Total | # of Opportunities | | | | # of Opportunities Total |
Industry	Jeff Smith	Ian McAllistair	Donna Jones	Ryan Taylor		Jeff Smith	Ian McAllistair	Donna Jones	Ryan Taylor	
Financial Services	1,024,100.00 USD				1,024,100.00 USD	27				27
Telecommunications	527,500.00 USD	0.00 USD			527,500.00 USD	17	4			21
Media & Entertainment	262,500.00 USD	1,061,200.00 USD	187,500.00 USD	2,099,200.00 USD	3,610,400.00 USD	15	29	23	53	120
High Technology	214,500.00 USD	39,000.00 USD	180,500.00 USD	1,407,000.00 USD	1,841,000.00 USD	10	14	19	39	82

Refresh - Print - Download

FIGURE 12-10. *Pivot table with column label totals after metric columns*

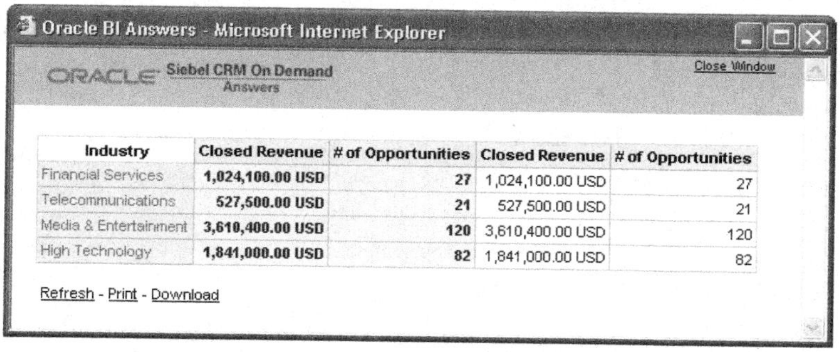

FIGURE 12-11. *Pivot table with total columns*

Column totals are really only applicable when you have split a metric into multiple columns by adding a database column to the Columns area and want to see a total across all of those columns. If you do not want to intermingle these individual total columns within the metric columns, you can choose to group all of your total columns together.

The At the Beginning option on the Totals menu creates a set of total columns before all of the individual metric columns, as shown in Figure 12-12.

The At the End option creates a set of total columns after all of the individual metric columns, as shown in Figure 12-13.

The default label on your total columns consists of the column name being totaled followed by "Total." You can change this if you like, along with the format of the label by again clicking the S button and selecting Format Labels. A typical Edit Format window opens, but with the addition of a Folder field at the very top of the window. Just like changing the label on the Grand Total row, enter a new label into the Folder field. The text you type into the Folder field is applied to all of your total columns, which could become confusing if you have multiple metrics in your pivot table, so you will probably want to keep the name of the metric in the total column. You can do this by entering the at sign (@) into your new label. Notice in Figure 12-14 that my total columns are named "Sum Total of" followed by the metric name. This is accomplished by typing **Sum Total of @** in the Folder field.

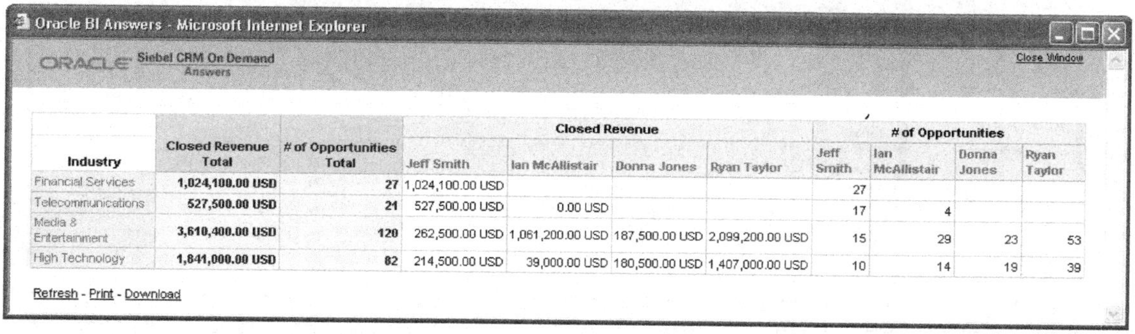

FIGURE 12-12. *Pivot table with measure label totals at the beginning*

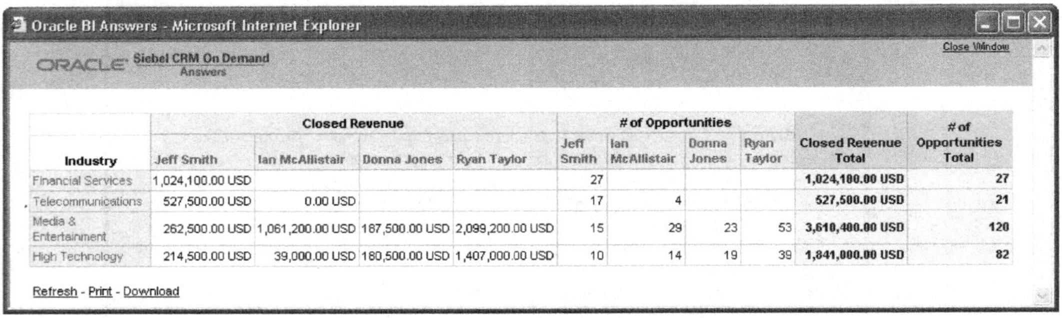

FIGURE 12-13. *Pivot table with measure label totals at the end*

The other formatting options for the label affect only the labels for the total columns. If you want to modify the measure labels (the column name, not the value name) of the metric columns, you can click the More Options button to open another menu (see Figure 12-15). Select Format Measure Labels to open an Edit Format window that allows you to format all of the measure labels. If you have not already formatted the total column labels, the format of the measure labels will also be applied to the labels on the total columns.

The More Options menu also includes an option to hide the measure labels. Select Hidden and the labels showing the name of the columns in the Measures area are hidden from sight in the pivot table. This option does not hide the labels on any total columns that you have added in the Columns area.

You can also format the values in the total columns by clicking the S button and selecting Format Values. Again, a typical Edit Format window opens, where you can format the font, cell, and border for the measure values in the total columns.

Adding Totals and Formatting the Sections Area

As you know, the Sections area allows you to split your pivot table into separate tables—one for each value in a column. Well, what if you want to have the entire pivot table for all values and

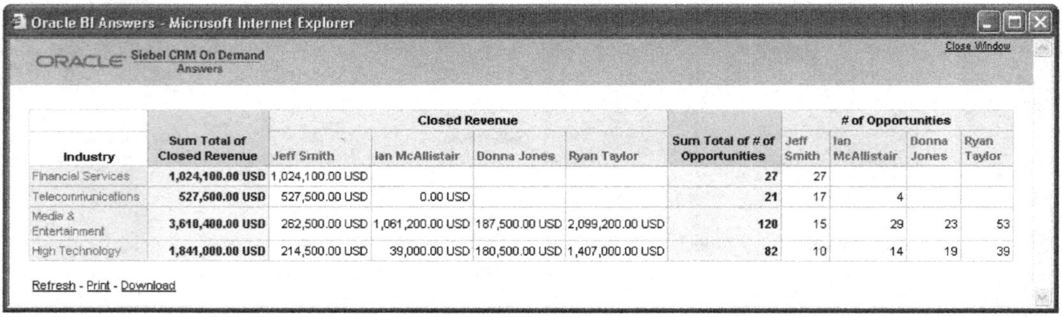

FIGURE 12-14. *Custom column total labels*

FIGURE 12-15. *More Options menu*

the individual tables? To the right of "Sections" in the Sections area, you see yet another S button. Click this button and you see the familiar Totals menu. Adding a total on the Sections area adds an additional pivot table to the view. This additional table is a summary of all sections. Choose the Before option to place this summary table before the other sections or choose the After option to place this summary table after the other sections. Figure 12-16 shows an example of a section total.

FIGURE 12-16. *Pivot table with section total*

The default label on this summary table is "All Sections." You can change this label by selecting the Format Labels option in the Sections area's Totals menu. The Folder field allows you to add your own label to the total table. The other format settings in the Edit Format window apply to this label as well. The Formatting Values option of the Sections area's Totals menu affects the values within the measures of your section summary table.

The second button in the Sections area is the Section Properties button. Clicking this button opens the Section Properties dialog box (see Figure 12-17), in which you can configure the display of column headings on the columns in your Sections area. You will also find options for inserting a page break and showing blank rows.

You have four options for displaying the column headings within your section. The column heading, by default, is not displayed, showing only the column value in the Sections area. If you want to display the column headings in the Sections area, click the radio button next to the location option of your choice. You can select Above, Left, or Before. Left and Before are very similar. Left places the column heading to the left of the column value, but treats the heading and the value as if they are in separate cells. If you are displaying multiple rows of values in the section, the headings and values will align across the rows. The Before option places the heading to the left of the value, separated by a space as if concatenated into a single value.

In the Options section of the Section Properties dialog box, the Insert Page Break field enables you to insert a page break between sections. Your page breaks are only in effect when you print the report to a PDF file. The Insert Page Break drop-down list will have at least four options, and more if you add more than one column to the Sections area.

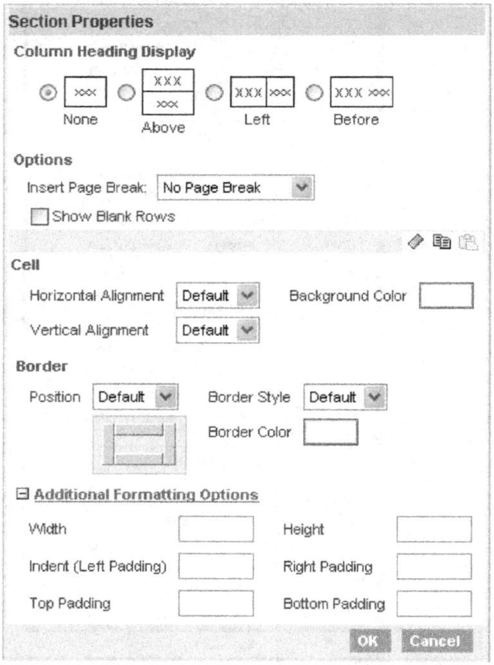

FIGURE 12-17. *Section Properties dialog box*

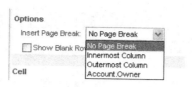

FIGURE 12-18.   *Insert Page Break drop-down list*

Figure 12-18 shows the drop-down list values in this field for a pivot table that contains three columns in the Sections area. No Page Break is the default setting. The next two values are Innermost Column and Outermost Column. The innermost column is the last column in the Sections area. The page break function inserts a page break after every unique section based on the column selected in this field. Uniqueness of sections is based on the section column values from the outermost column to the innermost column. Selecting Innermost Column in this field will guarantee that each section is on its own page.

You will also notice that each column present in your Sections area appears in the list of values for the Insert Page Break field. If you have more than two columns in your Sections area, you will have more than just an innermost column and outermost column to choose from. You can insert a page break after sections based on any column by selecting the column in this field. Remember that uniqueness is determined from the first column working inward, so selecting the second of three columns will group onto the same page all sections where the first two section columns are the same.

If you add to the Sections area a column that is blank on some of the records, you will have a section with no name. The Pivot Table view truncates out the space that would otherwise be occupied by a value. The difference is subtle, but checking the Show Blank Rows check box causes the pivot table to retain this space.

The format options in the Cell and Border sections affect the section header area above the table in each section. The line that appears by default above the section name is a top border on the Sections area. If you want to change or remove this border, make that change here. The Additional Formatting Options in the Section Properties dialog box affect the text area of the section header and does not change the size of the section header.

Adding Totals and Formatting the Pages Area

When you add a column to the Pages area, a drop-down list appears at the top of your pivot table that works like a filter. This page filter field enables you to dynamically change the content of the pivot table based on a selected value. The field contains only the values in the column. Suppose you want to also have the option of seeing all of the values in the one pivot table.

To the right of "Pages" in the Pages area, you see another S button. Click this button and you see the familiar Totals menu. Adding a total on the Pages area adds the All Pages option to the drop-down list, as shown in Figure 12-19. Since the pivot table will display the first page in the list when the report initially runs, if you select Before in the Totals menu, your pivot table will default to show all pages when the report runs. Selecting After places the All Pages option at the end of the list. The All Pages option is only available for the first column in the Pages area.

The formatting options have no effect here. The Pages area does not contain any headings or values of its own. The headings present here are elements of the columns in the Pages area.

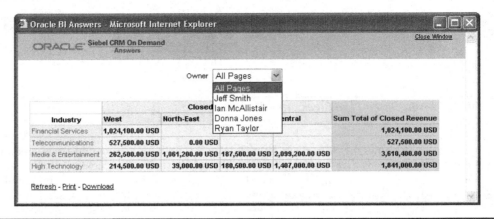

FIGURE 12-19.   *Page selector drop-down list*

Updating Content Properties

You may have noticed that there is a mostly blank area between the Sections area and Rows area and to the left of the Columns area. You cannot drop a column into this area. The only object here is a Content Properties button. Content in this case is defined as the Rows, Columns, and Measures areas of the pivot table. Click this button and the Content Properties dialog box opens (see Figure 12-20).

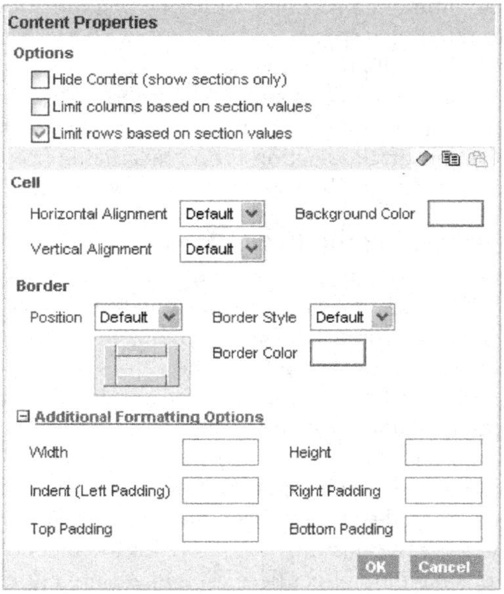

FIGURE 12-20.   *Content Properties dialog box*

At the top of this window, in the Options section, you find three check boxes, the third of which is checked by default. The first option here is to hide the content of the pivot table. This may seem like something you would never want to do, but it does serve a purpose, and you will see more of this option in the "'LayOUTside' the Box" section. When you check this check box, your pivot table will display only the Pages and Sections areas of your pivot chart. If you have not added any columns to your Pages or Sections areas, then your pivot table essentially disappears.

If you have added a column to your Columns area in your pivot table, you may have noticed that there are columns present that do not contain any data and are not needed in the pivot table. Another situation that leads to blank columns is a pivot table with the same column placed in both the Sections area and the Columns area, which is not unusual at all. The second check box under Options serves to remedy this design issue. When you choose to limit columns based on section values, any column that has no values in it will not appear in the section's pivot table. Compare Figures 12-21 and 12-22. In 12-21, I am designing a pivot table to show potential revenue by account type, with a separate section for each account type. In Figure 12-21, I am not limiting columns based on section values, and you see in the preview that I have a column for the account type of Prospect in the Customer section. Any record appearing in this section has an account type of Customer and will never have potential revenue listed under the Prospect type. Now look at Figure 12-22. Notice that the Prospect column has disappeared, but the columns in the pivot table have not changed. This happened because I chose to limit the columns based on section values.

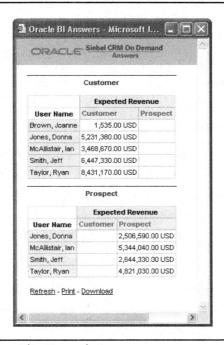

FIGURE 12-21.   *Pivot table not limiting columns*

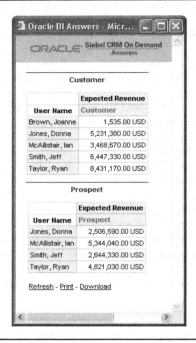

FIGURE 12-22. *Pivot table limiting columns*

The third check box under Options limits rows based on section values. This check box is checked by default, as it is unusual to want to show blank rows within your table. I have needed to uncheck this option in the past for a report that I was designing to replace a manual paper form. I needed to display all of the record type values, even if the row contained no data. Another reason to uncheck this option is for what many refer to as "negative reporting." Sometimes it is as important to see that a record is missing a value as it is to see the values associated with records.

Consider the simple table in Figures 12-23 and 12-24. These tables show potential revenue by account. Figure 12-23 shows only those records with potential revenue, because the third check box under Options was checked. When I uncheck this option, I get the pivot table shown in Figure 12-24 showing all accounts with and without potential revenue.

The formatting options in the Content Properties dialog box affect the entire content area. Again, the content area is the combined Rows, Columns, and Measures areas. Here you may add a background color to the entire content area, add a border, and adjust the alignment of the entire table. By default, pivot tables center themselves. Often it is more desirable to move the entire table to the left. You would make that adjustment here.

Formatting Columns in Your Pivot Table

So far this chapter has reviewed configuration and customization of your Pivot Table view on the canvas and area layers. There is another highly configurable area. The columns that you place in your pivot table all have a set of configuration options. Many of these options are dependant on which area the column resides in, and some are common across all areas.

FIGURE 12-23. *Pivot table limiting rows*

I will start with the formatting options that you will find on nearly every column in the pivot table, regardless of location. I will then describe the options that are specific, or at least somewhat different, for each of the areas.

Common Column Format Options

On each database column that you have added to your Pivot Table view, you will find up to three buttons next to the column name. All of the columns have a More Options button. Many have the Totals (S) button. You will also find that columns in any area other than the Measures area have a Sort button.

The availability of many of these buttons and the options beneath them is dependant on the area, and in some cases the location within the area, of the pivot table. There are, however, several options that are common across all columns.

Format Headings and Values   Click the More Options button and select Format Headings from the menu. This opens the Edit Format window. To change the heading on the column, type a new value in the Folder field. The remaining options in the Edit Format window also affect the heading for that column in your pivot table.

While the formatting affects only the heading on the column, if you adjust the width of the heading using the additional formatting options, the entire column, including the column values,

FIGURE 12-24.   *Pivot table not limiting rows*

adjusts according to the width setting. It is not possible to widen the heading without also widening the values. The inverse is true, as formatting the value width also affects the heading. If you adjust both the column heading width and the column value width, the larger of the two settings will control the width of the column. Concerning text alignment within the heading and values area, the width setting does affect the location of the center or left side of the column.

Click More Options and select Format Values to open the Edit Format window for the values portion of the column. I often find myself needing to apply the same formatting across many column headings or column values in my pivot tables. After formatting one heading the way I like, I click the copy icon in the upper-right portion of the Edit Format window and then paste my formatting into the other column headings.

Duplicate Layers   If you want to include one of your columns in your pivot table more than once, click the More Options button and select Duplicate Layer. This inserts an exact copy of the column into the same area. The copy will retain any formatting that you had applied to the original column before creating the duplicate. You can now move this duplicate to any of the other areas and apply formatting.

Duplicating a column is often quite useful when you want to show a column value in a pivot table section and rows, for instance, or want to include a measure in a pivot table twice with different aggregation rules.

Once you have added a duplicate, a new menu option becomes available on both the original and duplicate column. Click the More Options button and select Remove Duplicate to remove that copy of the column from the pivot table.

Remove a Column   If you click the More Options button and select Remove Column, you remove the column from the entire report. This means that you are removing the column not only from the pivot table, but from all other views too. If you select the Remove Column option, a confirmation dialog box appears confirming that this is what you really intend to do. Remember, if you want to remove a column from the pivot table only, drag it to the Excluded area.

Sort   In addition to the options in the More Options menu that are common to all columns added to a pivot table, every column outside of the Measures area has a Sort button. To override default sorting in your pivot table, click the Sort button on the column you want to sort on. Sorting within the pivot table is quite different from sorting in a normal table.

Sorting only impacts the area that contains the column. Sorting a column in the Pages area changes the order of the values in the page list box. Sorting a column in the Sections area affects the order in which the sections appear in the Pivot Table view.

In the Rows area, the grouping effect restricts the sort of column values within the confines of the column to the left. Consider the pivot table I am building in Figure 12-25. I am sorting on the third column in my Rows area. Notice that the values in this column sort only within the grouping of records based on the second column.

Formatting Columns in the Rows Area

A column's More Options menu changes based on the area of the pivot table to which the column is assigned. Columns in the Rows area have two additional options—Hidden and New Calculated Item. The Totals button appears on all but the rightmost column in the Rows area as well, providing the ability to add sub totals for the column values.

Hidden   Click the More Options button and select Hidden to hide a column in your pivot table. Just like hiding a column in a regular table, the column continues to affect the table but does not appear in the results. If you simply excluded the column from the report, the values within that column would have no effect on your pivot table.

You can still sort on a hidden column, which is useful if you want to sort by a specific column but want the values displayed in a location that would sort incorrectly based on the grouping of data.

New Calculated Item   The New Calculated Item option allows you to add a new value to a column. This value is usually a grouping of other values. For instance, suppose you have a column of U.S. states in your pivot table but want to group this data into areas rather than individual states, so that the data for NC, SC, GA, and FL is reported as part of a new value named "South." Click the More Options button and select New Calculated Item to open the Calculated Item dialog box (see Figure 12-26). Name your new item in the Name field. Notice that the available data values

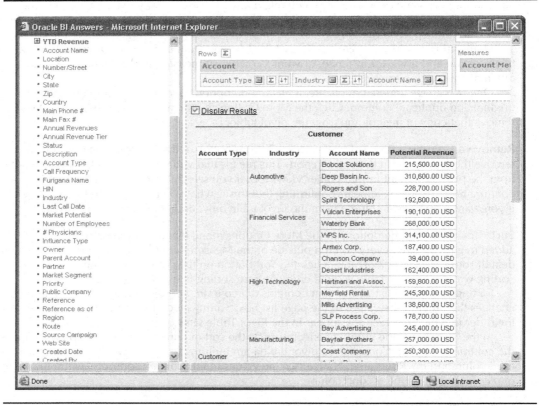

FIGURE 12-25. *Sorting rows in pivot table*

are listed on the right. To create a grouping of values into this new item, simply click each item in the list that you want to group together. The formula for the new item builds as you click these values. Each value is inserted into the formula surrounded by single quotes and separated with a plus sign.

The Format button in this dialog box opens a standard Edit Format window, allowing you to apply special formatting to this new calculated value within the column. If you check the Hide Details check box in the Calculated Item dialog box, the individual values that make up the calculated item will be hidden in the results.

The syntax for calculated item formulas is quite simple and allows you to create calculations of values and display them as new values in the pivot table. Column values are surrounded by single quotes and separated by an operator. Suppose you want to calculate commission amounts based on closed revenue in a table that shows closed revenue by industry for each sales person. Figure 12-27 shows such a table. The formula for my Commissions value here is

```
('Automotive'+'Consumer Goods'+'Financial Services'+'High Technology'+
'Manufacturing'+'Media & Entertainment'+'Retail'+'Telecommunications'+
'Travel & Transportation') *0.02
```

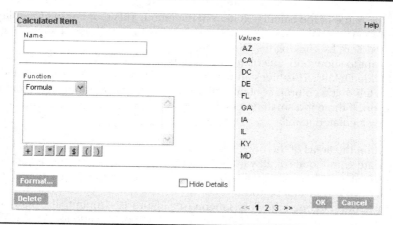

FIGURE 12-26.   *Calculated Item dialog box*

You can also use functions in your calculated item formulas. For instance, if you want to include a row that displays the range size of the measures in the pivot table, the following formula subtracts the smallest value in the column from the largest value in the column. Notice that the asterisk is used to identify all values.

```
MAX(*)-MIN(*)
```

Other useful formulas include average amounts and sum totals of specific rows:

```
AVG(*)
SUM('East'+'South')
```

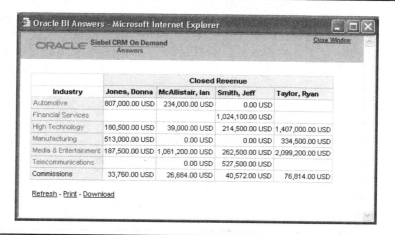

FIGURE 12-27.   *Commissions as a calculated item*

To make changes to a calculated item that you have created, click the More Options button and select the name of the calculated item in the menu. This reopens the Calculated Item dialog box, where you may make changes and then click OK to save those changes. You can also delete the calculated item by clicking the Delete button.

If you want to show only calculated items in your pivot table, click the More Options button and select Hide Details. This hides all values in the column except the calculated items.

You can tell that a column contains calculated items by examining the More Options button on the column. If there is a small box in the upper-right corner of the button, the column contains one or more calculated items.

Totals Within the areas of the pivot table, you can add totals for the columns within the area. These totals are grand totals of all values. On the specific columns, you can add subtotals for each column value. When you have two or more columns in the Rows area, all but the innermost column will have a Totals (S) button.

Click this button to open the Totals menu (see Figure 12-28). Initially, the None option is checked, indicating that no subtotals are included in the pivot table for the row. To add subtotals, select either the Before, After, At the Beginning, or At the End option. The Before option creates a total over each value in the column. The After option gives you a total row after each value (see Figure 12-29). The At the Beginning and At the End options group all of your subtotal rows together at the top or at the bottom of the table.

If you want to display a row label between each value in a column but do not want to show the totals, select the Labels Only (No Totals) option in the Totals menu. A blank row bearing the name of the column value is inserted into the table based on the location checked above.

The default label for the row total shows the row value followed by "Total." You can change this if you like, along with the format of the label, by again clicking the S button and selecting Format Labels. A typical Edit Format window opens, but with the addition of a Folder field at the very top of the window. Enter a new label into this field. You may also apply any formatting options to the font, cell, or border as you normally would.

If you want to retain the value name in the heading, you can use the @ wildcard to represent the value name. For instance, if you type @ **Sub Total** in the Folder field, your total row will display the value name followed by "Sub Total."

FIGURE 12-28. *Totals menu*

FIGURE 12-29. *Pivot table with subtotals*

You can also format the values in the total row by clicking the S button and selecting Format Values. Again, a typical Edit Format window opens, where you can format the font, cell, and border for the measure values in the total row.

Formatting Columns in the Columns Area

Similar to when working with columns in the Rows area, in the Columns area you gain the option for new calculated items and also the ability to add subtotals. The functionality is the same as described in the Rows area, but the location and purpose is somewhat different due to the location of the columns.

New Calculated Item In the Columns area, you will also find the New Calculated Item option on your More Options menu for the columns. I typically add a column to the Columns area to group data into specific columns. The values for these columns are not always exactly what I want to show in my pivot table. Sometimes there are values in the column that I do not want included.

The New Calculated Item gives me some flexibility here. Functionally, the Calculated Item dialog box is the same here as in the Rows area, but the applications are often a little different.

I find that I use the calculated items here as a filter more than for any other purpose. For instance, if I have a column of account types and want to only show a column for a couple of these account types, but do not want to filter the other types out of my report entirely, I can use the calculated item as a filter. I simply create a new calculated item by clicking the More Options button and selecting New Calculated Item. In the Calculated Item dialog box, I name the item (I often just type the name of the value I want to include) and then click the value on the right. I repeat this process to create all of the calculated items for each value. Once I have created my calculated items, I click the More Options button and select Hide Details. The final effect is a pivot table with a set of measure columns filtered to just the column values I want.

Of course, you can also use the calculated item to group data and perform special calculations as described previously with regard to formatting columns in the Rows area.

Totals When describing the pivot table areas earlier, I mentioned adding totals on the Measure Labels object. There, you saw that you can insert a total column for each measure column. The Totals button on the columns in the Columns area allows you to insert a total column for each value in a column when you have more than one column here. As you add columns, the order of the columns controls how the columns are displayed in the pivot table. The individual values for the second column are grouped beneath each value in the first column. Figure 12-30 shows a pivot table with two columns in the Columns area. Notice that the values of the second column (Account Type) are repeated for each value of the first (User Name).

All columns in the Columns area except the last column have a Totals (S) button. Click this button to open the Totals menu. Initially, the None option is checked, indicating that no subtotal columns are included in the pivot table. To add subtotals, select either the Before, After, At the Beginning, or At the End option. The Before option creates a total column before

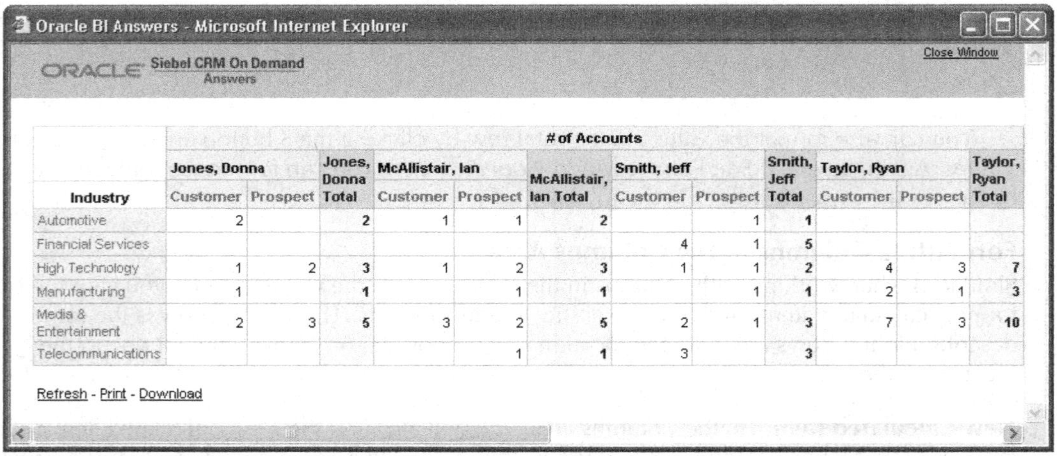

	# of Accounts											
	Jones, Donna		Jones, Donna Total	McAllistair, Ian		McAllistair, Ian Total	Smith, Jeff		Smith, Jeff Total	Taylor, Ryan		Taylor, Ryan Total
Industry	Customer	Prospect		Customer	Prospect		Customer	Prospect		Customer	Prospect	
Automotive	2		**2**	1	1	**2**		1	**1**			
Financial Services							4	1	**5**			
High Technology	1	2	**3**	1	2	**3**	1	1	**2**	4	3	**7**
Manufacturing	1		**1**		1	**1**		1	**1**	2	1	**3**
Media & Entertainment	2	3	**5**	3	2	**5**	2	1	**3**	7	3	**10**
Telecommunications					1	**1**	3		**3**			

FIGURE 12-30. *Pivot table with total on first column*

each value in the column. The After option gives you a total column after each value. The At the Beginning and At the End options group all of your subtotal rows together at the top or at the bottom of the table, respectively.

The default label for the column total shows the column value followed by "Total." You can change this if you like, along with the format of the label, by again clicking the S button and selecting Format Labels. A typical Edit Format window opens, but with the addition of a Folder field at the very top of the window. Enter a new label into this field. You may also apply any formatting options to the font, cell, or border as you normally would. Like before, if you want to retain the value name in the heading, you can use the @ wildcard to represent the value name.

You can also format the values in the total column by clicking the S button and selecting Format Values. Again, a typical Edit Format window opens, where you can format the font, cell, and border for the measure values in the total row.

Formatting Columns in the Measures Area

The More Options menu for columns in the Measures area contains some very different options from the other More Options menus. You can transform your measure values into percentages and indexes of portions of your data, change the way data aggregates, and display running totals. You could perform many of these calculations on the column directly in Step 1 of the Build and View Analysis window, but the formula required to group the data and perform the calculations is a bit more complex.

Show Data As   Click the More Options button and move your mouse to the Show Data As option. Another submenu opens showing three options (see Figure 12-31). By default, your measure columns are set to show the data values. You also see options here for Percent Of and Index Of, described next.

Move your mouse over the Percent Of option and you see another submenu with the following options for showing the column values as a percentage:

■ **Percent of Column**   Shows the calculated percentage of the column represented by the value in each row.

■ **Percent of Row**   When you have not added any columns to the Columns area, this option produces a calculated result of 100% for each row because you are calculating the percent of a row that a value represents with only one metric column in the row.

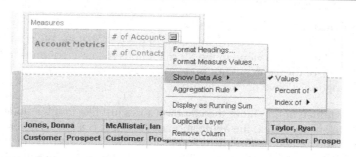

FIGURE 12-31.   *Show Data As menu*

When you are grouping data into column values, this option gives you the percentage that the column value represents within that row.

- **Percent of Section** Converts the column values into a percentage of the section. The values in the columns will total to 100 percent for each section of the Pivot Table view.

- **Percent of Page** Converts the column values into a percentage of the page represented by each value. All of the percentages in the entire Pivot Table view will total to 100 percent.

- **Percent of Column Parent** If you have multiple columns in the Columns area, this option gives you the percentage of the topmost column.

- **Percent of Row Parent** If you have multiple columns in the Rows area, this option gives you the percentage of the outermost row.

- **Percent of Layer** Allows you to select the exact column for which you want to see the percentage. This may be necessary when the desired column is not represented by the page, section, row parent, or column parent.

The Index Of option contains the same submenu options as the Percent Of option and provides the exact same functionality in a different format—the Percent Of option results in values reflected as percentages, whereas the Index Of option results in index values. So if you would rather see ".38" than "38%," use the Index Of option.

Aggregation Rule As described in Chapter 5, every column has an aggregation rule that controls how the column values calculate when shown in a subtotal or grand total. The aggregation rule defines how this amount is calculated.

You can use in the pivot table a different aggregation rule from the aggregation rule you apply to the column directly in Step 1 of the Build and View Analysis window. This allows you to duplicate columns and display different calculations for the same columns, for instance.

To set the aggregation rule on a measure column, click the More Options button and move your mouse to Aggregation Rule. A submenu displays showing all of the available aggregations rules. There are 12 values available for your pivot table measure column value aggregation. Table 12-1 provides an explanation of each of these values.

Display as Running Sum If you want to display your column values as a running sum across the rows of data, click the More Options button and select the Display as Running Sum option. The aggregation rule on the column affects this calculation too. An aggregation rule of Count coupled with the Display as Running Sum option results in a running count in the column.

Formatting Columns in the Sections Area

Columns that you add to the Sections area control the way that the pivot table breaks into smaller tables within the Pivot Table view. In the More Options menu of columns in the Sections area, you will find some of the same options previously described in other areas, in addition to a couple of new options I have not yet discussed.

Hidden The Hidden option hides the column values just like in other areas, but when the column is in the Sections area, the application of the effect is a little different. Since each section contains a separate table based on the columns in the Sections area, hiding the column here causes the value to disappear but retains the splits based on the values in the column. This potentially results in an unlabeled section.

Aggregation Rule	Effect
Default	Default aggregation uses the column's aggregation rule set back in Step 1. This option is used for all columns unless you make a change here.
Sum	The value in the pivot table reflects the total of all values that meet the criteria of each row and column in the pivot table. For instance, if your table shows revenue by owner and account type, each value in the table will be the sum of all values of the same account type owned by the same user. This option is not available for nonmetric data.
Min	The value in the pivot table reflects the lowest value in the dataset meeting the requirements of the row and column. For text values, this is the first value when sorted alphabetically. For date and time values, this is the earliest date and time in the column.
Max	The value in the pivot table reflects the largest value in the dataset meeting the requirements of the row and column. For text values, this is the last value when sorted alphabetically. For date and time values, this is the latest date and time in the column.
Average	The value in the pivot table reflects the average value of the column values in the pivot table. This option is not available for nonmetric columns.
First	The value in the pivot table reflects the first value in the dataset meeting the requirements of the row and column. This rule is particularly useful for date values, as it will show the earliest date in the dataset.
Last	The value in the pivot table reflects the last value in the dataset meeting the requirements of the row and column. This rule is particularly useful for date values, as it will show the latest date in the dataset.
Count	The value in the pivot table reflects the total number of values meeting the requirements of the row and column.
Count Distinct	The value in the pivot table reflects the total number of distinct values meeting the requirements of the row and column.
None	Setting the aggregate rule to None prevents a value from displaying in the Measures area.
Server Complex Aggregate	If the values in your metric columns are generated through some complex calculations within the report, you may find that using the Server Complex Aggregate aggregation rule will provide the desired results.
Report-Based Total	Not really an aggregation rule, the Report-Based Total option is enabled by default and indicates that the totals should only include the values in the report.

TABLE 12-1.   *Aggregation Rules*

Place Value in New Row   A good reason for hiding a column value here is if you want to split the table based on some criteria that you do not want displayed but you want to display the values in another column that you have included in the Sections area.

When you add multiple columns to the Sections area, it is the combination of these columns that determines what the section contains. Each unique combination of column values from each column results in a separate section. The column values are initially displayed on a single line separated only by a space. If you are displaying column headings in your sections, the headings and values are all strung together in a single line.

To show each value on a separate line in the section heading, click the More Options button on a column you want to move to the next line and select the Place Value in New Row option. The column value, and heading if displayed, moves to the next line in the section heading.

I take advantage of this option along with hiding the content area regularly for a special type of report that I describe in the "'LayOUTside' the Box" section.

Hide Repeated Values   When you have multiple columns in your Sections area, you will find that the first column value is repeated for each of the values in the second column. You may want to display the value from the first column in the first section, but then only show the value from the second column in the remaining sections until the next value in the first column is reached. To accomplish this effect, click the More Options button on the first column and select the Hide Repeated Values option.

New Calculated Item   As with the Rows and Columns areas, you will find the New Calculated Item option on your More Options menu for the columns in the Sections area. The Calculated Item dialog box gives you the same flexibility here as in the other areas.

I use calculated items in sections as a filter and for grouping to control what my sections contain. For instance, if I have a column of opportunity types and I want to only show a section for a specific type or group certain types together, I can use the calculated item. I simply create a new calculated item by clicking the More Options button and selecting New Calculated Item. In the Calculated Item window, I name the item and then click the values on the right that I want to include. Once I have created my calculated items, I click the More Options button and select Hide Details. The final effect is a pivot table with only the sections I want and the data I want in each section.

Totals   Just as you are able to add column totals in the Rows and Columns areas, the Totals button on the columns in the Sections area allows you to insert a summary section for each value in a column. You will need more than one column in the Sections area to have this option. As you add columns, the order of the columns controls how the sections are created and ordered in the pivot table. The individual values for the second column are combined with each value in the first column to form unique sections.

All columns in the Sections area except the last column have a Totals (S) button. Click this button to open the Totals menu. Initially, the None option is checked, indicating that no summary sections are included in the pivot table. To add a summary section, select either the Before, After, At the Beginning, or At the End option. The Before option creates a total section before each section containing a unique value in the column. The After option gives you a total section after the sections for each value in that column. The At the Beginning and At the End options group all of your total sections before or after all of the sections, respectively.

The default label for the summary section shows the column value followed by "Total." You can change this if you like, along with the format of the label, by again clicking the S button and selecting Format Labels. A typical Edit Format window opens, but with the addition of a Folder field at the very top of the window. Enter a new label into this field. You may also apply any formatting options to the font, cell, or border as you normally would. Like before, if you want to retain the value name in the heading, you can use the @ wildcard to represent the value name.

You can also format the values in the summary section by clicking the S button and selecting Format Values. Again, a typical Edit Format window opens, where you can format the font, cell, and border for the measure values in the section.

Formatting Columns in the Pages Area

Columns that you add to the Pages area control the content of the page selector drop-down list. The way in which this area uses column values is very different from the way in which the other areas use them, so it stands to reason that the options on the columns here are a little different too. In the More Options menu of columns in the Pages area, you will find some of the same options but with unique effects.

Hidden   The Hidden option hides the column values just like in other areas, but since the column values in the Pages area are displayed as values in a drop-down list, the application of the effect is rather counterproductive. Since the combination of column values determines the content of the page selector, hiding one of the columns causes repeating values in the drop-down list. I have never needed to do this.

If you are creating a separate drop-down list for each column, hiding a column results in an error because you must display at least one value per drop-down list.

Start New Page Dropdown   When you add multiple columns to the Pages area, it is the combination of these columns that determines what the pivot table page contains. Each unique combination of column values from each column results in a separate page. The column headings are initially displayed on a single line separated by a hyphen, and the values on the single drop-down list are also displayed hyphenated.

To create a new drop-down list for each column, click the More Options button on the column and select the Start New Page Dropdown option. A new drop-down list for the column appears on the next line in the Pages area of the pivot table.

New Calculated Item   As with the other areas, you will find the New Calculated Item option on your More Options menu for the columns in the Pages area. The Calculated Item dialog box gives you the same flexibility here as in the other areas, but the values appear in the drop-down lists. You can use calculated items in the Pages area to filter out pages or group data into single pages. The process for creating a new calculated item here is the same as in other areas of the pivot table.

Totals   Just as you can add column totals to create a summary section in the Sections area, you can also create summary page options in the page selector drop-down list.

All columns in the Pages area except the last column have a Totals (S) button. Click this button to open the Totals menu. Initially, the None option is checked. To add a summary page, select either the Before, After, At the Beginning, or At the End option. The Before option creates a page value in the list before each column value. The After option gives you the additional page value after each column value in the drop-down list. The At the Beginning and At the End options group all of your total pages before or after all of the values in the drop-down list, respectively.

The default label for the new value is the column value followed by "Total." You can change this if you like by clicking the S button and selecting Format Labels. A typical Edit Format window opens with the Folder field at the very top of the window. Enter a new label into this field. Like before, if you want to retain the value name in the heading, you can use the @ wildcard to represent the value name.

Since the label for the new page actually appears in the drop-down list, any format changes you make beyond the name are ignored. You can format the values in the summary pages by clicking the S button and selecting Format Values. Again, a typical Edit Format window opens, where you can format the font, cell, and border for the measure values in the section. When you display a summary page in the report, the data is formatted according to the settings here.

Pivot Charts

In the Edit View window for the Pivot Table view, you will find a Chart Pivoted Results check box and Chart Position field in the header bar. If you check this check box, a chart based on your pivot chart data is inserted into the Pivot Table view at the location selected in the Chart Position field. Most of the basic charts are available as a pivot chart, but there are some differences in how you format the charts. Bubble charts and scatter charts are not available as pivot charts.

There are some distinct advantages and disadvantages to pivot charts versus regular Chart views. This section addresses these differences and describes the formatting of pivot charts.

Inserting Pivot Charts

Pivot charts are based on the rows, columns, and measures in your pivot table. To insert a chart, click the Chart Pivoted Results check box. The default position for the pivot chart is to the right of the pivot table, but you can choose to place the pivot chart on the left, top, or bottom. You can also hide the pivot table and display only the charted pivot data.

One thing you will notice about pivot charts is that you do not select the columns you want to display and assign the axis on which column data displays. The control for this is in the layout of your pivot table. The location of the row data, column data, and measures differs by chart. Table 12-2 describes for each chart exactly where your pivot data appears in the charted pivot data.

Chart	Row Data	Column Data	Measures
Area	Bottom axis	Measure labels	Left axis
Horizontal bar	Left axis	Measure labels	Bottom axis
Vertical bar	Bottom axis	Measure labels	Left axis
Line	Bottom axis	Measure labels	Left axis
Line bar combo	Bottom axis	Measure labels 1st column—line 2nd column—bar	Left/right axis
Pareto	Bottom axis	Measure label 1st column only	Left axis 1st metric only
Pie	Measure label		Pie 1st metric only
Radar	Radar	Measure label	Left axis
Step	Bottom axis	Measure labels	Left axis

TABLE 12-2. *Data Placement in Pivot Charts*

Formatting Pivot Charts

Select the graph, type, and style for your pivot chart from the corresponding drop-down list, just like you would for a Chart view. Most of the chart controls for pivot charts are also the same as the controls available in the Chart view. Because Chapter 11 covered these controls in depth, this section provides only a brief review.

General Chart Properties Button

The leftmost button in the toolbar is the General Chart Properties button. Click this button to open the General Chart Properties dialog box, in which you can add a title to your pivot chart, specify how labels will appear, change the data format, and specify the size for the chart. The only tangible difference between the pivot chart and a normal Chart view has to do with the sizing of the chart. There are no slider bars for adjusting the size of the pivot chart. You must adjust pivot chart size in the General Chart Properties dialog box.

Axis Titles & Labels Button

The next button (second from left) is the Axis Titles & Labels button. Clicking this button opens the Axis Titles & Labels dialog box, which contains two or three tabs, depending on the chart type. The Left tab (and Right tab for a line bar combo chart) allows you to configure the title and label formats of the vertical axis. The Bottom tab also has a Title section and Labels section for modifying the title and scale labels of the bottom axis.

Axis Scaling Button

The next button is the Axis Scaling button. Clicking this button takes you to the Axis Scaling dialog box, which has one or two tabs, depending on the type of chart. A line bar combo chart, for instance, has a scale on the left vertical axis and on the right vertical axis. Both the Left and Right tabs contain the same fields but may have different settings within those fields. Here you can adjust the range of your axis scale and the number of major and minor tick marks. You can also add scale markers to your pivot charts.

Additional Charting Options Button

To the right of the Axis Scaling button is the Additional Charting Options button. Clicking this button opens the Additional Charting Options dialog box, which contains for tabs:

- **Grid Lines**   Change the color of the major and minor grid lines. Clicking the Override Defaults check box enables the check boxes on the tab that allow you to disable major and minor grid lines, both vertical and horizontal.

- **Legend**   Configure if and where your chart legend appears.

- **Interaction**   Select the type of interaction that will occur when a user clicks part of the chart.

- **Borders & Colors**   Set a color for your chart's background, text, and border.

Format Chart Data Button

Clicking the Format Chart Data button opens the Format Chart Data dialog box, where you can format the appearance of your chart data elements. On a pivot chart, the Format Chart Data dialog box contains two tabs. The Positional tab is the same as for the normal Chart view. On the Positional tab, you can specify the color and style for each series and each chart component.

The Conditional tab gives you a formatting option that you do not have with the normal Chart view. On the Conditional tab (see Figure 12-32), you will find each of the columns in your pivot chart listed on the left side of the tab.

Click the Add Condition button. A submenu appears that contains the list of columns in the pivot chart. Select the column to which you would like to add a conditional color format. A typical Create/Edit Filter window opens. Designate the operator and values for the condition and click OK. A new condition is added to the tab for the selected column. Click the color selector for the condition and select a color from the palate. Now, whenever the condition is met, the chart element representing that column will change to the specified color.

You can continue to add additional conditions to the column, change their order by using the arrow buttons, delete them by using the × button, and modify the condition by clicking the Filter button. Figure 12-33 shows the Conditional tab of the Format Chart Data dialog box with several conditions defined. Conditions are evaluated beginning at the top of the list, so order is important.

Advanced Properties Button

With the line bar combo and pie charts, you can make additional special formatting changes by clicking the Advanced Properties button. For the line bar combo chart, the Chart Type Special dialog box contains a single check box that allows you to synchronize the line and bar axis scales. For the pie chart, you can format the data values as a percentage of the total or the actual value represented by each wedge. You can also define what information is included in the data label. You can display the value only, the name only, or both the name and value.

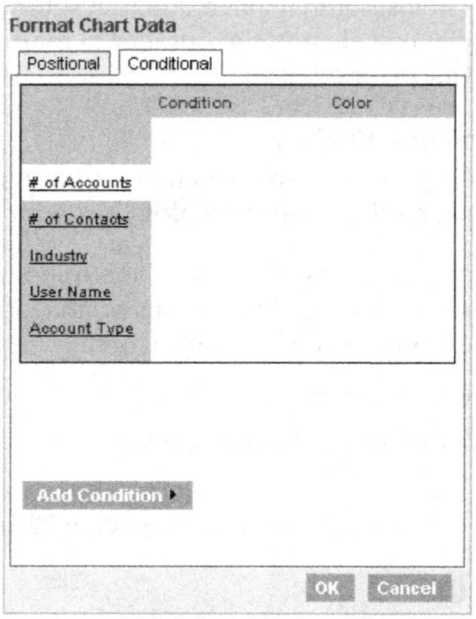

FIGURE 12-32. *Format Chart Data dialog box—Conditional tab*

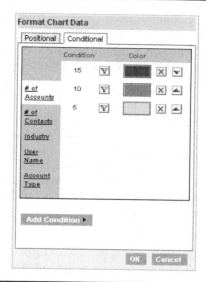

FIGURE 12-33. *Format Chart Data dialog box—Conditional tab with conditions*

"LayOUTside" the Box

In the beginning of the chapter I described the pivot table as an extremely versatile report view. I really enjoy working with the pivot table. It is the one view where imagination is given some room to roam. That being said, pivot tables are often the culprits behind poorly performing reports. Pivot tables can do a lot of things with your data, and naturally, the more you try to do in your report, the longer it will take to generate the report. In this section, I toss speed and performance aside and explore some alternative ways to use pivot tables to challenge the boundaries of standard reports.

I will begin with a few formatting tips and move into some more advanced, and somewhat unconventional, formatting of the Pivot Table view.

Formatting Tips

I have spent a lot of time formatting pivot tables in many different types of reports, and along the way I've picked up a few tricks. I have captured some of these for you here.

Turn Off the Preview

Every time you move a column in the Edit View window for the pivot table, the preview of the pivot table results refreshes. If you have many columns to move around, uncheck the Display Results check box (below the Rows area), and then move your columns around. Answers will not need to spend time and bandwidth refreshing the preview after every move. After rearranging the columns, turn the preview back on and verify that everything is as you want.

Format Width of All Columns at Once

If you ever need to format the width of all columns in a pivot table to the same width, you can do it very quickly using the alternate row formatting. Click the Pivot Table View Properties button and check the Enable Alternating Row 'Green-Bar' Styling check box. Set the Alternate field to All Columns. Next, click the View Format button and set the column width to the desired size. You may also want to change the background color for the green-bar styling and the content area to the same color if you do not want the green-bar shading.

Use Any Column as a Measure

Pivot tables typically show the metric columns on the right side of the table, but occasionally I need to display text data or date data between or after metric data. If you drop a nonmetric column into the Measures area, the data in the columns seems to disappear. This is due to the fact that those columns have a default aggregation rule of "None." Pivot tables aggregate data based on the arrangement of rows and columns and rely on aggregation rules to determine how to display this data. Simply change the aggregation rule on your text or date columns to an aggregation rule that is valid for text or date columns, such as "Max."

Use Summary Tables

I often use a simple pivot table at the top of my report rather than cluttering up the detail table with subtotals. A small summary table is also much easier to chart in a pivot chart. Experiment with adding columns to the Pages area in your summary tables too. This is a great way to save some real estate on the screen without losing the ability to report on multiple variables.

Inserting Sections Inside a Table

You know that you can create a separate table for each value in a column placed in the Sections area. What if you don't want separate tables but do want to section the data? Try this technique to separate your pivot data into sections without using the Sections area.

Place the column you want to use to segment your data in the first position of the Rows area. Duplicate this column and place the duplicate in the second position. Now all you have to do is add a total to the first column, checking the Before option and also checking the Labels Only option. This puts a header into the pivot table for each value. You can use the Format Labels option in the Totals menu to add borders, change colors, and so forth to get the look you want. Now, hide the first column by clicking the More Options button and clicking Hidden.

The duplicate column in the second position is still visible. You can add a total to this column using the After option to get section totals. Figure 12-34 shows a pivot table that I have formatted in this way.

Creating a Section-Only Record Detail Report

This trick may be the furthest from the proverbial box outside of which we are always instructed to think. I have had several customers insist on having data from rows presented in columns in their reports. Some have even wanted a means for printing details of a single record, but didn't want every single field like you might get with a Print Screen command. I have used this technique to overcome several such challenges, some quite small and some very large.

When I am presented with a need to display record data not in rows but more like a printed form, I turn to my trusty Pivot Table view. For this explanation, the form contains multiple sections and is about a page in size.

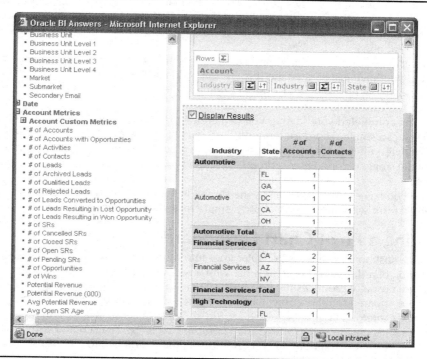

FIGURE 12-34. *Using Labels Only total as section heading*

Start by creating a report that contains every column you are going to need in your report. Add a column filter to allow only a single record into the report while building. A filter on an ID field is typically most effective. You will change the filter later. Ensure that all of your formulas are working the way you like by examining the Table view in Step 2 of the Build and View Analysis window, and then delete the Table view.

Insert a pivot table and immediately turn off the preview at the bottom. Trust me, you have a lot of columns to move around, and there is no point in waiting for the preview to refresh after every move. At this point, I find it is easiest to move all of the columns to the Excluded box. If you click the table heading to drag your columns, all of the columns under that heading move at once. This is much easier than dragging each individual column.

After excluding all of the columns, begin placing the columns for the first section of your form one by one into the Sections area. If your form has multiple columns of fields, place the fields into the Sections area in left-to-right order rather than going down one column and then down the next. You also need to drop a column into the Measures area. It does not matter which column you drop there. If you do not have an extra column, duplicate one from the Sections area and move it to the Measures area.

Next, click the More Options button on each column that should appear first in a row on your form, and choose to place the value in a new row. Open the Section Properties dialog box and add column headings if you like, and make any other formatting changes to the section that you like.

Click the Content Properties button, check the first check box in the Content Properties dialog box to hide the content of the pivot table, and then click OK. Now that you have all of your needed columns in the Sections area and have hidden the content areas, go ahead and turn the preview back on.

Format your column headings and values to get the spacing the way you want it on your form, and you have just created the first section. Add another Pivot Table view and repeat these steps to create the next section. Consider adding additional title views and placing them between the Pivot Table views to create section headings.

Having completed your layout, you can either go to Step 3 and create a prompt to allow the user to select a single record for the report, or you can go back to Step 1 and change the filter to an Is Prompted filter to facilitate navigating to the report, passing a single value into this filter to identify the single record. Filter prompts and report navigation are described in detail in later chapters.

Now you have a report similar to one shown in Figure 12-35, which looks more like a completed form with information about a single record than a report.

Creating a Pivot Chart Dashboard

Users love dashboards. The next chapter goes into more detail on creating a custom dashboard, but the look of a dashboard is achievable with a set of Pivot Table views. The Account History subject area usually produces the best results because there are many more relationships available compared to other subject areas, but any subject area will do as long as it contains the data you are after.

Pivot tables enable you to show small portions of a large data set, and with multiple pivot charts, you can show multiple different portions of the data. I like to create a set of very simple pivot tables and then chart the data in each, displaying only the chart.

Arranging this set of pivot charts as I have in Figure 12-36 makes for a nice dashboard-type display of many different, yet related, segments of CRM On Demand data.

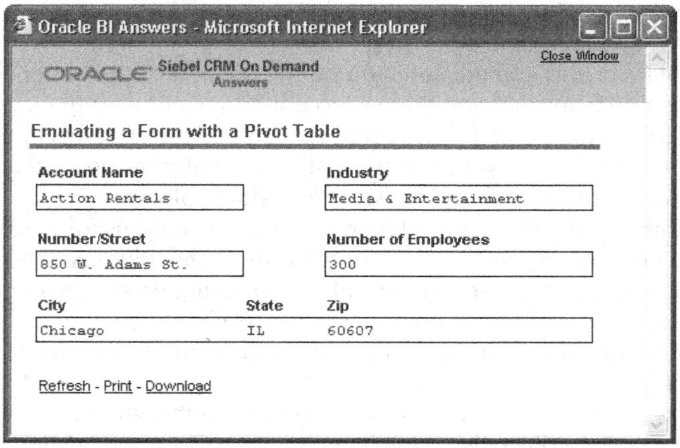

FIGURE 12-35. *Emulating a form with a Pivot Table view*

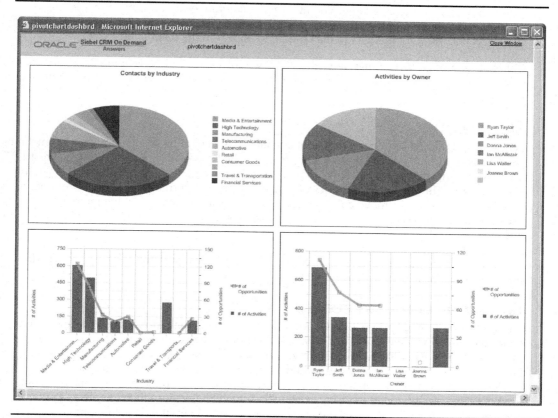

FIGURE 12-36. *Pivot table dashboard*

Troubleshooting

When you think about what pivot tables actually do, it is amazing to think that you can perform such complex data manipulations in a browser-based hosted application. Well, nothing is without limits, so there are some limitations. I will mention some of the limitations and issues I have encountered while working with pivot tables.

Pivot Table Requirements

The following are two specific rules (in the form of actual error messages) with which you must comply in order to successfully add a pivot table to your report. Most of the error messages that you receive when you run up against one of these requirements are fairly clear and easy to understand.

"You must add at least one measure."   If the set of columns that you add to the report in Step 1 includes metric columns, these columns automatically move to the Measures area of the pivot table. If you did not include any metrics in Step 1, then you will see this error message when configuring your Pivot Table view. You must add a column, even if it is not a metric, to the Measures area in order to create a pivot table. Remember that an aggregation rule on a nonmetric column is necessary for the data in the column to appear in the pivot table.

"At least one page layer must be visible."   If you place any columns in the Pages area of the pivot table, at least one column must be visible. You will see this error message if you hide all of the columns in the Pages area.

Slow Script

When I am working with a pivot table that contains many columns and a lot of data, I sometimes get a browser error telling me that a script is causing the browser to slow down (see Figure 12-37).

I see this most often when saving a formatting change to a heading or value and when the preview is refreshing. One obvious performance tip here is to turn off the preview. Another tip is to, whenever possible, remove columns from your analysis instead of placing them in the Excluded area. Of course, removing columns affects other views, so do this only when you know it is safe.

As far as the error message goes, I normally just click No and let the script finish doing what it needs to do. If your patience grows short, you can save your report and close and reopen the browser to clear out some virtual memory.

Governor Limit Exceeded

This error has nothing to do with state politics, though the thought does make me laugh. Pivot tables can handle a large amount of data, but there are limits to the number of columns and rows that a pivot table can display in a report. When you run or preview your report and you see Figure 12-38 where your pivot table should be, your pivot table has grown too large.

Receiving this error is not always a bad thing. I often build reports that rely on some filters to limit the data, but the report in design mode does not yet have those filters in place. Perhaps another report passes a value to the filter or a filter prompt limits the data. I recommend placing column filters in place in Step 1 to test your report design and get the layout just right, and then remove the temporary filters before deploying the report.

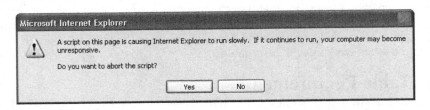

FIGURE 12-37.   *Slow script browser error*

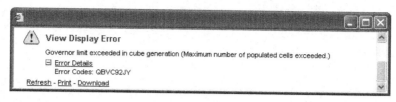

FIGURE 12-38.   *Pivot Table view error—governor limit exceeded*

Of course, if you see this error when you are really expecting a pivot table, and you are already filtering the data as much as you planned to, you need to scale back the pivot table. Some strategies here include removing unnecessary columns, using the Pages area to view data one page at a time rather than all pages at once, or splitting the data into separate tables or separate reports.

Assertion Failure

This error (see Figure 12-39) means there is a problem with a calculated item on one of your columns in the pivot table. This error appears in place of your pivot table in the preview or when you run the report.

If you construct a calculated item and use an incorrect syntax, you will see an error and be unable to save your calculated item. This error occurs when you have written a calculated item with the correct syntax but a predicate in the formula fails or does not agree with the data in the column.

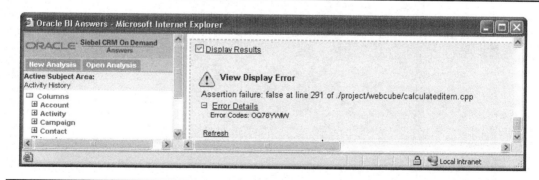

FIGURE 12-39.   *Pivot Table view error—assertion failure*

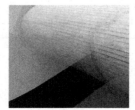

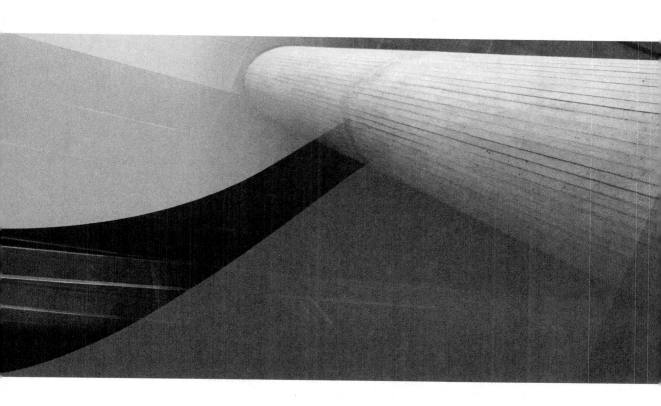

CHAPTER
13

Adding Advanced Views and Creating Custom Dashboards

I n addition to tables and charts, Answers On Demand includes some views that provide other means for delivering information to your users or adding more functionality to your reports. You can also create custom dashboards. A dashboard is a collection of reports that shares a common filter delivered on a single page. This functionality is new to CRM On Demand and is a welcome addition.

In this chapter, I describe the informational views and how to configure them. I also provide detailed instructions on several more advanced views that provide additional effects and functionality. Finally, I take you through the process of developing your own custom dashboard. As you go through this chapter, if you find that some of these views are not available in Answers On Demand, verify that your role has the Analytics Scripting privilege enabled as well as all of the Dashboard privileges.

Informational and Advanced Report Views

I am sure you have noticed that there are several other views available in the Add View menu that haven't been discussed yet. These views are discussed in this section.

NOTE
Many of your reports might use only the Title, Table, Chart, and Pivot Table views. Even if you never use a single view from this chapter, with the four views mentioned, you can create very powerful and engaging reports in Answers On Demand.

Informational Views

I have grouped together the first set of views as "informational" views because they do not really report data, but rather support the users' use and understanding of your reports. With these views, you can add instructions, copyright or confidentiality statements, policy statements, or any other static information you want to deliver along with your report.

You can also let users know how the report is filtered, what the different colors in a report mean, or that the report did not find any data to report. Think of these views as the supporting cast in your report. The data may be the star of the show, but these views pull the storyline together.

Active Filters View

Reports are filtered in many ways. Some filters are static and do not change each time a report runs. There are others that may be based on system variables or time variables. Other filters may be directed by the user passing a value from a prompt or navigation link. Regardless of how they become part of your report, filters are an integral component of most analyses.

Knowing what is *not* in a report is often just as important as knowing what is in a report. If you filter a particular industry out of a report that shows revenues by territory, it is probably going to be very easy for a user to draw an incorrect conclusion from this report unless you indicate in some way that the data is not all-inclusive.

To include in your report a view that will dynamically display a list of all filters currently applied to your report, click the Add View button in Step 2 of the Build and View Analysis window and select Active Filters. This inserts the Active Filters view at the bottom of your report. Figure 13-1 shows an Active Filters view with several variations of filters. Notice that the view here reads a lot like the filter's description in Step 1 of the Build and View Analysis window.

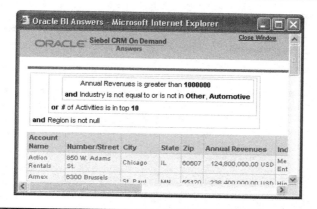

FIGURE 13-1. *Active Filters view*

Active Filters view formatting options are quite limited in this view compared to others. The Format View button opens an Edit Format window that gives you some options for background shading, borders, and some sizing. If you have an "is prompted" filter on your report, the Active Filters view shows the value passed to the filter. If no value is passed to the filter, the Active Filters view will not include the filter.

A potential problem with the Active Filters view is that a complex set of filters not only takes up a lot of report real estate, but also may be difficult for your users to understand. The language and structure of the filter descriptions can be confusing to someone who is not accustomed to reading them. This brings me to my Active Filters view simplification technique.

If your report contains a complex or confusing filter definition, you can simplify the Active Filters display by saving your filter and reapplying it. When you reapply the filter, insert the filter as a reference to the saved filter, replacing the complex filter with a simple reference. Now, your Active Filters view looks more like Figure 13-2. Notice that there is now a View link next to the

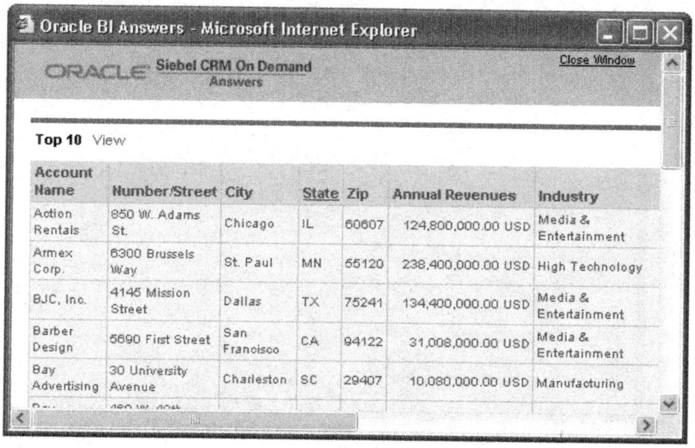

FIGURE 13-2. *Active Filters view with saved filter reference*

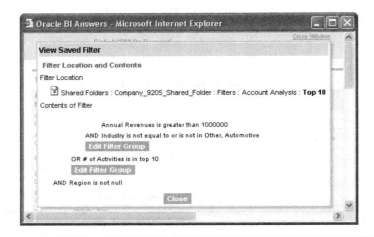

FIGURE 13-3. *Active Filters view details*

filter name. The user can click this link to see the details (see Figure 13-3) if they like, and the Active Filters view does not take much space away from your report.

Static Text View

The Static Text view is another simple view. This view does not draw from the CRM On Demand data for content or change based on any run-time variables. The Static Text view behaves exactly as its name implies.

Click the Add View button and select Static Text. This opens the Edit View: Static Text window (see Figure 13-4), where you can add the text you want displayed in your report. The Edit View

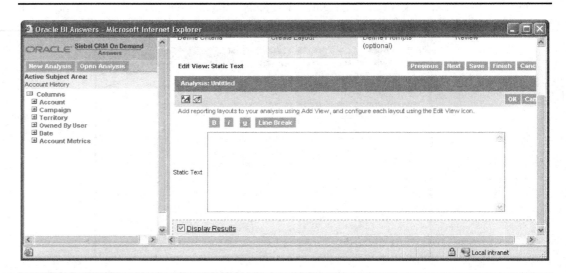

FIGURE 13-4. *Edit View: Static Text window*

Format	Open Tag	Close Tag	Example
Bold	[b]	[/b]	[b]Bold Text[/b]
Italics	[i]	[/i]	[i]Italic Text[/i]
Underline	[u]	[/u]	[u]Underline Text[/u]
Line Break		[br/]	Line Break[br/]

TABLE 13-1.   *Static Text Formatting Tags*

window has format buttons for bold, italic, and underline. These allow you to apply formatting to parts of the static text. Clicking the Line Break button inserts a line break tag at your cursor location.

The Static Text view uses formatting tags that are similar to HTML tags. Clicking one of the formatting buttons inserts the appropriate open and close tags. If you highlight the text you want to format before clicking a format button, the tags position before and after the highlighted text automatically. Table 13-1 shows the formatting tags accepted by the Static Text view.

You can combine tags to apply multiple formats. Simply place the open tags in front of the text and the close tags after the text:

```
[b][i][u]This text would be bold, italic, and underlined.[/u][/i][/b]
```

In addition to regular text, you can insert special characters into your static text using HTML entity names or numbers. Table 13-2 provides a sample of the most commonly used HTML entities. You can find a complete list of these codes with a simple Internet search.

Result	Description	Entity Name	Entity Number
¢	cent	¢	¢
£	pound	£	£
¥	yen	¥	¥
€	euro	€	€
§	section	§	§
©	copyright	©	©
®	registered trademark	®	®
×	multiplication	×	×
÷	division	÷	÷

TABLE 13-2.   *HTML Entity Names and Numbers*

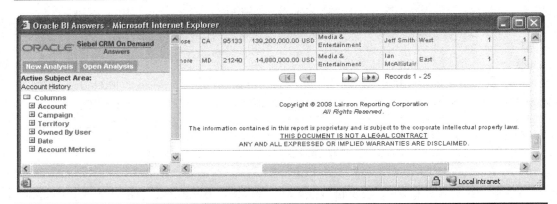

FIGURE 13-5. *Sample Static Text view*

The portion of the report shown in Figure 13-5 is a Static Text view containing a copyright statement. This example utilizes all of the formatting features just described. The code entered into the Static Text view is shown here as well:

```
[b]Copyright &copy; 2008 Lairson Reporting Corporation[/b] [br/]
[i]All Rights Reserved.[/i][br/][br/]
The information contained in this report is proprietary and is subject
to the corporate intellectual property laws.[br/]
[u]THIS DOCUMENT IS NOT A LEGAL CONTRACT[/u][br/]
ANY AND ALL EXPRESS OR IMPLIED WARRANTIES ARE DISCLAIMED.
```

Legend View

The more you change the background and text colors, the more likely you are to confuse your report users and potentially reduce the usability of your reports. This is particularly true when using conditional formatting and dynamic filtering to change the appearance of data. The Legend view enables you to add some clarity to your report formatting by inserting a static legend into your report (see Figure 13-6).

Click the Add View button and select Legend. This takes you to the Edit View: Legend window. Your legend is made up of three components. The title appears above the legend items. You can format the title font, background, border, and size using the Format window by clicking the Format button to the right of the field. The next component is the caption. Each legend item can have a caption to its left or right or have no caption at all. Choose the location for your captions in the Location field. You can also format the caption text by clicking the Format Captions button next to the caption's heading. The format properties you set here are applied to all captions in the legend.

The final component is the sample text. For each format that will appear in your report, you add an example in the legend. This may include images, text, or just a background color. Click the Add button to add additional entries. If you have added any text to the Sample Text field, when you click the Add button, the text from the previous sample is entered into the new Sample Text field automatically. You can change this text if you like.

FIGURE 13-6. *Edit View: Legend window*

You will also want to format each sample to reflect a particular format that will appear in your report. To finish off your legend, you can format the view by clicking the Format Legend Table button. In the resulting format window, you can adjust the alignment, background color, borders, and spacing for the legend table. In the Legend Items Per Row field, you set the number of legend entries to display in each row. This number can be as small as 1 item, creating a single column of legend values, or as large as 12, creating a legend that spans the width of the report.

Your Legend view can be a simple list of colored blocks, as shown in Figure 13-6, or can include caption and sample text to describe the format meanings in the report, as shown in Figure 13-7.

TIP
When appropriate, add a legend to your report that covers any conditional text as well as your charts. You can format chart data so that your colors and formats are consistent across all of your report views and then use a single legend to describe all of the view formats at once.

FIGURE 13-7. *Sample legend*

No Results View

When a report returns no results, users receive the window shown in Figure 13-8. This particular window is rather generic and only offers the current filters, if any, as an explanation for there being no data. Many users will naturally assume that the report is broken rather than understand that the result set is null. If you have a concern that your users will potentially encounter a null result based on filter prompts or other conditions, you can add a custom No Results view to your report. This view is only visible when the report does not produce any data.

To add a No Results view, click the Add View button, move to the Advanced submenu, and select No Results. The Edit View: No Results window (see Figure 13-9) is a very simple window with only two text fields.

Your No Results view can contain a headline and text of your choice. You cannot modify the format of either of these elements. To create the No Results view, simply enter text in one or both of these fields. The headline appears in a bold blue text and the text appears in regular black text (see Figure 13-10).

The No Results view appears only in Step 2 of the Build and View Analysis window, in the preview, or on the actual report when there are no results in your report. If you want to preview the No Results view, add an overly restrictive filter to your report. To make changes to the No Results view, click the Add View button and select Advanced | No Results again. You may have only one No Results view on each report.

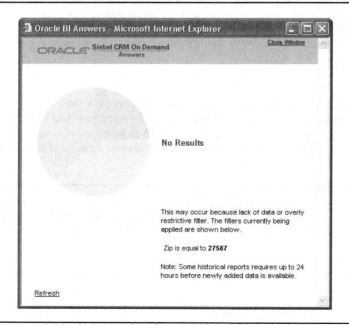

FIGURE 13-8. *Standard No Results window*

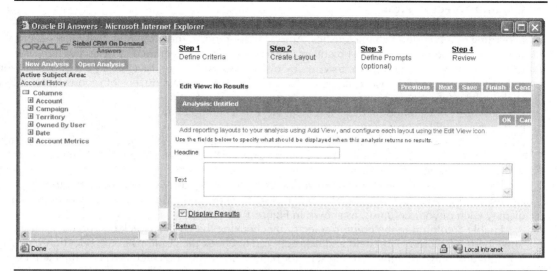

FIGURE 13-9. *Edit View: No Results window*

Advanced Views

This section provides information on using and formatting the following advanced views:

- **Column Selector view**   Allows report users to change the columns that appear in an analysis
- **View Selector view**   Allow report users to change the views on the report
- **Narrative view**   Allows report users to display multiple reports or virtually any HTML content
- **Ticker view**   Allows report users to scroll data across the report window

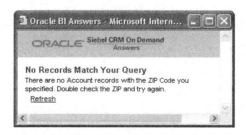

FIGURE 13-10. *Custom No Results window*

Column Selector View

Suppose you have been asked to produce a series of reports, each of which analyzes revenue according to a couple of characteristics. Among these reports, the only thing that differs is the way the revenue data is grouped by other columns. You have revenue by owner and territory, revenue by manager and region, revenue by owner and sales stage, revenue by account type and industry, and so on. This list could go on for pages and encompass dozens of reports, each with a slightly different organization of the same metrics.

Answers On Demand includes a special view that can potentially reduce your report library of dozens of single-purpose reports to a few multipurpose reports. The Column Selector view allows you to put some control in the users' hands, letting them select the columns they want to see in the report. You determine which column options to offer the users by enabling columns within the Column Selector view.

To add a Column Selector view to your report, click the Add View button, move to the Advanced submenu, and select Column Selector. The Edit View: Column Selector window will display each of your columns, as shown in Figure 13-11.

Enable a column in the column selector by checking the Enable check box on the column. This opens a Column Label field and instructs you to check the columns in the selection pane. You can add only columns from the selector pane. That means no calculated columns will ever be one of the optional columns in a column selector. The original column may have a customized formula.

Each column that you click is added to the list at the active column position, denoted by yellow shading. These columns will be listed in the column selector drop-down list in your report. The original column will be the default when your user first runs the report, and the added columns will be available in the column's drop-down list. Selecting one of the values in a column selector drop-down list replaces the current column with the selected column.

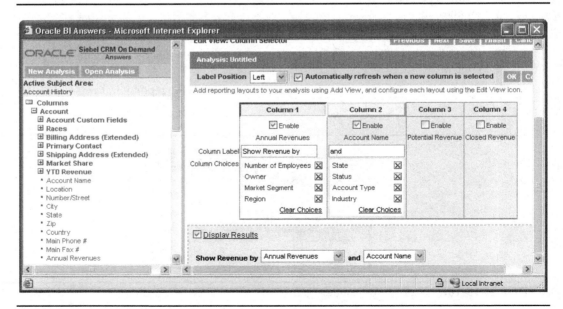

FIGURE 13-11. *Edit View: Column Selector window*

When entering the labels for your column selector, consider the column order. If it is the first column in a series, I recommend a label that begins a statement about what the report will contain. "Show Data by" and "Analyze Revenue Using" are a couple of good examples. If you are enabling additional columns, use a label that connects the two columns and completes the statement including the column names. "Show Data by Owner Within Each Territory" for instance. If the user changes columns, the statement built by combining the labels and columns still makes sense, such as "Show Data by Fiscal Year Within Each Industry."

The Label Position field in the title bar area allows you to specify the location for your labels—above or to the left. To the right of the Local Position field is a check box to set the report to automatically refresh when a new value is selected in a column selector column. My recommendation is that you leave this box checked if you are enabling only one column in your column selector. If the user can make changes to several columns, then it may be best to uncheck this check box. When you uncheck this option, a Go link is added to the view after the column selector fields. With the automatic refresh disabled, the user is able to make all of the column selections and then click the Go link to refresh the report. This keeps the report from attempting to refresh after each individual column selection, which can be rather annoying if there are several columns enabled.

You will not find any text format options while editing the Column Selector view, but after saving the view and returning to the Step 2 window, you will be able to format the view to apply alignment, background settings, borders, and size settings. Figure 13-12 shows a configured Column Selector view.

The column selector is actually replacing columns in your report when you select columns from a column selector. Formatting on the original column is not transferred to the new column. To apply formatting to the additional columns, you need to select each of your alternative columns

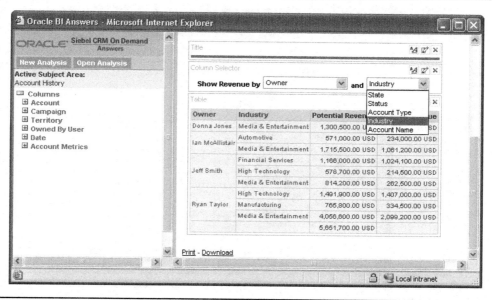

FIGURE 13-12. *Column Selector view*

in the preview in Step 2 of the Build and View Analysis window, and then navigate back to the Step 1 window. Now the columns shown in Step 1 will reflect the columns selected in Step 2. Format the column here. Repeat this process to format each of the columns in your report.

View Selector View

Another option for giving users some control over what they are seeing in your reports is the View Selector view. With a view selector, the user is able to select from a number of different views of the report data. Perhaps some users prefer to see the data charted at a summary level while others may need the details of a table. You could build a single report that displays all of these views, but that report would be large and difficult for your users to use effectively. Well-designed business intelligence delivers the data that your users need in order to understand their business and perform their business tasks effectively. More is not always more effective when it comes to reporting. Too much information can serve to obscure meaning rather than enhance it.

With the View Selector view, you can provide multiple views of data but allow the user to select the single view of their choice. The first step in implementing a view selector in your report is to build all of the views you plan to offer in the report. Once you have added all of the charts, pivot tables, and other views, you can add the View Selector view by clicking the Add View button, moving to the Advanced submenu, and selecting View Selector.

The Edit View: View Selector window (see Figure 13-13) is where you identify the views that you want to include in the view selector. The available views are listed in the Available Views list. This list includes all of the views on the report, including views that you may have created

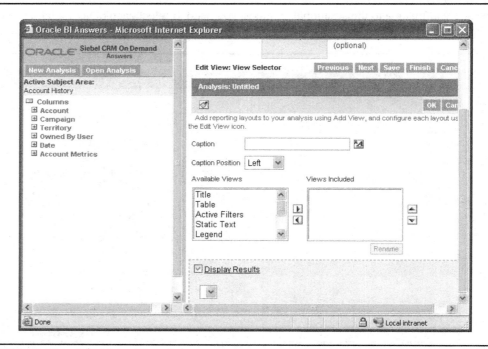

FIGURE 13-13. *Edit View: View Selector screen*

and subsequently deleted. To include views in the view selector, select the views from the Available Views list and click the arrow pointing to the right. Included views may be reordered by selecting the view in the Views Included list and clicking the up or down arrows.

Any views that you leave in the Available Views list will be displayed on the report at all times outside of the view selector, unless you have deleted the views from the layout. Notice that the names of the views do not give you much information about what the view contains. You can customize the name that appears in the view list by selecting the view in the Views Included list and then clicking the Rename button. The Rename dialog box contains a New Name field in which you can enter the desired name of the report view.

Above the Available Views and Views Included fields you find a Caption field and a Caption Position field. Use the Caption field to enter the text you want to appear with the view selector drop-down list. You may format this caption by clicking the Format button to the right. Use the Caption Position drop-down list to position this caption above, to the left, or to the right of the view selector. Click OK and the View Selector view is added to the bottom of your report. If you have not already done so, you may now delete the extra views from your report. The final result (see Figure 13-14) is a simple report with a view selector that allows your users to control which view is displayed, printed, or downloaded.

Narrative View

The Narrative view is the most open-ended of all the views. You can use a Narrative view to create letters, quotes, or invoices. You can use a Narrative view to embed other reports, web pages, or any HTML document. If you are skilled in HTML and JavaScript, you can do just about anything inside a Narrative view that you can do in any other web page.

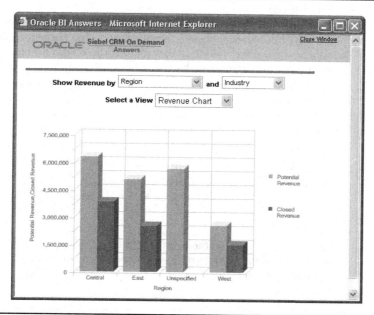

FIGURE 13-14. *Report with a view selector*

Obviously, I will not be able to describe every possible use of the Narrative view, but I will describe how the Narrative view works, and leave the rest to your imagination and ingenuity.

Add a Narrative view to your report by clicking the Add View button, moving to the Advanced submenu, and selecting the Narrative option. The Edit View: Narrative window contains five fields, listed and described in Table 13-3. Each of these fields, with the exception of the Rows to Display field, accepts HTML and JavaScript.

TIP
The Oracle CRM On Demand Customer Care Team is not able to troubleshoot custom HTML code and JavaScript. If you have trouble with your Narrative views due to your code, seek out a web developer for help.

The Edit View: Narrative window also has some buttons that insert formatting tags just like the Edit View: Static Text window. These tags are similar to HTML tags. Refer to the "Static Text View" section earlier in this chapter for more information; Tables 13-1 and 13-2 describe the formatting tags and HTML entities, respectively.

As you work with the Narrative view, you will find that some font formatting HTML tags have no effect. Font color and background colors are not affected by HTML tags. You can format the font used throughout the Narrative view by clicking the Edit Font Format button. Here you can set the font family, size, color, style, and effect. These settings are applied to all text in the Narrative view.

Field	Description
Prefix	The Prefix field accepts HTML. The content of the Prefix field appears at the top of the Narrative view in your report. The content of the Prefix field appears only once, which makes it a favorable field for embedding content from other URLs (such as the URL of another report in CRM On Demand).
Narrative	The Narrative field content repeats for every row in your report results. This is where you are able to pull data from the report table into the narrative text using references to the column number (@1 for column one, @2 for column two, and so on). Each "page" of narrative is 25 records in length.
Row Separator	The Row Separator field allows you to place some space, a horizontal line, or some text between each row of data in the narrative.
Rows to Display	The Rows to Display field takes an integer value to set the number of records from the report results to include in the Narrative view. This will cut off the results at the number of records specified, regardless of the number of records returned in the report.
Postfix	The content placed in the Postfix field displays after every 25 records and at the end of the Narrative view. The odd thing about this field is that the content will repeat for every 25 records regardless of how many rows you are displaying in the Narrative view.

TABLE 13-3. *Narrative View Fields*

Any text inside of heading tags will change color to match these settings, but the sizing is controlled by the heading tags.

After saving your Narrative view and returning to the Step 2 window, you can adjust the background color, text alignment, border, and spacing by clicking the Format View button on the Narrative view object. Figure 13-15 shows a sample quote developed using a Narrative view. The HTML code that I used to generate this Narrative view is shown next as an example:

```
<h2 align=center>Custom Guitar Picks Quote<br>
Guitar Strings n Things</h2>
<hr>
<b>CUSTOMER:</b> @1<br>
<b>LOCATION:</b> @2<br>
<b>PHONE:</b> @3<br>
<b>WEB SITE:</b> @4<br><br><hr>
We appreciate your business and guarantee this quote to be your exact final
charge. Your 100% satisfaction is also guaranteed with a full price return.
```

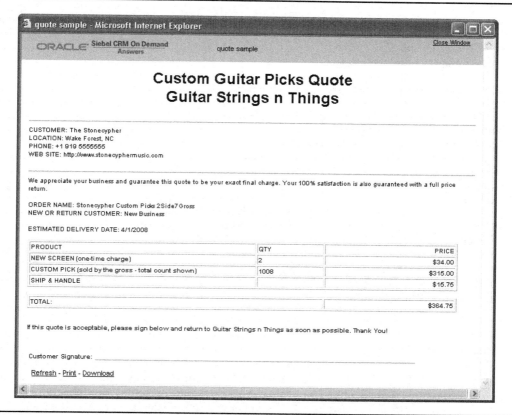

FIGURE 13-15. *Quote developed using Narrative view*

```
<br><br>
<b>ORDER NAME:</b> @5<br>
<b>NEW OR RETURN CUSTOMER:</b> @8<br><br>
<b>ESTIMATED DELIVERY DATE: @6<br><br>
<table border="1">
<tr>
<th width="350" align="left">PRODUCT</th>
<th width="100" align="left">QTY</th>
<th width="200" align="right">PRICE</th>
</tr>
<tr>
<td>NEW SCREEN (one-time charge)</td>
<td>@9</td>
<td align="right">@12</td>
</tr>
<tr>
<td>CUSTOM PICK (sold by the gross - total count shown)</td>
<td>@10</td>
<td align="right">@11</td>
</tr>
<tr>
<td>SHIP & HANDLE</td>
<td> </td>
<td align="right">@13</td>
</tr>
</table>
<BR>
<table border="1">
<tr>
<td width="455">TOTAL:</td>
<td width="200" align="right">@14</td>
</tr>
</table>
<br><br>
If this quote is acceptable, please sign below and return to
Guitar Strings n Things as soon as possible. Thank You!
<br><br><br>
<table>
<tr>
<td width="100" align="left">Customer Signature:</td>
<td width="500"><br><hr></td>
</tr>
</table>
```

Ticker View

Everyone has seen a stock ticker or news ticker on television or a web site. The Ticker view attempts to emulate this method of looking at data. The tickers that you can create in your report are not constantly updating like you might expect from a ticker, so this view may not be as exciting as you might think. Essentially, the ticker will scroll data of your choosing using a special HTML class that performs this function.

The Ticker view uses the Marquee HTML function, which works well in Internet Explorer but is unreliable in other browsers. Consider your users' browser applications when choosing to include a Ticker view in your report.

To add a Ticker view to your report, click the Add View button, move to the Advanced submenu, and select the Ticker option. The Edit View: Ticker window opens with a number of default values already set in most of the fields (see Figure 13-16). The Behavior field defaults to Scroll but can also be set to Slide or Alternate. Scroll moves data across the screen and then repeats. Slide moves data across the screen and stops. Alternate moves data across the screen and then reverses direction.

The Direction field controls the direction that the data moves across the screen. Left is the default direction, but your data may also move right, up, or down. The default width is 420 points. You can set the width and height to whatever size accommodates your data.

The remainder of the fields in the Edit View: Ticker window are HTML fields that you use to define and format the data in your ticker. Table 13-4 lists these fields and describes how to add text and data to the Ticker view.

Keep in mind that the Ticker view is a special HTML table and that you can use HTML tags to format the data that appears in your Ticker view.

The buttons below the text entry fields allow you to return to the default by clicking Set Defaults or clear all of the text fields by clicking Clear Fields. Click the Advanced button to open the Advanced Ticker Options dialog box (see Figure 13-17), in which you can set the number of loops your ticker will make. You may want to limit the number of loops for performance reasons. You can also set the scroll speed using the Scroll Amount and Scroll Delay fields. The default

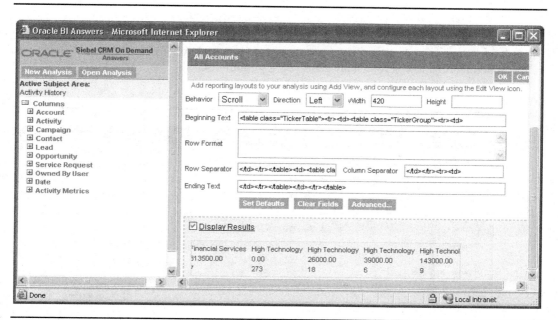

FIGURE 13-16. *Edit View: Ticker window*

Field	Code Explanation
Beginning Text	<table class="TickerTable"><tr><td> [1] <table class="TickerGroup"><tr> [2] <td> [1] Text inserted here appears above the ticker. [2] Text inserted here appears above the ticker in a second row.
Row Format	By default, every column in your report appears in the Ticker view. Adding any text to this field changes this default. Reference the columns using @n, where n is the column position. The following code will insert the first, third, and fourth columns in two rows (column 1 is in bold): @1 @3, @4
Row Separator	</td></tr></table> [3] <td> [4] <table class="TickerGroup"><tr><td> [3] Text inserted here appears at the bottom of each row, except the last one. [4] Text inserted here appears at the top of each row, except the first one.
Column Separator	</td></tr><tr><td> [5] [5] Text entered here appears before the data from the report columns, except the first column. This only works if you have not entered anything in the Row Format field.
Ending Text	</td></tr></table> [6] </td></tr></table> [6] Text entered here appears at the end of the last row of data.

TABLE 13-4. *Ticker View Fields*

Scroll Amount setting is 2, meaning that the text moves 2 pixels at a time. The default Scroll Delay is 1, meaning that the text moves every 1 millisecond. A high Scroll Amount gives you a faster scroll and a low Scroll Delay gives you a smoother scroll.

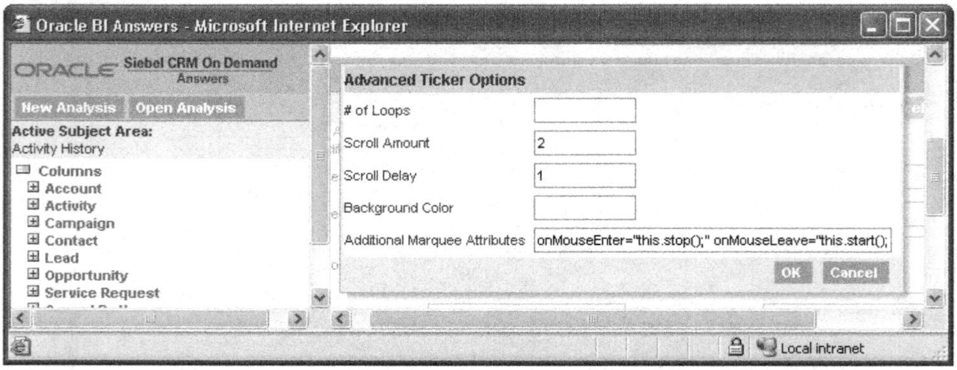

FIGURE 13-17. *Advanced Ticker Options dialog box*

Enter an HTML color code in the Background Color field to change the color of your ticker object. You can find a list of the thousands of supported color codes with a quick Internet search. Finally, the Additional Marquee Attributes field contains some code that causes the scroll to stop and restart when the mouse moves in and out of the ticker area. You may enter additional options here if you are familiar with this type of code. The following code added to the Additional Marquee Attributes field causes the text to fade in and out as it scrolls across the screen. This is not terribly useful, but serves as an interesting example.

```
style="Filter:Alpha(Opacity=100, FinishOpacity=0, Style=2, StartX=0,
StartY=90, FinishX=0, FinishY=0);"
```

Creating Dashboards

You can think of a dashboard as a container for reports. The dashboard enables you to combine multiple reports onto a single set of pages that shares a common filter. These reports may be from multiple subject areas. A dashboard can also serve as a launch page for multiple management summary reports, to make accessing multiple reports very convenient for your users.

In this section, I will describe the steps necessary to combine the reports you have developed into a dashboard. There are two sides to dashboard development. You of course have to develop the reports in Answers On Demand that you want to include in the dashboard. You also develop your dashboard filters in Answers On Demand. Outside of Answers On Demand, you create the dashboard on the Dashboard tab. You can think of the Dashboard tab as an extension of Answers On Demand because it interfaces with Answers On Demand to link the reports and filters into the sections of the dashboard.

Controlling Dashboard Access

As with reports, role-based access control mechanisms control which users can access and develop dashboards. Dashboards are public, so all users with access to the Dashboard tab can open a dashboard, but the reports inside of the dashboard are still subject to the user's report access. In order for you or another user to create public dashboards, the user role must have the Manage Dashboards privilege and Manage Custom Reports privilege enabled.

Constructing the Dashboard Filter Prompt

Start with the dashboard prompt that will filter the reports on your dashboard. You will continue to use Answers On Demand to construct the dashboard prompt. Getting to the Dashboard Prompt window is not entirely intuitive:

1. Begin as if you are creating a new report. Click the Design Analysis link on the Reports tab.

2. Click a subject area to open the Build and View Analysis window. It really does not matter which subject area you select; you are just trying to get to the Build and View Analysis window.

3. In the Build and View Analysis window, there are three buttons above the column selector list. Click the third button in this set, the Dashboard Prompt button. You may be asked whether you want to save your current analysis. If you happen to have been building a report and want to save it, click OK; otherwise, click the Cancel button.

4. A list of subject areas appears for you to select the subject area for the dashboard prompt. This time it somewhat matters which subject area you select. As you know, dashboards can contain reports from different subject areas, but to filter all the reports with a dashboard filter prompt, the prompt and all the reports you are filtering must have columns in common. Select the subject area for your dashboard prompt, and you arrive at the Dashboard Prompt window, shown in Figure 13-18.

You can set your dashboard prompt to affect the entire dashboard or just the page on which it appears. You make this selection in the Scope field. Now you can begin adding the columns to your dashboard prompt. You do this in exactly the same way you add columns to a report. Add a column from the column selector by clicking the column name.

The selected column appears in the Prompts section. Just as you can change the column formula for your columns in a report, click the Edit Formula button next to the column name to make changes to the column formula. Bear in mind that the prompt will filter all the reports in your dashboard only if the column is in each report, so change column formulas carefully and use the same formula you used in the reports populating the dashboard.

Each prompt contains a number of fields with which you can adjust the settings for the prompt, as listed and described in Table 13-5.

There is a Format View button in the upper-left corner of the Dashboard Prompt window that permits you to change the font, background, and border settings on the dashboard prompt. The three buttons on the other side of the window are the Preview button, Open button, and

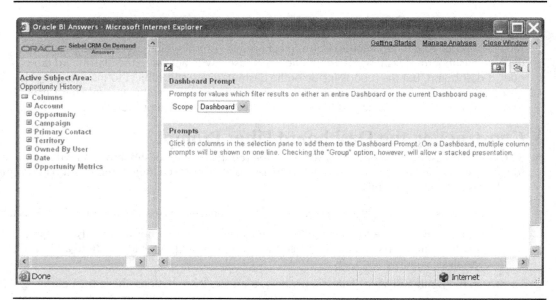

FIGURE 13-18. *Dashboard Prompt window*

Field	Field Description
Group	The Group check box appears when you have added two or more columns to your prompt. When you check the Group check box on a column, that column appears below the previous column in the prompt. When the Group check box is not checked, the column appears to the right of the previous column.
Operator	Each column needs an operator to determine how column values should be evaluated by the filter. Each column may use different operators. Which operators are available for each column depends on the data type of the column.
Control	Dashboard prompt columns may allow users to select a single value from a drop-down list, enter values directly, or select one or more values from a multi-select control. You also have the option of a calendar control for date and time columns. You can select one of these controls for each of your dashboard prompt columns in the Control field.
Show	Unless you selected the Edit Box control, the Show field allows you to specify which data will appear in the control for each column. The Drop-Down List control gives you the option to show all values or to show only the results of a SQL query. The default SQL query is a simple SELECT statement. If you are handy with SQL, you can modify this statement slightly to constrain the SELECT statement. Check the All Choices check box if you want to offer all possible choices in the control. The Constrain check box (available if you chose to show all values) will limit the choices based on the selection made in other prompt columns. The Multi-Select control gives you the same Show options minus the All Choices check box. The Calendar control only has the Constrain check box as a Show option.
Default To	The Default To field allows you to specify what value will initially appear in the prompt field when the dashboard is accessed. The options that appear here are Report Defaults, All Choices, Specific Value, Variable Expression, Server Variable, or SQL Results. Report Defaults defaults the column value based on default values in your reports. All Choices defaults the prompt column to "(All Choices)," which if unchanged does not filter the column at all. Specific Value allows you to specify a specific value for the column default. The next three options are available only in the Enterprise version of Answers. They are here for future enhancement to the hosted Answers On Demand version, and are not currently functional.
Set Variable	Set Variable is also a placeholder for future enhancement as the On Demand application continues to narrow the functionality gap between the hosted application and the enterprise application. Leave this field set to None.
Label	The Label field allows you to change the default label on the column. By default, the label is the name of the column.
Delete/Order	At the end of each column prompt, you will find a delete button with which you can remove the column from your prompt. You also find Up and Down arrow buttons with which you can change the order of the columns in your prompt.

TABLE 13-5. *Dashboard Prompt Column Fields*

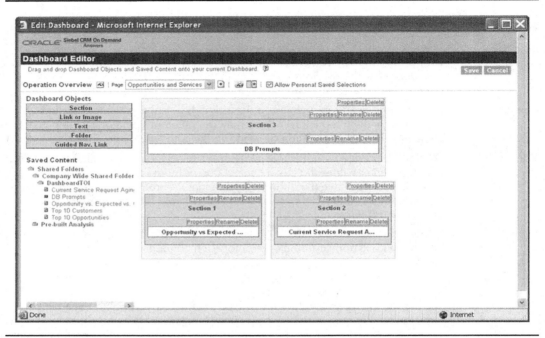

FIGURE 13-19. *Dashboard Editor window*

Save button. Figure 13-19 shows a Dashboard Editor window with several columns added. Figure 13-20 shows a preview of the same dashboard. Now that you have your dashboard prompt and your reports developed, it is time to put it all together.

Managing Dashboards

To get started, access the Dashboard tab. The standard prebuilt dashboards are listed in the Select Dashboard field. Any custom public dashboards are listed at the bottom of this pick list. To create a new dashboard or modify a custom dashboard, click the Manage Dashboards link.

The Manage Dashboards window (see Figure 13-21) lists all the custom public dashboards that have been created, if any. Dashboards listed here have three links to the left of the dashboard name. The Edit link opens the Dashboard Edit window, where you can change the name and description of the dashboard. The Delete link deletes the custom dashboard. The Design link opens the Dashboard Editor window, which is where you create and adjust the layout of your dashboard.

To create a new dashboard, click the New Dashboard button. This action takes you to the Dashboard Editor window, where you name your dashboard and optionally enter a description. Click the Save button to return to the Manage Dashboards window with your new dashboard listed. The next step is to add all the components to your dashboard.

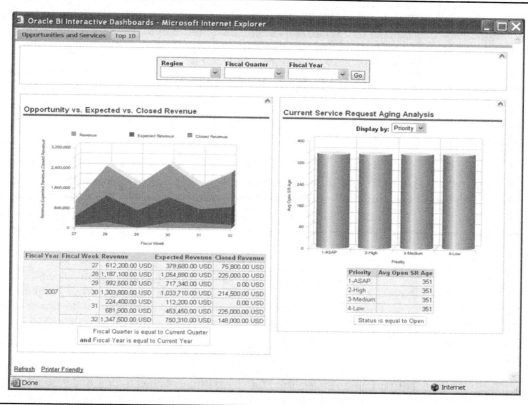

FIGURE 13-20. *Dashboard preview*

Adjusting Dashboard Layout

To begin populating your new dashboard, click the Design link next to your dashboard in the Manage Dashboards window. This takes you to the Dashboard Editor window. This is a window specific to dashboard layout, so let us take a moment to examine this window in detail.

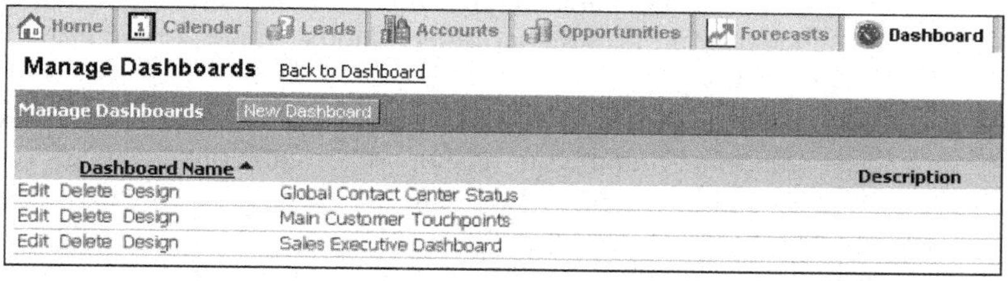

FIGURE 13-21. *Manage Dashboards window*

At the top of the window you see your dashboard name and, next to it, the Dashboard Properties button. To the right of the Dashboard Properties button you have the page selector and the Add Page button. Your dashboard can contain multiple pages in the form of tabs. A new dashboard has one page initially. The next button is the Print Control Settings button, which enables you to specify the page size and print orientation for a printed version of your dashboard. Finally, to the right of the Print Control Settings button is the Add Column button, which adds an additional column to the dashboard layout.

TIP
Limit your dashboard to two columns to avoid horizontal scrolling as much as possible.

On the left side of this window are the dashboard objects. You add objects to the dashboard by clicking the objects of your choice. Table 13-6 lists and describes each of the dashboard objects.

Dashboard Object	Description
Section	A Section object is an area that contains a report object in the dashboard. Sections may contain reports, text, or dashboard prompts. Your dashboard may contain as many sections as you like, but be mindful of how much users will need to scroll horizontally and vertically to view the content. You are limited to six reports per dashboard page. Consider adding pages if you have a lot of content to display in your dashboard.
Link or Image	The Link or Image object can contain a link to another URL. This may be a text link or an image link. From the dashboard objects, drag and drop a Link or Image object onto a section in the dashboard page. To set the URL for the object, click the Properties button to open the Link or Image Properties window.
	For a text link, type the display text for the link in the Caption field. You also use the Caption field to enter a caption for an image link. Set the position of the caption in the Position field. For an image link, enter the URL for the image in the Image field. Next, specify the result of clicking the text or image. Select Request or Dashboard and then click the Browse button to select the target to navigate to another dashboard. Select URL and enter the full path in the field to open another web site.
Text	Use the Text object to enter HTML-formatted text into your dashboard.
Folder	The Folder object allows you to place a folder structure on the dashboard that enables users to browse and select another report to run from the dashboard page.
Guided Nav. Link	Add a Guided Navigation Link object to your dashboard to provide a static or conditional link in your dashboard. A static link is always visible and a conditional link appears based on the results of another report. Click the Properties button on the object to specify the target URL for the link and the conditions that must be met for the link to appear.

TABLE 13-6. *Dashboard Objects*

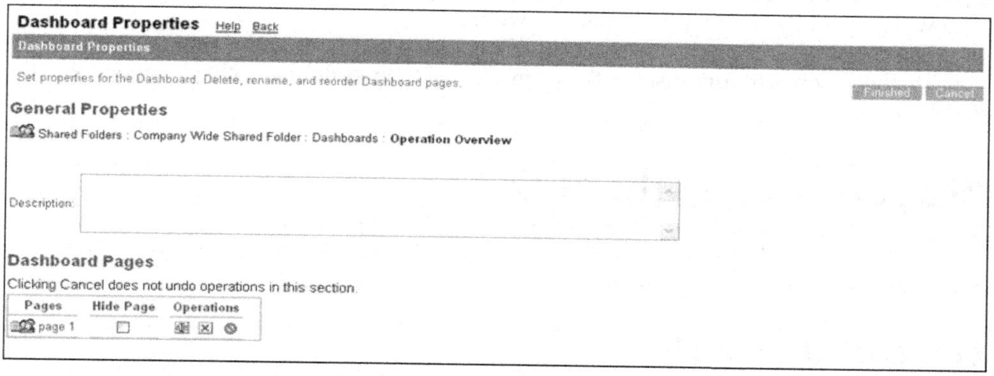

FIGURE 13-22. *Dashboard Properties window*

To adjust your layout, you can drag sections around the page. If you need a column break, click the Properties button on a section and select Break. You can add a column or page break here by selecting the break type and clicking OK. You can add columns by clicking the Add Column button. If you want to add a page, click the + button next to the page selector and enter a name for your page in the Page Name field. The page name will appear on the Dashboard tab.

Click the Dashboard Properties button to open the Dashboard Properties window (see Figure 13-22), where you can provide a description for your dashboard and see a list of all the pages in your dashboard. In the Dashboard Pages section, you can click the Rename button next to a page to enter a new name and description. You can also hide, delete, or add pages here.

It's time to add some saved content to the dashboard. The Saved Content section contains a directory structure of the shared folders in Answers On Demand. Expand the folders to find the reports that you want to add to the sections you have placed on your dashboard. Drag saved reports and prompts from the Saved Content area to the sections of the dashboard page. Once you have populated your dashboard sections with the desired content, click the Save button and your dashboard is displayed in the window. Close this window to return to the Manage Dashboards window. Your dashboard is now listed in the dashboard selector on the Dashboard tab.

All custom dashboards are listed below the standard dashboards on the Dashboard tab. You cannot limit the contents of the dashboard selector, so all users, regardless of role, will be able to select any dashboard. The reports within the dashboard are still subject to access control, so some users may see limited or no data based on their level of access.

Dashboard Design Considerations

It is very easy to overload a dashboard with many reports and objects to the point that the dashboard becomes difficult for your users to use. Avoid horizontal scrolling by limiting your dashboard to two columns and formatting the reports on the dashboard to around 380 points wide. The best reports for dashboards are those that summarize data into a small table with limited rows or single charts. Reports that are designed for presentation to management are typically best for dashboard use. Consider adding a link from the dashboard to a more detailed report rather than trying to get a large detailed report to appear in a dashboard.

The reports located on the first page of a dashboard all run at once when a user opens the dashboard. For performance reasons, consider placing on pages other than the first page complex reports that must process large volumes of data. Reports built on an Analytics (historical) subject area will perform better in a dashboard as well.

Do not place a report that contains prompts (discussed in the next chapter) on a dashboard. If you do, the report will run, display the prompt, and then open in another window outside of the dashboard.

"LayOUTside" the Box

Because CRM On Demand is a browser-based application and has advanced views that accept HTML and JavaScript, you can really step way outside the box with these views. This section describes a few of my favorite tricks.

Embedded Reports

Before it was possible to create a custom dashboard in CRM On Demand, this technique was a good way to create a pseudo dashboard. Now that you have custom public dashboard functionality, you do not need to employ this trick for a dashboard, but it has been useful to me for some complex reporting where I wanted to show data that just wouldn't come together nicely on a single report. One example that comes to mind is a report that includes both a top 10 list and bottom 10 list on the same report.

To embed another report inside of a report, you use the Narrative view. Since you are working in a web environment, each report has its own URL. You can take advantage of this by referencing the report's URL inside of an HTML IFrame.

NOTE
An IFrame (inline frame) is an HTML element that allows you to embed another HTML document inside the main document.

The first step is to find the URL for the report you want to embed. Access the Reports tab and run the report. Once the report has generated, right-click within the body of the report and selects the Properties option on the pop-up menu. The Address field in the Properties window shows the URL for the report. Only part of the URL is visible but, by using your mouse, you can select the entire URL and copy it to your clipboard.

Add a Narrative view to your report. Inside the Prefix field, you will place the report URL inside of an iframe tag. The format of the report URL is shown next. You could potentially type the URL in directly if you know all of the necessary elements of the URL, but copying and pasting is much easier.

```
<HOSTING POD REFERENCE>/OnDemand/user/analytics/saw.dll?
Go&Path=/shared/Company_<COMPANY NUMBER>_Shared_Folder/
<FOLDER NAME>/<REPORT NAME>&Options=rfd&Action=Prompt
```

Placing the report URL as the source inside of an iframe embeds the report inside the Narrative view. You will also want to size the iframe using the height and width tags. Other tags are available to control borders and scrolling, and more. A quick Internet search will provide a list of the available tags. Your final iframe code will look something like this:

```
<iframe src="/OnDemand/user/analytics/saw.dll?
Go&Path=/shared/Company_9999_Shared_Folder/EmbeddedReports/
AccountListReport&Options=rfd&Action=Prompt"
```

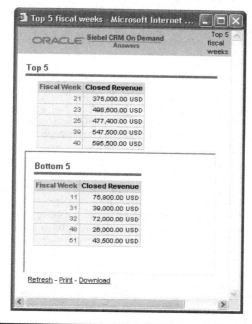

FIGURE 13-23. *Embedded report*

```
width=700 height =500>
</iframe>
```

Notice the &Options=rfd portion of the report URL. This tag, as shown here, indicates that the Refresh, Print, and Download links should be included with the report. You can set these options with the combination of the links you like, where **r** is Refresh, **f** is Print, and **d** is Download. You can also set this tag equal to "none" if you want to exclude all the links.

Figure 13-23 shows a sample report with another report embedded inside.

View Selector and Narrative Views

Using the same technique that I described for embedding reports, you can embed just about anything into a report. In fact, if you take this idea to extremes, you can create a single report that permits your users to do many of the web tasks that they regularly perform all day long at the office. Suppose you want to embed a Web Search page in the company web site home page. Let us also get a little crazy and embed a CRM On Demand New Account window inside the report.

Create a separate Narrative view for each web site that you want to embed. Use an iframe tag in the Prefix field as previously described. To insert a web site, the code in your Narrative view Prefix field will look something like this:

```
<iframe src=http://www.oracle.com height=700 width=800></iframe>
```

I mentioned adding a CRM On Demand New Account window in your report. I am not endorsing this method, but want to show that you can embed almost any web content in a Narrative view. Using the same method, you can embed the New Account, New Opportunity, New Task, or any of the other Create windows. The URLs for the common new record windows are shown here:

```
Appointment:  /OnDemand/user/AppointmentQuickCreate?OMTHD=New
Account:   /OnDemand/user/AccountQuickCreate?OMTHD=New
Contact:   /OnDemand/user/ContactQuickCreate?OMTHD=New
Lead:  /OnDemand/user/LeadQuickCreate?OMTHD=New
Opportunity:   /OnDemand/user/OpportunityQuickCreate?OMTHD=New
Service Request:   /OnDemand/user/ServiceRequestQuickCreate?OMTHD=New
Task:   /OnDemand/user/TaskQuickCreate?OMTHD=New
```

Once you have created all of your Narrative views, delete them from the layout. Add a View Selector view to the report and move the views into the Selected Views field. Rename each view and save the View Selector view to your report. Now, when users run your report, they will be able to select a page from the view selector and interact with the embedded web sites right inside your report.

Scrolling Charts

This next trick isn't terribly useful but it is an impressive bit of formatting that demonstrates how a little HTML knowledge can really enhance your report design. Suppose you have several charts that you would like to show in a report, but are having a hard time getting all of the charts in the layout…and your users are absolutely against using a scroll bar to move around the screen.

Create a report with all of the charts and remove all the views other than the charts. If possible, size all the charts to the same height. If it is not possible, at least make a note of the height of the tallest chart. Now arrange all the charts into a single row so that all the charts are beside each other and you have to scroll to the right to see all of the Chart views. Save this report and then run the report and get its URL.

Next, create a new report or open the report in which you want to show the charts. Add a Ticker view to this report. In the Row Format field, once again use the iframe tag to embed the other report into the ticker. Adjust the Ticker view height to accommodate your tallest report, and adjust the width of the Ticker view to the width of your report.

Now, the report that contains nothing but charts will scroll across the screen in this report. All the charts you wanted to show in your report will now scroll across the screen so that your users do not have to do the scrolling.

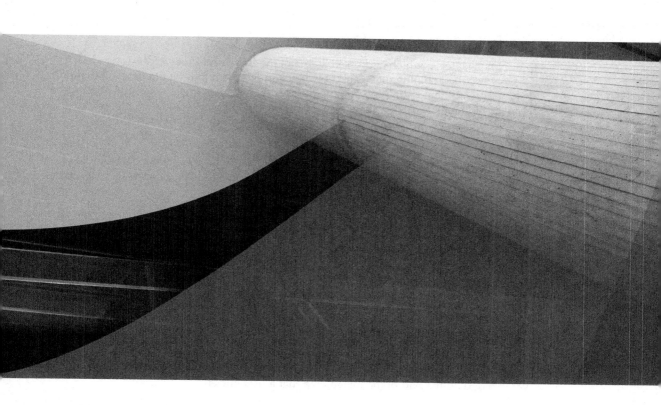

CHAPTER
14

Adding Filter Prompts
to Reports

n Chapter 4, which addressed Step 1 of the Build and View Analysis window, I described column filters and how you can use them to limit the data in the report. The problem with using column filters is that not every user wants the exact same report with the exact same data. Users have no control over filters placed directly on the columns.

With filter prompts, you can put the decision in the users' hands about what data should or should not appear in the report. In this chapter, I explain how to add filter prompts to your reports and configure the prompts to maximize control and efficiency.

Overview of Filter Prompts

Move to Step 3 of the Build and View Analysis window, shown in Figure 14-1, where you can add prompts that users see when they run the report. These prompts ask your users to specify which data to include or exclude from the report. As the report developer, you determine how the prompt is configured and what data, if any, the user is presented with to choose from.

There are two types of filter prompts:

■ **Column filter prompt** Provides the user with a dialog box in which they can enter or select values to populate the filter.

■ **Image filter prompt** Presents the user with an image map. The report filter contains a value based on the part of the image map that a user clicks.

The operators are identical to those you use in a static column filter that you apply directly to a column in Step 1. There are not quite as many operators available to the filter prompts. Table 14-1 provides some details about each of the available operators.

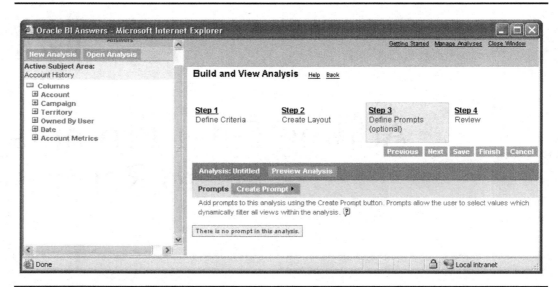

FIGURE 14-1. *Build and View Analysis window: Step 3*

Operator	Usage
* Prompt User	Allows the user to select the filter operator at run time. You cannot limit the operators available to the user. The list of operators available are different from the set of operators available when building a filter prompt. Table 14-2 shows the run-time operators available to users in a Prompt User filter prompt.
is equal to or is in	Limits results to records where the column matches the filter value(s) selected by the user.
is not equal to or is not in	Limits results to records where the column does not match the filter value(s) selected by the user.
is less than	Limits results to records where the column is lower (or earlier for date values) than the filter value selected by the user.
is greater than	Limits results to records where the column is higher (or later for date values) than the filter value selected by the user.
is less than or equal to	Limits results to records where the column is the same as or lower (or earlier for date values) than the filter value selected by the user.
is greater than or equal to	Limits results to records where the column is the same as or higher (or later for date values) than the filter value selected by the user.
is between	Limits results to records where the column is the same as or falls between the two filter values selected by the user.
is in top	Limits results to records where the column contains the top-ranked records. The filter value is a number indicating how many records to return.
is in bottom	Limits results to the bottom-ranked records. The filter value is a number indicating how many records to return.
contains all	Limits results to records where the column contains all of the filter values selected by the user.
contains any	Limits results to records where the column contains any of the filter values selected by the user.
begins with	Limits results to records where the column data begins exactly as described by the filter value selected by the user.
ends with	Limits results to records where the column data ends exactly as described by the filter value selected by the user.
is LIKE (pattern match)	Limits results to records where the column data matches the pattern described in the filter. You may use a single filter value, and that value may contain up to two percent-sign wildcard characters (%) to define the pattern.

TABLE 14-1. *Filter Prompt Operators*

Operator	Usage
is equal to or is in	Limits results to records where the column matches the filter value(s).
is not equal to or is not in	Limits results to records where the column does not match the filter value(s).
is less than	Limits results to records where the column is lower (or earlier for date values) than the filter value.
is greater than	Limits results to records where the column is higher (or later for date values) than the filter value.
is less than or equal to	Limits results to records where the column is the same as or lower (or earlier for date values) than the filter value.
is greater than or equal to	Limits results to records where the column is the same as or higher (or later for date values) than the filter value.
is between	Limits results to records where the column is the same as or falls between the two filter values.
is null	Limits results to records where the specified column contains no data.
is not null	Limits results to records where the specified column contains any data.
is in top	Limits results to records where the column contains the top-ranked records.
is in bottom	Limits results to the bottom-ranked records.

TABLE 14-2. *Run-Time Operators with a * Prompt User Filter Prompt*

When you select the * Prompt User operator in a column filter prompt, the user is presented with an Operator selection field as part of the filter prompt. The operators available at run time in a prompt, outlined in Table 14-2, are slightly different from those you can select when creating a column filter prompt.

Column Filter Prompts

To add a column filter prompt to your report, click the Create Prompt button in Step 3 of the Build and View Analysis window and select Column Filter Prompt from the menu. The Prompt Properties window (see Figure 14-2) opens, in which you specify exactly how your column filter prompt behaves when a user runs your report.

The top of the Prompt Properties window has two text entry fields. The text that you enter in the Caption field appears as the title of the prompt. The text you enter in the Description field also appears at the top of the prompt, but directly under the Caption. This is a great place to provide some instruction to the user.

The Filter On Column drop-down list contains all the columns in your report. Select the column you want to filter in this list. If you want to create a filter prompt for a column that is not in your report, click the column name in the Columns list on the left. This adds the column to the Filter On Column drop-down list but does not add the column to the report.

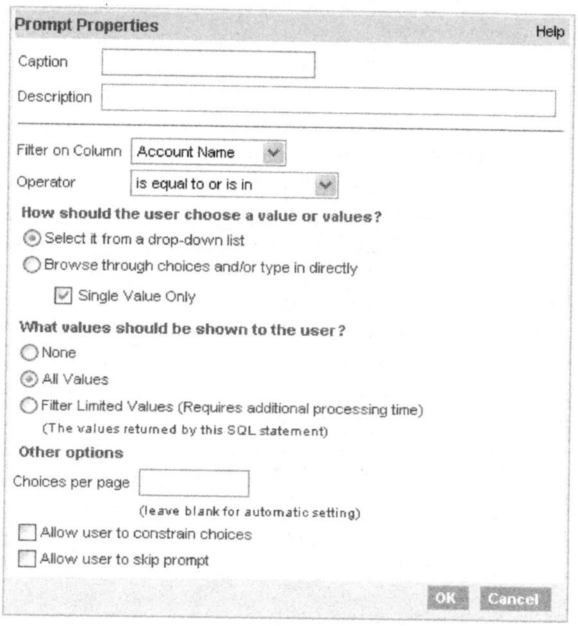

FIGURE 14-2. *Prompt Properties window*

In the Operator field, you select the operator that you want the filter to use. Figure 14-3 shows the list of available operators. If you need a refresher on the operators, refer to Chapter 4. The * Prompt User operator, found only on the filter prompt, makes an operator selection field part of the filter prompt. This allows the user to select an operator of their choosing.

Next in the window, you identify how users will select values for the column filter. There are two options here. First, you can provide a drop-down list of values. This option permits only a single value selection, so when you select this option, the Single Value Only check box is checked automatically. Figure 14-4 shows a filter prompt with the drop-down list value selector. This is the most simplistic column filter prompt. The other option for selecting values is to allow the user to browse through a list of values and select one or more values to include in the filter. Users may also type values in directly with this option—and may have to, depending on your selection in the next section of the Prompt Properties window. You may limit the prompt to accept only a single value by checking the Single Value Only check box, or leave the check box unchecked and allow multiple values. Certain conditions such as "is between" will not allow you to limit the number of values to one.

The next section of the Prompt Properties window asks what values the prompt should show to the user. Your options here are to show no values, show all values, or to show filtered values. If you select the None option, the user is forced to type a value into the value field for the filter prompt. The drawback to this is that the user must match spelling, capitalization, and punctuation exactly to effectively filter the report. This option is really only good for numeric columns, where such spelling errors are not a factor.

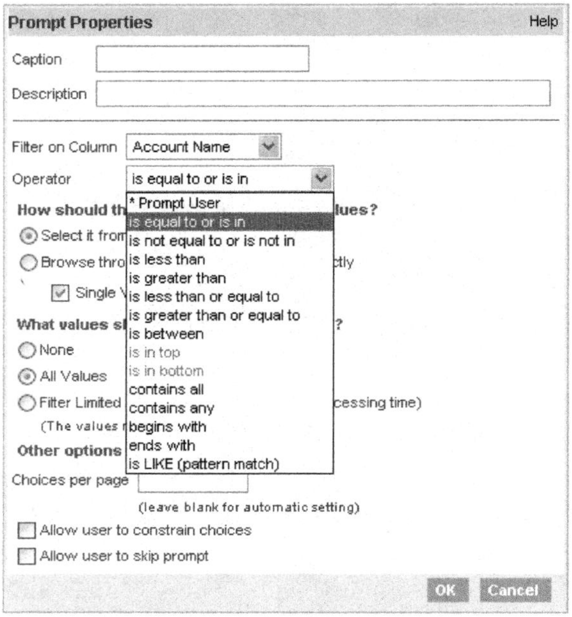

FIGURE 14-3. *Operator selector list in Prompt Properties window*

Choosing the All Values option causes the filter prompt to show all possible column values in the drop-down or value list selector. The drawback of this option is that values are made available that may not be available in the report data. Suppose you have a report that has a column filter on the Region column that limits the data to include only the East region but a column filter prompt on the State column shows all values. Your user will be able to select states outside of the East region, and the report will return no values.

The third option, Filter Limited Values, shows only the values that are available in the report results at that point. In other words, in the preceding example, the prompt on the State column would include only the states in the East region. The order of the filters is also a consideration.

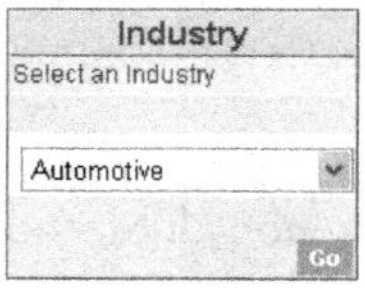

FIGURE 14-4. *Sample column filter prompt*

If your report has two or more filter prompts and your prompts are showing limited values, prompts will only show values that are valid given the selection in previous prompts. Limiting the values in the filter prompts may be best for your users, but comes with a performance cost. Each prompt limiting the values must run a query to populate the values list. If your dataset is large or you have a large number of prompts, you may detect slightly slower performance. To minimize this impact, order your prompts so that the prompts that will filter out the most data run first, so that subsequent prompts have less data to sort through to populate the values list.

In the Other Options section of the Prompt Properties window, you can specify how many values to show per page. If you have set the prompt to allow users to browse through the values, this option sets the number of values to show at one time. If you are using a drop-down list to present the values in your prompt, do not enter a number in the Choices Per Page field because this will limit the number of values in the drop-down list, and users will have no way to access values that are truncated off the list.

Checking the Allow Users to Constrain Choices check box adds two fields to the filter prompt that allow users to limit the values in the prompt. Users can select Begins With, Ends With, or Contains from the first Match field, and then enter a value in the next field to constrain the values to only those that match the condition. When you enable this option for a date column and choose to show no values, a calendar button appears next to the value fields so that users can click the calendar and select a date.

The final check box in the Prompt Properties window gives users the option of skipping the prompt. When a user skips a prompt, the report is not filtered on that column.

With so many options and combinations possible, attempting to craft a column filter to have the appearance you are looking for is often confusing. I have often heard from my customers that they have seen a filter prompt that looks like "this" but they only seem to be able to create a prompt that looks like "that." In an effort to add some clarity to the configuration of column filter prompts, the following list shows a sample result of each of the options that you can set on the Prompt Properties window.

* Prompt User Operator   Result sample:

Operator Selector Field

Drop-Down   Result sample:

Drop-Down List Field

Browse Values—Show None   Result sample:

Text Entry Field—No Values Showing

Browse Values—Show All/Filtered   Result sample:

Text Entry Field—Values Showing

Allow Constrain—Show All/Filtered—Text Field   Result sample:

Begins With Filter Field

Allow Constrain—Show None—Date Field   Result sample:

Date Entry Field with Calendar Button

Allow Constrain—Show None—Date/Time Field   Result sample:

Timestamp Field—No Calendar Button

Allow Skip   Result sample:

Skip Prompt Button

Back in Step 3 of the Build and View Analysis window, you will see all of your filters listed. Here you may click the Properties button to reopen the Prompt Properties window and change the properties of the column filter prompt. The next button deletes the prompt from the report. Using the up and down arrow buttons, you can set the order in which your prompts are presented to the user.

Click Preview Analysis to test your prompts. You will notice that each prompt is presented individually. You cannot group prompts or display more than one prompt at once, which you can do with the dashboard prompt.

Image Prompts

The other type of filter prompt available in Answers On Demand is the image prompt. An image prompt presents users with an image map. An image map is an image containing clickable areas that are linked to other pages. In the case of an image prompt, clicking an area of the image passes a value to a filter on a column in your report. An image prompt uses only the "is equal to or is in" operator. When a user clicks an area of the image map, the user is indicating that the report should include only the records with that specific selected value in the report.

I have to admit that I rarely build a report and think to myself that an image prompt would be perfect for this report. None of my customers has ever asked for one either, which is unfortunate, because I think the image prompt functionality offers a great bit of enhanced usability in a report. For example, imagine that you want to run a report about a particular part from one of your company's products. Rather than having to know the product code or exactly how to spell the name, you run a report that first shows a picture of each product. You click a product and get a diagram of the components of the product. You click a component and see an exploded view of the component that shows all of its parts. Click a part and you get a report based on that specific part.

Perhaps the reason this form of prompt is not very popular is that putting it together takes a bit more effort. However, once you understand the process, it is not very difficult. You may find that you need to employ the services of someone to assist with the graphics, and may also need some image-mapping software, which you can find at a low cost or cost free on the Internet. The process follows:

1. Use an image-mapping tool to draw and label the clickable areas on your image and produce map code in HTML.

2. Copy the resulting HTML code to your clipboard and return to the report you are building in CRM On Demand.

3. In Step 3 of the Build and View Analysis window, click the Create Prompt button and select Image Prompt. The Image Map Prompt Properties window (see Figure 14-5) appears.

4. Complete the Caption and Description fields, which serve the same purpose here as they do in the Prompt Properties window when creating a column filter prompt.

5. In the Image URL field, enter the URL for the image you plan to use for your prompt. This image should be located on a web server that all users running the report have

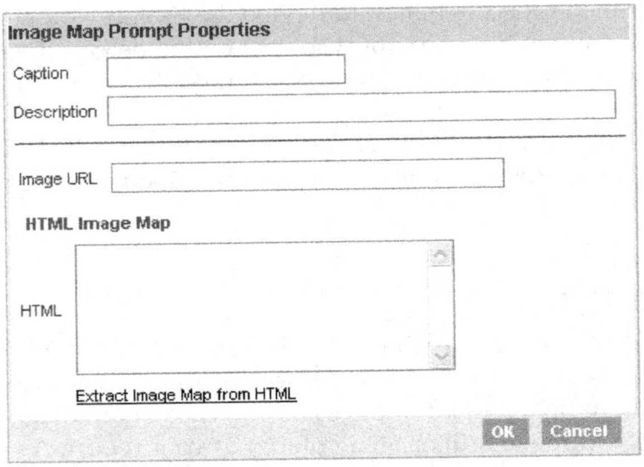

Image Map Prompt Properties

Caption

Description

Image URL

HTML Image Map

HTML

Extract Image Map from HTML

OK   Cancel

FIGURE 14-5.   *Image Map Prompt Properties window*

access to; otherwise, the image will not display, and your users will not be able to run the report properly.

6. Paste into the HTML field the map code that your image-mapping software generated. Ensure that your HTML code begins with <map and ends with </map>, as in the code shown next. If your code does not contain the HREF or TITLE elements, that is okay because you will have an opportunity to set these properties during the next step.

```
<MAP NAME="map1">
<AREA SHAPE="POLY" COORDS="611,298,621,317,611,330,586,351,566,337,
532,334,522,340,507,342,535,311" HREF="" TITLE="NC">
<AREA SHAPE="POLY" COORDS="557,388,519,342,536,336,566,338,584,352"
HREF="" TITLE="SC">
<AREA SHAPE="POLY" COORDS="509,418,553,413,560,389,518,341,491,345"
HREF="" TITLE="GA">
<AREA SHAPE="POLY" COORDS="472,414,479,428,501,426,507,437,520,425,
544,445,546,462,565,491,577,502,586,501,584,473,554,415,510,418,505,
413" HREF="" TITLE="FL">
<AREA SHAPE="POLY" COORDS="459,348,493,343,506,414,471,414,476,428,
461,426" HREF="" TITLE="AL">
<AREA SHAPE="POLY" COORDS="431,350,461,347,460,429,445,430,443,417,
417,417,424,396,420,375" HREF="" TITLE="MS">
<AREA SHAPE="POLY" COORDS="439,320,430,349,505,343,536,311"
HREF="" TITLE="TN">
</MAP>
```

7. Click the Extract Image Map from HTML link. The HTML Image Map section of the Image Map Prompt Properties window is replaced with an Image Areas table containing the image map information from the HTML code, a completed version of which is shown

in Figure 14-6. This information minimally includes completed Shape and Coordinates columns for each clickable area. To complete the image map definition, fill in the other three columns:

- **Area Title** Enter the text that will appear in the rollover pop-up for the area of the image map.
- **Column** Enter the analytical field reference for the column you are filtering.
- **Value** Enter the value that is passed to the column filter when the area of the image is clicked.

NOTE

If you need to make a change to the shape or coordinates, click the Change Image Map link to go back to the HTML.

8. Click OK to return to Step 3 of the Build and View Analysis window. The image prompt is listed in this window just like the column filter prompts are.

When the user runs the report, an image is presented that the user must click to pass a value to the filter. Figure 14-7 shows a sample image prompt in Answers On Demand.

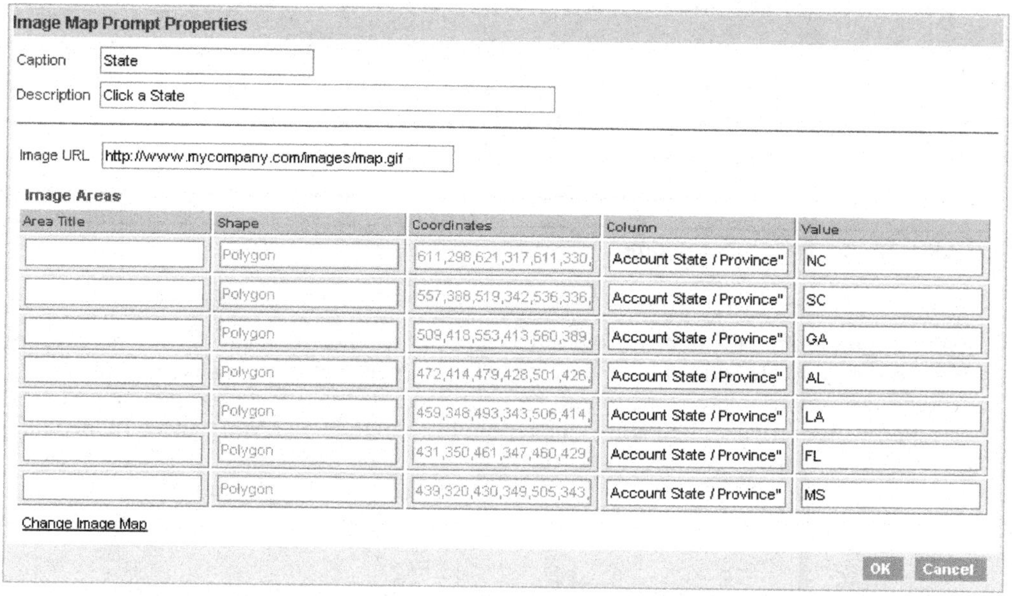

Image Map Prompt Properties

Caption `State`

Description `Click a State`

Image URL `http://www.mycompany.com/images/map.gif`

Image Areas

Area Title	Shape	Coordinates	Column	Value
	Polygon	611,298,621,317,611,330,	Account State / Province"	NC
	Polygon	557,388,519,342,536,336,	Account State / Province"	SC
	Polygon	509,418,553,413,560,389,	Account State / Province"	GA
	Polygon	472,414,479,428,501,426,	Account State / Province"	AL
	Polygon	459,348,493,343,506,414,	Account State / Province"	LA
	Polygon	431,350,461,347,460,429,	Account State / Province"	FL
	Polygon	439,320,430,349,505,343,	Account State / Province"	MS

Change Image Map

[OK] [Cancel]

FIGURE 14-6. *Image Map Prompt Properties window with mapping*

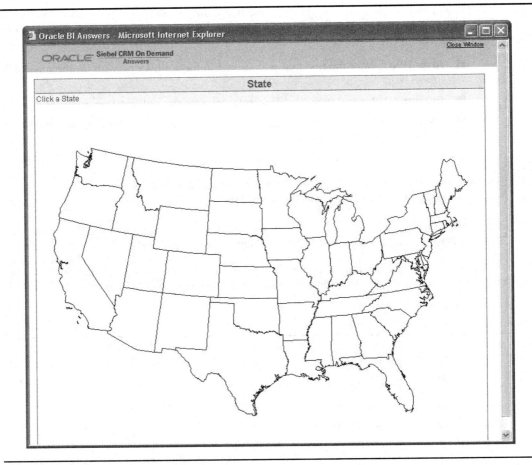

FIGURE 14-7. *Image map prompt*

There is no limit to the number of prompts that you can add to a report, but keep track of how many prompts a user will need to go through before actually getting to the report results. Too many prompts affects the usability of the report. You also increase the risk of users getting no results in their report with every filter you add to the report. Keep in mind that you may combine column filter prompts and image prompts.

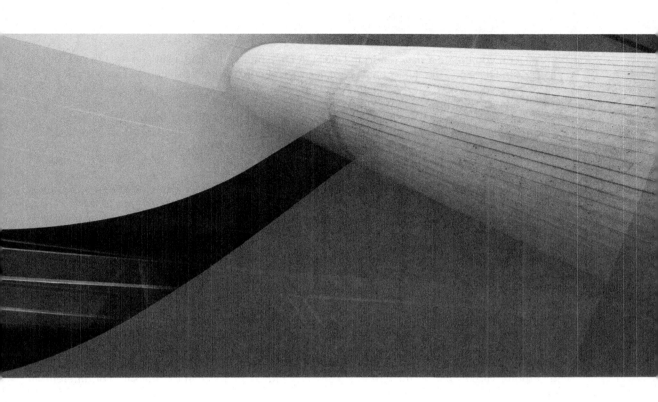

CHAPTER
15

Combining Reports

W hen you create a new report in CRM On Demand, you select a subject area in Answers On Demand. This subject area contains a set of columns from which you can pull data into your report. Most of the time, the subject area contains everything you need for a report. Sometimes you will find that the subject area doesn't quite give you access to all the data that you want in your report. Other times you might find that the data columns are there but, due to the configuration or data structure, you cannot get the data into a single report the way you want. It is those situations that bring us to combining reports.

If you are database savvy, you know something about joins between database tables. Typically, if a relationship does not exist in your database, you can create inner and outer joins to build those relationships. CRM On Demand is a hosted environment. The database does not reside on a server within your company or on your computer, so you cannot access the tables directly. The database techniques that you may be accustomed to using, such as adding and dropping tables and creating joins, are simply not available to you. You do not have direct access to the database structure of CRM On Demand.

To overcome the reporting limitations of disparate data in unrelated tables or the lack of related data in related tables, you can use multiple report queries to create the joins necessary to draw the required data for your report.

There are essentially two methods for using multiple reports to arrive at your desired result set. You can use one report to filter another, which is useful when you want to show data in one subject area based on results of a report based on another subject area. The other method has you combine reports into a single report. These individual queries can use the same or different subject areas.

In this chapter I explain how you can use multiple report queries, either as a filter or combined into a single report that is a combination of two or more reports.

Using a Report to Filter Another Report

You know that there are several ways to filter your report data. Among them, column filters, filters in formulas, filter prompts, and even using Pivot Table views. All of these methods rely on the same subject area on which you have based the report. Suppose you want to see the expected product revenue for accounts that have purchased products in the past. When purchased, products become account assets. The purchase price for an asset is stored in the Asset subject areas and the expected revenue amounts for products are stored in the Opportunity-Product subject areas.

To use a report of accounts with assets to filter a report of accounts with expected product revenue, you create two reports. First, you create a simple report with the Account ID column and a filter to identify only the accounts where the Purchase Price column is not null. This report, based on the Asset History Analytics subject area, returns only the account IDs for accounts with purchased assets.

First, you create your report based on the Opportunity-Product History subject area with all of the columns you want in your report. You then need to filter this report based on the

Asset History report. By holding down the CTRL key while clicking the Account ID column in the column list, you open the Create/Edit Filter window. To filter one report based on another, click the Advanced button and select Filter Based on Results of Another Request from the pop-up menu.

The Filter on Saved Request dialog box (see Figure 15-1) opens with the filtered column identified in the Column field. In the Relationship field, select the filter condition you want for the filter. The choices here are a little different from the filter conditions you have seen in other filters. The conditions listed here end with "any" or "all." Selecting a condition that ends with "any" indicates that a value must meet the specified condition for any value in the other report to be included in the report. Selecting a condition that ends with "all" indicates that a value must meet the specified condition for all values in the other report to be included.

Identify the report you want to use for your filter by clicking the Browse button and selecting the saved report that will serve as your filter. In the Use Values in Column field, select the field in the saved report that you are referencing with your filter. This is typically the same column that is identified in the Column field at the top of the Filter on Saved Request dialog box. Now the Filters section of the Build and View Analysis window shows something similar to the filter shown in Figure 15-2.

For performance reasons, you want your filter report to be as simple as possible. A report with a single column and filter, if possible, is best. Answers On Demand needs to run the filtering report behind the scenes in order to generate the filtered report. The filtering report does not display on the screen and is undetectable by users running the filtered report. Filter prompts, if on the filtering report, do not display and have no effect on the reports.

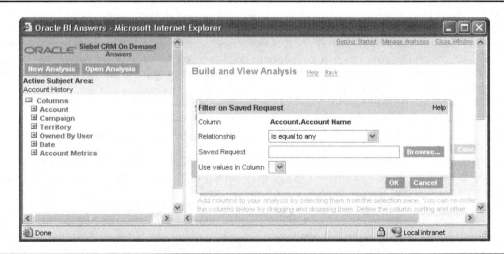

FIGURE 15-1. *Filter on Saved Request dialog box*

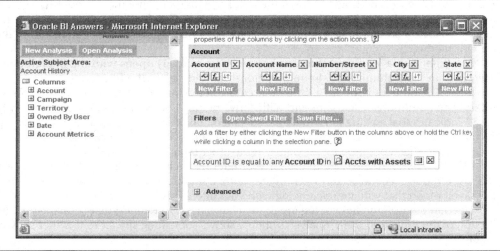

FIGURE 15-2. *Filter description for a filter on another report*

Combining Reports into a Single Report

There are several common situations in which you may find that you need a combined analysis. Some of these include not having access to all data columns in a single subject area, having data rows missing due to a natural inner join that causes the report to drop rows where no related value exists in another table, or having multiple columns of the same type that you want to display in a single column.

To create a combined analysis, first create a new report based on the most appropriate subject area, adding all the columns that you want to display in your report. It is a good idea to go ahead and set the order of the columns now, because it is a little more involved to do so after combining the report with another report.

In Step 1 of the Build and View Analysis window, expand the Advanced section at the bottom of the window. Click the Combine with Similar Analysis button to open a list of all subject areas (see Figure 15-3). You can select a different subject area or the same subject area you are already working with. Click the subject area of your choice.

The resulting window, shown in Figure 15-4, includes some new sections. The Set Operations section contains three links now: the Result Columns link, and Criteria links for your original report columns and the columns of your newly added report. The Columns section shows the columns in the report based on the selected link from the Set Operations section.

The Result Columns are columns that will display in the final report based on the combination of the criteria columns. You will notice that when you have selected Result Columns in the Set Operations section, each column shown in the Columns section has the Column Properties, Edit Formula, and Order By buttons that you are accustomed to seeing on your report columns. The formulas on the Result Columns are blank, however.

Click the first Criteria link and you will see the columns you originally added to your report. Notice that each column now contains only the Edit Formula button. The columns that will

FIGURE 15-3. *New criteria subject area list*

ultimately display in your report are the Result Columns, and the formula for each column is the combination of each criteria column in the same position. This explains why there is no formula at the Result Column level. For this reason, any additional criteria added to the combined analysis needs to contain the same number of columns as all other criteria and, in order for the columns to combine properly, each criteria column must be of the same data type as the other criteria columns in the same position.

If you have not yet added columns to a newly added criteria report, Answers On Demand displays a placeholder for each column as a dotted-line outline of the column (see Figure 15-4). Within the dotted outline, you may see a reference to the column present in that position of the Result Columns. To add criteria columns, click the column in the column selector list on the left.

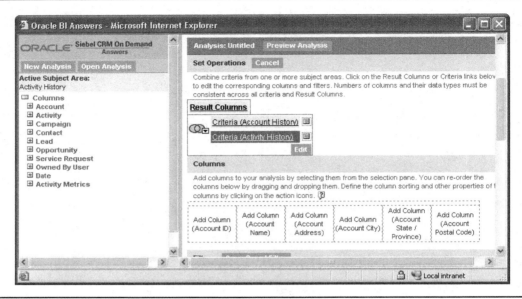

FIGURE 15-4. *Criteria without columns*

The column selector list shows the columns contained in the subject area of the criteria. If a criteria column is not in the correct position, you can drag it to the correct location just like you would in a regular report.

You may include as many criteria reports as necessary to extract the data you need for your report. This is rarely more than three or four reports, but I have created a union of 24 reports for a customer. To add an additional criteria report, click the Edit button and then select Create New Criteria from the pop-up menu. You can remove a criteria report by clicking the Edit button and selecting Cut from the pop-up menu.

You can also filter your criteria columns as you would within any other report. You cannot add a filter at the Result Columns level. If the same filter should be applied to all criteria, you need to add the filter to each set of criteria.

Mind Your Data Types

Each criteria report column that combines to populate a result column must be of the same data type. This usually poses no problems when you are actually combining data from similar columns in two criteria. Where the data type requirement tends to be a little more complicated are those situations in which you are combining one criteria column containing data and other criteria columns with no data. In other words, you need to include a null value in a criteria column.

Each column data type requires a specific method for inserting literal or null values. If you must have a null value in a nontext column, you can write a CASE statement that will always result in a null value. You may find that it is easier to use the CAST function to change the data type of a column to text, and then use single quotes to create a null value. Table 15-1 describes the column formula options for entering a literal value and creating a null value in your criteria reports.

Field Type	Data Type	Literal Value	NULL Formula
Check box Phone Picklist Text	Character	'Unspecified'	'' (two single quote marks)
Currency Integer Number Percent	Numeric	0	CASE WHEN 0 = 1 THEN 0 ELSE NULL END
Date	Date	DATE '1000-01-01'	CASE WHEN DATE '1000-01-01' = DATE '9999-09-09' THEN DATE '1000-01-01' ELSE NULL END
Date/Time	Timestamp	TIMESTAMP '1000-01-01 00:00:00'	CASE WHEN TIMESTAMP '1000-01-01 00:00:00' = TIMESTAMP '9999-09-09 00:00:00' THEN TIMESTAMP '1000- 01-01 00:00:00' ELSE NULL END

TABLE 15-1. *Literal and Null Value Formats*

Union Types

You can combine reports in four different ways. Depending on your needs, you will choose a Union, Union All, Intersect, or Minus combination method, or set operator, between each criteria. You identify the set operator between each criteria report using the selector to the left of the criteria report links. Click this button and a drop-down list opens, displaying each of the set operators. When you have more than two sets of criteria and choose different set operators between criteria reports, the criteria reports group together based on their set operator. This is quite similar to the effect of the And/Or setting between filter criteria. You can ungroup criteria reports by clicking the Edit button and selecting Ungroup. This section describes each set operator and provides an example of a report using each set operator.

Union Set Operator

The Union set operator combines two criteria showing all columns from the first criteria and all columns from the second criteria without duplication. Any rows that both criteria have in common are displayed only once. Duplicate rows, in other words, are displayed only once in the result set.

I often use this method when one of the objects in CRM On Demand contains multiple fields of the same type. Suppose you have configured opportunities with multiple currency fields to represent separate costs involved in an opportunity. You want a report that calculates the total of these costs for each opportunity, but you want to include each cost only in specific situations based on the customer type, sales person, date range, or a number of other columns. It is quite easy to build a filter on one report to isolate the records for the first cost field and build a filter on another report to isolate the records for the second cost field. The trouble you have here is that the filters are not the same for including each cost, and the CASE statement you would have to write to isolate this data is extremely daunting and complex.

Column	Opportunity Name	Owner	Cost Type	Cost
Criteria 1 (Opportunity History)	Opportunity. "Opportunity Name"	Employee. "Employee Name"	'Production Cost'	"- Revenue Custom Metrics".S_CUR_1
Criteria 2 (Opportunity History)	Opportunity. "Opportunity Name"	Employee. "Employee Name"	'Packaging Cost'	"- Revenue Custom Metrics".S_CUR_2

TABLE 15-2. *Union Report Sample Criteria*

In a case like this, you may find that it is much easier to combine the two reports. Create two criteria with the same subject area and the same columns except the cost fields. Each criteria report includes one of the two cost fields, each of which is located in the same position within the report. You also want to include a column that describes the cost of each criteria report. You need to do this to ensure that your report does not eliminate a row as a duplicate when the two cost fields contain the same number. Table 15-2 shows the columns in this report and their formula to help you understand the structure.

Notice that I have hard-coded values into the Cost Type column. Doing so ensures that each row is unique even when the cost values are the same within a single opportunity record.

Union All Set Operator

The Union All set operator combines two criteria showing all columns from the first criteria and all columns from the second criteria, including duplicates. Any rows that both criteria have in common are displayed twice. Duplicate rows, in other words, are not filtered out of the result set. One example that seems to come up frequently is the combination of account records and contact records, particularly in the healthcare industry, where there is often little distinction between accounts and contacts. If you want to create a report that combines this type of data and want to include duplicates in case a particular record exists as both an account and a contact, you use the Union All set operator.

Table 15-3 shows a sample column set for this type of combined analysis.

Column	Name	Phone	Last Visit Date	Service Type
Criteria 1 (Contact History)	Contact. "Contact Name"	Contact."Work Phone #"	Contact.INDEXED_ DATE_0	Contact. "Contact Type"
Criteria 2 (Account History)	Account. "Account Name"	Account."Phone Number"	"- Account Custom Attributes".INDEXED_ DATE_0	Account. "Account Type"

TABLE 15-3. *Union All Report Sample Criteria*

Notice in this example that every column contains a different formula and that two different subject areas are being used. Each column in the report is made up of two column formulas with the same data type. If the report should encounter a record from each subject area where the name, phone number, visit date, and service type are identical, the results will include the row twice.

This same analysis can be performed with the Union set operator, in which case duplicate records will be removed from the results. The addition of the ID column to this report would make each row unique, even if the other columns match, because the Contact ID will never be the same as the Account ID. In this case, either the Union or Union All set operator will deliver the same result set.

Intersect Set Operator

You can use the Intersect set operator to identify only the rows that are duplicated in your analysis. Using the previous example, the result set from Table 15-3 would include only those records where the name, phone number, visit date, and service type are identical. This method is useful when trying to identify duplicate records, either in the same subject area or in different subject areas.

Minus Set Operator

Use the Minus set operator to include only records from the first criteria report that do not appear in the second criteria report. Suppose you have a report that shows all opportunities and products. You want to remove from this list any opportunity for an account that has the same product listed as an asset. The criteria for this report might look something like Table 15-4 using the Minus set operator.

The result of this analysis will include only the accounts that have opportunities with products that they do not already own.

Set Operator Comparison Example

Many people find this concept of combining analyses difficult to master, so this section offers one more example of each set operator using the same datasets for each set operator method. Table 15-5 and Table 15-6 show the two datasets that I will combine with each set operator.

Now if you combine these two criteria reports into a single report, each set operator gives you different results. First, the Union set operator report contains the data shown in Table 15-7. The Union set operation combines the two datasets, removing duplicate records.

Column	Account Name	Product
Criteria 1 (Opportunity-Product History)	Account."Account Name"	Product."Product Name"
Criteria 2 (Asset History)	Account."Account Name"	Product."Product Name"

TABLE 15-4. *Minus Set Operator Sample*

Player Number	Age	Sport	Team
1	13	Golf	Chippers
2	14	Golf	Chippers
2	14	Bowling	Strikers
3	13	Basketball	Clippers
4	14	Basketball	Clippers
5	13	Golf	Chippers
6	14	Bowling	Strikers

TABLE 15-5. *Criteria Dataset One*

Player Number	Age	Sport	Team
1	13	Baseball	Strikers
2	14	Golf	Chippers
2	14	Bowling	Strikers
4	13	Basketball	Clippers
5	13	Baseball	Strikers
5	13	Golf	Chippers
6	14	Bowling	Strikers

TABLE 15-6. *Criteria Dataset Two*

Player Number	Age	Sport	Team
1	13	Golf	Chippers
1	13	Baseball	Strikers
2	14	Golf	Chippers
2	14	Bowling	Strikers
2	14	Bowling	Strikers
3	13	Basketball	Clippers
4	14	Basketball	Clippers
4	13	Basketball	Clippers
5	13	Golf	Chippers
5	13	Baseball	Strikers

TABLE 15-7. *Results of a Union Set Operation*

Player Number	Age	Sport	Team
1	13	Golf	Chippers
1	13	Baseball	Strikers
2	14	Golf	Chippers
2	14	Bowling	Strikers
2	14	Golf	Chippers
2	14	Bowling	Strikers
3	13	Basketball	Clippers
4	14	Basketball	Clippers
4	13	Basketball	Clippers
5	13	Golf	Chippers
5	13	Baseball	Strikers
5	13	Golf	Chippers
6	14	Bowling	Strikers
6	14	Bowling	Strikers

TABLE 15-8. *Results of a Union All Set Operation*

Table 15-8 shows the result of a Union All set operation on these two criteria reports. The Union All set operation simply puts both datasets in their entirety together.

Table 15-9 shows the result of an Intersect set operation on the two criteria reports. The Intersect set operation returns only these records that appear in both criteria reports.

Finally, Table 15-10 shows the result of a Minus set operation on the two criteria reports. The Minus set operation returns only these records in Criteria Dataset One (Table 15-5) that do not appear in Criteria Dataset Two (Table 15-6).

So far, I have described how a single set operation works with two criteria reports. Often, you will have a need to use more than two criteria reports and multiple set operations.

Player Number	Age	Sport	Team
2	14	Golf	Chippers
2	14	Bowling	Strikers
5	13	Golf	Chippers
6	14	Bowling	Strikers

TABLE 15-9. *Results of an Intersect Set Operation*

Player Number	Age	Sport	Team
1	13	Golf	Chippers
3	13	Basketball	Clippers
4	14	Basketball	Clippers

TABLE 15-10.   *Results of a Minus Set Operation*

Using Multiple Set Operations—Null Reporting

When you initially clicked the Combine with Similar Analysis button, you were prompted for the subject area of the next criteria report. After selecting the subject area, a second criteria report appeared in your analysis. To add additional criteria, you have two choices:

- For a criteria based on a subject area you do not yet have represented in your analysis, click the Edit button, select Create New Criteria, and select your subject area for the next criteria report.

- For a criteria based on a subject area already in your analysis, it is easier to copy an existing criteria report. Click the small button to the immediate right of the criteria report you want to copy, and select Copy from the pop-up menu. Next, click the button next to the criteria report that you want immediately before the new criteria report.

Regardless of which method you use to insert your criteria report, the set operator connecting the new criteria report will match the set operator of the previous criteria report. When you have more than two criteria reports in your analysis, and you change the set operator between a pair of criteria, the two criteria reports are grouped together. Figure 15-5 shows several groupings of criteria with different set operators.

You can use this grouping ability to your advantage. One use of multiple set operators is to report on null data. Suppose you want a report of the number of open activities for all of your accounts. Naturally, you would turn to one of the Activities subject areas to build this report. Now, if you add the Account Name column and the # of Open Activities metric column, you get a report of every account that has open activities. The problem here is that you want your report to include all accounts, and this report will only include the accounts with open activities.

A combined analysis is the only way to get a single report that includes all accounts (with and without related activities) along with the number of open activities. The hard part here is figuring out how to combine reports to get the data you want. You know it is easy to get a list of accounts and number of open activities for accounts with activities. That means all you need is a list of accounts without open activities to combine with the list of accounts with open activities.

If you created a report with just the Account Name column, your report would include all accounts. If you can somehow isolate the accounts without activities, you can combine this with the accounts with activities. If you think about the list of accounts you are able to create, you can come up with an equation:

Accounts with Activities + (All Accounts - Accounts with Activities)

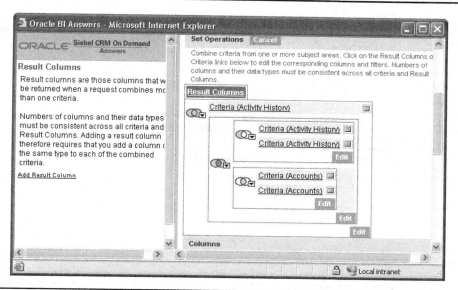

FIGURE 15-5.   *Criteria grouping*

Now you need to figure out how to create and combine these three reports. You know that you need the Account Name and # of Open Activities columns in your report, and that all reports need the same number of columns and the same column data types. You also know that you need three reports to get to the outcome you want, so start by creating a combined analysis that includes three identical reports containing Account Name and # of Open Activities. All three reports would return only accounts with activities.

The second report needs to include all accounts. To get that to happen, you need to remove whatever it is that is limiting your results to only accounts with open activities. If you remove the # of Activities metric, you should get all accounts in your report. You cannot remove the column, since all criteria reports need the same number and type of columns. You can remove the formula from the column and replace it with a static value. Since you need to maintain the correct data type, replace the formula in the second criteria report with a zero. This report will now return all accounts with a zero in the # of Open Activities column.

The third criteria report already returns only accounts with activities, but you have a different problem. The Minus set operator will only remove rows that are exact duplicates, and your second criteria report shows a zero in the second column for each account. This means you need to replace the numbers in the second column with zeros, but only include accounts that have open activities. You can accomplish this by replacing the formula in the second column with a zero and then adding an Is Not Null filter on the # of Open Activities column. By holding down the CTRL key as you click the column name on the left, you can add a filter to the report on a column that is not in the report. This will limit the results to accounts with open activities.

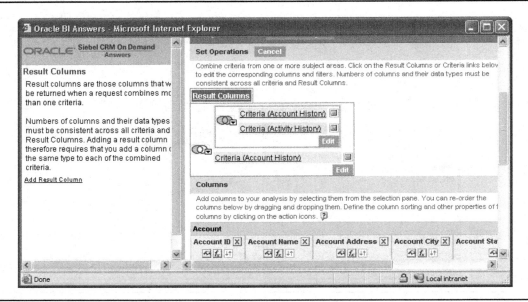

FIGURE 15-6. *Criteria for a Null Report*

Now, all you need to do is change the set operator between the second and third criteria report to the Minus option. Figure 15-6 shows how the criteria reports should appear. Table 15-11 shows the column formula for each criteria report.

When this report runs, Answers On Demand executes all three criteria reports to populate the result columns. You adjust all of your formatting and sorting of the data on the result columns. Often, the result column name changes to reflect a column reference or one of the column names from a criteria report. Click the Column Properties button on the result column and modify the column heading on the Column Format tab.

Report	Account Name	# of Open Accounts	Filter
1	Account."Account Name"	"Activity Metrics"."# of Open Activities"	None
2	Account."Account Name"	0	None
3	Account."Account Name"	0	"Activity Metrics"."# of Open Activities" IS NOT NULL

TABLE 15-11. *Criteria Report Formula*

Using a Combined Analysis to Filter Another Report

There are a couple of truths that you must respect when combining reports:

- A combined analysis requires that each criteria report contain the same number of columns and the same data types.

- The records in the result set for each criteria must match exactly, column-for-column, for a set operator to consider the data row as duplicates.

Given these two rules, combined analysis reports are far more successful and easier to construct when they are very simple and contain few columns.

When deciding that report requirements require a combined analysis, it is usually precipitated by a need to identify and take advantage of overlapping data or to combine disparate data into a single result set. A very effective use of combined analysis, then, is to create a simple report that combines criteria to arrive at a set of record IDs or other distinguishing value that you can use to filter another report that contains a robust data set with all the columns you want to display in a report.

Perhaps an example will help clarify this idea. Suppose you want a report that gives some account details, but you want to include only accounts that have purchased a product in the past, currently have an open opportunity, and also have an open service request. One effective way to create such a report is to first create a combined report with three criteria reports connected by the Intersect set operator. Each criteria report is filtered to include only the records you want. Table 15-12 shows the criteria report configuration for this report.

This report contains only one column and is made up of three criteria reports, each with a filter to include only account records that meet the desired criteria. The three criteria reports are combined with the Intersect set operator. The final result is a list of Account IDs for accounts with open service requests AND open opportunities AND at least one asset.

Next, you can create on the Account History subject area a report that contains all the account details that you need. Adding a filter on the Account ID column to include only those Account IDs that appear in your combined analysis will restrict the records to just those that have open service requests, open opportunities, and an asset.

Displaying Combined Data in a Pivot Table

One of the most frustrating challenges in creating a report that contains data from two or more subject areas is getting the record data to display on a single row per record. Often, when combining data in a report, you need to make some columns zero or blank in one criteria report

Report	Subject Area	Account ID	Filter
1	Service Request History	Account."Account ID"	# Open SRs is not null
2	Opportunity History	Account."Account ID"	# Open Opportunities is not null
3	Asset History	Account."Account ID"	# Assets is not null

TABLE 15-12. *Intersect Report Criteria*

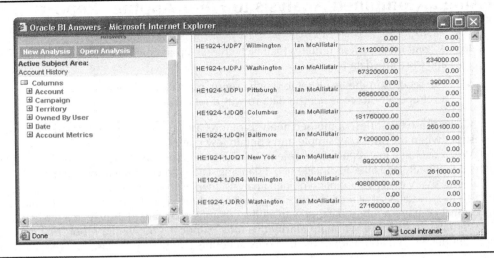

FIGURE 15-7. *Account Measures Union report—Table view*

and make some columns zero or blank in the other criteria report. The result is something like the report table shown in Figure 15-7. Notice that for some of the Account IDs, there are two rows of data, with some of the columns zero in one row and not the other.

With a result like this, you can often use a Pivot Table view to combine the results from each criteria report into a single row for each account. By placing the columns containing zeros into the Measures section of the Pivot Table view, you can take advantage of the aggregation rules on each column to total numerical data. You can sometimes use the Max, Min, First, or Last aggregation rules on date and text data types to get the same effect. This method is not always appropriate or effective with nonnumeric data when there are multiple values in a given column for a record. Figure 15-8 shows the Pivot Table view version of the analysis featured in Figure 15-7.

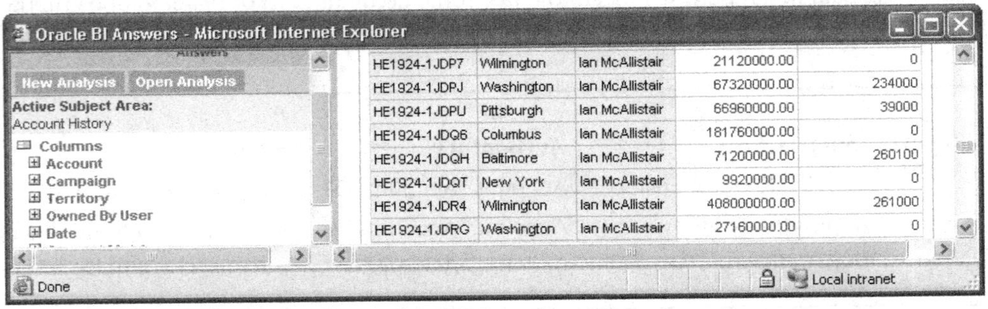

FIGURE 15-8. *Account Measures Union report—Pivot Table view*

Working with Result Columns

The result columns reflect the value of the criteria columns in each column position. The formula of all result columns at this point is blank. In any other report, if you wanted to use a function to perform an aggregation of some sort, you would simply edit the column formula. With a combined analysis, the result columns do not have a regular column reference to use in a column formula.

Every column in an analysis does have a Siebel Analytics Web (SAW) reference that you can use in a formula within your result columns. Each column in your report is referenced by "SAW_" followed by a number based on the column position. The first column is SAW_0. The second column is SAW_1. The third column is SAW_2. This pattern continues on, where the SAW number is one less than the column's position number.

You can take advantage of these SAW references to create calculations using the results of a combined analysis. Working with the same report as in the previous section, if you want to include a calculation that totals the four currency columns, you can do that with a formula in a result column. Before I explain how you add result columns, I want to first describe the approach you use to create these calculations.

Previously I explained that all the reports in the combined analysis must have the same number of columns and that those columns need to be the same data type. This is true for the criteria reports, but you can have additional result columns in your report. If you have more columns in your results than you have in your criteria, the extra result columns have nothing feeding data into them.

Generally, the same functions available for column formulas are available for use in the result columns. Rather than using an analytic column reference, you use the SAW references for the columns you want to include in your calculation. In order to aggregate column data, you need to also identify the column by which you are aggregating. For instance, MAX(SAW_3 BY SAW_0) returns the maximum value in the fourth column (SAW_3) for each value in the first column (SAW_0).

Going back to the previous report example, in order to get a total amount across all four revenue columns for each account, the formula in the additional result column is shown below.

```
MAX(SAW_1 BY SAW_0) + MAX(SAW_2 BY SAW_0) + MAX(SAW_3 BY SAW_0) +
MAX(SAW_4 BY SAW_0).
```

Now you just need to make a place for your calculated value. This is where additional result columns come into play. The result columns already present in your combined analysis contain the data from each of the columns in the criteria reports.

There are three methods for adding a result column to your report. I will explain the method that the developers of Answers On Demand intended, first. Select the Result Columns view by clicking the Result Columns link above the criteria reports. Now click the Add Result Column link in the area normally occupied by the list of columns in the current subject area. A new column is added at the end of the result columns row. This column is not present in any of the criteria reports, and therefore has no data feeding into it. If you try to move to Step 2 or preview the report at this point, you will see an error message, because the number of your report columns no longer matches across all criteria and result columns. You must provide a data source for the new result column, and you do this with a formula.

You may also hard-code values into a result column, just like you would for any other report column. It is not unheard of to create a combined report that has a calculated result column that aggregates each of the other columns in the report.

Result Column	SAW_0	SAW_1	SAW_2	MAX(SAW_2 BY SAW_0) / MAX(SAW_1 BY SAW_0)
Criteria (Account)	Account ID	Revenue	0	
Criteria (Assets)	Account ID	0	Price	

TABLE 15-13. *Combined Analysis Structure with Calculated Result Column*

There are a two other ways to add a result column that you may stumble across while exploring Answers On Demand. If you add a column to one of your criteria reports, a new result column is automatically added to contain the data from the criteria. If you then remove the column from your criteria report, the result column remains. To completely remove a column from a combined report, you must explicitly delete the criteria report column and the result column.

Another method that I have come across has you clicking one of the criteria reports, which opens the columns list on the left. While in this view, click over to Step 2 of the Build and View Analysis window. Now, click back over to Step 1. When I have done this, I've noticed that the list of columns is still available, yet the Step 1 view reverts to the result columns. Clicking a column at this point adds the column to the result columns and not to the criteria reports.

Either of the last two methods for adding a result column may stop working as I have described here, because they are not the intended functionality; but, as of this writing, they work perfectly well to add a result column to your combined analysis.

To help illustrate how the result columns work, Table 15-13 shows a representation of the result columns and criteria columns of a combined analysis.

Filtering Combined Analyses

Earlier in the chapter I described the process for using one report to filter another report. I also touched on filtering criteria reports in a combined analysis. To make explicit some of the implied points made earlier:

- You cannot add a filter to the result columns layer of a combined report. This means that to filter a combined analysis, you may need to apply your filter to each of your criteria columns. For instance, if the Account Industry column is on each of your criteria reports and you want to filter on industry, you need to add the industry filter to each of the criteria report. Adding a filter to only one of the criteria reports affects only the data within that specific query, so consider your filters carefully.

- It is not possible to add a filter prompt. If you attempt to add a prompt to a combined analysis, you receive a message stating that "Prompts are not currently supported for requests that combine criteria."

- If you happen to create a prompt on your report before you begin the process of adding additional criteria for the combined analysis, the prompt will remain on the report. When you attempt to run or preview the report, the results will consist of a view display error.

CHAPTER
16

Adding Interactivity
to Reports

raditionally, reports are documents that are spat out by a printer, photocopied, and distributed to the in boxes of everyone who should be interested...and then subsequently tossed in the trash or recycle bin by those who aren't interested. Those of us seeking a greener solution appreciate the ability to distribute reports electronically for display on the computer.

Either way, reports are traditionally very static documents that display the data that someone else decided to offer in the report. With Oracle CRM On Demand, you can take reporting to the next level. By giving your users more control over the reports, you can make a static information-delivery instrument an interactive experience.

There are many ways to interact with Oracle CRM On Demand reports. Some of these methods were described in previous chapters:

■ Chapter 12 presented interactivity in the Pages area of the Pivot Table view. Adding columns to the Pages area in a pivot table creates a drop-down list that allows users to filter pivot table data related to specific column values.

■ Chapter 13 presented the Column Selector view, which enables users to change the columns within the report.

■ Chapter 13 also covered the dashboard and dashboard prompts, which also provide some interactive filtering control over one or more reports.

These examples are only the beginning of the possibilities with report interactivity. Other interactive elements available include drilling down to refine report data, navigating to another report, navigating to another screen in Oracle CRM On Demand, and linking to other places outside Oracle CRM On Demand. Other interactive elements move you from other screens into a report. The overriding principal of interactivity in reports is accessibility. The more accessible we can make business intelligence, the greater the benefit of having that intelligence.

In this chapter, you will discover methods for turning your reports into an extension of the Oracle CRM On Demand application that provides users with a report that is more like a guided tour through your business data than a paper printout cluttering the desk.

Changing Default Drill-Down Behavior

You have probably noticed that some columns, when added to a report, are automatically drill-down links. There appears to be no consistency in the behavior of these drill-down links. Sometimes they cause additional data to appear in the report, and other times they seem to filter the report.

Typically, the key data columns and columns of data that have limiting subvalues on each object have some sort of default drill-down behavior. I'll use an example to explain what I mean by "limiting subvalues." Create a simple report that includes the Account Name and Country columns. You will find that your Account Name and Country data is drillable. Click an account name value in this report and the report refreshes to show only the clicked record with the addition of the Location column. The Account Name and Location columns now have no drill-down functionality, because this is the lowest level for the Account key data. Account uniqueness is identified by the Account Name and Location columns. The Location column is a sub-value of the Account. Since there are no additional key fields, you cannot drill any further.

The Country column in the report is still drillable. Click the country value and the same report returns with the State column added. Now both the Country and State columns are drillable. Click one of these values and the City column appears in the report. Click any of these columns again and the Zip Code column appears. At this point, you have reached the lowest level of address data and all columns are no longer drillable.

The column headings are also drillable. The effect of inserting the next column in the hierarchy is the same, but the report does not filter to a specific record. Instead, the additional column appears and the report still contains all the records.

Removing Default Drill-Down Behavior

The columns that have default drill-down interactivity are drillable unless you explicitly change the drill-down behavior. In Step 1 of the Build and View Analysis window, click the Column Properties button on a column to open the Column Properties window. On the Column Format tab, you will see the Column Heading Interaction and Value Interaction Type fields. Changing the values in these fields to No Interaction removes the default drill-down behavior from the column.

It is also possible to select the Drill value in these fields for columns that do not have drill-down functionality by default. I have not successfully added drill-down capability to any columns in this way, unless the column's default behavior includes drilling.

Drill-Down Charts

Drillable columns, when included in the Measures area of charts, also have drill-down capability, which is accessed by clicking the chart. The drill-down behavior is the same as drilling on values in a table. The values added to a report when you drill down on a column are added to all views in the report when you drill down on either table value or chart value.

To disable drill-down functionality on a chart, click the Additional Charting Options button in the Edit View Chart window to open the Additional Charting Options dialog box. On the Interaction tab, click the None radio button.

Navigating Between Reports

Another option for adding drill-down capabilities to a report is to enable the user to click a value in order to run and possibly filter the current or another report. This is a very flexible feature that allows you to create a series of connected reports. You could potentially enable a user to run a single report and then navigate to many other reports from within that report, essentially creating a menu of reports. You may want to develop a guided tour of sorts that has the user run a report and then navigate deeper and deeper into the data using the navigation functionality to move from summary reports to detail reports.

Simple Navigation—No Filters

To establish a navigation path from one report to another, you use the Navigate interaction setting on the column and/or chart. To set up a Navigate option on a report column, access the Column Properties window for the column in Step 1 of the Build and View Analysis window. On the Column Format tab, select the Navigate option in either of the navigation Type fields. Upon selecting Navigate, the Add Navigation Target button appears beneath the field (see Figure 16-1).

Click this button and two new fields and two new buttons appear beneath the Add Navigation Target button (see Figure 16-2). Click the Browse button to select a target report for the navigation. The selected report must be one that the user can normally access given their visibility settings. The Caption field allows you to apply a custom caption to the navigation link. When you add more than one navigation target to a report, the user sees a pop-up menu when they click the value in the report. The caption does not display if there is only one target. If you choose to leave the Caption field blank, the names of the target reports appear in the pop-up menu.

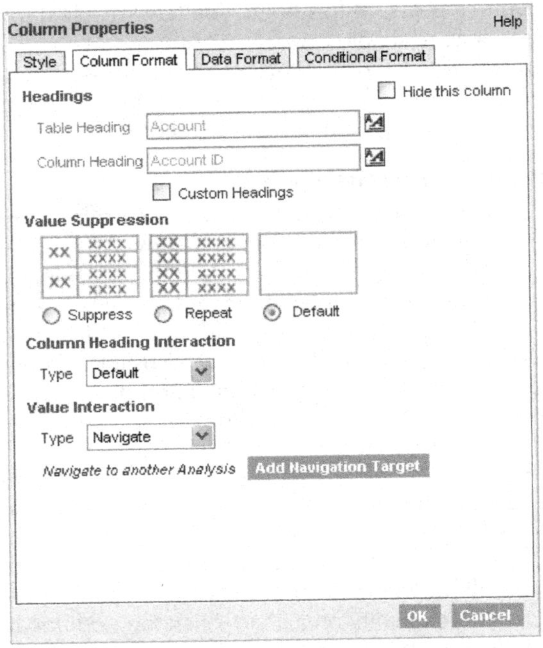

FIGURE 16-1. *Column Properties window—Column Format tab with Add Navigation Target button*

You can add navigation targets to both the column headings and column values. Navigation targets for the column headings and column values do not need to be the same. The simple navigation previously described runs another report but does not pass any values from the linking report to the target report. Actually, a more accurate statement is that the target report does not receive the data passed from the linking report. In order to use the navigation feature, you must modify the target report to receive the clicked value that passes from the linking report.

Navigating and Filtering

If your desired interactivity has your user click a value in one report in order to filter and run another report, the navigation portion of this interactivity is configured as described in the preceding section. In addition to configuring the navigation, you need to configure the target report to receive the filter value.

Open the target report, which you will have created before setting up the navigation interaction. Add a filter to the column that contains the data you plan to pass from the linking report. Set the condition on the filter to Is Prompted. This filter setting will have no effect on your report unless a value is passed to the report. You could potentially place an Is Prompted filter on every column, in which case that report would be unfiltered if a user runs it from the Reports tab. The same report, when the target of a column value navigation interaction, will filter to the records that equal the value clicked in the linking report.

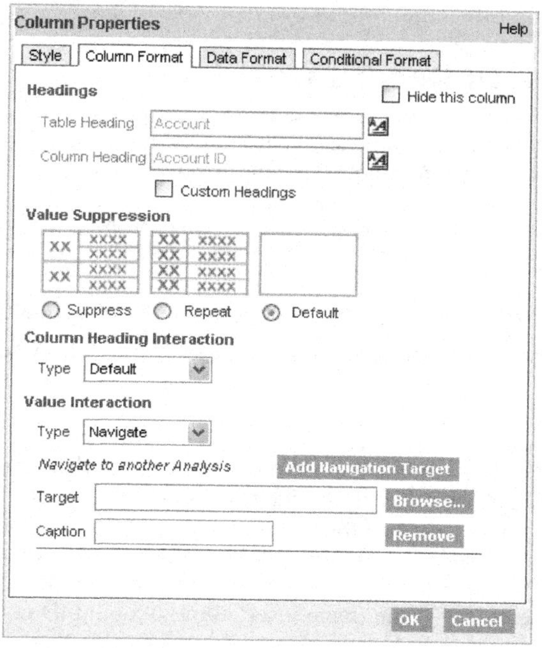

FIGURE 16-2. *Target navigation fields*

The same target report with the same filter accessed through a navigate interaction on a column heading will run unfiltered. This means that you can enable your users to filter the target report by clicking a value or simply run the target report unfiltered by clicking the linked column heading.

Using the Navigate Option to Filter the Current Report

The target of your navigate interaction need not be another report. You can use the navigate interaction to filter the current report by placing the Is Prompted filter on the same column as you place a navigate interaction targeting the very report to which you are adding the navigate interaction. When a user runs the report from the Reports tab, the report is unfiltered because no value is passed to the filter. When the user then clicks one of the interactive values in the report, the same report runs again, only this time the clicked value passes to the column filter and the report shows only records with values that match the clicked value.

Navigating from Charts

You can also set up your charts with the navigate interaction. By clicking a value represented in the Measures area of your chart, you may navigate to, or navigate to and filter, another report. To enable the Navigate interaction on a chart, click the Additional Charting Options button in the Edit View Chart window to open the Additional Charting Options dialog box. On the Interaction tab, click the Navigate radio button. The rest of the process is exactly like setting up navigation on a column. Click the Add Target Report button, browse for and select a report for the Target field, and enter a caption in the Caption field if you want to display something other than the report name when more than one target reports are defined.

Drilling Down to Record Details

Reports in Oracle CRM On Demand are delivered within the application and are interactive, making them an integrated part of the application. Given this tight integration of reports, it makes sense that users would be able to quickly and easily navigate between reports and other application windows.

It is possible to provide users with a drill-down path from a report to a record detail screen using one of two methods:

- **ActionLink method**   using an embedded ActionLink JavaScript
- **HTML method**   You build the link that builds the URL based on the selected data in the report.

ActionLink

Using an Action Link, users can navigate from a report to the detail record for a selected account, opportunity, contact, campaign, lead, service request, or user record. You configure columns with ActionLink functionality in Step 1 of the Build and View Analysis window. The first thing that you need to do to effectively enable an ActionLink is to insert the ID column for the object you are linking to. You need to position this column to the immediate right of the column that will contain the link. Notice in Figure 16-3 that I have inserted the Account ID column to the immediate right

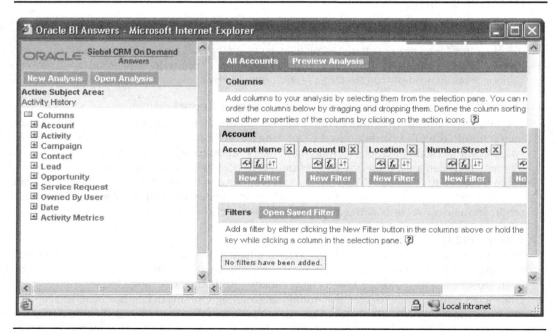

FIGURE 16-3. *Account ID column to right of Account Name column*

of the Account Name column. I would most likely format the Account ID column as hidden in my report, but the ID column must be there in order to properly pass the ID to the URL that will take you to the detail screen for that record.

Next, you open the Column Properties window for the column containing the values you want to use as a link to the detail screen. On the Style tab, expand the Custom CSS Style Options (HTML Only) section to expose the Use Custom CSS Style and Use Custom CSS Class fields, as shown in Figure 16-4. Check the Use Custom CSS Class check box and type **ActionLink** in the Use Custom CSS Class field.

With the ActionLink CSS class on the column, when a user clicks a value in the report, a URL is dynamically generated using the text in the column and the ID column. On the Data Format tab, change the format to Custom Text Format and enter the Action Link URL Code in the Custom Text Format field. The code for the Action Link has a very specific structure. Table 16-1 gives you the exact code that you should enter into the Custom Text Format field for each of the valid Action Class record types.

The resulting URL when a user clicks an action link follows the following format:

```
https://[SECURE SERVER SITE]/OnDemand/user/AccountDetail?
OMTHD=AccountDetailNav&OMTGT=AccountDetailForm&AccountDetailForm.Id=
[ACCOUNT ID FROM NEXT COLUMN]
```

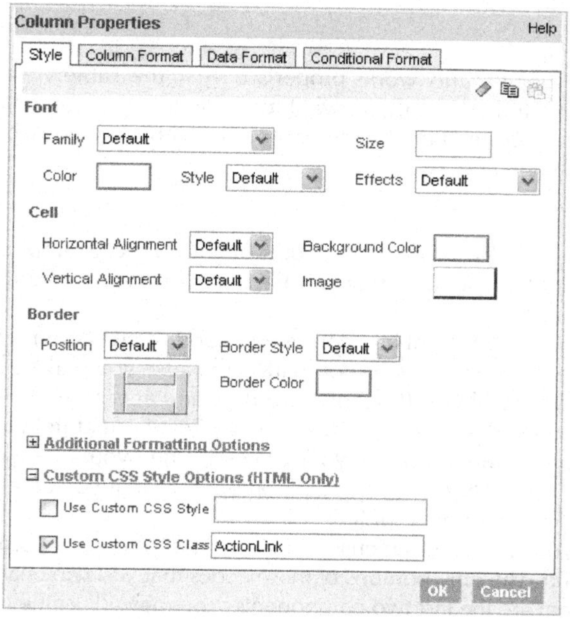

FIGURE 16-4. *Column Properties window—Style tab with ActionLink CSS class*

Record Type	Custom Text Format Code
Account	@[html]"<span onClick=\"javascript:LinkOccam (this, 'account');\ ">"@"</span>"
Opportunity	@[html]"<span onClick=\"javascript:LinkOccam (this, 'opportunity');\ ">"@"</span>"
Contact	@[html]"<span onClick=\"javascript:LinkOccam (this,'contact');\ ">"@"</span>"
Campaign	@[html]"<span onClick=\"javascript:LinkOccam (this, 'campaign');\ ">"@"</span>"
Lead	@[html]"<span onClick=\"javascript:LinkOccam (this,'lead');\ ">"@"</span>"
Service Request	@[html]"<span onClick=\"javascript:LinkOccam (this,'service');\ ">"@"</span>"
User	@[html]"<span onClick=\"javascript:LinkOccam (this, 'user');\ ">"@"</span>"

TABLE 16-1. *Action Link Text*

The ActionLink functionality works properly only in the Table view and only for the primary record types listed in Table 16-1. If you want to create a navigation link from a report to one of the other record types, or need the link to work from within a pivot table, you need to build the URL using the HTML method.

HTML Links

To create a link that works inside of a pivot table and links to objects that are not available with the ActionLink class, such as tasks and assets, you need to build the URL using a custom text format.

As you would with an ActionLink, you need to add the ID column for the record type you are linking to. This time the position does not matter, because you will be building the link on the ID column itself. Open the Column Properties window and access the Data Format tab.

The text that you need to insert into the Custom Text Format field is largely the same as the URL that you see in the Address bar of your browser when you access a detail screen in Oracle CRM On Demand. Table 16-2 describes the components that you enter in the Custom Text Format field to build the URL for this type of link.

In Table 16-3 you see a sample custom text format for each record type available to you in Answers On Demand. The only portions of these codes that you can change without risk of rendering the link nonfunctional are the last two components. You may adjust the target and the display text as described previously in this section.

Custom Text Segment	Description
@[html]	Indicates that the custom text format is HTML.
"<a href="	The beginning of the HTML hyperlink tag.
/OnDemand/user/AccountDetail?	The beginning of the URL. Notice that the http:// and https:// (secure server) address portions of the URL are assumed and are not necessary for the link.
OMTGT=AccountDetailForm	Identifies the target form of the URL.
&AccountDetailForm.Id=@	Identifies the record ID. The @ character in this code instructs Oracle CRM On Demand to use the ID in the column of the clicked record. This is why you must use the object's ID column in the report for this link.
target="_blank">	Indicates how you want the target form to open. The target tag can be one of four options: **target="_top"** within a link tag causes the page to load in the entire current window. **target="_parent"** is similar to target="_top" but opens the page in the immediate parent of a frame. Within On Demand, _parent and _top are the same. **target="_blank"** causes the link to open in a new browser window, leaving the report still open behind it. **target="_self"** loads the page within the same frame as the link.
"Account Details"</a>"	Provides the display text for the link and closes the tag. If you place an @ character between the quotation marks, the hyperlink shows the contents of the report cell, which is the record ID.

TABLE 16-2. *HTML Link Components*

Adding a New Record Link in a Report

Do you envision a process within your company whereby a user who runs a report and discovers that a needed record does not exist in the database can then create the new record in Oracle CRM On Demand? If so, consider this little trick for placing on your report a hyperlink that opens a new record edit screen in which to create the desired record.

Add a column to your report and replace the formula with a static value other than NULL. Now change the data format to a custom text format to create a URL for a new record form. You can place this column in the Sections area of a pivot table that is displaying sections only. This places a single link on the report that allows the user to navigate to a new record screen directly

Record Type	Custom Text Format Code
Account	@[html]<a href="/OnDemand/user/AccountDetail?OMTGT=AccountDetailForm&AccountDetailForm.Id="@ target="_blank">"Account Details"</a>
Opportunity	@[html]<a href="/OnDemand/user/OpportunityDetail?OMTGT=OpptyDetailForm&OpptyDetailForm.Id="@ target="_top">"Opportunity Details"</a>
Contact	@[html]<a href="/OnDemand/user/ContactDetail?OMTGT=ContactDetailForm &ContactDetailForm.Id="@ target="_top">"Contact Details"</a>
Campaign	@[html]<a href="/OnDemand/user/CampaignDetail?OMTGT=CampaignDetailForm&CampaignDetailForm.Id="@ target="_top">"Campaign Details"</a>
Lead	@[html]<a href="/OnDemand/user/LeadsDetailPage?OMTGT=LeadDetailForm &LeadDetailForm.Id="@ target="_top">"Lead Details"</a>
Service Request	@[html]<a href="/OnDemand/user/ServiceRequestDetail?OMTGT=ServiceRequestDetailForm&ServiceRequestDetailForm.Id="@ target="_top">"SR Details"</a>
User	@[html]<a href="/OnDemand/user/AppDrillDwnUserDetail?OMTGT=UserDetailForm&UserDetailForm.Id="@ target="_top">"User Details"</a>
Task	@[html]<a href="/OnDemand/user/TaskDetail?OMTGT=TaskDetailForm&TaskDetailForm.Id="@ target= "_parent">"Task Details"</a>
Appointment	@[html]<a href="/OnDemand/user/ApptDetail?OMTGT=ApptDetailForm&ApptDetailForm.Id="@ target= "_parent">"Appointment Details"</a>
Asset	@[html]<a href="/OnDemand/user/AssetDetail?OMTGT=AssetDetailForm&AssetDetailForm.Id="@ target="_top">"Asset Details"</a>
Product	@[html]<a href="/OnDemand/user/ProductDetail?OMTGT=ProductDetailForm&ProductDetailForm.Id="@ target="_top">"Product Details"</a>

TABLE 16-3.   *Custom Format Text for Detail Form Links*

from the report. Figure 16-5 shows an example of a report with several of these links. Table 16-4 shows the custom text formats for some of the new record screens.

Adding an Edit Record Link in a Report

By adding a similar HTML link on the record ID column in your report, you can also provide links to edit specific records directly from your report. Using the code shown in Table 16-5, you can add this functionality for nearly every record type.

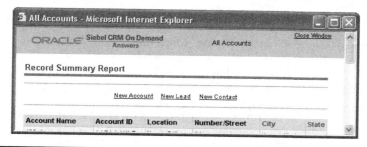

FIGURE 16-5. *Report with new record links*

Another Method for Record Links

There is another specific case in which neither of the preceding hyperlink formats will work. If you closely examine some of the screen URLs in Oracle CRM On Demand, you will find cases where the URL contains more than one record ID. The Opportunity-Product Edit screen, for instance, requires both the Opportunity ID and Product ID to correctly identify the opportunity-product relationship.

Action	Custom Text Format
Create a new account	@[html]"<a href="/OnDemand/user/DefAccountInsert? OMTGT=AccountEditForm" target="_blank"> "Create New Account"</a>"
Create a new contact	@[html]"<a href="/OnDemand/user/DefContactInsert? OMTGT=ContactEditForm" target="_blank"> "Create New Contact"</a>"
Create a new opportunity	@[html]"<a href="/OnDemand/user/OpptyCreateNewPageDefault? OMTGT=OpptyCreateEditForm" target="_blank"> "Create New Opportunity"</a>"
Create a new SR	@[html]"<a href="/OnDemand/user/DefServiceRequestInsert? OMTGT=ServiceRequestEditForm" target="_blank"> "Create New SR"</a>"
Create a new lead	@[html]"<a href="/OnDemand/user/DefLeadInsert? OMTGT=LeadCreateEditForm" target="_blank"> "Create New Lead"</a>"
Create a new campaign	@[html]"<a href="/OnDemand/user/DefCampaignInsert? OMTGT=CampaignEditForm" target="_blank"> "Create New Campaign"</a>"

TABLE 16-4. *New Record Custom HTML Text Formats*

Action	Custom Text Format
Edit an account	@[html]"<a href="/OnDemand/user/AccountEdit? OMTGT=AccountEditForm&OMTHD=AccountEditNav &AccountEditForm.Id=@ " target="_blank"> "Edit Account"</a>"
Edit a Contact	@[html]"<a href="/OnDemand/user/ContactEdit? OMTGT=ContactEditForm&OMTHD=ContactEditNav &ContactEditForm.Id=@" target="_blank"> "Edit Contact"</a>"
Edit an Opportunity	@[html]"<a href="/OnDemand/user/OpptyCreateEditPage? OMTGT=OpptyCreateEditForm&OMTHD=OpportunityEditNav &OpptyCreateEditForm.Id=@" target="_blank"> "Edit Opportunity"</a>"
Edit a Service Request	@[html]"<a href="/OnDemand/user/ServiceRequestEdit? OMTGT=ServiceRequestEditForm&OMTHD=ServiceRequestEditNav &ServiceRequestEditForm.Id=@" target="_blank"> "Edit SR"</a>"
Edit a Lead	@[html]"<a href="/OnDemand/user/LeadsEditPage? OMTGT=LeadCreateEditForm&OMTHD=LeadEditNav &LeadCreateEditForm.Id=@" target="_blank"> "Edit Lead"</a>"
Edit a Campaign	@[html]"<a href="/OnDemand/user/CampaignEdit? OMTGT=CampaignEditForm&OMTHD=CampaignEditNav &CampaignEditForm.Id=@" target="_blank"> "Edit Campaign"</a>"

TABLE 16-5. *Edit Record Custom HTML Text Formats*

The solution in this case is to use the concatenate function to build the necessary URL in the column formula. You use the HTML data format to interpret the text string in your formula into an HTML hyperlink. Since you build the URL in the column formula, you use the analytical field reference for the column in which to insert the record IDs.

The following is a sample formula that provides an Edit link in a report that takes the user from the Opportunity-Product report to the appropriate Opportunity-Product Edit screen. The second example provides a link to the Opportunity-Product Detail screen.

```
'<a href=/OnDemand/user/RevenueCreateEditPage?OMCR0='||
Opportunity."Opportunity ID" || '&OMTGT=RevnNewEditForm
&OMTHD=RevenueEditNav&OMCBO=Opportunity&OMRET0=OpportunityDetail
%3fOMTGT%3dOpptyDetailForm%26OMTHD%3dOpportunityDetailNav
%26ocEdit%3dY%26OpptyDetailForm.Id%3d' ||
 Opportunity."Opportunity ID" ||'%26OCTYPE%3dFORM_OCTYPE
%26ocTitleField%3dName&OCNOEDITTYPE=Y&RevnNewEditForm.Id=' ||
"Opportunity - Product"."Opty-Product Id" ||
' target=%22_blank%22>Edit</a>'
```

```
'<a href=/OnDemand/user/RevenueDetail?OMCR0='||
Opportunity."Opportunity ID" ||'&OMTGT=RevenueDetailForm
&OMTHD=RevenueDetailNav&OMCBO=Opportunity&RevenueDetailForm.Id='||
"Opportunity - Product"."Opty-Product Id" ||'&OMRET0=OpportunityDetail
%3focTitle%3dtest%2blead2%26OMTGT%3dOpptyDetailForm%26OMTHD
%3dOpportunityDetailNav%26ocEdit%3dY%26OpptyDetailForm.Id%3d'||
Opportunity."Opportunity ID" ||'&ocEdit=Y target=%22_blank%22>Detail</a>'
```

You will notice that the formula builds a text string in the form of an HTML hyperlink. By accessing the Data Format tab of the Column Properties window and changing the data format to HTML, the report will read this text as HTML and display the text just before the </a> tag as a hyperlink.

Another difference in the hyperlink here is the need for URL encoding that was not necessary with the other forms of navigation links. Because URLs read certain characters differently, it is often necessary to replace these characters in your URL with a code that does not confuse the URL into misreading the address. You will also encounter URL encoding in Web Link fields, described in the next section. Table 16-6 shows some of the most common URL codes that you will encounter in Oracle CRM On Demand.

Value	URL Encoding
space	%20
!	%21
"	%22
#	%23
$	%24
%	%25
&	%26
'	%27
(	%28
)	%29
*	%2a
+	%2b
,	%2c
—	%2d
.	%2e
/	%2f
:	%3a
;	%3b

TABLE 16-6.   *URL Encoding*

Value	URL Encoding
<	%3c
=	%3d
>	%3e
?	%3f
@	%40
\	%5c
_	%5f
{	%7b
|	%7c
}	%7d

TABLE 16-6. *URL Encoding (Continued)*

Navigating into Reports

So far I have discussed methods for navigating within a report, navigating between reports, and navigating from a report into the Oracle CRM On Demand application. In this section, I describe some methods for moving from within the Oracle CRM On Demand application windows into a report and displaying reports embedded in other windows within the application.

Because Oracle CRM On Demand is a hosted, browser-based application and reports are delivered as web pages, you can use a URL to open or embed a report.

Using Web Link Fields to Access Reports

A user with administrative access in Oracle CRM On Demand can create custom fields on the different objects. One of the field types available is the Web Link field. A Web Link field on a page layout provides a hyperlink that can link to another web page, either another Oracle On Demand screen or an external site. The special thing about the Web Link field is that you can insert record values inside the target URL identified in the Web Link field. This feature is often used to provide a link on an Account Detail screen to access a mapping web site, to pass account address data from the record to the web site to generate the map.

The basic steps for creating a Web Link field are given in Table 16-7. If you have trouble with this process or do not have the necessary access to create new fields and layouts, consult with your Oracle CRM On Demand administrator for assistance.

To use a Web Link field to access a report, you need to identify the URL for the report. The easiest way to do this is to run the report, right-click the body of the report, and select Properties from the pop-up menu to open the Properties window. The Address: (URL) field contains the URL for the report. Highlight all the text in this field and copy it to your clipboard.

I usually paste the URL to a text file for the next step. You will not use the entire URL, and will need to add several arguments to the URL to pass the necessary values to your Is Prompted

Step	Action	Result
1	Click the Admin Global link from any On Demand window.	Opens the Admin Homepage.
2	Click the Application Customization link.	Opens the Application Customization window.
3	Click a Record Type link in the Record Type Setup section.	Opens the Record-Specific Application Customization window.
4	Click the Field Setup link for the selected record type.	Opens the Fields window.
5	Click the New Field button.	Opens the Field Edit window.
6	Complete the Display Name field, Select Web Link in the Field Type drop-down list, and click Save.	Returns to the Fields window.
7	Click the Edit Web Link link next to the new field in the list.	Opens the Edit Web Link dialog box.
8	Select the way your target page should open. Enter the target URL in the URL field. The User Fields drop-down list and the record type-specific Fields drop-down list are used to insert field references in the URL field. These field references identify the places within the URL where values will be inserted to identify the record. After completing the screen, click the Save button.	Returns to the Fields window.
9	Click the Back to Application Customization link.	Returns to the Record-Specific Application Customization window.
10	Click the Page Layout link.	Opens the Page Layout window.
11	Click the Edit link next to the layout onto which you want to add your Web Link field.	Opens the Page Layout Wizard window.
12	Access Step 3 of the wizard and locate your Web Link field in the list on the left side of the screen. Use the arrow buttons to position your field on the layout. Click Finish.	Returns to the Page Layout window.

TABLE 16-7.   *Steps for Creating a Web Link Field*

column filter to run the report filtered on the current record. Initially, your URL will look something like this:

```
https://secure-ausomxaaa.crmondemand.com/OnDemand/user/analytics/saw.dll?
Go&Path%252fshared%252fCompany_00000_Shared_Folder%252fMy%2bReport
&Options=rfd&Action=Prompt
```

The first thing you need to change is the Action argument. Change Prompt to **Navigate**. This argument tells the browser that it should navigate to the designated web page when the user clicks the link.

Next, you need to indicate how many parameters should pass to the report filters, the condition for each, the columns receiving the values, and the values to pass. For this, you use a series of parameter tags, as described in Table 16-8.

Parameter Tag	Argument Description
&P0=	[Integer] Example: &P0=2 The number provided here identifies the number of parameters you are passing to the report.
&P1=	[Condition] Example: &P1=eq This parameter identifies the condition to use in the filter. The valid values follow: **eq** Equal to or in **neq** Not equal to or not in **lt** Less than **gt** Greater than **ge** Greater than or equal to **le** Less than or equal to **bwith** Begins with **ewith** Ends with **cany** Contains any (of the values in &P3) **call** Contains all (of the values in &P3) **like** Is like (Type %25 rather than the % wildcard) **top** In the top *n* (&P3 contains 1+*n*, where *n* is the number of top items) **bottom** In the bottom *n* (&P3 contains 1+*n*, where *n* is the number of bottom items) **bet** Between (&P3 must have two values) **null** Is null (&P3 must be 0 or omitted) **nnul** Is not null (&P3 must be 0 or omitted)
&P2=	[Column] Example: &P2= Account."Account ID"

TABLE 16-8. *Report Web Link Parameters*

Parameter Tag	Argument Description
&P3=	[Field] Example: &P3=%%%Row_Id%%% Use the Field drop-down lists to insert this field value variable into the URL. The field identifier will always be proceeded and followed by %%%. You may also use a static value here, such as 0 in case of the null condition.
&P4=	[Condition] for second value if needed.
&P5=	[Column] for second value if needed.
&P6=	[Field] for second value if needed.
	This pattern continues for each additional value: P7, P8, and P9 for the third value, P10, P11, and P12 for the fourth, and so on.

TABLE 16-8. *Report Web Link Parameters (Continued)*

Your completed Web Link URL will appear something like the following URL. This particular URL passes two values to a report with different conditions.

```
https://secure-ausomxaaa.crmondemand.com/OnDemand/user/ReportIFrameView?
SAWDetailViewURL=saw.dll?Go%26Path%3D%252fshared
%252fCompany_00000_Shared_Folder%252fAccount%2bProfile&Action=Navigate
&P0=2&P1=eq&P2=Account."Account Region"&P3=%%%Region%%%&P4=gt
&P5=Account."Number of Employees"&P6=500
```

Using a Web Link Field to Access a Report with Prompts

You can also use a Web Link field to run a report that contains prompts. The URL structure is slightly different, and you do not pass any values to the report. The key to a Web Link field that calls a prompted report is the AnalyticFieldReference argument placed at the end of the URL:

```
https://secure-ausomxaaa.crmondemand.com/OnDemand/user/ReportIFrameView?
SAWDetailViewURL=saw.dll?Go%26Path%3D%252fshared
%252fCompany_00000_Shared_Folder%252fAccountReport&Options=rfd
&Action=Navigate&AnalyticReportName=AccountReport
```

Creating a Custom Web Applet with a Report

Suppose you want to display some specific information, perhaps a chart, on a record detail page. You want this information to be specifically related to the current record that you are displaying on the screen. The solution is to embed your report into a custom web applet and add the applet to your homepage.

The basic steps for creating a web applet are given in Table 16-9. If you have trouble with this process or do not have the necessary access to create new fields and layouts, consult with your Oracle CRM On Demand administrator for assistance.

There are some specific design considerations when building a report that you intend to use as a custom applet. I typically eliminate titles and format the appearance of the report to look as much like a standard, related-item applet in Oracle On Demand.

Step	Action	Result
1	Click the Admin Global link.	Opens the Admin Homepage.
2	Click the Application Customization link.	Opens the Application Customization window.
3	Click a Record Type link in the Record Type Setup section.	Opens the Record-Specific Application Customization window.
4	Click the Web Applet link for the selected record type.	Opens the Applet List window.
5	Click the New button.	Opens the Custom Web Applet window.
6	Complete the required Name field and complete the fields necessary to reference and embed your desired web page, and then click the Save button.	Returns to the Applet List window.
7	Click the Back to Application Customization link.	Returns to the Record-Specific Application Customization window.
8	Click the Page Layout link.	Opens the Page Layout window.
9	Click the Edit link next to the layout onto which you want to add your web applet.	Opens the Page Layout Wizard window.
10	Access Step 4 of the wizard and locate your web applet in the Available Information list. Use the arrow buttons to position your applet in the displayed Information list. Click Finish.	Returns to the Page Layout window.

TABLE 16-9. *Web Applet Configuration Steps*

As with most reports and views, you want to keep your web applet report as simple as possible. That being said, I want to offer as an example the most extreme report-based web applet that I have built during my own consulting experience. This applet essentially combines nearly every complexity, which was necessary to meet the specific needs of my client.

The customer in this case wanted to replace the Product Revenue applet with one that provides a very specific set of data but still provides most of the functionality the Product Revenue applet offers. There are several challenges to building such an applet, including replicating the Edit and Delete links and providing the ability to add additional products to an opportunity from within the applet. I also wanted to provide information on quoted pricing, displaying only the total amount, while also providing line-item purchase prices.

The first step in building the applet is to create the report that the custom web applet will reference. This seems easy enough, and for most applets, it certainly is. In this particular case, I needed to build a combined analysis between the Opportunity-Product History subject area and the Opportunity-Products subject area, because the historical subject area contains the Opportunity-Product ID that is necessary when building the URL for the Edit and Delete links. The customer wanted to display any newly added products as well, so I needed the real-time subject area to provide information on records created the same day.

In the column for the Edit link, my column formula builds the URL for accessing the Opportunity-Product Edit screen and displays an Edit hyperlink to the left of each related record from the historical subject area:

```
'<a href=/OnDemand/user/RevenueCreateEditPage?OMCR0=' ||
Opportunity."Opportunity ID" || '&OMTGT=RevnNewEditForm&OMTHD=RevenueEditNav
&OMCBO=Opportunity&OMRET0=OpportunityDetail%3fOMTGT%3dOpptyDetailForm
%26OMTHD%3dOpportunityDetailNav%26ocEdit%3dY%26OpptyDetailForm.Id%3d' ||
Opportunity."Opportunity ID" || '%26OCTYPE%3dFORM_OCTYPE%26ocTitleField
%3dName&OCNOEDITTYPE=Y&RevnNewEditForm.Id=' ||
"Opportunity - Product"."Opty-Product Id" || ' target=%22_blank%22>Edit</a>'
```

The Delete link in a standard applet relies on some JavaScript to pop up a delete confirmation window and then delete the record when the user clicks OK. This seemed a bit risky to try to replicate in the report, and I am not even sure it would be possible without some complex coding, so I opted to have the Delete link navigate the user to the record detail screen so that the user can verify the record and then use the Delete button on the detail screen to delete a record. The formula for this column builds the URL for the Opportunity-Product Detail screen, which also needs the Opportunity ID and Opportunity-Product ID:

```
'<a href=/OnDemand/user/RevenueDetail?OMCR0='|| Opportunity."Opportunity ID"
||'&OMTGT=RevenueDetailForm&OMTHD=RevenueDetailNav&OMCBO=Opportunity
&RevenueDetailForm.Id='|| "Opportunity - Product"."Opty-Product Id"
||'&OMRET0=OpportunityDetail%26OMTGT%3dOpptyDetailForm
%26OMTHD%3dOpportunityDetailNav%26ocEdit%3dY%26OpptyDetailForm.Id%3d'
|| Opportunity."Opportunity ID" ||'&ocEdit=Y target=%22_blank%22>Delete</a>'
```

I also needed to add a column to the report to provide the Add functionality. I did this with a URL-building formula. This URL needs only the Opportunity ID in a couple of places to properly identify the opportunity to which the user is adding a product:

```
'<a href=/OnDemand/user/RevenueCreateNewPage?OMCR0='
|| Opportunity."Opportunity ID" || '&OMTGT=RevnNewEditForm
&OMTHD=RevenueNewNav&OMCBO=Opportunity&OMTGT%3dOpptyDetailForm
%26OMTHD%3dOpportunityDetailNav%26ocEdit%3dY%26OpptyDetailForm.Id%3d'
|| Opportunity."Opportunity ID" || '&OCNOEDITTYPE=Y&OCTYPE=
target=%22_blank%22>Add Product</a>'
```

On the layout of this report, I have only a single Pivot Table view. I used a pivot table here to facilitate the grouping of data. I also used the Sections area of the pivot table to display a single Add Unit link and the Total Quoted Price only once within the applet. I formatted the column heading and column values to replicate the appearance of a standard applet. This is easily accomplished by applying the appropriate background color to the heading and using an 11-point font with the appropriate color. For the values, I bumped the font up to 11 points and inserted a light-blue border at the bottom of each column cell. For your reference, the specific colors needed for this formatting using the Contemporary theme are offered in Table 16-10.

I placed an Is Prompted filter on the Opportunity ID column. This is the column for which I pass the current record's value so that the applet filters to show the correct related records.

To make the report display within the web applet, I used the Web Applet HTML field rather than the URL field. Technically, either may be used, but by using an iframe and HTML, you have a little

Applet Element	HTML Color Code
Heading background	#F8EBD7
Heading text	#835809
Value background	#FFFFFF
Value border	#C7DDF2

TABLE 16-10. *Color Codes for Custom Applet*

more control over the display of the report within the applet. A sample of the code I used to embed the report in the web applet follows:

```
<iframe src=/OnDemand/user/analytics/saw.dll?Go
&Path=%2fshared%2fCompany_00000_Shared_Folder%2fProduct+Applet&Options=r
&Action=Navigate&p0=1&p1=eq&p2=Opportunity."Opportunity+ID"&p3=%%%Id%%%
FRAMEBORDER="no" WIDTH="100%" HEIGHT=300></iframe>
```

Notice that the URL portion of the code looks exactly like the code would look for a web link, with the parameter values indicating from which report field to pass the value to the report filter. With the iframe tag, you can control the height and width. Notice also that the Options argument in the code is set to Options=r. This argument identifies which of the three standard report links (Refresh, Print, or Download) appears at the bottom of your report. Usually, for a web applet report, I set this argument to Options=none so that none of these links appears, but for this particular applet, I needed the Refresh link because my report queries a real-time reporting subject area. I point this out because simply refreshing the page will not refresh the report.

The web applet shown in Figure 16-6 is formatted as described above to appear very similar to the other applets in this window.

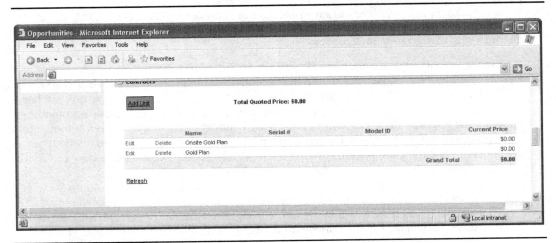

FIGURE 16-6. *Sample report web applet*

Displaying a Report on a Homepage

Designing a report for a homepage is similar to designing a report for a web applet in that you probably want a simple table or chart that summarizes data for a particular type of record, without titles and multiple views of data. The primary difference is in how you link the report to the homepage.

Click the Admin link to access the Admin Homepage. Click Application Customization to access the Application Customization window. From there, you may either click the My Custom Homepage Report link to make a report available on the main Homepage screen, or drill into a record type and click the Homepage Custom Report link to add a report to that particular record type homepage. Either path takes you to a screen that lists any existing homepage reports. On this screen, click the New Homepage Report button to access the Homepage Custom Report Detail window (see Figure 16-7).

In this window, you name the homepage report and then identify the path to the report. When setting the homepage report properties, you may choose single or double height and width. A double-wide report spans both columns of a homepage. If you choose the Height option Double, the report will be twice the height of other sections.

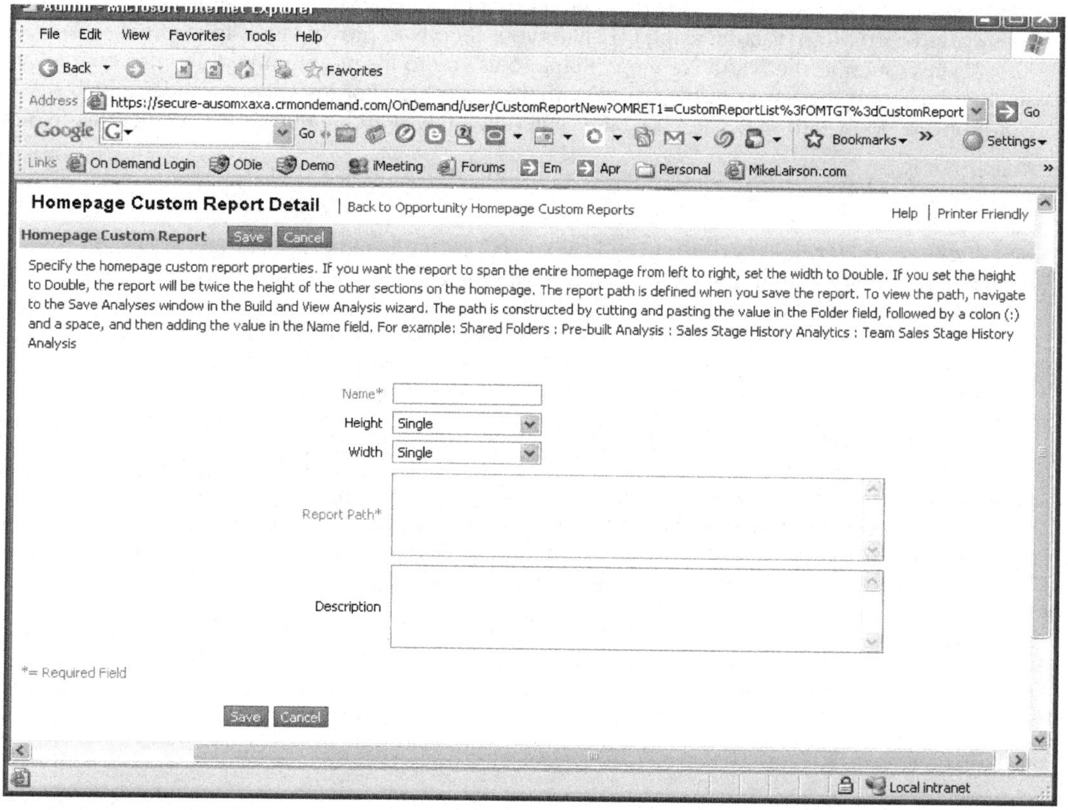

FIGURE 16-7. *Homepage Custom Report Detail window*

The path of the report is based on where you save the report. To determine the path, look at the Folder field when you are saving the report. You can copy and paste the value in the Folder field, followed by a colon and a space, and then type the name of the report shown in the Name field. Once saved, the homepage report is available for users to select for their homepage screen.

Embedding Reports on Web Tabs

Using custom web tabs is also a great way to make a frequently referenced report very easy to access and use. When you create a custom web tab in Oracle CRM On Demand, you are asked for the URL for the site that you wish to display within the tab. To display a report here, you simply provide the report URL as it appears within the Properties window. Notice in the sample URL that I left the action set to Prompt:

```
https://secure-ausomxaaa.crmondemand.com/OnDemand/user/analytics/saw.dll?Go
&Path=%2fshared%2fCompany_00000_Shared_Folder%2fSRAnalysis&Options=rfd
&Action=Prompt
```

Providing External Links

Up to this point in this chapter, I have described methods for navigating between reports, navigating into reports, and displaying reports in other areas of Oracle CRM On Demand. There is one more navigation method to discuss: using HTML in your reports to provide links to external sites.

A view, such as the Narrative view, that allows you to insert column values also enables you to pass values from the report results along with the hyperlink. For instance, consider a web site URL for a phone book web site. The URL, after entering a few search values, looks something like this:

```
http://www.somephonebooksite.com/search/FindPerson/?&firstname=Michael
&lastname=Lairson&zip=22222
```

Include an HTML hyperlink string in your report that inserts values from the report to create a link that passes values to the web site along with the URL. The format for this string looks something like this:

```
<a href=http://www.somephonebooksite.com/search/FindPerson/?
&firstname=@1&lastname=@2&zip=@5>Look Up Phone Number</a>
```

If you decide to employ this method to provide links to other web sites outside of Oracle CRM On Demand, be sure to include the target="_blank" argument so that the external site opens inside a new browser window; otherwise, the current Oracle On Demand session will be interrupted.

Enabling users to navigate through your analysis is a great way to add interest and usability to your reports and extend the Oracle On Demand application. In many ways, you are limited only by your imagination and HTML abilities.

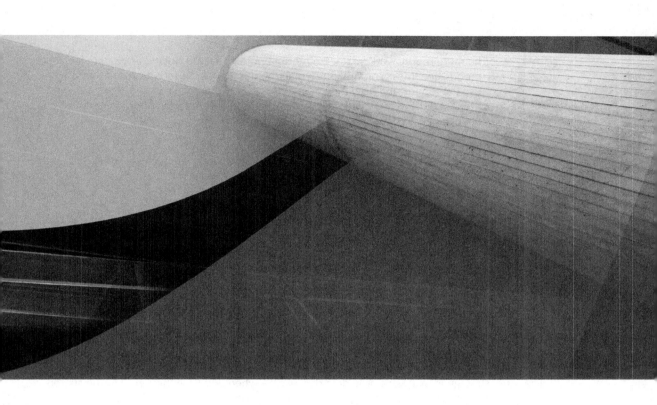

CHAPTER
17

Managing Reports and
Controlling Access

he more reports you create, the more important a good organization plan for your reports becomes. You obviously plan the design of your reports around who will use the reports and how they plan to use the reports. It makes sense to give some thought to how users will access the reports and which users should or should not have access to particular reports.

In this chapter, you will explore the mechanisms available for limiting access to reports, organizing your report library, and maintaining order in your report library.

Report Management

If you are the type of person who has dozens of shortcut icons on your computer desktop and whose My Documents folder contains hundreds of files but very few folders, then this chapter will be especially helpful to you. A systematic approach to report management not only helps you to make reports easy for users to find and run but also helps you to control which reports each user can access. Keeping a neatly organized report library is not a requirement, but it certainly is helpful.

The simplest strategies for organizing your report library are to use a clearly defined naming convention and to provide descriptions for each report. These two things alone can greatly enhance the report users' experience. For instance, if all the reports designed for your sales organization are named with a prefix of SALES, all the sales reports will appear together when the reports sort and anyone in sales will easily be able to locate the set of reports in which they are interested.

The other strategy is to always provide a description when you save the report to the shared reports area. This description might describe the content of the report, when the user should use the report, or what to do with the report. Consistent use of the Description field can provide your users with answers to common questions about the reports.

Organizing Reports

Beyond using a standard naming convention and description, you may find that you need a little more structure in your report library. Perhaps the naming convention isn't enough when you have a couple hundred reports that users must sort through to find the report they need. This section describes the processes for creating folders, renaming reports, moving reports, and copying reports to create an organizational scheme for your report library.

The processes that I describe in this section all take place in the Manage Analyses window. To access the Manage Analyses window, click the Design Analyses link on the Reports tab. This takes you to the Getting Started window, from which you click either the Manage Analyses link in the upper-right corner or the Manage Analyses button in the lower-right section.

Creating Folders

Oracle CRM On Demand reports are organized by default into two primary areas: the My Folders area and the Shared Folders area. Within the Shared Folders area, you initially have two directories, Company Wide Shared Folder and Pre-built Analysis directories. The Pre-built Analysis directory contains a number of additional folders that organize the prebuilt reports by topic area. You cannot change anything within the Pre-built Analysis directory, so I am not going to spend much time on it, but I do want you to notice that the folder structure here is an excellent example of a report organization strategy with topic area folders.

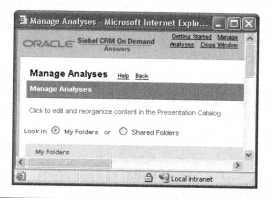

FIGURE 17-1. *Manage Analyses Look In radio buttons*

When you access the Manage Analyses window, shown in Figure 17-1, you have the option of viewing the My Folders area or the Shared Folders area. Select one of the Look In radio buttons to indicate which of these two areas you want to access.

The bottom portion of the window contains a list of the folders and reports within the area you have selected. You can click any folder listed there to access that folder and any folders and reports within it. To create a new folder, click the Create New Folder link in the section header. This takes you to the Create New Folder window (see Figure 17-2), where you enter a name for your folder in the Folder Name field and, optionally, a description in the Description field.

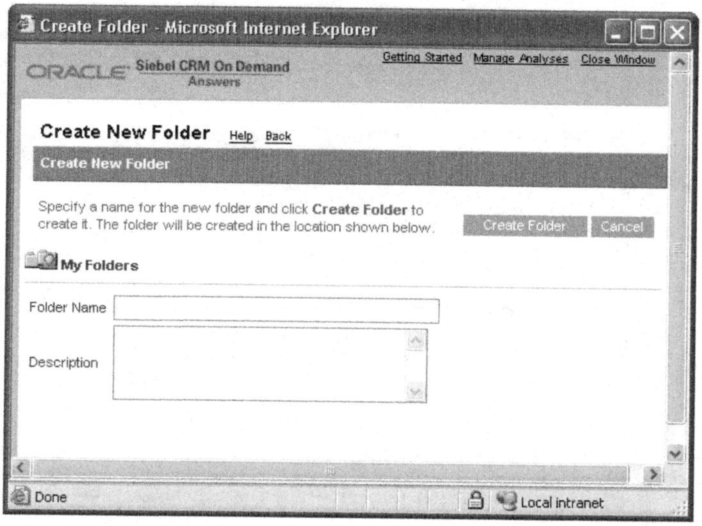

FIGURE 17-2. *Create New Folder window*

Click the Create Folder button and you return to the Manage Analyses window. You are now viewing the list of reports inside the folder you just created, which of course is empty at this point. To move up a level in the structure, click the link in the folder header for the higher-level folder.

Renaming Folders and Reports

In the Manage Analyses window, you will find three buttons next to each folder and report. The first (leftmost) of these three buttons is the Rename button. To change the name of a folder or report, click the Rename button next to the item you want to rename. This takes you to the Edit Item Name and Description window (see Figure 17-3), where you see two fields and a check box.

The Name field contains the current name of the folder or report. To give the item a new name, simply change the contents of the Name field. You may also add or change the description of the folder or report in the Description field.

If the report or folder is named in a navigation link in another report or Web Link field and you want to maintain this link after you change the name, make sure you check the check box to preserve references to the item. Click the Update button to commit the name change.

Copying and Moving Reports

The second of the three buttons next to each folder and report in the Manage Analyses window is the Copy/Move button. Clicking this button takes you to the Copy/Move Item window (see Figure 17-4), which shows you the folder structure of your report library. To copy a report, select the folder into which you want to place a copy of the report and then click the Copy button. Two reports with the same name cannot reside in the same folder, so if you attempt to copy a report into a folder that already contains a report by the same name, you are shown a presentation catalog error indicating that an item already exists with that name.

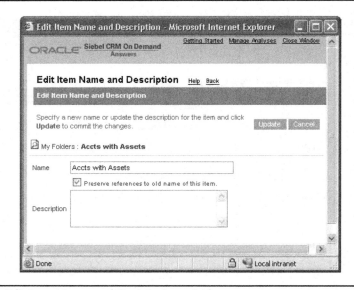

FIGURE 17-3. *Edit Item Name and Description window*

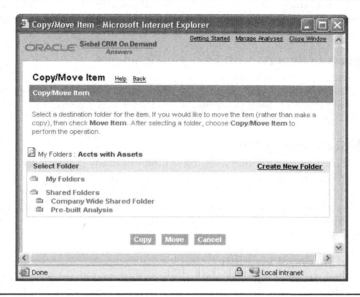

FIGURE 17-4.   *Copy/Move Item window*

Moving an item is exactly the same as copying, except that you click the Move button and a copy of the report does not remain in the original location.

Deleting Reports

The Delete button is the third button in the series of buttons next to each folder and report in the Manage Analyses window. Click the Delete button next to an item that you want to delete, and the window changes to show a confirmation message explaining that the item is about to be deleted and that any shortcuts to the item will become invalid. Click Yes if you are sure you want to delete the folder or report. An item deletion is irreversible.

Controlling Analytic Data Access

You can control data visibility in Oracle On Demand Analytics in a number of ways. This section provides an overview of these methods. Some of these methods require some level of administrative control within Oracle CRM On Demand, so, depending on your own access privileges, you may need to work with your company's system administrator to configure data access for your report users. The methods for data access include assigning user role privileges, assigning report folders to roles, using analytics visibility settings, using the Book of Business feature, and granting access through user delegation.

Controlling Access with Role Privileges

The privileges on each user role can impact the data that is visible to users within reports. The least restrictive setting for report data access has the Access All Data in Analytics privilege enabled on the user role. This privilege gives users unlimited access to all data across the entire company, regardless of other settings. Essentially, the Access All Data in Analytics privilege trumps all the other mechanisms for controlling report data access described in this section.

Limiting Access to Reports with Folder Assignments

You can limit user access to specific reports by creating the reports inside of, or moving the reports into, a folder that has been associated with one or more roles. When you associate a role with a folder, only the users with that role see the folder and the reports within the folder in the Company Wide Shared Folder directory.

Using Analytics Visibility Settings

You will find the Analytics Visibility setting on the company profile and the user profiles. The setting identified on the user profile takes precedence over the company profile setting, but if no analytics visibility setting is identified on the user profile, the company setting is used to control visibility. There are three settings in the Analytics Visibility field, listed and described in Table 17-1. You can set the visibility for the Reporting subject areas and the Analytics subject areas individually.

Using Book of Business Visibility

I like to think of the Book of Business feature as an additional filter for users of Oracle CRM On Demand. With the Book of Business feature activated for a company and the Look In selector displayed, a user assigned to one or more books can limit the data returned in a report to a specific book and any subbooks of the selected book.

Users may have a defaulted book in the Look In selector. The administrator can set this default by updating the Default Analytics Look In Setting field on each user's profile in Oracle CRM On Demand.

Using the Delegate User List

User delegation is another feature of the Book of Business that can affect the data that appears in your reports. If someone delegates to another user by adding them to their Delegated User list, the delegated user has the option of selecting the other user in their Look In selector. The delegated user then sees only the data visible to the other user in the report. Manager Visibility does not pass to the delegated user, however.

Visibility Setting	Description
Manager Visibility	Allows users to see their own data and any data owned by their subordinates. Managers see only records specifically owned by themselves and their subordinates. This does include private records.
Team Visibility	Allows users to see their own data and any records shared with them through team assignment (account and opportunity) and group assignment.
Full Visibility	Available only for the Analytics subject areas, combines the access provided by the Manager Visibility setting and Team Visibility setting.

TABLE 17-1. *Analytics Visibility Settings*

Analytics Performance Guidelines

One element of report management that permeates throughout the report design and development process is the management of report performance. I have mentioned some of these considerations along the way, but it is no accident that this particular topic is at the end of this book. In many places in this book, I have suggested ways to do some unusual things with reports. Some of my ideas are meant to take reporting in directions that the engineers behind this product probably never anticipated or intended. Pushing the limits of your reports does not come without cost, though, and sometimes that cost is in performance. For this reason, I want to close this book with some information on how to manage report performance.

Performance Guidelines

You must do everything in your power to both meet your users' reporting needs and maximize report performance. However, in some situations, you must make a trade-off between meeting users' reporting needs and maximizing report performance. In my opinion, meeting users' reporting needs is more important than maximizing performance. This section offers guidelines that you should follow whenever possible to keep report performance as high as possible while meeting your users' reporting needs.

Choose the Right Subject Area

Use an Analytics subject area whenever possible. The Analytics subject areas are built on the data warehouse, which is designed for reporting. Use the Reporting subject areas only when absolutely necessary to meet user needs.

A Report Is Not Always the Best Solution

When determining your users' needs for a report, consider that sometimes users think they need a report when a custom list or a data export is a better solution. If the proposed report includes data from only a single record type and does not require calculations or any type of data conversion, consider that a list may meet the user's needs better than a report would. If the proposed report contains many columns and is intended for downloading to a file, consider that a data export may be a better solution than a large report with many records.

The ID Is Key for Detail Reports

If your report is gathering detail information for individual records, include the record ID in the report. Hide it if you like, but the ID field is a key field and helps Answers On Demand gather the data quickly.

Two Reports Are Often Better Than One

It is not necessary to force every detail into a single report. A summary report will generate much faster, and by adding navigation to other reports or detail screens, you can still provide access to the detail data that the user needs. Usually, when a user wants to see a lot of detail, it is for one or a small number of records. A summary report with drill-down links allows the user to select exactly what they need to see and saves the report from having to collect all the details for many records at once.

The Higher You Go, the More You Can See

The president of a company usually has access to much more information than users at lower levels in the company hierarchy have access to. Think about how much data a report will include when an executive runs the report compared to when an individual contributor runs the report. You may find that you need to summarize data or include filter prompts to control the amount of data in the report.

The More You Combine, the Lower the Performance

If you consider that each criteria report in a combined analysis is actually a separate report and that each report runs at least one query against the data warehouse or database, it is easy to accept that a report with many set operators will generate a bit slower than one with only a few set operators. Design your combined analyses carefully to limit the number of queries to as few as possible, and expect combined reports to take a little longer to generate than your others take.

Simplify for Speed

Case statements, embedded reports, and HTML are examples of possible speed bumps affecting report performance. If you are using a lot of code in your reports, keep it as simple as possible. Excessive coding means more time to evaluate the code to generate the report.

If you have excluded columns in a pivot table that are not critical to your report, remove the columns. Even though the columns are excluded from the pivot table, they are still included in the query, and still require some processing time when the report generates.

No matter the type of report or the views included, keeping the report as simple as possible is always best for performance. I love creating impressive reports as much as, possibly more than, anyone. The reality is that meeting user needs with the best possible performance is usually far better than a flashy report that takes a long time to generate.

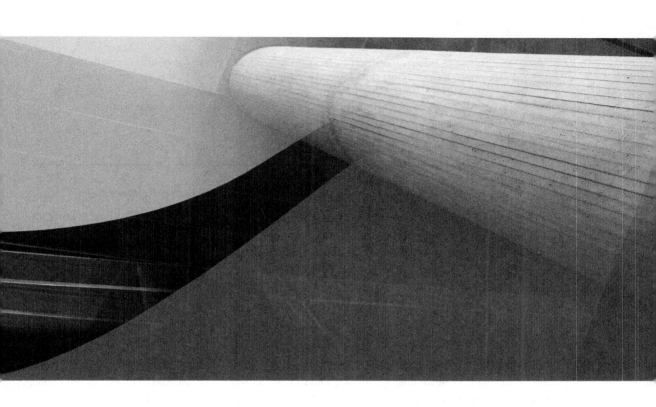

APPENDIX

Quick Reference

his appendix is intended to serve as a quick reference for nearly everything you need during report development. Much of the information here appears elsewhere in the book with examples and explanation, so the following table provides not only a directory to the tables in this appendix but also chapter references so that you can easily find more details.

Table	Table Name	Chapter Reference
Table A-1	Data Format Settings	Chapter 3
Table A-2	Column Filter Operators	Chapter 4
Table A-3	Aggregation Rules	Chapter 5
Table A-4	Formula Operators	Chapter 5
Table A-5	Date and Time Literals	Chapter 5
Table A-6	Session Variables	Chapter 5
Table A-7	Repository Variables	Chapter 5
Table A-8	Formula Functions	Chapters 5 through 9
Table A-9	Literal and Null Value Formats	Chapter 15
Table A-10	Action Link Text	Chapter 16
Table A-11	Custom Format Text for Detail Form Links	Chapter 16
Table A-12	New Record Custom HTML Text Formats	Chapter 16
Table A-13	Edit Record Custom HTML Text Formats	Chapter 16
Table A-14	URL Encoding	Chapter 16
Table A-15	Report Web Link Parameters	Chapter 16
Table A-16	Basic HTML Code	Chapters 8, 13, 14, and 16

Data Format Settings

Column Type	Data Format Option	Detail
Numeric data	Number	1 displays as 1.
	Currency	1 displays as $1.00. The currency symbol, negative format, thousands separator, and number of decimal places are based on Currency option selections.
	Percentage	1 displays as 1%. 0.25 displays as 0.25%.
	Month Name	1 displays as January. 12 displays as December. 13+ returns NULL.

TABLE A-1. *Data Format Settings*

Column Type	Data Format Option	Detail
	Month Name (Abbreviated)	1 displays as Jan. 12 displays as Dec. 13+ returns NULL.
	Day Name	1 displays as Sunday. 7 displays as Saturday. 8+ returns NULL.
	Day Name (Abbreviated)	1 displays as Sun. 7 displays as Sat. 8+ returns NULL.
	Custom	The # symbol represents the numeric data. As an example, with a custom format of Number #:, 1 returns Number 1:.
Date and time	Provided formats	The Format drop-down list provides dozens of available formats.
	Custom Format	MMMM = month name MM = 2-digit numeric month M = 1- or 2-digit numeric month d =1- or 2-digit numeric day of month dd = 2-digit numeric day of month dddd = Weekday name yy = Last 2 digits of year yyyy = 4-digit year HH = 2-digit hour using 00–23 hh = 2-digit hour using 01–12 H = 1- or 2-digit hour using 0–23 h = 1- or 2-digit hour using 1–12 mm = minutes ss = seconds tt = A.M. or P.M.
Text	Plain Text	Displays text just as it appears in the column row.
	Plain Text (Don't Break Spaces)	Displays text without truncating spaces.
	HTML	Treats text as HTML.
	HyperText Link	Places text inside a hyperlink HTML tag.
	HyperText Link (Prepend http://)	Places text inside a hyperlink HTML tag with http:// automatically inserted before the text.
	Mail-To Address	Places text inside a mailto hyperlink HTML tag.
	Image URL	Places text after the source argument inside an HTML image tag.
	Custom Text Format	Allows you to insert any text along with the text of the column row. Represent the data value with @.

TABLE A-1. *Data Format Settings*

Column Filter Operators

Operator	Valid Column Types	Usage
is equal to or is in	Text, numbers, or dates	Limits results to records where the column matches the filter value(s).
is not equal to or is not in	Text, numbers, or dates	Limits results to records where the column does not match the filter value(s).
is less than	Numbers or dates	Limits results to records where the column is lower (or earlier for date values) than the filter value.
is greater than	Numbers or dates	Limits results to records where the column is higher (or later for date values) than the filter value.
is less than or equal to	Numbers or dates	Limits results to records where the column is the same as or lower (or earlier for date values) than the filter value.
is greater than or equal to	Numbers or dates	Limits results to records where the column is the same as or higher (or later for date values) than the filter value.
is between	Numbers or dates	Limits results to records where the column is the same as or falls between the two filter values.
is null	Text, numbers, or dates	Limits results to records where the specified column contains no data.
is not null	Text, numbers, or dates	Limits results to records where the specified column contains any data.
is in top	Text, numbers, or dates	Limits results to records where the column contains the top-ranked records. The filter value is a number indicating how many records to return. When used on text columns, the ranking is the inverse of alphabetical order. Date ranking evaluates the latest date being first. Number ranking is highest to lowest value.

TABLE A-2. *Column Filter Operators*

Operator	Valid Column Types	Usage
is in bottom	Text, numbers, or dates	Limits results to the bottom-ranked records. The filter value is a number indicating how many records to return. When used on text columns, the ranking is the inverse of alphabetical order. Date ranking evaluates the latest date being first. Number ranking is highest to lowest value.
contains all	Text, numbers, or dates	Limits results to records where the column contains all of the one or more filter values.
contains any	Text, numbers, or dates	Limits results to records where the column contains any of the one or more filter values.
does not contain	Text, numbers, or dates	Limits results to records where the column does not contain any of the one or more filter values.
begins with	Text, numbers, or dates	Limits results to records where the column data begins exactly as described by the filter value.
ends with	Text, numbers, or dates	Limits results to records where the column data ends exactly as described by the filter value.
is LIKE (pattern match)	Text	Limits results to records where the column data matches the pattern described in the filter. You may use a single filter value, and that value may contain up to two percent-sign wildcard characters (%) to define the pattern.
is not LIKE (pattern match)	Text	Limits results to records where the column data does not match the pattern described in the filter. You may use a single filter value, and that value may contain up to two percent-sign wildcard characters (%) to define the pattern.
is prompted	Text, numbers, or dates	Limits results to records where the column data matches values passed to the report from another report. Use this operator when linking reports using report navigation.

TABLE A-2.   *Column Filter Operators*

Aggregation Rules

Aggregation Rule	Effect
Default	The Default aggregation rule for columns not listed in any of the Metric folders is None. The Default aggregation rule for columns from the Metrics folders is Sum.
Server Determined	When I have used this setting on nonmetric columns, the result is always the value in the first row of my table. Used with metric columns, the Server Determined aggregation rule returns a sum of column values in the table.
Sum	The Total row gives you the total of the column values in the table. Attempting to apply the Sum aggregation rule on a text or date/time column results in an error.
Average	The Total row gives you the average value of the column values in the table. Attempting to apply the Average aggregation rule on a text or date/time column results in an error.
Count	The Total row gives you the total number of values in the table column.
Count Distinct	The Total row gives you the total number of unique values in the table column.
Min	The Total row gives you the lowest value in the table column. For text values, this is the first value when sorted alphabetically. For date and time values, this is the earliest date and time in the column.
Max	The Total row gives you the largest value in the table column. For text values, this is the last value when sorted alphabetically. For date and time values, this is the latest date and time in the column.
None	Prevents a value in the Total row for the column.
Server Complex Aggregate	Returns the sum of column values from all records in the database. This aggregation rule ignores report filters.

TABLE A-3. *Aggregation Rules*

Formula Operators

Operator	Description
+	Add
−	Subtract
*	Multiply

TABLE A-4. *Formula Operators*

Operator	Description
/	Divide
||	Concatenate
( )	Parenthetical group
>	Greater than
<	Less than
=	Equal to
>=	Greater than or equal to
<=	Less than or equal to
<>	Is not equal to
BY	Connector indicating that the statement should apply for each value in another column
AND	Connector indicating that both statements must apply
OR	Connector indicating that at least one statement must apply
NOT	Connector indicating that a condition must not be met
IS NULL	Indicates that condition is met when formula returns NULL
IS NOT NULL	Indicates that condition is met when formula returns a value
,	Delimiter used to separate elements in a list

TABLE A-4. *Formula Operators (Continued)*

Date and Time Literals

Value	Literal Expression Format
Date	DATE 'yyyy-MM-dd'
Time	TIME 'hh:MM:ss'
Date and time	TIMESTAMP 'yyyy-MM-dd hh:mm:ss'

TABLE A-5. *Date and Time Literals*

Session Variables

Session Variable Syntax	Result
VALUEOF(NQ_SESSION. CURRENT_DT)	Current date and time
VALUEOF(NQ_SESSION.COMPANY_LANG)	Company's default language
VALUEOF(NQ_SESSION.COMPANY_TIMEZONE)	Company's default time zone
VALUEOF(NQ_SESSION.COMPANY_TMPLT_COUNTRY)	Company's default country
VALUEOF(NQ_SESSION.CURRENT_MONTH)	Current month
VALUEOF(NQ_SESSION.CURRENT_QTR)	Current quarter
VALUEOF(NQ_SESSION.CURRENT_YEAR)	Current year
VALUEOF(NQ_SESSION.DISPLAYNAME)	Current user's name
VALUEOF(NQ_SESSION.LAST_QTR)	Previous quarter
VALUEOF(NQ_SESSION.LAST_QTR_YEAR)	Year of previous quarter
VALUEOF(NQ_SESSION.LAST_YEAR)	Previous year
VALUEOF(NQ_SESSION.NEXT_QTR)	Next quarter
VALUEOF(NQ_SESSION.NEXT_QTR_YEAR)	Year of next quarter
VALUEOF(NQ_SESSION.NEXT_YEAR)	Next year
VALUEOF(NQ_SESSION.QAGO)	Last quarter
VALUEOF(NQ_SESSION.QTR_BEFORE_LAST)	Two quarters ago
VALUEOF(NQ_SESSION.QTR_BEFORE_LAST_YEAR)	Year of two quarters ago
VALUEOF(NQ_SESSION.REPLUSER)	Current user's email
VALUEOF(NQ_SESSION.USER)	Current user name
VALUEOF(NQ_SESSION.USER_ALIAS)	Current user's alias
VALUEOF(NQ_SESSION.USER_COMPANY_CURCY)	Company's default currency
VALUEOF(NQ_SESSION.USER_DEFAULT_CURCY)	User's default currency
VALUEOF(NQ_SESSION.USER_FISCAL_CALENDAR)	First month of current user's fiscal year
VALUEOF(NQ_SESSION.USER_LANG)	User's default language
VALUEOF(NQ_SESSION.YAGO)	Last year
VALUEOF(NQ_SESSION.YEAR_MINUS_THREE)	Three years ago
VALUEOF(NQ_SESSION.YEAR_MINUS_TWO)	Two years ago
VALUEOF(NQ_SESSION.YEAR_PLUS_TWO)	Two years from now

TABLE A-6. *Session Variables*

Repository Variables

Repository Variable Syntax	Result
VALUEOF(CRMODURL)	CRM On Demand URL
VALUEOF(CURRENT_WEEK_BEGIN_DT)	First day of this week
VALUEOF(CURRENT_WEEK_END_DT)	Last day of this week
VALUEOF(LAST_REFRESH_DT)	Date of last Analytics refresh
VALUEOF(LAST_WEEK_BEGIN_DT)	First day of last week
VALUEOF(LAST_WEEK_END_DT)	Last day of last week
VALUEOF(NEXT_WEEK_BEGIN_DT)	First day of next week
VALUEOF(NEXT_WEEK_END_DT)	Last day of next week

TABLE A-7. *Repository Variables*

Formula Functions

Function Syntax	Result
ABS(*n-exp*)	Returns the absolute value of a number.
ACOS(*n-exp*)	Calculates the arc cosine of a number.
ASCII(*char-exp*)	Converts a character to its numerical ASCII code.
ASIN(*n-exp*)	Calculates the arc sine of a number.
ATAN(*n-exp*)	Calculates the arc tangent of a number.
ATAN2(*n-exp, n-exp*)	Calculates the arc tangent of one number divided by another.
AVG(DISTINCT *n-exp*)	Averages distinct numbers.
AVG(*n-exp*)	Averages numbers.
BIT_LENGTH(*char_exp*)	Returns the length of a string, in bits.
BOTTOMN(*n-exp*,N)	Returns the requested number of bottom-ranked records.
CASE *exp1* WHEN *exp2* THEN *exp2* {WHEN *exp...* THEN *exp...*} ELSE *exp* END	Performs a single lookup and evaluates a series of WHEN expressions, applying the THEN expression upon encountering a WHEN expression that evaluates as true.

TABLE A-8. *Formula Functions (Continued)*

Function Syntax	Result
CASE WHEN *condition1* THEN *exp1* {WHEN *condition...* THEN *exp...*} ELSE *exp* END	Evaluates each WHEN condition and, if satisfied, assigns the value prescribed in the related THEN expression.
CAST(*exp*|NULL AS *datatype*)	Changes the data type of either a value or a null value to another data type (INT or INTEGER, SMALLINT, FLOAT, REAL, DOUBLE or DOUBLE PRECISION, CHAR or CHARACTER, VARCHAR, DATE, TIME, TIMESTAMP).
CEILING(*n-exp*)	Rounds a number to the next integer.
CHAR(*N*)	Converts an ASCII numeric code to its character.
CHAR_LENGTH(*string_exp*)	Returns the number of characters in a string.
CONCAT(*string_exp1, string_exp2*)	Concatenates two character strings.
COS(*n-exp*)	Calculates the cosine of a number.
COT(*n-exp*)	Calculates the cotangent of a number.
COUNT(*)	Counts the number of rows in a table.
COUNT(DISTINCT *expression*)	Counts distinct records.
COUNT(*expression*)	Counts records.
CURRENT_DATE	Returns today's date.
CURRENT_TIME	Returns the time that a report is run.
CURRENT_TIMESTAMP	Returns the date and time that a report is run.
DATABASE()	Returns the name of the Analytics database.
DAY(*date_exp*)	Returns the day of the month for a date.
DAY_OF_QUARTER(*date-exp*)	Returns the day of the quarter for a date.
DAYNAME(*date_exp*)	Returns the abbreviated name of the day of the week for a date.
DAYOFMONTH(*date_exp*)	Returns the day of the month for a date.
DAYOFWEEK(*date_exp*)	Returns the numeric day of the week for a date.
DAYOFYEAR(*date_exp*)	Returns the numeric day of the year for a date.
DEGREES(*n-exp*)	Converts radians to degrees.
EXP(*n-exp*)	Raises the value *e* to the specified power.
FLOOR(*n-exp*)	Rounds a number to the previous integer.
HOUR(*time_exp*)	Returns the hour portion of a time.

TABLE A-8. *Formula Functions (Continued)*

Function Syntax	Result
IFNULL(*exp, value*)	Replaces null values with another value.
INSERT(*string_exp1, location N, replace N, string_exp2*)	Inserts one string at a specific location of another string.
LCASE(*string_exp*)	Converts a string to lowercase characters.
LEFT(*string_exp, N*)	Extracts the specified number of characters from the beginning of a string.
LENGTH(*string_exp*)	Returns the number of characters in a string.
LOCATE(*string_exp1, string_exp2*)	Returns the numerical position of one string within another string.
LOCATE(*string_exp1, string_exp2, N*)	Returns the numerical position of one string within another string beginning from a specified position.
LOG(*n-exp*)	Calculates the natural logarithm of a number.
LOG10(*n-exp*)	Calculates the base 10 logarithm of a number.
LOWER(*string_exp*)	Converts a string to lowercase characters.
LTRIM(*string_exp*)	Trims leading spaces from a string.
MAVG(*n-exp,N*)	Calculates the moving average over a specified number of records.
MAX(*expression*)	Returns the largest value.
MEDIAN(*expression*)	Returns the median value.
MIN(*expression*)	Returns the smallest value.
MINUTE(*time_exp*)	Returns the minutes portion of a time.
MOD(*n-exp, n-exp*)	Returns the remainder when dividing two numbers.
MONTH(*date_exp*)	Returns the numeric month of a date.
MONTH_OF_QUARTER (*date_exp*)	Returns the numeric month of the quarter for a date.
MONTHNAME(*date_exp*)	Returns the abbreviated name of the month for a date.
MSUM(*n-exp,N*)	Calculates the moving total over a specified number of records.
NOW()	Returns the date and time that a report is run.
NTILE(*expression,N*)	Returns the rank within a segment.
OCTET_LENGTH(*char_exp*)	Returns the length of a string, in bytes.
PERCENTILE(*expression*)	Returns the percentile rank within a column.
PI()	Returns the number pi up to 12 digits.

TABLE A-8.   *Formula Functions (Continued)*

Function Syntax	Result
POSITION(*string_exp1 IN string_exp2*)	Returns the numerical position of one string within another string.
POWER(*n-exp, N*)	Raises the number to a specified power.
QUARTER(*date_exp*)	Returns the numeric quarter of the year for a date.
QUARTER_OF_YEAR(*date_exp*)	Returns the numeric quarter of the year for a date.
RADIANS(*n-exp*)	Converts degrees to radians.
RAND()	Returns a pseudo-random number between 0 and 1.
RANK(*expression*)	Returns the rank of each value.
RCOUNT(*expression*)	Returns the running count of records.
REPEAT(*string_exp, N*)	Repeats a character string the specified number of times.
REPLACE(*string_exp, string_exp to change, new string_exp*)	Inserts a character string in place of another character string within a string.
RIGHT(*string_exp, N*)	Extracts the specified number of characters from the end of a string.
RMAX(*expression*)	Returns the largest value encountered in current and all previous rows.
RMIN(*expression*)	Returns the smallest value encountered in current and all previous rows.
ROUND(*n-exp,N*)	Rounds a number to the specified number of digits.
RSUM(*n-exp*)	Returns the running total of current and all previous rows.
RTRIM(*string_exp*)	Trims trailing spaces from a string.
SECOND(*time_exp*)	Returns the seconds portion of a time.
SIGN(*n-exp*)	Returns –1, 0, or 1, indicating if a number is negative, zero, or positive.
SIN(*n-exp*)	Calculates the sine of a number.
SPACE(*N*)	Inserts the number of space characters specified.
SQRT(*n-exp*)	Calculates the square root of a number.
STDDEV_POP(*n-exp*) STDDEV_POP(ALL *n-exp*) STDDEV_POP(DISTINCT *n-exp*)	Returns the population standard deviation for a set of values in a dataset. Use ALL for all values in the dataset and DISTINCT to ignore duplicates.
STDDEV(*n-exp*) STDDEV(ALL *n-exp*) STDDEV(DISTINCT *n-exp*)	Returns the standard deviation for a set of values in a dataset using the population calculation of standard deviation. Use ALL for all values in the dataset and DISTINCT to ignore duplicates.

TABLE A-8. *Formula Functions (Continued)*

Function Syntax	Result
STDDEV_SAMP(*n-exp*) STDDEV_SAMP(ALL *n-exp*) STDDEV_SAMP(DISTINCT *n-exp*)	Returns the standard deviation for a set of values in a dataset using the sample set calculation of standard deviation. Use ALL for all values in the dataset and DISTINCT to ignore duplicates.
SUBSTRING(*string_exp* FROM *N* FOR *N*)	Creates a new string by extracting a portion of another string.
SUM(DISTINCT *n-exp*)	Adds all distinct values.
SUM(*n-exp*)	Adds the values.
TAN(*n-exp*)	Calculates the tangent of a number.
TIMESTAMPADD(*interval, integer, timestamp*)	Adds a number of intervals to a timestamp.
TIMESTAMPDIFF(*interval, timestamp1, timestamp2*)	Calculates the difference in intervals between two timestamps.
TOPN(*n-exp,N*)	Returns the requested number of top-ranked records.
TRIM(BOTH *char* FROM *string_exp*)	Trims a specified character from the beginning and end of a string.
TRIM(LEADING *char* FROM *string_exp*)	Trims a specified character from the beginning of a string.
TRIM(*string_exp*)	Trims leading and trailing spaces from a string.
TRIM(TRAILING *char* FROM *string_exp*)	Trims a specified character from the end of a string.
TRUNCATE(*n-exp, N*)	Truncates a number to the specified number of digits.
UCASE(*string_exp*)	Converts a string to all uppercase characters.
UPPER(*string_exp*)	Converts a string to all uppercase characters.
USER()	Returns the current user's login ID.
WEEK(*date_exp*)	Returns the numeric week of the year for a date.
WEEK_OF_QUARTER(*date_exp*)	Returns the numeric week of the quarter for a date.
WEEK_OF_YEAR(*date_exp*)	Returns the numeric week of the year for a date.

TABLE A-8. *Formula Functions*

Literal and Null Value Formats

Field Type	Data Type	Literal Value	NULL Formula
Checkbox Phone Picklist Text	Character	'Unspecified'	' ' (two single quote marks)
Currency Integer Number Percent	Numeric	0	CASE WHEN 0 = 1 THEN 0 ELSE NULL END
Date	Date	DATE '1000-01-01'	CASE WHEN DATE '1000-01-01' = DATE '9999-09-09' THEN DATE '1000-01-01' ELSE NULL END
Date/Time	Timestamp	TIMESTAMP '1000-01-01 00:00:00'	CASE WHEN TIMESTAMP '1000-01-01 00:00:00' = TIMESTAMP '9999-09-09 00:00:00' THEN TIMESTAMP '1000-01-01 00:00:00' ELSE NULL END

TABLE A-9. *Literal and Null Value Formats*

Action Link Text

Record Type	Custom Text Format Code
Account	@[html]"<span onClick=\"javascript:LinkOccam (this, 'account');\">"@"</span>"
Opportunity	@[html]"<span onClick=\"javascript:LinkOccam (this, 'opportunity');\">"@"</span>"
Contact	@[html]"<span onClick=\"javascript:LinkOccam (this,'contact');\">"@"</span>"
Campaign	@[html]"<span onClick=\"javascript:LinkOccam (this, 'campaign');\">"@"</span>"
Lead	@[html]"<span onClick=\"javascript:LinkOccam (this,'lead');\">"@"</span>"
Service Request	@[html]"<span onClick=\"javascript:LinkOccam (this,'service');\">"@"</span>"
User	@[html]"<span onClick=\"javascript:LinkOccam (this, 'user');\">"@"</span>"

TABLE A-10. *Action Link Text*

Custom Format Text for Detail Form Links

Record Type	Custom Text Format Code
Account	@[html]<a href="/OnDemand/user/AccountDetail? OMTGT=AccountDetailForm&AccountDetailForm.Id="@ target="_blank">"Account Details"</a>
Opportunity	@[html]<a href="/OnDemand/user/OpportunityDetail? OMTGT=OpptyDetailForm&OpptyDetailForm.Id="@ target="_top">"Opportunity Details"</a>
Contact	@[html]<a href="/OnDemand/user/ContactDetail? OMTGT=ContactDetailForm &ContactDetailForm.Id="@ target="_top">"Contact Details"</a>
Campaign	@[html]<a href="/OnDemand/user/CampaignDetail? OMTGT=CampaignDetailForm&CampaignDetailForm.Id="@ target="_top">"Campaign Details"</a>
Lead	@[html]<a href="/OnDemand/user/LeadsDetailPage? OMTGT=LeadDetailForm &LeadDetailForm.Id="@ target="_top">"Lead Details"</a>
Service Request	@[html]<a href="/OnDemand/user/ServiceRequestDetail? OMTGT=ServiceRequestDetailForm &ServiceRequestDetailForm.Id="@ target="_top">"SR Details"</a>
User	@[html]<a href="/OnDemand/user/AppDrillDwnUserDetail? OMTGT=UserDetailForm&UserDetailForm.Id="@ target="_top">"User Details"</a>
Task	@[html]<a href="/OnDemand/user/TaskDetail? OMTGT=TaskDetailForm&TaskDetailForm.Id="@ target= "_parent">"Task Details"</a>
Appointment	@[html]<a href="/OnDemand/user/ApptDetail? OMTGT=ApptDetailForm&ApptDetailForm.Id="@ target= "_parent">"Appointment Details"</a>
Asset	@[html]<a href="/OnDemand/user/AssetDetail? OMTGT=AssetDetailForm&AssetDetailForm.Id="@ target="_top">"Asset Details"</a>
Product	@[html]<a href="/OnDemand/user/ProductDetail? OMTGT=ProductDetailForm&ProductDetailForm.Id="@ target="_top">"Product Details"</a>

TABLE A-11. *Custom Format Text for Detail Form Links*

New Record Custom HTML Text Formats

Action	Custom Text Format
Create a new account	@[html]"<a href="/OnDemand/user/DefAccountInsert? OMTGT=AccountEditForm" target="_blank"> "Create New Account"</a>"
Create a new contact	@[html]"<a href="/OnDemand/user/DefContactInsert? OMTGT=ContactEditForm" target="_blank"> "Create New Contact"</a>"
Create a new opportunity	@[html]"<a href="/OnDemand/user/ OpptyCreateNewPageDefault? OMTGT=OpptyCreateEditForm" target="_blank"> "Create New Opportunity"</a>"
Create a new SR	@[html]"<a href="/OnDemand/user/DefServiceRequestInsert? OMTGT=ServiceRequestEditForm" target="_blank"> "Create New SR"</a>"
Create a new lead	@[html]"<a href="/OnDemand/user/DefLeadInsert? OMTGT=LeadCreateEditForm" target="_blank"> "Create New Lead"</a>"
Create a new campaign	@[html]"<a href="/OnDemand/user/DefCampaignInsert? OMTGT=CampaignEditForm" target="_blank"> "Create New Campaign"</a>"

TABLE A-12.   *New Record Custom HTML Text Formats*

Edit Record Custom HTML Text Formats

Action	Custom Text Format
Edit an account	@[html]"<a href="/OnDemand/user/AccountEdit? OMTGT=AccountEditForm&OMTHD=AccountEditNav &AccountEditForm.Id=@ " target="_blank"> "Edit Account"</a>"
Edit a contact	@[html]"<a href="/OnDemand/user/ContactEdit? OMTGT=ContactEditForm&OMTHD=ContactEditNav &ContactEditForm.Id=@" target="_blank"> "Edit Contact"</a>"
Edit an opportunity	@[html]"<a href="/OnDemand/user/OpptyCreateEditPage? OMTGT=OpptyCreateEditForm&OMTHD=OpportunityEditNav &OpptyCreateEditForm.Id=@" target="_blank"> "Edit Opportunity"</a>"

TABLE A-13.   *Edit Record Custom HTML Text Formats*

Action	Custom Text Format
Edit a service request	@[html]"<a href="/OnDemand/user/ServiceRequestEdit?OMTGT=ServiceRequestEditForm&OMTHD=ServiceRequestEditNav&ServiceRequestEditForm.Id=@" target="_blank">"Edit SR"</a>"
Edit a lead	@[html]"<a href="/OnDemand/user/LeadsEditPage?OMTGT=LeadCreateEditForm&OMTHD=LeadEditNav&LeadCreateEditForm.Id=@" target="_blank">"Edit Lead"</a>"
Edit a campaign	@[html]"<a href="/OnDemand/user/CampaignEdit?OMTGT=CampaignEditForm&OMTHD=CampaignEditNav&CampaignEditForm.Id=@" target="_blank">"Edit Campaign"</a>"

TABLE A-13. *Edit Record Custom HTML Text Formats (Continued)*

URL Encoding

Value	URL Encoding
space	%20
!	%21
"	%22
#	%23
$	%24
%	%25
&	%26
'	%27
(	%28
)	%29
*	%2a
+	%2b
,	%2c
-	%2d
.	%2e
/	%2f

TABLE A-14. *URL Encoding (Continued)*

Value	URL Encoding
:	%3a
;	%3b
<	%3c
=	%3d
>	%3e
?	%3f
@	%40
\	%5c
_	%5f
{	%7b
|	%7c
}	%7d

TABLE A-14. *URL Encoding (Continued)*

Report Web Link Parameters

ParameterTag	Argument Description
&P0=	[Integer] Example: &P0=2 The number provided here identifies the number of parameters you are passing to the report.
&P1=	[Condition] Example: &P1=eq This parameter identifies the condition to use in the filter. The valid values follow: **eq** Equal to or in **neq** Not equal to or not in **lt** Less than **gt** Greater than **ge** Greater than or equal to **le** Less than or equal to **bwith** Begins with **ewith** Ends with **cany** Contains any (of the values in &P3) **call** Contains all (of the values in &P3) **like** Is like (Type %25 rather than the % wildcard) **top** In the top *n* (&P3 contains 1+*n*, where *n* is the number of top items)

TABLE A-15. *Report Web Link Parameters*

ParameterTag	Argument Description
	bottom In the bottom *n* (&P3 contains 1+*n*, where *n* is the number of bottom items) **bet** Between (&P3 must have two values) **null** Is null (&P3 must be 0 or omitted) **nnul** Is not null (&P3 must be 0 or omitted)
&P2=	[Column] Example: &P2= Account."Account ID"
&P3=	[Field] Example: &P3=%%%Row_Id%%% Use the Field drop-down lists to insert this field value variable into the URL. The field identifier will always be proceeded and followed by %%%. You may also use a static value here, such as 0 in case of the null condition.
&P4=	[Condition] for second value if needed.
&P5=	[Column] for second value if needed.
&P6=	[Field] for second value if needed.
	This pattern continues for each additional value: P7, P8, and P9 for the third value, P10, P11, and P12 for the fourth, and so on.

TABLE A-15.   *Report Web Link Parameters (Continued)*

Basic HTML Code

Page Element	HTML Code
HTML basic document	<html> <head> <title>Document name goes here</title> </head> <body> Visible text goes here </body> </html>
Heading elements	<h1>Largest Heading</h1> <h2> . . . </h2> <h3> . . . </h3> <h4> . . . </h4> <h5> . . . </h5> <h6>Smallest Heading</h6>

TABLE A-16.   *Basic HTML Code (Continued)*

Page Element	HTML Code
Text elements	<p>This is a paragraph</p>
 (line break) <hr> (horizontal rule)
Logical styles	<em>This text is emphasized</em> <strong>This text is strong</strong> <code>This is some computer code</code>
Physical styles	<b>This text is bold</b> <i>This text is italic</i> <u>This text is underlined</u>
Links, anchors, and image elements	<a href="http://www.example.com/">This is a Link</a> <img src=" http://www.example.com/image.jpg" alt="Alternate Text"> <a href="mailto:webmaster@example.com">Send e-mail</a>
Unordered list	<ul> <li>First item</li> <li>Next item</li> </ul>
Ordered list	<ol> <li>First item</li> <li>Next item</li> </ol>
Definition list	<dl> <dt>First term</dt> <dd>Definition</dd> <dt>Next term</dt> <dd>Definition</dd> </dl>
Tables	<table border="1"> <tr> <th>someheader</th> <th>someheader</th> </tr> <tr> <td>sometext</td> <td>sometext</td> </tr> </table>
Frames	<frameset cols="25%,75%"> <frame src="page1.htm"> <frame src="page2.htm"> </frameset>
Comment	<!-- This is a comment -->

TABLE A-16. *Basic HTML Code (Continued)*

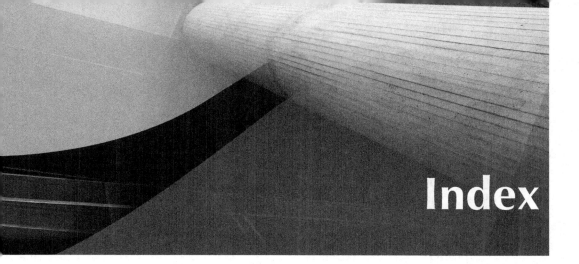

Index

GET OUR FREE SUBSCRIPTION TO *ORACLE MAGAZINE*

Oracle Magazine is essential gear for today's information technology professionals. Stay informed and increase your productivity with every issue of *Oracle Magazine*. Inside each free bimonthly issue you'll get:

- Up-to-date information on Oracle Database, Oracle Application Server, Web development, enterprise grid computing, database technology, and business trends

- Third-party news and announcements

- Technical articles on Oracle and partner products, technologies, and operating environments

- Development and administration tips

- Real-world customer stories

If there are other Oracle users at your location who would like to receive their own subscription to *Oracle Magazine*, please photocopy this form and pass it along.

Three easy ways to subscribe:

① Web
Visit our Web site at **oracle.com/oraclemagazine**
You'll find a subscription form there, plus much more

② Fax
Complete the questionnaire on the back of this card
and fax the questionnaire side only to **+1.847.763.9638**

③ Mail
Complete the questionnaire on the back of this card
and mail it to **P.O. Box 1263, Skokie, IL 60076-8263**

ORACLE®

Want your own FREE subscription?

To receive a free subscription to *Oracle Magazine*, you must fill out the entire card, sign it, and date it (incomplete cards cannot be processed or acknowledged). You can also fax your application to +1.847.763.9638. **Or subscribe at our Web site at oracle.com/oraclemagazine**

O **Yes, please send me a FREE subscription** *Oracle Magazine*. O No.

O From time to time, Oracle Publishing allows our partners exclusive access to our e-mail addresses for special promotions and announcements. To be included in this program, please check this circle. If you do not wish to be included, you will only receive notices about your subscription via e-mail.

O Oracle Publishing allows sharing of our postal mailing list with selected third parties. If you prefer your mailing address not to be included in this program, please check this circle.

If at any time you would like to be removed from either mailing list, please contact Customer Service at +1.847.763.9635 or send an e-mail to oracle@halldata.com. If you opt in to the sharing of information, Oracle may also provide you with e-mail related to Oracle products, services, and events. If you want to completely unsubscribe from any e-mail communication from Oracle, please send an e-mail to: unsubscribe@oracle-mail.com with the following in the subject line: REMOVE [your e-mail address]. For complete information on Oracle Publishing's privacy practices, please visit oracle.com/html/privacy.html

X _____   _____
signature (required)   date

name   title

company   e-mail address

street/p.o. box

city/state/zip or postal code   telephone

country   fax

Would you like to receive your free subscription in digital format instead of print if it becomes available? O Yes O No

---

YOU MUST ANSWER ALL 10 QUESTIONS BELOW.

① WHAT IS THE PRIMARY BUSINESS ACTIVITY OF YOUR FIRM AT THIS LOCATION? (check one only)

- ☐ 01 Aerospace and Defense Manufacturing
- ☐ 02 Application Service Provider
- ☐ 03 Automotive Manufacturing
- ☐ 04 Chemicals
- ☐ 05 Media and Entertainment
- ☐ 06 Construction/Engineering
- ☐ 07 Consumer Sector/Consumer Packaged Goods
- ☐ 08 Education
- ☐ 09 Financial Services/Insurance
- ☐ 10 Health Care
- ☐ 11 High Technology Manufacturing, OEM
- ☐ 12 Industrial Manufacturing
- ☐ 13 Independent Software Vendor
- ☐ 14 Life Sciences (biotech, pharmaceuticals)
- ☐ 15 Natural Resources
- ☐ 16 Oil and Gas
- ☐ 17 Professional Services
- ☐ 18 Public Sector (government)
- ☐ 19 Research
- ☐ 20 Retail/Wholesale/Distribution
- ☐ 21 Systems Integrator, VAR/VAD
- ☐ 22 Telecommunications
- ☐ 23 Travel and Transportation
- ☐ 24 Utilities (electric, gas, sanitation, water)
- ☐ 98 Other Business and Services _____

② WHICH OF THE FOLLOWING BEST DESCRIBES YOUR PRIMARY JOB FUNCTION? (check one only)

CORPORATE MANAGEMENT/STAFF
- ☐ 01 Executive Management (President, Chair, CEO, CFO, Owner, Partner, Principal)
- ☐ 02 Finance/Administrative Management (VP/Director/ Manager/Controller, Purchasing, Administration)
- ☐ 03 Sales/Marketing Management (VP/Director/Manager)
- ☐ 04 Computer Systems/Operations Management (CIO/VP/Director/Manager MIS/IS/IT, Ops)

IS/IT STAFF
- ☐ 05 Application Development/Programming Management
- ☐ 06 Application Development/Programming Staff
- ☐ 07 Consulting
- ☐ 08 DBA/Systems Administrator
- ☐ 09 Education/Training
- ☐ 10 Technical Support Director/Manager
- ☐ 11 Other Technical Management/Staff
- ☐ 98 Other

③ WHAT IS YOUR CURRENT PRIMARY OPERATING PLATFORM (check all that apply)

- ☐ 01 Digital Equipment Corp UNIX/VAX/VMS
- ☐ 02 HP UNIX
- ☐ 03 IBM AIX
- ☐ 04 IBM UNIX
- ☐ 05 Linux (Red Hat)
- ☐ 06 Linux (SUSE)
- ☐ 07 Linux (Oracle Enterprise)
- ☐ 08 Linux (other)
- ☐ 09 Macintosh
- ☐ 10 MVS
- ☐ 11 Netware
- ☐ 12 Network Computing
- ☐ 13 SCO UNIX
- ☐ 14 Sun Solaris/SunOS
- ☐ 15 Windows
- ☐ 16 Other UNIX
- ☐ 98 Other
- 99 ☐ None of the Above

④ DO YOU EVALUATE, SPECIFY, RECOMMEND, OR AUTHORIZE THE PURCHASE OF ANY OF THE FOLLOWING? (check all that apply)

- ☐ 01 Hardware
- ☐ 02 Business Applications (ERP, CRM, etc.)
- ☐ 03 Application Development Tools
- ☐ 04 Database Products
- ☐ 05 Internet or Intranet Products
- ☐ 06 Other Software
- ☐ 07 Middleware Products
- 99 ☐ None of the Above

⑤ IN YOUR JOB, DO YOU USE OR PLAN TO PURCHASE ANY OF THE FOLLOWING PRODUCTS? (check all that apply)

SOFTWARE
- ☐ 01 CAD/CAE/CAM
- ☐ 02 Collaboration Software
- ☐ 03 Communications
- ☐ 04 Database Management
- ☐ 05 File Management
- ☐ 06 Finance
- ☐ 07 Java
- ☐ 08 Multimedia Authoring
- ☐ 09 Networking
- ☐ 10 Programming
- ☐ 11 Project Management
- ☐ 12 Scientific and Engineering
- ☐ 13 Systems Management
- ☐ 14 Workflow

HARDWARE
- ☐ 15 Macintosh
- ☐ 16 Mainframe
- ☐ 17 Massively Parallel Processing

- ☐ 18 Minicomputer
- ☐ 19 Intel x86(32)
- ☐ 20 Intel x86(64)
- ☐ 21 Network Computer
- ☐ 22 Symmetric Multiprocessing
- ☐ 23 Workstation Services

SERVICES
- ☐ 24 Consulting
- ☐ 25 Education/Training
- ☐ 26 Maintenance
- ☐ 27 Online Database
- ☐ 28 Support
- ☐ 29 Technology-Based Training
- ☐ 30 Other
- 99 ☐ None of the Above

⑥ WHAT IS YOUR COMPANY'S SIZE? (check one only)

- ☐ 01 More than 25,000 Employees
- ☐ 02 10,001 to 25,000 Employees
- ☐ 03 5,001 to 10,000 Employees
- ☐ 04 1,001 to 5,000 Employees
- ☐ 05 101 to 1,000 Employees
- ☐ 06 Fewer than 100 Employees

⑦ DURING THE NEXT 12 MONTHS, HOW MUCH DO YOU ANTICIPATE YOUR ORGANIZATION WILL SPEND ON COMPUTER HARDWARE, SOFTWARE, PERIPHERALS, AND SERVICES FOR YOUR LOCATION? (check one only)

- ☐ 01 Less than $10,000
- ☐ 02 $10,000 to $49,999
- ☐ 03 $50,000 to $99,999
- ☐ 04 $100,000 to $499,999
- ☐ 05 $500,000 to $999,999
- ☐ 06 $1,000,000 and Over

⑧ WHAT IS YOUR COMPANY'S YEARLY SALES REVENUE? (check one only)

- ☐ 01 $500, 000, 000 and above
- ☐ 02 $100, 000, 000 to $500, 000, 000
- ☐ 03 $50, 000, 000 to $100, 000, 000
- ☐ 04 $5, 000, 000 to $50, 000, 000
- ☐ 05 $1, 000, 000 to $5, 000, 000

⑨ WHAT LANGUAGES AND FRAMEWORKS DO YOU USE? (check all that apply)

- ☐ 01 Ajax
- ☐ 02 C
- ☐ 03 C++
- ☐ 04 C#
- ☐ 13 Python
- ☐ 14 Ruby/Rails
- ☐ 15 Spring
- ☐ 16 Struts

- ☐ 05 Hibernate
- ☐ 06 J++/J#
- ☐ 07 Java
- ☐ 08 JSP
- ☐ 09 .NET
- ☐ 10 Perl
- ☐ 11 PHP
- ☐ 12 PL/SQL
- ☐ 17 SQL
- ☐ 18 Visual Bas
- ☐ 98 Other

⑩ WHAT ORACLE PRODUCTS ARE IN USE A▼ SITE? (check all that apply)

ORACLE DATABASE
- ☐ 01 Oracle Database 11*g*
- ☐ 02 Oracle Database 10*g*
- ☐ 03 Oracle9*i* Database
- ☐ 04 Oracle Embedded Database (Oracle Lite, Times Ten, Berkeley
- ☐ 05 Other Oracle Database Release

ORACLE FUSION MIDDLEWARE
- ☐ 06 Oracle Application Server
- ☐ 07 Oracle Portal
- ☐ 08 Oracle Enterprise Manager
- ☐ 09 Oracle BPEL Process Manager
- ☐ 10 Oracle Identity Management
- ☐ 11 Oracle SOA Suite
- ☐ 12 Oracle Data Hubs

ORACLE DEVELOPMENT TOOLS
- ☐ 13 Oracle JDeveloper
- ☐ 14 Oracle Forms
- ☐ 15 Oracle Reports
- ☐ 16 Oracle Designer
- ☐ 17 Oracle Discoverer
- ☐ 18 Oracle BI Beans
- ☐ 19 Oracle Warehouse Builder
- ☐ 20 Oracle WebCenter
- ☐ 21 Oracle Application Express

ORACLE APPLICATIONS
- ☐ 22 Oracle E-Business Suite
- ☐ 23 PeopleSoft Enterprise
- ☐ 24 JD Edwards EnterpriseOne
- ☐ 25 JD Edwards World
- ☐ 26 Oracle Fusion
- ☐ 27 Hyperion
- ☐ 28 Siebel CRM

ORACLE SERVICES
- ☐ 28 Oracle E-Business Suite On Dema
- ☐ 29 Oracle Technology On Demand
- ☐ 30 Siebel CRM On Demand
- ☐ 31 Oracle Consulting
- ☐ 32 Oracle Education
- ☐ 33 Oracle Support
- ☐ 98 Other
- 99 ☐ None of the Above

CPSIA information can be obtained
at www.ICGtesting.com
Printed in the USA
FSOW03n1953190716
22934FS